Popular American Recording Pioneers
1895-1925

HAWORTH Popular Culture
Frank W. Hoffmann, PhD and B. Lee Cooper, PhD
Senior Editors

New, Recent, and Forthcoming Titles:

Arts & Entertainment Fads by Frank W. Hoffmann and William G. Bailey

Sports & Recreation Fads by Frank W. Hoffmann and William G. Bailey

Mind & Society Fads by Frank W. Hoffmann and William G. Bailey

Fashion & Merchandising Fads by Frank W. Hoffmann and William G. Bailey

Chocolate Fads, Folklore, and Fantasies: 1000+ Chunks of Chocolate Information by Linda K. Fuller

The Popular Song Reader: A Sampler of Well-Known Twentieth-Century Songs by William Studwell

Great Awakenings: Popular Religion and Popular Culture by Marshall W. Fishwick

The Christmas Carol Reader by William Studwell

Media-Mediated Relationships: Straight and Gay, Mainstream and Alternative Perspectives by Linda K. Fuller

The National and Religious Song Reader: Patriotic, Traditional, and Sacred Songs from Around the World by William E. Studwell

Rock Music in American Popular Culture: Rock 'n' Roll Resources by B. Lee Cooper and Wayne S. Haney

Rock Music in American Popular Culture II: More Rock 'n' Roll Resources by B. Lee Cooper and Wayne S. Haney

Rock Music in American Popular Culture III: More Rock 'n' Roll Resources by B. Lee Cooper and Wayne S. Haney

The Americana Song Reader by William E. Studwell

Images of Elvis Presley in American Culture, 1977-1997: The Mystery Terrain by George Plasketes

Popular Culture: Cavespace to Cyberspace by Marshall W. Fishwick

The Classic Rock and Roll Reader: Rock Music from Its Beginnings to the Mid-1970s by William E. Studwell and D. F. Lonergan

Popular American Recording Pioneers: 1895-1925 by Tim Gracyk with Frank Hoffmann

Popular American Recording Pioneers
1895-1925

Tim Gracyk

with
Frank Hoffmann

Routledge
Taylor & Francis Group

LONDON AND NEW YORK

Transferred to Digital Printing 2008 by Routledge 2008
2 Park Square, Milton Park, Abingdon, Oxon, OX14 4RN
270 Madison Ave, New York NY 10016

The Haworth Press, Inc., 10 Alice Street, Binghamton, NY 13904-1580

Cover design by Jennifer M. Gaska.

The Library of Congress has cataloged the hardcover edition of this book as:

Gracyk, Tim.
  Popular American recording pioneers, 1895-1925 / Tim Gracyk, with Frank Hoffmann.
    p.   cm.
  Includes bibliographical references and indexes.
  ISBN 1-56024-993-5 (alk. paper)
    1. Music—United States—Bio-bibliography—Dictionaries. 2. Musicians—United States—Biography. 3. Popular music—United States—History and criticism. 4. Sound recording indus-try—United States—History. I. Hoffmann, Frank W., 1949- II. Title.

ML106.U3 G67 2000
781.64′092′273—dc21
[B]

                                                                              99-049825

ISBN 0-7890-1220-0 (pbk.)

Publisher's Note
The publisher has gone to great lengths to ensure the quality of this reprint but points out that some imperfections in the original may be apparent.

CONTENTS

ABOUT THE AUTHORS

Tim Gracyk, MA, is editor and publisher of the *Victrola and 78 Journal.* He has published widely on pioneers of the recording industry. He taught English for over a decade at Santa Clara University. He is currently completing a book about the early years of jazz and has overseen the reissue of vintage recordings on compact disc for record labels.

Frank Hoffmann, PhD, MLS, is the author of several Haworth titles including *Arts & Entertainment Fads, Sports & Recreation Fads, Mind & Society Fads,* and *Fashion & Merchandising Fads.* He is Professor in the School of Library Science, Sam Houston State University, Huntsville, Texas.

Acknowledgments

In 1995, I began systematically compiling facts that were scattered in catalogs, trade journals, newspaper clippings, hobbyist magazines, and other sources. As I gathered information about prolific recording artists, other collectors of vintage recordings donated the fruit of their own research, earning my lasting gratitude.

Frank Hoffmann, who is a professor of library science at the Sam Houston State University in Huntsville, Texas, donated summaries of dozens of Jim Walsh's articles, and I used these as foundations, adding information from a variety of other sources.

Special thanks go to Quentin Riggs, who decades ago corresponded with several of the artists discussed in this book. When he was a teen, Riggs met Billy Murray, Will Oakland, Walter Scanlan, Irving Kaufman, and others at a gathering of artists held at tenor John Bieling's home in Hempstead, Long Island on September 10, 1947. In the late 1960s, Riggs visited Olive Kline in her home in Pelham, New York, and visited Elliott Shaw at the singer's home in Sharon, Connecticut. For decades he helped Jim Walsh by providing information and photographs for *Hobbies* articles (Walsh often cited Riggs' help). Riggs has continued to assist researchers over the years. We exchanged hundreds of letters, and his support was invaluable from the project's beginning until its completion.

Brian Rust was working on yet another major discography, yet he always found time to answer my questions.

Many corrections and suggestions were made by Robert Olson, Jack Palmer, David Rocco, Dick Carty, David Banks, Bruce Vermazen, R.J. Wakeman, Martin Bryan, Tim Brooks, Allan Sutton, Martin Maas, Houston Maples, and Ronald Dethlefson. Others who helped include Dr. Lawrence Auspos, Nolan Porterfield, Bill Knorp, Jack Jenkins, Kurt Nauck, Stan Hester, Tom Mootz, Mike Sibley, Ron Pendergraft, Larry Jeannette, Tom Gervat, Richard Arsenty, Alan Mueller, Arthur Makosinski, and George Wagner.

I welcome comments, suggestions, corrections, and additional information. If you can help in some way, please contact me at:

Tim Gracyk
9180 Joy Lane
Granite Bay, CA 95746-9682
tgracyk@garlic.com

Introduction

This book covers artists who long ago made records of music that was "popular" in nature, as opposed to records of operatic arias, symphonic works, or concert pieces. It covers the recording industry's early decades, from the 1890s to the mid-1920s. Today we call this the acoustic era of the industry, since a preelectric method for recording was used, with musicians performing into a horn, not a microphone.

The word "pioneers" in the title is used loosely. Some writers reserve the term "pioneers" for musicians who recorded only in the 1890s or so, but I do not define the word so narrowly. From today's perspective, all artists who made records before 1925 seem to be pioneers of sorts, and with the introduction of the microphone in the mid-1920s, many of these artists were pioneers of the new electric era. "Pioneers" has several meanings. Artists new to the industry often have fresh ideas and help sweep away old musical trends. Paul Whiteman as well as Henry Whitter were true pioneers in the early 1920s, and innovations they introduced are discussed in this book. In short, the word "pioneers" is appropriate for all artists in this book since they made records long ago, and some were pioneers in a secondary sense in that they helped create new trends.

The year 1925, which marks the beginning of the electric recording era, is a convenient cutoff point. The earlier process required musicians to perform into a large horn or what some artists would later recall as being a funnel or tube. Studios were equipped with horns of all sizes, shapes, and lengths—some round, some square, some flared at the mouth. Horns were carefully selected to suit the orchestras or voices that would be recorded during a session. Sound was projected into a recording machine, which was usually in an adjacent room. The energy of sound waves activated a diaphragm attached to a stylus, which transferred vibration patterns to the surface of a blank recording disc or cylinder. Today this is called an acoustic recording process. Not all records issued after 1925 were made with a microphone. Columbia for four years continued to use nonelectric recording equipment for its budget-priced labels, including Harmony, Velvet Tone, and Diva.

HOW THIS PROJECT BEGAN

When I began collecting old discs and cylinders, I wanted to learn about the artists on these records. This was not easy since facts were scattered in out-of-print books, old company catalogs, and rare trade journals. Even many articles by Jim Walsh, who decades ago shared all he knew about artists he most admired, were difficult to locate. Nonetheless, I amassed reference materials, and compiling information into a single volume seemed inevitable.

Included are some artists who in the early 1890s made some of the earliest commercial records. Other artists covered began recording shortly after the turn of the twentieth century, when the industry was no longer in its infancy. Several artists with entries did not have sessions until the early 1920s, a few entries covering artists who made their first records as late as 1924.

Careers did not abruptly end with the advent of electric recording, and in some entries electric recordings are discussed. However, in the case of Paul Whiteman and a few others with very long careers, electric-era recordings are not discussed.

Franklyn Baur and Nathaniel Shilkret were arguably more popular in the electric era but each began recording in the acoustic era, Shilkret being especially busy as the leader of orchestras that made records for the Victor Talking Machine Company's foreign and ethnic market. Since no other book contains much information about Baur or Shilkret, I happily made room for them in this book.

Both Baur and Shilkret were active in studios when companies changed from acoustic to electric recording, and their observations about that transition are interesting. In an interview for the September 1927 issue of *Phonograph Monthly Review*, Baur discussed the different demands made on singers by the two recording processes:

> The invention of the electrical process was of greater significance than the average layman realizes. Not only are the finished records incomparably better from every standpoint, but the strain on the singer is immeasurably eased. A record can be made in exactly one-third the time it used to take, and no longer is it necessary for us to nearly crack our throats singing into that hated horn . . .

Shilkret wrote about the transition from acoustic to electric recording in the trade journal's May 1927 issue, pointing out difficulties at first with recording tenor voices: "The tenor voice gave us plenty of grief for a while. At first they sounded rather thick, like baritones. At times hollow; but all voices finally were conquered."

This book covers American artists who recorded Tin Pan Alley numbers, Broadway show tunes, ragtime, "coon" songs, "darkey dialect" stories, novelty numbers, quartet arrangements, parlor ballads, early jazz (sometimes called "jass"), blues, dance music, hymns, and early country. ("Coon" and "darkey" will offend some readers today, but long ago such terms were commonly used by record companies to describe some genres and therefore are cited a few times in this book.) Several here recorded some opera as well as "popular" material, with three examples from Victor's roster being Lucy Isabelle Marsh, Reinald Werrenrath, and Olive Kline. Books about opera singers overlook these fine singers, which is not surprising since they enjoyed no fame in opera houses, and I happily pay tribute to their studio work here. Their recordings issued on Victor's black, purple, blue, and red labels sold well.

Thousands made records—individuals, duos, trios, small and large ensembles—so obviously not all artists of the acoustic era could be included. In fact, we will never know the names of everyone featured on records. In the 1890s some regional companies recruited local talent, and not all catalogs and records have survived. Many early catalogs and records fail to identify artists, instead using generic terms such as "tenor" and "soprano," and the identity of some remain unknown.

Many artists recorded a few titles and never again entered a studio. Perhaps thousands of now-forgotten men and women made small contributions to the industry in the early decades. In contrast to such performers were the studio regulars, or professional recording artists, who were responsible for a vast number of titles. It is remarkable how much was recorded by a relatively small number of artists!

This book covers many of the incredibly prolific artists. I also selected as subjects for entries a manageable number of artists who did not record often but who left behind notable performances. Readers may discover that favorites are missing, and I regret that the omission of artists will strike some as glaring, but to cover all nonclassical acoustic-era recording artists of consequence was not possible, at least not in this first edition.

WHAT IS COVERED IN THE ENTRIES

Most entries give basic biographical information, such as where and when artists were born (if known), and where and when they died. They discuss when artists began recording and stopped, how much they recorded, what they were best known for, and which companies employed them. To do full justice to the long careers of artists covered here was not always possible. Omissions and errors were inevitable, and I hope in an expanded edition to address oversights and correct mistakes. Jim Walsh wrote in the August 1951 issue of *Hobbies:*

> A set of books the size of the Encyclopedia Britannica would be required to publish an exhaustive account of all the American performers who made records at some time from Edison's invention of the phonograph in 1877 to the advent of the electric recording in 1925. . . . When I wake in the middle of the night one of the things I worry about is the disconcerting knowledge that I could turn out an article a month for the next hundred years and still have left artists worth writing about at the end of my century of exertion.

Regrettably, Walsh did not compile that hypothetical set of books. He uses the adjective "exhaustive," and perhaps he was deterred because he thought such a project must be comprehensive. By setting more modest goals, I found that compiling information for this book was manageable and always enjoyable.

SOURCES OF INFORMATION

One of my goals is to preserve in this book much information that Walsh presented in the monthly magazine *Hobbies* from January 1942 to May 1985 as well as in earlier publications, such as the obscure *Music Lover's Guide*. Much information not documented in this book, such as real names of many singers as well as many dates of birth and death, came from Walsh's articles. Whenever possible, I examined the sources that Walsh consulted—trade journals, obituaries, and catalogs.

For many artists covered here, Walsh had written nothing—he had no interest in early dance bands and detested jazz. For these entries I worked more or less from scratch, taking information from a variety of sources, most of which I cite in the entries themselves. Fortunately, trade journals such as *Talking Machine World* and *Edison Phonograph Monthly* say much about the lives of record artists.

I regularly consulted these reference works:

1. *Berliner Gramophone Records: American Issues, 1892-1900* (Greenwood Press, 1995), compiled by Paul Charosh
2. *Edison Cylinder Records, 1889-1912* (APM Press, 1987), compiled by Allen Koenigsberg

3. Brian Rust's various discographies
4. *A Guide to Pseudonyms on American Records, 1892-1942* (Greenwood Press, 1993), compiled by Allan Sutton
5. *The Encyclopedic Discography of Victor Recordings: Pre-Matrix Series* (Greenwood Press, 1983) and *The Encyclopedic Discography of Victor Recordings: Matrix Series* (Greenwood Press, 1986), compiled by Ted Fagan and William R. Moran
6. *Edison Disc Artists and Records 1910-1929* (APM Press, 1985), by Ronald Dethlefson and Raymond R. Wile
7. *Edison Blue Amberol Recordings 1912-1914* (Stationary X-Press, 1997) and *Edison Blue Amberol Recordings 1915-1929* (APM Press, 1981), compiled by Ronald Dethlefson
8. *Edison Phonograph Monthly* as reprinted by Wendell Moore
9. *Show Music on Record: The First 100 Years* (Smithsonian, 1992), by Jack Raymond
10. *Moanin' Low: A Discography of Female Popular Vocal Recordings, 1920-1933* (Greenwood Press, 1996), compiled by Ross Laird
11. *Encyclopedia of Recorded Sound in the United States* (Garland Publishing, Inc., 1993), edited by Guy A. Marco

Talking Machine World, founded in January 1905 by Edward Lyman Bill as a trade monthly for America's talking machine industry, proved invaluable since it contains fascinating articles about artists' professional activities. At the back of each issue are "Advance Record Bulletins" listing discs and cylinders about to be issued by various companies.

Another trade monthly was *Phonograph Monthly Review*, first published in October 1926 and edited by Axel B. Johnson. According to an early editorial, "This magazine is to the United States what the 'Gramophone' is to Great Britain and bids fair in its splendidly edited pages to rival the 'Gramophone.'" The magazine catered to a new type of collector, namely the listener interested primarily in symphonies, concertos, and chamber music, but it covered various topics. Phonograph societies were formed at this time, which led to increased interest in the industry's early years. *Phonograph Monthly Review* was the first American publication to feature on a regular basis articles written by some writers interested primarily in old recordings and the industry's early years. It published the first substantive articles on such pioneers as Harry Macdonough, S. H. Dudley, and Anthony and Harrison.

I was able to borrow complete runs of a few trade journals, but for some elusive journals such as *The Phonoscope*, I was able to examine only a few issues. Published from November 1896 to June 1900, it called itself "a monthly journal devoted to scientific and amusement inventions appertaining to sound & sight." Even rarer are issues of *The Phonogram*, a monthly published in New York from 1891 to 1893. It called itself the "official organ of the phonograph companies of the United States."

THE BEGINNING OF THE RECORDING INDUSTRY

This book covers some of the earliest recording artists. Giving an exact date for when the recording industry began in earnest is difficult. Thomas A. Edison invented the phonograph in 1877, but the technology had to be refined before commercial recordings could be marketed. The industry was essentially born in early 1889 when sales franchises were established in various regions of the United States for Jesse H. Lippincott's North American Phonograph Company, a syndicate begun in July 1888. The *Proceedings of the 1890 Convention of Local Phonograph Companies* (reprinted in 1974 by the Country Music Foundation Press) establish that the industry was truly in its infancy in 1890. Specific recording artists are not named in the transcript of the proceedings. There were no "hit" records as early as 1890.

Edison at first anticipated that his invention would best serve business-men, especially for dictation. Edison himself recorded messages for friends via cylinders. But some companies shrewdly promoted cylinder technology for entertainment, and the general public eagerly deposited coins into the machines set up where crowds gathered. There was a steady demand for newly made cylinders, including new titles so the public would not weary of the same selections. This was before individuals had machines in their homes.

Page 17 of the June 1907 issue of *Edison Phonograph Monthly* quotes an 1889 memorandum in which Edison employee Charles Batchelor (in his own right an important inventor) writes of "enormous orders for musi-cal cylinders." Thomas A. Edison had replied to Batchelor, "We are mak-ing about 50 [records] per day and I am rigging up to furnish 300 daily. Please send orders (written) to Laboratory. We will book them, fill the orders by sending them to Phono. Co., and make charges so that we will not be out of pocket." The Edison trade publication then adds analysis, citing current production figures of 1907: "As we have manufactured as many as 110,000 Records in a single day recently, it follows that for every one produced when this memo was written, 2,200 have since been turned out in the same space of time!"

Two remarkable booklets listing early recordings are duplicated in Al-len Koenigsberg's *Edison Cylinder Records, 1889-1912*. One is titled *The First Book of Phonograph Records*. Compiled by Edison employee

A. Theo E. Wangemann (1855-1906), it lists records made from May 24, 1889, to April 23, 1892. The other, from January 1890, was issued by the North American Phonograph Company, itself established on July 14, 1888, by Jesse Lippincott after he secured the right to both the Edison and American Graphophone Company patents.

The earliest surviving commercial recordings, which are white wax and brown wax cylinders from the early 1890s, are incredibly rare (tinfoil recordings of earlier years—even more rare—were not commercial products, and they cannot be played without being destroyed). Many cylinders of this vintage in archives and private collections have deteriorated to such an extent that their contents are almost unrecognizable. Some brown wax cylinders and Berliner discs of the late 1890s that have survived are not much better (clean cylinders from this period on the right equipment deliver a more satisfying sound than Berliner discs of comparable condition).

It is a rare individual today who plays records of the 1890s for the pure joy of listening. Although some superb musicians perform on records of the 1890s, technology did not do justice to what was happening in the studio, and deterioration of original copies makes assessing performances even more difficult. However, such records are valuable because they open a window into an era. They allow us to hear how memorable songs were interpreted long ago; they help us understand how the industry got on its feet and how some artists who would record for many years began their careers.

WHAT WERE THE ARTISTS REALLY LIKE?

What motivated recording artists of the past? What were their personalities like? Which records most pleased them? Did they enjoy recording, or did they view it as just a way to earn money? How did they spend leisure hours? How did colleagues view them? For virtually all artists, such questions are impossible to answer today. We do know a little about the personalities of artists who met or corresponded often with Jim Walsh (it is interesting that many who were interviewed late in life by Walsh owned few or no copies of their old records). Walsh noted which artists were generous, courteous, and helpful to him, but this does not necessarily help us know their true personalities.

Letters, scrapbooks, and diaries of pioneering artists do not exist. Information about the private lives of some artists has been handed down from enthusiasts of earlier generations, but even when sources can be documented, interpretation is difficult and corroboration impossible. Consider Jim Walsh's reference to Billy Murray's feelings for Aileen Stanley on a cassette made in 1976 that reissues some Murray records: "Billy, I understand, had quite a crush on Aileen when their partnership first began, but it did not result in marriage." It is an interesting comment, but does it belong in this book? Is it worth quoting anywhere except here as an example of the problematic nature of isolated bits of information? We do not know Walsh's source. Did he hear it firsthand from Murray or from a third party? What we think we know about the personalities of the recording artists is sometimes hearsay, and little of it is repeated here.

Should entries include facts about artists that are not flattering to them? A mild example—hardly scandalous—is found in the March 27, 1924, edition of *The New York Times*, which reports that singers Van and Schenck "pleaded guilty . . . to a charge of illegal possession of liquor in the Silver Slipper Cabaret, Forty-eighth Street and Seventh Avenue, of which they were alleged to be part owners." This is not in their entry since I would be sorry if readers were to recall nothing about Van and Schenck except that the singing team evidently knew some bootleggers. Fortunately, we know more about Van and Schenck than what is reported in that *New York Times* article, but there is not enough information anywhere for a researcher today to say with certainty what the two singers were like as individuals.

RECORD SALES—NOT KNOWN TODAY

Although some entries identify specific records as being popular, entries do not cite numbers of copies sold since no reliable sales figures exist. We do not know what record was first to sell a million copies or two million. Some artists late in life bragged to reporters or correspondents that one of their records was first to sell a certain number, but companies had no reason to provide artists with exact or even approximate sales figures unless royalties were owed, and few artists who covered "popular" material were paid royalties. With sales figures known only to company executives, some artists may have concluded that they could guess at— even exaggerate—sales without risk of contradiction. After all, who could prove them wrong?

Sales figures not taken from primary sources lack credibility, but few documents related to sales of this period are available to researchers, largely because few such documents have survived. Company advertisements that made bold claims about sales have questionable value, and entries avoid presenting as fact what is clearly promotional hyperbole. A Columbia advertisement in the April 6, 1912, issue of *The Saturday Evening Post* proclaims that "The Herd Girl's Dream"—a violin, flute, and harp trio played by George Stehl (later Stell), Marshall P. Lufsky, and Paul Surth—had "the largest sale of any record in the world." It was genuinely popular, first on single-faced Columbia 3908, then on double-faced A587, finally on double-sided A1157. But as Jim Walsh points out in the April 1967 issue of *Hobbies*, Columbia executives did not have sales figures of competitors in the United States and abroad, so they were in no position to identify the world's best-selling record.

Consider how various sources discuss a record that was genuinely popular when issued in early 1920, "Dardanella," as played by Selvin's Novelty Orchestra on Victor 18633. In an article announcing that Ben Selvin had signed a three-year contract with Columbia, page 128 of the November 1927 issue of *Talking Machine World* states, "Ben Selvin has the distinction of recording the famous phonograph record of 'Dardanella' back in 1919, the record which sold more copies than any other up to the recent phenomenal success of Columbia's 'Two Black Crows' records." The trade journal does not indicate how it arrived at the conclusion that Selvin's disc was the best-selling record of the acoustic era. It is likely that Selvin himself was the article's primary source.

In the early 1960s RCA Victor employee Benjamin L. Aldridge wrote a brief history of Victor's early years after examining company files, and in his list of sales figures for some Victor records popular before 1927, he cites 961,144 as the number of copies sold. According to Aldridge, "Dardanella" was one of the company's best sellers but did not hit the million mark! (The list is duplicated on page lxii of Ted Fagan and William R. Moran's *Encyclopedic Discography of Victor Recordings: Matrix Series.*) Phil Hardy and Dave Laing's undocumented *Faber Companion to 20th-Century Popular Music* (Faber and Faber, 1990) claims that "more than six million copies" were sold and that "when Selvin retired in 1963, RCA-Victor presented him with a gold disc for its huge sales" (p. 708). Sadly, no source is cited for the six million figure, which seems exaggerated.

Examples of writers citing specific numbers for records sold but without mentioning sources are too plentiful. James Lincoln Collier states in his "Jazz" entry in *The New Grove Dictionary of Jazz* (St. Martin's Press, 1988) that "Three O'Clock in the Morning" performed by Paul Whiteman and His Orchestra "sold 3,500,000 copies, one for every other phonograph in the country" (p. 587). How he arrived at such figures—over three million for a disc, seven million for all phonographs—is a mystery. Aldridge does suggest that "Three O'Clock in the Morning" sold better than any other popular number cut by Victor. It tops his list at 1,723,034 copies sold. But this is the combined sales of the song as performed by four different Victor artists. The version by Joseph C. Smith and His Orchestra sold well, as did John McCormack's. (Collier's figure of seven million for phonographs is equally puzzling. Does this refer to all talking machines made from the 1890s to the mid-1920s? Phonograph manufacturers did not issue information about units sold, so estimating how many phonographs were in use during any given year is no simple matter.)

Though we cannot know how many copies of specific titles were sold, entries do state that certain records were relatively popular, and some entries even indicate what an artist's best-selling record was. One gets a sense for that after studying trade journals, examining boxes of 78s at swap meets, scrutinizing auction lists, and talking to other collectors about what records show up most often.

We can debate which versions or takes sold best, but collectors agree that some titles from the acoustic era pop up again and again. They include Richard Jose's "Silver Threads Among the Gold," Arthur Collins' "The Preacher and the Bear," Billy Murray's "Grand Old Rag [or Flag]," Len Spencer's "The Arkansaw Traveler," Nat Wills' " 'No News' or 'What Killed the Dog,' " Collins and Harlan's "Bake Dat Chicken Pie," Joe Hayman's "Cohen on the Telephone" (Columbia executive George Clarence Jell told Jim Walsh that over two million copies sold), Selvin's "Dardanella," Paul Whiteman's "Three O'Clock in the Morning" (some researchers have erroneously identified Whiteman's "Whispering" as his biggest seller), Wendell Hall's "It Ain't Gonna Rain No Mo'," and Vernon Dalhart's "The Prisoner's Song." Among Victor's Red Seal records that sold well, Alma Gluck's "Carry Me Back to Old Virginny" (74420), issued in mid-1915, may be easiest to find today. A good rule of thumb is that if one owns six copies of any one record after buying various collections, then the record was probably a huge seller.

Some secondary sources exaggerate the popularity of certain records, and such claims are not repeated in entries here. For example, a few jazz history books claim that "Tiger Rag" was the best-selling record of the Original Dixieland Jazz Band, but it is safer to assert only that it was the ODJB number most often covered by later bands. Collectors know from experience that several copies of the ODJB's "Margie," issued in early 1921, will turn up before a copy of "Tiger Rag" appears. "Tiger Rag" was genuinely popular but it was issued in August 1918, when wartime rationing of raw materials prevented the Victor Talking Machine Company from issuing huge quantities of any disc (shellac was diverted from the record industry for the making of munitions). Victor advertisements in early 1919 proclaimed, "Don't blame the dealer for the shortage of Victor products— the Government needed us!"

Some titles remained available in catalogs for a long period but that does not necessarily mean they sold well. George M. Cohan's "Life's a Funny Proposition After All" was available on Victor 60042 from 1911 until 1927, but it is not a common record. Admittedly, it is easier to find than Cohan's other six Victor discs. The two Nora Bayes records that remained available as late as 1925 in Victor's catalog (45123 and 45136) are among her rarest.

A few writers in recent years, following the example of Joel Whitburn's *Pop Memories: 1890-1954* (Record Research Inc., 1986), have cited precise chart numbers for early recordings—what records after being released were number one, number two, number three, and so on. It is a deplorable trend, and I never refer to chart positions. Primary sources provide no basis for assigning chart numbers. No company files tell us precise numbers; trade journals never systematically ranked records (dealers at times reported to *Talking Machine World* that certain records were selling well but this is meaningless—were some salesmen trying to create interest in merchandise that they wished would sell better?); record catalogs contain no information about sales; sheet music sales are irrelevant (sales figures cited on sheet music covers were often exaggerated).

At no time in the acoustic era was enough information compiled or made available about sales for anyone today to create accurate charts or rank best-sellers, and the further back in time we go, the more difficulty we have in identifying hits. Even if one had access to sales figures of the 1890s, a chart of hits means little for an era when records of many popular titles were made in the hundreds, not thousands or millions. Moreover, markets were regional, not national. For example, many "original" records were made and sold only by the Kansas City Talking Machine Company in 1898, while Peter Bacigalupi in San Francisco also marketed cylinders available nowhere else. All chart positions concerning records of the acoustic recording era are fictitious, and since they mislead novice collectors, they do much harm.

STATE OF TECHNOLOGY
DETERMINING WHO RECORDED

Entries rarely discuss technical developments, such as improvements in recording and playback equipment, yet the state of technology in any given year helped determine who recorded at that time. That is a point worth developing here.

In the 1890s male singers far outnumbered female singers, and trade journals at the turn of the century were frank about technology of the time not doing justice to female voices. When records of Minnie Emmett and Corinne Morgan were issued, promotional literature actually stressed that finally the female voice had been successfully recorded. The June 1903 issue of *Edison Phonograph Monthly* states, "It has always been a difficult matter to make successful Records of female voices, and after months of careful experimentation our Record Department has succeeded in getting perfect results in quartettes and duets. It is now at work on solos, and expects before long to list some very good songs by female voices." Contraltos and mezzo-sopranos were better served than sopranos, whose high notes were sometimes shrieks on early playback technology.

Edward B. Marks, recalling his experience of running the Universal Phonograph Company in the late 1890s, writes in *They All Sang* (Viking Press, 1935), "The women's voices never sounded right, but their names looked good in the catalog." Marks refers specifically to Lottie Gilson and Annie Hart. It is likely that other female pioneers were recorded in the 1890s mainly to add variety to catalogs. The January 1899 issue of *The Phonoscope* includes an advertisement in which the Lyric Phonograph Company (1270 Broadway, New York City) boldly declares itself the "only company making full toned record [sic] of the female voice." This refers to mezzo-soprano Estella L. Mann, shown in the advertisement singing into three recording horns (she owned and operated the company).

In short, anyone struck by how infrequently female singers were recorded in early years should consider the state of technology at the time. It was not sexist attitudes of the day that prevented women from entering studios, although some were pressured by husbands to give up recording careers. Elise Stevenson wrote to Jim Walsh in the late 1940s that her departure from the recording field while at the peak of her popularity was due to the wish of husband Rusling Wood, a businessman who asked that she concentrate on being a housewife and mother. The marriage of Grace Spencer in 1903 to Dr. Willard Foster Doolittle ended her recording career.

When speculating about why certain recording pioneers abruptly stopped recording or significantly reduced their output, we should consider that some may have owed their initial success to having the right voice in the right place at the right time. As time went on and technology improved, some artists became less essential to companies. It is difficult to prove, but this may apply to any number of singers—J. J. Fisher, for example. His was a good voice but he was never prominent on the concert stage (at this time virtually no prominent singers embraced the new recording medium, the sound being too crude to help anyone's professional reputation). His success around 1898 was undoubtedly the result of Fisher having not only a voice that recorded just right but the patience to make records. It is possible that his services were no longer in great demand by 1902 because of advances in technology. Improved equipment meant studios finally had their pick of any number of singers. Also, the permanent master, widely adopted at the time, reduced recording opportunities and therefore income for artists who had been earning a living by hopping from studio to studio. Fisher became an insurance salesman and real estate dealer.

In the 1890s, George J. Gaskin's voice could be duplicated better than most voices. Edward B. Marks writes in *They All Sang,* "Few voices reproduced well, and these, for some reason, were not always voices one should have wished to reproduce. . . . George had one of the best reproducing voices in the old phonograph days—one of the tiniest voices in the world." With improvements in technology at the recording and playback ends, studios in time could do justice to a great number of singers. Was Gaskin, with his "tinny" voice, judged dispensable? Gaskin later made Pathé and Rex discs, which is evidence of his willingness to record, but he was not an important or popular recording artist after 1904.

Dan W. Quinn's voice was one that happened to record well at a time when technology was crude. Quinn recounted how he began recording in early 1892 in a letter sent to Jim Walsh, who quotes it at length in "Reminiscences of Dan W. Quinn," published in the July 1934 issue of *Music Lovers' Guide:* "I was lucky enough to have a voice and style of singing that were just 'made' for recording. . . . I don't know what it was about my voice that made it 'go,' as I always sang quietly. There must have been some latent penetrating power." Quinn made records for many years but was most important in the 1890s, his popularity declining after the turn of the century.

Likewise, S. H. Dudley's voice was good but not extraordinary. As technology became more sophisticated, the baritone recorded less often. Did technical advancements lead to a reduced output? Recording technology by 1902 could do justice to any number of baritones, and more singers were willing to enter a studio. Dudley, using his real name, Sam Rous, had other talents and remained active in the industry—among other responsibilities, he wrote text for Victor catalogs and supplements.

Due to the state of technology in the industry's early years, stamina was more important than artistry. In the days before the permanent master, singers with the "right" voices who were willing and able to perform by the round—singing one song ten times in a row, then another song ten times, and so on—could earn a living. Year after year, some artists made new takes of the same popular songs. Nobody who listens to the recordings of George W. Johnson is likely to conclude that he was a first-rate singer or brilliant interpreter of song. He sang for virtually every company the same handful of titles over and over, with the advent of the permanent master record evidently bringing an end to his career. Johnson's willingness to perform those few songs so often (he recorded thousands of takes of "The Laughing Song") was the key to his success as a recording artist, not his artistry. Indeed, if artists of the 1890s attempted anything subtle in delivery, it could go undetected by the recording equipment. Of all the important recording pioneers, Johnson had the most limited repertoire.

Consider Silas Leachman. Walsh's article on Leachman in the July 1955 issue of *Hobbies* emphasizes the singer's strength as well as his versatility, which would have been important to a studio (again, George W. Johnson stands out as an artist who succeeded without being versatile). Walsh quotes an 1895 *Scientific American* article that had stated about Leachman,

[H]e has been practicing loud singing for four years. He has been doing this work until his throat has become calloused so that he no longer becomes exhausted after singing a short time. As soon as he has finished one song he slips off the wax cylinders, puts on three fresh ones without leaving his seat, and goes right on singing until a passing train compels him to stop for a short time.

Clearly Leachman's talents were not strictly musical. Walsh also quotes an article from the October 1905 issue of the English trade journal *Talking Machine News*. Linzey A. Willcox had written about Leachman, "I believe that musically his records were not a success, but for clearness of words they 'took on' tremendously." Later, Leachman was an inspector of personnel for the Chicago police. His *Chicago Tribune* obituary makes no mention of his records, his recording career evidently forgotten or deemed unimportant.

Just as 1925 was an important year in marking the transition from acoustic to electric recording, so 1902 was important because major companies at that time adopted the permanent master record. This made recording less lucrative for artists who in the 1890s had been paid to sing during any one session the same handful of songs over and over. Masters were used in the 1890s but they wore out after a few dozen duplicates were made. The gold-molded cylinder process finally adopted in 1902 for commercially issued cylinders was revolutionary, and disc companies developed ways of creating identical negative stampers—a copper master would be made from the original wax master (a process that destroyed the fragile wax master), a mother shell would be made from the copper master, and several stamper shells would be made from the mother. It was at this time that Victor adopted the matrix system and the "sunken," as opposed to "flush," Monarch label.

The permanent master meant that once a song was successfully recorded, an artist rarely needed to cover it again for a company. Sessions for some artists became less frequent, and a few may have given up their recording careers because the improved technology made this line of work less lucrative. It is interesting that in 1902 Frank C. Stanley gave up a banking job to be a professional singer. He obviously did not feel threatened by the advent of the permanent master. But others around this time did the opposite, leaving the recording field for more traditional work.

The state of technology determined who made records in another sense. For most of the acoustic era nearly all recording activity was done on the East Coast, especially in New York City, because it was not feasible to set up recording equipment in various cities, unlike today when modern technology makes it possible for artists to make quality recordings in any location. It is true that in the 1890s companies in various cities made original recordings, but such companies in San Francisco, Kansas City, and elsewhere stopped making their own "original" cylinders after the permanent wax master was adopted by the industry. From around 1900 to the early 1920s almost all commercial recording sessions were in New York City or in New Jersey (the Edison company had a studio in Orange; Victor had a studio in Camden). Artists who moved away from this area stopped making records, and American musicians who never traveled to New York or New Jersey were simply not recorded. That changed a little in the early 1920s when recording engineers began traveling to new locations with portable equipment.

CONDITIONS UNDER WHICH RECORDS WERE MADE

In considering technical matters, we must also remember that performing into a studio's horn was never like working on a stage. An ability or willingness to adjust to studio conditions helped determine who recorded often and who did not. In an interview for the March 23, 1913 issue of *Providence Journal*, Lucy Isabelle Marsh stated, "Singing to [make] records, or making canned music—you may call it that without giving offence, for, although it savors of slang, we ourselves use it in the recording laboratory—is not materially different from concert work after one has become accustomed to the *strange* environment . . ." (emphasis added).

The environment was "strange" even in that singers heard their own voices differently than in a large auditorium. This was due to the size and acoustics of a studio but also to the voice being projected into a horn.

Cupping a hand to the back of an ear helped a singer only a little in hearing his or her own voice. Relatively few musicians made enough recordings to grow accustomed to studio conditions. If the records of some stage celebrities who attended only a session or two are lackluster (some mementos of once-famous artists are indeed disappointing), it may be because these artists did not spend enough time in a studio to become comfortable in the relatively unusual recording environment.

Studios were bare and often stifling in those days before air conditioning. There was no audience to inspire brilliant performances, only a pianist who provided accompaniment. Soon after the turn of the twentieth century, house musicians provided accompaniment, and most of them were also near the horn, uncomfortably close to the featured singer (incidentally, accompanying musicians were seated in chairs of differing heights, some instruments being elevated so they would be recorded properly). Because they were crowded near the recording horn, musicians did not always have space for music racks. A photograph duplicated in the January 1983 issue of *Hobbies* shows that Columbia's studio had wires hanging from the ceiling, which were designed to hold musical scores; a different photograph in the May 1922 issue of *The American Magazine* again shows a studio (the same?) with such wires. For several reasons, accompaniment in a studio did not sound quite like that in a theater, at least not in early days. For example, an accompanying violinist used a Stroh violin, which had a specially attached diaphragm and horn (patented in 1899, the device was invented by John Matthias Augustus Stroh and manufactured by his son Charles).

To perform take after take under these conditions required patience. Multiple takes were often needed since there was no way to edit blemishes from a performances, no way to splice together different takes. A mistake—or a cough or sneeze from an accompanying musician within range of the recording horn—usually meant beginning again.

In the October 1954 issue of *Hobbies*, Aida Favia-Artsay quotes soprano Mabel Garrison, who began making records in 1916: "It was nerve-wracking! Every little imperfection—and not only due to singing—meant another recording. Sometimes everything would work out perfectly, but a violinist might slightly touch his violin with a bow, and the record would have to be done again." Actually, not every performance on issued records is perfect since mistakes are audible on some records. Even if musicians performed flawlessly, additional takes might be required because of problems at the recording end.

Victor's September 1917 catalog supplement includes an article titled "How Recordings Are Made in the Victor Laboratory," and it stresses how trying the recording process could be:

> There is only a bare auditorium stripped of every bit of unnecessary furniture. . . . Spoken directions cannot be given once the recording instrument is set in motion. . . . So communication between artist and operator is by signs. The artist who makes a record sings into the horn and sees nothing else except a bare wall and the face of the operator at a tiny window.

In later years artists would recall the difficulties of recording into the horn. Researcher Milford Fargo interviewed tenor Walter Van Brunt and quoted his words at an Edison National Historic Site gathering in October 1976:

> My voice evidently cut a little more than Ada's [Ada Jones was among his regular singing partners], and I would stand back of her shoulder. I'd put my arm around her lots of times. Especially where I was singing harmony I'd have to get back a little so I wouldn't drown Ada's voice out. When Ada would sing solo, she'd stand in; and when I had a solo part, Ada would move over. On the interludes between verses we'd both duck down to let the sound of the orchestra past us. Then we'd have to come up. We ducked down on the introductions and the tags. . . . If you had a headache, it wasn't so good. When we were both singing, then I'd put my arm around her and we almost had our heads together pointing right straight into the horn. It was just a small opening, and it was made out of a material that wouldn't vibrate. She would stand on a box [since] she was shorter. . . . Most companies had a music rack to put your stuff on. . . . You didn't hold [sheet music] because it would rattle.

STAGE CELEBRITIES VERSUS PROFESSIONAL RECORDING ARTISTS

For stars of the stage, fees earned for making records in the early years hardly made up for the undignified conditions. In an era before million sellers, record companies were unable to pay much. It is true that by 1904 Victor paid handsomely to sign opera luminaries and even assigned royalties, but such artists brought much-needed prestige to the fledgling industry, so the company wrote off high fees as an advertising expense.

In the 1890s some celebrities did make records, perhaps in some cases for the novelty of the experience—after all, it was the best way to hear one's voice as others heard it. The Berliner Gramophone Company somehow induced famous orators to make discs. For example, Chauncey M. Depew recited into the recording horn "A Story at a College Dinner" and two other orations, presumably repeating what he had said at some public functions. At this time Depew was president of the New York Central Railroad (he was later a U.S. senator), and any fees earned for making the records would not have motivated Depew. It is likely that someone—perhaps Fred Gaisberg—convinced Depew that his oratory skills should be preserved for posterity.

But Broadway stars naturally expected to be paid handsomely for their performances, and few made records in the 1890s. As recording and playback technology improved, and as prospering companies were able to pay larger fees, more Broadway celebrities made records, some having many sessions, such as Al Jolson, who was well paid. By 1910 most Broadway stars who made records earned royalties (Victor used a purple label for such artists, whereas studio singers who were issued on the regular black label earned flat fees for each session, or monthly salaries). But no stage performer of any renown during the industry's first two decades cultivated recording careers the way, for example, Frank C. Stanley or Len Spencer did. Stage celebrities could ill afford the time that a Stanley or Spencer spent in a studio.

It is important to recognize a distinction between stage personalities who happened to make some recordings when they found time in their busy schedules, and artists who made their living largely by recording regularly, perhaps finding a little time on the side for theatrical performances, vaudeville, or concert recitals. Few stars of the stage made records regularly. Exceptions are Bert Williams, Nora Bayes, and Al Jolson, but even their output is minuscule compared with that of Henry Burr, Harry Macdonough, Lewis James, Vernon Dalhart, Irving Kaufman, and others who, for a long time, earned a living by recording.

Many stage personalities had only a session or two. This is true of Jessie Bartlett Davis, who won fame in Reginald de Koven's *Robin Hood* and Victor Herbert's *Serenade*. She was among the first stage celebrities to record, making three Berliners on May 3, 1898. George M. Cohan cut ten titles for Victor on May 4, 1911, his only session during the acoustic era. The titles selected were minor Cohan compositions instead of genuine hits from his musicals, which partly accounts for poor sales, which in turn helps explain why he did not make more records. The famous Elsie Janis had a single session for an American company, performing three numbers in a Victor studio in 1912.

Several stars of the stage recorded too little, too late. The great Lillian Russell finally cut three titles on March 21, 1912. She was long past her prime, and nothing was issued at that time, although a dubbing of a test pressing for "Come Down Ma Evenin' Star" surfaced in the 1940s on the Collectors Record Shop label, owned by Jack Caidin. Eva Tanguay likewise was not in her prime when she finally recorded, in 1922, her famous "I Don't Care" from the Ziegfeld show *Follies of 1909*. Lillian Lorraine, who had introduced on stage many songs that became hits, waited until 1922 to take part in an ensemble performance for Vocalion 35010. Julia Sanderson was a musical comedy star early in the century but did not record until 1931, when she was married to popular recording artist Frank Crumit.

Various stars never made commercial recordings, including Fay Templeton (a great favorite of the vaudeville and legitimate stages), Anna Held (whose theme song was "I Just Can't Make My Eyes Behave"), Fritzi Scheff (who introduced "Kiss Me Again" in Victor Herbert's *Mlle Modiste*), Hazel Dawn (who introduced "My Beautiful Lady" in Ivan Caryll's *The Pink Lady*), Lina Abarbanell (star of *Madame Sherry* and other musical comedies), and Kitty Gordon (star of *The Enchantress* and other productions).

Stage celebrities at the turn of the twentieth century had any number of reasons for not recording, with undignified working conditions and low fees for sessions being only two of them. For much of the acoustic era record company executives had any number of reasons for not inviting every major stage artist to make records, including the fact that records made by prominent stage personalities did not always sell well (if performers earned royalties, their records were often priced higher than ordinary ones, which discouraged sales). When shopping for records of popular songs, the record-buying public did not insist that songs be covered by artists who had introduced the songs in Broadway shows or vaudeville. Sometimes a hit song was offered in a regularly priced series (featuring a studio artist) as well as in a higher-priced series (featuring the Broadway personality who originally popularized it). Record buyers usually picked the cheaper version. Exceptions are interesting. Many record buyers in 1917 paid a dollar for "Over There" sung by Nora Bayes on blue label Victor 45130 despite an American Quartet version being available on Victor 18333 for seventy-five cents. Actually, the American Quartet version also sold well, having the advantage of being issued in September, one month before the Bayes version. Enrico Caruso's version on one-sided 87294, priced at two dollars, also sold well! Companies relied more on studio regulars than on Broadway personalities for a number of reasons. Multiple takes were often required during a session, but the schedules of stage personalities did not always allow extra hours in a studio. They worked long hours in theaters, often giving matinee as well as evening performances. They were not always available exactly when companies wanted them and for as long as companies wanted them. It is worth noting that when May Irwin, Blanche Ring, and Christie Macdonald made time for a recording session, they cut only what they had already performed with success on stage. No time was spent in the studio mastering new material. Also, there was little risk in issuing material that had already been tested before audiences. Executives almost always turned to studio regulars to cover new material.

Companies did not restrict themselves to songs that had already been popular on stage. Two to three months were required for most recordings to be cut, processed, and distributed nationally, which was enough time for the typical hit to have peaked and to lose some popularity. Recording executives often wanted artists to cover songs hot off Tin Pan Alley presses or cut them even before the songs were published. A Universal Phonograph Company advertisement on page 18 of the January 1899 issue of *The Phonoscope* makes this bold announcement: "Albert Campbell, tenor, sings all the latest hits from manuscript copy before they are published and therefore before any other dealer can possibly supply them."

Companies routinely gambled on new songs, especially by established composers. They assigned new songs to studio regulars—that is, professional recording artists—as soon as the songs were published, hoping the songs would be popular by the time records were released months later or that the records themselves would make the songs popular. In the first decade of the twentieth century, studios relied heavily on two or three dozen singers who made their living mainly by recording. They include Billy Murray, Arthur Collins, Byron G. Harlan, Ada Jones, Henry Burr, Frank C. Stanley, and Steve Porter. The grooming of professional recording artists—men and women who were readily available to companies, presumably rested from their last recording session (in other words, not exhausted by a recent theatrical performance)—was a crucial development for the American industry. In the acoustic era this class of artists was probably unique to the American industry. In England and other nations, busy stage performers did most of the recording work.

Professional recording artists were told by company executives what songs must be learned for a coming recording session. Some evidently learned new songs at the recording studio, coached by house pianists (singers who could read music learned new material with ease; those who could not read music depended on others to teach them new songs). Artists would sometimes visit publishing houses in New York City to learn new songs. When the young Ed Smalle was employed in Harry Von Tilzer's music publishing house, he taught new songs to some recording artists and impressed Billy Murray enough for Murray to urge companies to record Smalle.

These artists were accustomed to being assigned new songs whereas stage celebrities must have been less open to suggestions about what to sing. Of course, professional recording artists might have made some suggestions about what songs should be recorded. Artists and recording directors probably worked together in deciding what material should be covered. Policies must have differed from company to company, some executives proving more flexible than others. But ultimately company executives, not artists, decided what songs were recorded.

When Theodore Morse published a new song, executives often turned to Collins and Harlan, who would quickly learn it and record it (whenever this duo learned a new song, they recorded it for as many companies as would pay them to perform it). Likewise, a new sentimental ballad might be given to Henry Burr, who was so busy in some years visiting studios of all companies that he probably recorded some songs on the day he was given the material to learn. Marion Harris, who was unusual in that she was as well-known for her stage work as for her records, sometimes recorded what had already proved successful for her on stage, and she was at other times given new and untested material. After several years Harris gave up recording to concentrate on stage work.

Since it was their way of earning a living, professional recording artists cheerfully performed anything that companies paid them to perform. Of course, executives, or A & R men, rarely selected wholly inappropriate material for any artist, though it did happen sometimes. Curiously, Columbia executives instructed the Original Dixieland Jazz Band to learn two new songs, "Darktown Strutters' Ball" and "Indiana," for recording purposes. The issued performances are lackluster, and the record did not sell especially well. Victor executives wisely allowed the band to record two of its own compositions, "Livery Stable Blues" and "Dixie Jass Band One-Step," and the resulting disc—the first "jass" record—was a huge success both commercially and artistically.

Artists who could learn new material quickly and then during a session meet high performance standards were engaged regularly by record companies. The importance to the industry in America of professional recording artists cannot be overstated.

We can place many singers in one of the following four categories: stage stars who attended only one session or recorded only occasionally during their heyday (George M. Cohan, May Irwin); stage stars who recorded often (Nora Bayes, Al Jolson, Bert Williams); performers who recorded often but enjoyed only moderate success on stage (Will Oakland, Walter Scanlan); and artists who recorded often but almost never performed before audiences (Harry Macdonough, Lucy Isabelle Marsh). We could make further distinctions. In the World War I era, a new type had emerged—singers who established their reputations through records and then were promoted as "famous record artists" when they toured (examples include Olive Kline, Reinald Werrenrath, and the Eight Popular Victor Artists).

It is worth noting that in Jim Walsh's many articles on prolific recording artists of popular material, not one was characterized as temperamental, at least not in the recording studio. Company executives were evidently willing to work closely with operatic stars, however difficult some might be, because of the prestige they brought to the label. It seems that executives were less willing to pamper stars of the popular stage. By employing a Harry Macdonough or Lucy Isabelle Marsh to record hits of musical comedies—instead of hiring those who introduced the songs on stage—many headaches were avoided. Macdonough did double duty in the 1910s, not only singing but supervising sessions in Victor's New York studio. With the possible exception of Henry Burr, Macdonough may have recorded more than any other singer from 1900 to 1920—often anonymously, as a member of trios, quartets, and choral groups—and he is one recording artist who was far too busy working in the Victor studio to sing in vaudeville or musical comedy (on Sundays he did sing as a church soloist). He is not to be confused with a singer of the same name who enjoyed success in musical comedy. The latter never recorded.

Of course, some stage personalities who had introduced popular numbers in musical comedies were hired to record songs associated with them, but companies were not often rewarded for going to this much trouble. Billy B. Van introduced in *Have a Heart* the song "Napoleon," with words by P. G. Wodehouse and music by Jerome Kern. The show opened on January 11, 1917, and Van recorded the comic song for Columbia A2307 on June 16, 1917. Van is a good example of an artist who enjoyed success in vaudeville and musical comedy but rarely recorded (his one other issued record was made for Victor in 1916). Meanwhile, Victor and Edison executives, recognizing the success of "Napoleon" in *Have a Heart*, en-

gaged studio regular Billy Murray to record it (Victor 18242; Diamond
Disc 50434; Blue Amberol 5346). The Columbia record may be more
interesting because it is a "creator record," and Columbia's engagement of
Billy B. Van may have helped sales around New York City, where *Have a
Heart* was performed with Van in the cast (he was dropped from the show
after three months, before it toured successfully). But in most towns in
America by this time, Billy Murray's name was better known than the
name Billy B. Van. In the end, no versions of "Napoleon" sold well.

Needing trained voices for musical comedy numbers, hymns, and parlor ballads, studio executives recruited many singers whose reputations
had been established in New York's prominent churches. The voices were
superb. The singers could read music and learn new material more or less
on the spot, with a minimum of rehearsal. Such singers did not request the
high fees that stage celebrities expected and were in no position to demand
special treatment.

That does not mean church soloists lacked respect or stature in the
musical community. Churches nurtured great singing, and record catalogs
in the 1910s and 1920s proudly named churches with which singers were
associated. It is significant that around the turn of the century most singers
who worked regularly as church soloists adopted pseudonyms when making records. Discs and cylinders delivered a relatively crude sound, and
being a record artist did not enhance a singer's professional standing in the
church community (the industry gained much-needed prestige as more and
more opera stars made records). This helps explain why William Stanley
Grinsted in the late 1890s adopted the name Frank C. Stanley for recording sessions. The young Grinsted had used his real name when recording
as a banjoist in the early 1890s, but later when he was establishing himself
as a church soloist—a "serious" singer—he employed a pseudonym on
records, reserving his real name for more important engagements. It explains why Harry McClaskey did not usually use his real name on records.
Instead, he became best known as Henry Burr.

ADVANTAGES OF EMPLOYING
PROFESSIONAL RECORD ARTISTS

One advantage of using professional recording artists, as opposed to
inviting stage celebrities to make records when they could spare the time,
is that singers who did enough studio work knew exactly what to do, even
where to stand. Lucy Isabelle Marsh states in the 1913 interview with the
Providence Journal:

Practice enables the soloist to gauge the distance at which she could stand from the end of the horn in order to produce the best results. It depends largely upon the quality of the voice. Some stand very close to the horn while others find that better results are obtained by standing a foot or more away. I have found that a foot is the proper distance for me . . .

Most artists who recorded regularly must have experimented at some point to determine what worked best for them in a studio. A test record even survives of diva Nellie Melba singing fragments from the opera *Hamlet* while standing at different distances from the horn.

Journalist Allison Gray reported in the May 1922 issue of *The American Magazine* that John McCormack sang within inches of the horn ("directly into the mouth of the horn") whereas Caruso stood six feet away. After enough sessions, regulars knew when to lean toward the horn (for low notes) and when to lean away to avoid blasting. They also learned, with experience, what other voices complemented theirs on records. Duos, trios, and quartets evolved as singers realized whose voices blended beautifully, at least on records.

Studios saved time, and therefore money, by employing artists who were accustomed to performing before a horn and whose voices were known as suitable for the technology of the time. Some performers who enjoyed only modest success on the stage had voices wonderfully suited for recording. Actually, the acoustic process for some voices was probably kind, perhaps downright flattering. The combination of horn resonance and lack of overtones could put a sort of glaze over the voice, making some voices on records sound more concentrated and uniform in production than those same voices might be during a concert. Likewise, voices that charmed and even thrilled live audiences did not always record well. Several singers who had enjoyed great success in opera insisted late in life that their records from decades earlier, especially from the acoustic era, gave only hints of their real voices, or were shadows of the real thing. Records made by Emma Eames, Lillian Nordica, and Olive Fremstad disappointed many who knew firsthand how these sopranos sounded on stage. The fame of professional recording artists was actually based upon how their voices sounded on records—with such singers we have only shadows of voices, but they are impressive shadows!

Some artists in the first decades of the twentieth century earned a living by making records, but it took extraordinary commitment. We can deduce from articles written by Jim Walsh, who met many artists in their retirement years, that most were comfortably well off but not actually rich. In a letter quoted in the May 1946 issue of *Hobbies*, Sam Rous describes to

Walsh the popularity of his records made under the name S. H. Dudley and concludes, "Too bad the days of royalties had not arrived!" Artists in Victor's classical Red Seal series did earn royalties, which made a difference in the life of at least one soprano. Page 64 of the January 1926 issue of *Talking Machine World* states:

> When next you play the Victor record, "Carry Me Back to Ol' Virginny," sung by Alma Gluck, sit back and revel in the thought that you helped pay for a twenty-one-room house on Park Avenue, New York. For it was from royalties of more than 1,000,000 reproductions of this record that Alma Gluck, in 1919, bought this house, for which she paid $127,000. This interesting bit of information came out in the real estate news recently, when Miss Gluck, now Mrs. Efrem Zimbalist, sold the property at a price of $300,000. The record was made in 1914, and to this day has large sales.

If royalties had been paid to artists who covered popular songs in the early years of the industry, several would have earned fortunes. On the other hand, companies such as Victor and Columbia were able to expand partly because records of artists such as Billy Murray and Henry Burr made money. As already stated, opera singers brought prestige to companies, but they were paid large fees for sessions in addition to royalties, so companies were lucky to break even after signing a diva. Most hit records were made by artists with less prestige. They made the business profitable.

Although a few became household names, professional recording artists were not famous in the way stage or opera celebrities were. Billy Murray, Arthur Collins, Ada Jones, and Henry Burr could walk down a busy street and go unrecognized, which was not true for Enrico Caruso. Newspapers did not report their comings and goings. In contrast to now-forgotten vaudeville performers whose photographs are on sheet music covers, their faces were not known to the general public unless record buyers studied record catalogs. Prior to the 1920s, music publishers viewed stage performers—never recording artists—as natural allies in making a new song a hit, so faces of professional recording artists were rarely on sheet music covers.

Consider how little Walter Van Brunt's fame as a phonograph artist meant in 1917 to Broadway promoters. The singer was urged to change his name to the more Irish-sounding "Walter Scanlan" around the time he appeared in Victor Herbert's *Eileen*. No effort was made to capitalize on whatever name recognition "Walter Van Brunt" might have had with audiences. His records sold well, but he was not a celebrity.

We must not overestimate the fame of those who made a living going from studio to studio, making hundreds of recordings. Some did have followings in that ordinary folks in towns throughout America knew their names and might ask for the newest releases of favorite artists, as opposed to buying records because of songs performed. But no performers of popular fare were "recording stars." Nobody was called a "star" in promotional literature, nobody had fan clubs, nobody was treated in the manner of pampered stars of the stage and of the growing motion picture industry. The Victor Talking Machine Company used labels of different colors to indicate different degrees of prestige enjoyed by artists, and the Red Seal series was reserved for artists who enjoyed the greatest prestige (it was generally reserved for celebrities of the operatic and concert stages). It is tempting today to say that Billy Murray, Ada Jones, Henry Burr, Vess Ossman, and others were recording stars of their day, but Victor issued them on regular black label records, which essentially meant that they were not "stars" in the eyes of company executives.

Nonetheless, the prolific recording artists of the acoustic recording era are important to researchers studying popular music of that era. Their records brought songs into American living rooms and can still be enjoyed today. To learn how the songs of Harry Von Tilzer, Paul Dresser, the young Irving Berlin, the young Jerome Kern, and other important composers were performed in their time, we naturally turn to the recorded work of Collins and Harlan, Billy Murray, Ada Jones, Henry Burr.

Although we should value information to be gleaned from sheet music and contemporaneous reviews of stage performances, I believe that America's popular music of the past is best understood by listening to recorded performances of the time. This book pays tribute to many artists who preserved for posterity the way America's popular music once sounded.

The Artists

American Quartet

The name "American Quartet" was employed by a few ensembles, but the group with this name that enjoyed the most popularity was formed in 1909 and originally consisted of first tenor John Bieling, second tenor Billy Murray, baritone Steve Porter, and bass William F. Hooley.

This quartet came into being soon after Billy Murray signed contracts that restricted his services to Victor for discs and Edison for cylinders. Jim Walsh writes in the February 1970 issue of *Hobbies:*

> For several years [Murray] had been singing frequently on Victor records with the assistance of the Haydn Quartet, but now it was decided there was a need for a foursome in which he would star. So John Bieling and Hooley were borrowed from the Haydn Quartet (in which, however, they continued to sing) and Porter was brought in from the Peerless, where he had been singing baritone.

Arthur Collins joined the Peerless as Porter's replacement. Victor christened this group the American Quartet while Edison called it the Premier Quartet (in 1919, when the group worked for other companies, it was sometimes called the Premier American Quartet).

Earlier groups with that name must be noted. The March 1899 issue of *The Phonoscope* establishes that John Bieling, Jere Mahoney, S. H. Dudley, and William F. Hooley recorded for Edison as the Edison Male Quartet, for Berliner as the Haydn Quartet, and for other companies as the American Quartet. The July 1899 issue of that publication indicated that a group making cylinders for Reed, Dawson and Company (located at

74 Cortland Street, New York, and 516 Broad Street, Newark) was "The Original American Quartet." Whether this group was the one cited in March is unknown.

Walsh notes that in 1900, after Harry Macdonough succeeded Mahoney as second tenor, the group was represented by its own manufacturing firm, the short-lived American Record Company, which specialized in producing cylinders as requested by customer order. The 1902 Edison Bell catalog listed a series of recordings credited to the American Quartet.

The name was on a number of early Victor discs. Fagan and Moran's *Encyclopedic Discography of Victor Recordings: Pre-Matrix Series* shows a quartet recording under the name American Quartet beginning in 1901. Members were tenor Albert C. Campbell, tenor W. T. Leahy, baritone S. H. Dudley, and bass William Hooley. By August 31, 1904, this quartet's records were no longer listed, and any of its titles remaining in the catalog were remakes by the Haydn Quartet.

When the American Quartet with Murray was formed in 1909, he must have seemed very young to the other members—he was thirty-one. Bieling was almost forty; Porter was forty-four; and Hooley was forty-seven. The American Quartet's debut release, "Denver Town," was recorded in February 1909 and was announced in Victor's May 1909 supplement. Composed by George L. Botsford and Harry Breen, this song was part of a cowboy trend that spread due to the popularity of Harry Williams and Egbert Van Alstyne's "Cheyenne" (Murray's recordings of it enjoyed brisk sales). Botsford arranged most of the material recorded by the American Quartet over the next several years.

The Victor supplement called the American Quartet "a new organization of male voices which makes its bid for popular favor with a 'cowboy' number, now quite in vogue. No praise for this new quartet is needed here, as the record speaks for itself—the voices being well-balanced, the words distinct and the music sung with spirit and precision."

First issued on a ten-inch single-faced disc (5683) priced at sixty cents, "Denver Town" was reissued several months later on double-sided 16521 along with "A Night Trip to Buffalo." The latter comedy sketch had first been recorded by one of the earlier variants of the American Quartet at the turn of the century and was redone by the Haydn shortly thereafter. Victor literature called the updated American version "much improved and funnier" than its antecedents.

The Edison company also selected "Denver Town" as the first release of the Premier Quartet, or Premier Quartette. Announcing its release in June on Standard 10155, the April 1909 issue of *Edison Phonograph Monthly* as well as the June 1909 installment of the *New Phonogram* called it "another cowboy song, telling how a cowboy wooed and won his bride. It is sung by a new combination of artists, including Will Oakland, John H. Biehling [sic], Billy Murray and W. F. Hooley. Unaccompanied." Walsh questioned the likelihood of Oakland participating in the session, noting that Oakland wasn't involved with the Victor recording, and that quartets never consisted of a countertenor, two tenors, and a bass. Baritones were so important to male quartets that when Porter could not show up for a session dedicated to new takes of "Casey Jones" by the American approximately one year later, orchestra leader Walter B. Rogers served as a last-minute replacement, taking the baritone role.

In December 1912 Edison's company introduced to the market disc phonographs and Diamond Disc records. Company executives made overtures to Victor, which still had Murray under exclusive contract for discs, about renegotiating the old arrangement. An agreement was reached and Murray's earliest credited Diamond Discs—"California and You," "I'm Goin' Back to Louisiana," and "My Croony Melody"—were released in the latter part of 1914 (he can be heard on a few earlier Diamond Discs but he is not credited). The Quartet's earliest Edison discs were issued several months later under the Premier name: "Tennessee, I Hear You Calling Me" (50233), "I'm on My Way to Dublin Bay" (50245), and "Moonlight Bay" (50258). They were recorded with tenor Robert D. Armour taking Bieling's place.

Bieling's throat problems brought change to the American Quartet. He had been a part of the first commercial recording group, the Manhansett Quartet, making cylinders with that unit by 1894. In early years he was in high demand as both a duet singer and as a quartet first tenor. This was at a time when many studio takes were necessary to produce sufficient copies of a recording to satisfy public demand. Macdonough described him as having "a voice in a million, to stand up under the work it did."

But Bieling's voice suffered from constant use. According to Quentin Riggs, the trouble began with the recording of Amberol 552, "A Cowboy Romance," credited to Len Spencer and Company. The September 1910 issue of *Edison Phonograph Monthly* indicates that the production was elaborate, being rendered "wonderfully realistic by the clatter of hoofs, the whinnying of horses, and the 'yipping' of the cowboys." Many takes were required, and making yipping sounds for hours caused Bieling's voice to suffer a strain from which it never recovered. The singer later in life assigned blame for his weakened voice to Edison studio manager W. H. A. Cronkhite, who was infamous among artists because he worked them hard to obtain perfect performances during sessions.

Bieling quit singing in mid-1913. His last Quartet record, "Floating Down the River" (Victor 17438), was recorded in June or July and released in November 1913. He was replaced in late 1913 by Robert D. Armour, a young tenor who had come to New York from his hometown of Mobile, Alabama, in 1909 to pursue a singing career. Armour stayed with the quartet until the middle of 1915, at which time he was replaced by John Young.

Armour sang on the following American Quartet recordings:

- "Rebecca of Sunnybrook Farm" (17534)
- "All Aboard for Dixieland" (17535)
- "Do You Take This Woman for Your Lawful Wife?" (17554)
- "It's a Long, Long Way to Tipperary" (17639)
- "When You Wore a Tulip and I Wore a Big Red Rose" (17652)
- "At the Mississippi Cabaret" (17650)

The last of these had each quartet member take a turn singing a solo line, which showed Armour's voice to good effect. The first verse begins:

Murray: I came to town just to take in the sights.
Porter: I heard about all the music and lights.
Hooley: I've seen each cafe.
Armour: Every cabaret.

Armour's last record with the American was "Back to Dixieland" (17783), issued in July 1915. He probably sang on all American Quartet releases for Victor between the number sequence 17534 and 17783. His involvement with the Haydn Quartet was evidently limited to the group's last two records, "The Woman Thou Gavest Me" (Victor 17544) and "'Cross the Great Divide" (Victor 17545), both released in April 1914.

In mid-1915 Victor recruited John Young to fill Armour's role in the American Quartet. Young had enjoyed success as the tenor "Harry Anthony" of the gospel duo called "Harry Anthony and James F. Harrison" (kiddingly termed "The Come-to-Jesus Twins" by Murray), in addition to singing in and managing the Criterion Quartet, whose other personnel included Horatio Rench, second tenor; George W. Reardon, baritone; and Donald Chalmers, bass.

The new edition of the Quartet enjoyed great success, beginning with its first Victor release, "War Song Medley" (17823). Walsh stated that virtually all of its recordings could be classified as "big sellers." They include:

- "America, I Love You"
- "Gasoline Gus and His Jitney Bus"
- "Goodbye, Broadway, Hello, France"
- "Keep Your Head Down, Fritzie Boy"
- "Oh Johnny, Oh Johnny, Oh"
- "Over There"
- "Where Do We Go from Here"

"Sailin' Away on the Henry Clay," issued on Victor 18353 in 1917, may be the first popular record on which a quartet sings lyrics that refer to barbershop quartet singing: "Hear that barbershop quartet a-harmonizin' . . ." The Quartet changed again when Hooley died October 12, 1918, in a New York City hospital. Hooley's decline in health had been relatively sudden. He attended a Victor recording session on August 1, 1918. Bass singer Donald Chalmers, a member of the Criterion Quartet like Young, was selected as Hooley's replacement.

After Murray became a freelance artist in 1918 the American Quartet recorded for virtually every company—not only Victor and Edison but Columbia, Okeh, Emerson, Pathé, and Vocalion. Walsh has noted a wide-ranging discrepancy in the names given the group by these companies. While most companies designated them as the "Premier American Quartet" (Pathé used the term Premier American Male Quartet), Columbia switched between "American" and "Premier American" and Okeh stuck with "American Quartet." The Aeolian-Vocalion recording of "Anything Is Nice If It Comes From Dixieland" was credited to the "Murray Quartet."

After a flurry of activity which lasted almost two years, the Murray-Porter-Young-Chalmers ensemble was abruptly retired as a recording entity. In the summer of 1920 Henry Burr, not only a singer of sentimental songs but an ambitious businessman, approached Murray with a proposition. Burr wanted to negotiate an exclusive contract with Victor, a package deal involving Murray and the Peerless Quartet members (Burr, second tenor; Albert Campbell, first tenor; John H. Meyer, baritone; and Frank Croxton, bass). The management agreed to a contract, and in the autumn of 1920 Murray and his associates became exclusive Victor artists. Murray and Burr were to receive $35,000 each per year, and Campbell, Meyer, and Croxton were to receive $10,000 each per year. According to the contract, the American Quartet would thereafter consist of Murray, Campbell, Meyer, and Croxton. The Peerless Quartet personnel would be unchanged.

With Murray exclusive to Victor beginning on July 1, 1920, Edison executives in mid-1920 assembled a new group of singers for its Premier Quartet, picking first tenor Charles Hart, second tenor Billy Jones, baritone Steve Porter (the only member from the old quartet), and bass Harry

J. Donaghy. Edison continued to use the Premier name. Donaghy told Walsh that the new quartet's first Edison recording was "Oh By Jingo! Oh By Gee!" It was released as Blue Amberol 4041 in August 1920, then on Diamond Disc 50666 in September. At least some record buyers must have recognized a change in the Premier's sound. The new ensemble was known on other labels as either the Harmonizers or Harmonizers Quartet. Never very popular, the Harmonizers disbanded by mid-1922. Diamond Disc 50944, featuring "Huckleberry Finn," was the last Premier Quartet record to be issued. It was released in September 1922 but had been recorded in 1917, so "Huckleberry Finn" features the voices of the original Premier Quartet.

The American became defunct just as Victor switched to the electric recording process. No electrically recorded performances would feature the name American Quartet. The Quartet's final release, "Alabamy Bound" (19680), was issued in August 1925. Two months earlier, Victor had begun issuing electric discs (without identifying them to the buying public as being electric), but "Alabamy Bound" was an acoustic recording, cut on May 20, 1925, in the New York City studio, which did not have electrical recording equipment as early as the Camden studio. The disc was in the catalog for only fourteen months.

Walsh questioned whether all records of the final edition of the American included Campbell, Meyer, and Croxton, saying:

> some of the "last ditch" American Quartet records sound to my ears more as if they had been made by Young, Murray, Porter, and Chalmers than by the later group. It sounds to me, for instance, as if Young, rather than Campbell, sings first tenor in "The High Brown Blues" and "The Little Red School House"; and the bass seems more like Chalmers than Croxton.

Researcher William R. Moran has confirmed that Walsh's suspicions were correct, and that Murray was indeed reunited with his old associates on the following dates: March 31, May 3, May 5, August 31, and September 13, 1922. Presumably the other American Quartet members were unavailable. Riggs notes that in addition to the above coupling (Victor 18904), at least two other titles were recorded in 1922 by the 1918-1920 formation of the group: "Some Sunny Day" (Victor 18903) and "Childhood Days" (Victor 18959).

Ash, Sam (August 28, 1884-October 21, 1951)

Born in Kentucky to parents who had emigrated from England, Samuel Howard Ash appeared in Broadway musicals from 1915 to 1931. The tenor was one of the principal players in Rudolf Friml's *Katinka*, which opened on December 23, 1915. He later appeared in *Doing Our Bit* (1917), *Monte Cristo, Jr.* (1919), and *The Passing Show of 1922.*

His most popular recording work was done for Columbia, the first two discs from that company featuring "Goodbye, Virginia," sung with a quartet (A1697), and "I'm Not Ashamed of You, Molly" (A1701). The latter song was cut during his first Columbia session (on December 17, 1914) whereas "Goodbye, Virginia," given an earlier catalog number, was cut a month later, on January 19, 1915.

He was at first exclusive to Columbia, whose catalogs beginning with the June 1915 edition state:

> The moment Mr. Sam Ash demonstrated in the Columbia Laboratories that he possessed [the] rare ability to sing popular music . . . the Columbia Graphophone Company made an exclusive contract with him. Mr. Ash sings songs of sentiment with a complete grasp of every musical value and with a beautifully clear natural voice. He has made his sudden and meteoric career before the best vaudeville footlights in the country . . .

"Rackety Coo," sung with Grace Nash on A1952, is a notable recording from 1916 since Ash introduced the song in Friml's popular musical show *Katinka.*

In 1917 he recorded Irving Berlin's World War I troop farewell song "Smile and Show Your Dimple" for Columbia A2425 and Little Wonder 756 (credited as "tenor solo"). The melody of this tune was recycled a generation later by Berlin for the more popular "Easter Parade." Jim Walsh estimates that Ash made more records for Henry Waterson's Little Wonder label, which used Columbia artists, than any other singer, with the possible exception of Henry Burr. As a solo artist, Ash made more Little Wonders than Burr, but Burr sang in many more duos, trios, and quartets.

He rarely cut duets with others, but a notable one is "Hello, Frisco!" made with Elida Morris on June 30, 1915 (Columbia A1801). Composed by Gene Buck and Louis A. Hirsch for the *Ziegfeld Follies of 1915*, the song commemorates the new transcontinental telephone hookup. Other duets issued by Columbia include "When You Were a Baby and I Was the Kid Next Door," made with Louise MacMahon (A1900), and "If You Only Had My Disposition," made with Edith Chapman (A1868). A duet partner on Little Wonders was Will C. Robbins. On Operaphone 1932 he sang "I'll Make You Want Me" with Helen Durant.

In 1916 he began making Emerson discs and soon afterward recorded for Pathé, Operaphone, Lyraphone, Okeh, Gennett, and Edison. By 1918 he worked for nearly every American record company with the notable exception of Victor. He recorded sentimental songs for the most part. On rare occasions he sang comic numbers, such as "I've Been Floating Down the Old Green River."

His records sold well from 1915 to 1921. Although he made records in 1922 for labels such as Puritan, Banner, Gennett, and Regal—his "Nelly Kelly, I Love You" was issued in December 1922 on Regal 9386—his recording activities had slowed considerably by this time.

Noteworthy from early 1922 is "The Sweetheart of Sigma Chi" on the Fraternity Record House label of Plymouth, Indiana. No record number is on the reddish-golden labels of the Fraternity disc, which is a Gennett client pressing. The top of the non-Ash side, which features the Taylor Trio performing the same number as an instrumental (matrix 7684a—the small letter "a" is typical of Gennett's matrix system), states, "Sig Song Series 1922." The song itself dates from 1912, with music by F. Dudleigh Vernor, lyrics by Byron D. Stokes (these Alpha Pi members were undergraduates when they wrote the song). Ash's rendition is probably the first vocal version on record, and the disc may have been sold only on a few college campuses. (In July 1923, Whitey Kaufman's Original Pennsylvania Serenaders cut an instrumental version for Victor 19115. By 1928 the song became widely known due to versions by Waring's Pennsylvanians, Gene Austin, and Ted Lewis.)

Vocalion 14534, issued in May 1923, features Ash singing "Love Sends a Little Gift of Roses." He did not record often after that but did make records as late as 1927 for Grey Gull. Probably the last records credited to Ash are Grey Gull 2369, 2374, and 2377. On Grey Gull and Radiex 2377, Ash sings "Love Is Just a Dream of You."

Later Ash played character roles in films (they include *Unmasked*, 1930; *Kiss and Make Up*, 1934; *Paris in Spring*, 1935; and *A Man Betrayed*, 1936) and operated a company in Hollywood called Ashcraft Industries, a supplier of woodworking hobbyist kits and supplies. He died in Hollywood of heart failure.

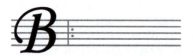

Baker, Elsie (September 27, 1886-April 28, 1958)

The contralto Elsie West Baker was born in Philadelphia to Carrie Ella (Greene) and William Drinker Baker. She began her recording career by making cylinders for a few companies—Thomas A. Edison, Inc.; the Cleveland-based U.S. Phonograph Company (which produced U-S Everlasting cylinders); and the Indestructible Phonographic Record Company (Montgomery Ward and Company issued these cylinders as Lakeside Indestructibles). Early in her career she also made Columbia discs, sometimes using the pseudonyms Edna Brown, Nora Watson, and Mabel West. But she ended up recording most often for Victor, becoming one of the company's most successful contraltos on the black as well as the semi-prestigious blue labels, eventually being issued as a Red Seal artist.

The 1914 Victor catalog states, "This young contralto has become one of the most valued members of the Victor vocal staff. . . . Miss Baker, who was a pupil of Dr. W.W. Gilchrist and Henry Gordon Thunder, of Philadelphia, and Oscar Saenger, of New York, has recently been secured by the fashionable Church of the Pilgrims in Brooklyn."

The 1920 catalog states:

> The ambition of Elsie Baker, she declares, is to live in a New England village—a modest ambition for a successful and brilliant artist. She comes of a Philadelphia musical family. She began at the piano as a child. . . . Unlike most singers, she believes the true school for the American voice is in the church, where she has had wide experience. She had made lengthened tours in concert and oratorio, and had many triumphs. Miss Baker is now soloist at St. Paul's M.E. Church, New York City.

Notices in *Musical America* and *The Musical Leader* also indicate that she was a successful recitalist, traveling widely to give performances. Victor's October 1918 supplement quotes Baker about her background as a church singer: "I began singing in church when I was fifteen years old, and I haven't missed a single Sunday since—except when on tour. I got six hundred a year for it when I was nineteen—don't you think that was a lot of money for a girl to make?"

Her first records were four-minute Edison Amberol cylinders: "Cradle Song" (930), issued in March 1912, and "Your Smile" (971), issued in April. Announcing the March release of her Edison debut record, the January 1912 issue of *Edison Phonograph Monthly* states, "Elsie Baker, a new Edison artist, is gifted with one of the rarest of contralto voices of remarkable depth in the lower and great brilliancy in the upper registers. . . . She has recently received flattering offers from two operatic impresarios and it is not unlikely that she may be heard in one of the leading opera houses in America." She never did perform in operas though she included operatic arias in concerts.

Another early Edison recording is "Pickaninny's Lullaby" (10552), issued in May 1912. In announcing its release, the March 1912 issue of *Edison Phonograph Monthly* states, "Miss Baker's first Standard Record is her favorite encore song which she gives in darkey dialect. It is a gem, and perfectly suited to Miss Baker's rich contralto voice . . ." It would be her only two-minute Edison cylinder. She recorded the same George W. Gage composition as U-S Everlasting cylinder 1499. Among several other titles cut for the U-S Phonograph Company are "Oh, That We Two Were Maying" (U-S Everlasting 1445), sung with Frederick Wheeler, and "See the Pale Moon" (U-S Everlasting 1533), sung with John Barnes Wells.

An unusual choice of song for this contralto was "Till the Sands of the Desert Grow Cold," issued as Indestructible 3308 and U-S Everlasting 1591. They may be the only records of a female singing this, which is normally performed by bass singers. Another title issued on an Indestructible cylinder is "All Night Long" (3295), which was originally issued on U-S Everlasting 1647. The two cylinder companies were separate but after the U.S. Phonograph Company folded in 1913, some U-S Everlasting molds went to the Indestructible company, which pressed records from the molds and sold them as their own.

On Rex 5018, issued in late 1913, she performs "Sing Me to Sleep." On Columbia A1383 the name Edna Brown is used for a duet with James F. Harrison (really Frederick Wheeler): "When It's Apple Blossom Time in Normandy." On Columbia A1455, issued in February 1914, Baker used the name Nora Watson for a duet with Henry Burr, "The Little Church Around the Corner." She again was Nora Watson for a duet with Harrison, "In the Candle Light" (Columbia A1483). These were perhaps the last records she made for a company other than Victor.

She became an important staff artist for Victor, making records as a solo artist but also as an anonymous member of the ensemble variously known as the Victor Light Opera Company, the Trinity Choir, and Victor Mixed Chorus. In her early sessions for Victor she recorded new takes of a few numbers covered years earlier by contralto Corinne Morgan, such as "Annie Laurie" (16388). Early Victor records credited to Elsie Baker include "Ye Who Have Yearned Alone" (17060) and "I Love You Truly" (17121).

A frequent duet partner for her Victor recordings was baritone Frederick Wheeler, usually identified as James F. Harrison at this time. Jim Walsh writes in the April 1978 issue of *Hobbies* that when they met for the first time, Baker told Walsh that she and Wheeler had been "sweethearts." She told Walsh, "Fred used to go out and get the [recording] dates, then we'd get together and make the records." The sweethearts broke up around 1917, after which they made no more recordings together.

Other male duet partners included Reed Miller (sometimes called James Reed), Charles Harrison, Elliott Shaw, Henry Burr, and Lewis James.

She was most often paired with soprano Olive Kline. The two sang duets on several records in Victor's blue label 45000 series; on several other discs, Kline as solo artist is featured on one side, Baker the other. Kline had been elevated from regular black label status to the more prestigious blue label series in June 1917. Baker followed with the release in December 1917 of "He Shall Feed His Flock" from Handel's *Messiah* (Victor 45144).

For music considered at the time to be nonserious, especially Tin Pan Alley hits and musical comedy selections, she adopted the pseudonym Edna Brown, using it from the beginning of her Victor career in the early 1910s into the 1920s. Early Victor records credited to Edna Brown include "I Want a Little Lovin'" (17067), "Please Don't Take My Lovin' Man Away" (17102), and "Daddy Has a Sweetheart and Mother Is Her Name" (17320). Her cousin, Robert G. Mitchell of Huntingtown, Maryland, suggests that "Edna Brown" combines names of two Philadelphia women: Baker had a cousin named Nellie Edna Greene who studied piano and voice under Baker, and a close friend of cousin Nellie was one Nellie Brown.

The name Edna Brown was used when she collaborated with Billy Murray, such as for "Some Sort of Somebody" (Victor 17992, 1916), and "Simple Melody" (Victor 18051, 1916). Later she was issued as Edna Brown when performing some duets with Charles Harrison, Elliott Shaw, Henry Burr, and Lewis James. Most recordings made with soprano Olive Kline were issued with the singers' real names, but an exception is "Underneath the Mellow Moon," recorded on April 10, 1923, issued as Victor 19071, and credited to Alice Green and Edna Brown.

Popular recordings include "I Love You Truly" (Victor 17121, 1912), "When You're Away" (with the American Quartet, Victor 17139, 1912), "Silver Threads Among the Gold" (Victor 17474, 1913), "Hush-a-Bye Ma Baby" (Victor 18214, 1917), and "Ka-lu-a" (with Elliott Shaw, Victor 18854, 1921).

"Dear Little Boy of Mine," originally issued on blue label 45161 as sung by Baker, was cut again by the contralto in Victor's early years of electric recording and issued on Red Seal Victor 4019. Its reverse side features Kline and Baker singing "Beautiful Ohio," a duet Olive Kline had recorded in the acoustic era with contralto Marguerite Dunlap (Victor 45161).

"Whispering Hope," a duet Baker recorded with Olive Kline in the acoustic era (17782), was also cut again by the same two singers in the early days of electric recording (19873). It was backed by a new take of "Abide with Me," also featured on the original disc. The original Kline and Baker record featuring the two hymns was popular despite the availability of "Whispering Hope" on Red Seal (87107) and "Abide with Me" also on Red Seal (87132), both recorded by the duet team of soprano Alma Gluck and contralto Louise Homer. The Kline-Baker electric version remained in the RCA Victor catalog into the 1940s, as did the Kline-Baker duet "I Know a Bank" (4085). Two titles sung by Baker as a solo artist remained available into the 1940s: "Silent Night" (19823) and "He Shall Feed His Flock" (4026) from Handel's *Messiah*.

Despite her considerable success as a recitalist and festival soloist, only a handful of Victor records credited to Elsie Baker featured operatic or oratorio work (an example is "My Heart at Thy Dear Voice" from Saint-Saëns' *Samson and Delilah*, Victor 16192), partly because contralto Louise Homer was a versatile and prolific recording artist for Victor's Red Seal series, working for Victor several years before Baker and continuing into Victor's electric era. The name Elsie Baker does not appear on Victor's acoustic-era Red Seal discs but by mid-1926, a year after the company had converted to electric recording, the company stopped issuing new items in the blue label series, and some Baker records were issued as Red Seal items, such as Coard's "The Gypsy's Warning" backed by Claribel's "Take Back the Heart" (4007). By elevating artists such as Baker, Kline, Richard Crooks, and others to the Red Seal roster in early 1926 (these records in the 4000 and 9000 series sold at first at the same price as old blue label discs, which was about half the price of most Red Seal discs), the company quickly expanded its selection of Red Seal records made by the new electric process.

From Charles Wakefield Cadman's *Shanewis*—the first American opera performed by the Metropolitan Opera Company for two consecutive seasons (the world premiere was on March 23, 1918, with Sophie Braslau as the title character)—Baker recorded "Spring Song of the Robin Woman," a Cheyenne ceremonial song bringing an end to winter, and "Her Shadow." These were issued on blue label electric Victor 45495—curiously, the label for "Her Shadow" fails to state that it is also from the opera. Baker told Phil Miller, one-time head of the Music Division of the New York Public Library, that she considered "Spring Song of the Robin Woman" to be her finest recording. G. Tilden Davis—composer of "By the Mississippi," recorded by Baker for Victor 45489—accompanies her on piano for the *Shanewis* arias.

The 1926 recording of "O Terra Addio," or Tomb Scene, from *Aïda* (1745), featuring Rosa Ponselle and Giovanni Martinelli, includes the voice of Baker in the brief but important role of Amneris (labels merely state,

"Duet with chorus and orchestra"). In the closing seconds of the opera, as the lovers expire, Amneris is heard praying, "Pace, pace . . . pace."

The Victor catalog of 1929 states, "It is probably safe to say that the name of Elsie Baker is familiar in every American home which possesses a talking machine. . . . Her voice is a pure contralto, of enviably smooth, even, rich quality, and her singing might be taken as a model of perfection." By the late 1920s she evidently worked often on radio. Issues of *Musical America* of 1929 list her for various broadcasts—she was featured with a string quartet and a baritone, one Theodore Webb.

She made several recordings in Victor's 24000 series in August 1935. One Baker recording appears to be from 1936. RCA Victor's 1937 Educational Catalog, in the "Songs—Rural Schools" section, shows Victor 25425 as sung by Anna Howard (a nom de disque for Lucy Isabelle Marsh), Ruth Carhart, and Elsie Baker.

She never married. She lived in Manhattan and died there "after a long illness," according to a brief *New York Times* obituary on page 29 of its April 29, 1958, issue. Her funeral was at Rutgers Presbyterian Church Chapel on West 73rd Street on April 30.

Baur, Franklyn (c. 1904-February 24, 1950)

Born in Brooklyn, this tenor was a church and concert singer around the time he began making records. He enjoyed his greatest success as a recording artist in the early years of the microphone, between 1925 and 1930, but he got his start in the business in the acoustic era. He was just out of his teen years when his first Victor recording, "If the Rest of the World Don't Want You" (19243), was cut in late 1923 and issued on February 22, 1924. Other acoustic-era Victor discs of Baur as a solo artist include "You're in Love with Everyone" (19368), "Deep in My Heart" (19378), and "Heart of a Girl" (19495).

He joined the Shannon Quartet in 1923, replacing Charles Hart, who aspired to be an operatic tenor (Hart cut opera arias for Edison around the time he left the quartet and in late 1923 was engaged by the Chicago Civic Grand Opera Company). Baur's voice can be heard on the Shannon's "Stars of the Summer Night" on a Victor disc made around the time of his first session as a solo artist, which suggests that joining the Shannon group paved the way to his solo recording career. Victor 19242, featuring the Shannons (with Baur), has a lower catalog number than Baur's first solo record (19243) but was issued on March 28, a month later than the solo disc. He remained with the quartet until 1927, and the young tenor must have learned much from the older quartet members, who were veteran performers. Likewise, the older members were influenced by Baur.

Charles Hart writes in the December 1958 issue of *Hobbies*, "Baur was instrumental in getting the boys to do jazz numbers and the name was changed in 1925 to the Revelers."

His earliest duet partner was Shannon member Elliott Shaw, who had been working regularly with Charles Hart up to this point. Shaw and Baur began singing vocal refrains on dance band records, such as "Arizona Stars" performed by the Troubadours on January 14, 1924 (Victor 19251). Baur and Shaw recorded duets for Gennett, such as "June Night" and "I Wonder What's Become of Sally" (5514), issued in October 1924. On Gennett 5543, issued in November 1924, Baur's partner is Marcia Freer for "When I Was the Dandy and You Were the Belle."

The tenor added a vocal refrain to "Counting the Days" when recorded by the International Novelty Orchestra on February 15, 1924, for Victor 19277. It was the first of many sessions on which he was vocalist for a Nat Shilkret ensemble.

The second company to issue a Baur record—that is, after Victor—was Columbia, which released "Watchin' the Moon Rise" and "Twilight Rose" on 106-D in June 1924. He would become an increasingly important vocalist for the company, with some numbers issued in 1925 on Columbia's newly launched budget label, Harmony, including "Let Me Call You Sweetheart" (52-H) with baritone Billy Travers (a nom de disque for Shaw).

The Aeolian Company, maker of Vocalion records, was another company that issued Baur titles in the acoustic era, beginning in November 1924 with Cliff Hess's "Beautiful Heaven," backed by another ballad, James Monaco's "I'm Forever Falling in Love with Someone" (14869). He began recording for Brunswick around this time and would become increasingly important to that label.

The September 1927 issue of *Phonograph Monthly Review* features an article about the singer, stating, "His singing career began a little over four years ago—when he was still under twenty!—when he was engaged as soloist at the Park Avenue Baptist Church of New York. . . . He began to make records almost simultaneously, at first for nearly a dozen various companies, then later for the three leading ones alone." The three companies alluded to are Victor, Columbia, and Brunswick.

Pseudonyms for Baur include Irving Post (Puritan), George Bronson (Regal and Banner), Sydney or Sidney Mitchell (Oriole and Banner), Joseph Elliott (National Music Lovers), and Ben Litchfield (Radiex, Grey Gull, and related labels—he was sometimes Charles Dale on these labels, a name used for various singers).

In 1926 his own name could be found on nearly a dozen labels, the three major ones (Victor, Columbia, and Brunswick) along with several minor ones. In January 1926, Gennett issued two titles: "The Lonesomest Girl in Town" backed by "I Wonder (If She Wonders Too)" (3167). In April 1926, "Just Around the Corner" was issued on Regal 8013 as well as Banner 1706, while "California Chimes" was issued on Domino 3673 as well as Banner 1701. Two titles issued on the Domino label in June 1926 are "Why Should I Cry?" (3709) and "Meet Me To-Night in Dreamland" (3711). In July, "Until You're Mine" was issued on Banner 1752 and Domino 3723. In early 1927 he recorded "Meet Me To-Night in Dreamland" for Emerson 7338. For a long period after that Emerson session, he recorded only for the three largest companies.

During his interview for the *Phonograph Monthly Review* article, Baur stated:

The invention of the electrical process was of greater significance than the average layman realizes. Not only are the finished records incomparably better from every standpoint, but the strain on the singer is immeasurably eased. A record can be made in exactly one-third the time it used to take, and no longer is it necessary for us to nearly crack our throats singing into that hated horn. . . . When the electrical system was first introduced, the recording rooms were difficult to sing in since they were "deadened," exactly like the broadcasting studio of today. But the phonograph people have learned some secret the radio does not know, and now the recording studios are no longer absolutely "dead," but are resonant and consequently infinitely easier to sing in.

In the mid-1920s he toured Europe with the Revelers, a new name for the Shannon Quartet. He sang with that group as late as March 25, 1927, for "So Blue" (Victor 20564) but on the reverse side of the disc, "Yankee Rose," Charles Harrison substituted for Baur. Harrison sang as first tenor other times in 1927. Baur recorded only a few times as a Revelers member in 1927, and James Melton replaced him by November—or possibly Harrison had replaced Baur and Melton replaced Harrison. The March 1927 issue of *Talking Machine World* reports that the Revelers, actually using the name Merrymakers, were heard on March 4, 1927, during the Brunswick *Hour of Music* broadcast over the National Broadcasting Company's Blue Network, and it includes a photograph of the singing group. Baur is named as a quartet member and is included in the photograph.

In the *Ziegfeld Follies of 1927*, which ran from August 16, 1927, to January 7, 1928, at the New Amsterdam Theatre, he sang "The Rainbow of Girls" and also, with Irene Delroy, the popular "Maybe It's You." Around this time he was especially busy in Victor's recording studios as a solo artist and dance band vocalist, though he also had Brunswick and Columbia sessions. It appears that his last session was for Victor on December 27, 1929, and his final Victor disc featured "With a Song in My Heart" backed by "Through" (22281), issued in early 1930.

He was the first singer to record selections from Jerome Kern's *Show Boat*. In mid-December, 1927, a few weeks after the show's premiere, he sang vocal refrains on performances by Nat Shilkret and the Victor Orchestra of "Why Do I Love You?" (December 13) and "Can't Help Lovin' Dat Man" (December 15), issued on Victor 21215.

Baur was the original "Voice of Firestone," or first resident soloist on the weekly coast-to-coast radio program that began as *The Firestone Hour* and was later named *The Voice of Firestone*. He was not only a regular on the show but the featured male vocalist on the program's first broadcast on December 3, 1928. His occasional recording partner Vaughn De Leath was the featured female vocalist on that debut broadcast. Sending greetings to listeners, both singers participated in a Firestone anniversary broadcast made on January 6, 1939.

He remained with Firestone until May 26, 1930, which marked the end of the 1929-1930 season. He was then dropped from the program—that is, his contract was not renewed—since Baur had tactlessly demanded his usual performing fee when asked to sing at a company function. Since Baur already earned a large salary from Firestone for his radio work, it had been expected that he would sing at the event without receiving additional compensation. For an unrelated reason the show went off the air for more than a year, returning on September 7, 1931, with other singers in place of Baur, including tenor James Melton and baritone Lawrence Tibbett, the latter remaining with the program until the spring of 1934. In 1934 tenor Richard Crooks, whose recording career also began like Baur's in early 1924, began his longtime association with the radio program.

Despite having a small voice, the ambitious Baur passed up further recording opportunities and radio work to study voice and French art song in Paris for over a year, returning for a recital at Town Hall in New York City on December 4, 1933, during which he performed works by Debussy and others. Critical responses were mixed, which evidently disheartened the singer. Immediately afterward, Baur, still in his twenties, retired from his singing career. He never married. He lived with a sister, Mrs. Marie Kuhlman, and at age forty-six died in the home in which he had been born.

Bernard, Al (November 23, 1888-March 6, 1949)

Alfred A. Bernard was born to Alfred and Katherine Bernard in New Orleans, probably on November 23, 1888 (this date comes from the

ASCAP Biographical Dictionary of 1952; his death certificate cites November 23, 1887). He attended St. Francis School and took a business
course at Jesuit College. His brother Joseph E. Bernard was also an entertainer, first in vaudeville and then in films.

The singer was known as Al Bernard, "the boy from Dixie." In popularizing songs with "blues" in the title, especially W. C. Handy numbers that
would eventually be recognized as classics, he was a pioneering artist. In
1919 he was the first singer to record "St. Louis Blues" and "Beale Street
Blues." In fact, he made his debut as a solo artist with "St. Louis Blues" on
Emerson 9163, issued in May 1919. In other ways he was a throwback to
an earlier era, especially in his use of black dialect and appearing on stage
in blackface. He worked in vaudeville before beginning his recording
career.

His first records were made in early 1919. Around the time he recorded
"St. Louis Blues" for Emerson, he also provided vocal refrains on dance
numbers issued by the Aeolian Company, maker of Aeolian-Vocalion discs.
Bernard sang on dance records cut by the Novelty Five, a Harry A. Yerkes
ensemble. The earliest titles with Bernard contributing a vocal refrain are
"Bluin' the Blues" (12117), "Don't Cry, Frenchy, Don't Cry" (12117),
"Shake, Rattle and Roll" (12124), and "I Want to Hold You in My Arms"
(12135). The first disc to feature Bernard's voice is Aeolian-Vocalion
12117, issued in May, and 12124 and 12135 followed in June. With the
Novelty Five he again cut Handy's "St. Louis Blues," and the rare Aeolian-
Vocalion 12148 was issued in July 1919. In 1919 as a solo artist he recorded
for Aeolian two more of his own compositions: "Sugar" and "Big Chief
Blues," issued on Aeolian-Vocalion 12191 in October.

He recorded for Edison around the time he recorded for the Aeolian
Company, and soon afterward he worked for Emerson, Okeh, and Gennett.
He recorded often for Edison, beginning on February 14, 1919, with
Middleton and Smythe's "Hesitation Blues," issued as Blue Amberol 3738
in June 1919 and Diamond Disc 50524 a month later. It was followed in
July 1919 by two Blue Amberol selections. Blue Amberol 3766 features a
1913 Leroy "Lasses" White composition called "Nigger Blues" (Bernard
later recorded with minstrel entertainer Lasses White for Columbia). Notwithstanding its offensive title, "Nigger Blues" is important for being one
of the first songs labeled "blues" to be published. George O'Connor had
recorded it in 1916 for Columbia.

Blue Amberol 3773 features "I Want to Hold You in My Arms," the
first of many duets by Al Bernard and Ernest Hare. "Nigger Blues" was
issued on Diamond Disc 50542 in August, a month after the Blue Amberol
version was issued. Likewise, "I Want to Hold You in My Arms," written

by J. Russel Robinson, was issued again later (in September) on Diamond Disc 50558.

As a solo artist he recorded the dice song "Shake, Rattle and Roll, Who's Got Me." It was issued in July 1919 on seven-inch Emerson 7503, a rare disc since Emerson stopped production of seven-inch discs at this time (the June issue of the company's trade journal, *Emersonian*, announced that soon all popular titles would be issued on nine-inch discs). A nine-inch Emerson disc from 1919 features "That's the Feller" (9227).

"Shake, Rattle and Roll, Who's Got Me" is also on Okeh 1235, issued in September and backed by Bernard singing Robinson's "Venus Blues," as well as Edison Blue Amberol 3854, released in November. On Gennett 4544, issued in September 1919, Bernard sings "Everybody Wants a Key to My Cellar" on one side while the tenor and the Kansas Jazz Boys perform an Original Dixieland Jazz Band number, "Bluin' the Blues," on the other.

Bernard recorded several Handy songs in this period but recorded "St. Louis Blues" most often. Handy, in his autobiography, *Father of the Blues* (Macmillan, 1941), acknowledges Bernard's help in popularizing it and recounts how Bernard took Handy's letter of recommendation to Thomas Edison, who "liked Al Bernard's test and immediately contracted for this blue song as well as other numbers that might be sung by the young Southerner." Bernard's Edison version was issued as Blue Amberol 3930 in March 1920 (almost a year after Emerson had issued a version) and then Diamond Disc 50620. When the company issued Bernard's Blue Amberol version, promotional literature stated that the song "is one of the real originals of the many songs of this character that have recently been greatly in demand." Accompanied by Carl Fenton's Orchestra, he sang it in late 1920 for Brunswick (2062).

He was the first to cut "Frankie and Johnny" successfully for an American record company (Gene Greene recorded it in London for Pathé in 1912), issued by Brunswick with "Memphis Blues" on the reverse side.

Bernard was often paired with Ernest Hare before that baritone teamed up with Billy Jones. The December 1919 issue of the Edison trade journal *Along Broadway* states that the two entertainers lived in Henri Court in New York City, Bernard's apartment above Hare's. "You're My Gal" (Diamond Disc 50607; Blue Amberol 3893), performed by Bernard and Hare, was written by Bernard, as was "See Old Man Moon Smile" (Blue Amberol 3881), issued in December 1919. Jim Walsh notes that Bernard and Hare were called Jack Clare and Frank Mann on Pathé, Skeeter Sims and Henry Jones on Regal.

One of Bernard's 1920 Brunswick releases is in the company's semi-prestigious purple label 5000 series: "Mississippi Bound," backed by the Al Bernard-Ernest Hare duet "Henry Jones" (5016), written by Bernard.

He recorded duets with Vernon Dalhart, including "I've Got My Habits On," issued on Edison Diamond Disc 50868 in 1921, and "I Want My Mammy," issued on Columbia A3520 in February 1922. They also cut "I've Got My Habits On" for Royal 10141, using the names Dalbert and Banning.

He made his Victor debut with "You Know What I Mean" backed by "Bell Hop Blues" (18644), issued in March 1920. During two sessions in 1921, on May 21 and June 7, he sang vocal refrains on four numbers recorded by the Original Dixieland Jazz Band, three of which were issued: "St. Louis Blues" (18772), "Royal Garden Blues" (18798), and "Dangerous Blues" (18798). Bernard provided a vocal refrain for "Satanic Blues" but it was rejected. He again sang a vocal refrain for "Dangerous Blues" when it was recorded by Bennie Krueger in mid-1921 for Brunswick 2109 (this would be, along with Mamie Smith's version on Okeh 4351, one of the earliest issued versions of the Spencer Williams song). Krueger also used Bernard for a vocal refrain on "Crazy Blues" (Brunswick 2077).

Bernard and pianist-composer-singer J. Russel Robinson formed a performing act called the Dixie Stars. The Record Boys featured Bernard, Robinson, and Kamplain (Sam Stept sometimes substituted for Robinson). Bernard and Robinson wrote some songs together from 1919 onward, Robinson composing the music, Bernard supplying lyrics. Bernard and Robinson's "Let Me Be the First to Kiss You Good-Morning" was cut by Jack Chapman and His Drake Hotel Orchestra on November 8, 1924 for Victor 19519. "Sam Jones Blues," written by Bernard, Robinson, and Roy Turk, was recorded by Bessie Smith on September 24, 1923 for Columbia 13005-D.

Page 75 of the October 1924 issue of *Talking Machine World* announced that the Dixie Stars had made their first Brunswick record, adding:

These two artists are not new to the recording game, Al Bernard having long been known to record fans through his records of negro dialect songs. Russell Robinson was for years the accompanist of Marion Harris, also a Brunswick artist and vaudeville headliner. The Dixie Stars . . . will appear during the next ten months at all the broadcasting stations.

Bernard also wrote songs with others, including Walter Haenschen, also known as Carl Fenton. Bernard wrote the lyrics for "Read 'em and Weep," Haenschen the music. Bernard, Jules Levy, and Paul Crane wrote "Spread

Yo' Stuff," recorded in 1921 by Daisy Martin for Gennett 4712. In 1923, Bernard's "Stavin' Change" was recorded by the Original Indiana Five for Perfect 14173 and by the Virginians for Victor 19189. Bernard and Jimmy Durante wrote "Papa String Bean" in 1923.

A rare twelve-inch disc from 1925 is Okeh 7002, credited to Al Bernard Minstrels. The selections—simply called "Part I" and "Part II"—were arranged by Justin Ring, Okeh's musical director. It was one of a dozen twelve-inch discs issued in Okeh's 7000 series, which featured early country artists such as Kelly Harrell, Fiddlin' John Carson, and Henry Whitter's Virginia Breakdowners. The exceptions are Conway's Band on Okeh 7001 and Bernard's minstrel company on Okeh 7002.

He had many sessions for the Grey Gull Record Company—maker of Grey Gull, Madison, Radiex, and other discs—between 1924 and 1930, when the company stopped production. Bernard covered a wide range of material—Tin Pan Alley, minstrel, even hillbilly. Inspired by Vernon Dalhart's success with hillbilly material, he cut such songs as "Little Brown Jug" (4093), "New River Train" (4150), "Cowboy's Lament" (4173), and "Oh Dem Golden Slippers" (4209). On some discs more authentic country singers were on the reverse of the Bernard side—an example is Gene Autry (as "Sam Hill") singing "Yodelin' Bill" on Grey Gull 4304. Bernard had a series of "Rufus Green" rural comic monologues on Grey Gull in the late 1920s.

In 1919 he married actress Gertrude Anderson. Late in life he lived at 305 West 45th Street in New York City. He died on March 6 in Manhattan's St. Clare's Hospital and was survived by his wife and two daughters. He was buried on March 9 in the Gate of Heaven Cemetery at Mt. Pleasant, New York. Some sources indicate he died on March 9, but Walsh, after examining a copy of Bernard's death certificate, corrected this in the March 1974 issue of *Hobbies*.

Borbee's "Jass" Orchestra

Led by pianist Ernest Borbee, this was among the earliest recording ensembles characterized as a "jass" group, the third after an Original Dixieland Jazz Band (ODJB) disc was issued in March 1917 by Victor and a Wilbur C. Sweatman and His Jass Band disc was issued in May 1917 by Pathé (the fourth group identified on records as a jass ensemble was Frisco "Jass" Band, an Edison group led by Rudy Wiedoeft). Though Columbia's first so-called jass group, Borbee's musicians in fact played dance music in a genteel fashion typical of its time. This was not the boisterous music of the ODJB, Sweatman, Earl Fuller, or others who played jass in this period.

The orchestra made its recording debut on February 14, 1917 with Josephine Vail's "It's a Long, Long Time" (a fox trot) and Harry Von Tilzer's "Just the Kind of a Girl You'd Love to Make Your Wife" (a one-step), issued on Columbia A2233 in July 1917. Columbia's next jass record was issued weeks later, on August 10. This was the Original Dixieland Jazz Band's sole disc made for the American company (A2297), featuring "Indiana" and "Darktown Strutters' Ball," cut on May 31, 1917.

Brian Rust's *American Dance Band Discography* gives the name Borbee's Tango Orchestra because Columbia files show that the band recorded as the Tango Orchestra at its first session. However, the label for Columbia A2233 gives the name as Borbee's "Jass" Orchestra. The band was evidently renamed a "jass orchestra" at the time of the disc's release to take advantage of the ODJB's success—both as a live act at Reisenweber's and also as a Victor recording ensemble—and the craze for the new dance music. It is unlikely that Borbee's musicians knew, when recording in mid-February, that they would be identified as jass musicians when their debut record was issued in July. In July Columbia also issued Prince's Band performing the Von Holstein and Sanders' hit "Hong Kong," identified on records as a "Jazz One-Step," probably the first time that "jazz"—as opposed to "jass"—appears on a label. Clearly Columbia executives wanted to exploit the jazz craze but had not successfully recorded any jass artists in early 1917. The ODJB had auditioned for Columbia in late January—it does not appear that the band recorded any numbers at that time.

On August 17, 1917, Borbee's "Jass" Orchestra recorded two additional titles for Columbia, "Paddle-Addle" (identified as a fox trot) and "The Ragtime Volunteers Are Off to War" (a one-step), issued as A2363 in November.

Rust's *Jazz Records 1897-1942* reports that Ernest Borbee recorded two titles as a member of the Original Georgia Five in 1923. For two of the five titles recorded by this band, the Original Georgia Five merely accompanies featured vocalist Arthur Hall. Borbee is otherwise an obscure figure. In *Jazz: The American Theme Song* (Oxford University Press, 1993), James Lincoln Collier states, "In view of some sixty years of grousing over the fact that a white group has the honor of making the first jazz record, it is worth noting that a black group, Borbee's 'Jass' Orchestra, was the first to *issue* a record with the word 'jazz' on it; the Borbee group, however, was by no means a jazz band." Actually, the word "jass" is on the label, not "jazz." Also, Borbee's Columbia disc was issued months after the Original Dixieland Jazz Band's first Victor disc (18255) was released in mid-April 1917 (Victor quickly placed this jass disc on the market, eager to take advantage of the ODJB's popularity at Reisenweber's). A photograph in Columbia's

September 1919 catalog of Borbee's "Jass" Orchestra (shown are five musicians—violin, piano, two banjos, and drums) establishes that the musicians were white.

Broderick, George H. (May 6, 1855-May 10, 1905)

Born in Philadelphia, Broderick was a noted bass singer of the 1880s and 1890s. He traveled to Europe with the Mapleson Opera Company. In 1885 he was Pooh-bah in the first American production of Gilbert and Sullivan's *The Mikado*, and his wife, Emma Mabelle Broderick, sang the principal contralto role of Katisha. He sang in other Gilbert and Sullivan light operas in New York, including *Ruddigore* and *The Yeomen of the Guard*.

Broderick had a bass voice of great beauty and power. He is featured on fourteen two-minute Edison Standard cylinders, two of them being recitations recorded in 1900: Thomas Buchanan Read's "Sheridan's Ride" (7694) and Rudyard Kipling's "Absent-Minded Beggar" (7649). The Kipling work was also recorded by Broderick for an Edison Concert cylinder (B359). He recorded twenty-three Concert (five-inch diameter) brown wax cylinders.

The first numbered record of the Consolidated Talking Machine Company—soon to be the Victor Talking Machine Company—features Broderick reciting Eugene Field's poem "Departure." Broderick recorded two takes of "Departure" on June 28, 1900, and at least one of these takes was issued when Eldridge R. Johnson, the company's owner, released his first batch of records, all seven inch, around August 1900. The disc is assigned catalog number A-1 (its matrix is also A-1). Records issued in this first batch of releases were the first ever to feature paper labels (Lioret had used them on the sides of celluloid cylinders earlier, and five-inch Berliners in Europe made from around 1889 to 1893 had rectangular labels on the back).

These early Victor discs state, "Improved Gram-o-phone Record, Manufactured by the Consolidated Talking Machine Company, Phil. PA." (The "Improved" probably refers to Johnson's new method of cutting masters in wax, instead of the zinc that Berliner used.) Johnson had not yet adopted the word "Victor" for his company. By November 1900 pressings of A-1 featured a newly designed label, with the words "Improved Record" prominent at the top and no reference to "Gram-o-phone." Takes 3 and 4 were recorded on November 3, 1900, and Take 3 was also issued on disc A-1 for later pressings (probably in 1901), possibly Take 4 also.

That Johnson's first numbered record features a recitation is not surprising since this was an era when reciting verse—on the vaudeville stage, at dinner parties—was commonplace. Johnson's employment of Broderick was natural given the fact that Broderick had been recording for Berliner at least as early as March 10, 1900, and that Johnson's company evolved from Berliner's. The fourteen titles Broderick recorded for Berliner consist of operatic arias ("Mephisto's Serenade" from Gounod's *Faust,* 01063), light opera numbers ("Gypsy Love Song" from Victor Herbert's *The Fortune Teller,* 01257), bass standards ("Down Deep Within the Cellar," 01053), and various popular songs of the day ("A Dream of Paradise," 01073). His interpretation of "Simon the Cellarer" (01064) reveals a flair for comedy.

What is unusual is that Johnson used Broderick primarily for recitations. With the possible exception of the rare "Yarn of the Dates" (01072—if this is a true yarn, it is recited), he had recorded no recitations for Berliner, a company that employed others for speaking performances, including Len Spencer, George Graham, David C. Bangs, John Terrell, and Russell Hunting. George Graham and William F. Hooley recorded several in late 1899. Paul Charosh's *Berliner Gramophone Records: American Issues, 1892-1900* (Greenwood Press, 1995) shows three recitations being recorded for the company in 1900, two by Press Eldridge and one by George Graham.

Broderick recorded nineteen separate titles for Johnson in five sessions, beginning on May 1, 1900, and ending on June 28, 1900. He returned once more, on November 3, 1900, to record new takes of previously recorded titles.

Whether the idea to record "Departure" was suggested by Johnson and his associates, or whether Broderick suggested it because it was in his performing repertoire, is impossible to say. The poem might have been chosen for recording purposes because of its brevity, ideal for a seven-inch disc. The recording lasts ninety-eight seconds. Johnson probably was familiar with Berliner recordings of "Departure." George Graham recorded it on June 17, 1896 (646) and again on November 5, 1899 (0704).

Most of his recordings for Johnson were made at a time when Johnson actually worked for Berliner. The Consolidated Talking Machine Company had not yet been formed.

Broderick's recitation of "Departure" was not his earliest recorded performance to be issued by Johnson's company. Some takes recorded during Broderick's earliest recording session for Johnson, on May 1, 1900, ended up on seven-inch discs with significantly higher numbers than A-1, including his renditions of "Friar of Orders Grey" (A-139) and de Koven's "The Armorer's Song" (A-141).

Moreover, Broderick performances were not the earliest to be issued by Johnson. The earliest recorded performance issued by Johnson appears to be on A-2, which features George Graham performing "The Colored Preacher," cut on May 14, 1900. Dan Quinn made a recording for Johnson as early as January 30, 1900 ("She Knew a Lobster When She Saw One") but it was not issued.

Why Johnson recorded Broderick in May 1900—a time when Emile Berliner's disc company was strong—is open to speculation. Frank Seaman would not file for the injunction that brought the Berliner company to a halt until June 25. S. H. Dudley recorded "The Colonel" (0929), from the show *Whirl-i-gig*, for Berliner on January 30, the day that Quinn recorded for Johnson. It is possible that the recordings were made at the same location, with Dudley recording during one part of the day and Quinn during another, but it is more likely they were made at different locations. Johnson did much experimentation, probably with Berliner's full support since only through experimentation could recording and playback technology be improved. Johnson's experiments could hardly have been a secret because he used many artists who worked regularly for Berliner. But it would not be surprising if Johnson's patent lawyer knew more about Johnson's experiments than Berliner.

That "Departure" is A-1 does not necessarily mean Johnson viewed it as better or more significant than other recordings available at the time. "Departure" may have become A-1 by a random process of assigning takes with release numbers, that process being unknown today. On the other hand, "Departure" was possibly selected for A-1 because the poem is about a young man saying farewell to his parents, the implication being that he is starting a new life (the opportunity for sound effects—a train whistling and moving on tracks—must have appealed to those making the recording). Here is a possible analogy to Johnson's new business venture, though it seems unlikely that the choice of "Departure" for A-1 has a special meaning. It was written by the now largely forgotten American writer Eugene Field, a newspaper man who wrote verse as well as stories. Although he died in Chicago on November 4, 1895, his work remained enormously popular at the turn of the century. However, Field's sentimental "Departure" was not well-known in 1900 and the twelve-volume set *The Writings in Prose and Verse of Eugene Field*, published by Scribner's, has no poem by this name. It may have been one of his uncollected newspaper verses or an excerpt from a longer work.

In the opening announcement, Johnson's company is not mentioned, although most other companies at this time used spoken announcements for company identification. Announcements on the earliest Zon-o-phones say "for the Zon-o-phone," with later ones saying "Zon-o-phone record!" But Johnson followed Berliner's practice of stating only title and performer. Spoken announcements on Berliners never mention the name "Berliner."

The following is a transcription of Johnson's first disc, featuring Broderick:

Eugene Field's poem "Departure"
Rendered by George Broderick

Well, Bill, shake hands and say goodbye
'Afore you go away
We hate to see you leave us
We'd much rather have you stay

Mother and me's gettin' old
We can't be with you long
She's been failing for some time now
And will never be as strong as she was
'Afore the ague laid her up so long in bed
And more than likely when you get back
You'll find your mother dead

Her cold lips were quivering
When you went to say goodbye
And tears splashed on her pillow
When she asked you to try
And be a good boy for her sake,
Bill, when you get far away
We hate to see you leave us
We'd much rather have you stay

[*Train whistle*]

Well, Bill, your train's a-comin'
Here's some stuff the children sent
Driftwood more than likely
And me and mother went
And had our pictures took
So as to give you one
To remember us by in the years
When we'll be dead and gone

And here's a little Bible mother sent to give to you
We didn't have much money
But I reckon it will do as well
As if we weren't poor
And had more change to spare
So take it, Bill, with mother's love
And try to keep it
Where it'll always be the handiest
When you get far away

We hate to see you go, Bill
We'd much rather have you stay
[*Sound of a train departing*]
Good-bye, Bill!
God bless him!

Johnson's recording career seems to have lasted less than a year, beginning and ending in 1900. He recorded for Edison, Berliner, Zon-o-phone,
and Johnson's fledgling Consolidated Talking Machine Company. Late in
1900 he moved to his wife's hometown of Aurora, Illinois, which ended
his recording work. But he continued to appear in stage productions with
great success. He was soloist for four years in Christ Episcopal Church in
Chicago. He suddenly took ill four weeks before his death. He died of
pneumonia at 3:40 a.m. on Wednesday, May 10, 1905, at his home. His
niece was Helen Broderick, a well-known film actress. Helen's son was
Broderick Crawford, a TV and film actor.

Burr, Henry (January 15, 1882-April 6, 1941)

This tenor was incredibly popular as a solo artist and was also important as a member of various duos, trios, and quartets. He probably recorded more selections than any other singer of the acoustic era. Not
surprisingly for one who recorded thousands of titles, he was remarkably
versatile. He was as deft with an upbeat tune such as "I Didn't Raise My
Boy to Be a Soldier," sung with the Peerless Quartet (Columbia A1697),
as with a sentimental favorite such as "In the Shade of the Old Apple
Tree." He won fame for singing the latter type of material.

He was born Harry Haley McClaskey in St. Stephen, New Brunswick,
Canada—the town is on the St. Croix River opposite Calais, Maine. He
was raised at 10 Armstrong Street. In 1895, at age thirteen, he was known
well enough as a boy tenor to appear with the St. John Artillery Band at the
opening of the city's annual Exposition. He attended Mt. Allison Academy

at Sackville, New Brunswick. His father, Alfred McClaskey, was a candy and tobacco dealer.

His first important concert was on April 14, 1901, when he appeared at the St. John Opera House with Scottish soprano Jessie McLachlan (she made some Berliner discs in Glasgow in September 1899 and other records in England in late 1903—early literature about Burr misspelled the name as "Maclachlan").

On September 30, 1901, Metropolitan Opera baritone Giuseppe Campanari arrived in McClaskey's part of Canada to perform at the St. John Opera House. Asked to listen to McClaskey's beautiful voice, Campanari—who afterward became a recording artist for Victor, Columbia, and Edison—insisted that the young man go to New York for musical training. The singer quit working at his father's business and traveled to New York for further voice instruction. While a student, McClaskey rose to the position of tenor soloist with the Grace Methodist Episcopal Church choir. Promotional literature reprinted in Ronald Dethlefson's *Edison Blue Amberol Recordings 1912-1914* states that the singer (called Irving Gillette on Edison records) "toured Canada in Scotch repertoire. For the last ten years [he] has been tenor soloist at the Church of the Incarnation, New York."

Henry studied with noted teacher John Dennis Meehan (sometimes spelled Mehan) and later Ellen Burr. He adopted the latter's name in tribute when he began making Columbia records.

Burr began his recording career with Columbia in 1902 or 1903. At this time the company did massive rerecording to take advantage of improved technology. Some Columbia discs bearing Burr's name have master numbers suggesting that they were made in 1901, but the Burr performances were remakes of numbers originally sung in 1901 by others. Tim Brooks reports that the earliest master that seems to be originally by Burr is 1351, "My Dreams," from mid-1903. In 1903 he recorded a song associated with Lillian Russell from the popular show *Twirly-Whirly*, "Come Down Ma Evenin' Star" (Columbia disc 1405 and cylinder 32174; Mina Hickman had earlier recorded this for Columbia disc 955), and he cut Neil Moret's popular "Hiawatha" (disc 1406; cylinder 32175). Another successful early Columbia disc was "The Holy City" (60). Harry Macdonough is on the earliest pressings of "The Holy City," Albert Campbell on some later pressings, and Burr on still later pressings though the Burr recording was made early enough to feature a spoken announcement (J. W. Myers also recorded "The Holy City" for the company but this version was issued as Columbia 149).

None of his Victor discs open with spoken announcements since by mid-1903—more than a year before Burr's debut with the company—Victor had discontinued the practice of opening performances with announcements. Columbia used announcements for a longer period, and Columbia discs made early enough to feature Burr's own spoken announcements include "Old Folks at Home" (174), "Ben Bolt" (208), "Absence Makes the Heart Grow Fonder" (221), "My Old Kentucky Home" (320), "For All Eternity" (846), and "Silver Threads Among the Gold" (1810).

His earliest record for Edison's National Phonograph Company was Standard 8827, issued in November 1904. The Edison company consistently used the pseudonym Irving Gillette for the tenor, and some other companies used this name at times, including Columbia and Rex. The October 1904 issue of *Edison Phonograph Monthly* states, "'Shine On, Oh Stars' is a ballad of the higher order in which Irving Gillette makes his bow to the Phonograph public. Mr. Gillette has a cultivated voice of a fine tenor quality as all who hear this Record will admit." At this time Edison also issued Irving Gillette on Standard 8853, "The Star of Bethlehem."

For the next few years, the Edison company issued Gillette cylinders regularly. Although he became increasingly popular, he worked less often for the company by the time the company marketed Diamond Disc and Blue Amberol products. As a solo artist, Burr was issued on only one Diamond Disc: "Sing Me the Rosary" (80132). The team of Campbell and Gillette was issued on several Blue Amberols but not on Diamond Discs. After a disagreement with Edison executives (Jim Walsh believed that the dispute was about how much Burr should be paid), Burr never sang for that firm again. The final Gillette recording for Edison was "When the Angelus Is Ringing" (Blue Amberol 2428), issued in October 1914. At this time the final Campbell and Gillette duet on Blue Amberol was issued: Fisher's "When It's Moonlight on the Alamo" (2422).

His first Victor session was on January 4, 1905, and two performances from that session were issued in March: "Loch Lomond" (single-sided 4240, later issued on double-sided 16062—Burr redid this for Victor in early 1919) and "Daddy" (single-sided 4239; Burr redid it on February 24, 1909, and this was issued on double-sided 16314). His next Victor session was four months later, on April 7, and especially popular from this session was Van Alstyne's "In the Shade of the Old Apple Tree" (single-sided 4338; Burr redid it for Victor on June 5, 1908—decades later one of the Victor takes was issued on Montgomery Ward M-8128, falsely labeled "electrically recorded"). Months earlier, Burr had recorded this for Edison, and this wax cylinder (8958), issued in April 1905, sold well. Burr enjoyed success with other Van Alstyne compositions, including "Won't You Come Over to My House" and "Old Pal."

Victor valued Burr in early sessions for singing airs of Scotland. In the three Victor sessions of 1905, he recorded, along with "Loch Lomond," the songs "Ye Banks and Braes o' Bonnie Doon" (4426), "John Anderson, My Jo" (4557), and "Scots, Wha' Hae' wi' Wallace Bled" (4558).

Burr was on virtually all American labels of the acoustic era, including the early disc labels Talk-o-phone, Imperial, Busy Bee, Eagle, and American. The July 1906 Zon-o-phone catalog shows Burr singing "Please Come and Play in My Yard" (21) and the popular "Teasing" (24). As a solo artist he made a couple dozen U-S Everlasting cylinders. He cut duets for that company with not only Albert Campbell but John H. Meyer, who used the pseudonym John Wilbur.

Burr was successful from the onset, becoming especially important to Columbia around the time that the career of a once-prolific tenor—George J. Gaskin—was in rapid decline. Burr served Columbia in the early years of the century much as Harry Macdonough served Victor. Both were tenors whose performances of ballads such as "Absence Makes the Heart Grow Fonder" sold well, as did their records of hymns. In 1905 the *Talking Machine News*, a trade journal published in London, praised one of Burr's gospel hymns and added, "We count Mr. Burr one of the foremost recorders of today."

He was a member, with Frank C. Stanley and Elise Stevenson, of the Metropolitan Trio and the Manhattan Mixed Trio.

Around 1903, Burr replaced second tenor James K. Reynard in the Columbia Quartet, which then also consisted of first tenor Albert Campbell, baritone Joe Belmont, and bass Joe Majors. Belmont and Majors left around the time Reynard did, so for a few years after 1903 the quartet was Campbell, Burr, baritone Steve Porter, and bass Frank C. Stanley. In late 1906 the quartet began recording for other companies in addition to Columbia, and called itself the Peerless Quartet, which became probably the most successful vocal group of the acoustic era, with only the American Quartet rivaling at times the Peerless in popularity. Until his sudden death of pneumonia in late 1910, bass Frank C. Stanley managed the quartet. Burr then managed the group.

For several years, after Stanley's death the Peerless consisted of Albert Campbell, Henry Burr, Arthur Collins (who replaced Porter in 1909 when that baritone joined the American Quartet), and John H. Meyer (Stanley's replacement). Campbell reported to Jim Walsh that Collins finally left (probably in early 1919) because the baritone and Burr could no longer get along. Collins sometimes sang lead on Peerless recordings, which added variety to the quartet's records, but after Collins left, Burr sang lead on nearly all Peerless recordings. Frank Croxton joined the Peerless soon after Collins' departure, taking the bass part. John H. Meyer, who had been singing bass, assumed the baritone part. The American Quartet had been going through changes in personnel around this time, and from 1920 onward the Peerless and American quartets were identical aside from second tenor Burr in the Peerless and second tenor Billy Murray in the American.

When the Peerless members worked as a minstrel troupe on records, Burr played a stuttering minstrel and was addressed by the other performers as "Harry," his real first name. Labels did not actually use the Peerless name, but the four quartet members made many minstrel records, especially from 1908 to 1913. Typical examples are "Virginia Minstrels" on Victor 35095, "North Carolina Minstrels" on Victor 35307, and "Missouri Minstrels" on Victor 35321.

From around 1906 to 1910, Burr cut many duets with Stanley, who had earlier used tenor Byron G. Harlan as a recording partner—presumably the success of Collins and Harlan brought an end to pairings of Harlan and Stanley. In the 1909-1910 period, Edison issued a new Stanley and Gillette duet almost every month. A couple of years after Stanley's death in late 1910, Burr made several Columbia recordings with Edgar Stoddard, who was really baritone Andrea Sarto. One successful duet was "There's a Girl in the Heart of Maryland" (A1360). Sarto's real name was used on a later duet with Burr: " 'Cross the Great Divide" (A1480).

After Stanley's death, Burr also began working regularly with fellow tenor Campbell, and for over a decade the team of Campbell and Burr enjoyed a popularity matched by few other duos of the acoustic era (years earlier they had cut a duet—"While the Old Mill Wheel Is Turning" was issued on Columbia 3453 in October 1906, then reissued on A588). Notable performances include "Take Me to Roseland, My Beautiful Rose" (Victor 17339), "Piney Ridge" (Columbia A1827), "Always Take a Girl Named Daisy" (Victor 17438), "Carry Me Back to My Carolina Home" (Victor 18975), "Those Days Are Over" (Victor 18877), "Angel Child" (Victor 18903), and "At the End of the Road" (Victor 19530). The final Campbell-Burr duet recording appears to be "I Need Thee Every Hour," made in the early months of electric recording, probably on July 2, 1925 (Burr and Campbell were in Victor's Camden studio on this day as members of the Peerless Quartet and Sterling Trio). The new take of "I Need Thee Every Hour" was issued on Victor 19884, replacing their old take of the Lowry hymn on Victor 16255.

Campbell and Burr normally recorded sentimental numbers. Unusual for the duo was "Theda Bara, I'll Keep Away from You," issued on Pathé 20021 in late 1916. They were the only artists to record this song about the silent film star, whose real name was Theodosia Goodman. She became famous as a "vamp" in the 1915 motion picture *A Fool There Was*.

Burr recorded duets with many other artists such as Elise Stevenson, Ada Jones, Helen Clark, Marcia Freer, Jean Sterling, Frank Croxton, and John H. Meyer. Despite a long association, Burr recorded with Billy Murray only one duet issued in the United States: "I Wonder Where My Baby Is Tonight?" It was recorded on December 12, 1925. The label of Victor 19864 calls the performance a "duet with piano" but adds that Burr and Murray are "assisted" by tenor Carl Mathieu (the reverse side features the tenor who was quickly eclipsing Murray and Burr in popularity—Gene Austin). In 1919, during a Canadian tour, Burr and Murray harmonized beautifully in a studio on "They're All Sweeties," issued only on Canadian Victor 216068. In 1926 Burr and Murray worked together on "My Dream of the Big Parade" (Victor 20098) but they do not sing together—Murray provides a recitation and Burr sings as a member of the Peerless.

On November 18, 1913, Campbell and Burr joined Will Oakland to record the successful "I'm On My Way to Mandalay" (Victor 17503). It is probably the first time that a record was made of three tenors (Oakland was a countertenor). On June 24, 1914, they cut an additional three titles for Victor. Labels identify the trio as "Oakland-Campbell-Burr."

The popular Sterling Trio, consisting of Meyer, Campbell and Burr, recorded for many labels from 1916 to mid-1920, then exclusively for Victor from late 1920 to 1925. The trio's final Victor disc was issued in October, 1925: "Down Deep in an Irishman's Heart" (19749). It was backed by Burr singing "Sweet Little Mother of Mine." When Burr, as manager of the Peerless Quartet, dropped Campbell and Meyer in the fall of 1925, the latter two singers took the name The Sterling Trio and made recordings for Gennett in 1926, using another tenor instead of Burr. The new Peerless Quartet consisted of first tenor Carl Mathieu (1894-1973), second tenor Burr, baritone James Stanley (1881-1963), and bass Stanley Baughman (1892-1963). This was the Quartet featured with the Eight Popular Victor Artists that toured from 1926 until it disbanded around 1928.

In late 1910 the Columbia Phonograph Company issued a ten-inch "Special Demonstration Double-Disc." The label of the record, which has no catalog number, states, "This Record is NOT For Sale." The company charged dealers ten cents for each copy, supposedly to cover handling expenses, and dealers were authorized to give away copies "free of charge except the incidental costs of packing and delivery." One side features the Columbia Male Quartette singing Geibel's "Kentucky Babe" with Burr as second tenor (this was also issued on Columbia A866), and Frank C.

Stanley spoke on the other side, praising the quality of Columbia's double-sided records, which had been introduced to the trade two years earlier.

In late 1913, the newly named Columbia Graphophone Company issued a second demonstration record though this time the word "demonstration" is not on the label. Instead, the label states "Special Price for Advertising Purposes only," and a price of twenty-five cents is boldly printed to the right of the spindle hole. This is among the most common discs featuring Burr. One side features solo artist Burr singing J. C. Macey's "Good Night, Little Girl, Good Night," the reverse side featuring an unidentified man giving a briefer version of Stanley's 1910 talk. He states about the Burr performance, "The other side of this sample Columbia record affords the best possible evidence of the quality of Columbia recordings."

When the Pathé Freres Phonograph Company, which was the American branch of the French firm Pathé Freres Compagnie, began recording in the United States in the spring or summer of 1914, Burr sang for the company, using the name Irving Gillette. Early Pathé discs featuring Burr have etched labels instead of paper. An example is Pathé 5015, featuring "The Song That Stole My Heart Away" and "In the Heart of the City That Has No Heart" (Burr cut the latter song for other companies in 1914). Until becoming exclusive to Victor in mid-1920, he worked steadily for the Pathé company, his real name—"Harry McClaskey"—often given on labels.

Burr was issued on many small-diameter discs of the World War I period. Although seven-inch discs had been common when discs were first marketed, they had been phased out by 1906, ten-inch discs becoming standard for popular music. The Little Wonder Record Company of New York, founded by Henry Waterson of the music publishing firm Waterson, Berlin and Snyder, introduced single-sided 5½ inch discs in October 1914. Short in musical duration (they play for about a minute and a half), they sold for ten cents. The first Little Wonder featured Henry Burr singing the 1848 song "Ben Bolt." He had recorded this over a decade earlier as a Columbia artist, with that early recording featuring piano accompaniment. On the Little Wonder disc, Burr is backed by an orchestra. Little Wonder discs were pressed by Columbia but songs were recorded specially for Little Wonder release. Singing solo and as a member of duos, trios, and quartets, Burr was on more Little Wonder releases than any other singer.

Victor most often used the name Henry Burr for the tenor but sometimes identified him as Harry McClaskey. Columbia used the name Burr most often but also used the names Irving Gillette (usually for duets with female singers, including Ada Jones, Helen Clark, and Frances Fisher) and Harry McClaskey (not surprisingly, this was used for some songs with

Irish themes, such as "The Lament of the Irish Emigrant" and "What an Irishman Means by 'Machree'"). Most companies issued the tenor as Burr, but Allan Sutton's *A Guide to Pseudonyms on American Records, 1892-1942* (Greenwood Press, 1993) lists these other pseudonyms: Henry Gillette (Crescent), Alfred Alexander (Pathé), Shamus McClaskey (Emerson), Robert Rice (Emerson), Harry Barr (Harmony), Frank Knapp (Harmony), Harry Haley (Banner and Cameo—"Haley" was the tenor's middle name), and Al King (Oriole).

In mid-1916 Burr formed with Fred Van Eps the Paroquette Record Manufacturing Company, which beginning in December 1916 released etch-label double-faced Par-o-ket records. These seven-inch discs sold for twenty-five cents (thirty cents "in the West," thirty-five in Canada). Advertisements advised that the records "should be played with sapphire needles to secure the best results" and "should be played at a speed of 80 revolutions per minute." The company also made and sold attachments that allowed the records to be played on machines designed to play only lateral-cut records. Artists included Rogers' Military Band, Campbell and Burr (sometimes singing as "Webster and Gillette"), Collins and Harlan, Louise and Ferera, John H. Meyer, and the Van Eps Banjo Band. Burr naturally recorded many titles for the company, sometimes as Irving Gillette, but he continued to record heavily for other companies as well.

The company's business office was at 47 West 34th Street, New York City. Page 76 of the January 1917 issue of *Talking Machine World* reports, "The company's factory and laboratory are located in the Bush Terminal Building, Brooklyn, NY, and although 6,500 square feet of space have been occupied for some months past, it has been found necessary to considerably enlarge the general manufacturing facilities . . ."

To run the Par-o-ket laboratory, Burr and Van Eps turned to John Kaiser, an associate with much experience in the industry. In the late 1890s Kaiser managed the New York brown wax cylinder firm Harms, Kaiser and Hagen; he made recordings, notably "Casey" monologues, for a few companies from the mid-1890s through the turn of the century; and beginning around 1909 he helped manage the U.S. Phonograph Company, maker of U-S Everlasting cylinders. Walter B. Rogers, after several years working as Victor's musical director, served as Paroquette's musical director. The company recorded and pressed its own records.

Related to Par-o-ket records were blue-labeled Angelophone Record discs. As the name suggests, a hymn is on each seven-inch Angelophone disc, the reverse side having an etched label and featuring a spoken "Hymn Talk." Perhaps all titles were sung by Burr himself. One example is #63, "How Can I Keep from Singing?"—Burr is curiously identified as a baritone.

Few machines were equipped to play these vertical-cut records, so it is not surprising that the Paroquette firm soon suspended operations. The December 1917 issue of *Talking Machine World* is the last issue to list new Par-o-ket releases. The May 1918 issue of the trade journal announced a public auction of the firm's assets, including 30,000 Par-o-ket discs, to be held in Brooklyn on May 22.

Burr was briefly a music publisher. The January 1919 issue of *Talking Machine World* reports:

> The talking machine trade will be interested to know that Henry Burr . . . has organized the Henry Burr Music Corp., with offices at 1604 Broadway, New York. Associated with Mr. Burr is Lieutenant Gitz-Rice, the very successful song writer who has recently been responsible for "Keep Your Head Down, Fritzie Boy," and other hits.

The formation of the short-lived company was also noted in the *New York Dramatic Mirror*. Burr helped write at least one song that was recorded by a major company. "Stand Up and Sing for Your Father an Old Time Tune," sung by Billy Murray in 1921 for Victor 18784, is credited to Henry Burr and Ray Perkins. According to surviving concert programs, Perkins wrote the words and music of the "Opening Chorus" used by the Eight Famous Victor Artists in the early 1920s when they performed before audiences.

For the first two decades of Burr's recording career he sang for virtually every record company. In late 1920, when he was arguably at the height of his career, Burr became exclusive to a company for the first time. Page 62 of the November 1920 issue of *Talking Machine World* states:

> Of great interest to all Victor dealers and Victor record enthusiasts is the announcement made by the Victor Talking Machine Co. that the popular record artists Albert Campbell, Henry Burr, John Meyer and Frank Croxton will, after November 1, be exclusive Victor artists. These singers have scored a tremendous success through their records and in person in almost every large city in the country, singing as the Sterling Trio, the American Quartet and the Peerless Quartet.

This followed a similar arrangement with Billy Murray, who was exclusive to Victor from July 1, 1920, to July 1, 1927.

Possessing unissued Burr performances from previous sessions, a few companies released new Burr titles after he became exclusive to Victor. Columbia had recorded enough of Burr, the Sterling, and the Peerless to continue releasing new titles into mid-1921. Okeh 4537, featuring Burr singing "Little Town in the Ould County Down," was issued in April 1922.

Burr enjoyed success as touring artist and leader of the group known by 1918 as the Popular Talking Machine Artists, in 1919 as the Peerless Talking Machine Artists as well as the Eight Victor Record Makers, in 1920 as the Eight Famous Victor Artists, and from mid-1923 onward as the Eight Popular Victor Artists. The July 1923 issue of *Talking Machine World* is the last with an advertisement for the Eight Famous Victor Artists, and the August issue includes an Eight Popular Victor Artists advertisement. The name was probably changed from "Famous" to "Popular" so audience members knew in advance that the group did not include Red Seal artists, many of whom also toured to give concerts. The first touring group to include Burr was formed sometime around 1915 and also consisted of Albert Campbell, John H. Meyer, Arthur Collins, Billy Murray, Byron G. Harlan, "Banjo King" Vess Ossman and composer Theodore Morse, who was a skilled pianist. Appearances were carefully coordinated with Victor dealers nationwide.

A printed program that survives of the Peerless Record Makers at the Williamsport High School Auditorium in Pennsylvania on April 17, 1917, names Ira Hards as manager. An advertisement on page 80 of the January 1918 issue of *Talking Machine World* cites Clinton Woodward as manager, but until 1925 most advertisements for the ensemble list Philip W. Simon, owner of the P. W. Simon music stores, as manager.

A full-page advertisement on page 50 of the August 1918 issue of *Talking Machine World* cites Burr as manager: "Write for particulars, H.H. McClaskey, Mgr., 102 West 38th Street, New York City." It seems Burr and Simon were co-managers, at least for some years. The group's singers in later years referred to Burr as its manager. Burr clearly functioned as musical director and may have eventually managed the touring group without Simon. Jim Walsh writes in "The Funny Side of the Phonograph World," published in the May 1952 issue of *American Record Guide*, "The organization was managed by Henry Burr. . . . Usually, when traveling by train from one engagement to another, the elephantine Mr. Burr kept much to himself, worrying about how his genuinely beautiful voice would sound that night." Walsh adds later in the article, "But he was not a good public speaker. His manner was hesitant and he was easily flustered." Murray served as master of ceremonies during concerts.

Page 78 of the April 1919 issue of *Talking Machine World*, reporting on the success of a concert given on April 7 in Pittsburgh, suggests that Burr was musical director of the group while Simon attended to business matters:

One of the most important events in talking machine circles in Pittsburgh . . . was the appearance of the Peerless Talking Machine
Artists, headed by Henry Burr. . . . They were in western Pennsylvania for ten days and gave nine concerts, which were liberally patron-
ized. . . . Much credit is due P.W. Simon, the well-known Victrola
dealer of Uniontown, Pa. . . . Mr. Simon gave personal attention to
the arrangements and bookings . . .

Surviving concert programs of 1924 list Simon as manager, at 1674
Broadway, New York City. Later programs list Burr as manager (the same
address is given) though an article titled "Victor Record Makers' Concert
Company" in the March 1919 issue of *Voice of the Victor* gives Burr's
address as 145 East Lincoln Avenue, Mount Vernon, New York.

By September 1925, the personnel changed dramatically, though the
change was not announced in *Talking Machine World* until January 1926.
The new touring group consisted of old members Burr, Murray, Silver, and
Banta along with new members Carl Mathieu (first tenor), James Stanley
(baritone), Stanley Baughman (bass), and Sam Herman (xylophone). This
new Peerless first recorded on October 23, 1925 (Victor 19827). Campbell, Meyer, and Croxton were joined by Charles Harrison to form another
Peerless Quartet—and Campbell, Harrison, and Meyer sang as the Sterling
Trio. An advertisement for this alternative Peerless was included in the
September 1925 issue of *Talking Machine World*, with Croxton identified
as manager. To compete with Burr's touring group of eight performers,
Croxton lined up several artists and called this group the Peerless Entertainers. This new group, available for bookings in the New York City area,
consisted of Croxton's Peerless Quartet, saxophonist Rudy Wiedoeft,
pianist-composer Lieutenant Gitz Rice (he recorded "Fun in Flanders" in
1918 with Burr for Victor 18405), and baritone Arthur Fields.

For a brief period, Burr shared ownership of a banjo factory with
virtuoso Fred Van Eps. Page 158 of the June 1921 issue of *Talking Machine World* announces, "A new instrument firm to be known as the Van
Eps-Burr Corp. has been formed under the laws of the State of New York
with a capital of $50,000. The incorporators are H.H. McClaskey,
M.T. Kirkeby and F. Van Eps."

Dance music was gaining in popularity, and Burr contributed a vocal
chorus to some dance band records, including one of the earliest to feature
a vocal refrain: "Mickey" (Victor 18532), featuring Joseph C. Smith's
Orchestra. This was recorded on January 28, 1919. Later Burr sang refrains for Art Landry's "Sleepy Time Gal" (recorded on November 10,
1925; Victor 19843), Roger Wolfe Kahn's "Somebody's Lonely" (May 13,
1926; Victor 20059), Philip Spitalny's "When You Waltz with the One

You Love" (October 6, 1926; Victor 20260), and Nat Shilkret and the Victor Orchestra's "Why Should I Say That I'm Sorry?" (April 28, 1927; Victor 20615). But this style of singing was different from what had made Burr popular for over two decades.

Burr's popularity was in decline from the mid-1920s onward, demonstrated by fewer recording sessions than in previous years, and by 1928 he recorded sporadically. As a solo artist he made few records in the electric era. The last Peerless Quartet title issued by Victor was "Old Names of Old Flames" (21079), recorded on November 11, 1927. On this day Burr's final recording for Victor as a solo artist was made, but "Mother, I Still Have You" was not issued. The last Victor disc to feature Burr's name on the label was a duet with Homer Rodeheaver: "Where the Gates Swing Outward Never" (Victor 21337). It was recorded on May 1, 1927, but issued over a year later in June 1928. The Henry Burr Octet, personnel unknown, attended a Victor session on January 2, 1927, but nothing was issued.

Burr's photograph rarely was featured on sheet music covers, but in 1927 a color photograph of Burr was published on the cover of "The Daughter of Sweet Adeline," with words by Al Dubin and Willie Raskin, music by Ted Snyder. The sheet music was published by Henry Waterson Inc., and Burr was probably friendly with Waterson himself—certainly they knew each other since Waterson had owned the Little Wonder Record Company. The 1927 song was never recorded.

Burr ceased being exclusive to Victor by the summer of 1928. On June 14, 1928, he had his first Columbia session in several years. As "Irving Gillette," he cut two sentimental numbers for Harmony 671-H. He made a few children's records for Brunswick, with titles including "The Night Before Christmas" (4093), "Jack and the Beanstalk" (4094), "The Three Bears" (4094), and "Wagsey Watermelon" (4095). He sang "Memories of France" and "Out of the Dawn" on Brunswick 4045, issued in late 1928. A Columbia recording was issued in February 1929: "Cross Roads" backed by "Love Dreams" (1649-D). He made a few records issued on Harmony (Columbia's budget label), Cameo (this was owned by Henry Waterson), and Banner.

He continued to tour with the group known by the mid-1920s as the Eight Popular Victor Artists, and that group even made two MGM Movie-Tone short films in late 1928 or early 1929, probably shot on the same day. For copyright purposes, two prints of *At the Club* were deposited with the Library of Congress on February 4, 1929. A surviving script shows that after some introductory material, James Stanley performs "Gypsy Love Song" and then pianist Frank Banta plays "Novelette." The group disbanded around 1929.

On January 28, 1929, he contributed to a twelve-inch Victor disc featuring the "Minstrel Show of 1929" (35961), credited to the Victor Minstrels ("Male voices with orchestra"), which consisted of Burr, Billy Murray, Frank Crumit, James Stanley, and others. Burr sings the chorus of "By the Light of the Silvery Moon," and though this is among his final recordings, his voice shows no sign of deterioration. In December 1929 and January 1930 he cut for Columbia twelve electrical remakes (matrix numbers W1784 through W1795) of titles originally issued on Harper-Columbia small children's discs. Titles include "The Dairyman" and "Who Killed Cock Robin?" These late Burr performances were issued on rare small-diameter black label Columbia Bubble Books discs (labels state "Bubble Books That Sing"), with two titles—"Cock Robin and Jenny Wren" and "The Sandman"—also issued on Velvet Tone 8000.

Burr worked regularly in radio in the late 1920s as a performer but also as a producer. He had performed on radio much earlier, making a radio broadcast in 1920 from Denver. Burr sang into a microphone improvised from a wooden bowl containing an inverted telephone transmitter. The fact that the broadcast was heard in San Francisco made newspaper headlines on the West Coast. Even before this, Burr was credited for making the first "transcontinental broadcast"—he sang from New York and telephone wires carried his voice to diners wearing headphones at a Rotary dinner in California.

Otherwise he was not a radio performer in the early 1920s, partly because Victor did not permit artists who were exclusive to the company to perform on radio. This policy changed in 1925, and the Eight (with the final lineup) performed on radio for a year or so on the Goodrich Zippers program. Turning to the production side of broadcasting, Burr spent two and a half years in charge of *Cities Service Hour*, one of network radio's first music programs. It was first heard in 1927 over NBC and was characterized in newspaper listings as a "Semi-classical program." The August 10, 1935, issue of *Stand By!*, a radio weekly, featured Burr on its cover and stated, "Feeling there was a place and a need for greater showmanship in radio, Henry formed 'Henry Burr, Inc.' in 1928. This organization produced many of the big commercial network programs of the time. . . . Henry also originated the *Cities Service* program and produced it for two years."

Page 33 of the December 10, 1929, issue of *Musical America* reports that on November 25, 1929, Burr began a new job in New York City as director of the Artist's Bureau of the newly organized Columbia Broadcasting Company. He was evidently responsible for securing artists for performances. He began this work soon after the stock market crash—he had lost a considerable amount of money. He evidently worked in radio in the early 1930s only as a producer.

He enjoyed a mild comeback as a singer from the mid-1930s to 1941, performing regularly as a member of the WLS (Chicago) National Barn Dance troupe, which was broadcast over NBC every Saturday evening. Others on the show included Lulu Belle and Scotty, Joe Kelly, Eddie Peabody, and the Hoosier Hot Shots. Identified as "The Dean of Ballad Singers," he remained with the show until about six weeks before his death. At this time Burr and his wife lived in a spacious Chicago apartment. The show's sponsor was Alka-Seltzer, and the company distributed in 1937 a small Alka-Seltzer Songbook. A photograph of a graying Burr is on the first page, and the three songs associated with Burr in the songbook are "I'll Take You Home Again, Kathleen," "When You and I Were Young, Maggie," and "Silver Threads Among the Gold." A surviving transcription of the show from September 21, 1940, includes two performances by Burr, who sounds tired.

He married Cecilia Niles, a concert singer. During Burr's early years in New York he rented a room in the home of Dr. and Mrs. Niles. While Burr was living with them, the doctor passed away. Some time later, on June 6, 1910, Burr married the widow, Cecilia Niles, who was fifteen years older than the singer. Despite the difference in their ages, Burr was devoted to Cecilia. The August 10, 1936, issue of the radio weekly *Stand By!* stated, "Many listeners will recall the anniversary program which was broadcast in honor of the Burr silver wedding day, June 6, 1935." They had no children but Burr was devoted to his stepdaughter, Marguarite. Burr was on tour when his stepdaughter died, and upon learning the news, he canceled the rest of the Eight Famous Victor Artists tour and rushed back home.

After suffering for months from cancer, Burr died in Chicago on April 6, 1941, and was buried three days later at the Kenisco Cemetery, Westchester County, New York. Cecilia died in Chicago on September 17, 1954, and is buried near her husband. Also buried there is stepdaughter Marguarite, a small flat stone marking her spot.

Collins, Arthur (February 7, 1864-August 3, 1933)

The baritone Arthur Collins was among the half dozen most prolific recording artists during the acoustic era, with nearly every American company employing him as a solo artist, as a member of the duo Collins and

Harlan, and as a member of quartets and minstrel companies. Known for singing "coon" and "ragtime" songs in black dialect, he was closely associated with the comic song "The Preacher and the Bear," which he recorded for many companies. One trademark was a short laugh, often interjected between lines in songs. But his repertoire was not limited to "coon" songs. His Peerless Quartet work alone establishes that he was a versatile baritone.

In the December 1942 issue of *Hobbies*, Jim Walsh attributed Collins' popularity to these qualities:

> There probably has never been a sweeter, more naturally musical baritone voice than his. . . . Then, too, Arthur Collins managed invariably to get into the wax the impression of a warm, lovable personality. The unctuous sound of his chuckles in dialect work is unfailingly charming. His negro [sic] heroes usually were in hard luck, but they bore up bravely and saw the funny side of their own misfortunes.

Arthur Francis Collins was born in the home of his grandfather, Reverend Joseph Perry (a chaplain in the U.S. Navy), on Gerard Avenue in Philadelphia. The oldest of ten children, he was about fourteen when his father—Captain Arthur Collins, a devout Quaker—retired from seafaring occupations and bought a home in Barnegat, New Jersey, where he opened a country store. This information was given by Collins' wife to Walsh, who reported it in the November 1942 issue of *Hobbies*.

Collins joined the lifesaving station on the New Jersey coast. By seventeen he was singing at church festivals and concerts, and his parents sent him to Philadelphia to take voice lessons. He joined the Old King Company, an unsuccessful touring company. He then joined a company starring Fay Templeton, but this company also failed. He next sang in summer operas in St. Louis and eventually toured with Francis Wilson in *Merry Monarch* and *The Lion Tamer*, remaining with Wilson for ten years, according to the October 1916 issue of *Edison Phonograph Monthly*.

In 1895 in New York City's St. Timothy's Episcopal Church he married an Irish-born singer named Anna Leah Connolly (May 18, 1867-May 14, 1949), and Collins left show business to study shorthand, typewriting, and bookkeeping. Around 1898 the marriage produced a son. Page 65 of the September 15, 1918, issue of *Talking Machine World* features a photograph of a proud Collins "saying good-bye to son," with twenty-year-old Sergeant Arthur Perry Collins taking leave in uniform, headed for France.

Collins went to work for a cigar company but resigned after six months when his right arm became lame. After recovering, he worked for the

De Wolf Hopper Company, singing in the musical comedy *Wang*, and soon received a letter from Edison's National Phonograph Company inviting him for a trial recording.

He went to Orange, New Jersey, at the earliest opportunity. The singer's wife reported to Walsh that the date was May 16, 1898. Early numbers recorded include "Every Night I See That Nigger Standing Round" (5404) and "Happy Days in Dixie" (5407). On Edison recordings he was often accompanied by Vess L. Ossman, such as on the popular "All Coons Look Alike to Me," recorded in late 1899 and issued as Edison Record 7317. He also recorded "All Coons Look Alike to Me" to the banjo accompaniment of William Stanley Grinsted, who was called George S. Williams when he worked as a banjoist in these years (he was later known to record buyers as singer Frank C. Stanley). One of his most popular numbers in the earliest years was Thurland Chattaway's "Mandy Lee," recorded in early 1900 for Edison (7404) and in two sessions for Victor in that year.

Walsh states in Ronald Dethlefson's *Edison Blue Amberol Recordings 1915-1929*, "By a hasty count, which may be off a few notches, he made, from 1898 to 1912, no fewer than 227 solo two-minute cylinders, including both brown wax and the louder and less fragile Gold Moulded type, introduced in 1902. . . . the team [Collins and Harlan] recorded approximately sixty-five Blue Amberol duets."

Collins is mentioned for the first time in the trade journal *The Phonoscope* in the February 1899 issue. It is noted that he was among the artists making Giant Tone cylinders. He probably made cylinders for a few other small firms around this time.

He began making Berliner discs on November 25, 1899, recording at that first session "My Hannah Lady" (0754), "I've Just Received a Telegram from Baby" (0753), "All I Wants Is My Black Baby Back" (0756), "Mandy Lee" (0757), and others. He cut "I Don't Allow No Coons to Hurt My Feelings" for Berliner 0887 on January 13, 1900, and around this time (probably at the same session) recorded "You're Talking Ragtime" (0888), a song composed by the Beaumont Sisters. He recorded over fifty titles for Berliner's National Gramophone Company. Although most are "coon" songs or ragtime numbers, a few titles from 1900 indicate his versatility, such as "The Mick Who Threw the Brick," "The Blue and the Gray" (associated around that time with Richard Jose, who sang it often on vaudeville stages), and "On the Road to Mandalay" (the date is too early for this to be the Oley Speaks composition; it was probably the Walter W. Hedgecock version of Kipling's verse set to music).

Collins' rendition of "My Girl's an Hawaiian Maiden" is performed in the "coon" style. It is one of the first times "Hawaiian" appears on a record

(John Terrell had recorded "My Honolulu Lady," Berliner 1924, a year earlier).

Since he worked regularly for Berliner, it was natural that he was among Victor's earliest artists, recording often in its first year. His first session for Eldridge R. Johnson's new company was on July 20, 1900, and he recorded seven titles, accompanied by a pianist. He returned the next day to record another eight titles, this time accompanied by the Metropolitan Orchestra, and it appears that Collins was the first singer on Victor records accompanied by more than piano. Some selections cut during early sessions had already been performed by Collins for Berliner's National Gramophone Company, but new titles included a rube number titled "Old Bill Jones" (162) and Paul Dresser's patriotic "The Blue and the Gray" (164).

Collins' wife reported to Walsh that the singer preferred the term "The King of Ragtime Songs" to "coon singer." Nonetheless, he was regularly marketed as a "coon singer" in trade publications. The December 1904 issue of *Edison Phonograph Monthly*, announcing the January 1905 release of "Abraham" on Standard 8873, states, "'Abraham' is Arthur Collins' coon song contribution for the month." His wife also reported to Walsh that Collins "particularly loved to sing the old plantation-type of music, especially the Foster songs. 'Old Black Joe' was his masterpiece and audiences all over the country demanded it always."

The May 10, 1901, catalog for Zon-o-phone lists nine titles sung by Collins, mostly "coon" songs, such as "Coon, Coon, Coon" (9900).

For a year before teaming with Byron G. Harlan, Collins had a partner in tenor Joe Natus. They made nineteen Edison cylinders in 1901-1902 and several Victor recordings. One Victor recording session was on March 5, 1902, during which the two sang Cole and Johnson's "Tell Me Dusky Maiden" (1296), among other songs. The June 1903 *Edison Phonograph Monthly* announces that "I Must Have a Been a Dreamin'" (Standard 7850), sung by Arthur Collins and Joe Natus, would be "hereafter . . . sung by Collins and Harlan."

Collins was one member in the short-lived Edison ensemble called the Big Four Quartet, which recorded five titles issued in 1901. Harlan was one of the quartet's tenors (Natus was the other; A. D. Madeira was bass), and it is possible that Collins and Harlan first sang together at a recording session as members of this Edison quartet.

Collins was the first to record the song that would become Bert Williams' signature song, "Nobody," with music by Williams and words by Alex Rogers. Announcing the September release of the Collins version on Edison 9084, the August 1905 issue of *Edison Phonograph Monthly* states, "The song fits Mr. Collins like a glove. The story is of a coon for whom nobody does nothing, therefore he does nothing for nobody. Nobody told him that the tobasco [sic] sauce wasn't catchup [sic], in fact 'nobody' told him 'nothing,' causing him lots of trouble." Williams recorded "Nobody" nearly a year later for Columbia.

One song written by Bert Williams was recorded by Collins but never by Williams himself: "That's a Plenty" (Columbia A724).

A Theodore Morse song that Collins popularized was "When Uncle Joe Plays a Rag on His Old Banjo," which led to a nickname for Collins. Walsh reports in Dethlefson's *Edison Blue Amberol Recordings 1915-1929* that Collins was "so dark and swarthy that in after years his recording artist friends called him 'Old Joe, the Pirate,' taking 'Joe' from the title of one of his most popular records. . . . The 'Pirate' alluded to Collins' sailing career as well as his complexion." Walsh continues with this observation on the size of the two: "His partner Harlan was taller and equally fat, and Billy Murray once annoyed them during one of their public performances by introducing them as the 'Half-Ton Duo.'"

Collins remained popular as a solo recording artist. He helped popularize the Thomas S. Allen song "Any Rags?" For Victor he cut it on October 26, 1903. He recorded it earlier for Edison, and the October 1903 issue of *Edison Phonograph Monthly* states, "A monthly list without a coon song by Arthur Collins would be like a play with a prominent actor missing. Mr. Collins' November selection, No. 8525, is 'Any Rags.'" The song's title refers to a junkman's business cry ("Any rags, any bones, any bottles today?"), not to ragtime songs—though Collins recorded many of these, such as "Bill Simmons" and "Ragtime Don't Go with Me No More."

Perhaps more than any other acoustic-era recording artist, Collins recorded many numbers by black songwriters, including Ernest Hogan ("All Coons Look Alike to Me"), Will Marion Cook and Joe Jordan ("Lovie Joe"), J. Rosamond Johnson and Bob Cole ("There's Always Something Wrong"), Cecil Mack and Chris Smith ("All In, Down and Out"), Alex Rogers and Bert Williams ("Nobody"), and Henry Creamer and John Turner Layton ("The Cute Little Wigglin' Dance").

Collins recorded "The Preacher and the Bear" soon after it was published in 1904. Normally credited to Joe Arzonia, the song was actually written by George Fairman (1881-1962) of Front Royal, Virginia. In 1955 Fairman wrote to Jim Walsh that in 1902 or 1903, shortly after he composed it, he sold for $250 all rights to the song to Arzonia, owner of a cafe in which Fairman played piano, adding that songwriter Arthur Longbrake was a frequent patron of that cafe. Longbrake, who established the Eclipse Music Company, shares credit with Arzonia on sheet music, which sold well when published by the Joe Morris Music Company. Eager to repeat the success of "The Preacher and the Bear," Collins cut other songs composed by Longbrake, enjoying mild success with "Nobody Knows Where John Brown Went" and "Brother Noah Gave Out Checks for Rain." He had less success with Longbrake's "Parson Jones' Three Reasons."

Collins first cut "The Preacher and the Bear" in early 1905, with Zon-o-phone 120 being the first record of it to be issued (in April 1905). It was issued as two-minute Edison Standard 9000 in May 1905. In announcing its release, the April 1905 issue of *Edison Phonograph Monthly* twice gives the name Arzonia as "Arzoma" and then simply summarizes what the song narrates, with nothing suggesting that Edison executives anticipated great sales for it.

He recorded it for Columbia around this time for cylinder 32720 as well as disc 3146 (they were issued in June), and Collins delivers these words on the disc version:

A preacher went out a-huntin'
'Twas on one Sunday morn
I thought it was against his religion
But he took his gun along
He shot himself some very fine quail
And one big frizzly hare
And on his way returning home
He met a great big grizzly bear
Well, the bear marched out in the middle of the road
And he waltzed to the coon, you see
The coon got so excited
That he climbed a persimmon tree
The bear sat down upon the ground
And the coon climb'd out on a limb
He cast his eyes to the Lord in the sky
And these words said to Him:

Oh Lord, didn't you deliver Daniel from the lion's den?
Also delivered Jonah from the belly of the whale and then
Three Hebrew chillun from the fiery furnace?
So the Good Book do declare
Now Lord, if you can't help me
For goodness sakes, don't you help that bear!

[SPOKEN] Now, Mr. Bear, let's you and I reason this here thing out together [growl]—nice bear! [growl]—good old bear [growl]—Say,

Mr. Bear, if I should give you just one nice big juicy bite, would you go away? [growl] Oh, you wouldn't, eh? Well, I'll stay right here!

When the Edison company issued the first batch of four-minute wax Amberol cylinders on October 1, 1908, an expanded "Preacher and the Bear" was included (Amberol 18). The September 1908 issue of *Edison Phonograph Monthly* announces, "This comic coon song has run second in popularity to none in the list of Edison two-minute Records. . . . Our new Amberol Record gives an extra verse, chorus, and scene." When the Edison Amberol cylinder gave way to the Blue Amberol in November 1912, the popular song was issued as Blue Amberol 1560, and it remained a steady seller. The February 1919 issue of *Edison Amberola Monthly* lists "eighteen Amberol Records that head the best sellers for the year 1918," and Blue Amberol 1560 is included.

He recorded it for Victor on May 9, 1905 (single-sided 4431 was issued in September), and in 1908 returned to the Victor studio for a new take (double-sided 17221 features the 1908 take). He sang it for virtually every company, including small firms that sprang up in the World War I years. For example, he sings it on Majestic 105, issued in January 1917. During the acoustic recording era, Collins was the only American singer to record "The Preacher and the Bear." Remarkably, Columbia as late as 1921 offered two versions on disc—A307 and A2290 (the former was dropped at the time Columbia's 1922 catalog was printed). All other Collins titles had been dropped from the Columbia catalog aside from "Railroad Rag." Riley Puckett was the first American artist aside from Collins to cut it for a record company—in December 1925, shortly after Collins' retirement, Puckett cut it for Columbia 15045-D. Al Bernard sang it for Brunswick, Romeo, and Vocalion. Ernest Hare cut it for Federal. Albert Whelan recorded it in England. The Golden Gate Quartet sang a gospel arrangement of it during an RCA Victor session on August 4, 1937. In 1947 Phil Harris enjoyed a hit with the song on RCA Victor 20-2143—lyrics were changed slightly, with substitutions found for the word "coon."

"The Preacher and the Bear" as performed by Collins was available to record buyers as late as 1941 on Montgomery Ward M-8128. It was the same performance that had been issued in 1908 on Victor 17221 and was listed in the hillbilly, or country, section of the mail-order catalog from 1933 to 1941, which indicates that rural audiences were especially fond of the number. On Columbia A293, Collins sings "The Parson and the Turkey," a successor to the famous bear song.

Collins as a solo artist never used a pseudonym, although when Harlan recorded as a solo artist pseudonyms were occasionally used—Cyrus Pippins, Deacon Treadway, Bert Terry, and others.

Collins joined the Peerless Quartet in 1909 when Steve Porter left to join the American Quartet. Collins remained with the Peerless for a decade and toured with a group known in the World War I era as the Record Makers, later as the Victor Record Makers (after Collins had left, it was called the Eight Famous Victor Artists, then the Eight Popular Victor Artists). With this touring group Collins performed at concerts some solo numbers (invariably giving as an encore "The Preacher and the Bear"), some songs with partner Harlan, and some tunes as a member of the Peerless.

In the Peerless Quartet, Collins sometimes sang the lead, such as on "Pull for the Shore" (Victor 17667), a song ostensibly about a boat stuck in a storm but really about a girl and a handsome suitor at sea engaging in too much petting for a father's comfort. This song by Jeff Branen and Edward O'Keefe may have brought back memories to Collins, who had spent much time on the sea in early years.

He left the Peerless and the Victor Eight troupe around 1919. The March 1919 issue of *Voice of the Victor* lists Collins as a member, and page 125 of the May 1919 *Talking Machine World* includes Collins when listing names of the "Popular Record Makers" touring in May. He was evidently not always present for Peerless recordings. Some Columbia records made in 1917 include bass Frank Croxton, with Meyer singing baritone instead of Collins. One of the last Peerless records featuring Collins is a World War I specialty titled "A Battle in the Air." Backed by "A Submarine Attack Somewhere at Sea," it was issued on Columbia A2626 in November 1918. The label gives composer credit for "The Battle in the Air" to Albert Campbell, Arthur Collins, and Theodore Morse. Campbell and Collins presumably wrote the dialogue spoken on the record. Campbell later reported to Walsh that Collins could not get along with manager Henry Burr.

From 1916 to 1920, Collins sang several numbers with lyrics about jazz, such as "Old Man Jazz," issued as Blue Amberol 4093 in October 1920. Promotional literature states, " 'Old Man Jazz' is a colored song, between whose lines we listen to jazzy music from clarinet, trombone, drum and other instruments. Their notes are certainly enlivening. Arthur Collins is a master in recording this song."

No Collins performances were issued on lateral Brunswick discs though he was on at least one green-labeled Canadian-issued vertical Brunswick disc of the World War I period. It features "The Ragtime Volunteers Are Off to War" and "The Darktown Strutters' Ball" (5175).

On October 20, 1921, during an Edison Tone Test demonstration at the Princess Theater in Medina, Ohio, Collins exited the stage in the dark so the audience could guess whether the singing heard came from the singer himself or a Diamond Disc machine, and the baritone suffered serious injuries when he fell through a trapdoor accidently left open. After a recovery period, he made a solo recording for Gennett—"I Ain't Got Enough for to Pass Around" (4866), issued in June 1922—and more recordings with Harlan for Edison.

The last reference in *Talking Machine World* to a Collins and Harlan performance is in the December 15, 1925, issue, which reports that they gave a concert in Muncie, outside Indianapolis, in early December "under the auspices of the Edison store."

Until mid-1926 Collins lived in New Jersey. The November 1919 issue of *Edison Amberola Monthly* includes a photograph of Collins "giving one of his cows the 'once over' down on his farm." According to Walsh in the January 1943 issue of *Hobbies*, Collins "specialized in breeding fancy horses and cattle." When he retired in 1926, Collins moved to Tice, Florida, with his wife. He was independently wealthy by this time, Collins' wife having made wise investments over the years, according to Walsh. His voice remained strong despite a weakened heart, and he sometimes sang at Masonic meetings in the Ft. Myers area. Walsh learned about how Collins died from the singer's wife: on August 3, 1933, he was sitting on a bench with his wife under his beloved orange trees, put his head on her shoulder, and quietly passed away.

Collins and Harlan

This was the most successful duo of the acoustic era. Jim Walsh states in the December 1942 issue of *Hobbies*, "Together they constituted what was probably the most popular team of comedians in the history of the phonograph. Only Billy Jones and Ernest Hare, who came along many years later, might have been able, at the height of their careers, to dispute the claim." Collins and Harlan came to be largely identified with black dialect work but they were not limited to this. They sang comic songs in various dialects, performed rube skits, and recorded songs satirizing trends of the day.

Before teaming with tenor Byron G. Harlan, baritone Arthur Collins had a partner in tenor Joe Natus for a year. Collins and Natus made nineteen Edison cylinders in 1901-1902 and several Victor recordings. Around this time Collins sang in an Edison ensemble called the Big Four Quartet, which recorded five titles issued in 1901. Harlan was one of the quartet's tenors; Natus was the other; A. D. Madeira was bass. It is possible that Collins and Harlan first sang together as members of this Edison quartet. By 1903 Natus was no longer recording for Edison. The June 1903 *Edison Phonograph Monthly* announces that "I Must Have a Been a

Dreamin'" (Standard 7850), sung by Arthur Collins and Joe Natus, would be "hereafter . . . sung by Collins and Harlan." Collins and Harlan made new takes of various titles originally cut for Edison by Collins and Natus.

The first time Arthur Collins was paired with Byron G. Harlan for a Victor recording session was on October 31, 1902, which happened to be Harlan's first Victor session. Collins and Harlan recorded five titles, including "The First Rehearsal of the Huskin' Bee" (1723), a "rube" skit. Many of their early recordings are rube sketches with songs, such as "Closing Time in a Country Grocery" (Victor 1728) and "Two Rubes in a Tavern" (1727), and they continued recording rural comedy for years, Harlan performing it into the 1920s. Harlan recorded these same three titles with Frank C. Stanley, who wrote the sketches.

Collins and Harlan were again paired a day later, on November 1. A session held March 3, 1903, is noteworthy since Collins recorded duets with Natus, then recorded with Harlan. It was the last Victor session for the team of Collins and Natus. Natus made Victor discs for another two years but only solo recordings, mostly of popular ballads. Natus' last Victor session was on April 28, 1905.

Among the first cylinder companies the duo worked for was the Lambert Company, with "Jerry Murphy Is a Friend of Mine" issued around 1903 on blue Lambert 935. Collins and Harlan's first Edison cylinders were "Down Where the Wurzburger Flows" (8238) and "Troubles of the Reuben and the Maid" (8239), issued in late 1902. They recorded many "rube" skits for Edison. "Way Back" (9803), issued in February 1908, is about an Uncle Josh visit to New York. It was made for Edison when Cal Stewart recorded exclusively for Columbia.

In 1903 Collins and Harlan recorded "Hurrah for Baffin Bay," issued as a Victor DeLuxe disc and as Edison 8447. Composed by Theodore Morse, it was in the Broadway musical *The Wizard of Oz*. The duo would have close ties with Morse, often recording his compositions. In the World War I period they even performed at concerts with Morse accompanying on piano. The April 1957 issue of *Hobbies* duplicates a photograph of Morse standing on a stage with Collins, Harlan, and other Victor artists who gave a concert in April 1917 in Wilkes-Barre, Pennsylvania.

Walsh reports in the December 1968 issue of *Hobbies* that the duo sang "what may have been the last Victor Monarch record to have a spoken announcement. . . . It was 2451, and the title was 'It Was the Dutch.'" This Theodore Morse song was recorded on September 11, 1903, with Collins doing the announcement. The next four Victor numbers, 2452 through 2455, were Billy Murray's first Victor discs and are unannounced.

Another change in the industry around this time was a shift from piano to orchestral accompaniment. The January 1904 issue of *Edison Phonograph Monthly*, announcing the release of "I Ain't Got No Time" on Edison Standard 8621, states, "This Record is also made with orchestra accompaniment, and with No. 8608 ["Barney," another Collins and Harlan duet] are the first Records ever made at the Edison Laboratory with such accompaniment."

On July 29, 1907, Collins and Harlan recorded for Victor a Morse song titled "In Monkey Land" (5270), and their Edison recording of the same number (Edison 9700) was issued in October, 1907. The song begins:

Where breezes blow in monkeyland
Up in a banyan tree
There lived a pretty monkey maid
Loved by a chimpanzee

Their recordings of Morse's "Down in Jungle Town" in 1908 sold very well (issued as Edison 9941 in July 1908; issued as Victor 16805). The popularity of "In Monkey Land" and "Down in Jungle Town" helped create a brief craze by 1909-1910 for "monkey" tunes, with labels referring to "jungle" songs ("Down in Jungle Town" was popular enough for Nat Wills to record a parody for Edison and Victor in 1909). In 1903 Morse had composed "Up in a Coconut Tree," sung by Billy Murray, but it was not as popular as later jungle tunes. Similar songs recorded by Collins and Harlan include Morse's "The Family Tree" (Victor 5361), George Meyer's "Underneath the Monkey Moon" (Edison 10367), Morse's "Down in Monkeyville" (Victor 17501; Edison Blue Amberol 2141), Morse's "On a Monkey Honeymoon" (Victor 16426), Morse's "The Jungle of Jungle Joe" (Columbia A967), and Dempsey and Schmid's "Moonlight in Jungle Land" (Victor 16483). As late as 1914 the duo had a hit about chimps with "The Aba Daba Honeymoon," music by Walter Donovan, words by a young Arthur Fields.

An important Victor session took place on May 9, 1905. As a team, Collins and Harlan recorded numbers that were popular—"Tammany" (baritone S. H. Dudley, as "Frank Kernell," also cut this for Victor) as well as "Take A Car"—and both made records as solo artists, with Collins performing the incredibly successful "The Preacher and the Bear" (4431). Another performance from 1905 that proved durable was of Paul Dresser's "Nigger Loves His Possum." First cut on November 7, 1905, and originally issued as single-sided Victor 4560, it remained available for over two decades. Fagan and Moran's *Encyclopedic Discography of Victor Recordings: Matrix Series* indicates that Collins and Harlan recorded it again on January 27, 1922, which is remarkable since Victor had dropped the duo in 1918. Victor regularly found substitute artists when cutting new takes if artists who had originally made the records no longer worked for the company, but in this case executives must have decided that no other artists could perform the song in a manner that would satisfy the public, so they were forced to call back Collins and Harlan. Collins was at the time recovering from a late 1921 accident.

Around 1906 Collins and Harlan joined Billy Murray and Steve Porter to form the Rambler Minstrel Company. This team recorded for various companies and also performed at New York social events such as club dinners.

Comic patter is exchanged in many Collins and Harlan recordings, with Collins often addressed as "Henry" or "Sam" and Harlan called "Mandy" (in many "coon" duets, Harlan impersonates a female—what Victor catalogs call "a darky wench"). Collins' voice is usually the first heard on a Collins and Harlan recording. It was typical in tenor-baritone duets for the baritone to lead. On rare occasions they harmonize from the beginning. The team is identified on labels as "Collins and Harlan," though an exception is the Columbia disc featuring their "On the Good Ship Whip-Poor-Will" (A1850), which cites Harlan first: "Byron G. Harlan and Arthur Collins."

Walsh suggests in Dethlefson's *Edison Blue Amberol Recordings 1915-1929* that Collins viewed his own contribution as more important to the duo's success than Harlan's. Billy Murray had reported to Walsh:

> Do you know that after Collins and Harlan had worked together for years and years, poor Harlan found out that Collins was trying to double-cross him by going to managers of the different recording sessions and insisting that, instead of the fees for making duets being divided equally between them, he should get two dollars to Harlan's one. Collins argued that he was "the strong man of the team" who made their records sell and should be paid accordingly.

The duo's first four-minute cylinders were "Don't Go Away" and "Nigger Loves His Possum," made available on October 1, 1908, when Edison's four-minute wax Amberol cylinder made its debut. The two minute version of Paul Dresser's "Nigger Loves His Possum" had proved so popular that Collins and Harlan sang it as one of their first four-minute Amberols. Edison literature states, "[It is c]onsidered by many to be Collins and Harlan's best duet. This 'classic' could not possibly have been left off the first list of Four-Minute Records."

A departure from the many "coon" duets recorded in 1909 was "Ting Ting Sang," issued by Edison's National Phonograph Company on Standard 10286 in January 1910. The November 1909 issue of *Edison Phonograph Monthly* calls it, "A pleasing proof of the versatility of these popular artists. Into this comic duet, which is a Chinaman's recital of his brother Tang Tang Sang's sporty propensities in contrast to his own superior virtues, they inject a surprising amount of comedy. . . ." Words were by Henry S. Creamer, with music by Tom Lemonier.

Collins and Harlan, always freelance artists, were steadily engaged by record companies for over two decades. When the duo found a song well-suited for their talents, they would sing it for Victor, then Columbia, then Edison—or in some other order—and then perhaps for Emerson, Pathé, and others. Titles closely associated with the duo include Yellen and Cobb's "Alabama Jubilee," Fields and Morse's "Auntie Skinner's Chicken Dinner," Dumont's "Bake Dat Chicken Pie," Fields and Donovan's "The Aba Daba Honeymoon," and Piantadosi's "Melinda's Wedding Day."

The word "swing" was rarely used to describe music in the industry's early decades, but the January 1907 issue of *Edison Phonograph Monthly* uses it when announcing the release of "Bake Dat Chicken Pie" on Standard 9499: "It has the old-fashioned swing that keeps your feet moving, and Collins and Harlan sing it as though they had the chicken and couldn't wait till it was baked." The song's lyrics perpetuate stereotypes that would offend most modern listeners. It was written by Frank Dumont, leader of a minstrel troupe based in Philadelphia called Dumont's Minstrels. Collins and Harlan were the only singers to record it during the acoustic era (Uncle Dave Macon cut it for Vocalion in 1927), and they cut it for various companies, even as late as 1920 for the Arrow Phonograph Corporation (Arrow 515).

They were not limited to "darky" duets, as some labels characterized such songs. They sang comic songs in various dialects, such as Italian in "My Brudda Sylvest" (Edison 10013, 1908). "The Old Grey Mare" and "My Wife's Gone to the Country" are devoid of racial or ethnic stereotypes. Numbers sung without ethnic dialect include "Come Along, Little Girl, Come Along" (Columbia 3241, Edison 9028), which was promoted as a "summer waltz song"; "Do the Funny Fox Trot" (Victor 17649; Columbia A1626), which satirizes the dance craze inspired by Irene and Vernon Castle; "Those Charlie Chaplin Feet" (Columbia A1780; Little Wonder 170), which celebrates the silent film comedian; and "The Kid Is Clever" (Victor 18014, Columbia A2008), which satirizes vaudeville.

On May 23, 1911, they were first to record Irving Berlin's "Alexander's Ragtime Band." When issued on Victor 16908 in September, it was coupled with Eddie Morton's performance of "Oceana Roll," cut on July 12, several weeks after Collins and Harlan had cut the Berlin song. That Victor did not release the Berlin number at the earliest possible date and that it was placed on the disc's "B" side suggests that nobody in the record industry had great expectations for the song. Prior to this the young Berlin had hits with such songs as "That Mesmerizing Mendelssohn Tune," "Stop! Stop! Stop! (Come Over and Love Me Some More)," "Grizzly Bear," and "My Wife's Gone to the Country (Hurrah! Hurrah!)"—for two of these titles, Berlin shared credit with others—but several other Berlin songs recorded by 1911 sold poorly.

The choice of Collins and Harlan for "Alexander's Ragtime Band" was natural. They had recorded more Berlin songs up to this point than any other artists and were known for singing songs with syncopated melodies—what Tin Pan Alley called ragtime—as well as songs with ragtime as the subject of lyrics. In 1910 they had cut an Irving Berlin-Ted Snyder song titled "Alexander and His Clarinet" but Columbia and Indestructible versions sold poorly. Industry executives must have recorded with some trepidation yet another Berlin song with "Alexander" in its title. "Alexander's Ragtime Band" did catch on, which may have surprised some in the recording industry. Berlin's new song had not been especially popular in the early months it was performed by stage artists. Copyright had been assigned to the song on March 18, 1911. Vaudeville headliner and musical comedy star Emma Carus introduced it on stage for the first time on April 17, according to Charles Hamm in *Irving Berlin* (Oxford University Press, 1997). Hamm writes on page 133, "It was not until mid-August that the Snyder Company [the song's publisher] acknowledged the song and its success. A full-page ad in *Variety* for August 19 calls it 'The Song Sensation of the Century . . .'"

Victor catalogs from 1912 to November 1917 ended up promoting "Alexander's Ragtime Band" and Morton's "Oceana Roll" by using this particular disc—or these two titles—to illustrate to catalog users how Victor's alphabetical system worked. Because all song titles and artists in the catalog were listed alphabetically, the catalog proudly proclaimed itself to be "A catalogue without indexes or page numbers . . . or rather, it is all index. . . ." The record remained available for a decade, dropped in December 1922 when Victor's 1923 catalog was printed.

Evidently Victor had trouble satisfying demand for "Alexander's Ragtime Band" in late 1911. Victor's January 1912 supplement announces the release of the song as played by the Victor Military Band on Victor 17006 and states, "It seems impossible for the Victor Company to furnish enough records of this great popular success to supply the demand, and therefore, to supplement the Collins and Harlan and Snyder Medley records, there is offered here a spirited band version—and it may be described as a 'corker'!"

Collins and Harlan soon recorded "Alexander's Ragtime Band" for other companies. They had hits with other Irving Berlin compositions, including "Snookey Ookums," "Everybody's Doin' It Now," "When That Midnight Choo Choo Leaves for Alabam'," "Down in Chattanooga," and "That International Rag."

The record slip included with Blue Amberol 1591, featuring Percy Wenrich and Jack Mahoney's "Buddy Boy" and issued in November 1912, states, "Collins and Harlan have sung together for years, always with increasing popularity, until to-day we may safely say that they have no superiors in their chosen field of rag-time coon shouts." As late as 1912 some in the industry still spoke of ragtime and "coon" songs as the same.

One indication of the duo's value in 1912 to the firm Thomas A. Edison, Inc. is that the first numbered Diamond Disc is Collins and Harlan's "Moonlight in Jungleland," backed by Collins' "Below the Mason-Dixon Line." Numbered 50001, it is the beginning of the Diamond Disc popular series.

Both singers remained in demand as solo artists. On Collins' "That Baseball Rag" (Victor 17377), Harlan makes an uncredited contribution in shouting the line, "You run like an ice wagon."

The duo's output was interrupted in late 1911 and early 1912 when Harlan suffered from typhoid fever and pneumonia. During Harlan's recovery, Collins recorded solo for Victor and teamed with tenor Albert Campbell for Zon-o-phone and Columbia discs. An example of a Collins and Campbell duet is "In Ragtime Land" (Columbia A1098). As a solo vocalist working with banjoist Vess L. Ossman, Collins cut "In Ragtime Land" for Victor 17126 on June 3, 1912.

Collins and Harlan sang before audiences as part of a touring ensemble formed in late 1916 or early 1917. In the February 1965 issue of *Hobbies*, Walsh describes a photograph of the Record Maker Troupe in Troop's Music Store at Harrisburg, Pennsylvania, in April 1917. The artists included Collins, Harlan, Vess L. Ossman, Albert Campbell, and songwriter-pianist Theodore Morse. A program that survives of the Peerless Record Makers at the Williamsport High School Auditorium in Pennsylvania on April 17, 1917, lists Collins and Harlan as performing "Bake Dat Chicken Pie."

The May 1917 issue of *Talking Machine World* lists members of what is called the Phonograph Singers: Collins, Harlan, Campbell, Morse, Henry Burr, Billy Murray, John H. Meyer, Frank Croxton—the fact that Ossman's name is missing suggests he stopped touring with other recording artists by this time. The May 15, 1917, issue of *Talking Machine World* announces a "new singing act now touring the Eastern States and featuring the well-known record makers, Billy Murray, Henry Burr, the Sterling Trio, Peerless Quartet, Collins & Harlan, with Theodore Morse as pianist." Later issues of *Talking Machine World*, which featured full-page advertisements of the group, used other names, and it seems names for the group varied from location to location. The Phonograph Singers evolved into the Popular Talking Machine Artists, the Popular Record Makers, the Peerless Record Makers, the Eight Famous Record Artists (this is the name used in June 1920, around the time five artists became exclusive to Victor), the Eight Famous Victor Artists, and finally the Eight Popular Victor Artists. Collins and Harlan left in mid-1919.

On December 1, 1916, Collins and Harlan were the first recording artists to refer to the new music called jazz, or "jas." For the Edison company they recorded various takes of "That Funny Jas Band from Dixieland." The lyrics by Gus Kahn and music by Henry I. Marshall were copyrighted on November 8, 1916:

> Howdy Sal—glad to see you honey
> Hello gal—got a roll of money
> Don't be late on our way [to]
> Some cafe with lots of pep and ginger
> There's a place
> You'll go wild about its dancing space
> Wouldn't be without it
> But if you go you'll stay alone
> Just to hear the jas band play!
>
> CHORUS: Oh honey dear
> I want you to hear
> That harmony queer
> When you listen to
> Mad musicians playing rhythm
> Everybody dancing with 'em!
> Oh, hold me close in your arms
> I'm in love with your charm and
> The funny jas band from Dixieland

This was issued in April 1917 as Blue Amberol dubbing 3140, then as Diamond Disc 50423 in July 1917 (Blue Amberols could be processed more quickly than Diamond Discs). The duo recorded the song for Victor on January 12, 1917, and in April "That Funny Jas Band from Dixieland" was also available on Victor 18235. A few months earlier they had cut "The Two-Key Rag," issued on Victor 18128 in November 1916. Their delivery for the two Victor performances—one being their last with "rag" in the title, the other being their first to refer to jazz—was similar though the musical interlude on the "jas" number is wilder.

The Edison and Victor records of Collins and Harlan satirizing jazz were issued before the first jazz record was released. The first time Victor literature refers to this new music ("jas") is in the April 1917 monthly supplement announcing the new Collins and Harlan disc. Victor announced the Original Dixieland Jazz Band's first disc (18255) in its May supplement. Collins recorded it as a solo number for three companies— Pathé (20143, issued in May 1917), Operaphone (1936, issued in May 1917), and Empire (6250, issued in December 1918, two years after the song was recorded for Edison).

Collins as a solo artist recorded a few songs about jazz whereas Harlan never did. An example is Chris Smith's "Get a Jazz Band to Jazz the Yankee Doodle Tune" on Emerson 7222, issued in October 1917. Collins recorded Brockman's "Ephraham's Jasbo Band" for Par-o-ket 84, issued in April 1917, and Emerson 7140, issued in May 1917. "Keep Jazzin' It, Ras" was issued as Emerson 7385 in September 1918. "Old Man Jazz" was issued as Blue Amberol 4093 in October 1920. The duo recorded "Everybody's Jazzin' It" for Victor (18303; issued September 1917). Their version of "Every Day's a Holiday in Dixie" (Emerson 9125) is characterized as a "Southern Jazz Melody" on the label.

For small companies Collins often recorded songs that he had earlier recorded with Harlan for major labels. An example is Collins singing "Alabama Jubilee" for Domestic. Harlan, as solo artist, never recorded numbers associated with the team Collins and Harlan.

Pseudonyms were evidently not used for the duo. Collins as a solo artist never used one, though Harlan as solo artist was occasionally issued under a pseudonym—Cyrus Pippins, Deacon Treadway, Bert Terry, and others.

Collins and Harlan's decline in popularity is notable from 1918 onward. They recorded for nearly every company but no longer for the two largest companies, Victor and Columbia. Their form of delivery, so familiar to record buyers, had become dated, which was made all the more obvious by many young singers making their recording debuts around this time. Popular music also changed during World War I, though the duo tried to adjust to these changes, covering material that reflected popular trends, including Hawaiian numbers. But they also continued to record material of earlier times, such as "coon" duets and rube numbers.

When their performance of "Dancing Down in Dixie Land" was issued on Diamond Disc 50402 in May 1917, the jacket for the disc more or less announces that new types of music had made the team old-fashioned:

> Since the craze for modern dances started these old-time darky tunes have been crowded into the background. Years ago, when the cake walks were in vogue, and when real ragtime was at its height, this sort of piece was quite common. . . . Among the Collins and Harlan records you will find practically every sort of comic song. They really made their reputation, however, among Phonograph owners, with pieces in the negro dialect, and so on this record you hear them at their best.

Victor and Columbia stopped recording new numbers of Collins and Harlan in 1918, both companies issuing the last new record by the duo in October. The singers did return to Victor on January 27, 1922, to record a new take of "Nigger Loves His Possum," and this take is on some pressings of Victor 17256. The two continued touring into 1919 with the Popular Record Makers. *Talking Machine World* indicates Collins and Harlan remained in the touring group until at least May 1919. However, Collins did not record with the Peerless Quartet as late as this.

Presumably the two largest companies stopped recording Collins and Harlan because the duo's style was dated (their Edison Tone Tests cannot be the reason since that began a full year after Victor and Columbia dropped them). War songs dominated popular music in 1918, and executives may have concluded that such songs are most credible when performed by artists who sound young enough to serve in the armed forces. Collins and Harlan had been famous a generation earlier and were clearly aging. Victor and Columbia looked to younger artists—Al Bernard, Ernest Hare, Van and Schenck—to record material that might have been well-suited for the talents of Collins and Harlan.

Curiously, the 1921 Columbia catalog states about the duo, "Their work is in its particular way quite unique and inimitable and a Columbia monthly list without at least one record by them would seem incomplete." No Columbia monthly list had included a new Collins and Harlan title for some time when this catalog was printed around September 1920.

Their last Victor disc as well as the last Columbia featured "When Uncle Joe Steps into France" (Victor 18492; Columbia A2599):

> When Uncle Joe steps into France
> With his ragtime band from Dixieland
> See the soldiers swaying

When Uncle Joe starts playing
A raggy ditty, so sweet and pretty.
When they play "The Memphis Blues"
They will use a lot of shoes
And fill them full of darky gin.
They'll rag their way right to Berlin
When Uncle Joe steps into France
With his ragtime regiment band

Victor issued it as a "B" side, with the "A" side featuring one of Victor's new and young singers, Marion Harris. The duet seems an up-to-date number in that it refers to the European conflict, but it is largely a sequel to a song popularized by Collins years earlier, "When Uncle Joe Plays a Rag on His Old Banjo" (Victor 17118), which probably also inspired a 1916 song popularized by the Peerless Quartet (with Collins) titled "When Old Bill Baily Plays the Ukulele" (Victor 17904—Nora Bayes sings it on Victor 45099).

About "Uncle Joe Steps Into France," the October 1918 Victor supplement states, "The Jazzing in the accompaniment is entirely in the spirit of the words." Music is by Billy Winkle, words by Bernie Grossman. It was issued in the same month Columbia issued its last Byron G. Harlan solo disc, "Bobby the Bomber" (A2587). Another World War I song recorded by the duo is titled "Big Chief Kill a Hun," evidently a sequel to the popular "Indianola." It was issued on Okeh 1113 in December 1918, a few weeks after the Armistice.

Collins and Harlan in these years—roughly 1917 to 1919—recorded regularly for small companies then emerging, including Domestic, Okeh, Emerson, Empire, Paramount, Operaphone, and Gennett. Songs from this period cut for more than one company include "Everything Is Hunky Dory Down in Honky Tonky Town," "Three Pickaninnies," "Everything Is Peaches Down in Georgia," "Down in Jungle Land," "There's a Lump of Sugar in Dixie," and "Good-bye Alexander."

When Paramount issued its first discs in early 1918 (they were vertical cut), Collins and Harlan were among its artists. Their rendition of "Everybody's Crazy 'Bout the Dog Gone Blues" was issued in April as Paramount 2049. The duo was included in the first Okeh catalog, issued in October 1918. As a solo artist for Paramount and Okeh, Collins recorded some Bert Williams material, in keeping with the public's association of Collins with "darky" humor.

The duo recorded often for Pathé. Their version of Von Tilzer's "Stop, Look, Listen to the Music of the Band" (20463) is curiously coupled with a Noble Sissle performance. Pathé issued "I Want a Jazzy Kiss" (22382) in

July 1920 (the Edison version, Blue Amberol 4133, appeared in December, with Diamond Disc 50940 following in 1922). Backed by the Van Eps Banjo Orchestra, Collins without Harlan often sang for Pathé and other companies.

Also issued during this period are "Sipping Cider Thru a Straw," on Operaphone in September 1919, and "Thipping Thider Thru a Thtraw," the same song with a more comical spelling, on seven-inch Emerson 7536 as well as nine-inch Emerson 9207. "Bake Dat Chicken Pie" appeared in March 1920 as Lyric 5215, backed by "Coon Loves His Possum." In June 1920, Pathé issued a disc of the duo singing "Way Down Barcelona Way" (4132). In September 1920, Okeh also released a disc of the duo singing this (4132) and in October Gennett issued the same title (9069).

In 1919, the duo signed an Edison contract, agreeing to travel widely and conduct Tone Test Recitals, designed to demonstrate that Diamond Discs re-created voices with such fidelity that audiences would be unable to tell the difference from the voices of the performers on stage with their voices on Edison discs (artists carefully sang at the same volume level as the phonographs, never in full voice). The earliest reference in *Talking Machine World* to Collins and Harlan on a Tone Test tour is on page 109 of the November 1919 issue. A photograph shows the two standing with William Reed, identified as "their recital conductor," in front of Thomas A. Edison's birthplace in Milan, Ohio.

In any case, the two had been important to Edison's National Phonograph Company from the duo's formation in 1902, and they were ending their career with Edison's company, now called Thomas A. Edison, Inc. As a solo artist, Collins made a recording for Gennett in 1922, and Harlan recorded as a solo artist for a few companies—Gennett, Okeh, and Brunswick—but as the team Collins and Harlan, they recorded only for Edison in the 1920s, their last ones made for Edison in 1924.

The team's career—and Collins' life—almost came to a premature end on October 20, 1921, during a Tone Test demonstration at the Princess Theater in Medina, Ohio. Exiting the stage in the dark, the baritone fell through a trapdoor accidently left open. By mid-1923 Collins had sufficiently recovered to leave his home and join Harlan for a long tour of the West.

The Edison company released records by the duo until late 1924. The last Collins and Harlan disc is Diamond Disc 51423, "Any Way the Wind Blows (My Sweetie Goes)" backed by "Liver and Bacon." These were not issued as Blue Amberols.

A late reference to the team in *Talking Machine World* is in the December 15, 1924, issue: "Collins & Harlan, popular Edison artists, gave a concert in Muncie [Indiana] the past week under the auspices of the Edison store, which was well received." Another late reference to the duo in the trade journal is on page 172 of the January 1925 issue: "Collins & Harlan, the famous singing team, assisted by William Reed, star flutist and saxophonist, will start in Cleveland on January 5 and continue giving concerts in the Middle West section." The final reference to the duo in the trade journal is on page 150 of the March 1925 issue: "Collins and Harlan began a [Tone Test] tour of the Philadelphia section on March 21."

Their recording career as a duo was over by the advent of electrical recordings. Researcher Ronald Dethlefson discovered in the Henry Ford Museum a letter dated January 18, 1926, that suggests Collins and Harlan did some radio work in the 1920s. Arthur Collins writes to Thomas Edison:

> I take the liberty of writing to you, to ask if you think Mr. Ford would be interested in, or could use Mr. Harlan and myself in his Broadcasting Programme each week. It occurred to us that he being an exponent of Old Time and clean dancing, might look with favor on singing songs of the same type. We are very desirous of affiliating with some *good* concern, and knew that a word from you would help us in this new field. While we were on tour for you, our Broadcasting in the West met with a great deal of success, and with excellent criticisms everywhere. We hope you are enjoying the best of health . . .

Collins signed the letter and then added "Always Edison Artists." Collins' address at the time was 362 Washington St., Hempstead, Long Island, New York. Harlan lived in West Orange, not far from the home of Thomas A. Edison. Clearly the duo was eager to continue working, but it is unknown if anything came from this request to Edison to help them secure radio—or "Broadcasting"—work.

Columbia Stellar Quartet

Founding members of the Columbia Stellar Quartet in late 1913 were tenors Charles Harrison and John Barnes Wells, baritone Andrea Sarto, and bass Frank Croxton. In 1915 Wells was briefly replaced by Henry Burr, who in turn was replaced by Reed Miller (after Miller left around 1920, Harrison switched from first tenor to second tenor—the singer who filled the first tenor slot for late records is unknown). Columbia catalogs state, "This quartette sings together only for the Columbia Company, and each new record is a veritable sensation." The group's first Columbia disc featured "Sally in Our Alley" backed by "The Girl I Left Behind Me" (A1440), issued in January 1914 and only briefly available.

Catalogs describe the extensive experience of each singer in choral societies and oratorio work, and the "stellar" adjective was appropriate given the fame of the members as concert singers. But record buyers could have easily confused the group with the similarly named Columbia Male Quartet (or Columbia Quartette), which other companies called the Peerless. After the Columbia Stellar Quartet was formed, Columbia itself began to use the Peerless name fairly regularly for Columbia discs featuring performances by the better established quartet led by Henry Burr, no doubt to prevent record buyers from confusing the Columbia Stellar Quartet and the Columbia Male Quartet. However, until 1918 the company did occasionally use the Columbia Quartette name instead of the Peerless name.

The quartet consisting of eminent concert singers was called the Columbia Stellar Quartet for standards and the Broadway Quartet for popular songs (on A2055, the Stellar name is used on one side, the Broadway name on the other). Before the Broadway name was coined in late 1915, the Stellar name was used for performances of some popular songs, such as Percy Wenrich's "When You Wore a Tulip and I Wore a Big Red Rose" on A1683. Curiously, the name Columbia Stellar Quartet (instead of Broadway Quartet) was used in 1921 on A3377 for the Walter Donaldson composition "My Mammy"— the song that Al Jolson made famous in *The Jazz Singer.*

The quartet was most active during the World War I period, perhaps enjoying its greatest success in 1918 when several new recordings were issued during most months. It recorded many sentimental favorites, including "Annie Laurie" (A1491), "Just Before the Battle, Mother" (A2246), and "Kathleen Mavourneen" (A5899). The Columbia Stellar Quartet functioned for Columbia much as the Orpheus Quartet did for Victor, even in assisting featured solo vocalists. In the Columbia studio the quartet assisted such singers as Oscar Seagle, Margaret Keyes, and Lucy Gates. As late as April 13, 1922, the quartet assisted Rosa Ponselle on "Little Alabama Coon."

The final session with Croxton as a member took place before November 1, 1920, when the bass became exclusive to Victor. "Ye Olden Yuletide Hymns" was issued in December 1920 on A2993. Several records were made in 1921. The last one credited to the Columbia Stellar Quartet was "Nearer, My God, to Thee" on A3469, and in February 1922 "Georgia Rose" as sung by the Broadway Quartet was issued on Columbia A3513 (despite the reverse side featuring Al Jolson singing "Yoo Hoo," it was only briefly available). Aside from Harrison, the singers on these late records are not known. Around 1927 Harrison organized a quartet with a similar sound and repertoire, the American Singers.

Conway's Band

Patrick Conway was born in Troy, New York, in 1865. According to Edison's *Amberola Monthly* of February 1921, "he began his musical career while working in a carriage factory, where a fellow worker sold him a cornet, agreeing, at the same time, to teach him how to play on it." Victor catalogs report that he was "an instructor in band music at Cornell University before he became director of the Ithaca Band, Ithaca, NY, 1895, which has since developed into 'Conway's Band,' known from coast to coast of America." He directed the Cornell Cadet Band until 1908. In that year he renamed the Ithaca Band to Patrick Conway and His Band, always called Conway's Band on Victor records.

His was a professional civilian band that sometimes toured but never as widely as Sousa's or Liberati's. Like most other famous bands characterized as "military bands," including Sousa's, it was a concert—never a marching or parade—band. In August 1903 Conway's Ithaca Band played the first of many Willow Grove Park concerts in the Chelten Hills part of Philadelphia, where prominent bands and symphonies played each summer from May 1896 onward. Renamed Conway's Band, it returned to Willow Grove Park many times, as late as 1925. It played season after season at Young's Million Dollar Steel Pier in Atlantic City. In 1915 it played for ten weeks at the Panama-Pacific Exposition in San Francisco. The January 1917 Victor supplement includes a photograph of Conway's Band, consisting of about forty musicians, during its San Francisco engagement. Instead of employing musicians year-round, he generally assembled musicians on a "pickup" basis to play for summer engagements. His reputation was such that he was able to engage excellent musicians, including cornet soloist John Dolan and saxophonist H. Benne Henton. In 1919 he added a winter engagement in Florida.

Conway's Band recorded a wide variety of numbers, including ragtime, waltzes, marches, cakewalks, musical show and popular song medleys (a medley was often called a "medley fox trot" or "medley one-step"), one-steps and two-steps, overtures, and parodies. Conway's Band recorded for Victor from 1912 to 1918, and it was, along with the Victor Military Band, important for providing music appropriate for several new dance steps of this era. Many labels state, "For dancing." The band's first session was in July of 1912, and soon afterward "Before the Mast" and Hernandez's "The United Service March" were issued on Victor 17154. For the next few years the band generally recorded for a week or two in the summer months, presumably during a lull in concert engagements.

Victor's December 1915 supplement, announcing the release of three twelve-inch discs, states, "Conway's Band furnishes the dance music for this month, and lively music it is, to be sure . . . all records of great volume and played in perfect rhythm. . . . No home in which dancing is enjoyed should be without these fine Fox Trot and One-Step records."

The band was also important for recording military band selections, many of which were promoted for serious listening purposes, not dancing. Victor's January 1917 supplement, announcing the release of Victor 18182, states:

> "The American Trumpeter March" starts out with a dash and a swing that will surely delight the heart of all lovers of band music. The bugle-like trumpet calls and rattling drums in the middle section are thrilling to hear. The "All American March" is no less spirited. The shrill notes of the piccolo are used to advantage, and in both numbers there are plenty of what Irvin S. Cobb chooses to call soul-stirring "um-pahs." Conway's Band is noted for its brilliance and precision of execution—qualities that put life into a march.

The band's recording of M. L. Lake's "Evolution of Dixie" (35600) is called by the Victor supplement of February 1917 "an amusing diversion in which the famous old melody is made to appear in many different ways." Tempos change too much for this to be suitable as dance music. That same month, Victor promoted the Conway Band recording of Neil Moret's "Jolly General March" (35608) as "offered for use in schools," perfect "for marching, calisthenics, penmanship and all kinds of rhythm drills."

The final Victor session was in the summer of 1918. Military band records sold well during the time America was at war, but demand dropped when the war ended. By 1919 military band records had lost popularity among dancers, who preferred the new sound of jazz bands and especially society orchestras such as Joseph C. Smith's.

Page 121 of the July 1919 issue of *Talking Machine World* reports, "Capt. Conway rendered invaluable service to the Aviation Corps of the United States Army during the past war as a bandmaster, and in recognition of this service he was recently appointed a Captain in the Aviation Corps."

In 1919 Conway's Band began recording for other companies, including Starr-Gennett, Pathé, and Paramount, but most often for Thomas A. Edison, Inc. and the Otto Heineman Phonograph Supply Company, maker of Okeh discs. On Pathé 40173 the band performs Thomas's "Raymond Overture." The first Conway's Band Edison release was Blue Amberol 3805, issued in August 1919: Hall's "Tenth Regiment March." A photograph of the distinguished-looking Captain Patrick Conway graces the cover of the September 1919 issue of *Edison Amberola Monthly*. The band's first Diamond Disc featured a Spanish March by Chapi titled

"Bunch of Roses" (50557), issued in February 1920. In the next few years the band was issued on fifteen Diamond Discs and twenty Blue Amberols.

Conway's earliest numbered Okeh record features Hadley's "To Victory March" backed by Weldon's "Gate City March" (1240), issued along with four other vertical-cut Okeh discs. The September 1919 issue of *Talking Machine World* includes a full-page Okeh advertisement announcing the release of the five discs featuring "Capt. Patrick Conway and His Famous Conway Band." In October Okeh began issuing lateral-cut discs, and over forty more Conway titles would be issued.

According to the March 1922 issue of *The Musical Observer,* Conway agreed to move from Syracuse back to Ithaca to direct the Ithaca School of Band Instruments, affiliated with the Ithaca Conservatory of Music. In 1924 he founded the Conway Military Band School in Ithaca and devoted his energies to the school for the few remaining years of his life. He died in 1929.

De Leath, Vaughn (September 26, 1896-May 28, 1943)

Vaughn De Leath was born in Mount Pulaski, Illinois, as Leonore Vonderleath, and her performing name was based upon her real last name, which was probably too German to be suitable for an entertainer in post-World War I America. "Von" became "Vaughn," and "-derleath" was simplified to "De Leath." Raised in California, she attended public schools in Pomona as well as Riverside and then attended Mills College in Oakland. Nicknamed "The Original Radio Girl" and "The Radio Girl," De Leath—occasionally given as DeLeath, deLeath, and de Leath—performed on countless broadcasts from the early 1920s to the mid-1930s. Radio history books suggest that she was before a radio microphone in December 1919 or January 1920 in the laboratory of inventor Lee De Forest, performing for dozens of listeners (the first station with regular broadcasts would not be established until late 1920). Details about her radio debut are murky—sources conflict not only on the date but on what she sang. In 1939 she was a television pioneer.

She sang in a crooning style (sometimes with a little-girl affectation) that was best captured in the electric era, but she made many recordings in the acoustic era, beginning in 1920. She could croon in an alto range or sing in a very high soprano voice. Irving Settel writes in *A Pictorial History of Radio* (Grosset & Dunlap, 1960, p. 58) that her crooning style "was imposed on her by the limitations of the radio equipment of the day, since the high notes of sopranos often blew out the delicate tubes of the transmitters."

Page 136 of the March 1922 issue of *Talking Machine World* discusses her early years:

> Miss De Leath's rise to popularity has been unusually rapid, for ten years ago she was playing the piano and leading the High School Orchestra in the evening in one of the Los Angeles theatres. The quality of her voice attracted the attention of several Los Angeles musical critics, and by sheer hard work she soon advanced rapidly in the musical world.

The article adds, "While in Detroit [in early 1922] Miss de Leath sang over the radiophone, accompanied by Paul Specht's Society Serenaders."

Her recording debut was "I Love the Land of Old Black Joe" from the revue *Ed. Wynn's Carnival*. Issued as Blue Amberol 4097 in October 1920, this was her only Edison record issued in the early 1920s. Six years later she returned to the Edison studio and worked regularly for the company, with the first of over forty Diamond Discs issued in early 1927. She is featured on the last numbered Diamond Disc: "Oh! Susanna" and "Honey, I'se A-waitin' Jes' Fo' Yo'" (52651), issued on November 1, 1929. The latter song was composed by De Leath.

Announcing the release of her Blue Amberol of 1920, Edison promotional literature states, "Vaughn de Leath's voice is well adapted to the colored accent. Her enunciation is so good that every word is intelligible."

After making this single Edison recording she worked regularly for the General Phonograph Corporation, making Okeh records beginning in late 1920 with "I'm a Little Nobody That Nobody Loves" (4292), issued in May 1921. For that label, and its Odeon subsidiary, she sometimes used the name Mary Miller. The July 1921 issue of *Talking Machine World* announced that she "signed a contract to make Okeh records exclusively. . . . Miss De Leath's voice is an exceptionally rich contralto which lends itself admirably to recording. . . . In addition to her recording activities, Miss De Leath is one of the composers on the staff of Irving Berlin, music publisher, and several of her numbers have attained considerable success."

She composed many songs, with a couple published as early as 1912. De Leath compositions that enjoyed moderate success include "It's a Lonely Trail" and "At Evenside." "Drowsy Head" featured the music of De Leath and the lyrics of Irving Berlin, and it was published in 1921 by Berlin's music company. Her composition "New Orleans" was recorded by

Mamie Smith for Okeh 4630 in 1922. Page 142 of the March 1922 issue of *Talking Machine World* lists Okeh artists who were enjoying success on radio, such as on a February 17 program, and new De Leath compositions are mentioned: "Miss de Leath was a prominent factor in the program. . . . The final number on the program was the 'Star-Spangled Banner,' by all of those present, but before that number was given Miss de Leath sang her latest compositions, 'New Orleans' and 'Cover Me With Kisses.' At the close of the program Miss de Leath was congratulated upon the success of the concert . . ." Page 54 of the May 1922 issue states, "Miss Vaughn De Leath, well-known contralto and exclusive Okeh artist, has just composed a new selection entitled 'Say It By Radio.' At the recent Brooklyn radio show Miss De Leath's new song was given an enthusiastic reception . . ."

Page 126 of the August 1922 issue of *Talking Machine World* reports, "Miss Vaughn De Leath . . . recently conceived a unique idea for her radio program. This plan involved singing a duet with herself from the WJZ station [in Newark, New Jersey], with the assistance of one of her Okeh records."

Her exclusive contract with Okeh evidently lasted only a year since in June 1922 she made her first Gennett recordings: "I'm Just Wild About Harry" (4905) and "Nobody Lied" (4907). She intermittently made Gennett records until 1927. Later in 1922 she also recorded for Pathé and Arto, then made no more records until mid-1923 when she recorded for Federal. In New York City's Belasco Theatre on November 28, 1923 she was in the opening cast as Signora Calvaro in *Laugh, Clown, Laugh*.

There was another gap in her recording activity until early 1924, when she returned to Gennett to record "Lazy" and "Waitin' Around" (5425). She recorded little in 1924, only a session each for the New York Recording Laboratories, Emerson, and Columbia. Two more sessions for Columbia followed in 1925, as well as two for Plaza. For her Columbia debut on December 22, 1924, she cut "Nobody Knows What a Red Head Mama Can Do" and "I Ain't Got Nobody to Love" (271-D). She made Columbia records as late as October 1928.

In mid-1925, De Leath may have signed a contract to be exclusive to Cameo since for the next year she was only on that label, all discs using the name Gloria Geer ("Geer" was her married name). On small labels and budget labels her performances were frequently issued under other names, including Mazie Green (Silvertone), Madge Thompson (Challenge), Angelina Marco (Harmony), Jane Kennedy (Oriole, Jewel, and Conqueror), and Mamie Lee (Parlophone).

When May Singhi Breen recorded "Ukulele Lessons, Part 1 and Part 2" for Victor 19740 on July 27, 1925 (with her husband Peter De Rose at the piano), De Leath was used briefly as vocalist. Months earlier, on April 6, 1925, she had cut "Ukulele Lady" for Columbia 361-D. She also made a few comedy and children's records in the mid-1920s.

In mid-1926 she returned to the Gennett studios, and from this point on until late 1929 De Leath was incredibly busy as a recording artist, appearing on many labels—Columbia, Edison, Okeh, Brunswick, Victor, Grey Gull, and more. She provided vocal refrains for various dance bands, including those led by Nat Shilkret, Paul Whiteman, Ben Bernie, Herb Gordon, Bill Wirges, Louis Katzman, and B. A. Rolfe.

She recorded "The Man I Love" a few times in 1928: for Columbia 1241-D, Brunswick 3748, and Columbia 50068-D with Paul Whiteman (in mid-1928 she also worked with Whiteman's ensemble on the NBC radio show *Columbia Phonograph Hour*). On January 7, 1928, she was perhaps the first female to record "Can't Help Lovin' Dat Man" from Jerome Kern's *Show Boat* (Columbia 1284-D). Edison promotional literature from this time characterized De Leath as especially deft with upbeat songs. Announcing the August 1927 release of Diamond Disc 52073, featuring "Baby Feet Go Pitter Patter" and "Yep! 'Long About June," the Advance Notice of New Edison Disc Record Releases (Weekly Bulletin No. 27) stated:

> Have you ever noticed how small children love to listen when Vaughn DeLeath is singing? . . . Miss DeLeath can sing almost any kind of song and make it charming, but her best songs are selections like these two, where every line is bubbling over with love and joy. . . . You can almost see her playing with children while she sings . . .

After a November 1929 session, she did not record again until 1931 when she had two sessions for Crown. She made no other recordings in the 1930s aside from some children's songs issued on Victor's budget-priced Bluebird label. She continued to work on network radio and even ran a nightclub in Stamford, Connecticut.

She was a resident soloist on the popular *Voice of Firestone* radio show, which was broadcast coast-to-coast each Monday evening beginning in the late 1920s. She was the featured female vocalist on the program's first broadcast on December 3, 1928, with Franklyn Baur being the featured male vocalist on that debut broadcast. Both singers participated in a Firestone anniversary broadcast made on January 6, 1939. By this time she was unable to secure work on the networks and settled for engagements on local radio programs.

On May 3, 1924, she married Livingston Geer, a portrait painter. They divorced in 1934. She married again in 1936. She died in Buffalo, New

York, on May 28, 1943. Her sister, Alma Cunningham of Los Angeles, had been named as sole beneficiary.

Denny, Will F. (c. 1860-October 2, 1908)

A native of Boston, the tenor Will Denny performed on vaudeville stages and recorded prolifically in the first decade of the commercial recording industry, specializing in comic numbers. He began recording in 1890. An article titled "Famous Record-Makers and Their Work" in the December 1891 issue of *The Phonogram* states:

> Mr. W. F. Denny, who has been employed by the New England Phonograph Company for over a year, early developed a talent for popular music, and appeared first as a public singer at the Academy of Music, where he sang with great success the then popular song "The Pretty Red Rose." Shortly thereafter he became a member of the "Quartette Club" of Philadelphia.

The New England Phonograph Company was established in 1890 in the Boylston Building in Boston. The 1891 article, duplicated in the Fall 1971 issue of *Association for Recorded Sound Collections Journal*, also states:

> After the termination of Mr. Denny's contract with this company he began to "star," visiting all the best theatres and music halls in the country. Mr. Denny's voice is a tenor of pure tone and much pathos, and his articulation is extremely wonderful. As a vocal record maker it is claimed he has no equal in this country, and although his services have been sought by others, he has devoted his spare time entirely to the New England Phonograph Company.

He was best known for singing topical and "coon" songs, able to sing at a fast pace with the words remaining distinct. He also recorded parodies, such as "Parody on 'Because'" (Edison 7379). He rarely recorded the standards or sentimental numbers covered by such colleagues as George J. Gaskin, Harry Macdonough, and Albert Campbell. In the early 1900s he may have viewed Billy Murray as a rival comic tenor, both singers notable for versatility and clear enunciation. Denny's recording career was in decline when Murray began recording for Edison, Victor, and Columbia in 1903.

Most of his pre-1900 recordings are Edison and Columbia cylinders. He began recording for Columbia in 1897 or early 1898 (he is not in the June 1897 catalog). Columbia's 1898 catalog lists a few dozen Denny titles, many with a British flavor, such as "A Pity to Waste It" (6325) and

"What Ze English Call Ze" (6351). An 1899 catalog of cylinders duplicates an agreement dated May 1, 1898, indicating that Denny, along with
more than a dozen others who signed the agreement, was exclusive to
Columbia. The arrangement lasted a year.

He made over two dozen Berliners. He cut a handful of titles in July and
August of 1897, and then nearly two years passed before returning on May
2, 1899, evidently as soon as his exclusive arrangement with Columbia
had expired. He was one of the last singers to record for Berliner. Within
weeks of his last session, the company was essentially forced by an injunction to cease production.

Typical Edison numbers are "Naughty Banana Peel" (7154) and "My
Ebony Belle" (7980), issued as brown wax cylinders. "Ain't Dat a
Shame?," with words by the prolific John Queen and music by Walter
Wilson, is sung by Denny on Edison 7875 at a pace that allows for two
verses and two rounds of the chorus. He was a more imaginative singer than
most of his generation and worked harder at injecting variety into comic
performances. When singing the chorus of "Ain't Dat a Shame?" a second
time, Denny yodels as he implores, "Won't you open that door?" He ends
the song by speaking the words, "Open that door—let me in, honey, will
ya?" Such an impromptu ending was atypical for this early period.

Denny recorded regularly for Edison up to 1903, with the Harry Von
Tilzer "coon" song "Trixie" issued as 8552 in December 1903. He did not
return to the company until 1906. The April 1906 issue of *Edison Phonograph Monthly*, announcing the May release of Standard 9278, states, " 'At
the Minstrel Show, No. 4,' by the Edison Minstrels introduces William F.
Denny in his great monologue entitled 'A Matrimonial Chat.' A bright,
crisp comedy talk of the kind that is always entertaining . . . concluding
with the topical song, 'It's All a Matter of Taste,' with orchestra accompaniment." As a solo artist, he recorded at that time only Seymour Furth's
"Nothing Like That in Our Family," issued on Standard 9306 in July.
Announcing its release, the May 1906 issue of *Edison Phonograph
Monthly* states, "Topical songs have always been his forte and this selection is similar in character." Denny recorded the same song for Columbia
cylinder 32919 and disc 3368.

In 1907, Edison issued final Denny titles in four consecutive months:
Cobb and Edwards' "Ask Me Not" (9551; issued in May), Dave Reed's
"You'll Have to Get Off and Walk" (9568; issued in June), Joe A. Budd's
"Tale of the Bucket" (9598; issued in July) and Reed's "My Word! What a
Lot of It!" (9620; issued in August). The subject of "My Word! What a Lot
of It!" is champagne, the first taste of which leads the song's subject,
Chauncey, to a hasty proposal and disastrous marriage.

According to Fagan and Moran's *Encyclopedic Discography of Victor Recordings: Pre-Matrix Series*, Denny recorded twenty-four takes for Victor on September 11, 1901. It was his only Victor session. Ten titles were covered, each one recorded for a seven-inch disc and a ten-inch disc. Denny had recorded the same songs for other companies. For example, Denny had recorded "Oh! Don't It Tickle You?" for Columbia in 1898 and Edison in 1899.

He worked most often for Columbia in his final years (his last record for the company was "You'll Have to Get Off and Walk," issued in July 1907). He made Zon-o-phone discs in this period, and his last records were Zon-o-phone discs. A Zon-o-phone catalog dated May 10, 1901, lists five titles sung by Denny. For Zon-o-phone he made one of the earliest records of "Meet Me in St. Louis, Louis" (5934). His last Zon-o-phone was "All the Girls Look Good to Me" (1048), issued in July 1908.

He worked in vaudeville and died in Seattle on October 2, 1908, while touring the Pantages Circuit. The October 10, 1908, issue of *Variety* reports, "Denny's illness began September 22, when he suffered a sudden seizure in his dressing room at Pantages Theater, Seattle. He was immediately rushed to Providence Hospital in that city, but paralysis seemed to have developed, and although he soon recovered consciousness, death followed . . ." He was buried in Philadelphia.

Dudley, S. H. *(January 15, 1864-June 6, 1947)*

S. H. Dudley may have been the most popular baritone to record at the turn of the century, his output by 1900 exceeding that of baritone J. W. Myers. Dudley was in the right place at the right time in the sense that his voice suited the crude recording devices of the time better than most. As a featured solo artist he was in studios regularly from 1898 to 1904, after which there is a noticeable drop-off. In a letter to Jim Walsh quoted in the May 1946 issue of *Hobbies*, Dudley even calls himself the Bing Crosby of 1900, stating that "more records were sold of Dudley, Kernell, duets, quartets, than of any other singer of the time." Dudley adds, "Too bad the days of royalties had not arrived!" The Bing Crosby analogy is misleading since Dudley records did not dramatically outsell those of Arthur Collins, Harry Macdonough, and a handful of other pioneers.

He was born Samuel Holland Rous in Greencastle, Indiana. His father was a professor at Asbury College and then a superintendent of county schools, a position that required constant moving. Rous wrote to Walsh in a letter transcribed in the May 1946 issue of *Hobbies*, "I never even went through high school, but was forced to get a job at 13 when my father lost his hearing and could no longer teach. Then I jumped into opera without ever having a single voice lesson!" He had at least one brother since Walsh reports in the June 1963 issue of *Hobbies* that the Rous of the cylinder company Burke & Rous, of 334 Fifth Avenue, Brooklyn, New York, "was the brother of Sam Rous."

The singer adopted the name S. H. Dudley as a stage name early in his career, and this is the name used for most of his Berliner, Victor, and Edison records. Some cylinders from 1898 and early 1899 give the name S. Holland Dudley, including Excelsior cylinders—the three principal Excelsior artists in 1898 were Dudley, Roger Harding, and William F. Hooley. But from mid-1899 onward the shorter "S. H. Dudley" was used on records. On a few Victor discs, he is identified as Frank Kernell, such as on "The Whistling Coon" (1982). When making duets with bird imitator Joe Belmont, he also used the name Kernell. His real name, Samuel Holland Rous, appears as the byline for some editions of *The Victor Book of the Opera.*

He spent some early years of his career singing opera with touring companies, including the Boston Ideal Opera Company. By 1890 he was touring with the Grand English Opera Company, which featured American soprano Emma Juch. Surviving program notes from productions given in Los Angeles on December 26 and 27, 1890, list "S. H. Dudley" for minor baritone roles in *Faust* and *Rigoletto.* By 1895 he toured with the Tavary Grand English Opera Company. His wife was Sofia Romani, a soprano in several of the opera companies with which Dudley toured. He also took on dramatic roles under the direction of Charles Frohman.

Walsh states in the October 1962 issue of *Hobbies* that the Edison Quartet (or Edison Male Quartette) was organized "about 1894 to make soft brown wax cylinders. Original members were Roger Harding, J. K. Reynard, S. H. Dudley, and William F. Hooley." Presumably none of these cylinders have survived. An 1896 Edison Quartet photograph once owned by John Bieling and duplicated in the September 1979 issue of *Hobbies* includes Dudley. Dudley recalled for Walsh in a 1931 letter quoted in the January 1944 issue of *Hobbies* that Steve Porter, putting together a quartet for recording, recruited Dudley as a second tenor. This is curious since Porter is absent from Walsh's list of original Edison quartet members, but if Porter did recruit Dudley, then 1894 may be too early a date for the quartet's formation or at least for Dudley's participation.

He became important as baritone for the Edison Quartet and Haydn Quartet. Dudley's signature is etched in several Berliner discs of the Haydn Quartet, and Dudley added the word "manager" after his name (an example is 021, "Nearer My God to Thee," recorded on March 23, 1899). He recalled in the 1931 letter that in the earliest days at the studio he sang "simple old-fashioned stuff—Old Oaken Buckett [sic]; Hail, Jerusalem—

but the singing position was decidedly cramping, as the crude methods of recording made it necessary for us to bump our heads close together." Soon he made his first solo record for Edison, recalling for Walsh that it was "The Chili Widow."

The earliest known discs to feature Dudley as a solo artist are Berliners from 1898, perhaps the first being "Tramp, Tramp, Tramp" (157), cut on June 10, 1898. Two weeks later he recorded two duets with Roger Harding (Berliners 3006 and 3014). He was prolific for the company as a solo artist, cutting over fifty titles. He made five Berliners with Harry Macdonough, with whom he sang often in the Haydn Quartet.

The Gramophone Minstrels (really the Haydn Quartet) made a few Berliners on March 28, 1900, and Berliner 01134 has handwritten on the master, "Introducing 'The Old Log Cabin in the Dell,' by the entire company, and 'How I Love My Lou,' by S. H. Dudley the phenomenal baritone." Since Dudley himself signed Berliners when Haydn discs were prepared (many Berliner artists signed the masters), this inscription on the Gramophone Minstrels disc was probably written by him. Early Victor literature for 509, featuring the Georgia Minstrels, states, "Introducing 'How I Love My Lou' by Mr. Dudley, the phenomenal baritone."

"The Merry Whistling Darkey" is featured on Standard 9502, and for the Edison company to release cylinders featuring Dudley as solo artist as late as March 1907 is surprising given Dudley's executive responsibilities at Victor by this time. It is also surprising since Dudley wrote to Walsh in a letter quoted in the May 1946 issue of *Hobbies* that Victor at first allowed the new executive to make Edison cylinders but that "after another year, they bought off my Edison privilege." Announcing the cylinder's release, the January 1907 *Edison Phonograph Monthly* states, "Mr. Dudley shows that he has lost none of his skill as a whistler. It is some time since he has made a solo Record for our lists." It was his last for Edison.

The Dudley recording to remain longest in the Victor catalogue was the popular "Red Wing," sung with Harry Macdonough and still available as late as 1925 on Victor 17233 though recorded two decades earlier.

Despite his earlier experience singing opera, Dudley was valued in studios for singing popular tunes of the day, including patriotic, marching, and "coon" songs. The opera background turned invaluable when Dudley later compiled *The Victor Book of the Opera*. Some selections are identified as "topical songs" on labels, such as "The Man Behind" from the show *The Medal and the Maid*. He recorded this in early 1904 as both a ten-inch disc (Monarch 2681) and twelve inch (Deluxe 31197). He was also one of four singers to popularize on disc "Meet Me in St. Louis, Louis" in 1904. Others were Billy Murray, Will F. Denny, and J. W. Myers.

He was versatile in studios, equally skilled as solo artist, whistler, member of a duet (often teamed with tenor Harry Macdonough or John Bieling), and quartet member. He was comfortable singing sentimental ballads (he harmonizes beautifully with Harry Macdonough on "Sweet Adeline") and comic tunes of the day.

One such comic number is "Not by a Dam Side" (Victor 1090), recorded on different dates, beginning November 9, 1901, and, finally, on September 22, 1903 (he also recorded it for Edison as Standard 7977). The song describes a young man eagerly showing his bride-to-be the home he has bought, but the house is near a mill's dam and she protests that she could never live near a dam. The humor resides in this "little maid" uttering "dam" often and vehemently:

> Not by a dam side
> Will I live with you
> Not by a dam side
> Would your love be true
> You promise me your tender care
> You say that we'll be happy there
> My love with you I'll ever share
> But not by a dam side

Dudley's diction is excellent.

Oaths were sometimes slipped into comic songs at this time. Another one is in Dudley's "Miss Helen Hunt," which offers the punch line "Go to Helen Hunt for it" (recorded in 1899 for Edison, in 1900 for Victor). On May 23, 1900, Dudley cut another song with "dam" in the title: "Yuba Dam," issued as seven-inch 36 (he cut it again for Victor on July 26, 1904, and also cut it for Edison as Standard 7178). The song is described in the Improved Gram-o-phone catalog as "A very funny play on the Western town of that name." The humor resides in listeners hearing the oath "you be damned." Yuba City in California suffered a century ago from water running over the banks of the Feather and Yuba rivers, but in fact no Yuba Dam existed.

The name S. H. Dudley is important for two different researchers: those interested in early recordings and those interested in early black musicals. The two S. H. Dudleys—one white, the other black—were both pioneers in their own ways but they should not be confused. That two performers of the same generation shared this name is only a coincidence. The white S. H. Dudley had already adopted it as a stage name before the black S. H. Dudley gained popularity. The latter was born Sherman Houston Dudley (May 12, 1872-February 29, 1940), and he used his initials for his stage name. He was perhaps best known as a leader of the touring vaudeville and musical comedy company called The Smart Set. One successful Dudley show was *His Honor the Barber* (the Ford Dabney song "That's Why They Call Me Shine," simply called "Shine" on various recordings, is from this 1910 show). This Dudley also composed songs with Chris Smith. The two men who used the name S. H. Dudley probably never met.

Dudley ceased recording regularly as a solo artist around 1903 to take on important responsibilities as assistant manager of the Victor Artist and Repertoire Department. Calvin C. Child was nominally responsible for all artists (Child also had considerable experience in the industry—he supervised Columbia sessions in the 1890s when the company was headquartered in Washington, DC and had worked for other early companies), but Child worked most closely with Red Seal artists, and Dudley supervised sessions producing "popular" Victor records (this job later went to John Macdonald, or "Harry Macdonough").

He did make contributions to sessions after 1903. He was master of ceremonies for a series of Christy Minstrel performances cut in 1907. He continued serving as Haydn Quartet baritone until Reinald Werrenrath replaced Dudley in 1909, at which point Harry Macdonough became the quartet's manager. Curiously, Victor catalogs as late as 1925 continued to identify the quartet members as "Bieling, Macdonough, Dudley, Hooley" and to include Dudley's photograph. A 1912 Victor catalog shows Dudley as a member of the Victor Light Opera Company, though it is not likely that he contributed to such ensemble recordings as late as 1912. He probably sang on some of the ensemble's earliest recordings. It is possible that uncredited performances on Victor Light Opera Company productions were his last on disc.

Walsh wrote about Dudley in three issues of *Hobbies*: January 1944, February 1944, and May 1946. Long before these articles, Walsh wrote "Reminiscences of 'S.H. Dudley'" for the January 1932 issue of *Phonograph Monthly Review*, based partly upon a letter sent by Dudley to Walsh in 1931. According to the letter, Dudley became around 1903 the executive who selected "each month 50 to 100 numbers for the monthly bulletin" and who made sure "that artists were engaged to sing them." Moreover, he had to "test all the new records, sometimes 500 a month" and "scout for new singers."

As assistant manager of the Victor Artist and Repertoire Department, Dudley each year compiled for Victor its alphabetical record catalog, which itself was based on the Victor monthly supplements that Dudley wrote from 1903 to 1916 or so (James E. Richardson succeeded Dudley as editor of Victor supplements and catalogs).

He deserves recognition as author of *The Victor Book of the Opera*, or, as some editions are titled, *The Victrola Book of the Opera*. The book was first published in 1912 and sold for 75 cents. It was expanded in 1913, the blue-covered second edition being by far the rarest of the many editions. The first three editions were published without credit to any author, but a name was given when the fourth edition was issued in 1917: Samuel Holland Rous.

The book was really an elaborate advertisement for Victor products, listing by number and price the discs on which Victor artists perform notable arias. In *The Victor Book of the Opera*, illustrations are plentiful; opera summaries are accurate and well-written; arias are sensitively translated; the selection of operas is broad, with many modern and obscure operas included. Books came in protective boxes.

He wrote decades later to Walsh that Victor in 1919 awarded the retiring executive a pension on condition that Dudley would not join a rival company. He established a home in Europe but also traveled widely for the rest of his life, writing to Walsh, "We spend six months in our little apartment in Monaco and in the summer explore the mountain passes in our trusty Renault. . . . In 1927 a trip around the world broke the monotony—and another book could be written about some adventures while trying to see something of the virgin jungles of Sumatra."

He continued working on *The Victor Book of the Opera* until around the mid-1930s. Even after he stopped working on editions, many of his summaries continued intact in late editions although his name is nowhere mentioned. Conductor and author Charles O'Connell revised the ninth edition so that photographs of new Victor Red Seal artists replaced old illustrations. Also, additional operas were included and a few new summaries supplanted the old.

Dudley died in Los Angeles on June 6, 1947. According to a directory of births and deaths compiled by Walsh for the December 1961 issue of *Hobbies*, Dudley's wife, Sofia, died there one day later.

Europe, Jim (February 22, 1880-May 9, 1919)

James Reese Europe was born in Mobile, Alabama, to a father, Henry J. Europe, who had been born into slavery. As a boy, Europe had shown talent on piano and other instruments. When he was nine, his family moved to Washington, DC, where he continued private music lessons. He lived for a time only houses away from John Philip Sousa and must have known, while living in the nation's capital, the excitement that Sousa and his famous U.S. Marine Corps Band could generate.

Around 1903, the young man moved to New York City, the best place for an ambitious musician—just as one generation later a young Duke Ellington would move from Washington, DC, to take his chances in the bigger city. Skilled at violin, piano, and mandolin, Europe in time earned the respect of the city's finest African-American musicians and composers. By 1905 he worked with Ernest Hogan in performances of musical comedy, later with the successful songwriting team of Bob Cole and J. Rosamond Johnson. Working with lyricist Cole, Europe in 1908 contributed to the Cole and Johnson show *The Red Moon* a comic song titled "I Ain't Had No Lovin' in a Long Time," and this was popular enough to be recorded (baritone Bob Roberts sings it on Columbia A604). Europe soon directed orchestras and choruses for musical shows featuring all-black casts. He also served as musical director for S. H. Dudley's Smart Set, an important black touring ensemble.

Of the many black musicians Europe counted among his friends at that time, only Bert Williams and his partner George Walker had made recordings. Opportunities for members of his race to record did not improve until Europe himself had a contract with the Victor Talking Machine Company. In fact, he would become the first African American to lead his own band on records issued by a major company. But that was still a few years away.

When Ernest Hogan suffered a breakdown around 1908, Europe helped organize a special performance so proceeds could be given to Hogan. The participating musicians formed a club, calling themselves the Frogs. Europe's inclusion in this elite group of black entertainers indicates how far the young man had come in just a few years.

In 1910, Europe helped establish the Clef Club for friendly meetings of musicians but more importantly as a union and booking office. It organized for the first time in New York City a large pool of African-American musicians from which employers could hire ensembles for dances and other events. The Clef Club's headquarters at 134 West 53rd Street even had modern technology to ensure that no job opportunities were lost—a telephone was installed. Until this time the city's black musicians were at a disadvantage because no efficient organization was in place to expedite their hiring.

To publicize the Clef Club, Europe organized a performance to be given on May 27, 1910, at Harlem's Manhattan Casino, 155th Street and Eighth

Avenue. He organized other events to advertise the wide-ranging talents of the black musical community. The next one, held on October 20, 1910, featured Europe's own "Clef Club March" and Henry Creamer's "Clef Club Chant." The Clef Club Symphony Orchestra was made up of over one hundred instruments, including eleven pianos.

Within two years, Europe was convinced that Clef Club musicians were ready for a Carnegie Hall performance, and on May 2, 1912, Clef Club acts performed for a sold-out house. It was a triumph for Europe, who had persevered despite others' objections that racial prejudice could mean disaster. He would later return to Carnegie Hall, leading musicians for annual concerts of the Negro Symphony Orchestra.

In 1913 Europe enjoyed even greater success through his work with husband and wife dancing team Vernon and Irene Castle, known on vaudeville stages and in Broadway shows. The Castles and Europe's Clef Club musicians were thrown together when hired for a private party, with Europe providing accompaniment for the dancing couple. The music was heavily syncopated, with instrumentation atypical for the time. The Castles found the music ideal for their routines and thereafter performed often with Europe's Exclusive Society Orchestra. The Castles opened a dance school called Castle House, where Europe's musicians regularly played and where his own compositions were featured. Europe also directed musicians at a nightclub operated by the Castles.

Association with the Castles made Europe's name well-known in New York society. Irene Castle later recalled in her autobiography *Castles in the Air* (Doubleday, 1958), "It was we who made colored orchestras the vogue of Fifth Avenue. We booked Jim Europe's orchestra, the most famous of the colored bands. Jim Europe was a skilled musician and one of the first to take jazz out of the saloons and make it respectable. All of the men in his orchestra could read music, a rarity in those days."

Wealthy patrons danced to this music endorsed by the Castles. Musicians who played in what was collectively called Europe's Orchestra, also called the Tempo Club, were steadily employed. In late 1913 Europe had resigned from the Clef Club to form his own Tempo Club.

Sheet music of waltzes and tangos composed by Europe with his associate Ford Dabney sold well. Various society bands organized by Europe were farmed out for formal dances. *The Evening Post* on March 13, 1914, identified Europe as "the head of an organization which practically controls the furnishing of music for the new dances." In this article Europe is quoted as saying, "I have between 150 and 187 musicians I can call on for work in the symphony orchestra, and I am continually adding to their numbers . . ." Never before had black musicians enjoyed such respect in New York City.

With the Castles in early 1914, Europe helped popularize the new fox-trot, introduced as a slow dance. It became a standard, outliving the turkey trot, grizzly, bunny hop, and steps with similar animal names. The fox-trot would be adopted by men in service as their favorite since the dance, when simplified, was relatively easy to master. In a 1920 letter to Noble Sissle, Irene Castle states that Europe was "the first to suggest the slow tempo used for the fox trot." Europe is quoted in the *New York Tribune* as saying, "The fox trot was created by a young negro of Memphis, Tenn., Mr. W. C. Handy, who five years ago wrote 'The Memphis Blues.' . . . Mr. Castle has generously given me credit for the fox trot, yet the credit . . . really belongs to Mr. W. C. Handy."

Eager to capitalize upon the popularity of the Castles, executives of the Victor Talking Machine Company invited Europe to make records. Europe's Society Orchestra recorded four titles for the company on December 29, 1913, and another four on February 10, 1914. Victor marketed the performances as dance music for the home, and labels state "For Dancing." Some labels even add, under the name Europe's Society Orchestra, "Recorded under the personal supervision of Mr. and Mrs. Vernon Castle." Victor advertisements proclaimed, "The Tango, Maxixe, Turkey Trot, Hesitation, Boston, One-Step, Two-Step—all are represented, and the selections are those now most in demand in dancing circles."

Victor promotional literature indicates that Europe was enjoying great success:

> During the past three seasons Europe's Society Orchestra of negro musicians has become very popular in society circles in New York and vicinity, and has played for social affairs in the homes of wealthy New Yorkers and at functions at the Tuxedo Club, Hotel Biltmore, Plaza, Sherry's, Delmonico's, the Astor and others. Mrs. R.W. Hawksworth, the famous purveyor of amusements for society, used the Europe players regularly, and they have recently been engaged to play for Mr. Vernon Castle, the popular teacher and exponent of modern dances.

Victor literature further states, "The success of this organization is due to the admirable rhythm sustained throughout every number, whether waltz, turkey trot or tango; to the original interpretation of each number; and to the unique instrumentation, which consists of banjos, mandolins, violins, clarinet, cornet, traps and drums." Around this time *The Sunday*

Press dubbed Europe "the Paderewski of syncopation," alluding to a famous classical pianist.

Europe's best-selling Victor disc may have been "The Castles in Europe One-Step" backed by "Congratulations Waltz" (Victor 35372), issued as a twelve-inch disc. It is not a common record but did remain in Victor's catalog for five years. Curiously, "The Castles in Europe One-Step" was retitled "Castle House Rag—One-Step" by the time the disc was listed in Victor's May 1914 catalog (versions with the original title, available for only a few months in early 1914, are scarce). Victor dropped from the catalog the other three Europe discs after one year.

In early 1914 Europe signed a contract with the Castles to tour England, France, and other countries, with forty black musicians to be led by Europe, but the declaration of war changed those plans. Vernon Castle, who had been born in England, volunteered to serve in the British Aviation Corps (he died in a plane accident in Texas on February 15, 1918). Although regular public performances of Europe and the Castles ended in 1915, Europe's various dance orchestras were in demand. Along with providing music for wealthy clients, he conducted performances in 1915 of a new black musical comedy, *Darkydom*, but this had a short run.

Around the time that Europe's work with the Castles ended, Noble Sissle and Eubie Blake became important to him. Sissle took a letter of introduction to the bandleader in the spring of 1916 and was invited to work in Tempo Club orchestras. Sissle soon convinced Europe to send for pianist Blake, then working in Baltimore. Sissle and Blake had met in 1915. The three remained close until Europe's death.

On September 18, 1916, Europe enlisted in the 15th New York Infantry. Noble Sissle joined a week later. Eubie Blake, with slim chances of being an officer as Europe was (Sissle would also become an officer in 1918), did not join the Army but instead proved invaluable by taking over administration of Europe's music business. When the nation was at war half a year later, thousands joined in a mass movement, but why Europe joined as early as he did is puzzling. At this time President Wilson was working to keep America officially neutral, so war fever does not explain it. The bandleader possibly joined for altruistic reasons, believing that a National Guard unit would be beneficial for Harlem as a community, but it is debatable whether Europe's enlistment set a good example for others in his community. Racial segregation was standard in the U.S. Army, and African-American enlisted men were routinely insulted and assigned dirty work. Army tradition prohibited black regiments from joining American combat divisions, and the 15th Infantry in 1918 participated in the fighting only after being assigned to the 16th Division of the French army (it was then renamed the 369th U.S. Infantry Regiment).

Joining the Army did not mean an end to Europe's work with society orchestras, at least not at first. Enlisting had nothing to do with his musical ambitions. It was only after Europe joined that a commanding officer proposed that a band be formed. Europe was initially cool to the idea.

Europe passed an officer's exam and was about to take command of a machine gun company when Colonel William Hayward induced Europe to organize a military band. Money was allocated for recruiting talented musicians. Within the year, Lieutenant Jim Europe and the 15th Infantry Regiment were in France. The band earned a superb reputation by entertaining countless soldiers, officers, and French civilians. Jim Europe, his band members, and the rest of the 15th Infantry Regiment then went bravely to Givry-en-Argonne for military training (Europe learned to operate French machine guns) and then to the trenches, soon fighting with the French 161st Division against the German army—and fighting heroically. They were nicknamed "Hellfighters" after proving themselves in battle.

Officers high in command concluded that a top-quality band would be invaluable for troop morale, so the lieutenant and his musicians were called away from the front in August of 1918. Europe, who had not led the band since February, again conducted for the benefit of thousands in camps and hospitals. One song performed was "On Patrol in No Man's Land," written by Europe, Sissle, and Blake. Sissle later recalled that Europe played it at the piano while the band made the sound effects of a bombardment.

> What the time? Nine?
> Fall in line
> All right, boys, now take it slow
> Are you ready? Steady!
> Very good, Eddie.
> Over the top, let's go
> Quiet, quiet, else you'll start a riot
> Keep your proper distance, follow 'long
> Cover, brother, and when you see me hover
> Obey my orders and you won't go wrong
> There's a Minnenwurfer coming—look out [bang!]
> Here that roar [bang!], there's one more [bang!]
> Stand fast, there's a Vary light [German rocket flare]
> Don't gasp or they'll find you all right
> Don't start to bombing with those hand grenades [rat-a-tat-tat-tat]
> There's a machine gun, holy spades!

Alert, gas! Put on your mask
Adjust it correctly and hurry up fast
Drop! There's a rocket for the boche barrage
Down, hug the ground, close as you can, don't stand
Creep and crawl, follow me, that's all
What do you hear? Nothing near
Don't fear, all is clear
That's the life of a stroll
When you take a patrol
Out in No Man's Land
Ain't it grand?
Out in No Man's Land

Newspapers reported what was happening to Americans overseas, but here the experience of battle is shaped in artistic form. Although thousands of songs were written about the war, mostly by songwriters who participated in no battles, nothing else in American popular song at that time was like "On Patrol in No Man's Land." However, the song enjoyed no popularity. No other musicians covered it, and Europe's recording of it did not sell well.

After the Armistice, Europe and his men were among the first African-American soldiers to enter a disarmed Germany. They were members of the most famous black unit of the war, and Americans were eager to hear Europe's band in 1919 upon its return to the United States. Europe also had a contract with the Pathé Frères Phonograph Company. This New York company, enjoying a special arrangement with a French firm, was making inroads in the American disc market.

Europe's music on Pathé discs is different from that of Europe's Society Orchestra issued on Victor discs five years earlier. The musicians were different; popular music had changed; instead of making dance records, he now worked in a military band tradition, conducting different instruments than in earlier years. Whereas none of the Victor recordings featured vocals, some Pathés feature singers Noble Sissle and C. Creighton Thompson. Moreover, different recording technology was used. It is unfortunate that his final discs are vertical-cut recordings. At the time the records were issued, hill-and-dale technology was quickly losing favor with record buyers. By 1920 nearly all talking machines were made for lateral-cut discs, which meant that equipment for playing Pathé discs became relatively scarce in subsequent years. Had his records been made with lateral-cut technology, they might have enjoyed more popularity and his name might have been better remembered by subsequent generations.

After four recording sessions—three in March of 1919, one in May—the Pathé company proudly issued a special flier announcing new titles: "Eleven records of the world's greatest exponent of syncopation just off the press." In bold type, the flier announced, "Jim Europe's jazz will live forever." Sadly, the music became relatively obscure. Although the style features syncopation and more jazz effects than other military bands offered, Europe's musicians perform more in a military band tradition than in the new jazz idiom. Nonetheless, Europe is a significant prejazz artist or transitional figure, the most important African-American musical leader in the period when ragtime was on the wane but before the reign of King Oliver and Louis Armstrong. He employed musicians who later became fine jazz performers, notably Dope Andrews and Herb Flemming.

Two jazz-oriented performances are "That Moaning Trombone," composed by Clef Club member Tom Bethel, and W. C. Handy's "Memphis Blues," each having a swing and freedom that virtually no other military band at the time attempted. Europe's arrangements showcase the fine trombone section though other band sections are heard distinctly, even the tubas.

Lyrics of some songs recorded for Pathé give form to the experience of returning home from the war. "How 'ya Gonna Keep 'em Down on the Farm?" questions whether America's young men can resume normal lives after celebrating victory in Paris. In "All of No Man's Land Is Ours," a soldier whose ship has docked phones a loved one. "My Choc'late Soldier Sammy Boy" evokes a Victory Parade for returning heroes, the kind in which Europe and his musicians proudly marched. Two other songs celebrate a return to the South after the war.

Europe suffered a fatal stabbing two days after his band recorded six titles for Pathé on May 7, 1919. There was no clear motive for the backstage attack during a concert in Boston's Mechanics Hall. Accounts differ, but it seems that Europe reprimanded Herbert Wright for the drummer's unprofessional habit of walking on and off stage while other acts performed. Wright was already simmering from what he perceived as favoritism, feeling the bandleader never blamed Steven Wright for mistakes but only criticized Herbert (together, Steven and Herbert Wright made up the "Percussion Twins"—they shared a surname but were not related). When Europe ordered Wright to leave a dressing room, the unstable drummer produced a penknife and stabbed the bandleader in the neck. Others in the room, including Noble Sissle, were unable to stop Wright. Europe was rushed to City Hospital but he soon died.

Sissle declined an agent's suggestion that he succeed Jim Europe by taking a fifteen-piece band on tour. He instead worked with Eubie Blake in vaudeville. *Variety* on June 27, 1919, reported that songs performed live by the duo included "Mirandy" and "On Patrol in No Man's Land," which had earlier been recorded for Pathé. Soon composer Blake and lyricist Sissle, with the black comedy team of Flournoy E. Miller and Aubrey Lyles, created the musical comedy *Shuffle Along*, which opened on May 23, 1921. A milestone in black entertainment, it appealed to both black and white audiences and opened many doors in the 1920s for black entertainers.

Favor, Edward M. (1856-January 10, 1936)

Born Edward M. Le Fevre in New York City, he was on stage in the 1880s and achieved fame in the early 1890s as a Broadway comedian during the long run of E. E. Rice's *1492* at Wallack's Theater. Around 1893 he recorded from this hit musical "The King's Song" (Columbia cylinder 6544). From another popular show of this period, *Ship Ahoy*, he recorded "The Commodore Song" (North American 772). The opening spoken announcement states, "Edison Record 772, 'The Commodore Song' from *Ship Ahoy* as sung by the original commodore Mr. Edward M. Favor, now of Rice's *1492* Company." These may be the first "creator" records, or records featuring songs from musical shows as sung by an original cast member. He was principal comedian with Klaw and Erlanger, the Shuberts, and other prominent managers.

He formed a team with his wife, Edith Sinclair. They were vaudeville headliners and also starred in musical comedies. The March 1909 issue of *Edison Phonograph Monthly* announces the release of "Casting Bread Upon the Waters" (Amberol 119) and identifies the performers as Edward M. Favor, Edith Sinclair, and Steve Porter. It states, "Until Mr. Favor entered the comic opera field he and Mrs. Favor were widely known in vaudeville as Favor and Sinclair."

He was by the late 1890s one of the most popular recording artists. He made records at a dollar a "round" between periods of filling vaudeville dates, working for virtually all companies. Billy Murray later recalled seeing Favor sing into eight cylinder phonographs at the headquarters of Bacigalupi Brothers, Edison wholesale distributors for the Western states, in 1897. Favor, who was then appearing at the Orpheum Theater, made an indelible impression on Murray. The veteran recording artist would cup his hands behind his ears to determine whether the tone was hitting the horn straight in the center.

Numbers from early in Favor's recording career include "Say Au Revoir, But Not Goodbye" (North American 858; 1894) and "My Best Girl's a New Yorker" (Columbia 2107; 1895). For Edison he recorded comic titles such as "Hamlet Was a Melancholy Dane" (8400, taken from the show *Mr. Bluebird*), "I Think I Hear a Woodpecker Knocking at My Family Tree" (10313) and "Who Threw the Overalls in Mrs. Murphy's Chowder?" (7697). Labels often identify him as "Ed. M. Favor."

He recorded sixteen titles for Berliner from 1897 to 1899. Representative is "Oh, What a Beautiful Ocean" (0537), recorded on September 22, 1899.

He possessed a high Irish voice, and his records include many Irish songs and nonsense ditties, the latter often taking the form of limericks. These include "Mr. Dooley," recorded in 1902 (Columbia 876, Edison Standard 8125), and "Fol-the-Rol-Lol," recorded for various companies, including Victor on March 16, 1906. Announcing the November release of Standard 9404, the September 1906 issue of *Edison Phonograph Monthly* states:

> "Jingles, Jokes and Rhymes," by Edward M. Favor, is a Record that includes three verses and two choruses of a topical song written by Benjamin Hapgood Burt and sung with orchestra accompaniment. Mr. Favor has made a great success with songs of this character, some of his Records in the past year being among the largest sellers we have had.

A song with an Indian theme, recorded during the March 16, 1906, Victor session, is Gus Edwards' "Pocahontas" (4683). This was recorded during an Indian song craze inspired by "Hiawatha" (1902) and "Navajo" (1903).

Favor was among the first around 1899 to make records sold by Frank Seaman's National Gramophone Corporation (3 and 5 West 18th Street in New York City), a subsidiary of the Universal Talking Machine Company. Its Zon-o-phone discs would soon compete with Berliners in the disc market. Favor began his association with Victor when it was called the Consolidated Talking Machine Company, his first session for Eldridge R. Johnson's new company taking place on July 26, 1900. He recorded "What Do You Think of Hoolihan?" and four other titles issued on seven-inch discs.

Favor recorded for Victor as late as 1911, his three final titles for that company being "Conversations," "Just for a Girl," and "The Dublin Rag" (with the American Quartet). He recorded for Edison "Conversations" as well as "The Dublin Rag."

In a 1968 interview with researcher Leo Kimmett, a former Edison employee named Clarence Ferguson recalled his friendship with Favor:

> One time Edward Favor spent about two hours at my home listening to his own records. He had never heard them after they had been made. I asked him why he did not have a phonograph. He said he had bought a Gem at one time from Edison and had it sent to a niece in Cliffside, New Jersey. "But," he said, "I never owned one because my wife and I were never home enough."

As a popular entertainer, Favor traveled constantly.

Ferguson also recalled Favor saying he earned $50 from Edison for singing for a cylinder "but the same song for Victor or the Columbia disc he would get from $150 to $200. . . . Singing for a disc record he had to shout to the top of his voice to record on the disc." This would leave Favor hoarse, which is why he demanded more. Favor was evidently recalling his early discs, probably Berliners. He told Ferguson that when recording for Edison he could sing in a natural voice.

Announcing the release of "Romance and Reality" on two-minute Standard 9760, the December 1906 issue of *Edison Phonograph Monthly* states:

> The mere reading of this title will bring pleasure to hosts of owners of Edison Phonographs, for Mr. Favor has always been a great favorite and he has not been able for some time to make a Record for us. Mr. Favor's position as a comic opera artist of wide fame keeps him on the road a large part of the time and it is only when he returns to New York that we can get him to sing for the Phonograph. This song is one of the hits in "Fascinating Flora." Mr. Favor scored nightly with it for many weeks at the Casino, New York.

Favor's popularity was in decline before double-faced records were introduced in 1908. Among his last two records were Blue Amberols featuring "My Best Girl and Me" (1510), from the musical comedy *My Best Girl*, and Gillen's "If They'd Only Move Old Ireland Over Here" (2391), from the Blanche Ring vehicle *When Claudia Smiles*. The latter number, his final Edison recording, was issued in September 1914. Favor was far more important to Edison as a cylinder artist during the era of brown wax cylinders and Standard Records. He did not make Diamond Discs.

Around 1914 he also recorded "On the 7:28," a train song issued on Rex 5251 (the song was written by Stanley Murphy and Henry I. Marshall, who soon afterward wrote "On the 5:15"). Rex issued "Indoor Sports" (5254) at the same time, and this was probably Favor's last record. He remained active in theater through the early 1930s. For example, he appeared in 1933 as grocer James Caesar in a production of *John Ferguson* at the Belmont Theater in New York City. He was successful with his impersonation of Amos Gashwiler, the country storekeeper, in the Broadway production of *Merton of the Movies*. Favor died in Brooklyn on January 10, 1936. His wife died on November 27, 1942.

Fenton, Carl (Walter Haenschen)
(November 3, 1889-March 27, 1980)

No individual musician was actually named Carl Fenton. Carl Fenton's Orchestra was led by conductor-arranger Walter Gustave ("Gus") Haenschen, whose own name was evidently judged ill-suited for commercial recordings. Indeed, *Talking Machine World* at various times gave his name as Haenchen, Hanschen, and Henchon. During his long career, Haenschen did not use the name Carl Fenton except insofar as it was a simple name to put on record labels.

In 1973, he was interviewed by researcher Cecil Leeson (1902-1989), a concert saxophonist who in the 1970s taped his conversations with musicians who had been active a half century earlier. Haenschen explained that when he searched for a suitable recording name at the beginning of his tenure with the Brunswick-Balke-Collender Company, he thought of the town Fenton, Missouri, which is on the Meramec River and near his hometown of St. Louis. The name was picked at random. As he put it, "How do you find a name? Just pull it out of a hat." He recalls that "Carl" may have been suggested by "the girls in the [Brunswick] office . . . somebody thought it sounded good."

Haenschen was born in St. Louis. The January 15, 1920, issue of *Talking Machine World* states that Haenschen graduated from Washington University in St. Louis in 1912. He recalled for Cecil Leeson in the 1973 interview:

I had a typical college orchestra which got pretty popular. So I was quite a busy guy in the dance field in those early days and there was a transition about that time from the old waltz and two-step era to the more modern, let's call it a jazz era, which then in those days we didn't dare to use the word—the word was rather taboo in circles.

But St. Louis had a very large black population and among them were lots of tremendous musicians. . . . I knew Scott Joplin. . . . Having met some of these men, I frequented some of the so-called dives where these men played and [I] learned, as probably one of the earlier white boys, how to play "rags" and get the feeling of that rhythm.

In 1912 he published "The Maurice Glide," named after dancer Maurice Mouvet. It was recorded by the Victor Military Band (Victor 17592), among others.

A skilled pianist, he made private recordings a few years before working for Brunswick. A single-sided disc in Columbia's "Personal Record" series is "Sunset Medley" (60782) played by "W. Gus Haenschen" on piano and "T. T. Schiffer" on drums, the date May 1916 printed on the label itself. Another selection from this session is "Country Club Melody" (60781). Later in 1916, W. G. Haenschen's Banjo Orchestra recorded at least four titles in the Personal Record series: "Honky Tonky" (61068), "I Left Her on the Beach" (61069), "Maple Leaf Rag" (61070), and "Admiration" (61071). The label for the disc featuring W. H. Tyers' "Admiration" states, "Made by W. G. Haenschen's Banjo Orchestra, St. Louis, MO." "Fox-trot" is added under the title. The four titles were possibly cut in early September 1916 when Haenschen and his musicians were in New York City to make test records for the Victor Talking Machine Company (nothing was issued by Victor).

Page 52 of the August 1916 issue of *Talking Machine World* includes an article about Haenschen, then a manager of the Victrola department of a prominent St. Louis store, and it appears to refer to the May 1916 records:

Another feature of Mr. Haenchen's [sic] business career is that he sells records made by himself. Recently he and a part of his orchestra had several records made by the Columbia personal service department and he has had quite a run on these. They are chiefly his own compositions, several of which have enjoyed good sale throughout the country.

The article states that he was "the newest recruit to the talking machine selling game in St. Louis . . . he is manager of the Victrola department of the Vandervoort Music Salon."

The January 15, 1920, issue of *Talking Machine World* again identifies Haenschen as a composer: "He has composed several songs, one of which was the sensation of the 1914 Follies, where it was known as 'Underneath the Japanese Moon.'" The song was recorded by a few artists in 1914, including Irving Kaufman (Victor 17699).

Haenschen recalled in the 1973 interview that in the 1920s he had compositions published under pseudonyms because intense company rivalry meant that any song credited to Haenschen would have been "shunned" by competing record companies. A popular song in 1921 was "Na-Jo," with music credited to saxophonist Rudy Wiedoeft and "Walter Holliday," one of Haenschen's pseudonyms (lyrics were supplied by George O'Neil). The Benson Orchestra of Chicago recorded it on April 15, 1921 (Victor 18779), and others recorded it. A song that gives composer credit to "Haenschen" is "Read 'em and Weep," included in the show *Come Seven*. Al Bernard was the song's lyricist, and Bernard recorded the song for Edison Blue Amberol 4164, issued in January 1921, and Actuelle 022437.

He stated: "One of the things that still sells is a tune called 'Rosita,' which I did . . . under the name of Paul Dupont, and I still get royalties from that thing, after all these years." The song "La Rosita," words by Allan Stuart and music by Paul Dupont, was published by the Sam Fox Publishing Company in 1923. Part of its success by late 1923 was because the number was played in motion picture theaters during showings of a film by that name directed by Ernst Lubitsch and starring Mary Pickford. It was recorded by many, including the International Novelty Orchestra in late 1923 (Victor 19218), D. Onivas and His Orchestra in 1924 (Pathé Actuelle 036057—"D. Onivas" was Pathé musical director Domenico Savino), Victor Red Seal soprano Rosa Ponselle in 1925 (HMV DB872), Lee Morse in 1927 (Columbia 1082-D), Eddie South and His Alabamians in 1927 (Victor 21151), Tommy Dorsey and His Orchestra in 1939 (Victor 26333), Benny Goodman and His Orchestra in 1941 (Columbia GL-523), Jimmy Dorsey and His Orchestra in 1941 (Decca 3711), and the Four Aces in 1953 (Decca 28393).

At least for part of the 1910s he juggled a performing career with his job as manager of the talking machine department of the large Scruggs, Vandervoot & Barney store in downtown St. Louis, making enough of a reputation for *Talking Machine World* to note in its September 1918 issue that "Gus Hanschen [sic] . . . enlisted in the engineering department of the army recently." The article gives the following background information on the musician who would become a key Brunswick executive within two years:

Mr. Hanschen is a graduate engineer, but had never followed that business. After he left school he continued his music studies, and before he entered the talking machine business he was locally famous as an exponent of ragtime music and he managed and led an orchestra that was extremely popular during the dancing revival. For the last two years his orchestra supplied music for the open air dances given by the city in the parks.

In 1919, soon after Brunswick executives judged the time ripe for the company to introduce its own discs in the American market, Haenschen began to manage the Popular Records Department. Frank Hofbauer, who had earlier worked for Edison, was Director for Recording Rooms. Walter B. Rogers was "General Musical Director." Haenschen later recalled in his 1973 interview being offered the position around July 1919: "I went into the Navy and I was away for almost two years and when I came back I was met in New York by the head of the Brunswick group and was offered the job."

He led Brunswick's house band consisting of studio musicians, with personnel varying from session to session, and his group of musicians was among the first to record for Brunswick, cutting sides in October 1919. "Karavan" and "Romance" were issued in 1920 on Brunswick 2011, one of the first in Brunswick's popular music series, which began at 2000. "La La Lucille" and "My Cuban Desire" were issued on Brunswick 2012.

Early Brunswick record catalogues included a small photograph of the Carl Fenton Orchestra. On records and in catalogs, the band was called either the Carl Fenton Orchestra or Carl Fenton's Orchestra, never Carl Fenton and His Orchestra. Haenschen states in the 1973 interview that in the early 1920s

> almost all of [the] orchestras of Brunswick were pretty much the same men. . . . We did the dance tunes always with the same pick up group. One or two men changed maybe—a different trumpet to give it a different style. And then we had names that were called Fenton's Orchestra when it was Rudy Wiedoeft's Orchestra, with usually the same men—or Bennie Krueger and then that name would be put on.

Carl Fenton's Orchestra only occasionally played in public, usually to promote new Brunswick retail establishments. For example, the first page of the August 1921 issue of *Talking Machine World* announces the opening of a store in Lowell, Massachusetts, and states, "Carl Fenton's Orchestra, exclusive Brunswick artists, and one of the country's leading dance orchestras, appeared at the opening of the Bungalow Shop, and played to capacity audiences throughout the day." Haenschen states in the 1973 interview that violinist Rudy Greenberg led the orchestra in public.

In the interview he indicates why musicians in Ray Miller's orchestra at the time it began recording for Brunswick in 1923 differ from musicians used by Miller for earlier Okeh and Columbia records:

You want to hear something about Ray Miller? That was my orchestra too . . . I put every man in there. . . . Ray was a good drummer, but that's where it stopped. We hired—this is all Brunswick now, when I say "we," it's Brunswick—we hired all the men and they stayed with Ray for several years. Even very popular players would make that their permanent stock and he did an awfully good job for Brunswick. I mean we sold a lot of Ray Miller records.

In the early 1920s Haenschen did arrangements for several Brunswick recording groups, though pianist Tom Satterfield was arranger for the Ray Miller Orchestra and trombonist Carroll Martin was arranger for the Isham Jones Orchestra, Brunswick's top dance band.

He worked closely with many record artists. The label for "Jean," performed by Isham Jones Rainbo Orchestra on Brunswick 5012, states, "Piano Passages by Alfred Eldridge and Carl Fenton," and other early Brunswick labels state, "Orchestral arrangement by Walter Haenschen." Some Brunswick labels of the mid-1920s state, "Under direction of Walter Haenschen." An article by David Wallace on the Happiness Boys in the February 1937 issue of *Popular Songs* credits the Brunswick recording manager for bringing together the two singers: "It was Gus Haenschen, now a noted orchestra leader but then recording manager for Brunswick records, who suggested that Billy Jones and Ernie Hare pool their talents." That was probably in late 1920.

Talking Machine World articles confirm that Haenschen worked closely with various Brunswick artists. When Paul Ash and His Syncopated Orchestra was recorded by Brunswick in August 1923 in San Francisco, Haenschen traveled to the West Coast to supervise sessions (that month's issue of *Talking Machine World* discusses on page 130 this special recording arrangement and gives his name as "Henchen"). The April 1924 issue states on page 104 that Haenschen was in St. Louis, along with Brunswick recording engineer C. Hancox, "for the sole purpose of recording the inimitable Jolson with Gene Rodemich's Orchestra, and also Isham Jones' Orchestra, which journeyed from Chicago to record with Al. There were also several new numbers recorded by the [Mound City] Blue Blowers." Jolson recorded with Rodemich on March 13 and with Jones on March 14, and the Mound City Blue Blowers recorded "San" and "Red Hot" on these two days (Frank Trumbauer, who had a home in St. Louis, joined for these sessions). Various discographies cite Chicago as the recording site, but the sessions clearly took place in Haenschen's home city of St. Louis. Jolson was in the city appearing in *Bombo* at the Jefferson Theatre.

The January 1925 issue reports on page 28 in an article on Nick Lucas, "In his recording work Mr. Lucas has been coached by Walter Haenschen, musical director of the Brunswick recording laboratories, and his first record shows that this training has been of great value." Haenschen's name is cited frequently in the journal, and it is possible Haenschen himself supplied the trade journal with information about Brunswick artists.

Page 140 of the May 1925 issue of *Talking Machine World* reports:

> Walter Haenschen, one of the chiefs of the Brunswick recording laboratories, surprised his friends recently by deserting the ranks of bachelors and "committing" matrimony. Mr. Haenschen was married to Miss Rose Anna Genevieve Hussey, and they are now away on a honeymoon trip to California. It is understood that this trip will also be utilized by Mr. Haenschen in the interests of Brunswick recordings, and it is expected that when he arrives on the Coast he will arrange for new recordings by Abe Lyman and other orchestras . . .

His wife had been on the Brunswick staff as executive assistant to Milton Diamond.

In early 1925 the Brunswick-Balke-Collender Company was left out when Western Electric granted patent rights for its new electrical recording method to the Victor Talking Machine Company as well as the Columbia Phonograph Company. Victor began making electrical test recordings in late February 1925. Brunswick engineers, aware that such technology would give a marketing advantage to competitors, collaborated with engineers of the Radio Corporation of America, the General Electric Company, and the Westinghouse Electric and Manufacturing Company to adapt a "Light-Ray" electrical recording method for phonograph records. Haenschen was in the studio often when Brunswick experimented with electric recording throughout April and early May, 1925.

The first electric recording to be recorded and then eventually issued in the company's popular series was Brunswick 2881, cut on April 15 and featuring Brunswick Hour Orchestra performances. The "Advance Record Bulletins" in the June 1925 issue of *Talking Machine World* establishes that 2881 was issued in July and notes, "Under Direction of Walter Haenschen." Record buyers at that time would not have known that this was cut by an electric process. Labels did not identify early electric discs as being improved products, and since equipment designed for playing electric discs would not be marketed until late 1925, no announcements about electric discs were made in the summer of that year.

Haenschen remained with Brunswick until mid-1927. The March 1927 issue of *Talking Machine World* reports the success of a March 4 radio broadcast of the Brunswick Hour of Music and notes, "The Brunswick Concert Orchestra, under the direction of Walter G. Haneschen [sic], accompanied the vocal and instrumental solos." Page 100 of the July 1927 issue of *Talking Machine World* announced his resignation from the company:

> Walter G. Haenschen, musical director of the Brunswick Recording Laboratories, New York, since 1920, resigned from the Brunswick organization July 1. Mr. Haenschen is one of the most popular members of the recording and musical fraternities, and is also well known in the radio broadcasting field, having inaugurated in 1925 the "Brunswick House of Music." He is planning to take a complete rest during the Summer and will announce his future plans in September.

Page 19 of the January 1928 issue of *Talking Machine World* announced the appointment of William F. Wirges "as recording director of the Brunswick Laboratories in New York." Louis Katzman became musical director and was promoted to recording laboratory manager in January 1929.

The October 1927 issue of *Talking Machine World* announced that Haenschen had become "recording director" of the Sonora Phonograph Company, recently purchased by former Brunswick director P. L. Deutsch. It adds, "There will also be established at the New York offices modern and thoroughly well-equipped recording laboratories under the direction of Walter G. Haenschen, who was for many years identified with Brunswick recording and who is recognized internationally as one of the most prominent authorities on present-day recording." Nothing came of the announced plans to issue discs on a new Sonora label.

Sometime after April 1927 violinist Ruby Greenberg (Haenschen recalled that the name was "Rudy" but other sources give the name as "Ruby"), who had played as a member of Carl Fenton's Orchestra and other Brunswick house orchestras, purchased the rights to use the Carl Fenton name and recorded a number of sides for Gennett Records in 1927, 1928, and 1929.

Haenschen remained active in the musical field, devoting his energy to radio work. He served as musical conductor on *Voice of Firestone* broadcasts and helped the careers of Frank Munn as well as Jessica Dragonette. By 1929 he was musical director for Sound Studios of New York, Inc. (50 West 57th Street, New York City), maker of World Broadcasting Company transcription records. The first recorded syndicated radio program series began in 1928, and Sound Studios was formed to meet a new demand for transcription records.

Page 619 of Thomas Calvert McClary's article "Electrical Transcription for Broadcast Purposes" in the January 1932 issue of *Radio News* states:

> Gustave Haenschen and Frank Black, vice-presidents of Sound Studios, high priests of the broadcast program and creators of such out-

standing achievements as the Palmolive, General Motors, Chase & Sanborn . . . and many other famous national broadcasts, are credited with having been largely responsible for the high quality of art in the better electrical transcription field.

He continued doing radio work for many years.

In his 1973 interview with Leeson, Haenschen states, "When I left Brunswick . . . this very intense radio activity started. We had six or seven dates a week on radio and making records was sort of forgotten. . . . I think one of the big mistakes in my life was that I sort of pushed that aside. . . . I made very few records for myself and never put out a record with my name on it."

On page xxi of Rosa Ponselle's autobiography, titled *Ponselle: A Singer's Life* (Doubleday, 1982), co-author James A. Drake identifies himself as a former professor and administrator at Ithaca College in New York "where the late Gustave Haenschen, a pioneer recording executive and popular musical director on radio, had commissioned a colleague and me to begin an oral history project for entertainment industry pioneers." Under the aegis of the Haenschen Collection, Drake and Haenschen in the mid-1970s recorded detailed interviews with over a dozen songwriters and performers active between the world wars, including Irving Caesar, Ben Selvin, Benny Goodman, Jan Peerce, and Elizabeth Lennox. Haenschen's collection of radio scripts, orchestrations, and personal papers are located at Ithaca College, where he served on the Board of Trustees for over two decades.

Ferera, Frank (and Helen Louise)

Frank Ferera introduced steel guitar and slide guitar playing to an audience that was literally worldwide since many of his recordings were issued outside the United States. He had more recording sessions than any other guitarist from 1915 to 1925.

He was not the first Hawaiian guitarist to record. That was probably Joseph Kekuku, the steel guitar's reputed inventor (credit has also been given to James Hoa and Gabriel Davion), who performed with Toots Paka's Hawaiian troupe on Edison cylinders, both two- and four-minute, announced in the December 1909 issue of *Edison Phonograph Monthly.* Another predecessor was W. K. Kolomku, whose guitar solo of "Hawaiian Melodies" was issued on Victor 65341. But Ferera was the first guitarist to enjoy success as a recording artist, his name a familiar one in the catalogs of virtually all record companies of the World War I era and 1920s. His style of playing was a forerunner of bottleneck playing on blues records and "steel" playing on country records, and his popular records must have influenced many guitarists of his generation.

Hawaiian music had been recorded as early as the 1890s but was neither popular on the mainland nor influential until the World War I era. The first important group of authentic Hawaiian performances issued on records was made by the American Record Co. of Springfield, Massachusetts and New York City. By 1904 some Hawaiian troupes were performing in mainland cities including New York, where American's Hawaiian recordings apparently were made in late 1904 or early 1905. Over two dozen performances were issued on a series of 10 $^5/_8$ inch blue single-sided "Indian label" discs. Titles include "Waikiki Kamehameha" (030939) and "Moani Keala" (030964). The American Record Company catalog dated September 1905 introduces the Royal Hawaiian Troubadours as "an orchestra and double quartet of native Hawaiians whose music has charmed America. . . . The Troubadours are in the United States on an educational tour. . . . By special arrangement we have secured the following list of the first and only records made by Hawaiians in America."

Shortly before World War I, interest in Hawaiian music was sparked by Richard Walton Tully's 1912 Broadway play *Bird of Paradise*, starring Laurette Taylor. The Hawaiian Quintette from the show even recorded for Victor the play's incidental music. Also significant was the appearance in 1915 of Keoki Awai's Royal Hawaiian Quartette at the Panama-Pacific International Exhibition in San Francisco. In late 1915 Victor began issuing Hawaiian discs on a monthly basis by such artists as Pale K. Lua and David Kaili (members of the Irene West Royal Hawaiians), and the Toots Paka Hawaiian Troupe. By 1916 all companies recorded Hawaiian or pseudo-Hawaiian numbers.

An article titled "Hawaiian Music Universally Popular," included in the September 1916 issue of *Edison Phonograph Monthly*, asks:

Two years ago what did the public know about Hawaiian Music, Ukuleles, Hula Hula Dances? Since then Hawaiian music and American versions of it have taken the United States by storm. . . . For years travelers who returned from Hawaii brought stories of the strange and beautiful music that the natives played on their Ukuleles, but it was not until Tully's opera "The Bird of Paradise" was produced that musicians gave any serious attention to the instrument and its music. This opera, with its wonderful setting of exotic music, however, brought the Hawaiian instrument into prominence. . . . A few months ago its music was translated to the American public through the medium of Hawaiian-American ragtime and since then it has sprung into universal popularity.

The jacket of Diamond Disc 50392, which features Louise and Ferera, points to another source for the interest in Hawaiian music:

Many music lovers have searched in vain for the cause of sudden passion for Hawaiian music, which struck the United States about 1915 and '16. Perhaps the cause may be found in the Panama-Pacific Exposition at San Francisco, where many Hawaiian singers and dances were heard by thousands of tourists who visited the fair. . . . The Hawaiian Guitar is rather similar to our own instrument of the same name, except that it is played by running a steel crosspiece over the strings instead of pressing them down.

Steel guitar virtuoso Frank Ferera—called Palakiko Ferreira on early Edison recordings (some of his Edison records were credited to Palakiko's Hawaiian Orchestra)—was born on June 12, 1885, in Honolulu to Mary and Frank Ferreira. He left for the mainland around the turn of the century. It has been said that he never returned to the islands, but there is evidence he visited them in the 1918-1919 period.

Frank Ferera was featured on the cover of the December 1916 issue of *Edison Phonograph Monthly*, and an article states:

Frank Ferera . . . has the distinction of being the one who first introduced the Hawaiian style of playing the guitar into the United States. It was in 1900 that he brought the first ukelele [sic] here and commenced to charm vaudeville audiences with the weird and plain-tive effects he produced. For quite a while he had the field to himself. . . . It is said that the Hawaiian style of playing the guitar was originated by a Portuguese sailor. Perhaps this has something to do with the tendency that Mr. Ferera had toward the ukelele for he, although of Hawaiian birth, is of Portuguese descent. He was musical even in his childhood.

His first wife was named Eva Perkins, but they divorced. He married a young woman from Seattle named Helen Greenus, who played ukulele as well as guitar. The two performed widely in vaudeville as Helen Louise and Frank Ferera. When Hawaiian records became incredibly popular in 1916 and 1917, Louise and Ferera recorded prolifically, benefitting from the sudden craze for Hawaiian records but also providing fuel for the craze with their many records featuring charming, always polished, but never flashy performances.

Interpretation was at times staid but their intonation was clean and accurate, which is important in steel guitar playing since performers must rely on a good sense of pitch when sliding a bar of steel along strings. Ferera's sliding glissandos punctuated by staccato melody lines were mostly played on the high melody string to achieve the greatest volume his instrument was capable of. This was typical of other steel guitar players of the time. Acoustic guitarists accustomed to performing for large audiences before the days of microphones had to forfeit all subtlety and delicate nuances.

More than any other artists, they supplied what the record-buying public wanted at the time in the way of Hawaiian music. The public was excited by the novelty of steel guitar, especially in combination with ukulele—there was no special demand for songs that originated in Hawaii or songs performed in an authentic Hawaiian manner. Ferera was a crossover artist from the beginning. In fact, the debut record of Louise and Ferera featured a Stephen Foster song. The duo often recorded songs that had originated in Hawaii but at other times recorded songs by Tin Pan Alley composers, only some of which include "Hawaii" in the song title, others being hits of the day such as "Missouri Waltz" (Pathé 20344).

Louise and Ferera made their recording debut in New York City for Columbia in late July 1915. The four songs recorded were "My Old Kentucky Home," "Medley of Hawaiian Waltzes," "Honolulu Rag," and "Kaiwa Waltz." The first two songs were issued as Columbia A1814, which remained in the catalog until 1929.

For Edison, Frank Ferera made his recording debut as a solo artist. Blue Amberol 2685 was issued in September 1915: "(a) Ua Like No Alike; (b) Medley of Hawaiian Hulas." The record is credited to Palakiko Ferreira. Edison literature states, "The crying, haunting quality of Hawaiian music is the leading feature of this record. . . . The artist plays on the Hawaiian guitar. His first selection was composed by the former Queen of the Hawaiians, next he plays a medley of Hawaiian Hula Dances." *Edison Phonograph Monthly* did not use the name Frank Ferera until its November 1916 issue. Edison released no further recordings of him in the remaining months of 1915, instead issuing in October 1915 the work of Hawaiian guitarists William Smith and Walter K. Kolomoku.

The first Victor disc of Louise and Ferera was issued in November 1915: "On the Beach at Waikiki—Medley" backed by "Moe Uhane Waltz" (17880). Releases that soon followed include Victor 17892 ("My Bird of Paradise" and "Kawaihau Waltz") and 18087 ("Maui Aloha—One Step" and "Pua Carnation"). Their Victor records sold well though they competed with releases of another Victor duo, Pale K. Lua and David Kaili.

For a vaudeville team of singers—tenor Horace Wright and soprano Rene Dietrich—the team of Louise and Ferera provided guitar and ukulele accompaniment on Victor recordings, such as on Wright and Dietrich's vocal versions of "On the Beach at Waikiki" (18132), "Song to Hawaii" (18159), and "My Own Iona" (18171). On a few records they provided accompaniment for the popular Sterling Trio, such as for "On the South Sea Isle" (18113), composed by Harry Von Tilzer, and "My Lonely Lola Lo (In Hawaii)" (18171). They often provided accompaniment for popular singers when they recorded songs with "Hawaii" in the title, including Sam Ash, Joseph Phillips, William Wheeler, and the Peerless Quartet.

Victor issued in April 1917 a disc of Louise and Ferera performing the Tin Pan Alley number "Yaddie Kaddie Kiddie Kaddie Koo" backed by the duo performing Sonny Cunha's "Everybody Hula" (18240). They recorded "Yaddie Kaddie Kiddie Kaddie Koo" for Pathé around this time. It was issued as Pathé 20158 in June 1917, the same time "Palakiko Blues" was issued as Columbia A2214. In 1917 they made recordings for virtually every company, including Victor, Columbia, Edison, Gennett, Pathé, and Imperial.

Around 1917 Pathé issued a demonstration record, and the narrator states in the middle of his sales pitch, "The Pathé repertoire of recording is acknowledged to be the finest in the world. Pathé reproduces each and every tone faithfully. Hark to the delicate tones of the Hawaiian guitar and ukelele, played by Louise and Ferera." At that point the two musicians play briefly.

Their Edison recording debut, as Helen Louise and Palakiko Ferreira, was "Medley of Hawaiian Airs—No. 1," issued on Blue Amberol 2917 in July 1916. This was followed in August by the release of "Hilo March" on Blue Amberol 2927. The two songs were then issued back-to-back on Diamond Disc 50354. Within the year Edison issued on Blue Amberol several recordings of Ferera, usually accompanied by Helen Louise. In September Edison issued two Blue Amberols featuring the team: "Hapa Haole Hula Girl" (2956), composed by Sonny Cunha, and "Medley of Hawaiian Airs—No. 2" (2941).

Ferera managed the Waikiki Hawaiian Orchestra, which often recorded for Edison, but neither Edison literature nor labels credit Ferera for leading the orchestra.

With Sam Kainoa on ukulele, the team of Louise and Ferera recorded "Waiu Lulilui," issued on Columbia A2077 in November 1916, soon followed by "Hawaiian-Portuguese Tango" on Columbia A2119. Dubbing the duo Helena and Palakiko, Emerson in December 1916 issued these recordings: "Li-ke No Li-ke" (796), "Kalima Waltz" (5137), and "Hawaiian Hula Medley" (5138). Emerson continued issuing Helena and Palakiko discs in

1917. Par-o-ket records made in late 1916 were issued in February 1917: "Kilima Waltz" (52) and "Ukulele Blues" (54).

The popular "Along the Way to Waikiki," written by Gus Kahn and Richard Whiting, was issued on Columbia A2362 in November 1917. Several Pathé discs issued in 1917 have the Louise and Ferera Waikiki Orchestra on one side, the Louise and Ferera Hawaiian Troupe on the other.

On Imperial 5483, "Sweet Lei Lehua," issued in September 1917, they are joined by Irene Greenus, misspelled "Greenis" in the August issue of *Talking Machine World* ("Introducing Hawaiian singer and whistler"). In June 1917 Irene had joined the two for a Pathé recording of Alau's "One Two Three Four," which was finally issued in February 1918 (20285). Irene Greenus was one of Helen Louise's three sisters from Seattle, the other two being Grace and Cecelia. The duo's use of Irene as vocalist instead of a Hawaiian is one indication that they were, as recording artists, not committed to preserving on record an authentic Hawaiian sound. Another is their readiness to record instrumental versions, arranged for Hawaiian guitars, of Tin Pan Alley hits. On Columbia A2509, Louise, Ferera, and Greenus even perform the Neapolitan standard "O Sole Mio."

Records of Louise, Ferera, and Greenus were issued for the next few months on Imperial discs. Imperial 5493, "Maui Waltz," was issued in October. Imperial 5505, "One Two Three Four," was issued in November 1917.

On Pathé 20215, also issued in November 1917, Irene Greenus provides vocals for the famous "Aloha Oe." Several more Pathé discs would be issued, many credited to vocalist Irene Greenus, with accompaniment by the Louise and Ferera Hawaiian Orchestra (sometimes called the Louise and Ferera Waikiki Orchestra) noted in smaller type on the label.

On Empire 5529, issued in January 1918, Irene Greenus provides a vocal for "Moana Girl." The team of Frank Ferera, Helen Louise, and Irene Greenus is called the Hawaiian Trio on some labels. Louise, Ferera, and Greenus recorded several titles for Columbia around this time, including A2916, "In the Heart of Hawaii," for which Greenus played banjo. Irene evidently stopped performing around 1918 though recordings would be issued for a few more years. According to an article in the December 19, 1919, edition of *The Seattle Daily Times*, Irene Greenus lived in Seattle at that time as Mrs. Irene Lilliam Johnstone.

Louise and Ferera did not record as often in 1918 as they had in 1917, perhaps partly due to touring engagements, perhaps also due to the demand for war songs, which far exceeded that for any other type of music. Their final Victor recording was issued in November 1917: "Aloha Land" backed by "Hawaii I'm Lonesome for You" (18380). For these two numbers Louise and Ferera are joined by the Athenian Mandolin Quartet. In December 1918, Edison released a Blue Amberol featuring the Waikiki Hawaiian Orchestra, "with Louise and Ferera," performing the song "Hawaiian Breezes Waltz" (3616).

In 1919 Louise and Ferera recordings were issued mainly by Empire, Gennett, Paramount, Columbia, and Lyric. Numbers recorded for Gennett in mid-1919 include "Hilo March" and "Kilima Waltz." Empire 61101, featuring Margis's "Valse Bleue" and Pestalozza's "Ciribiribin," was issued in May 1919. These were probably taken from Pathé or Operaphone masters. Aeolian issued the team of Louise, Ferera, and Greenus performing "Wailana Waltz" (12147) in July. Two distinctly non-Hawaiian numbers—"Christmas Waltz" and "La Paloma"—were issued on Empire 61104 in August. Empire 61105, with "whistling and singing by Irene Greenus," was issued in September. Empire 61106 was issued in October. Performances by the Louise and Ferera Waikiki Orchestra of the songs "Ciribiribin" and "La Paloma" would later be issued in 1921 on Olympic 16103, with "Ciribiribin" also appearing on Supertone 16103.

According to the December 19, 1919, issue of *The Seattle Daily Times*, Helen Louise Ferera vanished during a ship voyage:

> Mystery veils the disappearance of Mrs. Helen Louise Ferera, 32 years old, daughter of Mr. and Mrs. Albert E. Greenus, 1616 Summit Ave., from the steamship President of the Pacific Steamship Company last Friday while the vessel was steaming from Los Angeles for San Francisco. Mrs. Ferera had taken passage in Los Angeles with her husband bound for Seattle. She left the stateroom they occupied at 4 o'clock in the morning and as she did not return, thorough search of the vessel was made, but she could not be found.

The ship's captain reported that the ship was sailing in "fine weather with the sea as smooth as a mill pond." But her father reported to the newspaper, "There was a strong wind blowing Friday morning when my daughter left her stateroom and we believe she was washed overboard." He also stated, "My daughter had been in Honolulu, with her husband, for about a year for her health . . . She had been wanting to come home for some time, but was not able to obtain passage until recently. She arrived in San Francisco last month and I met her there. Then she decided to go to Los Angeles to spend the holidays when she disappeared." The article says nothing more that would indicate whether an accidental fall or suicide more likely accounts for her disappearance.

Her father's statement that she was in Honolulu "for about a year" accounts for a gap in recording from July 1918 (a Columbia session) to mid-1919 (a Gennett session). His chronology is curious since the duo did make Gennett recordings in New York City in mid-1919. His statement that she "was not able to obtain passage" could refer to a shortage of ships traveling between Hawaii and the mainland during America's fighting in World War I. Such an interpretation would put them in Hawaii in late 1918 or early 1919, not late 1919.

Frank Ferera recorded for most companies in the 1920s, and his new partner in early 1920 was Anthony Franchini. Victor 18669 featuring this duo was issued in June 1920, with "Wild Flower" on one side, and "Alabama Moon" on the other (this is credited to the Hawaiian Trio—George Hamilton Green joins the two guitarists). Aeolian 14055 was issued in June 1920, with Frank Ferera and Anthony Franchini performing "Wild Flower" on one side, and Ferera and David Kaile performing "Hawaiian Smiles" on the other. The team of Ferera and Franchini were on one side of Columbia A2916, issued in June 1920, the team of Louise, Ferera, and Greenus on the other (Greenus plays banjo—the matrix number, 77886, indicates it had been recorded years earlier).

Okeh 4107 featuring the team of Frank Ferera and Dave Kaili was issued in July 1920, as was Okeh 4116, which featured Ferera and Franchini performing "Wailana Waltz" and "Beautiful Hawaii" (4116). In August, Ferera and Franchini's "Hawaiian Twilight" and "Drifting" were issued on Pathé 22391. Their recording of a Ferera composition, "Honolulu Bay," followed on Pathé 22398. In September, Columbia issued the duo on A2950 and Gennett issued the duo on 9055. In the early 1920s they also recorded for Emerson, Regal, Paramount, Brunswick, Mandel, Globe, and Lyric.

Olympic 16103, issued in July 1921, is credited to Louise and Ferera, though Helen Louise had been dead for a year and a half. Olympic, a company formed in 1921, perhaps was able to issue recordings made several years earlier by using Pathé masters. As late as November 1923, with A3522, Columbia issued a Louise and Ferera recording ("My Sweet Sweeting"), backed by a Ferera and Franchini number ("My Hawaiian Melody"). In the same month Columbia issued a dozen other titles performed by Ferera, mostly as leader of Ferera's Hawaiian Instrumental Quartet. A3560 featured the team of Ferera, Franchini, and Green (probably George Hamilton Green).

In the 1920s Ferera continued to be a featured soloist on other artists' records. In 1920 and 1921 he contributed to records made by Paul Whiteman and His Orchestra (Victor 18721, 18801, and 18826). Along with whistler Margaret McKee on "Honolulu Eyes" (18721), he was probably the first non-Whiteman musician to be included on Whiteman releases.

Ferera and Al Bernard made a single Edison Diamond Disc (51299) and they recorded in the mid-1920s for other companies. On both sides of Aeolian 14744—"Twenty-Five Years from Now" and "De Ducks Done Got Me," issued in April 1924—he not only accompanies vocalist Bernard but shares composer credit with Bernard. The two recorded "It Ain't Gonna Rain No Mo'" for Cameo and Paramount.

He made several recordings with Vernon Dalhart joining on vocal refrain. One Edison recording made in May 1924 and issued on Diamond Disc 51361 in August (then issued as Blue Amberol 4898 in September) helped popularize "hillbilly" music: Frank Ferera accompanied Vernon Dalhart as he sang and played harmonica on "The Wreck on the Southern Old 97." Dalhart was sufficiently encouraged by the recording's success to record it again for Victor—without Ferera. The Edison recording was successful and Victor 19427 was even more so, becoming one of the decade's most popular discs.

Ferera made a few records on which he plays only ukulele, such as "Hawaiian Medley" and "Maui Waltz" on Pathé 020833, issued in December 1922.

One of the most unusual artists that Ferera and Franchini accompanied was Virginia Burt, who made her recording debut with Okeh discs in early 1922. Page 103 of the February 1922 issue of *Talking Machine World* states:

> Miss Burt is well known to theatre-goers throughout the country, and she possesses the unusual gift of being able to produce in her throat tones resembling with marvelous accuracy the notes of a steel guitar string. When producing her melodies of the guitar in combination with the famous Hawaiian guitar artists Ferera and Franchini, it is almost impossible for the hearer to believe that it is not a third guitar playing.

By the mid-1920s Ferera recorded less often with Franchini, instead working with John K. Paaluhi (Franchini had begun working with a guitarist named Dettborn). One of the first Harmony discs (17-H), introduced to the trade in September 1925, features Ferera and Franchini on one side ("Dreamy Hawaii"), Ferera and Paaluhi on the other ("Dark Hawaiian Eyes"). The team of Ferera and Paaluhi made a single Diamond Disc, with "St. Louis Blues" on one side, "Southern Blues" on the other (51616). Around this time, in 1925, Ferera and Paaluhi recorded "St. Louis Blues" for Gennett. The two recorded for many companies from 1925 to 1933.

Ferera, working alone, cut "St. Louis Blues" and "In the Heart of Hawaii" for Columbia 339-D. Issued in June 1925, these were among the first performances recorded with Columbia's new electric recording process. Two Columbia discs made with the electric process (326-D and 328-D, both featuring Art Gillham) have lower catalog numbers.

With the advent of electrical recording, Ferera's later work reflects more harmonic complexity and dexterous work with his picking hand and use of the steel. On Brunswick 4731, Ferera, who uses the pseudonym Palakiko, performs the steel guitar standard "Maui Chimes," issued simply as "Maui." Ferera's playing flows with a relaxed confidence as he performs the chimes interlude using finger harmonics.

From 1928 to 1930 Annette Hanshaw sang refrains for numbers recorded by Frank Ferera's Hawaiian Trio (these were issued on Cameo, Perfect, Harmony, Clarion, and other labels), and "Maui Chimes," cut on January 11, 1929, sold well. Ferera recorded often in the 1920s as leader of Frank Ferera's Hawaiians. Representative is "Honolulu Home Sweet Home," issued on Banner 2156. On Gennett he was leader of Frank Ferera's Hawaiian Quartette, which featured guitars, cello, and flute.

In the mid-1920s he recorded for Victor and other companies with guitarist Paaluhi, the last Victor session being held on May 20, 1926, during which they recorded "Kilima Waltz" (20131). They are given equal credit on the Victor label, but they do not share equal billing on all records. For example, Columbia 492-D, featuring the Ferera composition "Drowsy Moon" backed by Sheridan's "My Hawaiian Evenin' Star," is credited to Frank Ferera, with smaller type citing Paaluhi for guitar accompaniment.

On July 24, 1931, Frank Ferera's Hawaiian Trio recorded, with Jack Miller as vocalist, two titles that were issued on Harmony, Velvet Tone, and Clarion: "When the Moon Comes Over the Mountain" and "Beautiful Love." He continued to record into late 1933, around which time he recorded "Dreaming," issued on Crown 3533 and Montgomery Ward M-1019, credited to Frank Ferera and His Hawaiian Trio.

By the late 1920s a new generation of steel guitarists with more dazzling performing techniques—they include Sam Ku West, Sol Hoopii, M. K. Moke, and Ben Nawahi—made Ferera's guitar work seem simple and perhaps dated.

Ferera died on June 26, 1951. He was survived by his third wife, Ruth, and two children, Frank Ferreira III and Mary Ferreira.

Fields, Arthur (August 6, 1888-March 29, 1953)

Arthur Fields was born Abe Finkelstein in Philadelphia to Mortimer and Elizabeth Finkelstein. He spent his early years in Utica, New York, singing solos as a boy in church. He was a professional entertainer by age eleven or so, singing illustrated songs (as the singer performed, colored slides with images related to a song's theme were projected on a screen) with Ray Walker at Wackie's Theater on Coney Island. Around age seventeen he toured with the Guy Brothers Minstrel Show.

His friend George Graff, the successful lyricist, wrote to Jim Walsh in 1953:

> Around 1907-08 [Fields] helped form a vaudeville act—Weston, Fields and Carroll—one of the earliest, and possibly the first, Rathskeller acts. Eddie Weston was a veteran performer and a few years older than Arthur and Harry Carroll, who were about 19 at the time. The act was a great success and headlined the Keith Circuit until Weston died. Fields and Carroll worked together for a while. They were both writing songs and Carroll had a couple of pretty big hits.

With partners other than Fields, Carroll wrote "The Trail of the Lonesome Pine," "By the Beautiful Sea," "I'm Always Chasing Rainbows," and other popular numbers.

Perhaps the first genuine hit of Fields the songwriter was "On the Mississippi." He wrote the music in 1912 with Harry Carroll; Ballard MacDonald supplied lyrics. It was recorded by the American Quartet for Victor 17237, Billy Murray for Blue Amberol 1637, Collins and Harlan for Columbia A1293, and Prince's Orchestra for Columbia A1307.

Fields sometimes composed music and other times provided lyrics to music written by others. In 1914 he supplied lyrics for "Aba Daba Honeymoon" (music by Walter Donovan), his most popular song. It was revived in the 1950 MGM film *Two Weeks With Love*, soon followed by the release of a popular Debbie Reynolds and Carleton Carpenter MGM record (30282), and Fields earned around $10,000 in royalty fees in 1951. The song was first popularized on records made in late 1914 by Collins and Harlan (Victor 17620, Edison Diamond Disc 50192, Blue Amberol 2468).

Another huge seller for Collins and Harlan was a Theodore Morse tune with lyrics provided by Fields: "Auntie Skinner's Chicken Dinner." Various versions recorded by the duo—for Victor, Columbia, and Edison—sold well. The song was reworked into "Mammy Blossom's 'Possum Party," with similar lyrics and the same basic melody, Fields and Morse again credited as the song writers. It was cut by Collins and Harlan for various companies, including Edison and Paramount.

Fields also supplied lyrics to "It's a Long Way to Berlin but We'll Get There" (music was by Leon Flatow), which he recorded for Edison and Columbia. The Columbia label (A2383) gives only Flatow credit for writing the song, following the practice of listing composer but not lyricist. The cover of the November 1917 issue of *Edison Amberola Monthly* features a photograph of Fields, and page 12 states, "At a recent benefit performance at the New York Hippodrome three copies of 'It's a Long Way to Berlin but We'll Get There,' by Arthur Fields, brought $500, $50 and $50. The proceeds were turned over to a relief fund."

Fields collaborated with Morse on "When I Get Back to My American Blighty," sung by Fields on Victor 18495, issued in October 1918. Another decade passed before Fields was listed as a songwriter on records, one song being "I Got a Code in My Dose," written with Fred Hall and Billy Rose. It was recorded by Fred Hall and His Sugar Babies for Okeh in 1929, Fields providing vocals.

In late 1914 Fields began his recording career. He cut mostly Irving Berlin songs at first, which suggests that the two songwriters were friendly. On Victor 17637 he made his debut with Berlin's "Along Came Ruth," a ballad interpolated into Holman Day's play of that name. The song was cut on September 2 and issued in November 1914 (he cut nothing else for Victor until late 1918—it appears he was exclusive to Columbia in 1915 and 1916). On September 19 he recorded it for Columbia, issued as A1612 in December, and in the Columbia studio at some point, perhaps on the same day, cut a shorter version for Little Wonder 21. He also cut it around this time as Indestructible cylinder 3346. His one other Indestructible cylinder was 3344, featuring "Stay Down Where You Belong." He cut this Berlin tune for Columbia A1628 on October 26, 1914, and—probably during the same session—for Little Wonder 46. He cut Berlin's "If I Had You" for Little Wonder 43 but not for Columbia (Henry Burr sings it on Columbia A1562), an instance of an artist cutting a song strictly for Little Wonder release.

The baritone recorded many songs of a topical nature. "Stay Down Where You Belong" fit the country's antiwar mood in late 1914 and 1915 (in it, the devil urges his son to remain "down below"—in Hell—rather than venturing up to the earth's surface, where Europeans were fighting viciously), and when America was later engaged in the European conflict, Fields cut songs that reflected the nation's commitment to victory. Interestingly, the popular "Let's Bury the Hatchet" on Columbia A2617 at first seems to call for peace until the title line is completed in the song's chorus: "Let's bury the hatchet in the Kaiser's head." This remained in Columbia's catalog even after the war was over.

Another example of a song with topical lyrics is "San Francisco" (Columbia A1699), recorded in 1915 to promote the Pan-American Exposition:

Go on and start your fair
The whole world will be there
Send out your invitations
Don't forget the foreign nations

Make them stop their plottin'
All will be forgotten
When they're turkey-trotting to a Yankee melody
We'll mend that map of Europe
We'll end that scrap in Europe
At that San Fran-Pan American Fair.

On March 15, 1917, Fields recorded "Everybody Loves a 'Jass' Band," and when this was issued in July 1917 on Diamond Disc 50439, its disc jacket stated, "Do you love a 'Jass' band? Doubtless you would if you knew what one was. You'll know all about it when you have heard this song. 'Jass' bands are all the rage this year in the 'Lobster Palaces' along Broadway."

A song associated with the singer is Bob Carleton's 1918 tune "Ja-Da," which Fields recorded for Victor, Columbia, Edison, and other companies. Victor originally announced to dealers in an advance list of records printed on December 31, 1918, that "Ja-Da" would be issued in March 1919 on the "B" side of Victor 18522, with the "A" side featuring Fields singing a comic stuttering song titled "Oh Helen!" (the list calls it "a good successor to Geoffrey O'Hara's 'K-K-K-Katy'"). "Ja-Da" in fact was issued on 18522 but Billy Murray's "Alcoholic Blues" was on the "A" side. Victor executives obviously judged at the last minute that the song was potentially offensive since stuttering in the chorus reduces the name "Helen" to "hell" and the word "damsel" to "damn." Other companies did issue versions. Fields sings "Oh Helen!" on Edison Diamond Disc 50518 and Lyric 5138. Ray Cummings, who wrote much promotional literature for Edison, states on the Diamond Disc jacket for the song, "There's something the matter with you if you can't laugh at it. And I don't very well see how anyone could be offended at it either for it isn't profane and it isn't vulgar."

In 1918, as America suffered heavy casualties in Europe, Fields recorded mostly songs that reflected the nation's involvement in the European conflict. Although he had enjoyed only moderate success as a recording artist from 1915 to 1917, by 1918 he was the right singer for the times. Many of these records were incredibly popular, some remaining available into the 1920s, a few available as late as 1925. Whereas the May 1918 Victor catalog listed only Fields' "Along Came Ruth" of 1914 and offers no biographical lines, the 1919 catalog lists five more selections, including "When I Send You a Picture of Berlin" (18474) and "Oui, Oui, Marie" (18489). Irving Kaufman recorded a competing version of "Oui, Oui, Marie" on Columbia A2637, but Fields' version proved the more popular. Fields also recorded it for Pathé 20424.

Victor's 1919 catalog states, "When America entered the war, [Fields] promptly placed himself at the service of his country, and did great work in recruiting the old Seventy-first Regiment." He became exclusive to Emerson beginning in September 1919, but Victor for a few years afterward kept in its catalog Fields' records with World War I themes. Victor's 1922 catalog lists fifteen titles sung by Fields. Victor catalogs include this cryptic line in a paragraph introducing the singer to readers: "He has gained honestly the great reputation he now enjoys." In catalogs and on labels the company called him a tenor from 1915 to 1925.

Fields recorded steadily for Columbia from 1914 to 1919, and Columbia kept his discs in its catalog for a few years after he became exclusive to Emerson, offering fifteen titles sung by Fields in its 1921 catalog, two of which duplicated titles that Fields also cut for Victor—the popular "Ja Da" and Irving Berlin's "Oh How I Hate to Get Up in the Morning."

Columbia identified the singer as Eugene Buckley when it issued in July 1918 his performances of "K-K-K-Katy" and "Good Morning Mr. Zip-Zip-Zip" on A2530, the label identifying each song as a "camp song," the two songs being genuinely popular among soldiers. Columbia's use of a pseudonym for the singer at this time is puzzling since in July it also issued "The Yanks Started Yankin'" coupled with "Hunting the Hun" (A2528), credited to Arthur Fields.

The name Buckley was again used in February 1919 with the release of "Would You Rather Be a Colonel with an Eagle on Your Shoulder, or a Private with a Chicken on Your Knee?" (A2669)—the reverse side is credited to Arthur Fields and the Peerless Quartet. He cut the same song for Pathé 22018, with credit given to Arthur Fields. However, earlier than Columbia's use of the pseudonym Eugene Buckley was Pathé's use of Roy Randal on some labels, such as "It's Not Your Nationality" on 20103. Months later, Pathé used the name Eugene Mack for some of the baritone's releases (20200 and 20201, among others). In the 1920s dozens of names were used for Fields on various labels for dance band records (he provided vocal refrains for many), hillbilly discs, and others.

Fields recorded many titles for Pathé, including "When I Send You a Picture of Berlin" (20413), Meyer's "If He Can Fight Like He Can Love, Good-Night Germany!" (20391), Moret's "Mickey" (22077), and "You'll Find Old Dixie Land in France" (20445).

He was among the first to record for the new Aeolian-Vocalion label. A catalog issued in 1918 by the Aeolian Company states:

> Those who have enjoyed Arthur Fields' agreeable voice in vaudeville productions will be interested in his first Vocalion records, which include two clever patriotic song-hits of his own composition—"It's

A Long Way to Berlin, But We'll Get There" (Fields-Flatow) and "Throw No Stones" (Fields-Morse). Mr. Fields is a member of the 71st Regiment, and has been featuring these selections in a recruiting campaign for the State—assisted by several other enlisted stage favorites and fifty soldiers.

Fields provided vocals on some recordings made for Aeolian-Vocalion by Ford Dabney's band, such as "Johnny's in Town" (12101), recorded in early 1919. Though black singers such as Bert Williams had recorded to the accompaniment of white musicians in recording sessions, this may be the first instance in a recording studio of a white vocalist singing to the accompaniment of black musicians. It is among the first dance records to feature a vocal refrain.

In 1919 Fields helped popularize Walter Donaldson's comic "How 'Ya Gonna Keep 'em Down on the Farm?" (Victor 18537), in which doubts are expressed about whether America's young men can resume normal lives upon returning from Europe. Fields' Victor disc competed with a Nora Bayes version on Columbia. Victor backed Fields' "How 'Ya Gonna Keep 'em Down on the Farm" with a title that opens in a similar way: "How Are You Goin' to Wet Your Whistle?," a song about prohibition, sung by Billy Murray.

Jack Kaufman, Irving Kaufman, and Arthur Fields signed a contract with the Emerson Phonograph Company on September 18, 1919, to record "exclusively for the Emerson record library for a period of three years," according to page 44 of the October 1919 issue of *Talking Machine World*. Together, the three singers sang as "The Three Kaufields." The trio had begun making Emerson discs months earlier, one title being "Oh You Women" (9205), issued in August 1919. A photograph shows the three signing contracts in the office of Arthur Bergh, Emerson's recording manager (when Victor Emerson left Columbia to begin his own company, he induced violinist Bergh to leave Columbia for the new company). The accompanying article states, "Arthur Fields is well known from coast to coast as he has appeared on every big-town vaudeville stage in the United States and Canada. He will soon start an extensive tour which will bring him into the leading vaudeville houses in the Eastern States, where he is a prime favorite."

Page 146 of the January 1921 issue of *Talking Machine World* states, "Arthur Fields is being headlined in the Loew circuit, a unique feature of his tour consisting of a film showing him making records in the recording studios of the Emerson Co. This film is exhibited in every house prior to and during his appearance." Though the October 1919 issue of *Talking Machine World* had reported that he was committed to Emerson for three years, his status as an exclusive Emerson artist must have ended in the summer of 1921 since he contributed a vocal refrain to "In My Tippy Canoe," cut by the Hackel-Bergé Orchestra for Victor 18783 on June 21, 1921, and sings "Sunnyside Sal" on Arto 9075, issued in August 1921. As a featured solo artist, he cut "Anna in Indiana" for Victor 18774, issued in August. The last Victor recording featuring Arthur Fields as solo artist was issued in December 1921, "Who'll Be the Next One (To Cry Over You)?" (18821).

Page 45 of the January 1923 issue of *Talking Machine World* announces, "The Arthur Fields Song Shop has been opened in the Hotel Theresa Building, 125th street and Seventh avenue, New York City. In addition to talking machines and records a full line of sheet music and musical instruments is carried. The formal opening on January 2." Briefly available in that year were Arthur Fields Melody Record records, which were lateral discs produced by the Fletcher Record Company. Labels state, "Made exclusively for Arthur Fields song shops—N.Y.C." Fields was the sole artist issued on this label, with material duplicated from Fletcher's Olympic label. One disc features Fields singing James Monaco's "You Know You Belong to Somebody Else" backed by "I Gave You Up" (1514). Another features him singing "Crying for You" backed by "Wanita" (1516).

The September 1923 issue of *Talking Machine World* states, "A petition in bankruptcy has been filed against the Arthur Fields Song Shop, talking machine dealer, with a store at 2094 Seventh avenue, New York City. The liabilities of the concern are placed at $14,973; assets unknown."

Talking Machine World advertisements establish that in early November 1925 Fields joined a newly formed group of artists called the Peerless Entertainers. Available for bookings in the New York City area, it consisted of the Peerless Male Quartet managed by Frank Croxton (the four singers were Albert Campbell, Charles Harrison, John Meyer, and Croxton), pianist-composer Lieutenant Gitz Rice, saxophonist Rudy Wiedoeft, and Fields. Croxton established the touring group soon after leaving Henry Burr's Eight Popular Victor Artists, but the group was not heavily engaged.

Fields sang over fifty selections issued on Edison Diamond Discs and Blue Amberol cylinders. His first Diamond Disc, "Honolulu, America Loves You" (50414), was issued in 1917 during a craze for songs about Hawaii. The craze for a different music is reflected in Fields' "Everybody Loves a 'Jazz' Band" (Diamond Disc 50439), issued in 1917 a few months after the Original Dixieland Jass Band recorded the first jazz record (Victor 18255).

In contrast to the relatively brief time Fields recorded for Columbia and Victor, he returned regularly to the Edison studio for over a decade. He made no Edison recordings in 1925, but from April 1926 to September 1927 he provided vocal choruses on one or both sides of fourteen Diamond Discs.

Fields was nominal head of a band for some Perfect sessions, with the band called Arthur Fields and His Orchestra, probably featuring Fred Hall's musicians. Banner in 1929 recorded Arthur Fields and the Noodlers, really a Fred Hall group. Fields and Hall, whose real name was Fred Arthur Ahl, worked closely together, making many records beginning with "Lay Me Down to Sleep in Carolina," issued on Emerson 3068 in September 1926. It is possible they met at the Emerson studio since they both recorded often for Emerson in 1926. Hall's group at the time was Fred Hall and His Roseland Orchestra. As a singer of vocal refrains for Fred Hall ensembles, Fields was issued in the late 1920s on Bell, Okeh, Banner, Domino, and Duophone, among other labels.

Fields worked closely with Hall even on radio. Fields' wife Selma wrote to Jim Walsh on April 12, 1953, that Fields and Hall "did the first hill-billy radio show at N.B.C. for Rex Cole, sponsored by General Electric. It was called 'The Rex Cole Mountaineers.' Arthur always called it 'The Times Square Hillbillies.' He had a terrific sense of humor. After five years with Cole they did a morning show called 'The Streamliners.'" Hall and Fields wrote songs which they published as Piedmont Music.

From 1928 to 1932 Fields and musicians led by Hall often cut hillbilly material, most of it written by Fields and Hall (their "Calamity Jane" was even recorded a few times by Vernon Dalhart). The Grey Gull Record Company turned regularly to Fields to cover hillbilly material and, to a lesser extent, the Plaza Music Company did the same. Fields even cut new takes of "Wreck of the Old 97" for Grey Gull when the master for an earlier performance by Vernon Dalhart, who was closely associated with the song on various labels, proved to be unusable. Dalhart's version (matrix 2343) had been briefly available on Grey Gull 4131, and the same record number was used on the Grey Gull label for Fields' later take (2511). The Fields performance was issued under four different names on the various Grey Gull Record Company labels such as Radiex, Globe, and Supreme: Jeff Calhoun (which was the name the company previously used for Dalhart), Arthur Fields, Vel Veteran, and Mr. X. Like other Grey Gull pseudonyms, "Mr. X" was used for a number of vocalists though it was used most often for Fields.

Representative hillbilly numbers cut by Fields include "The Terrible Mississippi Flood" (Grey Gull 2334), "Floyd Collins' Fate" (Grey Gull 4086—this was also on Madison 1607, the pseudonym "James Cummings" used), "In the Baggage Coach Ahead" (Grey Gull 4090—also on Sunrise 33015, the name "Jack Ramsey" used), and "Hallelujah I'm a Bum" (Grey Gull 4228—also on Madison 1642, the name "John Bennett" used). Names given for Fields and Hall when they performed hillbilly material for records or radio broadcasts include Fred "Sugar" Hall & His Sugar Babies (used for novelty as well as hot dance records), Eddie Younger and His Mountaineers (on Velvet Tone labels), Jim Cole's Tennessee Mountaineers, Sam Cole & His Corn Huskers, and Buck Wilson & His Rangers.

He cut over 160 songs of all types for the Grey Gull Record Company in its 2000 series and others. In 1927 and 1928 he probably recorded more for Grey Gull as a solo artist than for any other company. Radiex 2337 features Fields singing "Plucky Lindy," one of many tributes recorded around this time about aviator Charles A. Lindbergh (Vernon Dalhart had nearly a monopoly on such songs in recording studios, though others who cut songs with Lindbergh themes include Irving Kaufman, Jack Kaufman, and Vaughn De Leath).

Like Irving Kaufman, Fields in the 1920s sang vocal choruses on numerous dance band recordings, working with studio musicians such as Red Nichols and the two Dorsey brothers. Bands include Bailey's Lucky Seven, the Vagabonds, the Alabama Red Peppers, Fred Hall and His Sugar Babies, Sam Lanin, California Ramblers, and the related Little Ramblers. These were issued on such labels as Gennett, Romeo, Pathé Actuelle, Perfect, and Harmony.

He had three Gennett sessions in 1929, producing a total of eight sides issued on Gennett, Champion, and Supertone. He also provided vocal refrains for a group called the Tin Pan Paraders.

His late work for Edison was released in the electric 52,000 Diamond Disc series as well as in the short-lived lateral-cut series. Five late Edison discs are credited to Arthur Fields and His Assassinators, and they feature Hall on piano and musicians who normally worked with Hall. Not typical for the time, harmonica is played on some of these dance band recordings. The last Edison Diamond Disc featuring Fields as a solo artist was issued in November 1928: "King for a Day" coupled with "Yascha Michaeloff-sky's Melody" (52406). Edison lateral-cut "Needle Type" records were introduced in mid-1929, and two feature Fields and His Assassinators on both sides, 14061 and 14075. Edison promotional literature dated October 18, 1929, in announcing the release of 14061, speaks of "Art [sic] Fields himself doing the vocal honors." Promotional literature dated November 1, 1929, states about 14075, "*Piccolo Pete* is the biggest novelty dance hit of the day. The Assassinators have executed it in a murderous manner." The reverse side of Needle Type 14075 is "I Can't Sleep in the Movies Any More," written by Fields, Hall, and Van Cleve.

For Victor on May 13, 1932, he recorded six titles with Fred Hall, using the name "Gunboat Billy and the Sparrow." These hillbilly performances were issued on Victor 23698, 23714, and 24024.

He made some recordings in the World War II era, including "Der Fuehrer's Face" on Hit 7043, credited to Arthur Fields and His Orchestra. Poking fun at the Axis powers in the 1940s must have seemed, to the man who sang "When I Send You a Picture of Berlin" and similar songs for an earlier generation, like old times. On Hit 7021, Fields sings "I Found a Peach in Orange, New Jersey."

George Graff wrote to Walsh that when Hall and Fields stopped working together around 1941, "Arthur started the Arthur Fields Publications. . . . The hymns he sang back at Utica as a boy had made a great impression on him and we decided to write some sacred songs. This was a labor of love for both of us and we wrote and published forty or more hymns which we called 'Hymns of Happiness.' "

Around 1946 he moved from New York to 1931 McKinley St., Hollywood, Florida. The illness of his wife Selma required the move to Florida. There he had his own radio program over WKAT, Miami, called the *Arthur Fields Program*. He died in a fire on March 29, 1953, at the Littlefield Convalescent Home at Largo, Florida. He had been admitted to the nursing home some time after suffering a stroke on March 11. His wife wrote to Walsh about Fields' final days as well as his early years in the entertainment field, and excerpts of her letter dated April 12, 1953, are in the June 1953 issue of *Hobbies*.

Fisher, J. J. (c. 1866-c. January 1923)

Baltimore-born John J. Fisher worked for many early companies, including Edison's National Phonograph Company (over two dozen titles on cylinders), Berliner's Gramophone Company (nearly three dozen titles on Berliner discs), the National Gramophone Corporation (nearly a dozen Zon-o-phone discs), and Eldridge R. Johnson's new company, which was not yet named the Victor Talking Machine Company at the time Fisher had two sessions. Fisher recorded twenty titles for Johnson's company on December 5 and 6, 1900.

His recording career probably began in early 1897. The April 1897 issue of *The Phonoscope* announces that a "new baritone" named J. J. Fisher had begun to make records that were a "great success." He was perhaps most closely associated with Columbia. He worked often for that company in the late 1890s, and Columbia kept Fisher in its catalog longer than other companies, even reissuing on a double-sided disc Fisher performances recorded years earlier. As late as 1904 he recorded for Columbia, whose June 1, 1904 list of new recordings includes two cylinders of Fisher singing sacred numbers: "I Heard the Voice of Jesus Say" (32503) and "Face to Face" (32505).

An early ten-inch Columbia disc featuring Fisher is "For All Eternity" (711). His final recordings were made either for Columbia or Zon-o-phone.

As early as May 10, 1901, Zon-o-phone listed in its catalog fourteen titles sung by Fisher, and he must have returned to that company's studio since nine-inch green label Zon-o-phones featuring Fisher were issued, which means some of his discs for that company were made as late as 1904. Ten-inch Zon-o-phones were issued in early 1905, and none featuring Fisher are known to have been made.

An 1898 Columbia catalog notes his "basso-cantante voice of unusual power, range and sweetness." Included in the 1898 catalog is "Down Deep Within the Cellar," traditionally associated with bass singers. One early ten-inch Climax disc of "The Wearing of the Green" (194) says "bass" on the label, and the spoken announcement identifies Fisher as the singer. On many other recordings Fisher is labeled a baritone.

He stopped recording for Edison by early 1903. The June 1903 issue of *Edison Phonograph Monthly* announces, "Hereafter, all Records of the following titles will be sung by Arthur Clifford instead of J.J. Fisher. 7011. Love's Sorrow. 7735. I'll Be Your Sweetheart. 7654. Believe." Arthur Clifford was a nom de disque for baritone George Alexander. According to the January 1923 issue of *Talking Machine World*, Fisher late in life was an "insurance and real estate dealer."

Exploring the possibility that Atwood Twitchell on Zon-o-phone discs may be a pseudonym, Jim Walsh writes in the October 1956 issue of *Hobbies:*

> I know too little of Fisher to deliver a positive pronouncement, but a 1904 *Columbia Record* [catalog] seems to dispose of him as a possibility. It says that he had just returned to record making after several years spent in other business, and was "singing better than ever." Presumably, then, he wasn't recording in the Twitchell era of 1901-02.

He died in December 1922 or early January 1923 of a stroke at age fifty-six in his home at 1907 Park Avenue in Bridgeport, Connecticut. He was survived by his wife Maude and two brothers.

Frisco "Jass" Band

In 1917 the Frisco "Jass" Band cut nine titles for Edison, all issued on Blue Amberol as well as Diamond Disc. It was among the first to make records marketed as "jass." Jaudas' Society Orchestra was the only Edison group to make an earlier recording characterized as jass. The Frisco "Jass" Band was formed in early 1917 by Rudy Wiedoeft soon after he arrived in

New York City. According to the July 1917 issue of *Edison Amberola Monthly*, the band "is now playing engagements at Montmartre, New York's famous midnight cafe, the Winter Garden and the leading summer resorts near New York." Presumably the word "Frisco" was chosen to reflect that the musicians were from California. The band had no connection with Edison xylophone artist and vaudevillian Lou Chiha Frisco.

At its first session—on May 10, 1917—the Frisco "Jass" Band cut "Canary Cottage" and "Johnson 'Jass' Blues." In 1916-1917 Wiedoeft had played in the pit for Oliver Morosco's production of *Canary Cottage* as the touring show headed for the East Coast (it finally opened in New York City in the Morosco Theatre on February 5, 1917). "Canary Cottage"—a medley of the show's popular songs, written by Earl Carroll—was an obvious choice for the band's first session. Announcing its August release, Edison promotional literature characterized it as "a rattling One-Step melody from the tunes of the musical show 'Canary Cottage,' played in typical 'Jass Band' style." No cornet was featured, which was unusual for a jass ensemble at this time.

"Johnson 'Jass' Blues" was issued first on Blue Amberol 3254 in September 1917, then a few months later on Diamond Disc 50470. It was named after the song's composer, Arnold Johnson, who was also the band's pianist (beginning in the early 1920s he made Brunswick records under his own name). By 1920 lyrics were added to Johnson's melody, and the song was transformed into the popular "O," recorded by Billy Murray and others. The reverse side of Diamond Disc 50470 features "Umbrellas to Mend," notable for a band member shouting "umbrella!" at intervals and for remarkable percussion work.

Additional titles include "Pozzo" and "That's It." Promotional literature for "Night Time in Little Italy," recorded on June 4, 1917, and issued as Blue Amberol 3286 in October, states, " 'Jazz' Bands are all the rage now. This one is typical. The piece it plays is a very successful popular song, given here in Fox-Trot rhythm."

The November 1917 issue of *Edison Amberola Monthly* promoted the December release of "Yah-De-Dah" on Blue Amberol 3337 by stating, "The utter abandon displayed by a Jazz Band constitutes the greatest charm of this newest and smartest addition to modern dance music." Other Edison promotional literature added, "No players ever before played like this; hear them once and the Frisco Jazz Band will have you fascinated for life. Incidentally you'll fox-trot as never before to this music." (In late 1917 the company dropped quote marks from the band's name and, like other record manufacturers, switched from "Jass" to "Jazz." "Yah-De-Dah" was recorded on July 26, 1917, and issued on Blue Amberol months afterward. It was finally issued on Diamond Disc 51081 in December

1922. The reverse side featured "All I Need Is Just a Girl Like You," which had been recorded by the band on August 2, 1917.

Earl Fuller's Famous Jazz Band/Rector Novelty Orchestra

By 1917 Earl Fuller led a society dance band at Rector's Restaurant in New York City. On Victor, Columbia, Emerson, and Edison records that sold well from 1918 to 1920, Fuller ensembles helped popularize dance band trends of that period.

For several of his earliest sessions, Fuller led a small jazz ensemble dubbed on record labels Earl Fuller's Famous Jazz Band, which was probably formed at the suggestion of Victor executives eager to duplicate the success of the Original Dixieland Jazz Band's first disc, made in late February of 1917. Due to various grievances, the ODJB severed ties with Victor for a year after making its first record, instead cutting titles for Columbia and the new Aeolian-Vocalion label. Earl Fuller's hastily assembled jazz group filled the void, enabling Victor later in 1917 to meet a sudden demand for jazz music.

Earl Fuller's Famous Jazz Band consisted of Walter Kahn on cornet, Harry Raderman on trombone, Ted Lewis on clarinet (before Fuller's first session Lewis had been playing with Arthur Stone's Syncopated Orchestra), and John Lucas on drums. Photographs on sheet music suggest Fuller played piano on these dates, though Ernie Cutting may have been the pianist on records (as on other jazz records of the period, the piano on Fuller discs is the least audible of the instruments). It was one of the first bands to imitate the Original Dixieland Jazz Band, though the Frisco "Jass" Band made an Edison recording on May 10, 1917, a little earlier than Fuller's jazz ensemble.

"Slippery Hank" and "Yah-De-Dah," cut during the group's first session on June 4, 1917, were issued on Victor 18321 in September 1917. These jazz performances are notably loud, and the musicians use instruments for comic effects. Victor's September 1917 supplement states:

A terrific wail from the trombone starts "Slippery Hank" (F. H. Losey) on his glide, and the rest of the Jazz Band noises are in kind. And if you think these are all the noises available for a Jazz Band, turn the record over and listen to "Yah-de-dah" (Mel. B. Kaufman). The sounds as of a dog in his dying anguish are from Ted Lewis' clarinet. Notice the two little chords at the end of each number. This is how you know for certain that a Jazz Band is playing.

Ending a number with these "two little chords" was a practice introduced by the ODJB on records.

His jazz discs sold well, especially "The Old Grey Mare" backed with "Beale Street Blues" (Victor 18369), and, on Victor 18394, "Coon Band Contest" (a rag composed by trombonist Arthur Pryor and recorded by banjoist Vess Ossman as well as Sousa's Band as early as 1900) backed with "Li'l Liza Jane," written by Countess Ada de Lachau and arranged by J. L. Burbeck.

Historian and critic Gunther Schuller has mixed feelings about the band, writing on page 184 in *Early Jazz* (Oxford University Press, 1968), "The band's ricky-tick rhythms and cornetist Walter Kahn are very hard to take today. Moreover, its performances are structurally monotonous in their exact repetitions. Nevertheless, the band had a crude sort of excitement . . ." The now-forgotten discs helped define and popularize a new music, jazz. They influenced young people who would later, in the 1920s, make important recordings.

In 1918 Earl Fuller's Famous Jazz Band recorded for Edison several numbers with titles that refer to the new music, including "Jazzbo Jazz" and "Jazzin' Around." The August 1918 issue of *Edison Amberola Monthly* characterizes "Jazbo Jazz One-Step" on Blue Amberol 3554 as "a real, red-hot jazz dance of the most ultra modern variety," and this may be the first time that a jazz record is promoted as "hot." The jacket for Diamond Disc 50541, featuring Fuller's own composition "Jazz De Luxe," states that the band "was organized just at the time the jazz music became popular in New York, and through its playing of jazz music in Rector's Restaurant, New York City, Earl Fuller's Band became famous." Promotional literature for the same number on Blue Amberol 3610 states, "Until you have heard one of Earl Fuller's 'symphonies in rhythm' you are a novice in the art of appreciating Jazz."

Fuller's orchestra, called Earl Fuller's Rector Novelty Orchestra, recorded for Columbia over two dozen dance numbers from mid-1917 to early 1919. Each number features a xylophone played by Teddy Brown. The songs recorded for the last Columbia sessions incorporated musical themes suggesting exotic lands. Titles of such fox trots include "Sweet Siamese" (A2712), "Egyptland" (A2722), "Mummy Mine" (A2722), "Singapore" (A2686), "Out of the East" (A2686), and "Spaniola" (A2697). Notable jazz numbers are "Graveyard Blues" and "Sweet Emalina, My Gal," issued on Columbia A2523. Other titles include the one-step "Howdy" (written by "Ted and Josh," which may be Ted Lewis and another band member) and "Russian Rag" (A2649).

An advertisement on page 67 of the February 1920 issue of *Jacobs Orchestra Monthly* identifies Fuller as president of the American Musicians Syndicate, Inc., with an office at 1604 Broadway in New York City.

Fuller managed various dance ensembles. Labels for Pathé records made in 1919 by Joseph Samuels' Orchestra identify Earl Fuller of the Cafe de Paris as manager of the band.

By 1921, his ensemble was called Earl Fuller's New York Orchestra on Edison Diamond Discs and Blue Amberols. The same name was used on two Olympic discs issued around the same time, though the misleading pseudonym Haynes' Harlem Syncopators was used when "Melody in F," originally on Olympic 15118, was issued on Black Swan 2058.

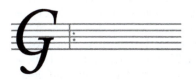

Gaskin, George J. (February 16, 1863-December 14, 1920)

George Jefferson Gaskin was born in Belfast, Ireland. After emigrating to the United States as a youth, he sang in churches and vaudeville. He probably started his recording career in 1891. A booklet titled "The First Book of Phonograph Records," compiled by Edison employee A. Theo E. Wangemann and duplicated in Allen Koenigsberg's *Edison Cylinder Records, 1889-1912*, shows Gaskin recording eighteen titles on August 3, 1891, for Edison's North American Phonograph Company. He is accompanied on piano by Edward Issler. Two titles are given twice: "Slide, Kelly, Slide" and "Drill, Ye Tarriers, Drill." In years to come Gaskin would sing both of these many times for other companies. The same booklet later shows Gaskin recording titles on June 2, 1891 (curiously, this is an earlier date). Only a few other singers who recorded this early would still be making records a decade later. Two others in this select group were Joseph Natus and George W. Johnson.

For the rest of the 1890s Gaskin performed often for most companies, covering all types of music—comic, sentimental, patriotic, sacred, even operatic ("Ah! I Have Sighed to Rest Me" from Verdi's *Il Trovatore*). Nicknamed "The Irish Thrush," he also sang Irish tunes. He was probably the most popular recording artist of the decade.

In the April 1928 issue of *The Gramophone*, Fred Gaisberg recalls the singer's early career:

> George J. Gaskin, who styled himself "The Silver-Voiced Irish Tenor," possessed a repertoire that ranged from the sacred and soulful

song to the popular vaudeville ditty. . . . It was a positive education to observe the facility with which he could switch over from the religious emotion he displayed during 10 rounds of a hymn to 20 hilarious rounds of "Maggie Murphy's Home." Secrets will out, and we discovered that the success of this transformation was mainly due to a quiet glass of lager imbibed offstage.

That Gaskin called himself a "Silver-Voiced Irish Tenor," at least according to Gaisberg, is interesting since Gaskin may be heard shouting on many early cylinders. The 1894 catalog of the United States Phonograph Company (87-91 Orange Street, Newark, New Jersey) states, "Every record is loud and ringing in tone, each word and syllable distinct, as if Mr. Gaskin were in the room with his audience. For horn use no vocals compare with these in loudness." On page 97 of the December 1943 issue of *Gramophone*, Gaisberg recalled that Gaskin was "one of the half dozen male singers with a voice clear and powerful enough to record." Edward B. Marks writes in *They All Sang* (Viking Press, 1935), "George had one of the best reproducing voices in the old phonograph days—one of the tinniest voices in the world." He knew Gaskin's work well because Marks and Joseph W. Stern ran in New York City the Universal Phonograph Company, for which Gaskin made cylinders.

The Phonograph Record and Supply Company ("Laboratory, 97, 99 & 101 Reade Street, New York") proudly announced Gaskin recordings in a supplementary list issued around August 1896. With Gaskin's photograph gracing the cover, it states, "We are pleased to inform our patrons that we have secured the services of this famous Tenor, and have now in stock a full line of his songs. These records are marvels of loudness, distinctness, brilliancy of tone, and execution. They possess all of the qualities essential to perfect reproduction through either horn or hearing tube." The tenor gave his signature to this statement dated August 6, 1896, and duplicated in the supplementary list: "I beg to advise my many friends among the users of the Phonograph, that I have made special arrangements with the PHONOGRAPH RECORD & SUPPLY CO., of No. 97 Reade Street, New York, to sing for them all of the selections listed below, and hereby authorize them to publish this fact over my signature."

Representative recordings include "Drill, Ye Tarriers, Drill" (North American/New Jersey), "Slide, Kelly, Slide" (North American), "O Promise Me" (New Jersey), "After the Ball" (New Jersey), "The Fatal Wedding" (New Jersey), "Sweet Marie" (New Jersey), "We Were Sweethearts, Nell and I" (Columbia), "The Sunshine of Paradise Alley" (Columbia), "She May Have Seen Better Days" (Columbia), "Down in Poverty Row" (Berliner), "On the Benches in the Park" (Columbia), "Sweet Rosie O'Grady" (Edison), "On the

Banks of the Wabash" (Columbia), "Break the News to Mother" (Columbia), "She Was Bred in Old Kentucky" (Columbia), "My Old New Hampshire Home" (Columbia) and "My Wild Irish Rose" (Columbia).

Gaskin's popularity peaked around 1896-97. The Columbia cylinder catalog in 1896 listed forty-one consecutively numbered recordings (2001-2041) under his name, and the company's June 1897 book lists many more. An 1899 catalog of cylinders duplicates an agreement dated May 1, 1898, indicating that Gaskin, along with more than a dozen others who signed the agreement, was exclusive to Columbia. The arrangement lasted a year. At some point Gaskin and John Bieling recorded tenor duets for Columbia, calling themselves Gaskin and Livingston. It was possibly the first tenor duo to make records.

Gaskin was among the first artists to be featured on Berliner discs, starting in 1894. He recorded often for the company in its earliest years, until the spring of 1897. He then made no discs until he returned two years later, in the spring of 1899.

He continued to record regularly into the early years of the 1900s, especially for Columbia, making discs for that company as late as 1904, such as "Bedelia" (1609). Afterward, Billy Murray recorded new takes of several songs originally recorded for the company by Gaskin. Zon-o-phone's May 19, 1901, catalog lists nine discs by the tenor (9811 through 9820, with the number 9818 not used). He never recorded for the Victor Talking Machine Company. Gaskin's voice, suitable for work with crude recording apparatus, was evidently less in demand by the century's turn when equipment was more sophisticated.

Around 1904, he stopped recording for over a decade. Using the name George Gaskin (no middle initial), he made a double-faced disc for Pathé around 1916: Claribel's "Come Back to Erin" backed by Balfe's "Killar-ney" (29115). According to *Variety*, he died of heart failure at his home at 42 W. 56th Street, New York on December 14, 1920.

Golden, Billy (June 9, 1858-January 29, 1926)

Billy Golden was born William B. Shires (note Shire, as some sources report) in Cincinnati, Ohio, to John and Elizabeth (Rust) Shires. The jacket for Edison Diamond Disc 50054 states that he was

> raised in St. Louis, where he became a butcher boy in the Union Market. He started his career in 1874, doing a black-face talking act in vaudeville. He was very successful in this for four years, at which time he joined John Merritt, the team being known as Merritt and Golden. About this time he originated the famous "cane pat," now so

popular with all buck dancers. Golden next became a member of Bailess and Kennedy's "Brightlights" vaudeville act, and here he introduced "Turkey in the Straw" to the public, starting the song on its career of fame . . .

Edward Le Roy Rice states in *Monarchs of Minstrelsy* (Kenny Publishing Company, 1911):

Billy Golden (Wm. B. Shire) started theatrically in 1874 with Frank Merritt as a partner, remaining with him one year. In 1875 he joined Billy Draiton, and for ten years they appeared in all parts of the United States as Golden and Draiton. In 1885 with his wife, May Golden, played for several seasons as The Goldens; later this alliance was augmented by Dick Schalpan. Mr. Golden retired in 1900 to enter hotel life in Washington, D.C., where he remained three years. September 25, 1904, he joined Joe Hughes as the team of Golden and Hughes, and as such they are now playing.

Elsewhere in his book Rice states that they were teamed in 1907, which seems a more likely date.

In the 1890s the comedian worked for nearly all companies, beginning with Columbia in 1891. In the early years, before the invention of master records, he cut some songs hundreds of times by the "round."

In his autobiography *The Music Goes Round* (Macmillan, 1942), Fred W. Gaisberg recalls an important introduction in 1894 to Emile Berliner (the two would work closely together for years) and gives credit to Golden: "It was Billy Golden who one day in Washington asked me if I would go with him to see a funny German who had started experimenting with a flat disc talking machine record and wanted to make some trials." Golden was among the first "name" entertainers to make Berliner discs. He cut "Rabbit Hash" on August 24, 1895 (635).

His biggest success was "Turkey in the Straw," considered by Jim Walsh to be one of the four great comic masterpieces of the industry's acoustic recording era, the others being Arthur Collins' "The Preacher and the Bear," Billy Murray's "Casey Jones," and Len Spencer's "Arkansaw Traveler." "Turkey in the Straw" is associated with Golden more than any other recording pioneer, though Arthur Collins recorded it in 1900 and Vess Ossman played it on banjo in 1902 as part of a "Medley of Old-Timers" (Victor 1358). Ossman rerecorded "Turkey in the Straw" on later occasions.

Another popular Golden number was "Bye-Bye, Ma Honey." Columbia's 1898 catalog of cylinders lists this as 7711, along with six other Golden titles. The catalog states, "Golden's negro delineations are always interesting—inimitable, and side-splitting."

For various companies Golden also recorded "Yaller Gal" and "Sisseretta's Visit to the North." Announcing the release of "Sisseretta's Visit to the North" on two-minute Standard 9369, the August 1906 issue of *Edison Phonograph Monthly* states that this

> is the first Record that Mr. Golden has made for our catalogue in some time. He comes back with renewed vigor and makes this vaudeville specialty perhaps better than anything he has previously done. This record is a combination of talking, laughing and singing. Sisseretta is so fat that it is hard to tell her from a round-house. She made a trip to the North and the talking part of the Record tells in a laughable manner of what happened.

Prior to 1908 Golden worked mostly as a solo artist, although he did record at least one skit for Berliner on June 22, 1897, with patent medicine salesman George Graham: "Negro Oddity" (732). A Berliner catalog promotes the disc with these lines: "A Street conversation by Graham and Golden. Golden's great coon laugh is frequently heard in this record."

Golden recorded eight titles for Edison in 1899 with Arthur Collins, including three titles that Golden also recorded as solo numbers: "Bye-Bye, Ma Honey," "Roll on de Ground," and "Rabbit Hash."

As years passed, Golden did little singing, instead mostly working with partners in the exchange of minstrel-derived, or blackface, comic dialogue (a little singing is included on some records that mainly feature dialogue). Golden and stage partner Joe Hughes began making records in late 1908 with "Shipmates," cut for Columbia, Victor, and Edison. The recording team of Golden and Hughes was first in a long line of two-man comedy teams that delivered jokes in black dialect, the popularity of such humor on records peaking in the late 1920s with such teams as Moran and Mack ("Two Black Crows" on Columbia), Correll and Gosden ("Sam 'n' Henry" and then "Amos 'n' Andy" on Victor), Green and Floyd ("Pork & Beans" on Cameo), and LeMaire and Swor ("Sweet William and Bad Bill" on Brunswick).

Hughes was born Joseph Sovey (or Savory) in Chicago on March 21, 1863, and raised in St. Louis. He had been associated with Haverly's Minstrels and the Keith and Proctor vaudeville circuits. The team of Golden and Hughes was formed on September 24, 1907, according to a summary of Hughes' career in Rice's *Monarchs of Minstrelsy*. The duo enjoyed success in vaudeville as well as on records. Popular titles include "Whistling Pete," "Clammy Green," and "My Uncle's Farm." A successful twelve-inch Victor disc from 1916 was "Jimmy Trigger Returns From the War" (35518), which features the team of Golden and Hughes, backed by "Curiosity Hunt," which features Golden and Marlowe. The sketch "Bear's Oil" was also a big seller as Edison Diamond Disc 50054.

After performing with Golden for several years, Hughes retired from the entertainment field for a time to tend a farm in Milford, Massachusetts. From 1915 to early 1917 Golden worked mostly with Jim Marlowe. This team made records not only for Columbia, Victor, and Edison (as had Golden and Hughes) but also for Pathé, Paroquette, and Canadian Brunswick. Marlowe died of pneumonia on March 21, 1917, at St. Vincent Hospital in New York City, and his death was noted in the May 1917 issue of *Edison Amberola Monthly*.

For a year and a half, beginning in mid-1917, Golden worked with comedian and singer Billy Heins, who had made Zon-o-phone discs and other records nearly two decades earlier. One popular Golden and Heins Victor disc features "A Trip to Paradise" backed by "The Death of Towser" (35641), recorded on May 24, 1917. ("The Death of Towser" was issued on Imperial 5500 in October 1917.) Another twelve-inch Victor disc features "In a Bird Store" and "Up for Sentence" (35659).

Golden and Heins made two Columbia discs. "The Colored Recruit" on Columbia A2551, issued in August 1918, is a sketch that includes the song "If They Let Me Use My Razor in This War," itself an updated version of a tune recorded years earlier by Len Spencer titled "If They'd Only Fought with Razors in the War." Two of the four songs issued by Columbia around this time were given new titles in 1928 ("The Colored Recruit" was retitled "The New Recruit"; "Up for Sentence" was retitled "A Day in Court") and reissued on Columbia's budget labels, credited to "Jones and Crawford." In 1917 Golden and Heins also made two twelve-inch Victor discs as well as a few Diamond Discs. Their skit "A Scheme to Enter Heaven" was issued on Imperial 5478 as well as Rex 5478 in September 1917.

In 1919 Golden was reunited with his old partner Hughes. They cut for Columbia the popular "Fishing and Drinking" and "Back Home on the Farm," issued on A2859 in April 1920. The label for Pathé 20460, which features "Back Home on the Farm" and "The Bell Boys," characterizes the duo as "Humorous Comedians." Curiously, the label for Okeh 4201, which also features "Back Home on the Farm" and "The Bell Boys," cites the name William Hughes (it was issued in January 1921). They recorded for Edison such numbers as "Who Stole the Chickens?" and "Back Home on the Farm," the latter being issued on Diamond Disc 51082 in December 1922. The last sessions for Golden and Hughes were in 1920.

Golden, working alone, recorded in 1921 for Edison "A Scene on the Old Plantation," largely a reworking of his old "Rabbit Hash" skit, which he had recorded for Edison as early as 1898 as a brown wax cylinder

(4014). The updated skit incorporated references to prohibition. Among Golden's last recordings are two monologues, "The Mocking Bird" and "Uncle Josh's Birthday," issued on Emerson 10291 in September 1922. "The Mocking Bird" was also issued in December 1922 on Banner 2062.

He performed in vaudeville into the 1920s. Page 163 of the November 1923 issue of *Talking Machine World* states, "Billy Golden, who has been known for so many years to hundreds of vaudeville fans and whose talking machine records are familiar to thousands, paid daily visits to the Victor record department of the Platt Music Co. while he was filling an engagement at the Orpheum last month." The Platt music shop was next to the Orpheum Theater in Los Angeles. He died in an apartment at 835 West 179th Street in New York City on January 29, 1926, according to his death certificate, dated that day (some sources erroneously state January 30). He was buried in Kensico Cemetery on February 1.

Green Brothers

The Green Brothers were not the first to make xylophone recordings (that was probably A. T. Van Winkle, who made North American cylinders with Edward Issler in 1889), but brothers Joe Green (1892-1939) and George Hamilton Green (1893-1970) were important recording artists when popular music underwent a transformation around 1917-1921. The two xylophone artists—sometimes performing together, other times working individually—recorded for nearly every company. They also played marimba, vibraphone, harpaphone, bells, and chimes. A younger brother, Lew Green (1909-1992), was also a professional musician, playing guitar and banjo. All were born and raised in Omaha, Nebraska.

Their musical talents were encouraged by their father, George Green, who was a prominent bandmaster. Page 6B of the July 18, 1915, edition of *The Omaha Daily News* reports:

> Thirty years ago, on July 4, 1885, George Green first began to play with the band known for twenty-five years as George Green's band. In the thirty years the band has played for four presidents, Cleveland, McKinley, Roosevelt, and Taft, playing "Hail to the Chief" at least once for each. As well known as George is as a bandmaster his two sons promise to become even better known. Joe Green now is playing as tympanist and drummer with Bohumir Kryl's concert band of Chicago. During the winter he appeared in vaudeville with his brother George Green Jr., who has been declared by critics to be the best xylophonist soloist in the world. The latter is playing this summer in an orchestra in Michigan and will return to vaudeville this winter. He

plays classical selections of the xylophone using six or eight hammers, a feat that critics say no other musician has been able to accomplish. Both boys began their musical careers by playing with their father's band when very young. George Jr. made his first public appearance when eight years of age by playing a xylophone solo with the band.

The March 25, 1917, edition of Omaha's *World-Herald* states about George:

Only a few years ago, while he was a pupil in Lake school, the boy made his musical debut at a Sunday afternoon concert in Hanscom Park, when he played a solo upon a xylophone which he had constructed himself out of odds and ends of wood and metal. . . . George is only twenty-two years old now. For six years he was a pupil of the late Sigmund Landsberg, studying piano. Later he decided to take up trap-drumming and at eighteen he was highly proficient in this work. His drumming turned him toward bell and xylophone playing . . .

The February 1917 issue of *Edison Amberola Monthly* gives a simliar account of George's musical background:

Being brought up in an atmosphere of music, he acquired the rudiments of a musical education very early and at the age of eleven years was proficient on a xylophone that he himself had made. When he was thirteen years old he began a study of the piano and for six years he worked under Prof. Sigmund Landsberg of Omaha. While studying piano, he decided to take up trap drumming and at eighteen he was highly proficient in his work. His drumming turned him toward bell and xylophone playing and within two years he had attained a degree of technical proficiency that enabled him to enter vaudeville.

The June 1919 issue of *The Music Messenger* states that Joe "started his musical career when a boy in a picture house as a drummer. He afterward went to Chicago, and while there studied drumming under the great tympanist, Joseph Zettelman, of the Chicago Symphony Orchestra."

Joe traveled as a member of Sousa's Band from 1915 to 1919. In 1914 George entered vaudeville. The November 21, 1914, edition of *The New York Clipper* notes the appearance of Green and Hodek (a pianist) at Chicago's Great Northern Hippodrome Theatre. Within a year he earned such titles as "World's Fastest Xylophonist" and "Speed King of Xylophonists." By late 1916 he was a member of Earl Fuller's Rector's Novelty Orchestra (Fuller around this time served as his manager) as well as a vaudeville and concert artist. In late 1916 he also began recording. His first Edison recording, Blue Amberol 3115, was issued in March 1917: Franz von Suppé's "Light Cavalry Overture." His xylophone playing is accompanied by orchestra. This was followed in May by the release of Kreisler's "Caprice Viennois" on Blue Amberol 3155, and then in June Edison issued the Suppé overture "Morning, Noon and Night in Vienna" (Blue Amberol 3182). His first Diamond Disc (80349), issued in July 1917, featured "Light Cavalry Overture" backed by the march from Wagner's *Tannhäuser*. He recorded only classical and semiclassical pieces in his first year; thereafter, he also played jazz compositions for Edison and other companies.

George Hamilton Green composed many songs that he recorded as a solo artist and with others, including "Fluffy Ruffles," "Greased Lightning," "Vanity Fair," "Watermelon Whispers," "Social Life," and "Log Cabin Blues." Joe Green composed "I'm Always Smiling."

In 1918, he recorded for other companies, including Emerson and the newly established New York Recording Laboratories, Inc, which produced Paramount records. "Venetian Love Song" backed by Dvořák's "Humoresque" was issued as Paramount 30022 on May 20, 1918. This Dvořák tune as arranged for dancing by Ford Dabney was sometimes called "Castle Valse Classique." Green joined pianist Victor Arden and saxophonist F. Wheeler Wadsworth to form the All Star Trio, which began recording in 1918.

Joe Green's debut as a solo record artist appears to be on Okeh 1137, issued in April 1919. He performs on xylophone the Byron Gay song "Sand Dunes." The two brothers—performing as soloists, working together, and performing with others—made many records in the Okeh studio under the supervision of director Fred Hager, who in the autumn of 1923 left the recording industry to serve as manager of the Greens.

The two Green brothers became a recording team in early 1919. Their performance of Wallace's "Hindustan" was issued on Okeh 1155 in April 1919. In May 1919, a disc by the Green Brothers Xylophone Orchestra was issued by Pathé featuring George Hamilton Green's own "Vanity Fair" backed by "Egyptland" (22066). In that month Emerson issued three performances by the Emerson Xylo-Phiends, a Green Brothers ensemble (George Hamilton Green's composition "Shake Your Shoulders" is on Emerson 9166). Another version of "Shake Your Shoulders" was issued in July on a smaller Emerson disc (7506), backed by "Sensation."

The Green Brothers' Novelty Band is introduced as "another new Victor dance band" in Victor's June 1920 supplement. Issued on 18667 are the fox trots "La Veeda" and "Desert Dreams." The supplement states, "The orchestra is largely made up of brass instruments, the sweet, clear tones of cornets being used with quite thrilling effect. Other brasses sustain the harmony, through which there tinkle the steel-blue notes of xylophone."

When Diamond Disc 52410 was issued in late October 1928, Edison promotional literature stressed that record buyers prefer "a good novelty dance tune" over "a good dance tune," adding that the "Green Brothers have long been specialists in dance novelty."

Throughout the 1920s they made discs as the Green Brothers' Xylophone Orchestra, Xylophone Band, Novelty Orchestra, Marimba Orchestra, even Mellorimba Orchestra. They played in hundreds of groups in recording studios and on the radio. Page 134 of the April 1927 issue of *Talking Machine World* reports that George was on an extensive tour sponsored by the Leedy Manufacturing Company, maker of Leedy drums, banjos, and xylophones. Visiting various cities, he played concerts in large hotels. Joe died in 1939 following an operation. George soon afterward retired from the music business and worked as a cartoonist from his Woodstock, New York home. He died in 1970.

Hager, Fred (December 31, 1874-March 3, 1958)

Fred Hager was born Frederick Wallace Haga in New Milford in Susquehanna County, Pennsylvania. He worked for many companies and was known as Frederick W. Hager, Fred W. Hager, F. W. Hager, and Fred Hager. A March 1901 catalog of Edison "Concert" cylinders lists him as Wallace Fredericks, adding "Frederick Wallace Hager" in parenthesis. Two decades later, he even used the name Milo Rega. "Rega" is essentially Hager's name spelled backward.

The February 1920 issue of *Jacobs' Orchestra Monthly*, which includes an article about Hager in its series called "Famous Bandmasters in Brief," states that since the father was leader of the town band, "it was quite natural that the youthful Hager should become interested in music, and at an early age he began the study of the violin." The family moved to New

York City in 1882. The article states, "In his earlier years he had won a free scholarship at the National Conservatory of Music which was then under the direction of the noted Dvořák. . . . In 1896 he branched out as a band leader and soon controlled nearly all the political affairs in his immediate home district (the Bronx) . . ."

The July 1898 issue of *The Phonoscope* states, "He studied under Prof. F. Hermann for several years, after which he received a term of free scholarship at the National Conservatory of Music. He then studied [for three years] with Carl Heuser, a prominent violinist of New York City. . . . Mr. Hager has the distinction of being the youngest bandmaster of merit in New York City, having procured a contract to furnish a band [Hager's American Military Band] for a public park when he was but 21 years of age. . . . Mr. Hager has recently gone into the phonograph field and is at present engaged by Messrs. Harms, Kaiser and Hagen." The January 1899 issue of *The Phonoscope* lists Hager among artists making cylinders for Harms, Kaiser, and Hagen, located at 18 East 22nd Street, New York City.

He made violin solos on brown wax cylinders in the late 1890s and Jim Walsh states Hager "has generally been considered the first violinist to make commercial records." Walsh writes in the March 1965 issue of *Hobbies*, "He was Charles D'Almaine's only rival as a cylinder record violinist when the 20th century began."

The May 10, 1901, catalog for Zon-o-phone records, issued by the National Gramophone Corporation, cites Frederick W. Hager as "Winner of the First Prize (Gold Medal) at the Pittsburgh Exposition, 1898, for the best Violin Record. After months of patient experimenting, we are able to give the public a violin record, that never has been equaled." It then lists twelve violin discs featuring Hager, including 9060: "Scene De Ballet. A marvelous and excellent record. . . . Every note is clear and sweet. This is a most difficult selection to record as it is four or five notes higher than usually used for recording purposes, and takes in the full register of the violin." Around this time Hager also worked for Columbia.

The article in *Jacobs' Orchestra Monthly* states:

> From soloist with the leading companies—including the Columbia for two years, the Zon-o-phone for six years and the Edison for two years—he next became director of both band and orchestral recording for the various companies. He attained prominence as director of the Edison Concert Band—a position that he held for two years, but which was relinquished to try a venture in the publication of popular numbers under the firm name of Helf & Hager.

Hager composed hundreds of numbers, the most successful being "Laughing Water." Published in 1903, the song was meant to suggest music of American Indians, and is similar in that regard to Neil Moret's 1901 "Hiawatha" (which started a craze for "Indian" tunes) and Egbert Van Alstyne's 1903 "Navajo." "Laughing Water" was issued on Edison Standard 8532, Columbia cylinder 32283 and discs 138 and 1571, Victor 31135 (Pryor's Orchestra), Victor 35017 (Victor Band), and Victor 2713 (Harry Macdonough). Hager himself led the Edison Concert Band when it recorded "Laughing Water" in 1903.

Other Hager compositions issued on Edison two-minute wax cylinders include "Gleaming Star" (9218), "Passion" (9309), and "Minerva" (9327). Hager's "Toy Shop Symphony" and his "Christmas Morning with the Kiddies" were recorded by the Peerless Orchestra and issued on Diamond Disc 50381. Byron G. Harlan sings Hager's "Captain Baby Bunting" on Edison Standard 9508 and Hager's "Georgia Skip" on Victor 18038. Arthur Pryor's Band performs Hager's "The Boy and the Birds" on Victor 19192, and the New York Military Band performs it on Blue Amberol 3736. "When I'm a Sergeant Man" is sung by Collins and Harlan on Pathé 30280. "In the Valley of Sunshine and Roses" is sung by Henry Burr on Okeh 4140. Conway's Band performs Hager's "Echoes of the Marne" on Okeh 4541, issued in March 1922.

From 1905 to 1909 Hager and J. Fred Helf, who wrote many popular songs, operated the Helf & Hager Company, a sheet music publishing firm with headquarters on West 28th Street in New York City. One of the biggest hits published by the company was "Everybody Works But Father" (1905), a song originally composed in England by Charles W. McClintock but with new words added by Jean Havez when published in America. Many Hager compositions were published by this firm (a non-Hager song published by the company in 1905 was "The Message of the Old Church Bell," with music by Manuel Romain, a tenor who would later make many records). By early 1910 Helf ran the J. Fred Helf Publishing Company.

When he stopped directing the Edison Concert Band is unknown though he worked for Edison's National Phonograph Company as late as 1904 since "Blue Bell," featuring the team of Albert Benzler and Frederick W. Hager on bells and xylophone, was issued on Standard 8829 in November 1904.

He directed Zon-o-phone house bands and orchestras around the time he directed Edison as well as Columbia house bands (early Zon-o-phone discs were sold by Frank Seaman's National Gramophone Corporation, a subsidiary of the Universal Talking Machine Company). The May 10, 1901, catalog for Zon-o-phone records gives composer credit to Hager for

"Zon-o-phone March" and states, "This march was written and dedicated to us especially for the Zon-o-phone by our musical director." Most of the early Zon-o-phone discs to feature the house orchestra give credit to the Zon-o-phone Orchestra, but later many Zon-o-phone releases refer to "Hager's Orchestra." In the January 1966 issue of *Hobbies*, Jim Walsh recalls Hager telling Walsh years earlier that "The Jolly Coppersmith" on Zon-o-phone 9175 outsold all other band and orchestra records issued by the company around 1901 "because the banging on the anvil and other noises were so loud they drowned out the scratch."

In late 1907 Eddie King succeeded Hager as musical director of performances issued on Zon-o-phone discs (by this time the discs were made by the Universal Talking Machine Manufacturing Company, a Victor subsidiary). After his few years in the music publishing business, Hager returned to the recording industry as director from 1910 to 1912 of the Boston Talking Machine Company, maker of hill-and-dale Phono-Cut discs. From 1912 to 1914 he was the Keen-O-Phone Company's director. From around 1914 to 1917 he was director of the Rex Talking Machine Corporation, which pressed Rex, Imperial, and Fraad discs. The Keen-O-Phone company had its recording studio in Philadelphia, as did Rex, which succeeded the liquidated Keen-O-Phone Company. Charles Hart writes in the December 1958 issue of *Hobbies*, "In 1915 I returned to New York and . . . made a test record some months later for a small, short-lived company called the Perma. Fred Hager was the manager." Nothing is known about Perma records, which are extremely rare, but the fact that Hager was manager suggests they may have been pressed by Rex.

In an article on singer Ellen Beach Yaw for *The Record Collector* (December 1955) researcher Antonio Altamirano quotes a letter by the retired Hager about circumstances regarding Yaw's Keen-O-Phone sessions, and Hager mentions that during Keen-O-Phone sessions he sometimes led members of the Philadelphia Symphony Orchestra, who were hired to provide accompaniment for singers; sometimes members of the Boston Symphony traveled to Philadelphia for sessions. It is not known if Hager remained as musical director when the Imperial Talking Machine Company acquired Rex in May 1917. Many Rex discs feature "Hager's Band" and "Hager's Dance Orchestra." His compositions on these discs include "The Song Thrush" (5070) and "A Bird Intermezzo" (5416). The Rex Talking Machine Corporation recorded some artists who had been prolific in earlier years but whose output had dropped off dramatically. They then resurfaced in the World War I years as Rex artists, including Bob Roberts, Edward Favor, and J. W. Myers. Hager may have recruited old friends from his Zon-o-phone, Columbia, and Edison years to record for Rex.

He was musical director for the Otto Heineman Phonograph Supply Corporation, maker of Okeh discs, for several years beginning in 1918 (the company's name was changed to the General Phonograph Corporation on October 1, 1919). Page 95 of the May 1918 issue of *Talking Machine World* announced that the first Okeh records, which were vertical cut, would be introduced at a trade show in early June and also identified Hager as musical director, so it is likely that he joined the company in early 1918.

He met recording engineer Charles L. Hibbard around the turn of the century at Edison's National Phonograph Company, and the two worked closely together into the 1920s. Hibbard also worked on Keen-O-Phone, Rex, and Okeh records when Hager was musical director for those labels, and he remained with Okeh after Hager left the company, assisted by sound engineer Peter Decker.

Hager supervised the August 10, 1920, Okeh session at which Mamie Smith recorded the influential "Crazy Blues," permitting black musicians to accompany the featured singer—the first time that had happened in the Okeh studio. Accompanied by Okeh house musicians, Smith had made her Okeh debut in February with "That Thing Called Love" and "You Can't Keep a Good Man Down."

During Okeh sessions in the early 1920s Hager led bands issued under such names as Hager's Dance Orchestra and Hager's Novelty Orchestra. He worked closely with Justin Ring, who was born in 1876 and died in Florida in January 1963. Hager and Ring had worked together as early as 1899. In 1903, Justus Ringleben Jr. (Ring's real name) was listed as arranger on sheet music for Hager's "Laughing Water," which was followed in 1904 by Hager's "Handsome Harry," Ringleben again credited as arranger. Hager led the Edison Concert Band in a recording of "Jovial Joe," composed by Ringleben and issued on Standard 8838 in late 1904.

Issued in late 1922, Okeh 4705 features two Christmas "novelty" numbers titled "Rocking Horse Parade" and "Grandma's Music Box," the first performed by Hager's Concert Orchestra, the second by Ring & Company. Composer credit on each is given to "Ring-Hager." Okeh 4395 features the Rega Dance Orchestra performing "Oriola," credited to "Ring-Hager." Okeh 4463 features Hager's Concert Orchestra performing "Christmas Memories," with composer credit given to Ring and Hager, and it is backed by "Adeste Fideles" performed on chimes "rung by James A. Hager," perhaps a brother. Okeh 4921 features the Hager and Ring composition "Gloria," played by Vincent Lopez and His Orchestra. Lewis James sings the Ring-Hager song "By the Babbling Brook" on Edison Diamond Disc 80503 and Blue Amberol 3807. Clyde Doerr and His Orchestra cut Ring and Hager's "Swanee Smiles" for Victor 18981 on August 29, 1922.

Page 142 of the March 1922 issue of *Talking Machine World* discusses Okeh artists who enjoyed success on a February 17 radio program: "The entire program of the evening was given by Okeh artists, with Fred W. Hager, musical director of the Okeh laboratories, in charge of the event." Page 96 of the May 1922 issue states, "Another Okeh radio party was held on Wednesday, April 26, at Bedloe's Island broadcasting station under the direction of Fred W. Hager, recording director of the General Phonograph Corp. Quite a number of well-known Okeh artists were on the program . . ." The reference here to Hager as "recording director" and other references in the trade journal around this time to Hager as "general manager" of the recording laboratories suggest a promotion from musical director.

Page 48 of the July 1923 issue of *Talking Machine World* announces that Hager, as "director of the Okeh recording laboratory," traveled to Chicago to make "a number of special recordings for the Okeh library." The practice of moving recording equipment to other cities was new for the company (as late as May 1923 the Chicago-based Guyon's Paradise Orchestra had traveled to New York City for sessions). Okeh executive Ralph S. Peer and engineer Charles Hibbard joined him in Chicago. Working closely with Elmer A. Fearn, president of the Consolidated Talking Machine Company (an important Okeh distributor based in Chicago), the men recorded King Oliver's Jazz Band (on June 22 and 23) and Erstine Tate's Vendrome Orchestra (on June 23). Louis Armstrong was one of Oliver's musicians, and records made at the June 22 and 23 sessions are important contributions to jazz. Months earlier Oliver's musicians had recorded for Gennett, but the Okeh records were of far better quality. Nobody at the time would have realized that these sessions produced records of historic importance. Their intention was simply to produce "race" records that would sell well, especially in Chicago's South Side. The records did sell well, leading to additional Okeh sessions in Chicago in October.

Months later, Hager retired from the record industry. Page 131 of the September 1923 issue of *Talking Machine World* announces the appointment of Arthur Bergh as successor to Hager, "who had resigned from the company's service." No reason is given for Hager's resignation, but it is worth considering that the record division of the General Phonograph Corporation had changed dramatically in the years since Hager began as its musical director. Hager's talents were well suited for the company when it began making Okeh records in 1918 since at first Okeh records offered conventional fare, but by 1923 the company had found a niche in the industry as a supplier of race and hillbilly records. Ralph S. Peer, who excelled at discovering new talent for Okeh's race and hillbilly markets, became increasingly important to the company, and Clarence Williams was musical director for many sessions during which race records were made. Hager's talents may have been less valued by the company as it went in new directions in the 1920s.

Bergh, who had earlier served as recording director for other companies, including Emerson, served as Hager's successor for only a year, leaving the Okeh position to serve as general manager of Columbia's recording laboratories beginning on November 15, 1924. Page 186 of the November 1924 issue of *Talking Machine World* announces the appointment of Hager's long-time associate Justin Ring "as director of the Okeh recording laboratories" but later issues of the trade journal cite Ring as Okeh's musical director (Tommy Rockwell was appointed manager of the Okeh recording laboratories in January 1927). By 1930 Ring's name appeared on Banner and other American Record Corporation labels and later Ring led musical groups that recorded for Decca.

Upon leaving Okeh, Hager managed the Green Brothers (xylophonists Joe and George Hamilton Green), who had made many Okeh records under Hager's supervision. For a long time he lived in Bayside, Long Island, New York, though Walsh reports in the January 1951 issue of *Hobbies* that Hager at that time lived in Northport, New York. Hager died in Dunedin, Florida.

Happiness Boys

The team of tenor Billy Jones and bass-baritone Ernest Hare, known as the Happiness Boys, recorded frequently throughout the 1920s, enjoying success on various labels, major and minor. They were also famous as radio artists.

Fred Rabenstein, who was paymaster for the Edison company for years, told Jim Walsh that Jones met Ernest Hare in the Edison recording studios. If they did meet here for the first time, it must have been in 1920, with nothing by the duo successfully recorded at that time. Jones and Hare made their first Edison record on June 25, 1921, and Edison promotional literature dated December 1921, announcing the release of "Down at the Old Swimming Hole" on Blue Amberol 4391, states, "To our knowledge, they have not been paired before." But the Edison session took place a few months after their first Brunswick session.

Jim Walsh cites in the June 1974 issue of *Hobbies* what Rabenstein recalled about that first meeting:

[T]hey had amused themselves by singing opera in a burlesque fashion, as they did in their 1922 record of "Operatic Syncopation" . . . They seemed to have everything in common except that Jones was a bachelor (he took a wife after his mother's death) and Hare was married, with a little girl named Marilyn, who was to serve for a short time as Jones's singing partner after her father's death in 1939. Hare was six years older to the day than Jones; both had mothers whose maiden names were Roberts; both were five feet and seven inches tall; both had voices of operatic calibre that perfectly complemented each other, and both had had operatic experience.

An article by David Wallace on the Happiness Boys in the February 1937 issue of *Popular Songs* credits Brunswick's recording manager for bringing together the two singers:

It was Gus Haenschen, now a noted orchestra leader but then recording manager for Brunswick records, who suggested that Billy Jones and Ernie Hare pool their talents. Their first record [together] was "All She'd Say Was Mmm-mmm-mmm" [sic] and it sold so well they immediately found themselves in the money. They made records for 16 phonograph companies. On December 13, 1923, as "The Happiness Boys," Billy and Ernie broadcast on their first commercial program. Their job was to advertise the Happiness Candy Stores, over WEAF. They started at $100 a week for the team and $15 a week for their accompanist. They were the Happiness Boys for five and a half years. In 1928, Jones and Hare became the highest paid singers in radio. They received $1,250 a week as the Flit Soldiers for singing over WJZ and 25 stations. The following year they became the Interwoven Pair, which they remained for two years.

Their teaming up seems almost inevitable since in 1920 Jones made records for the same companies as Hare—Brunswick, Okeh, Pathé, Gennett, and others. They first sang together on Brunswick 2063, "All She'd Say Was 'Umh Hum,'" issued in March 1921. As "Reese Jones," Billy Jones as a solo artist had recorded this earlier for Edison (Blue Amberol 4149).

They did not record together again for a few months, Hare still having a partner in Al Bernard (their "Change Your Name, Malinda Lee" was issued on Olympic 14110 in August 1922). In the spring of 1921 Jones and Hare recorded "I Like It" for Okeh 4325, which was issued in July. Also in July Brunswick issued "Nestle in Your Daddy's Arms" backed by "Down Yonder" (2101).

On October 18, 1921, they were on radio for the first time, broadcasting over WJZ from a Westinghouse factory in Newark, New Jersey—probably the first time a program was broadcast in the metropolitan New York area. They would become radio stars of the 1920s. (Fortunately, in the early 1920s they were not exclusive to Victor or Brunswick. These companies prohibited their artists from performing for radio audiences, as Ward Seeley reported in "Will the Great Artists Continue?" in the June 1923 issue of *The Wireless Age*.)

From mid-1922 onward they made records as a duo on a regular basis, but each continued to have sessions as a solo artist and each continued to contribute vocal refrains to dance band records. They were never exclusive to any record company. Records of the duo made from 1921 to early 1924 do not use the name Happiness Boys but instead cite the names Billy Jones and Ernest Hare (usually in that order), or pseudonyms for the two singers were used. They became known as the Happiness Boys because as radio entertainers they were sponsored—beginning in August 1923—on Manhattan's WEAF by the Happiness Candy Stores, owned by Irving Fuerst.

The name Happiness Boys was first used on a label on Victor 19340, issued on June 20, 1924: "Hard Boiled Rose" backed by "Oh! Eva." *Talking Machine World* used the name Happiness Boys for the first time on page 99 of the June 1924 issue, which features a full page ad for the duo's version of "Hinky Dinky Parlay Voo" on Columbia 132-D. Edison literature first used the name Happiness Boys on its August 1924 release sheet of new Blue Amberol cylinders. In announcing the release of "Down Where the South Begins" on Blue Amberol 4892, the list states, "North or South, East or West—everywhere, this rollicking song by Jones and Hare (The Happiness Boys) will brighten many an evening." Other companies continued to use the name of Jones and Hare for some time, some eventually adding "The Happiness Boys" in parenthesis.

From the early to mid-1920s the comic duo was regularly accompanied by studio orchestras, but from 1925 to 1929 Dave Kaplan often provided piano accompaniment. On the duo's first electric Victor disc (19718), featuring performances cut on July 1, 1925, Kaplan assists the singers, and the disc's labels give credit to him in a conventional way: "Piano Accomp.—Dave Kaplan." Soon afterward Victor labels for Happiness Boys discs stated, "Dave Kaplan at the piano." Throughout the 1920s Kaplan directed Edison house musicians on popular numbers (Cesare Sodero supervised anything classical in nature), with many performances credited to Kaplan's Melodists. By mid-1927 he began using the name Dave Kaplan with His Happiness Orchestra. Kaplan worked for Edison exclusively except when he joined Jones and Hare in other studios to provide accompaniment.

By 1924 the Happiness Boys adopted "How Do You Do?" as their radio theme song. They maintained a business office at 1674 Broadway in New

York City. The peak years of their popularity as record artists were probably 1925 to 1927. It is possible that by 1928 their many performances on radio adversely affected sales of their records, with members of the public deciding that they did not want records of Jones and Hare with songs that they were also performing on radio.

They were among the first to make electric recordings, even cutting one song—"I Miss My Swiss"—for both Victor and Columbia in the early weeks of the new electric era. They were important Edison artists throughout the 1920s, the last Jones and Hare Diamond Disc (52598) being issued on July 5, 1929. Their final record was made in 1930, with Victor 22491 featuring the talking skits "The Happiness Boys Going Abroad" and "The Happiness Boys in London" (Hare's last record made as a solo artist was issued in 1932). In 1930 they appeared in a Vitaphone short titled *Rambling 'Round Radio Row with Jerry Ward—Introducing the Happiness Boys, Billy Jones and Ernie Hare*.

They continued working on radio in the early 1930s, the name of the duo changing as sponsors changed. Their popularity waned, and network activities evidently ceased in 1932. *Radio Guide* during the winter of 1933-1934 shows Jones and Hare working as "The Taystee Loafers," on WOR on Monday, Wednesday, and Friday at 8:15. Sponsored by the Taystee Bread Company, the show was probably not syndicated. The orchestra was The Taystee Breadwinners, directed by Ben Selvin.

An article by James A. McFadden titled "Pioneers of Radio Forgotten" on page 13 of the August 13, 1936, edition of the *San Francisco Examiner* suggests that by this time the duo worked in relative obscurity. McFadden asks, "What has happened to those folks that pioneered the world of radio entertainment? . . . The names of Morton Downey . . . the 'Happiness Boys' Billy Jones and Ernie Hare, John and Ned . . . come to our mind."

Sponsored by the Gillette Safety Razor Company, they returned to network radio (CBS) in 1936, on Sundays performing with Milton Berle and others on the *Community Sing* program (the studio audience was directed in community singing). From that time until 1939, they were called "The Gillette Gentlemen." For three weeks during the illness that led to Hare's death on March 9, 1939, his sixteen-year-old daughter Marilyn substituted for him on radio. She also worked with Jones briefly after her father's death. Jones remained a bachelor most of his life, finally marrying, in 1937, a woman named May. Carrying in his pocket a script for a radio program scheduled for the next day, he died of a heart attack on the evening of November 23, 1940, while walking in New York City's Times Square, near 1627 Broadway at Fiftieth Street (his office was at 1674 Broadway).

Harding, Roger (1858-August 29, 1901)

The Irish-born tenor Roger Harding worked steadily as a featured soloist on records and as a member of duos, the Spencer Trio, and male quartets from early 1897 or so until his untimely death in 1901.

Early in his performing career he toured with musical comedy and opera companies. He was also with Sam Devere's Own Company, a popular minstrel company led by blackface banjoist Sam Devere. Diverse experiences as a stage performer evidently helped him be a versatile recording artist. He cut sentimental songs (his own "Pretty Kitty Doyle" from 1897 is one example), lullabies ("Tom Dixon's Lullaby" on Berliner 1753), comic numbers (including "coon" songs such as "I Don't Care If You Nebber Comes Back" on Berliner 1783), musical comedy hits ("How I Love My Lou" from *Pousse Café* on Berliner 1864), and opera (with soprano Minnie Emmett he recorded "Home to Our Mountains" from Verdi's *Il Trovatore*).

He made recordings for the two large cylinder companies of the late 1890s—Edison and Columbia—and also for small companies. All of his cylinders were brown wax. Five Harding titles are listed in Columbia's June 1897 catalog, which states, "Mr. Harding's specialty is the rendition of high-class ballads and vocal numbers from the standard operas. He possesses a clear, high tenor voice of remarkable range and singular sweetness." Columbia's 1898 catalog includes no Harding selections. Numbers in the early 2000 series were reserved for him as an Edison artist in the late 1890s, ranging from 2001 ("Ah, I Have Sighed to Rest Me") to 2053 ("You'd Better Stay at Home").

He made discs for Berliner and later—during a single session on June 10, 1901—for Eldridge R. Johnson's fledgling Consolidated Talking Machine Company, which months later was incorporated as the Victor Talking Machine Company.

He was a songwriter as well as a singer. At least nineteen songs by Roger Harding were published between 1891 and 1900. Early ones were published by major firms, such as M. Witmark & Sons. Several were published in 1900 by his own small publishing firm. No Harding compositions were genuinely popular, though several were recorded for Columbia by the tenor as well as by colleagues George J. Gaskin and Steve Porter. Harding sings a bit of his "My Sunny Southern Home" toward the end of Victor 3450, a record titled "A Southern Dialect Story—I've Been Down in Old Kentucky."

Like several other recording artists of the 1890s, he was an ambitious businessman. The February 1899 issue of *The Phonoscope* states, "Fred Hylands, Roger Harding, and Steve Porter are the enterprising young men who have recently organized a song publishing company under the name

of the Knickerbocker Music Publishing Co." Hylands and Harding collaborated on at least two songs published in 1899 by Hylands, Spencer &
Yeager (Harding wrote the lyrics, Hylands the music). Likewise, Harding
and Porter collaborated on a song, "My Love's the Same," published in the
same year by the firm. It is not known what songs were published by the
short-lived Knickerbocker company.

In the October 1897 issue of *The Phonoscope* he placed an advertisement for his own cylinder company located at 18 East 22nd Street in New
York City, but the company lasted only a month or so. The next issue of
the trade journal announced that the Excelsior Phonograph Company had
purchased Harding's plant, with Harding remaining as general manager.
No cylinders made by Harding's company are known to have survived.
The August 1898 issue of *The Phonoscope* reports that William F. Hooley
had succeeded Harding as the Excelsior's manager, though Harding remained with Excelsior as one of its three main artists, the other two being
S. H. Dudley (at that time known as S. Holland Dudley) and Hooley.
These three singers were probably members of the Excelsior Quartette.
Page 11 of the January 1899 issue of *The Phonoscope* reports that the
company had moved to the Dewey Building at 5 East 14th Street.

Page 16 of the January 1899 issue of *The Phonoscope* quotes a June 27,
1898, letter by Harding endorsing a new product of the Greater New York
Phonograph Company:

> I have given the fibre diaphragm you so kindly sent me a thorough
> test, and found it all you claim it to be. It gives a smooth, loud
> reproduction without blast, takes away the nasal quality, and is
> equally as good for reproducing purposes. I am sure that all phono-
> graph dealers will recognize its merits upon the first trial. Sincerely
> yours, Roger Harding.

His address is given as the Musical Phonograph Record Company,
57 West 24th Street. That Harding's letter was used for testimonial purposes suggests that he was well-known to readers of the trade journal.

His professional activities are mentioned in various issues of the trade
journal. The November-December 1897 issue of *The Phonoscope* lists him
among the personnel of the Greater New York Quartet, which also included
Steve Porter, Len Spencer, and a singer whose last name was "Depew" (the
trade journal gave only last names, but this would not have been Chauncey
Depew, who made a few Berliner discs around this time—this prominent
orator and railroad magnate was not likely to sing in a quartet for brown
wax cylinder companies). The Greater New York Quartet afterward underwent personnel changes, though Harding and Porter evidently remained.

Harding performed in various quartets. At some point he was a Man-hansett Quartette member. Jim Walsh states in the October 1962 issue of *Hobbies* that original members of the Edison Male Quartette, formed in the mid-1890s, were Roger Harding, J. K. Reynard, Dudley, and William F. Hooley. This evolved into the Haydn Quartet. Dudley and Harding recorded a duet for the Berliner Gramophone Company on the same day as the Haydn's debut for the disc company—on June 27, 1898—which suggests that Harding was a Haydn member at that time.

Colleagues who matched Harding in versatility and ambition—Porter, Dudley, Hooley, Len Spencer, Harry Macdonough, and a few others—would become increasingly important to a continually growing record industry. Harding's premature death of a viral infection (Victor's February 1902 catalog states that he died "very suddenly") removed from the industry a potentially major artist.

Harlan, Byron G. *(August 29, 1861-September 11, 1936)*

Byron G. Harlan was perhaps best known as half of the comic duo Collins and Harlan, but he made many records without Arthur Collins. As a tenor soloist, he specialized in sentimental ballads and also recorded many rube numbers, sometimes with partners other than Collins.

He was born in Kansas as George Byron Harlan. An Edison catalog states that his birthplace was Lynn, Kansas, but Harlan's widow reported to Jim Walsh that the singer was born in Paris, Kansas. His father, George Winchester Harlan, moved the family to Sioux City, Iowa to begin a brick business, then moved the family to Canton, South Dakota, where he operated an overland stage.

The young Byron G. Harlan joined touring companies. Walsh writes in the March 1965 issue of *Hobbies:*

> He got his first chance in . . . show business when Gus Brigham, a traveler for "the Yanes Piano House," heard him singing while he was working as a hotel clerk in South Dakota, and told the manager of the Hess Opera Company about him. Harlan became a member of the Newton Beers' "Lost in London" company, then was with Hoyt's "A Texas Steer" for three and one-half years . . .

According to the October 1916 issue of *Edison Phonograph Monthly:*

> [I]t was not until he was twenty-four years old that he went to Chicago and studied music. . . . After gaining valuable theatrical experience by his appearances in opera, he accepted a part with Otis

Harlan in *A Texas Steer*. Later he became a producer and had a company of his own. His singing of "coon" and "rag" songs gained him much renown and when the phonograph came into general use he became an Edison artist.

The statement that he was famous for singing "coon" and "rag" songs is curious since he almost never recorded such songs as a solo artist, in contrast to his partner Arthur Collins.

Harlan formed his own "Lost in London" theatrical company and by 1899 he reached Orange, New Jersey. Walter Miller, Edison's recording director, invited Harlan to make cylinders. Harlan's first record may be "Please, Mr. Conductor, Don't Put Me Off the Train," issued as Edison 7219 in the autumn of 1899. From the beginning he was associated with sentimental numbers, and he continued to record such numbers for years. Announcing the March 1906 release of "Once Upon a Time" on Standard 9235, the February 1906 issue of *Edison Phonograph Monthly* states, "Mr. Harlan's identification with songs of this character has been almost forced upon him by the public, which has always been prompt to show its appreciation of his conception of songs telling of the sadder things of life, such as 'Please, Mr. Conductor' (our Record No. 7219) and 'Always in the Way' (our Record No. 8501)."

Reporting on a patent for an early "puzzle" record, Allen Koenigsberg on page 70 of *The Patent History of the Phonograph* (APM Press, 1990) states: "An interleaved double-volute disc was applied for by R. Klein as early as March 1904 (814,053, with 1/5 assigned to Byron G. Harlan . . .)."

Harlan settled in Orange for the rest of his life and was a personal friend of Thomas A. Edison. Walsh writes in "The Funny Side of the Phonograph World" published in the May 1952 issue of *American Record Guide*, "When Byron was married, the inventor gave him the then latest model Edison cylinder phonograph as a wedding present, and when Mr. and Mrs. Harlan's daughter was graduated from high school, he presented her with an Official Model Diamond Disc instrument."

Harlan is featured on several Edison Concert-size cylinders. Produced from 1898 to 1901, these are five inches in diameter. Titles include "The Blue and the Gray" (B461), "Will I Find My Mamma There?" (B462), and "Please, Mr. Conductor" (B463).

Walsh states in Ronald Dethlefson's *Edison Blue Amberol Recordings 1915-1929*, "Harlan's list of two-minute solos didn't equal Collins' in number, but by my count, he made 132 brown wax and Gold Moulded before the two-minute records were discontinued in 1912."

Harlan made no Berliners and his first disc may be Columbia 55, "In the House of Too Much Trouble." Another early Columbia disc featuring

Harlan is "He Laid Away a Suit of Gray to Wear the Union Blue" (326). Other discs followed a Victor session on October 31, 1902, and on this date he also was teamed with Arthur Collins, perhaps for the first time (in the previous year, Collins cut duets with tenor Joe Natus). Collins and Harlan recorded five titles during that Victor session, including "The First Rehearsal of the Huskin' Bee" (1723), a rube skit.

In his early years of making Edison cylinders Harlan had several recording partners aside from Arthur Collins. Around 1902-1903, Harlan recorded ten Edison selections with whistler Joe Belmont. From 1901 to 1909 he made fifty Edison recordings with fellow Orange resident Frank C. Stanley, including many rube skits, and the two recorded for other companies, including a sacred number, "Almost Persuaded" on ten-inch Zon-o-phone 92. Civil war duets with Frank C. Stanley sold well, such as "Tramp! Tramp! Tramp!" (Victor 16531, 1910). He was paired often with Steve Porter in rube sketches. His earliest regular partner was bass A. D. Madeira. In fact, an Edison ensemble called the Big Four Quartet combined the duo Harlan and Madeira with the duo Collins and Natus, and from this sprang eventually the team of Collins and Harlan.

A novelty tune recorded in 1901 by Harlan, Stanley, Joe Belmont, and the so-called Florodora Girls was "Tell Me, Pretty Maiden" (Columbia 31604). The names of the Florodora Girls singing on this are not known.

As a singer of sentimental songs, he was especially successful with "child" ballads, or songs with lyrics featuring a child's point of view. Announcing the April release of "Captain Baby Bunting" on Standard 9508, the February 1907 issue of *Edison Phonograph Monthly* states, "Mr. Harlan occupies an almost unique position in the talking machine world as a singer of these songs." Successful records of sentimental numbers include "Hello Central, Give Me Heaven" (Edison 7852; 1901), "Where the Morning Glories Twine Around the Door" (Columbia 3282, Victor 4616; 1905), "Wait Till the Sun Shines, Nellie" (Edison 9130, Columbia 3321; 1906), and "School Days" (Edison 9562, Victor 5086; 1907).

Comic material he recorded as a solo artist was mostly rube material, a notable exception being the Gus Edwards song "My Cousin Caruso" from the 1909 show *Miss Innocence* (Columbia A714).

A popular rube song cut by Harlan is "They Gotta Quit Kickin' My Dawg Aroun'." He was the only recording artist associated with it, and versions on Victor 17065 and Columbia A1150 sold well. Edison issued versions in two-minute cylinder format and four-minute wax Amberol format. Announcing its June release on wax Amberol 1023, the April 1912 issue of *Edison Phonograph Monthly* states, "The Missouri Houn' Song, as this selection is familiarly known in the Ozarks, though by no means a new song, has attained national prominence during the last few months. Its sudden popularity is due to its adoption by the Champ Clark cohorts as a presidential campaign slogan." Cy Perkins is credited for the music, Webb M. Oungst for lyrics. Perkins was actually Carrie Bruggerman Stark, daughter-in-law of ragtime music publisher John Stark.

It was among the first records he made after recovering from a serious illness in 1911. During this time Collins was teamed with Albert Campbell. The January 1912 issue of *Edison Phonograph Monthly*, announcing the March release of "I Want to Be Down Home in Dixie" performed by Collins and Harlan on Amberol 948, states, "Mr. Harlan is just getting around again after his long illness, and his voice sounds fresher and more pleasing than ever."

In the 1910s Harlan as a solo artist recorded fewer sentimental numbers than before. Songs with child or "kid" themes remained fashionable for female singers such as Irene Franklin and Frances White (their material was comic) but not for male singers. Companies increasingly relied upon Will Oakland and Manuel Romain for sentimental material, and Harlan as a solo artist performed mostly as a rube singer. He made a few recordings under the name Cyrus Pippins, such as a rube number written by William McKenna titled "Cyrus Pippin's Wedding Day" (Victor 16836; Columbia A967). Other pseudonyms used on rare occasions include Deacon Treadway (for some Pathé discs), Bert Terry, Byron Holland, Chester Lincoln, and Cy Stebbins.

Especially popular in 1918 was the rube number "Long Boy," written by William Herschell and Barclay Walker. It is about a new recruit named Hiram who bids farewell to his family as he leaves for the battlefields of Europe:

> Good-bye, Ma!
> Good-bye, Pa!
> Good-bye, mule,
> With your old hee-haw!
> I may not know
> What the war's about
> But you bet, by gosh,
> I'll soon find out

Victor issued this in January 1918 (18413), stating in its supplement, "There is some realistic talk as he says good-bye to his friends and to the farm stock and promises to bring something back for his sweetheart." Harlan also sang the song with the Peerless Quartet for Columbia A2409. A less characteristic solo number recorded for Columbia is "Bobby the

Bomber" (A2587), issued around May 1918. It tells of Bobby Kline, a pitcher on a baseball team who joins a bomb brigade and uses his pitching skills to kill Germans.

Victor and Columbia stopped recording him by 1919, but Harlan was a solo artist on a few Diamond Discs around this time. One featured a rube song that Harlan had recorded for several other companies, "I'm a Twelve O'Clock Fellow (In a Nine O'Clock Town)," issued in 1919 as Diamond Disc 50566.

In 1919 Harlan enjoyed success with "How 'Ya Gonna Keep 'Em Down on the Farm," which he recorded for Edison, Pathé, Emerson, Okeh, and Gennett. Since it is a rube song, companies naturally turned to Harlan to record it. Thereafter his recording career was in decline, and no records made by Harlan in the 1920s sold well.

In the early 1920s he worked often for the General Phonograph Corporation, maker of Okeh discs. Okeh 4429, issued in December 1921, featured Harlan singing two rube songs: "I Ain't Nobody's Darling" and "Down Where I Belong." Page 142 of the March 1922 issue of *Talking Machine World* lists Okeh artists who contributed to a February 17 radio program, and Harlan is identified as an Okeh artist specializing in "rural interpretations and songs." Page 96 of the May 1922 issue identifies Harlan as among the Okeh artists under the direction of Fred W. Hager, recording director of the General Phonograph Corporation, who contributed to a radio program of April 26.

As a solo artist, he made a Gennett recording issued in July 1922: "Who Tied the Can on the Old Dog's Tail?" (4866). It was backed by Arthur Collins singing "I Ain't Got Enough for to Pass Around."

Harlan made some Uncle Josh records after the death of Cal Stewart, originator of the Uncle Josh character, and during the period when Arthur Collins was recovering from an injury. Harlan performed "Uncle Josh Buys an Automobile" and "Uncle Josh at the Circus" on Okeh 4517, issued in March 1922. He performed "Uncle Josh on the Radio" (writing credit is given to Cal Stewart and Fred Hager—Stewart died in 1919, and Hager evidently revised an old Uncle Josh skit) and "Uncle Josh Patents a Rat Trap" (writing credit is given to Jack Baxley) on Okeh 4686, issued in December 1922. He also recorded skits for the Brunswick label in the early 1920s. In July 1923, Brunswick issued "Uncle Josh at the Circus" and "Uncle Josh Buys an Automobile" (2431). One year later, in July 1924, Brunswick issued "Uncle Josh Playing Golf" and "Uncle Josh on the Aeroplane" (2626). Harlan also made some recordings with Billy Jones and Ernest Hare.

Researcher Ronald Dethlefson reports that Harlan made experimental, unissued recordings for the Edison company on October 18, 1926. These were probably electrical. Harlan is on electrical Grey Gull 4255 (also Radiex 4255) with Harlan E. Knight (who wrote the sketch in 1916 for Columbia A1838) and Steve Porter, performing "Greetings in Bingville." Harlan and Porter cut "Uncle Si and Hiram Swapping Horses" and "Uncle Si at [the] Village Barber" (Grey Gull 4230)." Harlan, Knight, and Porter perform "The Trial of Josiah Brown" on Grey Gull 4256. Around this time Harlan also made electrical recordings of Uncle Josh monologues for Gennett, and performances issued on Silvertone and Supertone discs were credited to "Byron Holland."

On June 22, 1904, the singer married Ethel Van Horn, who was at that time a nineteen-year-old school teacher. They met in a boarding house in Orange. Walsh reports in "Reminiscences of Collins and Harlan," published in the October 1934 issue of *Music Lovers' Guide*, that Harlan lost his savings during the Depression. Collins, in contrast, was well off in his retirement. Walsh reports in the March 1943 issue of *Hobbies*, "On September 11, 1936, Mr. Harlan died of a heart attack in the bathtub at his home in Orange." He was survived by his wife and a daughter.

Harris, Marion (c. 1896-April 23, 1944)

This Broadway, vaudeville, and cabaret headliner made many popular records in the World War I era and early 1920s. She was among the first to cover Creamer and Layton's "After You've Gone" (1918), Isham Jones' "I'll See You in My Dreams" (1925), Jones' "It Had to Be You" (1924), and George Gershwin's "The Man I Love" (1927). Her recordings helped establish several songs as standards, including "I Ain't Got Nobody," "Look for the Silver Lining," "Tea for Two," "I'm Nobody's Baby," "Some Sunny Day," "There'll Be Some Changes Made," and "I'm Just Wild About Harry." She cut over 100 issued titles for Victor, Columbia, and Brunswick.

Between making her first acoustic disc in 1916 and her first electrical disc in 1927, Harris evolved from vaudeville "shouter," in the tradition of Sophie Tucker and Nora Bayes, to crooner. She began by recording mostly comic songs, blues, and Tin Pan Alley songs about blues as well as about the new music known as "jass." Toward the mid-1920s she made records that indicated a greater versatility and by the late 1920s her voice was much different from earlier years, with Harris singing in the more intimate manner of torch singers such as Ruth Etting and Helen Morgan. Her late recordings suggest Harris had more vocal training than these singers.

She was born Mary Ellen Harrison in 1896, at least according to obituaries, which themselves were based on press releases approved by Harris in the years she was active in show business. The month and day are unknown, and even the year is open to question. No researchers have located a birth certificate. Jim Walsh reports in the August 1963 issue of *Hobbies* that her 1944 death certificate gives her father's name as James Harrison, but nothing is known of him nor of her mother.

Her background is obscure, and she may have wanted it to remain unknown. Decades ago many Americans looked down upon those who performed on stage, and few would have said that working in vaudeville was a respectable way for a young woman to earn a living. Harris may have been one of the many performers from middle-class backgrounds who were evasive or deceptive about their roots to avoid embarrassing family members.

Newspaper obituaries state that she was born in the small town of Henderson, Kentucky, but no documents relating to a Mary Ellen Harrison exist in Henderson County, Kentucky. The singer is said to have been the granddaughter or grandniece of "Senator Harrison of Kentucky," but Kentucky never had a Senator Harrison. Other sources, such as Columbia's 1922 catalog, say she was the granddaughter of "General Harrison of Civil War fame." That war produced on both sides several generals named Harrison.

Columbia's September 1920 supplement states, "Marion Harris is a Kentucky girl and a descendant of Benjamin Harrison." The reference may be to the Benjamin Harrison who signed the Declaration of Independence, though most readers would infer that the Harrison here was the twenty-third President of the United States. Page 14 of the December 1933 issue of the British publication *Rhythm* specifically states that she was related to the president:

> Marion Harris was born in Henderson, Kentucky, and is a direct descendant of President Benjamin Harrison. She started her stage career at the age of fourteen, but a theatre manager in Chicago, amused at the pigtails she wore, told her to have her hair dressed and come back. She did, and started on a career that has led her to a headline position in radio, record and theatres in all parts of the world.

This information undoubtedly came from the singer's own press agent.

Harris was clearly not a direct descendant of President Harrison, who had a son and two daughters (one of the daughters, Elizabeth, was not even born until 1897). Hugh Brogan and Charles Mosley's *American Presidential Families* (Macmillan, 1993) does not include a Mary Ellen Harrison among President Harrison's descendants. Columbia's 1922 catalog states, "Marion Harris, who really is Mary Ellen Harrison, is a granddaughter of the late General Harrison of Civil War fame." If she had been related to the president, it is curious that the Columbia catalog refers only to this connection with a General Harrison. Possibly the claim that she was related to President Harrison originated with an imaginative press agent and by the 1930s the myth grew to the bold claim that she was a direct descendant.

One obituary reports that in 1910, when Marion was fourteen, her parents sent her to a Chicago convent that was a boarding school and she evidently ran away from it. According to another obituary published on April 26, 1944, in *Variety*, "Miss Harris began her theatrical career by singing with colored slides that motion pictures houses used to use, and it was in an obscure theatre that the late Vernon Castle discovered her. She was brought to New York by Charles Dillingham and opened in [the] latter's star-studded production of 'Stop, Look, and Listen.' . . ." Irving Berlin's *Stop! Look! Listen!* was one of 1915's most successful shows.

An early press notice is in the *New York Telegram* dated January 7, 1916: "The latest addition to the cast of the new *Midnight Frolic*, which is to be produced in about a week, is Marian [sic] Harris. When *Stop! Look! Listen!* began its career in Philadelphia, Miss Harris was prominent in the cast. In fact, it was she who originally sang 'I Love a Piano' and other favorite numbers. For some reason her engagement abruptly terminated, and they do say—but that's another story. At any rate, Miss Harris, who comes from the West, will get a New York hearing with the Ziegfeld company."

Harris is cited in the *New York Telegram* nineteen days later in a review of Flo Ziegfeld's new *Midnight Frolic*. Under the heading "Miss Harris Speedily Scores," a reviewer reports, "A newcomer was Marian [sic] Harris and in two numbers she sang her way into immediate favor. Miss Harris is of the Blossom Seeley type of singer, possessed of pleasing voice and ingratiating personality." Her name is misspelled as "Marian" elsewhere, including on the sheet music for the 1917 "Sweet Daddy" (the cover calls this song "the only real jazz song"). Her photograph was used several times on sheet music covers.

Her first recording, "I Ain't Got Nobody Much," was made on August 9, 1916, and was issued as Victor 18133 in October. The 1915 classic song is sometimes known as "I Ain't Got Nobody (And Nobody Cares for Me)" and may be regarded as an early theme song for Harris since she recorded it for Victor in 1916; Columbia on April 21, 1920; and Brunswick in early 1923. The song has a complicated history, which is reflected by Victor and Brunswick citing Spencer Williams and Roger Graham as composers while the Columbia disc credits "Warfield." David Jasen's *Tin Pan Alley* (Donald I. Fine, Inc., 1988) reports that Charles Warfield and David Young had copyrighted the song as "I Ain't Got Nobody" (the "Much" is missing) in 1914, and it is not clear which set of composers deserves song credit.

Harris also sang "My Syncopated Melody Man" during that first Victor session on August 9, but the take was rejected. During her fourth recording session (on November 17—three months later) she sang this again and it was issued as Victor 18152. Lyrics are typical of songs Harris recorded in these early years:

> If you should ever happen to be down my way
> And you want to hear a fellow who can play
> On an old piano
> In a raggy manner
> Stop in old Savannah any day
> He is always fooling with the ivories
> Liking funny syncopated harmonies
> There is nothing sweeter
> Than the raggy meter of his melody
> My syncopated man
> Plays a rag like no one can
> When he sits down at that piano . . .

Victor's February 1917 supplement states, "If you like ragtime, you can get all you want from 'Syncopated Max,' who has 'a way of his own,' according to Marion Harris in 'My Syncopated Melody Man,' written and composed by Blanche Merrill and Eddie Cox." The supplement is incorrect—Harris sings "syncopated man," not "Syncopated Max." The disc's reverse side features Spencer Williams' "Paradise Blues," with lyrics by Walter Hirsch about blues piano:

> Down old Mobile way
> In a cabaret
> There sits Ragtime Lew
> He can show you how to "blue"
> On that piano . . .
> Honey, don't play me no op'ra
> Play me some blue melody
> I don't care nothing 'bout *Carmen*
> When I hear that harmony . . .

An example of her early association with jazz is her mid-1917 recording of Gene Buck and Dave Stamper's "When I Hear That Jazz Band Play" (Victor 18398) from Ziegfeld's *Midnight Frolic*. Announcing its release, the December 1917 Victor supplement states: "'Say what you will, you cannot keep still while they're playing,' is the verdict Marion Harris sings regarding the Jazz Band, and it is true." Other songs about jazz recorded by Harris are Merrill and Jerome's "Jazz Baby" (Victor 18555), Wendling's "Take Me to the Land of Jazz" (Victor 18593), and Morgan's "I'm a Jazz Vampire" (Columbia A3328). The melody and lyrics of the 1920 tune "I'm a Jazz Vampire" owe much to the successful 1919 "Jazz Baby."

The September 1, 1918, edition of the *Kansas City Star* reported that Harris was part of Madame Sarah Bernhardt's company during the French actress's 1918 tour. It alludes to Harris' recording success in glowing terms that suggest the work of a press agent:

By singing two songs in a big musical show in New York, [Harris] took the honors away from the star of the production! That sounds like it might have been Ray Samuels, but it wasn't. It was Marion Harris on the same bill this week with Mme. Sarah Bernhardt at the Orpheum. It might be said that Miss Harris's voice is better known in the home than the theater because there are probably few owners of talking machines who have no record of her voice. She specializes in "rag" songs. This is her second season in vaudeville.

Variety on November 22, 1918, confirms that Harris was only beginning to gain recognition: "Marion Harris, comparatively new to New York vaudeville, may be said to have stopped the show. Tall, very blonde, her locks dressed in an original fashion, she is an animated picture of youthful vivacity." A Newark newspaper characterizes a performance given months earlier in January this way: "Songland's newest production, Marion Harris sang her way into the hearts of the typical Newark audience and in addition to the word 'newest' can add 'best.'"

The April 1919 issue of *Talking Machine World* lists Harris among Victor artists who entertained at that year's annual banquet of the trade organization Talking Machine Men, Inc., some other artists being Henry Burr, Billy Murray, and Arthur Fields. The Van Eps Quintet provided dance music.

Harris moved from Victor to the Columbia Graphophone Company in early 1920, making her Columbia debut with "Left All Alone Again Blues" (A2939). Harris recorded for Columbia many songs with "blues" in the title, including the W. C. Handy tunes "St. Louis Blues" (A2944),

"Memphis Blues" (A3474), and "Beale Street Blues" (A3474). Page 27 of the July 1920 issue of *Talking Machine World* announces her new status as a Columbia artist and states, "Since the advent of the 'Blues' type of song she has risen to pre-eminent height as a singer of this character song. In fact, she is known as 'The girl with the voice which chases the "blues" away by singing them.'"

In his autobiography, *Father of the Blues* (Macmillan, 1941), W. C. Handy refers to Harris moving from Victor to Columbia, though Handy does not name the companies:

> Marion Harris, celebrated white blues singer, left a recording company that objected to her making a record of *St. Louis Blues*. Miss Harris had used our numbers in vaudeville for a long time, and she sang blues so well that people hearing her records sometimes thought that the singer was colored. When she signed with another company that permitted her to select her own material—often from our catalogue—one of the managers of this company [Victor] got hot under the collar.

Handy's autobiography has many inaccuracies, so one may view with skepticism his suggestion that Harris left Victor because of a conflict over "St. Louis Blues." It is possible that Victor executives turned down requests by Harris to record Handy tunes, but Handy's passage almost suggests that Victor would not record Handy compositions. The company often recorded them, beginning with the Victor Military Band recording "The Memphis Blues" on July 15, 1914. In 1921, a year after Harris left Victor, the company issued the Original Dixieland Jazz Band performing "St. Louis Blues," which enjoyed success. Harris did record "St. Louis Blues" within her first month at Columbia, after recording five other titles. She evidently was partial to "St. Louis Blues," recording it again in early 1923 for Brunswick (2395).

Every number Harris recorded in her last five sessions for Victor, from July 18 to November 18, 1919, went unissued. Her earliest Columbia takes also were unissued.

Elaborate, full-page advertisements in *Talking Machine World* publicized that she was exclusive to Columbia. The company's advertisement department provided dealers with Harris posters, window streamers, hearing room hangers, and cardboard cutouts. Columbia instructed its dealers to declare in shops that August 28 to September 3, 1920, was Marion Harris Week.

Many of her Columbia discs sold well. Bandleaders providing accompaniment included Charles A. Prince and Paul Biese. The 1922 Columbia catalog states:

> When asked how she came to choose negro songs for her type, Miss Harris guessed, "It just came naturally. When you first get over stage fright your one instinctive thought is to please. In order to please you must do your best, and you usually do best what comes naturally. So I just naturally started singing Southern dialect songs and the modern blues songs, which closely resemble the darky folk songs."

The catalog includes a photo.

Harris remained with Columbia for two years, shifting to the Brunswick-Balke-Collender Company in August 1922. She may have made this change because Columbia was financially troubled at this time, in contrast to Brunswick's steady growth as a record manufacturer. Brunswick was arguably more successful in recording her voice than the earlier companies. Her first Brunswick disc, made with the Isham Jones Orchestra, featured "My Cradle Melody" backed by *Shuffle Along*'s "I'm Just Wild About Harry" (Vaughn De Leath recorded this months earlier for Gennett). On Brunswick discs she is often accompanied by Carl Fenton's Orchestra. Aside from a single Victor disc made in 1927, Harris was an exclusive Brunswick recording artist for almost a decade.

At first Brunswick categorized its new artist as a comic singer. The January 1923 Brunswick supplement states, "Marion Harris, the ever-applauded Comedienne, is up to her habitual tricks of making the world laugh." The 1923 Brunswick catalog stresses her appeal as a blues artist:

> A supreme artist in her own particular field is Marion Harris, vaudeville's darling, known from coast to coast as "the Queen of Blues Singers." Her voice has a sweetness and sympathy of deep appeal and her charming prettiness and good humor always bring the maximum of encores on the Keith Vaudeville Circuit where she is a headliner. . . . Harris usually wins the house to the point of stopping the show and the popularity of her records may be judged by the fact that one of them broke all records for number of copies sold. Miss Harris records for Brunswick exclusively.

It is not clear which Harris disc sold so well.

By 1925, Brunswick promoted the singer in its catalog as a versatile artist, stating:

> Marion Harris, the inimitable, enjoys the enviable position of being a reigning favorite in American vaudeville. Her great popularity is due

to a magnetic personality added to a charming and fascinating voice which has a very deep appeal. As a singer with great emotional qualities, she is unsurpassed. Miss Harris is largely responsible for the rapidly increasing demand for popular vocal records. Her splendid Brunswick Records of unusual, though artistic interpretations, are much called for by her many enthusiastic and exacting admirers.

She recorded for Brunswick regularly from August 1922 to April 1925. Many of her early Brunswicks feature the type of songs she had recorded for Victor and Columbia, and even some late Brunswick discs, such as her jazzy 1924 "Charleston Charlie," share much with her 1916 "My Syncopated Man." But for Brunswick she also recorded romantic and sentimental songs, sometimes singing to piano accompaniment after an orchestral introduction, which allowed Harris to sustain notes, sing softly, and achieve greater intimacy (this is in contrast to her Victor recordings with steady orchestral accompaniment that encouraged Harris to belt out songs). Titles that show this intimacy include the 1923 "I've Been Saving for a Rainy Day" (2470) and the 1924 "Jealous" (2622).

Her last acoustically cut Brunswick number shares little with the earlier comic and blues work, instead foreshadowing the crooning style that would be fashionable in the late 1920s. She sings very slowly in waltz time the tune "When You and I Were Seventeen," sustaining notes as in no earlier recording.

Just as Brunswick shifted to the electrical recording process, she took a hiatus from her recording career, with stage work and especially family taking precedence. In 1924 Harris married Rush B. Hughes, a stage actor, occasional silent film actor, radio performer, and cousin to industrialist Howard Hughes. Her father-in-law was Rupert Hughes, best-selling novelist, biographer, musicologist, and senior editor of the *Encyclopaedia Britannica*. Within a few years the marriage produced two children: Rush B. Hughes, Jr. (known as Sonny) and Mary Ellen.

Hughes was approximately nineteen at the time of the marriage, nearly ten years younger than Harris. The marriage lasted three years. Page 33 of the June 29, 1927, edition of *Variety* reports that Marion Harris and Rush Hughes were maritally estranged—when Harris had her attorney draw up a separation agreement, Hughes refused to sign. A divorce soon followed. Page 26 of the July 11, 1928, edition of *Variety* includes a denial by Hughes of rumors that the two had remarried.

In the late 1940s a supper club entertainer named Marilyn Williams won some publicity by identifying herself as the daughter of Marion Harris and actor Robert Williams, who died in 1931. Nothing is known of any connection between Harris and Williams aside from the claim of this entertainer, who is not credible since she gave to the press various statements that were untrue, such as that her father was British (Robert Williams was born in Morgantown, North Carolina), that her mother worked as a nude dancer in 1918, and that her mother died at the Waldorf-Astoria.

In the 1920s Harris remained popular as a stage artist. She performed often at the Palace in New York City, usually guaranteeing a sold-out house in this prestigious vaudeville theater. *The New York Times* reviewed several of her Palace appearances. In 1927 Harris enjoyed great success in Broadway shows, first in *Yours Truly*, which opened on January 25, and then in *A Night in Spain*, which opened on May 3 (Harris may not have been in the opening cast). The latter ran for 174 performances and featured, among others, Helen Kane and Aileen Stanley.

In 1929 Harris was in Philadelphia's stage production of *Great Day!* but was not in the Broadway cast. She sang the classic "More Than You Know" in that show. She returned to Broadway in 1930 in *The Second Little Show.*

By the time she returned to a recording studio in the electrical era, her singing style had changed. Popular music itself had changed, and Harris kept pace with new trends. Her first electrical recording is something of an anomaly. She had a single Victor recording session in Chicago on December 8, 1927. The two songs recorded were issued as Victor 21116: "Did You Mean It?" and, on the "B" side, "The Man I Love." Victor was evidently eager for Harris to record "Did You Mean It?" This very popular song was composed by Phil Baker, Sid Silvers, and Abe Lyman, and Baker himself plays accordion on the Victor recording. Harris introduced the song in the Broadway show *A Night in Spain*. Abe Lyman recorded the song months earlier, on September 5 (Brunswick 3648). Others recorded it before Harris, notably Nat Shilkret's Virginians on November 25, 1927, with Lewis James as vocalist. Whereas Shilkret performs it at a quick pace, Harris is very much a torch singer, and her performance is superb.

Harris was among the first to record "The Man I Love." Hers may be the first issued recording of Gershwin's classic. Adele Astaire sang it on stage in Philadelphia as early as 1924, but the song was removed from the show *Lady, Be Good!* before it hit Broadway because early audiences had given the ballad a lukewarm reception. It was added to the 1927 out-of-town tryouts for *Strike Up the Band* but was again dropped. The song enjoyed greater success outside the theater than in any show. Gershwin himself credited Helen Morgan for popularizing it in New York, but Morgan never recorded it. Gene Austin may have been the first to cover it in a studio, but his performance of September 15, 1927, went unissued. Others who recorded it soon after Harris include Sam Lanin's Famous Players, Grace Hayes, and Sophie Braslau.

Finally in Chicago in late 1929, Harris made her first electrical discs for Brunswick, the company with which she had enjoyed great success years earlier. By the time they were issued the industry was suffering from the Depression and the discs did not sell well.

In 1928 Harris began a brief film career, with Metro-Goldwyn-Mayer promoting her as "The Songbird of Jazz." She was in at least two early shorts with sound and one feature-length film. In an MGM Metro-Movietone filmed in the summer of 1928, she sings "I'm Afraid of You" and "We Love It." The singer opens with a rhyming prologue about how she lacks a song, then picks up a phone to hear Irving Berlin on the other end (or so the audience is told) recommending "I'm Afraid of You." Accompaniment is provided by an unidentified pianist, possibly Jack Austin. In this early period of sound film recording, when pre- and postscoring were mostly unknown, song and dance acts were filmed live throughout the duration of the act. For the 1928 Harris short, two cameras were used, one in a full shot, the other in a medium close-up. This was a sound-on-disc production, not sound-on-film.

Another short, "Gems of MGM," was filmed in 1929 but was not released until 1931. Harris sings Whiting and Moret's "She's Funny That Way," usually known as "He's Funny That Way" when sung by female vocalists. Harris sings it as "I'm Funny That Way." The cast includes the Brox Sisters and comedian Benny Rubin.

The July 1929 issue of *Photoplay* mentions Harris in an article about the motion picture industry's new practice of "voice doubling" or "dubbing":

> [G]ood singing voices are not always easily found. One reason for this is that persons of marked vocal accomplishments are frequently reluctant to double. They are afraid their voices will be recognized, that it will cheapen them. A notable case in point was that of Marion Harris, the vaudeville headliner, who turned down an offer of $10,000 from Universal, according to one of her representatives, to substitute her voice for a film player, presumably in "Broadway."

Broadway was an all-talkie musical.

MGM cast her in a supporting role in *Devil May Care*, a musical hit of 1929. Ramon Novarro and Dorothy Jordan are the two principals who fall in love. The film is set in France, opening at Fontainebleau with the April 11, 1814, abdication of Napoleon, whose withdrawal to Elba and subsequent landing in Provence are important to the film's plot. Harris's role is pivotal, and she is a convincing actress. She also sings in the film, notably

"If He Cared," which she never recorded. The film's most popular tune, "Charming," is sung by leading man Novarro. Leo Reisman and His Orchestra recorded this and "The Shepherd's Serenade," also from *Devil May Care*, on November 29, 1929, with Frank Luther providing vocals. Music of all three songs was by Herbert Stothart, words by Clifford Grey.

In the September 1963 issue of *Hobbies*, Jim Walsh quotes a newspaper clipping from around 1930 that states Harris "is still contracted to Paramount to make a few pictures . . . ," but no titles are known. A *Photoplay* issue from this period states that Harris was offered more film work because of her success in *Devil May Care*, but additional film work did not interest her.

In America in the early 1930s Harris was in radio shows broadcast over the WEAF-NBC network. The network billed her as "The Little Girl with the Big Voice" (the "little" here need not be taken literally—a 1918 review characterized Harris as tall). She was a guest on other programs, such as Rudy Vallee's *The Fleischmann Yeast Hour* on December 10, 1931. Her last known performance on the *Fleischmann Hour* was on August 10, 1933. She also performed with the Ipana Troubadours on radio.

In early 1931 Harris performed in London and in subsequent years returned to England for long engagements, mostly working at the Café de Paris though she also was in the show *Evergreen*. She made records with Billy Mason and His Hotel de Paris Orchestra in 1931 and 1932. Especially popular was "My Canary Has Circles Under His Eyes" (Columbia DB-453). "Is I In Love? I Is" (Columbia DB-822), with the line "Oh gosh, oh gee, gee whiz," has a coyness more typical of Helen Kane's work than Harris'. She gives a characteristically polished performance singing Walter Donaldson's "An Ev'ning in Caroline," which features unusual Hawaiian guitar accompaniment. She did various BBC broadcasts from 1932 to 1934.

The last known reference to an engagement is on page 5 of the April 11, 1936, edition of the British trade journal *Radio Review*, which states, "Marion Harris, famed torch-singer of radio and cabaret, has returned to the limelight after an absence of a year and seven months. She has recently completed a month's engagement at the Café de Paris . . . Marion met with big success at this rendezvous of critics—yet it was her first appearance since her accident, when she fell and broke her jaw."

By the late 1930s she had evidently retired from show business. She married a London theatrical agent named Leonard Urry. In late 1943 or early 1944, their home on Rutland Street in the Knightsbridge section of London was destroyed by a German rocket bomb. She returned to America to recuperate from this traumatic experience, her husband remaining in

London. She was hospitalized at the Columbia-Presbyterian Medical Center from February to April 15, 1944, according to the *New York Daily Mail*. When she had sufficiently recovered to leave the hospital, she moved into the Hotel Le Marquis at 12 East 31st Street, taking the room under the name Mrs. M. E. (Mary Ellen) Urry.

Some of Harris' old Broadway friends made contact with her at the Hotel Le Marquis during the week she was there. These included vaudevillian Rose Perfect and the former Ziegfeld queen Peggy Hopkins Joyce. On Sunday, April 23, 1944, Harris spoke on the telephone with Joyce to make dinner plans for the following week. The *New York Daily Mail* states, "Then, apparently, she fell asleep while smoking a cigaret." The time was around 6:00 p.m. *Variety* on April 26, 1944, reports, "According to police, the singer had gone to bed with a lighted cigaret that ignited the mattress. Not disclosed whether she died of burns or suffocation." The body was identified by Joyce and Perfect. *The New York Times* reported in a short article on April 25, 1944, two days after the accident, that "the one-time singing star was known to millions through her recordings and later she starred in 'A Night In Spain.'"

Haydn Quartet/Hayden Quartet

One of the three most popular quartets of the acoustic recording era (along with the Peerless and American), the Haydn Quartet made many records from 1898 to 1914. The March 1899 issue of *The Phonoscope* establishes that members at that time were John Bieling, Jere Mahoney, S. H. Dudley, and William F. Hooley. The name "Haydn" was chosen in memory of composer Franz Joseph Haydn. The quartet's repertoire shared nothing with Haydn's works, but quartets were sometimes named after famous composers. Other examples include the Mozart Male Quartet, which made Berliner discs in late 1896; the Mendelssohn Mixed Quartet, which made Victor discs in 1902; the Handel Mixed Quartet, which made a Victor disc in 1906; and the Gounod Mixed Quartet, which made Okeh discs.

Quartet members evidently did not know the standard pronunciation of "Haydn" since the quartet's name was always pronounced to rhyme with "laden." In 1912 spelling of the quartet's name was actually changed to "Hayden" to conform to the pronunciation that members had been using, and the Pronunciation Table at the back of Victor catalogs gives different pronunciations for the names Haydn (the composer is "High-dn") and Hayden (the quartet is "Hay-den").

By June 1899, according to that month's issue of *The Phonoscope*, the Haydn consisted of Fred Rycroft, Bieling, Dudley, and Hooley. Berliner

01304—perhaps the last Berliner disc issued—features the Haydn, and inscribed on its surface is this statement: "Solo by Mr. Rycroft, with Quartet accompaniment and chorus." This refers to Fred Rycroft, and the performance is from mid-1900. When Mahoney contracted inflammatory rheumatism in 1899, Harry Macdonough replaced Mahoney, as Macdonough himself wrote to Jim Walsh in 1931. But Rycroft was also used during some sessions after Mahoney's departure. By 1900 both Macdonough and Rycroft were in the Haydn, Bieling absent from the quartet for a short time. Rycroft was a manager for M. Witmark & Sons, the music publishing company.

The quartet made its Berliner debut on June 27, 1898, with Hattie Starr's "Little Alabama Coon" (870) and made around seventy Berliners. Dudley was the group's manager. His signature is etched on the surface of several Berliner discs featuring the quartet, and Dudley added the word "manager" after his name. An example is 021, "Nearer My God to Thee," recorded on March 23, 1899. Since Dudley and tenor Roger Harding recorded a duet for Berliner on the same day as the Haydn Quartet's debut for the company, it is likely that Harding was one of the quartet's tenors at this session.

The Haydn seems to have recorded as the Gramophone Minstrels for a few Berliners on March 28, 1900. Berliner 01135 features first the group and then Harry Macdonough (minstrel records go back and forth from ensemble work to solo work), and 01136 features the group and then William F. Hooley. Berliner 01137 features Dudley and 01138 again features Hooley. Berliner 01134 has etched on its surface, "Introducing 'The Old Log Cabin in the Dell,' by the entire company, and 'How I Love My Lou,' by S.H. Dudley the phenomenal baritone." As already stated, Dudley himself signed Berliners when Haydn discs were prepared (many Berliner artists signed the masters), and it is likely that this was also written by him.

In the late 1890s the group recorded for Edison as the "Edison Male Quartette." It made its Victor debut with "Negro Wedding in Southern Georgia" on October 26, 1900. This was issued as seven-inch A-42 and was recorded again two years later for ten-inch Monarch release. The quartet then recorded regularly for Victor for years. It made early Zon-o-phone discs for Frank Seaman's National Gramophone Corporation, a subsidiary of the Universal Talking Machine Company. A typical title is "Massa's in the Cold Cold Ground" (9257).

In 1902 the quartet went to England for about three months to make records. Around that time the Haydn Quartet signed a contract to make, in the United States, discs exclusively for Victor and cylinders exclusively for Edison, with the Edison contract expiring in late 1907. Thereafter, the quartet worked only for Victor.

Although in 1909 Victor placed two members of the Haydn personnel—Bieling and Hooley—in a newly formed American Quartet (which also consisted of tenor Billy Murray and baritone Steve Porter), Bieling and Hooley continued to record with Macdonough and Dudley as the Haydn. Dudley left the quartet in 1909 and was replaced by Reinald Werrenrath. Curiously, Victor catalogs as late as 1925 continued to identify quartet members as "Bieling, Macdonough, Dudley, Hooley" and to include Dudley's photograph.

The Hayden (which was the new spelling after 1912) stopped recording in early 1914, with Victor 17544 and 17545—issued in April—being perhaps the last discs to feature new titles (17544 features "The Woman Thou Gavest Me"; 17545 features "'Cross the Great Divide"—each performance is credited to "Harry Macdonough and the Hayden Quartet"). Curiously, labels for "On the Banks of the Wabash" on 17397 give credit to the American Quartet though Harry Macdonough sings from beginning to end, three others joining for a final chorus—this is a performance by the Hayden Quartet, not the American. In 1912, Macdonough, Hooley, Werrenrath, and tenor Lambert Murphy had formed the Orpheus Quartet. This was the Hayden Quartet without John Bieling—instead, Murphy is first tenor.

Victor recording logs indicate that occasionally there were substitutions of singers late in the Hayden's career. For example, on January 23, 1914, a quartet consisting of Macdonough, Robert D. Armour, Steve Porter, and Wilfred Glenn recorded a new take of a song that had been a popular seller for years, "The Church Scene" from *The Old Homestead.*

Many Hayden records remained in the Victor catalog into the 1920s, with "In the Sweet By and By" and "Lead, Kindly Light" listed up through the 1930 catalog.

Victor recordings include "Blue Bell" (16179), "Down in the Old Cherry Orchard" (5331), "Lonesome" (5743), "Put on Your Old Gray Bonnet" (16377), "School Mates" (16548), "Lady Love" (16366), "Where the Southern Roses Grow" (16167), and "When the Snowbirds Cross the Valley" (31590). The company's August 1906 supplement revealed that "Nearer, My God, to Thee" (109) was the quartet's best-selling disc up to that point.

Hunting, Russell (May 8, 1864-February 20, 1943)

Born in West Roxbury, Massachusetts, Russell Hunting eventually became more important to the industry as a businessman than performer. As a young man he was a dramatic actor in the Boston Theater Company and in the early 1890s enjoyed success with cylinders of "Michael Casey" Irish comedy skits, for which he frequently assumed multiple parts and supplied various sound effects. Titles include "Michael Casey at the Telephone," "Casey at the Klondike Gold Mines," "Casey Exhibiting His Panorama," "Casey Joins the Masons," "Casey as the Dude in a Street Car," and "Casey at Denny Murphy's Wake." From late 1895 to late 1897 he made over a dozen Berliners, including "Casey as Judge" (612) and "Casey as Chairman of Mugwump Club" (615).

"Michael Casey Taking the Census," cut for various companies, was among the most popular in the series. Edison's National Phonograph Company had James H. White (known on records as Jim White) cover it in 1902, years after Hunting had introduced it. Soon after Hunting left the United States in 1898 to work in England, other artists—Joseph Gannon, Jim White, John Kaiser, George Graham—recorded Casey skits.

In 1897 advertisements cited Hunting as manager of the Universal Phonograph Company in New York City (he was succeeded by Mitchell Marks). The company had a recording studio at 21 East 20th Street, near its parent firm, Joseph W. Stern and Company, at 45 East 20th Street. The publishing firm established the cylinder company in hopes that records would create hits of songs owned by the publishing company.

In late 1896 Hunting founded the trade journal *The Phonoscope*, which called itself "the only journal in the world published in the interest of Talking Machines, Picture Projecting and Animating Devices, and Scientific and Amusement Inventions appertaining to Sound & Sight." The publication lasted until December 1899, but Hunting edited only the first couple dozen issues, his last being October 1898. Emil Imandt succeeded him as editor.

Jim Walsh writes in the November 1981 issue of *Hobbies*, "Near the end of the 19th century, Hunting got into trouble which caused him to leave America hurriedly and take up residence in England." Hunting worked in England for years, beginning in London as director of the Edison Bell Consolidated Phonograph Co., Ltd. In late 1904 he founded, with Louis Sterling, the Sterling Record Company, Ltd. (Sterling was managing director, Hunting the manager of the recording department), which by April 1905 was renamed the Russell Hunting Record Company, Ltd. Notwithstanding the name change, the company's products were called Sterling records.

By May 1908 Sterling and Hunting had sold their interest in the cylinder company, which failed in late 1908, and by October Hunting was Pathé's chief recording director. He made the rounds in visiting Pathé studios in Paris, London, Milan, Brussels, Amsterdam, and St. Petersburg and other Russian cities.

In 1914 Hunting returned to the United States to help establish an American branch for the French company, opening a recording laboratory at 18 West 42nd Street in Manhattan and a pressing plant at 10-34 Grand Avenue in Brooklyn. For the American firm Pathé Frères Phonograph Company, which he helped manage into the early 1920s (Eugene A. Widmann was president until he was succeeded in July 1921 by W. W. Chase, and H. N. McMenimen was managing director), Hunting resumed his recording career as a recitalist. Some labels identify him as "elocutionist." He revived several Casey skits and recited popular verse, including Whittier's "Barbara Frietchie," Miller's "The Dying Soldier," and Riley's "Old Man and Jim." On a few numbers he was reunited with Gilbert Girard, the imitator of animal sounds (he had made records with Girard two decades earlier). He also revived a descriptive sketch that he first recorded in England during the Boer War years, originally calling it "The Departure of the Troopship." In late 1917, working with a chorus and band, he recorded this as "Departure of the First U.S. Troops for France" (Pathé 20125).

Summarizing events at a New York City convention of Pathé jobbers, page 129 of the October 1917 issue of *Talking Machine World* describes Hunting's responsibilities:

> One of the pleasing events of the evening was the appearance of Russell Hunting, of "Casey" fame. Mr. Hunting, who is recording director for the Pathé interests abroad, and who is recognized as one of the industry's foremost authorities, is at present spending some time in this country, making his headquarters at the Pathé recording laboratory in New York. He gave several of his popular "Casey" numbers in his inimitable fashion and then surprised his audience with a dramatic poem which brought back recollections when he was a prominent figure in Shakespearean productions.

Page 1 of the January 1921 issue of *Talking Machine World* identifies Hunting as "chief recorder for the Pathé Freres Phonograph Co. in this country."

On March 19, 1888, he married Mary Ann Lawrence, and the marriage produced three children: Bessie Marie (1889), Henry Lawrence (1892), and Russell Emerson (1897). He evidently spent most of the 1920s and 1930s in Paris to supervise recording activities in various European studios but returned to the United States shortly before World War II because his health failed. His wife and two sons survived him (his daughter died in infancy). He is buried in Westchester, New York. His son Russell Hunting

Jr. was active in the industry by the 1920s. Page 1 of the January 1921 issue of *Talking Machine World* identifies him as "head of the recording department for the Nipponophone Co., Ltd., of Yokohama, Japan," and later issues of the trade journal indicated that he worked for the Music Master Corporation and the Pooley Company.

Jones, Ada *(June 1, 1873-May 2, 1922)*

Ada Jones was the leading female recording artist in the acoustic re-cording era, especially popular from 1905 to 1912 or so. Her singing range was limited but she was remarkably versatile, able to perform vaudeville sketches, sentimental ballads, hits from Broadway shows, British music hall material, "coon" and ragtime songs, and Irish comic songs. She was known for an ability to mimic dialects.

Victor catalogs listed roles at which she excelled: "Whether Miss Jones' impersonation be that of a darky wench, a little German maiden, a 'fresh' saleslady, a cowboy girl, a country damsel, Mrs. Flanagan or an Irish colleen, a Bowery tough girl, a newsboy or a grandmother, it is invariably a perfect one of its kind." Until 1921, Columbia catalogs paid this tribute:

> Miss Jones is without question the cleverest singer of soubrette songs, popular child ballads and popular ragtime hits adaptable for the soprano voice now recording for any Company. She is also one of the most popular singers in the record field and her records have been heard in all quarters of the globe. Her duet records with Mr. [Walter] Van Brunt, unique and entertaining as they are, have also come in for unlimited popular approval.

Despite this high praise in Columbia's 1921 catalog, only six of her Co-lumbia records were available at that time, and only one of the six ("Cross My Heart and Hope to Die") was a solo effort.

She was born in her parents' home at 78 Manchester Street in Oldham, Lancashire, England. Her father, James Jones, ran an inn, or public house, named The British Flag (the original building no longer stands). Her mother's maiden name was Ann Jane Walsh. Ada was baptized on June 15 in Oldham's St. Patrick's Church as Ada Jane Jones. Her birth was registered on August 18, 1873. The family moved to Philadelphia by 1879 (documents show that a brother was born there in that year). Her mother died and her father remarried. Ada's stepmother, Annie Douglas Maloney, encouraged Ada to make stage appearances, and "Little Ada Jones" was on the cover of sheet music in the early 1880s. One example is the sheet music for Harry S. Miller's "Barney's Parting" (1883). The January 1921 issue of *Farm and Fireside* duplicates an 1886 photograph showing Ada Jones as "Jack, a stable boy with song."

According to Milford Fargo during a presentation about Jones at the 1977 Conference of the Association for Recorded Sound Collections, cash disbursement books at the Edison National Historic Site (no recording logs of this period exist) suggest Ada's stepmother had been hired to make or mend drapes for the Edison company. The Jones family at that time lived nearby in Newark, New Jersey. It is likely that at the studio she saw an opportunity for her talented stepdaughter. In any case, Ada's earliest recordings were brown wax cylinders made for Edison in late 1893 or early 1894. Two surviving cylinders are "Sweet Marie" (North American 1289), a song by Raymon Moore, and "The Volunteer Organist" (North American 1292). The piano accompaniment is presumably by Edison's house pianist, Frank P. Banta. A male does the announcement for each record.

They are among the earliest commercial recordings of a female singing as a solo artist. Even earlier than Jones was "Miss Lillian Cleaver, the phenomenal contralto of the Howard Burlesque Co."—she is included in an 1892 New Jersey Phonograph Company catalog described by Jim Walsh in the October 1958 issue of *Hobbies*. Though Jones would later win fame as a performer of comic numbers, these two early numbers are not comic. The sentimental "Sweet Marie" had been introduced in the show *A Knotty Affair*, which opened in New York in May 1891. Composed by Raymon Moore, its lyrics are meant for a male singer:

> I've a secret in my heart, Sweet Marie
> A tale I would impart, love to thee
> Ev'ry daisy in the dell
> Knows my secret, knows it well,
> And yet I dare not tell, Sweet Marie
> When I hold your hand in mine, Sweet Marie
> A feeling most divine comes to me
> All the world is full of spring,
> Full of warblers on the wing
> And I listen while they sing Sweet Marie

Come to me, Sweet Marie, come to me
Not because your face is fair, love to see
But your soul so pure and sweet,
Makes my happiness complete
Makes me falter at your feet, Sweet Marie

It is not known whether the song was already in Jones' repertoire or whether Edison recording executives, believing that sentimental numbers best suited female singers, picked this song for what was probably her recording debut. Jones was in the show *A Knotty Affair* in December 1893, but the song was sung on stage by its composer, Moore. In any case, this early recording gives no hint of her comic talents.

Jones may have recorded other titles at this time, such as whatever was issued on North American 1290 and 1291, but they are not known to have survived. Shortly after her recording debut, the North American Phonograph Company went into receivership—in August 1894—and this evidently ended the first phase of her recording career. A decade would pass before she recorded again.

Meanwhile, other female singers made discs and cylinders but nearly all had very short recording careers and virtually none sang comic numbers regularly. Columbia's November 1896 cylinder catalog lists fourteen titles performed by contralto Maud Foster—titles include "I Want Yer, Ma Honey," "I Don't Want to Play in Your Yard," and "Mamma Says It's Naughty"—but Foster is absent from the company's June 1897 catalog, so her recording career was decidedly shortlived. Berliner artists of the late 1890s include Laura Libra, Virginia Powell Goodwin, Edna Florence, Dorothy Yale, Grace McCulloch, Florence Hayward, Maud Foster, Mabel Casedy, and Annie Carter. These were trained singers and mostly sang light opera selections or sentimental parlor songs. Few made records after 1900. With the exception of Edna Florence, these vocalists did not work for Eldridge R. Johnson's new Consolidated Talking Machine Company (this soon evolved into the Victor Talking Machine Company) when Emile Berliner was forced by an injunction to stop making discs. (Florence Hayward did make Victor discs in 1905 and 1906.) This is surprising since many of Berliner's male vocalists did work for the new company.

A predecessor to Jones in specializing in comic numbers was Marguerite Newton, known in her youth as "The Little Annandale" (she died on January 1, 1942). Newton recorded over twenty titles for Edison, including "Kiss Your Goosie Woosie" (4606) and "De Cakewalk in the Sky" (7143).

Beginning in 1902, Corinne Morgan was among the first female singers to record regularly, mostly duets with Frank C. Stanley. She sang sentimental fare, not comic numbers. Even a rare "coon" number, sung with Stanley—" 'Deed I Do"—is characterized in the June 1903 *Edison Phonograph Monthly* as being "of a sentimental character." Announcing the release of Standard 8427, "The Lord's Prayer" and "Gloria" as sung by a quartet featuring two male voices (Frank C. Stanley and George M. Stricklett) and two female (Morgan and one Miss Chapell), the June 1903 issue of *Edison Phonograph Monthly* frankly admitted the limitations of technology at that time: "It has always been a difficult matter to make successful Records of female voices, and after months of careful experimentation our Record Department has succeeded in getting perfect results in quartettes and duets. It is now at work on solos, and expects before long to list some very good songs by female voices."

When the September 1903 issue of *Edison Phonograph Monthly* announced an October release of one Morgan title, it again acknowledged that technology up to that point had not done justice to female singers: "A fourth feature for October is the listing of one of the best Records ever made by a woman's voice. It is No. 8499, 'Happy Days,' and is sung by Miss Corrinne [sic] Morgan, with violin obligato . . . It is sung by Miss Morgan with entire absence of all objectionable features of Records made by women's voices . . ."

It was perhaps for the best that Ada Jones ceased to make recordings for a decade. If she had made more in the 1890s, they likely would have been commercial failures for technical reasons, or recording executives might have selected for her too many sentimental numbers, preventing Jones from standing out. In 1905, when her recording career began in earnest, the time was right for this comic singer. She was extremely successful and for a long time was unique, the only female to record as regularly as Billy Murray, Henry Burr, Arthur Collins, and a handful of other artists.

Meanwhile, throughout the 1890s Jones continued to develop as an entertainer. As a stage performer, she specialized in singing while colored slides were projected—it was the heyday of the illustrated song. She evidently worked steadily and continued to be featured on sheet music covers, but she was by no means a famous entertainer yet. Soon she would be the first female singer to win fame on the basis of recordings.

Billy Murray reported in the January 1917 issue of *Edison Phonograph Monthly*, and then later to Jim Walsh, that he was responsible for Jones making her Columbia recording debut in 1904. It happened when Murray was recording a duet with Len Spencer. Victor Emerson, then supervisor of Columbia recording sessions, was appalled by Murray's imitation of a female and insisted that a woman play the female role. Murray states in the Edison trade journal:

I can get away with some pretty high notes, but there were a couple in that song that I couldn't reach on tiptoes . . . So I told the director about the girl I had heard in the Fourteenth street museum [Huber's] and suggested that she be given a try-out. He told me to bring her around. I did, and she made just as big a hit with everybody else as she did with me. . . . Some one has spread the impression that Ada Jones is in private life Mrs. Billy Murray. We *are* married but *not to each other.*

Walsh writes in the June 1947 issue of *Hobbies*, "According to Dan W. Quinn, Spencer 'hot-footed it down to Huber's museum' and obtained Miss Jones' services just a day before Quinn made her a similar offer." That Quinn entertained thoughts of forming a partnership with Jones is interesting since he normally did not sing with others, and his own recording career ended around the time that Jones' blossomed.

Huber's Palace Museum, sometimes called Huber's Fourteenth Street Museum, was located at 106-108 East 14th Street in Greenwich Village, New York City. Entertainment "museums" were divided buildings, with one stage for freak acts and another for variety shows. Not a high-class establishment, Huber's often featured performing monkeys and Unthan, the "armless wonder" who played piano with his toes. Harry Houdini performed at Huber's before enjoying widespread acclaim as an escape artist. Several shows were given each day and entertainers worked hard at museums. Huber's was known in New York City for its variety of acts, but it was not a leading vaudeville house and did not feature top-name entertainers. Huber's closed in July 1910.

Jones undoubtedly welcomed the opportunity to make recordings. Performing before live audiences must have been difficult since she was subject to epileptic seizures. No medication at this time could control epilepsy.

In the February 1917 issue of *Edison Amberola Monthly*, she stated, "The first record I made was a duet with the late Len Spencer. It was a rendition of the once popular song called 'Pals,' and was one of the famous 'Jimmie and Maggie' series of records. My first solo was 'My Carolina Lady,' a song that swept the country when 'coon' songs were in vogue."

It is interesting that she cites "My Carolina Lady," music by George Hamilton and words by Andrew B. Sterling, as her first recording. It was issued in March 1905 as Edison Standard 8948 (her Victor version was released in September). She may not have recalled the solo recordings of the 1890s or may not have believed that those old brown wax cylinders were worth mentioning. In announcing its release, the February 1905 issue of *Edison Phonograph Monthly* states, " 'My Carolina Lady' serve[s] as an introduction to the Phonograph public of another new singer in Miss Ada Jones, who has a charming contralto voice. Miss Jones sings this selection in a style all her own, with a dainty coon dialect and expression, that claim your interested attention at once." She is called a contralto here—she was at different times identified as a mezzo soprano, contralto, and soprano ("soprano" was used most commonly by companies). She is called "Miss Ada Jones," though in Manhattan on August 9, 1904, she had married Hughie Flaherty. Her Edison debut recording was followed in April 1905 by "He's Me Pal" (8957), by Gus Edwards and Vincent Bryan, for which she takes on a Bowery accent.

In May, Edison issued Jones performing a "coon" song: "You Ain't the Man I Thought You Was" (8989). The April 1905 issue of *Edison Phonograph Monthly* states, "Miss Jones' coon dialect will be found very entertaining. . . . A coon dialect by the female voice is something new in our recent supplements."

Around this time her first Columbia recordings were issued, and though she recalled in 1917 that "Pals" was her first record (it was issued as Columbia disc 3148), Columbia discs with earlier numbers include "The Hand of Fate" (3050, with Len and Harry Spencer) and "Mr. and Mrs. Murphy" (3108, with Len Spencer). The first Columbia cylinder of Spencer and Jones was "The Hand of Fate," issued as Columbia cylinder 32623 (again, Len's brother Harry is an assisting artist) and she recorded "The Hand of Fate" for Victor in late 1904, several months before recording "Pals" (on May 3, 1905) for the company. It is likely that "The Hand of Fate" was the beginning of her second recording career, not "Pals."

In April 1905, the team of Jones and Spencer is cited for the first time in an Edison trade publication. The April issue of *Edison Phonograph Monthly* announces the May release of the Ted Snyder song "Heinie" on Standard 8982 (they recorded it as Columbia 3206 around this time), calling it a "Dutch vaudeville specialty." This was followed in June by the release of Jones and Spencer performing "Ev'ry Little Bit Helps" (9016). On various records the two imitated Bowery toughs (on the popular "Peaches and Cream," Spencer was a "newsy" named Jimmie, Jones being his "goil"), German immigrants, Western ranch workers (as in the skit "Bronco Bob and His Little Cheyenne"), African Americans, and others. Most of their so-called vaudeville specialties or vaudeville sketches (some Victor labels use the term "descriptive specialty") were written and arranged by Spencer himself. He was influenced by others' vaudeville routines, but his skits were not performed in vaudeville.

For the next few years, a new Jones or Jones-Spencer performance would be issued regularly by Edison. Often the company included in a new Advance List, issued each month, both a Jones performance and a Jones-Spencer skit. In May 1910, Edison released a Jones performance ("By the Light of the Silvery Moon," on which she is assisted by a male quartet), the Jones-Spencer routine titled "The Suffragette," and the Jones-Murray duet titled "Just a Little Ring From You"—busy at this time with other companies as well, she was at the peak of her popularity! Jones and her husband Hugh Flaherty lived in Manhattan at 150 W. 36th Street until 1910, so visiting the Edison studio in lower Manhattan and various midtown studios was easy. They then moved to Huntington, Long Island.

She did not play an instrument. Unable to read music, she learned songs by ear. In an unpublished letter dated March 12, 1982, researcher Milford Fargo gives this information about the singer when answering a question posed by Ronald Dethlefson about Jones' handwriting:

> Actually she did not have very good script and rarely wrote her own letters because she was aware of it. She had meager formal schooling and was content to let her stepmother write for her. Len Spencer (of the Spencerian handwriting family) often signed autographs for her on pictures and documents in the Edison and Columbia files. Also, her writer friend, Elizabeth Boone, composed letters and copy for her and often sent them in her own writing.

Her first Victor discs were issued shortly after the company switched from the "Monarch" label to the "Grand Prize" label (beginning in January 1905, "Grand Prize" surrounded the center hole of new discs, and "Victor Record" replaced "Monarch Record" on ten-inch discs). Her first Victor session took place on December 29, 1904, and Spencer was her partner on two selections: "Reuben and Cynthia" (4304) and the burlesque melo-drama "The Hand of Fate" (4242). As a solo artist, she recorded on that day two "coon" songs, only one of which was issued: "Mandy Lou, Will You Be My Lady-Love?" (4231). It was issued in March 1905, the same time that Henry Burr's first Victor disc was issued. Both Burr and Jones would become important Victor artists, and despite differences in style they eventually recorded some duets.

Ada gave birth to her daughter Sheilah (sometimes spelled Sheelah by reporters) on January 14, 1906. This was her only child. She worked in the final trimester of her pregnancy, making Victor recordings as late as December 15, 1905, and returned to work relatively soon after giving birth. On March 16, 1906 she recorded for Victor the song "Henny Klein" as well as skits with Len Spencer.

Though Billy Murray claimed credit for "discovering" Jones at Huber's in 1904, Murray and Jones were not paired immediately. When Murray and Jones finally recorded together, probably beginning at Victor on November 2, 1906 (they cut "Wouldn't You Like to Flirt with Me?" and "I'm Sorry"), the pairing was incredibly popular. Murray and Jones became one of the three or four most successful duos of the acoustic era. Their first Edison recording was Standard 9659, "Will You Be My Teddy Bear?" issued in August 1907. Their first Columbia cylinder was "You Can't Give Your Heart to Somebody Else and Still Hold Hands With Me" (33088). Their first Columbia disc was "I'd Like to See a Little More of You" (3612). Before this, Jones and Murray had joined Frank C. Stanley for "Whistle It" (3589).

The Jones-Murray pairing became exclusive to Victor and Edison after Murray signed a joint contract with those companies in 1909. Their most successful cylinder recording for Edison was probably "Rainbow" (Standard 10049), issued in January 1909. This Percy Wenrich composition (with lyrics by Jack Mahoney) was part of a craze at the time for "Indian" songs, and Jones recorded similar songs with Murray, including "Blue Feather" (Standard 10162), "Silver Star" (Amberol 940), and the very popular "Silver Bell" (Standard 10492; Amberol 576).

Other notable Jones-Murray recordings issued by various companies include "Be My Little Baby Bumble Bee," "The Boy Who Stuttered and the Girl Who Lisped," "Smile Smile Smile," "When We Are M-A-R-R-I-E-D," "Wouldn't You Like to Have Me for a Sweetheart," "I'm Looking for a Sweetheart, and I Think You'll Do," "I've Taken Quite a Fancy to You," and "The Belle of the Barbers' Ball" (popularized on stage by female impersonator Julian Eltinge with the Cohan & Harris Minstrels, according to the February 1910 issue of *Edison Phonograph Monthly*).

The March 1909 issue of *Edison Phonograph Monthly* states, "Scarcely less popular than Miss Jones' solo Records are those made with the assistance of Mr. Murray, himself one of the best of the Edison artists. The duet Records by Miss Jones and Mr. Murray are eagerly sought for in each month's list." By this time sales of Jones and Murray duets significantly exceeded sales of Jones and Spencer records. The July 1909 issue of *Edison Phonograph Monthly* stresses that the team of Jones and Murray had no competitors: "Miss Jones and Mr. Murray have the field absolutely to themselves so far as comic love duets are concerned—they have no near rivals."

Probably because of high demand for Murray and Jones duets, she worked only occasionally with Spencer by 1909. The last Edison cylinder credited to Ada Jones and Len Spencer is wax Amberol 670 featuring "The Crushed Tragedian," issued in May 1911. Jones also contributed to

"Uncle Fritz's Birthday," credited to Len Spencer and Company and issued on wax Amberol 700 in June 1911. But so closely linked were the names of Jones and Spencer, who died in late 1914, that several editions of the Victor catalog, beginning in 1915, state at the end of the biographical sketch for Jones, "The recent death of the popular and genial comedian, Mr. Spencer, is regretted by a host of friends and admirers."

Because Murray in 1909 became exclusive to Victor for disc recordings and to Edison for cylinders, Jones needed another singing partner when working for other companies, and she relied mostly on a young Walter Van Brunt, especially during Columbia sessions. Many Lakeside, Oxford, United, and Indestructible records feature the duo of Jones and Van Brunt. They stopped working together in mid-1914 because the tenor signed an exclusive contract with Edison. Van Brunt later recalled in a taped interview with Milford Fargo that he found Jones to be easy to work with, stressing that he could not recall ever having a disagreement or exchanging a cross word.

Other recording partners include Henry Burr, Billy Watkins, Will C. Robbins, George Wilton Ballard, George L. Thompson, M. J. O'Connell (he used the name "Harry Dunning" for their Rex duets), and Billy Jones. With Byron G. Harlan she recorded "How 'Ya Gonna Keep 'Em Down on the Farm" (Diamond Disc 50518). Harlan was among the prolific artists in record studios during the years Jones was popular, but the two did not often work together. Though she was well-known for performing "coon" songs, she never recorded a duet with the artist best known for "coon" songs, Arthur Collins.

She continued to work with Cal Stewart until his death in 1919. Especially successful was "Uncle Josh and Aunt Nancy Putting Up the Kitchen Stove," recorded for several companies. It was renamed "Uncle Josh and Aunt Mandy Put Up the Kitchen Stove" when an Emerson master was used for a Radiex pressing (4082), and Cal Stewart was identified on the Radiex label as "Duncan Jones."

In contrast to colleagues with various pseudonyms, she was issued only as Ada Jones. Unlike most other singers, Jones performed for years without rivals, without singers of similar talents seriously threatening her popularity. From 1905 to 1915 many comic female singers were introduced to record buyers. The most talented included Helen Trix, Clarice Vance, Maude Raymond, Elida Morris, Irene Franklin, Stella Tobin, Stella Mayhew, and Dolly Connolly (more obscure are Amy Butler, Lilian Doreen, Elen Foster, Marie Hoy, June Rossmore, and Ethel Costello). Each singer's recorded output was minuscule compared with Jones'. Stage work, which often included making tours on vaudeville circuits, undoubtedly prevented a few from cultivating recording careers, whereas Jones in this period devoted all efforts toward making records.

Dorothy Kingsley on two Edison Standard cylinders sounds remarkably like Jones. On Zon-o-phone 1078 Kingsley even performs a song that Jones recorded for various companies, "Do You Know Mr. Schneider?" However, Kingsley's career was too brief for Jones to have worried about her as a rival. Kingsley was not a pseudonym for Jones. Documents at the Edison National Historic Site show that Jones was paid $1950 for the business year ending on September 30, 1908; Kingsley was paid $85 for making two cylinders. Otherwise nothing is known today of Kingsley except that she also made a few Victor, Zon-o-phone, and Indestructible records around the same time she worked for Edison. As little is known of Madge Maitland, who made one Edison cylinder, "Is Everybody Happy?" on 9210. The January 1906 issue of *Edison Phonograph Monthly* reports that she is "well known on the vaudeville stage" and states, "Miss Maitland's coon dialect has never been excelled by an Edison singer." But Maitland's recording career began and ended with this one cylinder, posing no threat to Jones.

Anna Chandler was introduced to Edison record buyers almost as a Jones rival. Announcing her second cylinder, "I Want Everyone to Love Me" on wax Amberol 770, the July 1911 issue of *Edison Phonograph Monthly* states, "Six years ago we 'discovered' Ada Jones. Today she is recognized as a leader in Phonograph circles wherever civilization extends. Our latest 'discovery' is Anna Chandler, who six years hence will certainly be equally as well-known and universally liked." But Chandler records did not sell well.

In a rare instance of a company remaking a record that had originally featured Jones, Columbia in late 1920 used Gladys Rice, assisted by the Harmonizers, to redo "All Night Long," originally issued in 1913 on A1297 as performed by Ada Jones assisted by the Peerless Quartet. The same catalog number was used for the 1920 remake. The choice of Rice, whose voice was very different from that of Jones, is surprising, especially since Jones herself was available in 1920—at least she was still making records for other companies. Possibly companies by the World War I era viewed Rice, who was also versatile, as a kind of successor to Jones. It is worth noting that around 1916 the Edison company turned increasingly to Rice and used Jones less often.

Popular discs featuring Jones as a solo artist include "Waiting at the Church" (Victor 4714, 1906), "I Just Can't Make My Eyes Behave" (Columbia 3599, 1907), "The Yama-Yama Man" (with the Victor Light Opera Company, Victor 16326, 1909), "I've Got Rings on My Fingers" (Columbia A741, 1909), "Call Me Up Some Rainy Afternoon" (with the American Quartet, Victor 16508, 1910), "Come, Josephine, in My Flying Machine" (with the American Quartet, Victor 16844, 1911), "Row! Row! Row!" (Victor 17205, 1913), and "By the Beautiful Sea" (with Billy Watkins, Columbia A1563, 1914).

Jones recorded Maurice Stonehill's "Just Plain Folks" for several companies. One of her most popular numbers, its lyrics are about an aged couple who visit a son for the first time in years, and the couple are disappointed that the wealthy son resents the visit. Edison issued it on two-minute Standard 9085 in September 1905, Columbia soon following. On wax Amberol 286, a longer version was issued in September 1909. Early Blue Amberols had record slips, and none had less text than the one included with Blue Amberol 1771, which gives chorus lines and nothing else:

> We are just plain folks, your mother and me
> Just plain folks like our own folks used to be
> As our presence seems to grieve you
> We will go away and leave you
> For we're sadly out of place here
> 'Cause we're just plain folks.

Walsh writes in the May 1977 issue of *Hobbies:*

> The late Fred Rabenstein, who was Edison's paymaster, told me that Ada Jones "never bothered to learn a song until she came to the studio to make the record," and this annoyed Walter Miller, the recording manager. On one of her "takes" of the Diamond Discs of "Snow Deer," she sings "snow bird" at one point where she should say "deer," and surprisingly the error was allowed to go uncorrected.

Edison promotional literature hailed her versatility. The July 1908 issue of *Edison Phonograph Monthly* announces the September release of "Hugo" (9928) and states:

> Here is more proof that Ada Jones' versatility has no limit. This charming entertainer can sing an Irish song "to beat the Dutch," and then turn right around and sing Dutch to beat the Irish. That may seem like a very difficult feat, but there will be no room for doubt after hearing "Hugo," which is her latest Dutch dialect song.

When her recording of "O'Brien Is Tryin' to Learn to Talk Hawaiian" was issued on Diamond Disc 50402 in May 1917, the jacket for the disc praises her comic talents and suggests she was at the top of her profession: "Ada Jones is without a peer singing comic songs. You'll laugh at these ridiculous words even when you have heard them many times, and you will always find the tune irresistible. Miss Jones is one of the best known of all comic song singers. As a dialect singer she is unique."

In reality, her career suffered when popular music changed in the World War I era, leaving her with only the occasional session, usually for small companies such as Rex and Empire. Recording engagements became less frequent around 1915, though Columbia engaged Jones regularly into 1916. One indication of her decline in popularity is that, as a solo artist, she is on only six Diamond Discs, which is a contrast to the many Standard and wax Amberol cylinders she made for Edison prior to the introduction of Diamond Disc technology. When she did go to the Columbia, Edison, or Victor studios, she was sometimes given only bit parts in ensemble pieces.

Around this time she began traveling and making personal appearances, which became her chief source of income. It could not have been lucrative. In the June 1972 issue of *Hobbies*, Walsh describes a Jones concert he attended in his hometown of Marion, Virginia, in 1922. In the early 1920s Marion "had less than 4,000 population," and the concert was given in the Smyth County courthouse, not a theater.

By 1917 new recording artists such as Marion Harris, Van and Schenck, and Gladys Rice made Jones's delivery seem old-fashioned. In the late 1910s and early 1920s, a new generation of female recording artists regularly recorded "blues," or at least Tin Pan Alley songs with "blues" in the title, but Jones never recorded any song with "blues" in the title. When her recording (with Billy Murray) of Harry Von Tilzer's "Don't Slam That Door" was issued as Blue Amberol 3135 in April 1917, it was advertised as a "conversational coon duet." "Coon" songs were decidedly old-fashioned by this time.

In an attempt to keep up with the times, she recorded a few songs about the war, such as Solman's "We'll Keep Things Going Till the Boys Come Home," issued on Imperial 5513 in December 1917, and Berlin's "They Were All Out of Step But Jim," issued as Okeh 1008 in July 1918. The Heineman Phonograph Supply Co. began issuing Okeh records in mid-1918 and she recorded a handful of titles for the company, joining George L. Thompson for three titles.

She recorded "She's Back Among the Pots and Pans Again" in late 1917. It was issued on Empire 5526 and Imperial 5526 in February 1918, the reverse side of both discs featuring Byron G. Harlan singing "Long Boy."

In 1917 she recorded songs for the new Gennett hill-and-dale record label, made by the Starr Piano Company. The Raymond Hubbell song "Poor Butterfly" was enormously popular throughout 1917 (with words by John Golden, it was introduced in 1916's *The Big Show* at the Hippodrome Theatre in New York), and on Starr/Gennett 7603 Jones sings the comic "If I Catch the Guy Who Wrote Poor Butterfly," issued in August 1917. Others issued between November 1917 and March 1918 include "Cross My Heart and Hope to Die" (7603), "Don't Slam That Door" (7607), and "Says I to Myself, Says I" (7637), and "I'm Old Enough for a Little Lovin'" (7637).

The Edison company continued to engage Jones, though not as regularly as in earlier years. The company by this time relied far more upon Helen Clark and Elizabeth Spencer for popular songs, and Gladys Rice became increasingly important to Edison. Rice was even paired often with Billy Murray, Jones' traditional partner.

No new Jones material was recorded for Edison between June 1914 and May 1915. There is a large gap in Blue Amberol releases featuring Jones as a solo artist. Blue Amberol 2409 featured her singing Monckton's "Bedtime at the Zoo," issued in September 1914, but then no new Blue Amberols of Jones were issued until two years later, with "If I Knock the 'L' Out of Kelly" (2940) released in September 1916. This is in contrast to new Jones cylinders being issued nearly every month during her heyday in the Standard and wax Amberol period. She did contribute to three performances issued between Blue Amberols 2409 and 2940. Blue Amberol 2777 features Gilbert Girard "and Co." Blue Amberols 2912 and 2914 feature the Metropolitan Mixed Chorus. Jones helped but was given no label credit. She also did remakes of "The Pussy Cat Rag" and "Uncle Josh's Huskin' Bee" in 1915.

Walsh reports in the June 1960 issue of *Hobbies* that when a new performance of "The Golden Wedding" was needed for Diamond Disc release, it was recorded on January 25, 1918, with Jones' twelve-year-old daughter playing the role of a granddaughter. (According to researcher Milford Fargo, Sheilah died sometime in the 1930s.)

Jones recorded Harry Von Tilzer's "Bye and Bye" with Billy Murray, and this was issued as Blue Amberol 3545 in September 1918. It was the last Blue Amberol to pair Jones and Murray.

The April 1918 issue of *Talking Machine World* (p. 13) reported that rumors were being spread that Jones had died:

Ada Jones, like Mark Twain, objects to being reported dead, and the veteran talking machine artist was quick to deny the latest rumor of her demise in the following letter: "I have often been reported dead. I even had a double who has been singing throughout the country, using my name, as 'Ada Jones, the phonograph artist.' I have just been out with a troupe of phonograph artists giving several entertainments where I was introduced as 'Ada Jones, the mother of the phonograph.' Which made me feel very ancient, I assure you. Cordially yours, Ada Jones, Long Island."

It is impossible to say how widespread such rumors were or even know if rumors were spread at all. This report of such a rumor—and, with it, the proclamation that she is in good health—must have been judged by everyone at the time as excellent publicity, especially since Jones had begun to tour. Incredibly, the March 1908 issue of *Edison Phonograph Monthly* speaks of a similar rumor: "A report has apparently gained considerable circulation in the Middle West to the effect that Miss Ada Jones died recently. There is absolutely no foundation for the report. Miss Jones is in good health and is making Records for us each month." The July 1910 issue of *Edison Phonograph Monthly* refers to the same rumor: "The persistency with which the report makes its appearance is exceedingly annoying to Miss Jones, and we are bothered by frequent requests for contradiction or confirmation of it."

From 1918 until her death she gave concerts, usually in small towns. Page 138 of the July 1918 issue of *The Voice of the Victor* states, "Ada Jones and the Shannon Four recently appeared in concert in Roanoke, Virginia, under the auspices of the Roanoke Cycle Company." The January 1919 issue of *Talking Machine World* reports on its front page that on December 26, 1918, the singer "sang several coon and character songs" in the Opera House in Pottstown, Pennsylvania. Others who performed were the Shannon Four as well as the McKee Trio. The trade journal by 1919 rarely used the term "coon" for songs since such music was long out of fashion by this time.

Page 75 of the March 1919 issue of *Talking Machine World* reports:

R. L. Hollinshead, manager of the talking machine department of the Clark Music Co., this city [Syracuse, New York], believes in keeping his customers familiar with the various record artists in order to maintain their interest in their machines. With that end in view he recently conducted a very substantial concert with Miss Ada Jones, one of the veterans among the recording artists, as the chief attraction. Miss Jones sang several character songs, for which she is noted, and also sang an Italian character duet with Mr. Hollinshead, entitled "I'll Take You Back To Sunny Italy." Mr. Hollinshead sang several songs, and there was demonstrated an Edison Re-Creation of a song by Jones and Murray, to show the remarkable reproduction of the

human voice. The concert was one of a series which the Clark Music
Co. is giving free to the public . . .

It is not clear where the "concert" took place, but talking machine departments of stores often served as concert halls.

Jones and Murray had their last hit as a duo with "When Francis Dances
with Me" (Victor 18830), composed by Benny Ryan and Sol Violinsky,
who was really Sol Ginsberg. It was recorded on August 25, 1921, and
finally issued in January 1922, too late for the Christmas season. Victor
executives probably had no great expectations since Jones records in recent years had been slow sellers. Brisk sales of the record can probably be
attributed to the song's success in vaudeville. The music stops at one point
for an exchange of comic dialogue, which was typical of recordings of a
previous generation, such as on many Collins and Harlan recordings. By
the 1920s, comic singers sometimes exchanged dialogue before music
began—as Billy Murray and Aileen Stanley do on several numbers, such
as "Whatdya Say We Get Together" (Victor 20065), and as the Happiness
Boys do—but not often in the middle of a song.

This was Jones' last Victor disc. She cut the same song with Billy Jones
for Edison on September 6, 1921. It was issued on Diamond Disc 50852 in
December 1921 and Blue Amberol 4404 in January 1922. The last song
she recorded was "On a Little Side Street," singing it with Billy Jones for
Edison (Diamond Disc 50852; Blue Amberol 4404). She also cut it as a
solo artist for Okeh 4439, which was issued in December 1921—she is on
one side of Okeh 4439 while a pioneer of radio, new recording artist
Vaughn De Leath, is on the other. Jones also recorded the song for Victor
but takes were rejected.

During most of her recording years she resided in Huntington Station,
Long Island, New York. She died of uremic poisoning (kidney failure) in
Rocky Mount, North Carolina, on May 2, 1922, while on a performing
tour. The town's newspaper, *The Evening Telegram*, had announced days
earlier that Jones and her company would put on a show at the local Palace
Theater on Saturday evening. Her touring company consisted of obscure
artists—violinist Beth Hamilton; pianist and soprano Mabel Loomis; and
one "Armstrong," identified as a "man of mystery, who will entertain by
moments of mystifying and being funny." A feature-length motion picture
and two-reel comedy were also scheduled for the evening's entertainment.

The newspaper reported days later that on the Monday after the Rocky
Mount performance (she had sung "Oh Lordy" and "You Ain't the Man,"
among other numbers), Jones had collapsed in her hotel room. She had
been booked for a Monday evening performance in the town of Tarboro,
and the other members of her company found her semiconscious shortly

before noon on Monday when they stopped at her room before departing for the train station. She was taken to the local St. Mary's Hospital on Tuesday morning and died that night. Her remains were shipped to New York for burial.

Walsh reports in the June 1972 issue of *Hobbies* what Jones researcher Milford Fargo learned in 1958 from the singer's longtime housekeeper, Rosina Mackie—namely, that Jones had been reluctant to begin the tour. Page 172 of the June 1922 issue of *Talking Machine World* includes a short article under the heading "Death of Miss Ada Jones"—she was still identified as "Miss" despite her many years of marriage. Her husband Hugh Flaherty died on July 9, 1961, outliving his first wife by nearly four decades. He had met Jones in a theatrical rooming house at 82 East 10th Street. Walsh reports in the November 1961 issue of *Hobbies* that Flaherty, who had been born in County Kerry, Ireland, "worked vaudeville routines and danced 'solo' with the Byron Spahn traveling tent show. Ada was the feature of the Spahn show, singing with illustrated song slides."

Performances by Jones, who always worked as a freelance artist, were issued on these domestic labels: Aeolian-Vocalion, American, Aretino, Busy Bee, Central, Clear Tone (single-faced), Cleartone (double-faced), Clico, Climax, Columbia (she recorded the most titles for this company), Concert, Cort, Crescent, D & R, Diamond, Eagle, Edison, Emerson, Empire, Excelsior, Faultless, Gennett, Harmony, Harvard, Imperial, International, Lakeside, Leeds, Lyric, Manhattan, Marconi, McKinley, Medallion, Mozart, Nassau, Okeh, Operaphone, Oxford, Paramount, Pathé Actuelle, Pathé Freres, Perfect, Playerphone, Puritan, Radiex, Radium (made by Leeds & Catlin), Remick Perfection, Rex, Rishell, Siegel Cooper, Silver Star, Silvertone, Square Deal, Standard, Star, Sun, Symphonola, Symphony, Talking Book, Thomas, United, Victor, and Zon-o-phone. She evidently made no Little Wonder discs—very few female artists did make them, exceptions being Elida Morris and Rhoda Bernard (this comedienne made Yiddish and Italian dialect records around 1916).

Jose, Richard (June 5, 1862-October 20, 1941)

Richard Jose was one of the best-selling artists of the Victor Talking Machine Company during the years the company issued discs labeled "Monarch" and then "Grand Prize." Although Victor issued nothing new from Jose after 1906 (he recorded exclusively for this company), several Jose selections remained in the Victor catalog until 1919, including "Silver Threads Among the Gold," a song closely associated with Jose in his life. One number remained in the catalog as late as 1922: "Abide with Me," which had been recorded on February 23, 1906 (Victor 16660).

He was the first singer to be identified on records as a countertenor, though he may have not have been the first to make records. Harry Leighton is identified as an "alto" in a mid-1890s cylinder catalog described by Jim Walsh in the January 1982 issue of *Hobbies*. Edward Le Roy Rice states in *Monarchs of Minstrelsy* (Kenny Publishing Company, 1911) that Leighton—born in Bradford, England—"has a peculiarly pleasing high-tenor voice."

Most of Jose's discs, including the earliest with Monarch and Deluxe labels (Victor used these words on early ten-inch and twelve-inch discs, respectively), identify him as "counter-tenor" though on some labels Jose is identified as "tenor." It does not appear that Jose was billed as a counter-tenor in minstrel shows or vaudeville. The origins of the term "countertenor" are not clear, but it may have referred to a voice part ("against the tenor"). In the earliest organum were contratenor altus (high against the tenor) and contratenor bassus (low against the tenor). Countertenors are sometimes called altos because they originally sang alto parts (alto meaning "high"). A countertenor's pitch is similar to the female contralto's.

Whereas nearly all modern countertenors rely on falsetto, which is a "head voice" with little or no chest resonance, Jose as well as recording artist Will Oakland achieved an unusually high range without reliance on falsetto, using full lung power. Each singer was a naturally high-placed tenor (another singer with such a range was Russell Oberlin, leading American countertenor of the 1950s and 1960s). Jose could color the tone of his voice in a way that is difficult for anyone using falsetto. No singer relying on falsetto could have produced the volume needed to fill concert halls, as Jose did for decades. Newspapers at the time insisted that Jose had the voice of a boy, but it should be added that he could project his voice and be heard throughout an auditorium as no boy soprano could. His was an extraordinarily rare voice.

A slim book titled *"Silver Threads Among the Gold" in the Life of Richard J. Jose* was written and self-published by Grace M. Wilkinson four years after Jose's death (February 8, 1945 is given as a copyright date). The biography was written in the late 1930s with the help of Jose, who states in a one-sentence preface dated January 12, 1939, in his own handwriting, "This biography written in collaboration with Grace M. Wilkinson is an authentic record of my life and the only one which has my approval for publication." Only once does Wilkinson refer to Jose as a countertenor: "His popularity in vaudeville as a contra-tenor was very much like that of Caruso in Italian grand opera." Almost nothing is said about Jose's singing techniques, but his range is noted: "Mr. Jose's compass was from D above middle C to E above high C." The book also notes that when he sang

"Goodbye, Dolly Gray," Jose's principle "working note was high 'D,' two half-steps above the sacred high 'C' of Italian tenordom."

The countertenor voice was much valued centuries ago (as was the castrato), especially in the 1600s and early 1700s. English composer Henry Purcell was reportedly a countertenor. But such singing went out of fashion for various reasons, and no singers of the nineteenth century won fame as countertenors with the exception of Jose at the end of the century. His recording career was brief—from 1903 to 1906—but his concerts were popular years before and after his recording sessions. Will Oakland enjoyed a much longer recording career, and when Oakland ceased making recordings in the 1920s, no other countertenors made recordings in America during the 78 rpm era. In England in the 1940s, Alfred Deller (a baritone who employed falsetto) won new respect among singers and voice enthusiasts for the high male voice. Deller's first recordings were made in 1949 for HMV.

Oakland began recording in 1908, two years after Jose's last Victor recordings were made. Oakland was inevitably compared with Jose for much of his career, even by the Edison company when it promoted Oakland's Edison work. Literature for Oakland's "Dear Old Girl," issued in 1913 as Standard 2075, states, "Richard Jose, the phenomenal contra-tenor, was the first to feature the song, and from its first performance it was a decided success." This is a rare instance of one company referring to another company's exclusive artist. Perhaps eager to exploit the success of first Jose and then Oakland, Columbia sometimes labeled Manuel Romain a countertenor, despite the fact that Romain was a regular tenor. Countertenor Frank Coombs began recording in 1910 but never approached the popularity of Jose or Oakland.

Jose was like a Horatio Alger character—a penniless boy rises to the top of his profession, enjoying renown and even fortune. His wife Therese (he married Therese Shreve of Carson City, Nevada on July 20, 1898) recalled in an article written for her newsletter *The Pony Express* that Harry Von Tilzer presented her with "a huge sunburst diamond broach" in gratitude because her husband made a hit of the 1900 song "A Bird in a Gilded Cage." She claimed Charles K. Harris likewise gave her a diamond necklace in gratitude for her husband's help in popularizing "After the Ball." However, Harris claimed in his autobiography *After the Ball: Forty Years of Melody* (New York: Frank-Maurice, Inc., 1926) that Jose, who was at that time with the Primrose and West Minstrels, insisted that the composer should push "Kiss and Let's Make Up," and Harris gives no credit to Jose for popularizing "After the Ball." Much of what Therese wrote late in her life is inaccurate, and her recollections of such gifts from Von Tilzer and Harris are not wholly credible.

In *They All Had Glamour* (Julian Messner, Inc., 1944), Edward Marks lists many Paul Dresser songs that Jose helped popularize. Therese Jose stated that her husband at one point was in the publishing business with Dresser. Oscar Lewis' history of San Francisco's Palace Hotel, titled *Bonanza Inn* (Alfred A. Knopf, 1939), tells of an Examiner reporter late for an interview with the famous conductor Walter Damrosch because the reporter had been detained elsewhere by the beauty of Jose singing to the accompaniment of Dresser himself. The reporter was too caught up in the music—"hypnotized," he announced—to be on time. The reporter's first words to the famous Wagnerian conductor were of praise for the beauty of Jose singing Dresser's "A Mother's Grave."

Evidence of his popularity is found in various sources. *The History of Boston Theatre*, published in 1908, reports that when Jose left a Boston stage on the night of April 5, 1891, after singing encore after encore, the happy audience rose en masse and likewise left the theatre—despite the fact that several other numbers remained on the program.

He was born in England in Lanner, a Cornish village. His birth certificate, according to British researcher David Ivall, shows that Jose was born on June 5, 1862. Various sources give later dates, but these rely on statements by Jose or his wife, both of whom wished him to seem younger than he was. Jose's wife cites 1869 in her account of the singer's life in a 1968 edition of *The Pony Express,* though a 1978 edition of the same corrects the year to 1862. The singer's 1941 death certificate cites 1872, off by ten years. About the singer's parents, Wilkinson refers to a home built in Lanner by Captain James Francis and writes, "In this home, all of Captain Francis' children were born. His daughter, Elizabeth, . . . was now being courted by a young Spanish miner, Richard Jose. His ancestors had come from Spain to work in the tin mines at Cornwall."

Jose's baptismal record is dated September 17, 1862, and gives the surname as "Joce." This is a phonetic spelling and indicates how Jose is pronounced in Cornwall, where it is an ordinary name. Although Victor catalogs give a Spanish pronunciation ("hoh-zay") and the singer evidently adopted this pronunciation at some point in his career, this name in Cornwall is pronounced to rhyme with "rose"—that is, "Joe's." There is no accent mark in the large "Jose" on the singer's tombstone, but Jose himself used an accent mark when signing his name.

Richard Jose senior was a copper miner who died in late 1876. After the father's death, the son, the eldest of five children, emigrated to Nevada in search of an uncle. Some accounts depict him as a mere boy when he emigrated, a myth Jose himself and later his wife Therese promoted, with Jose's obituary in *The Billboard* giving the age as eight. However, he was fourteen or possibly older when he emigrated. He never located the uncle but found a home in Nevada among Cornish miners who welcomed the fellow emigrant. He became an apprentice to William J. Luke, who was a Reno blacksmith with a business at Fourth and Sierra streets.

Jose was largely untrained as a singer. Although the singer's wife recalls that Jose's father played the organ and sang in the village church, the only real instruction may have been in Jose's teen years when one Bishop Whitaker arranged for singing lessons in Reno.

Some sources suggest that Jose's career began in Sacramento with Charlie Reed's Minstrels while Edward Le Roy Rice states in *Monarchs of Minstrelsy:* "His first professional appearance was with Charley Reed's Minstrels in San Francisco, March 2, 1886. He remained with Reed until the season ended, April 10, following. A few weeks later he joined Birch and Cotton's Minstrels for a brief road trip." Wilkinson states, "Mr. Jose never blacked his face during the many years he sang in the minstrels nor did he ever parade on any street."

But Jose had considerable experience earlier in Reno and elsewhere. A reporter from Virginia City, one Alfred Doten, kept a detailed journal, and *The Journals of Alfred Doten: 1849-1903,* published in three volumes in 1973, refer several times to Dick Jose's early singing career.

Doten's first reference to Jose is in the entry for February 16, 1885. This is the earliest known reference to Jose aside from documents regarding his birth and baptism:

> Dicky Jose a young man about 19 yrs old & resident of Reno came up with the Reno Guard, as a member, & having one of the finest tenor voices I ever heard, he favored us with several popular ballads, with others to accompany him—After the funeral was over he was at the Hole-In-The-Wall saloon, Capt Avery's, and sang, & the bands also played there.

Rice states in *Monarchs of Minstrelsy,* "In September, 1886, he joined Lew Dockstader's permanent minstrel company in New York; here he remained about three years." *Annals of the New York Stage* also reports that Jose's success in New York began in September of 1886. Dockstader's company performed a comic number titled "Jim the Penman," with Jose playing Ag, a daughter.

But Doten's journal entries suggest that Jose traveled in the summer months. On July 4, 1887, two years after first mentioning Jose, Doten again refers to Jose, calling him "Reno's favorite tenor" and writes, "In response to encores and vociferous calls he sang 'Grandfather's Footsteps' in his clearest, sweetest, most sympathetic voice, and was rapturously applauded."

In his entry of August 5, 1887, Doten writes about Jose performing with a female singer: "Dickie has a peculiarly beautiful tenor and alto voice—a mezzo tenor, as it were. She about 19 or 20 & he a little older." This is a rare reference to Jose singing with a partner. He sang as a solo artist when recording for Victor.

In 1891, while in Virginia City, Doten notes that Jose at that time was with Thatcher's Minstrels. Twelve years lapse before Doten's journals again speak of Jose. In Carson City, Doten gives this entry on August 18, 1903: "Richard J, otherwise Dicky Jose with his star company of minstrels—30 or 40—arrived on morning train from Virginia [City] where they played last evening to crowded house. . . . Dicky Jose told me today that he weighs 247 pounds—About 35 yrs old—" He was actually over forty. Jose was to make his first recordings a few months later.

Jose appeared on New York stages regularly from 1886 onward, being an important addition to Denman Thompson's successful *The Old Homestead* a few years after the play was first presented in 1886. He was engaged with *The Old Homestead* for eight years, afterward joining William H. West's Minstrels. He formed his own minstrel company about 1901 or 1902, according to Rice (Doten confirms this), but soon left minstrel work for vaudeville.

In 1887 Jose won a gold medal in a competition at the Academy of Music on 14th Street in New York City.

According to his wife, Therese, Richard Jose received a special salute from Teddy Roosevelt in 1898 as his Rough Riders, riding down Broadway on the way to Cuba, stopped to hear Jose sing Dresser's "Goodbye, Dolly Gray" from an elevated platform. Wilkinson's book claims Jose's singing to the enthusiastic troops occurred in Tampa, Florida.

He was at this time well known as a singer of ballads. At the turn of the century Jose's photograph was often featured on the covers of sheet music, almost always for sentimental songs, many of them variations of "Silver Threads Among the Gold." For example, the sheet music cover of Thurland Chattaway's 1901 "I've Grown So Used to You" features "R. J. José."

Fagan and Moran's *Encyclopedia Discography of Victor Recordings: Matrix Series* shows that Jose made his first recording on October 27, 1903. The song was "Silver Threads Among the Gold," published in 1873, with music by Hart Pease Danks and lyrics by Eben Eugene Rexford. Wilkinson reports that Victor Talking Machine Company executives hesitated paying $100 for Jose to record a song that was already old.

This appears to be the first recording of "Silver Threads Among the Gold," which is noteworthy since no other song was covered so often in the acoustic recording era. The first Edison version was issued in December of 1905 (9162), sung by soprano Marie Narelle. The December 1905 issue of *Edison Phonograph Monthly* states, "There have been constant requests for this ballad and doubtless our friends have often wondered why it has not been listed before, but to have it by Miss Narelle is well worth waiting for."

The early ten-inch version of the song, Victor 2556, is not to be confused with the better-selling twelve-inch version, Victor 31342. Jose sang Rexford's popular song five times for the company. On December 8, 1904, Jose redid "Silver Threads Among the Gold" and Victor pressed this as a ten-inch record, reusing the number of the version made a year earlier. On December 10, two days later, Jose recorded the twelve-inch version, and though Jose sang additional versions in later years for Victor, apparently none were improvements since they were not issued. The 1904 version stayed in the Victor catalogue for years.

His last recording session was on September 16, 1909, but nothing was issued from this. His last Victor records are from February, 1906.

During a 1907 interview with the *San Francisco Examiner*, Jose was asked about any secret to singing into a horn for recording purposes. "Secret!" exclaimed the countertenor.

> It's the most secret thing in the world—for the singer. You're locked all alone with the band in a big bare room. Your back is to the musicians and your face to a bleak blank wall through which protrudes a solemn horn. A bell rings—one. That is to get ready, for the receiving instrument is so sensitive that if you moved your sleeve against your coat the sound would register. Somebody outside presses the button—two. The band starts the prelude, then you sing, turning neither to the right nor left, always looking and singing into that protruding horn. And you can't even let out a breath after your last note; you must close your lips on it and wait for the little whir within the horn to cease.

It is surprising that Victor issued nothing new from Jose after 1906. While it is true that some Jose selections are extremely rare, which indicates that they sold poorly, several Jose titles continued to sell well for over a decade. It is not known why he stopped making records. It is possible that Jose, who toured heavily, was away from New York City so often that company executives came to rely on others for Jose's type of material. His decline as a stage and recording artist probably stemmed from a serious injury. Jose suffered a blow to the head in 1906 (the date is unknown but it was presumably after the February 1906 Victor session). His convalescence was undoubtedly very long and it is possible that he never fully recovered. According to a 1978 issue of *The Pony Express*, in

1906 a stage curtain fell on Jose with such force that stitches were required in his scalp. Therese Jose recalls that at this time the singer's "black hair turned perfectly white overnight." (In the late 1940s she had reported to Jim Walsh that the accident occurred in 1905 but she later cited 1906.) For whatever reason, studios engaged countertenor Will Oakland, tenor Henry Burr, and others for the type of material Jose had been recording.

In 1905-1906 he headed the Richard J. José Grand Concert Company, making stops in various cities to give concerts in auditoriums, and the accident may have happened during this tour. Surviving concert programs indicate that the music for these concerts was provided by a group of English musicians called The Fuhrer String Quartet, led by Conrad W. Fuhrer.

Wilkinson suggests the accident happened at the end of Jose's third year on the Keith Circuit:

> At the end of the third year while playing with Keefe & Keefe in a New York theatre, a heavy iron bound drop fell from the theatre, and hit his head, laying it open from his brow to the back of his head. Dick Jose battled death for many weeks at the hospital. This accident forced him to cancel a three-year contract to sing in Europe. On recovery his hair, which had been black, turned silver white.

Throughout the 1910s Jose toured with a small company that presented a "pastoral play" titled *Silver Threads Among the Gold.* Rice reports that Jose first produced the play in December 1909. Wilkinson states that Pierce Kingsley was its author. Jose did not leave the theatre until 1919, according to Bess Johns, a niece living in Butte, Montana.

Around 1915, the K & R Film Company, named after owners Pierce Kingsley and R. R. Roberts, made a six-reel film with Jose titled *Silver Threads Among the Gold.* In an unusual gimmick during the age of silent pictures, the singer stood in the wings of theatres that showed the film and sang along to match the motion of lips on the screen. Along with the title song, Jose sang "Every Night a Prayer Is Said" and "Where Is My Wandering Boy?" This was the company's first film and, on June 5, 1915, it was the first to be shown at Madison Square Garden as a motion picture theater. The singer's voice must have been powerful to fill this hall. No copy of the movie is known to exist.

The film's producers issued in 1915 a publication oddly called *The Kanr Journal,* and it included an article titled "The Life Story of Richard J. José." Walsh quotes from it in the April 1950 issue of *Hobbies.* Among other unlikely details, it reports that Jose as a boy soprano "sang before the crowned heads" of England.

Jose was eventually appointed Assistant Enrolling and Engrossing Clerk of the California Legislature. During the 1930s he served as Deputy California Real Estate Commissioner under first Ray L. Riley and then Edwin T. Keiser. He sang occasionally in his retirement years, including appearances on radio's *Shell Hour.* On radio he performed numbers that by this time would have been regarded by listeners as nostalgic tunes. In fact, at the turn of the century Jose was singing many songs of an earlier generation. An irony of Jose's hit "I Cannot Sing the Old Songs," recorded for Victor in 1905, is that many songs were already old by the time he recorded them. He had helped popularize "With All Her Faults I Love Her Still" in 1888, almost twenty years before recording it as Victor 31171.

Jose made electric recordings in San Francisco for the small MacGregor and Ingram Company around 1930. The company made personal records—that is, for a fee it recorded musicians (often nonprofessionals) and pressed small quantities of records for the artists themselves to distribute. The company's name first appears in San Francisco phone books in 1930 and is listed again in 1931. In 1932 the company changed its name to MacGregor & Sollie, which survived until 1937 and was an early and prolific West Coast transcription company. Jose was approaching seventy when he recorded for the last time "Silver Threads Among the Gold" and "When You and I Were Young, Maggie." Curiously, one side of his electric disc is number 449 and the other is 441. A sticker on the back of some copies states, "Obtainable from the exclusive representatives, Schwabacher-Frey, 735 Market St., San Francisco off Grant Ave." Researcher David Banks reports that the Schwabacher & Frey office was in the Russ Building at 235 Montgomery. The 735 Market Street address was the Schwabacher & Frey Stationary Co. (Printers & Bookbinders), and it is likely that Jose autographed copies of his disc at the stationary store.

Jose lived at 795 Sutter Street in San Francisco for decades until his death at age seventy-nine on October 20, 1941. He had no children. He was buried in Olivet Memorial Park, Colma, California.

Kaufman, Irving (February 8, 1890-January 3, 1976)

The tenor Irving Kaufman was probably the most recorded singer between 1914 and 1930, his busiest years being in the late 1920s. He began his career by making records as a featured singer, but in the mid- to late 1920s he also contributed vocal refrains to dance band recordings for many labels. Labels of some band dance records give credit to Irving Kaufman, but pseudonyms were also frequently used. On many labels the simple phrase "vocal chorus" is used, with no name given for the singer.

Kaufman reported years later that the major companies gave permission for him to record for smaller firms as long as pseudonyms were used. In fact, Columbia was the only major company to engage Kaufman in the late 1920s—by this time he no longer made records for Victor—and Columbia itself employed various pseudonyms for the singer. Kaufman rarely knew at the time he attended a session what name would be used on a label afterward. Jim Walsh writes in the November 1962 issue of *Hobbies* that when Kaufman's wife would ask, "Well, who are you going to be today— George Beaver, Frank Harris, or who?" the reply was, "What do you care, as long as the check is made out to Irving Kaufman?" Kaufman said in a 1974 interview published in John and Susan Edwards Harvith's *Edison, Musicians, and the Phonograph* (Greenwood Press, 1987, p. 56), "I had so many different voices that half of the time my wife would say, 'Who are you going to be today?' I would say, 'I won't know until I get to the studio.'"

He was born Isidore Kaufman to Barnett and Lena (Cohn) Kaufman in Syracuse, New York. His father was a Russian immigrant who made a living as a butcher. Irving was the youngest of seven children. His siblings were Jacob ("Jack"), Harry, Charles, Phillip, Ida, and Tillie. Jack and Phillip also made recordings.

Announcing Kaufman as an exclusive Emerson artist, page 44 of the October 1919 issue of *Talking Machine World* gives this background information: "Irving Kaufman . . . started his career as an entertainer when only eight years of age. He was then a boy tenor with the 'Jenny Eddy Trio,' and a few years later was the principal soloist with Merrick's Band of fifty pieces, which accompanied the celebrated Forepaugh and Sells Circus." Irving had little formal education. Before reaching his teen years, he joined the Forepaugh and Sells Brothers Circus and sang during acts as a circus band played. A few years later he sang in movie theaters between silent films being screened. In 1911 in New York City he worked as a song plugger for the sheet music giant Leo. Feist, Inc.

His first record was a Blue Amberol cylinder issued in July 1914, "I Love the Ladies" (2328), composed by Jean Schwartz. The May 1914 issue of *Edison Phonograph Monthly* states:

> This record is the first that Irving Kaufman has made for Edison owners. Mr. Kaufman, born in Syracuse, NY, comes from a very

musical family, being one of the famous "Kaufman Bros.," known in vaudeville throughout the United States and Europe. His clear tenor voice has received much careful training under Professor Samoiloff of Carnegie Hall, New York. His first stage appearance was at the tender age of seven, when with the "Jennie Eddie Trio" he appeared in vaudeville. He was the leading soloist with Merrick's Band for some time, and has filled many other engagements.

Notwithstanding the trade journal's claim that he received "much careful training," Kaufman late in life told researcher Quentin Riggs that he had only two lessons from Samoiloff.

In the 1974 interview published in *Edison, Musicians, and the Phonograph*, Kaufman stated:

> About 1911 I had been making the round of Victor, Columbia, and all the other seventy-five-cent record companies, and I couldn't get my nose into any one of those doors. . . . So finally, as a last resort, I went to the Edison Company at 75 Fifth Avenue . . . and asked them if I couldn't make a test. They said, "We don't need anybody now, but if you want to go ahead, you can go in the other room and have somebody play for you. Let's see what you can do." (p. 54)

Days later an executive phoned Kaufman to announce that Thomas Edison himself was impressed by the test record, Edison reportedly saying, "You'd better sign that boy up; he's got a good voice."

Perhaps beginning in 1913, Kaufman was a member of the Avon Comedy Four, a vaudeville act that was most popular around the World War I era. The ensemble, which consisted of Kaufman, Harry Goodwin, Charlie Dale, and Joe Smith, sang and performed comic skits for Victor, Columbia, and Emerson. Victor catalogs claimed that the group "is well known in every city where there is a Keith's Theatre." (Benjamin Franklin Keith was creator of the vaudeville circuit, opening a number of theaters for vaudeville artists beginning in the 1880s, and though he died in 1914, B. F. Keith theaters thrived for years afterward, with the B. F. Keith office booking vaudeville acts regularly into hundreds of theaters by the 1920s.)

Kaufman's earliest Victor record was "They Don't Hesitate Any More" (17561), cut in early 1914. Other Victor titles from 1914 include "Hands Off" (17589), "Fatherland the Motherland" (17636), and Irving Berlin's "Always Treat Her Like a Baby" (17636). He continued making Victor discs for several years, his last being "You're Just the Type for a Bungalow" and "Don't Throw Me Down" (18811), issued in December 1921. Some remained available in the Victor catalog after the singer ceased making discs for the company, with "California and You" (17613) lasting longer than others, available from 1914 to 1925.

During the World War I era he recorded for various small companies. He sings "My Fox Trot Wedding Day" on Fraad 5280, a rare Rex product of 1916 (he also cut this for Victor 17923). He sings "On the Beach at Waikiki" on Rex 5484, issued in 1917. In early 1919 the tenor recorded several titles for the Indestructible Phonographic Record Company. Cylinders include "K-K-K-Katy" (3441), "Mickey" (3448), "Chong" (3453), and "Alcoholic Blues" (3461).

His first Columbia record, "The Greatest Battle Song of All" (A2040), was issued in September 1916, and within the year several Columbia discs featuring Kaufman titles were available. The company issued in September 1919 a disc of Kaufman singing "Take Your Girlie to the Movies" (A2756), the reserve side featuring Arthur Fields singing "Pig Latin Love." Kaufman and Fields were similar in being incredibly prolific in studios during their long careers, recording for virtually all the same labels in roughly the same years (both started recording in 1914), each one adding vocal choruses in the 1920s to countless dance band recordings. On other Columbia discs, Fields is on one side, Kaufman on the other, such as Fields' "Jim, Jim, I Always Knew That You'd Win" coupled with a Kaufman performance of a song with one of the longest titles from the period: "You'll Have to Put Him to Sleep with the Marseillaise and Wake Him With an Oo-La-La" (A2679).

The trio of Irving Kaufman, Arthur Fields, and Jack Kaufman recorded around this time as Three Kaufields. Among other songs, they recorded a 1919 composition by Jim Europe, Noble Sissle, and Eubie Blake titled "Good Night, Angeline" (Emerson 10166). The trio also performed on stage. Page 152 of the May 1919 issue of *Talking Machine World* introduces the group as the Kaufield Trio (records call the group the Three Kaufields) and explains how the trio was formed:

Their advent as a trio was somewhat of an accident. The three singers were in the recording room of the Emerson Co., while Harry Marker, chief recorder of the company, was waiting to make test records of some new singers. When he asked if the singers were ready, Mr. Field [sic] answered yes, and as a practical joke the three popular artists advanced to the horn without preparation, a song was decided upon on the spur of the moment and the test was recorded. When Mr. Marker saw what was taking place he continued the recording, put the wax master through as a test, and the result was so surprising and startling that the Emerson Co. immediately engaged the trio to sing a series of songs.

Irving Kaufman left the Avon Comedy Four and soon afterward worked in the Lee and J. J. Shubert production of *The Passing Show of 1918*, replacing original cast member Charles Ruggles. He left that show when his brother Phillip died, a victim of the flu epidemic. The death left Jack Kaufman without a partner (Phillip and Jack had recorded as the Kaufman Brothers), so Irving teamed up with Jack in 1919. Together, they made Emerson records into the early 1920s. Page 151 of the September 1923 issue of *Talking Machine World* shows the two men together in a full-page Emerson advertisement. The partnership dissolved in late 1923, though they reunited briefly in 1927. Irving was in the Winter Garden production of *The Passing Show of 1919*.

Jack Kaufman, Irving Kaufman, and Arthur Fields signed a contract with Emerson on September 18, 1919, to record "exclusively for the Emerson record library for a period of three years," according to page 44 of the October 1919 issue of *Talking Machine World*. A photograph shows the three men signing contracts in the office of Arthur Bergh, Emerson's recording manager (he would later direct Okeh's recording laboratories, beginning in September 1923, and then Columbia's, beginning on November 15, 1925). An accompanying article states, "Irving, together with his brother Jack, has been engaged to appear in leading roles in the forthcoming 'Ziegfeld Follies of 1920.'" Although he purportedly signed to record only for Emerson for three years, Kaufman was exclusive to that company for around two years. It is possible that he was a freelance artist before three years had passed because Emerson, like Columbia, suffered severe financial problems by late 1921.

Through the leasing of masters, some Emerson performances—solo numbers as well as duets with brother Jack—were issued on other minor labels, perhaps beginning with Banner 1004 ("Ain't Nobody's Darling"— Arthur Fields is on the reverse side), which was among the first batch of Banner discs issued in late 1920. The pseudonym "Billy Clarke" is used on some Banner and perhaps all Regal releases featuring Kaufman in 1922 and 1923 (Regal was Emerson's budget label, introduced in 1921, and the spelling is "Billy Clark" instead of "Clarke" on at least two Regal discs— Jack Kaufman often was issued as "Bert Green"). It was the first of many pseudonyms to be used on the tenor's records, with perhaps no others used until 1925. He was featured on many releases during Banner's first two years, then for two years beginning in late 1923 was on no Banner releases, and in 1926 again became important to the label as well as to the related Domino label.

His status as an exclusive Emerson artist evidently ended by the summer of 1921 since at that time he cut new titles for Columbia. "What I Want to Do Doodle Do for You," cut on July 19, was not issued but "Ten

Little Fingers and Ten Little Toes" was released on A3477 in December. He contributed a vocal refrain to a Hackel-Bergé Orchestra performance of "Yoo-Hoo" cut on August 31, 1921, which was issued on Victor 18802 in November. As a featured solo artist, Kaufman recorded two titles for Victor in 1921—"Don't Throw Me" and "You're Just the Type" (18811)—and curiously never made another Victor disc. By late 1921 he was also working for Arto, Clarion, Aeolian, Gennett, and others.

At this time he worked steadily in vaudeville, notably on the Keith Circuit. Page 146 of the January 1921 issue of *Talking Machine World* states, "Irving and Jack Kaufman are being headlined in the Keith circuit and have been honored by being brought back to New York territory eight times within the last three months." Emerson's February 1921 list of records states, "It certainly is significant when an act is 'headlined' and brought back to the Big City several times during a season, as is the case with the Kaufman act on the Keith circuit."

The brothers also did promotional work for Emerson. Page 26 of the May 1923 issue of *Talking Machine World* reports:

A clever tie-up was made recently by the talking machine department of Frederick Loeser & Co, big Brooklyn, NY, department store, when Irving and Jack Kaufman, popular Emerson artists, appeared at the store and sang a number of songs which they have recorded for the Emerson. On the platform with the artists was placed an Emerson phonograph and when the artists had completed a song a record of the same number was played on the instrument.

Though no longer exclusive to Emerson, which was reorganized after going into receivership in 1922, Irving and Jack Kaufman continued to be important Emerson artists through 1923. Page 151 of the September 1923 issue of *Talking Machine World* shows the two brothers standing side by side in a full-page advertisement that hails Emerson's product for being the "ONLY RECORD on the market today which is being sold universally at FIFTY CENTS retail." But Irving's association with this label soon ended. Page 159 of the October 1923 issue of *Talking Machine World* reports that on October 1, Kaufman signed to record exclusively for the Aeolian Company, maker of Vocalion discs, often called "Vocalion Red records" by the trade journal. He had made Vocalion discs as early as 1921, when he stopped being exclusive to Emerson, and he continued to make Vocalion records after the Brunswick-Balke-Collender Company bought the record division of the Aeolian Company in late 1924. Vocalion discs were Brunswick products beginning in early 1925.

In late 1925 he again recorded for various companies. Page 161 of the January 1926 issue of *Talking Machine World* states, "The Plaza Music Co., manufacturer of Banner and Domino records, announces that Irving Kaufman, well-known record artist, will in the future contribute monthly releases to these catalogs." The first Kaufman releases to follow this announcement were "Too Many Parties and Too Many Pals" on Banner 1668/Domino 3641 and "I Wish That I'd Been Satisfied with Mary" on Banner 1669/Domino 3637, all issued in February 1926. In the late 1920s the names "George Beaver" and "Frank Hollis" were used for him on some Banner labels though on many Banner releases the name Kaufman is used.

He worked steadily for Columbia from late 1925 to late 1930, even serving as master of ceremonies when Columbia's annual luncheon and dance for employees was held in late November 1926 at the Hotel McAlpin (musical entertainment was provided by the Happiness Boys, the team of Jack Kaufman and Al Campbell, Frank Banta, Nathan Glantz, Johnny Marvin, and others). In the autumn of 1926 Columbia acquired the Okeh record division of the General Phonograph Corporation, and thereafter Kaufman was often on Okeh releases, sometimes as "George Beaver." Page 86 of the December 1927 issue of *Phonograph Monthly Review* includes a photograph of Kaufman standing before a microphone with sheet music in hand. He is surrounded by Okeh executives, including engineer Charles L. Hibbard, recording manager Tom Rockwell, and music supervisor Justin Ring.

Victor and Edison had never used pseudonyms for Kaufman. He worked for these two companies in his early career only, and pseudonyms became common for Kaufman later, especially from 1925 to 1930. The pseudonyms were always less Jewish-sounding than his own name. From the mid- to late 1920s Kaufman was issued under such names as Noel Taylor (Okeh), Charles Dickson (Oriole), Charles Vaughn (Broadway), and Pete Killeen (Pathé, Perfect). Grey Gull and other labels issued Kaufman under some "house" pseudonyms—for example, the names "Vel Veteran" and "Mr. X" were used for not only Kaufman but other singers.

The name Irving Kaufman was frequently used for the Harmony label when he performed as a featured singer. The pseudonym "Confidential Charlie" was used on this budget label when Kaufman performed in the style of Whispering Jack Smith and other crooners. He was not Columbia's "Whispering Billy Day," as some writers have speculated. Page 129 of the May 1927 issue of *Talking Machine World* features a photograph of radio artist Day and identifies the new Columbia artist as "a headline entertainer at such metropolitan night clubs as the Castillian Gardens, the Avalon Club, and The Fifth Avenue Caravan Club, and appeared in the first Fox Movitone [sic] picture."

Columbia file cards establish that other names used for Kaufman as a featured singer on Harmony include Jack Wilson and, for a total of three discs (six selections) featuring hillbilly material, Ned Cobben. Names used for him as a dance band vocalist on Harmony and related budget labels by 1927 include Tom Frawley, Marvin Young, Robert Wood, Jimmy Flynn, Arthur Seelig, Jim Andrews, and Harry Brady.

From 1926 onward, on Columbia's regular line of popular records (as opposed to any budget series), he was mostly identified as "Frank Harris" when performing as a featured singer, beginning with "Five Foot Two, Eyes of Blue" on 526-D, his first Columbia disc in three years. On one disc issued in January 1927 (780-D), he was "Allan Jordan," and on another issued in late 1928 he was "Tom Edwards" (1354-D). He was "Harris" when he sang with Vaughn De Leath for a few sessions from 1926 to 1928, which are rare instances of Kaufman working with a female singer.

When contributing vocals to dance band performances issued in the full-price line of popular records, he was sometimes "Frank Harris," but other times, beginning with discs released in 1927, "Vincent Van Tuyl." Despite his many sessions, only a few times was Kaufman's name on a Columbia label of this period. One example from 1927 is "Roam On, My Little Gypsy Sweetheart" (1088-D), with Kaufman providing a vocal refrain on a Knickerbockers performance. Columbia undoubtedly attempted to disguise his identity with this new name because some record buyers would have hesitated to pay full price for records credited to a singer whose name was found often on cheap records.

He helped popularize many songs of the 1920s, but the record-buying public never associated him with hit numbers the way Wendell Hall was associated with "It Ain't Gonna Rain No Mo'" and Vernon Dalhart with "The Prisoner's Song." When Kaufman records sold well, it was more because record buyers wanted particular songs than because Kaufman was featured. To identify his best-selling record would be difficult.

As a featured singer on records (as opposed to a contributor of vocal refrains for dance bands), Kaufman in the 1920s could be characterized as a singer with a talent for covering songs that others had popularized. For example, soon after Vernon Dalhart had a hit in 1925 with "The Prisoner's Song," Kaufman covered it for Harmony, Columbia's budget label (Dalhart himself cut it for Columbia's regular 75-cent label).

Likewise, Al Jolson enjoyed great success with "Sonny Boy" on the Brunswick label, but since Jolson was exclusive to Brunswick, Columbia turned to Kaufman to cover the hit. Kaufman, a good Jolson imitator, sings it on the Harmony label at least twice, once as a featured singer with credit given to Irving Kaufman, and again as a vocalist for Ernie Golden and His

Orchestra (the pseudonym "Arthur Seelig" is used). "There's a Rainbow 'Round My Shoulder" was another song cut by Kaufman for the Harmony label—as a featured artist on 771-H, also as a dance band vocalist on 749-H—after Jolson popularized it in the film *The Singing Fool* as well as on Brunswick 4033. On Domino 4392 and other records he sings two numbers from Jolson's 1929 film *Say It with Songs*: "Little Pal" and "Why Can't You?" He covered many other songs popularized by Jolson.

It is clear from the sheer number of his sessions that recording directors viewed him as dependable and professional. They relied heavily on Kaufman because on dance band numbers he delivered, with a minimum of rehearsal or preparation, vocal choruses that were considered strong by the standards of that time. From 1922 to 1926 he was only occasionally used as a vocalist on dance records, mostly for Vocalion (he was exclusive to the company for a few years), usually for Ben Selvin ensembles. For vocal refrains, other studios in the mid-1920s turned regularly to such singers as Billy Murray, Vernon Dalhart, Ernest Hare, Billy Jones, and Arthur Hall (in 1925 Hall may have been the busiest of all singers who contributed refrains to dance band records). But when Kaufman was again a freelance artist, he worked more often in studios providing choruses for dance band records than any other singer, with Arthur Fields a close second. His three busiest years in studios were 1926 through 1928.

He could perform in the studio immediately after being handed a copy of a song that was new to him. This was despite a minimum of formal musical training. In his 1974 interview he speaks of only two lessons at Carnegie Hall with Russian vocal teacher Lazar S. Samoiloff, and he told Quentin Riggs the same. The cylinder slip for Kaufman's first Edison cylinder, "I Love the Ladies," may exaggerate his training in saying that Kaufman "received much careful training under Professor Samoiloff of Carnegie Hall, New York." The jacket for Diamond Disc 50524, "Don't Cry, Little Girl, Don't Cry," states, "Irving Kaufman possesses a beautiful, rich tenor voice which has received much careful training."

About song preparation, Kaufman stated in the interview, "I knew nothing about what I was going to sing until I got to the studio. Then they'd hand me a copy of the song and say, 'This is what you're singing.'" He was paid a flat fee each time he recorded, never royalties.

He sang on some discs of the late 1920s that interest jazz enthusiasts today because of instrumentalists used on sessions, including Bix Beiderbecke. Kaufman provided vocals on "There Ain't No Land Like Dixieland to Me" and "There's a Cradle in Caroline," which were coupled on Harmony 504-H, and "Just an Hour of Love" and "I'm Wonderin' Who," coupled on Okeh 40912. Beiderbecke played cornet on these numbers recorded on September 29 and 30, 1927. Saxophonist Frank Trumbauer was present at the sessions. Kaufman on March 3, 1928, again provided vocals for sides that today interest Beiderbecke fans: "Oh Gee! Oh Joy!" (Harmony 611-H) and "Why Do I Love You?" (Harmony 607-H). He provided vocals for orchestras led by Ben Selvin (these include the Knickerbockers, the Kensington Serenaders, and the Harmonians), Sam Lanin (this includes the popular Bailey's Lucky Seven), Lou Gold, Adrian Schubert, Fred Rich, Don Voorhees, Jerome Conrad, Ben Bernie, Ted Bartell, and Joe Candullo.

His voice was well-suited for the acoustic recording process, his words clear to listeners. With the introduction of the microphone to the recording process, a new crooning style of singing became popular, and Kaufman adjusted his voice accordingly. Working as "Frank Harris" for Columbia's regular popular series soon after the company adopted the new Western Electric recording system, he often sang softly into the microphone, this voice being very different from the one he projected for acoustically cut records. Examples of Kaufman holding back on dance records can be found on the Columbians' "Buy, Buy for Baby" (Columbia 1661-D; 1928) and The Travelers' "Am I Blue?" (Okeh 41259; 1929). But he was important to studios that converted late to the electric process, singing into the acoustic horn into the late 1920s for Columbia's budget releases (Harmony, Velvet Tone, Diva) and other budget labels.

Not many Kaufman performances were issued on the Brunswick label (he was often on the company's Vocalion label, acquired by Brunswick in late 1925), but Brunswick 4508—issued on December 12, 1929—is notable because the two numbers conducted by Louis Katzman and sung by Kaufman have Jewish themes: "My People" is backed by "Say a Prayer for Palestine."

In 1930, he was in a motion picture short, *The Inquiring Reporter*, that showcases his mastery of various dialects.

He continued to work for various companies through 1930, with sessions for Columbia discs (especially budget releases) being most frequent. Then sessions for commercial records essentially ended. An August 22, 1930, session with bandleader Ben Selvin, who had been using Kaufman regularly for years, may been have his last for Selvin. A session on December 12, 1930, may have been his last with bandleader Lou Gold. A session on December 19, 1930, appears to be his last with Sam Lanin.

With record companies hit hard by the Depression, he instead worked regularly in nightclubs and then on radio, a medium that made full use of his talent for changing voices and imitating dialects.

During the mid-1940s Kaufman recorded numbers to be broadcast on *Music Hall Varieties*, a radio show with a "Gay Nineties" theme. Several dozen songs were pressed for the NBC-produced Thesaurus Orthacoustic, a radio transcription label, and the transcription discs were sold to stations (other artists included Joe E. Howard, Beatrice Kay, and Aileen Stanley). Identified as a baritone, he is accompanied by the Music Hall Varieties Orchestra, which used original arrangements. The songs were popular ones of the 1900 to 1920 period, few of which had been recorded by the young Kaufman. Titles include "Alexander's Ragtime Band" (recorded on July 3, 1946 and pressed on Record 1362), "Bedelia," "Under the Bamboo Tree," "My Wife's Gone to the Country," and "Oh, You Beautiful Doll." He was in top vocal form and the best available recording technology was used. Kaufman himself told Quentin Riggs that he would be happy if future generations judged him by these Thesaurus recordings, which are unfortunately rare.

Promotional literature for the radio show states, "Kaufman is well-remembered for a five year coast-to-coast network stint as 'Lazy Dan, The Minstrel Man' and his many characterizations on top network and local programs. He is a master dialectician specializing in Irish, Jewish, Scotch, Negro, Italian and Chinese."

After World War II, many small record companies sprang up, and he made the occasional 78 rpm recording as late as 1947, the last being "The Curse of an Aching Heart" coupled with "Think It Over Mary" (originally issued on the Sterling label; also issued on the Bennett label). Around this time he also recorded for Sterling some Yiddish comedy songs, including "Moe the Schmo Makes Love" and "Moe the Schmo Takes a Rhumba Lesson."

On radio, he was sometimes accompanied by his wife Belle Brooks, an accomplished organist and pianist. In fact, she worked as a pianist for Edward B. Marks' music publishing company when they met in 1928. They married in 1929 and had a daughter, Carole. From a previous marriage to Sarah Lazarus, whom he married in 1915 and who died in 1927, he had two children: Eleanor and Lawrence.

He performed in Broadway stage productions, including Kurt Weill's *Street Scene* in 1947 (it was a speaking role), and in nightclubs until a heart attack in 1949 put an end to such professional engagements. He moved to Florida, and later to California. On August 20 and 21, 1974, he recorded in his California home eight songs for a two-album set that also reissued some of his old recordings, which means that Kaufman's recording career spanned six decades, from 1914 to 1974. Titled *Reminisce with Irving Kaufman*, the LP was only briefly available. He lived at 49-305 on Highway 74 in Palm Desert.

He died in Indio, California, a month before his eighty-sixth birthday.

Kline, Olive *(July 7, 1887-July 29, 1976)*

This concert soprano recorded often as a solo artist, Lyric Quartet member, and Victor Light Opera Company member. She also sang in duos and trios. She made records exclusively for the Victor Talking Machine Company, beginning in 1912 and ending in 1935. In contrast to many singers invited to make records after they had already established themselves as concert artists, she used a successful recording career as a springboard for a successful concert career. She sang opera arias in concert but did not sing in operatic productions.

Her concert engagements were often reviewed in *Musical America* and *Musical Leader* from the mid-1910s onward, one review stating:

> Since her debut in 1914, when she sang a "Traviata" aria and "Vissi d'Arte" on the same program with Titta Ruffo in Detroit, this Schenectady girl has found her place with the foremost concert artists of the day . . . Following Lucy Marsh at the Madison Avenue Reformed Church, then succeeding Anna Case at the Church of the Pilgrims in Brooklyn, Miss Kline was recently re-engaged at the Collegiate Church, where her immediate predecessor was Florence Hinkle.

Victor's 1922 catalog states, "Until a year or so ago she was a member of one of the highest-salaried quartets in the history of American church music, at the West End Collegiate Church in New York. Declining an offer to appear in opera, she nevertheless gave up this position to devote her entire time to concert work and the making of Victor records."

She was born in Amsterdam, New York. Though sources give different dates, her birth certificate establishes that she was born on July 7, 1887. When she was around ten, her family (she had two brothers) moved to Schenectady, where her father worked as a General Electric employee. She began high school in Schenectady and then went to St. Agnes Girls' School in Albany, New York. Kline's father played piano and encouraged his daughter to pursue a concert career as a pianist, but finally her vocal talents became evident. Her first vocal teacher was Herbert Wilbur Greene, and she paid tribute to this teacher by adopting the nom de disque Alice Green for some recordings ("Alice," close to "Olive," was a natural choice). She was later instructed by Herbert Witherspoon.

Established as a soloist in prominent churches, she began recording as a solo artist in mid-1912 (she may have participated anonymously in ensemble recordings before this). In a February 16, 1976, interview with Merritt F. Malvern (the interview was recorded but never transcribed or made public), she recalled how Harry Macdonough, a member of the church quartet in which Kline was a substitute singer, invited her to make records: "A tenor was . . . the manager of the Victor office in New York, and during the sermon he wrote me a little note that said, 'How would you like to come down on Tuesday and make a test record for the Victor company?' Well, of course, I almost fell off my chair, I was so excited."

The first Olive Kline record featured "Spring" (Victor 17135), issued in September 1912. For the next few years she was issued on black label Victors and, beginning in 1917, on blue also. Her name is not on purple label Victors, which means that in the hierarchy of Victor singers in the early 1910s, she was not at the beginning of her Victor tenure placed as highly as fellow soprano Lucy Isabelle Marsh, which is also reflected by much of the material she was given to sing. After 1926 Kline was on some Red Seal Victors (as "Olive Kline") as well as on some black label discs (as "Alice Green").

She was a versatile artist, recording hits from musical shows ("Chu Chin Chow" from the show of that name), hymns ("Jesus, My Saviour," sung with Elsie Baker), lullabies ("Ma' Little Sun Flow'r—Good-night!"), art songs (Gounod's "Serenade"), ditties for children (six short selections were often offered on ten-inch discs in this series), and opera arias ("The Shadow Song" from *Dinorah*—she sang this at concerts). She recorded with tenor Harry Macdonough the famous "Miserere" from Verdi's *Il Trovatore*, a remake of a Harry Macdonough-Elise Stevenson version that had been popular years earlier. It was translated to English, so the title is given as "Ah! I Have Sigh'd to Rest Me" (35443). But she also recorded, in Italian, selections from *Madama Butterfly* and other operas.

The name on her early black label Victor discs, including those of light opera numbers, such as the 1913 "Say Not Love Is a Dream" from Lehár's *Count of Luxembourg* (35266), is Olive Kline. The same name is on all of her blue label Victors, beginning with "Lo, Here the Gentle Lark" and "Ma Curly-Headed Babby [sic]," issued on Victor 45115 in June 1917. Starting in late 1915, for songs of a decidedly popular nature, beginning with the duet "They Didn't Believe Me" (credited to "Alice Green—Harry Macdonough," Victor 35491), she was issued on some black labels as Alice Green. In 1916, which was probably her busiest year as a recording artist, and continuing to June 1917, she was sometimes issued as Olive Kline on black label Victors (such as in the trio of Kline, Wheeler, and Dunlap) but more often as Alice Green (even for solos from Handel oratorios issued on Victor 35623 in May 1917).

Upon being elevated to blue label status in June 1917, the soprano was no longer issued on new black label discs as Olive Kline, with the exception of "Whispering Hope" backed by "Abide with Me" on electrically recorded Victor 19873, a remake of an earlier record. Into the 1920s she continued to be issued as Olive Kline on blue label discs and as Alice Green on black label discs.

Among the many Green discs are "Hello Frisco!" (with Reinald Werrenrath, billed as "Alice Green—Edward Hamilton," 17837), "Rackety Coo!" from the musical comedy *Katinka* (17954), "Here Comes Tootsi" from *Around the Map* (17974), and "The Land Where the Good Songs Go" (credited to "Alice Green—Charles Harrison," 18410). Examples of duets recorded in the 1920s and issued under the name Alice Green on black label Victor discs are the 1923 "Honeymoon Time" (with Lewis James), the 1923 "Underneath the Mellow Moon" (with Elsie Baker using the nom de disque Edna Brown), and the 1925 "Listen to the Mocking Bird" (with Lambert Murphy singing as Raymond Dixon). Only sometimes were duet partners of "Alice Green" also assigned pseudonyms.

She recalled during her retirement years that when issued as Alice Green she was paid no royalty, whereas she received royalties for discs issued under the name Olive Kline. A big seller in 1920 was blue label Victor 45201, featuring the Egan-Whiting composition "The Japanese Sandman" backed by Cole Porter's "An Old-Fashioned Garden" from the show *Hitchy-Koo*. She recalled receiving more in royalties for that disc than for any other.

Regular recording partners were contralto Elsie Baker, tenor Harry Macdonough, and tenor Lambert Murphy. Kline and Baker's version of "Marcheta" (Victor 45309), recorded on April 4, 1922, was popular. The acoustic version of "Whispering Hope," recorded with Baker (Victor 17782), was so popular, despite competition from a Red Seal version recorded by Alma Gluck and Louise Homer, that it was rerecorded on September 22, 1927 (Victor 19873), again backed by "Abide with Me." This electric version remained in the RCA Victor catalog into the 1940s.

Into the electric recording era she sang a wide range of material. Though no credit is given on the label of Victor 6693, on April 7, 1927, she assisted bass Feodor Chaliapin in the Death Scene from Jules Massenet's opera *Don Quichotte*. Again uncredited on a label, she is featured on Paul Whiteman's "Selections From Show Boat" (Victor 35912), made on March 1, 1928. Her brief contribution as solo vocalist of "Why Do I Love You?" is followed by trumpet solos from first Henry Busse and then Bix Beiderbecke. Later on the record she briefly sings "Make Believe" with tenor Lambert Murphy.

She made few recordings after 1928. Perhaps her last recording as a member of the Victor Light Opera Company was made on June 28, 1929, when she sang in a medley from the show *Follow Through*. In the 1930s she made a few black label records for Victor's Educational Catalog. She sang on radio in the 1920s and 1930s.

She was known as "Ollie" to friends. She married Dr. John Walter Hulihan in 1919, moved at that time to Pelham, New York, and resided there until her death. Page 13 of the July 30, 1976, edition of *The New York Times* briefly notes her death, identifying her as a "soprano who recorded for Victor Records as Olive Kline" and giving her age as eighty-nine.

Lanin, Sam (September 4, 1891-May 5, 1977)

Few dance band directors presided over as many recording sessions in the 1920s as Sam Lanin, who never actually played an instrument during sessions, aside from drums during some of his early ones. Sometimes his name was cited on record labels—Sam Lanin's Dance Orchestra, Lanin's Famous Players, Lanin's Red Heads, Lanin's Arcadians—but dozens of non-Lanin names were also used for studio groups he assembled. Occasionally his name was used for recording ensembles that he did not personally supervise.

He was important to the record industry not for specific titles—no one Lanin record was a huge hit—but for the sheer quantity of records made under his supervision. He may be best remembered today for the superb musicians who at some point worked under him, including Miff Mole, Tommy Dorsey, Jimmy Dorsey, Manny Klein, Jack Teagarden, Jimmy McPartland, Bix Beiderbecke, Benny Goodman, Eddie Lang, and Bunny Berigan. Nick Lucas played banjo and guitar during some Lanin sessions before Lucas became a Brunswick artist in late 1924. Lanin gave much session work to a young Red Nichols beginning in 1923 and helped Nichols in 1925 with the formation of the Red Heads, renamed the Five Pennies in 1926.

In the 1920s, it was common practice for bandleaders such as Lanin when coordinating sessions to send telegrams to musicians a day before a scheduled session, instructing each to be at a certain studio at a certain time. Musicians for these pickup groups showed up without knowing what new popular songs would be scheduled for recording at that session. Lanin was paid by a record company for sessions, and he in turn paid the musicians.

Many of the musicians hired by Lanin were also used during sessions supervised by Ben Selvin, Nathan Glantz, Adrian Schubert, and Lou Gold.

Most of his sessions produced dance records featuring popular songs of the day that were given tasteful yet conservative arrangements. He was not an innovator but instead helped popularize musical trends begun by others. Some Lanin sessions featuring small ensembles produced good jazz records, though none are of extraordinary interest to the jazz historian.

He was born into a Jewish family headed by Benjamin and Mary Lanin. Sources differ on whether he was born before or after the parents emigrated from Russia to the United States. He was raised in Philadelphia. Younger brothers Jimmy, Howard, and Lester also became dance band directors. Born on July 15, 1897, Howard led dance orchestras in Philadelphia and made recordings beginning in 1923. He died in that city on April 26, 1991. As a society bandleader, Lester enjoyed his greatest success in the 1950s.

When a child, Sam studied violin and later took up clarinet. By 1912 he played clarinet in Victor Herbert's Orchestra (one source states that he was a timpanist). He joined the Navy in World War I but remained in the States, serving the military as a skilled musician. Sam led a dance band in Philadelphia upon his return from military duty and by the end of 1918 played in New York City's new Roseland Ballroom on Times Square at Broadway and 51st Street. Roseland was opposite Madison Square Garden (it was moved decades later to 52nd Street) and was the nation's most prestigious dance hall during the years that Lanin's dance orchestra (along with various other dance bands) was featured.

His first issued record, featuring two numbers cut for the Columbia Graphophone Company on April 28, 1920, was credited to Lanin's Roseland Orchestra. That he made his recording debut with a major record company is noteworthy since most of his sessions in subsequent years produced records issued by minor as well as budget labels, important exceptions including Ipana Troubadours sessions for Columbia from the mid-1920s to early 1930s. Soon after cutting titles for Columbia he recorded for Okeh and by late 1920 made Emerson records. At some point in the 1920s he worked for possibly every American record company, though the name Sam Lanin was never on Brunswick or Victor discs. In 1925 Victor issued a few Howard Lanin and His Benjamin Franklin Hotel Orchestra records, but logs indicate that Sam Lanin was the director.

By mid-1921 he began an association with the Starr Piano Company, often leading a dance ensemble called Lanin's Famous Players on the company's Gennett label. At least for some sessions he may have provided direction for a smaller group of skilled jazz musicians identified as

Bailey's Lucky Seven on some Gennett records, Ladd's Black Aces on others. (The names are misleading since there was no "Bailey" and the groups recording under this name did not always have seven musicians. No black musicians were in Ladd's Black Aces.) Lanin's Southern Serenaders was another name for a small group that played jazz. The personnel of Lanin groups constantly changed, though trumpeter Phil Napoleon (his real name was Filippo Napoli) was present at most sessions. Other regulars in the early 1920s were Miff Mole and Jules Levy Jr.

He contributed a vocal refrain when Ladd's Black Aces cut "Shake It and Break It" in August 1921 for Gennett. This was uncharacteristic of Lanin, though when Lanin's Southern Serenaders, consisting of the same musicians, cut the song around this time for Emerson, he sang a refrain for this also.

His dance band had its final Roseland engagement in May 1925, a month after his new Ipana Troubadours made its radio debut. His Roseland orchestra had played on WHN radio as early as 1923, so Lanin was one of the first "name" bandleaders to broadcast, and after leaving Roseland he worked steadily on network programs. Sponsored by the Bristol-Myers Company, which made Ipana toothpaste, he led the Ipana Troubadours, popular on radio each Wednesday evening and on Columbia's full-priced series of popular records. The names Broadway Bell-Hops, the Westerners, Sam Lanin and His Orchestra, and others were used for Columbia's budget labels.

The orchestra was first heard on April 8, 1925, on stations WEAF and WOO, and the first Ipana Troubadours recording session was on October 30. Photographs establish that orchestra members wore distinctive uniforms, but of course radio audiences could not see the clothing. Direct advertising was not allowed on WEAF at this time, but borrowing the sponsor's name for the orchestra's name was an effective form of indirect advertising.

Lanin's name is prominent on Ipana Troubadours discs: "S. C. Lanin—Director." A Columbia session on December 28, 1928 is notable because a young Bing Crosby, who at that time was under contract to Paul Whiteman, contributed vocal refrains for "I'll Get By As Long As I Have You" and "Rose of Mandalay" (Columbia 1694-D). It was a case of a good singer being on loan from one Columbia bandleader to another. A month later, on January 25, 1929, Crosby had a session with Lanin and His Famous Players. Joe Tarto decades later told researcher Stan Hester that he had been the arranger for Crosby's sessions with Lanin. Other Lanin arrangers included Einar Swan, Frank Ludlow, and Franz Jackson.

The Ipana Troubadours had their last radio broadcast in January 1931, according to the January 14, 1931, edition of *Variety*, but Lanin continued to use the name for several more months for concerts and Columbia recording sessions. He led ensembles for other record companies, even making Hit of the Week discs for the Durium Products Corporation, using the name Sam Lanin's Dance Ensemble. In July 1931 Lanin began leading his Pillsbury Orchestra for the *Pillsbury Pageant* radio program each Friday night over New York City's WABC. Of course, the music industry around this time suffered terribly from the Depression. Recording sessions became infrequent for musicians and many radio shows, even popular ones, were abruptly ended because sponsors cut expenditures.

After the Pillsbury radio show was cancelled in March 1932, Lanin found other radio work and made many transcriptions on the Associated label until 1937. He retired early, having built up considerable wealth from years of hard work. He died in Hollywood, Florida in 1977. His wife was named Sadye.

Macdonough, Harry (March 30, 1871-September 26, 1931)

Of Scottish descent, Harry Macdonough was born in Hamilton, Ontario, Canada, as John Scantlebury Macdonald. During the two decades he was active as a recording artist, the tenor was perhaps the most popular ballad singer to make records aside from Henry Burr, also a tenor from Canada. Determining who made more records before 1920 would be a challenge since both Macdonough and Burr worked regularly as solo artists and also within duos, trios, quartets, and larger ensembles.

He first made cylinders for the Michigan Electric Company in Detroit. In a letter written to Jim Walsh dated February 9, 1931, he states that these cylinders "were not sold but merely used in their 'Phonograph Parlor' on the slot machines in use at that time." The June 1920 issue of *Talking Machine World* states he "spent his early business life in Detroit."

John Kaiser, who recorded "Casey" monologues and later served as a U.S. Phonograph Company executive, helped Macdonald enter the record business on the East Coast. After Macdonald made a test record in October 1898 at the New York studio of Harms, Kaiser & Hagen, Kaiser himself played the test record for Walter H. Miller, then Edison's recording manager. As a result, Macdonald began making commercial recordings at the Edison laboratories in West Orange, New Jersey, on October 17, 1898. His first Edison recordings included "The Lost Chord" (6504), "Good-Bye, Sweet Dream, Good-Bye" (6500), and "Mary Quite Contrary" (6510). Macdonough wrote to Walsh:

> At my first session I made twelve selections, for which I received $9.00. The regular rate was at that time $1.00 per song but being a beginner I was supposed to be satisfied with anything they chose to pay me and, as a matter of fact, I was. That $9.00 seemed pretty big pay for the afternoon and I had no complaint. However, shortly after that they paid me the regular rate of $1.00 per "round" as it was described in those days. Each morning or afternoon session consisted of 30 "rounds," consisting of five or six songs selected from the repertoire on the list in proportion to their selling qualities; sometimes it would be "The Holy City" ten times; "Mid the Green Fields of Virginia" five times, with the other fifteen divided up among the songs of which they needed additional masters. At that time they made five masters at each performance of a song and from each master they could make from twenty-five to seventy-five duplicates before the master wore out. When the masters were worn out they had to have more made at once. "The Holy City" was the outstanding seller and had to be done over more than any other selection. It paid the rent for many years.

Miller objected to the first name of "John" as not being "romantic enough" and told the singer, "You're Harry Macdonald from now on." However, on the first cylinder by the singer, the last name had been mistakenly printed as "Macdonough." The tenor later explained why he continued using this name: ". . . I was completely indifferent to what they called me. I thought then that record-making was a sort of lowdown business, anyway." It is a curious explanation for a name change since "Harry" seems no more romantic than "John," but the singer reported this to Walsh without any hint of jesting.

His assumed name led to some embarrassment since a veteran theatrical comedian named Harry Macdonough was mistakenly asked to sing ballads when on stage. The recording artist wrote to the stage artist a letter of apology because, as he later told Walsh, "I felt that if I told him the truth, that I had never heard of him before I appropriated his name, I would only be adding insult to injury." A friendly understanding was reached, the only inconvenience being the tendency of each to receive the other's mail. Since John Macdonald never worked as a stage performer—he sang in churches—all references in theater literature from the 1890s and later to Harry Macdonough concern this stage artist, never the recording artist. In

1899, for the cylinder company Harms, Kaiser, and Hagen, the tenor used the name Ralph Raymond.

As a solo artist he recorded in 1899 and 1900 a few dozen titles for Berliner. His first Berliner session was probably on October 7, 1899. Titles recorded on that day include "One Night in June" (0560), "The Girl I Loved in Sunny Tennessee" (0561), and "Rock of Ages" (0565). For Berliner, he recorded with baritone S. H. Dudley an additional three titles and with soprano Florence Hayward eleven more titles.

In 1900 the tenor made discs for Eldridge R. Johnson's newly formed Consolidated Talking Machine Company, soon to be called the Victor Talking Machine Company. He recorded more titles for the company in its first year than any other solo artist (S. H. Dudley was the company's second busiest singer in that year). In fact, only Sousa's Band recorded more titles for Johnson's company in its first year. The Metropolitan Orchestra, sometimes listed as the Victor Orchestra, recorded almost as many titles as Macdonough.

Though he recorded nearly a dozen duets with Florence Hayward for Berliner, the tenor was not paired with a female during his first year with Victor (Hayward would not record for Victor until 1905). From July 1901 to 1903 he made Victor records with soprano Grace Spencer (1872-1952). He and Spencer had worked together for other companies as early as 1900. Her marriage in 1903 to Dr. Willard Foster Doolittle ended her recording career.

In 1901, as a Victor artist, Macdonough recorded many duets with bass A. D. Madeira. For Edison sessions from 1904 to 1906 he was paired a dozen times with John H. Bieling.

At the turn of the century he recorded for the National Gramophone Corporation, maker of Zon-o-phone discs. Its May 10, 1901, catalog lists eight titles sung by Macdonough as a solo artist as well as five duets by Macdonough and "Miss Spencer"—that is, Grace Spencer.

From about 1901 to 1904 he was a Columbia artist. On Climax Record 272 he sings "Just As the Sun Went Down" with S. H. Dudley. "Blue Bell," composed by Theodore Morse, was issued on June 1, 1904 on cylinder 32515. A few Busy Bee cylinders, made by Columbia for the O'Neill-James Company of Chicago, feature Macdonough, such as "Dainty Little Ingenue" (221).

He made cylinders for Burke & Rous, of 334 Fifth Avenue, Brooklyn, New York around 1903-1904 and is listed in the company's catalog.

He was perhaps the first vocalist to record "Hiawatha," issued on Edison 8424 in July 1903. He recorded it for Victor on May 26, 1903 (2351). This song by Neil Moret (whose real name was Charles N. Daniels) was originally published in 1901 as an instrumental, and James O'Dea added lyrics in 1903. It was incredibly popular and started a Tin Pan Alley trend of "Indian" songs. In early 1904 Macdonough recorded another song in this genre, Harry Williams and Egbert Van Alstyne's popular "Navajo" (Edison 8640).

Macdonough wrote to Walsh that soon after he began making records, he was asked to join the Edison Quartet. At that time it consisted of first tenor John Bieling; second tenor Jere Mahoney; baritone S. H. Dudley; and bass William F. Hooley. Macdonough replaced Mahoney (tenor Fred Rycroft instead of Macdonough sang during some sessions in 1900), and the four men sang together for a decade (Dudley was finally replaced by Reinald Werrenrath), employing the name Haydn Quartet when singing for Berliner and Victor. In 1902 the ensemble toured England.

Announcing the release of "Softly and Tenderly" (9367), sung by Macdonough and a new soprano, the August 1906 issue of *Edison Phonograph Monthly* states, "Miss Florence Hinkle was heard last month as one of the Edison Mixed Quartette, although her name was not given. Mr. Macdonough is an Edison veteran. This is the first time they have sung together for an Edison Record."

For Edison and Victor he recorded often as a member of various minstrel companies. The last Edison record to feature him as a solo artist—probably his final record for any company aside from Victor—was "The Tale the Church Bell Tolled" (9522), issued in April 1907. For years up to this final cylinder, a new Macdonough record had been issued by Edison nearly every month. Since by this point he had taken on executive responsibilities for Victor, it is surprising that he still worked for Edison. As a member of the Edison Quartet, he made cylinders into 1908, with a new take of an old number, "The Old Oaken Bucket," issued in September ("made over by the same talent," according to *Edison Phonograph Monthly*).

He recorded as a member of both the Lyric Quartet and the Orpheus Quartet, participating in recordings that he supervised as head of Victor's New York recording studio. The former group, founded in 1906, originally consisted of bass Frank C. Stanley, soprano Elise Stevenson, and contralto Corinne Morgan. The Orpheus, formed in 1912, also included tenor Lambert Murphy, baritone Reinald Werrenrath, and bass William F. Hooley. Macdonough was a member of the Schubert Trio (along with Stanley and Stevenson), which recorded a religious composition in 1906, and the Lyric Trio (including Hooley and Grace Spencer), active in the early years of the century. He was also a member of the Victor Male Chorus, the Trinity Choir, the Victor Mixed Chorus, and the Victor Light Opera Company.

Walsh quotes in the October 1959 issue of *Hobbies* a letter he received from Lambert Murphy which indicates that the two tenors had been close:

"I was particularly interested in the fine things you had to say of Jack Macdonald who was an intimate friend over many years. In fact his family and mine spent their summers together for at least ten years, both at Ogunquit, Maine, and at Munsonville, New Hampshire."

If the many records of the Orpheus Quartet and similar groups with Macdonough are considered, one may conclude that the tenor was Victor's most recorded singer prior to 1920. He was also among its most versatile, contributing to minstrel records during some sessions, singing opera and light opera in others. Year after year, Victor catalogs stated that Macdonough's "correct method of singing and the clearness of his diction have supplied excellent model records in various classes."

Duet partners over the years included, along with those already mentioned, S. H. Dudley, Frank C. Stanley, Elise Stevenson, Olive Kline, George P. Watson, Corinne Morgan, Elsie Baker, and Lucy Isabelle Marsh (as "Anna Howard"). Olive Kline in the 1970s recalled for record collectors that Macdonough had asked her to make Victor records after hearing her sing in a church in which Macdonough was also a featured soloist.

Page 205 of the June 1920 issue of *Talking Machine World*, in announcing Macdonald's appointment as Victor's sales manager, states that he was

> an influential member of the Victor laboratory staff for about sixteen years, and for the past ten years has been in charge of the New York laboratory where he has been responsible for engaging all popular talent including orchestras and similar organizations. He has also been charged with the makeup of the monthly bulletins and the choice of the selections to be listed, a distinctly important work involving a thorough understanding of the status of the popular music of the day, as well as of retail trade conditions. He has been a close student of the copyright laws, and has carried on negotiations for the Victor Co. with the music publishers.

For years, Macdonald was partly responsible for what was issued on black label, or "popular," Victor records—what songs were recorded and how musical artists performed them. In *The Story of the Original Dixieland Jazz Band* (Louisiana State University Press, 1960), Harry O. Brunn indicates that Macdonald made important decisions involving Victor's first jazz records, confirming that he was responsible for numbers recorded in the New York studio. Brunn, who wrote the book after extensive interviews with Nick LaRocca, reports that Macdonald suggested the title "Barnyard Blues" as a substitute for "Livery Stable Blues." Macdonald came up with the title "Fidgety Feet" for one ODJB selection and "'Lasses Candy" for another. Macdonald and Eddie King were responsible in 1920 for saxophonist Bennie Krueger joining the ODJB at sessions. Brunn reports that Macdonald insisted that vocalist Al Bernard be added for some numbers recorded in 1921. King became responsible for recording activities in the New York studio after Macdonald left it in mid-1920 to work as Victor's sales manager, but Macdonald as sales manager was in a position to dictate whether vocal refrains be added to dance band numbers.

In the 1910s he handled executive duties while maintaining a heavy singing schedule as a soloist and member of ensembles, solo records appearing less frequently after 1916 because his duties as a Victor executive were so demanding. His two final recordings as a solo artist were "Good-bye, Mother Machree" (18488), issued in September 1918, and "It's Never Too Late to Be Sorry" (18516), issued in February 1919.

Macdonough sings on what is perhaps the first dance band record to feature a vocal refrain: "Smiles" (18473), featuring Joseph C. Smith's Orchestra. It was recorded on June 3, 1918, and issued in August. Nearly two months later, he was a member of the trio that sings the vocal refrain on Smith's "Mary" (18500), recorded on July 29, 1918. These were recorded in Victor's New York studios at a time when Macdonough was responsible for recording activities there. The fact that Macdonough provided vocal refrains during sessions for which he was responsible suggests he trusted himself to deliver exactly the performance necessary for a commercially successful record.

Among his final contributions as a tenor to an issued recording was the vocal refrain on Joseph C. Smith's "Peggy" (18632), recorded on September 25, 1919, and issued in February 1920. On October 1, 1919, he sang the refrain for a Smith composition titled "Lovely Summertime," but the take was rejected, "Lovely Summertime" instead being issued as an instrumental. His promotion to sales manager meant the end of a long recording career.

Page 122 of the January 1923 issue of *Talking Machine World* announced that effective January 8, 1923, he was associate director of the Artists and Repertoire Department, a job that meant he would "divide his time between duties at Camden and New York and travel in the interest of the record catalog . . ." He was direct assistant to Calvin G. Child. The article states that Macdonald was Victor's sales manager "for the past two years" (Frank K. Dolbeer, who had been head of Victor's Traveling Sales Department, succeeded him) and "before becoming sales manager at the Victor factory, was in charge of the recording rooms in New York."

The October 1923 issue of *Talking Machine World* announced the retirement of Victor executive Calvin G. Child, adding, "J. S. Macdonald has been appointed to the important position of manager of the artists and repertoire department of the Victor Co. and will henceforth assume the administrative duties formerly falling on Mr. Child." Months after Victor's Oakland plant became operational in 1924, Macdonald traveled to the West Coast. The January 1925 issue of *Talking Machine World* reports on page 156, "J. S. Macdonald, head of the recording department of the Victor Talking Machine Co., left Camden on January 8 for a visit to the Pacific Coast where he will inspect the new recording and pressing plant in Oakland, Cal. . . . E. [Eddie] J. King, of the New York Recording Laboratories of the Victor, will also make a trip through the West shortly."

In October 1925, Macdonald left Victor to become director of recording studios of the Columbia Phonograph Company, guiding artists through the company's early Viva-Tonal recording years. Page 6 of the November 1925 issue of *Talking Machine World* states:

> John S. Macdonald, who has been associated with the Victor Talking Machine Co. for twenty-four years, has joined the Columbia Co. to take charge of the entire recording department. The Columbia recording department has grown so large it has become necessary to organize it on a more efficient scale than hitherto. Arthur Bergh, who has done wonderful work and is largely responsible for the improved Columbia recording will now concentrate on the musical end of the department. . . . Mr. Macdonald becomes the executive head of that department.

A year after Macdonald left Victor for Columbia, Edward T. King did the same. King had assisted Macdonald in the 1910s when the latter managed Victor's New York recording studios, and King succeeded Macdonald, producing Victor dance and popular vocal discs in the 1920s. Page 42 of the November 1926 issue of *Talking Machine World*, which announces the move to Columbia, states that King had been with Victor for twenty-one years (some of those years would have been spent supervising Zon-o-phone sessions), and before that time had been with Columbia. Given their long association in the Victor studios, Macdonald may have persuaded King to defect to Columbia. They worked closely together as Columbia managers, as suggested by page 102 of the December 1926 issue of *Talking Machine World*, which announces the imminent release of performances recorded in Chicago of Ted Lewis, Paul Ash, Ruth Etting and others: "J. S. Macdonald, assisted by Eddie King, gave his personal supervision to the recording of the new Columbia numbers."

An article titled "J. S. MacDonald Is Feted by Associates" in the July 1929 issue of *Talking Machine World* indicates his high standing in the industry:

On June 3, Keene's Old English Chop House, New York City, was the scene of a Bon Voyage dinner and entertainment given to J. S. MacDonald, recording director of the Columbia Phonograph Co., by a group of his associates. Mr. MacDonald's itinerary abroad includes France, Switzerland and the most interesting portions of the Continent. Beside many of his co-workers, there were present at the dinner a number of the brighter lights of the music composing and publishing world. . . . The merriment was ably handled by such well-known stage and recording stars as Ruth Etting, Eddie Walters, Charles W. Hamp, Ethel Waters, and Mary Dixon—all exclusive Columbia artists. Among the other mirth-provokers were Mamie Smith, one of the first "blues" singers, and Fatima and Cleopatra. Rube Bloom, composer and pianist, served capably on the keyboard . . . Mr. MacDonald sailed on the "De Grasse" of the French Line and will return on the "Tuscania."

He was Columbia's recording director when he died at age sixty of a heart attack in his New York home.

Marsh, Lucy Isabelle (April 10, 1878-January 20, 1956)

Born in Ithaca, New York, the lyric soprano Lucy Isabelle Marsh began singing in church choirs and traveled to Paris to study under teachers Trabadello and Baldelli. Upon returning to the United States she studied singing under John Walter Hall and soon made her only appearances on an operatic stage during the 1904-1905 Metropolitan Opera Company season as a Flower Maiden in Wagner's *Parsifal* (a relatively minor role—the production's star soprano was Lillian Nordica). She was a leading soprano for New York City's Madison Avenue Reformed Church and the Temple Bethel, and into the 1930s she performed for audiences, but Marsh is an example of a trained singer who became widely known and respected because of recordings, not live performances.

In 1908, she recorded three titles for Columbia, the most successful being "The Glow-Worm" (3791, reissued as A435), a Paul Lincke composition featured in the 1902 German operetta *Lysistrata* but introduced in America by May Naudain in the 1907 musical comedy *The Girl Behind the Counter*. The other Columbia recordings were duets: "Are You Sincere?" (A584), with Henry Burr, and the Kiss Duet from Oscar Straus's *Waltz Dream* (A437), sung with Berrick Von Norden (misspelled as "Van" Norden in catalogs and on Lakeside Indestructible 70503—the tenor's real name was Berrick Schloss).

In 1909, she began working for Victor Talking Machine Company and thereafter never recorded for another company. Her Victor debut was "Angels Ever Bright and Fair" from Handel's *Theodora* (35075). Issued in May 1909, it remained available as a black label disc until 1925 and is a rare instance of the name Lucy Isabelle Marsh on a black label disc. Another black label record is "Every Little Movement" on single-sided Victor 5784, a duet with Harry Macdonough, and on this she is identified as "Lucy Marsh." Though a fine performance, it was available only briefly, almost immediately replaced by a version sung by Inez Barbour and Reinald Werrenrath, which sold extremely well (the same catalog number was used). Perhaps her new status among Victor artists in early 1910—her records were to be issued on purple label discs—had something to do with its replacement.

Victor's single-sided purple label series—a middle ground between the prestigious Red Seal and regular black labels—was introduced in February 1910 with over a dozen Harry Lauder discs. The series was reserved for certain artists exclusive to Victor. With "My Hero" on ten-inch Victor 60012, recorded on February 21, 1910, Marsh was the second artist featured in the new series (Nora Bayes was third). Marsh became one of the series' most important artists, even becoming, with the possible exception of Lauder, the best-selling artist in that series. In 1916 Victor ceased issuing new titles on ten-inch purple label discs and in 1920 ceased issuing new titles on twelve-inch purple label discs, instead issuing new titles on its double-sided blue label series. Although various Victor titles remained available on single-sided purple label discs until 1925, such as George M. Cohan's "Life's a Funny Proposition After All," by the 1920s all Marsh titles still in the Victor catalog were on double-sided blue label discs.

With tenor John McCormack she recorded two operatic duets—"Parlemoi de ma mere" from *Carmen* (May 1, 1913) and "O terra addio" from *Aïda* (April 9, 1914)—and this elevated her to Red Seal status twice during the acoustic recording era. On post-1910 black label discs featuring the soprano, Victor used the pseudonym Anna Howard, such as for "At Siesta Time" from *Chu Chin Chow* (18424), issued in February 1918.

A versatile artist, she recorded musical comedy hits and light opera numbers ("To the Land of My Own Romance" from Victor Herbert's *The Enchantress*, "Song of Love" from Sigmund Romberg's *Blossom Time*), sentimental songs (Carrie Jacobs-Bond's "Just A-wearyin' for You"), oratorio ("With Verdure Clad" from Haydn's *Creation*), opera ("O patria mia" from Verdi's *Aïda*), standards (Moore's "The Last Rose of Summer"), waltzes ("Parla Waltz," "Swallows Waltz," "Amoureuse Waltz"), and lullabies ("Pickaninny Sleep-Song").

One of her most popular records was "Italian Street Song" from Herbert's *Naughty Marietta* (Victor 60031), introduced in stage productions in 1910 by soprano Emma Trentini, a famous member of Oscar Hammerstein's Manhattan Opera Company. Marsh cut it on December 5, 1910. Also highly successful was "My Beautiful Lady" from Ivan Caryll's *The Pink Lady*, which had been introduced at New York's New Amsterdam Theatre on March 13, 1911, by Hazel Dawn (born Hazel Tout in Ogden City, Utah), who never recorded. The waltz "My Beautiful Lady" was successful first as a single-sided disc in Victor's purple label series (60040) and later as Victor blue label 45193, which features "My Hero" from Oscar Straus's *The Chocolate Soldier* on its "A" side (originally issued as purple label 60012—the composer's name is misspelled "Strauss").

She regularly sang in ensembles such as the Victor Light Opera Company and the Trinity Choir. Though a few artists sing solo for brief periods on each recording in Victor's "Gems" series, performances go uncredited. Another very popular record was of the Victor Opera Trio performing, in English, the Trio from Gounod's *Faust* (purple label 60097, reissued as blue label 45182). The three singers are probably Marsh, Harry Macdonough, and Reinald Werrenrath.

Victor's October 1911 supplement, announcing the release of Chaminade's waltz "Summer" (70051), states, "Miss Marsh's brilliant vocal waltzes have set a new standard, and have been among the most successful of all Victor records. The flawless technique, the absolute purity of the soprano tones, and her perfect intonation are all in evidence here . . ."

After marrying Dr. Walter Colwell Gordon in 1910, she moved to Providence, Rhode Island. Reviews of her concerts indicate she adopted Lucy Marsh Gordon as her professional name—she did local concert work, never touring widely—but Victor continued issuing her on purple, blue, and red labels as Lucy Isabelle Marsh, sometimes Lucy Marsh.

Articles dated January 21 and 30, 1925, in the *Providence Journal* of Providence, Rhode Island, discuss the soprano making her radio debut on January 29 of that year in New York City (others on the program were Miguel Fleta and the Flonzaley Quartet), and she continued doing radio work for several years.

In the early electric era Marsh, like a number of other Victor staff artists, cut new takes of numbers that had sold well in the acoustic era, beginning with Adolphe Adam's "Holy Night." On the acoustic and electric versions she is assisted by other Victor staff artists—the Lyric Quartet on the former, the larger Trinity Choir on the electric. The acoustic version had been issued as blue label Victor 45145 in December 1917 ("Soprano and Mixed Quartet with Organ and Chimes") with early pressings featuring the Lyric Quartet on the "B" side singing "Silent Night, Holy Night," but since an accompanying organ drowns out voices—except Marsh's—this side was replaced within months by the Trinity Choir singing it. The electric version of the same Christmas hymns, issued on blue label Victor 45519 (the label of side "A" states "Soprano with mixed voices and organ"—chimes are no longer mentioned), remained in the catalog long enough for late pressings to feature RCA Victor's double circular design, which succeeded the scroll label—this was unusual for a blue label disc. In late 1940 the company reissued it on red label V-4534 and made no more records with blue labels.

Her duet with Royal Dadmun of "Song of Love" from Sigmund Romberg's *Blossom Time*, recorded with the electric recording process, was issued as Red Seal 4013. In the acoustic era, on blue label Victor 45304, the two singers had enjoyed success with this number.

Uncredited on labels, she continued to work as a Victor Light Opera Company soloist. Victor album C-1, a set of Red Seal discs featuring Victor Herbert melodies, contains her electrical version of what had been her best-selling record in the acoustic era, "Italian Street Song." Red Seal album set C-9, featuring music of Rudolf Friml, includes Marsh singing "Giannina Mia" on the *Firefly* selections, and she is heard as soloist in the *Rose Marie* and *Katinka* selections. The other soprano on this set is Gladys Rice.

From 1927 to 1936, as Anna Howard, she recorded children's songs which were issued in the regular 20000 popular series—black label as opposed to Red Seal and blue label. Her accompanist at these sessions was usually house pianist Myrtle C. Eaver. One late Victor session took place on March 23, 1932, which produced "Songs for Children," issued on Victor 22992 and 22993. Her final Victor recordings date from 1936. The 1937 Educational Catalog, in the selections for Elementary Grades (Primary), lists children's songs issued on 25423 and 25424 as sung by Anna Howard. Victor 25425 is shown as sung by Howard, Ruth Carhart, and Elsie Baker.

Residing at 118 Princeton Avenue in Providence, she raised two sons, Calvin and Walter, who would become doctors like their father. She continued performing into the mid-1930s, usually for private and charity entertainments. She died at her Providence home at age seventy-seven.

Murray, Billy (May 25, 1877-August 17, 1954)

Billy Murray was arguably the most popular recording artist of the acoustic era, with sales of his records probably exceeding those of any other artist. Only a few other singers, such as Henry Burr and Harry Macdonough, may have recorded more titles than Murray, who often worked as a solo artist but was equally comfortable in duets, trios, quartets, and quintets. Though most famous as a singer of comic songs, he also recorded love songs, sentimental ballads, patriotic numbers, hits from Broadway musicals, vaudeville skits, and refrains for dance band numbers. His ability to adapt to changing musical trends resulted in heavy session work from 1903 until the advent of electric recording, and though his popularity was in decline from the mid-1920s onward, he continued to make records regularly until the onset of the Great Depression, even returning to studios in the World War II era to cut a few final titles.

William Thomas Murray "squalled for the first time in 1877" in Philadelphia, according to an article attributed to Murray and titled "My Twin—The Phonograph" in the January 1917 issue of *Edison Phonograph Monthly*. It is the only account close to an autobiographical sketch, though the article was probably written for him after he was interviewed by the company's advertising department. He points out that he was born in the year Edison invented the phonograph, adding, "I didn't do very much for ten years after that; but neither did the phonograph . . . I can understand just why Mr. Edison did not make any attempt to improve or market the phonograph he invented in 1877 until 1887 . . . I was not ready to sing for it, that's all."

Murray's parents, Patrick Murray (born in 1849) and Julia Kelleher Murray, appear to have emigrated as young adults from County Kerry, Ireland. The family moved from the East to Denver, Colorado. To reflect his Colorado upbringing, Victor catalogs nicknamed him "The Denver Nightingale." Billy's parents allowed him to join Harry Leavitt's High Rollers Troupe as an actor in 1893, reports Jim Walsh in the April 1942 issue of *Hobbies*. Harry Leavitt was a touring impresario.

In 1897, Murray and Matt Keefe visited the Bacigalupi Brothers in San Francisco. Murray cites an earlier year in "My Twin—The Phonograph," but the fact that one song recorded was first published in 1897 suggests he was off by a year. Murray states:

> In 1896 I was trouping with a minstrel show, and finally landed in "Frisco." The Edison Jobbers in San Francisco were Bacigalupi Brothers, and one of the members of the firm, or one of their customers, attended a performance at which Matt Kief [sic], the famous minstrel, and myself sang "The County Mayo" ["The Lass From the County Mayo"] . . . As a result, Matt and I were engaged to go to the store and make some records of the song. At that time many dealers had devices by which eight records could be made at once, and Matt and I were set to work in front of one of these.

No Bacigalupi cylinders by Murray are known to exist. Murray soon joined the Al. G. Field Greater Minstrels as a blackface singer and dancer.

Alfred Griffith Hatfield formed in 1886 what would in time be called the Al. G. Field Greater Minstrels. With headquarters in Columbus, Ohio, Field advertised his company as "the largest and most complete organization of its kind in the world." An advertisement in the February 22, 1902, issue of *Billboard* indicates that Field's stage production called *The Roof Garden: A Night in New York* was an elaborate affair, with "100 people on the stage in this production."

When the troupe reached New York City, Murray made the rounds of record companies in the metropolitan area. According to Walsh in the May 1942 issue of *Hobbies*, Murray came armed with letters of introduction from the Edison distributor in San Francisco, testifying that cylinders made there for local distribution had been successful and that he was a "natural" recording artist. Murray secured an engagement with Edison's National Phonograph Company almost immediately.

His first Edison recordings, possibly the first Murray records to be marketed nationwide, were released in August 1903. The July 1903 issue of *Edison Phonograph Monthly* announced the August release of the "coon" songs "I'm Thinkin' of You All of de While" (8452) and "Alec Busby, Don't Go Away" (8453). It also calls Murray "a new man on our staff of entertainers." The performances were probably recorded in June 1903. He cut the same two titles for Victor in September, though no Victor takes of "Alec Busby, Don't Go Away," a song by Hughie Cannon, were issued. Murray became closely enough identified with Dave Reed's "I'm Thinkin' of You All of de While" for his photograph to be featured on some editions of the sheet music (Victor Monarch labels give the title as "I'm Thinkin' of You all o' de While"). In 1902 his photograph had been featured on covers of sheet music for "A Little Boy in Blue," with words by Raymond A. Brown and Theodore F. Morse. He never recorded the song, which was covered by several artists in 1902—before Murray's recording career began. His photograph rarely was featured on sheet music covers, perhaps fewer than a dozen times in his long career.

At this time, artists such as Harry Macdonough, Arthur Collins, Byron G. Harlan, the team of Collins and Harlan, Albert Benzler, Frank C. Stanley, and the Edison Concert Band recorded so regularly for Edison's National Phonograph Company that a new title featuring each artist was issued virtually each month, year after year. The young Murray joined these veterans, a new cylinder being issued nearly each month, year after year. Other release dates and titles from his first year as an Edison artist include the following (after each song title is a genre type cited in Edison promotional literature, followed by the cylinder number):

- September 1903—"I Could Never Love Like That" ("Coon song"), 8477
- October 1903—"Won't You Kindly Hum Old Home, Sweet Home to Me?" ("Coon song"), 8521
- November 1903— "Under a Panama" ("Coon song"), 8541
- December 1903: "Bedelia," ("Irish coon serenade"), 8550
- December 1903: "Up in the Cocoanut Tree" ("Love song of the co-coanut grove"), 8564
- January 1904: "Under the Anheuser Bush" ("Waltz song with orchestra accompaniment"), 8575
- January 1904: "Mary Ellen" ("Irish coon serenade with orchestra accompaniment"), 8597

It is possible that Columbia records featuring Murray were made slightly earlier, but Murray himself told researcher Quentin Riggs that his initial East Coast recordings were made for Edison in 1903. Murray began recording for Columbia in that year but the month is unknown. No Columbia logs from this period have survived. Murray sings on Columbia records that have relatively early catalog numbers, but original release dates for those catalog numbers do not indicate when Murray began recording for Columbia since in these years the company often changed artists for subsequent takes but kept the same catalog numbers. For example, Murray sings "The Way to Kiss a Girl" on cylinder 4275, a remake of a number first recorded for the company by George J. Gaskin. On some pressings of Columbia disc 1163 and cylinder 32099, Murray sings "Tessie You Are the Only, Only, Only," a Will R. Anderson song that first became popular when interpolated into the 1902 show *The Silver Slipper*, starring Edna Wallace Hopper. Versions of "Tessie" had been issued before Murray's first Edison cylinders were released—another tenor sang the early takes. Take Five is by Murray.

Another example of Murray cutting a title that had been cut earlier by another artist is "Has Anybody Seen Our Cat?" on Columbia 1008. Will F. Denny had been the original vocalist, and when later pressings of the disc featuring Murray's take appeared, Denny's name remained on the label, presumably because reusing the old label saved Columbia some money. Denny's recording career declined rapidly as Murray's career gained momentum, and there may be a connection. Murray was skilled at performing the type of comic songs that Denny had long been recording, and being new to the industry, Murray may have even demanded less in payment than established artists such as Denny. Examples of songs cut by both tenors—for competing companies—include "Meet Me in St. Louis,

Louis," "The Whole Damm Family," and "Nothing Like That in Our Family."

Murray's first Victor session was on September 2, 1903, and the following titles were cut (some takes from that session were rejected and the issued takes were from slightly later sessions):

- B-386, "I'm Thinkin' of You All o' de While" (2467)
- B-387, "Alec Busby, Don't Go Away" (unissued)
- B-388, "Won't You Kindly Hum Old Home, Sweet Home to Me" (unissued)
- B-389, "Up in a Cocoanut Tree" (2453)
- B-390, "My Little 'Rang Outang" (2454)

He returned to the Victor studio on September 10, 1903, to make additional takes of these songs as well as to record two new ones: "I Never Could Love Like That" and "Under a Panama." The company, heralding him as a "new singer of coon songs whose records are unusually clear," issued four discs in November 1903:

- "I Never Could Love Like That" (2452)
- "Up in a Cocoanut Tree" (2453)
- "My Little 'Rang Outang" (2454)
- "Under a Panama" (2455)

Murray also made Columbia cylinders late in 1903, and they include:

- "It Takes the Irish to Beat the Dutch" (32355)
- "Under a Panama" (32356)
- "General Hardtack on Guard" (32357)
- "Plain Mamie O'Hooley" (32367)
- "Mary Ellen" (32368)
- "The Girl You Love" (32369)
- "Dear Sing Sing" (32374)
- "Lazy Bill" (32376)
- "Under the Anheuser Bush" (32384)

Labels on the Columbia discs of "It Takes the Irish to Beat the Dutch" (single-sided 1647) and "Under the Anheuser Bush" (single-sided 1676) identify Murray as a baritone! His cylinder version of "Meet Me in St. Louis, Louis" was issued on Columbia 32488 on June 1, 1904, and some surviving copies are brown wax cylinders, which is noteworthy since Columbia began marketing black wax cylinders in August 1903, and only a few titles were issued on brown wax cylinders as late as June 1904.

In his early years, Murray cut popular songs of the day for any label willing to pay for his services. Songs Murray recorded in 1903-1904 for more than one company include "It Takes the Irish to Beat the Dutch" (Columbia, Victor), "Ain't It Funny What a Difference Just a Few Hours Can Make" (Columbia, Victor), "Meet Me in St. Louis, Louis" (Columbia, Edison, Victor), "Alexander" (American, Edison), and "Teasing" (Columbia, Victor).

In his first year Edison promotional literature characterized Murray as a singer of "coon" songs. Announcing the August release of Edison Standard 8765, the July 1904 issue of *Edison Phonograph Monthly* states, "'Alexander' is Billy Murray's monthly coon song contribution." But it was soon clear that he could sing nearly any type of popular song. He became associated with George M. Cohan songs, beginning with "Yankee Doodle Boy" on Standard 8910 in February 1905. It was followed in April by the release of 8954, "If Mr. Boston Lawson Has His Way," also from Cohan's show *Little Johnny Jones*. By mid-1905 Victor advertised that Murray's disc of "Yankee Doodle Boy" (cut for that company on December 2, 1904) was the top-selling record in its history.

In the summer of 1906 the tenor's version of Cohan's "The Grand Old Rag" on Victor 4634 succeeded Richard Jose's "Silver Threads Among the Gold" as the company's best-selling disc up to that point. Victor's March 1906 supplement had identified the Jose item as Victor's best-selling disc, but the Murray record sold well that summer and for years afterward. Murray cut it for the company on February 6, 1906, six days before Cohan's *George Washington, Jr.* opened in New York City, and cut it for other companies around this time. Nearly all of his versions have the original words: "You're a grand old rag, you're a high-flying flag . . ." Soon after Cohan's show opened at Herald Square Theater, some people—including reviewers—objected to "rag" in a song about the American flag, ignoring the context in which Cohan had placed the word (the chorus expresses respect, and in the show a war veteran carries a flag that is tattered and worn—a rag). Cohan revised the chorus, with some printed versions of the song merely changing "rag" to "flag," thereby weakening the chorus with repetition, others having the words, "You're a grand old flag tho' you're torn to a rag . . ."

After a year or so of issuing the record as "The Grand Old Rag," Victor changed the title on labels and in catalogs to "The Grand Old Flag" but continued to make pressings from one of the February 1906 takes, so even on late Victor pressings Murray sings the original words. The Edison company issued a Murray version on black wax cylinder 9256 in April 1906 as "You're a Grand Old Rag" (this was the song's full title), but by

January 1907 and thereafter it was "You're a Grand Old Flag" on cylinder rims and in catalogs.

In 1906 "Cheyenne" was also a big seller. Other popular Murray recordings in these early years include "Give My Regards to Broadway" (Columbia 3165; Edison 9095; Zon-o-phone 140), "In My Merry Oldsmobile" (Victor 4467; Columbia 3564 and 33063), and "Everybody Works But Father" (Victor 4519).

Though Murray credited himself in the January 1917 issue of *Edison Phonograph Monthly* with "discovering" Ada Jones in 1904 at Huber's Museum and recommending her for recording work, Murray was not paired immediately with Jones. She instead worked closely with Len Spencer. When Murray and Jones finally worked together, probably beginning with a Victor session on November 2, 1906 (they recorded "Wouldn't You Like to Flirt with Me?" and "I'm Sorry"), their voices blended wonderfully, and the duo became incredibly popular. The first Edison recording of Murray and Jones was "Will You Be My Teddy Bear?" (Standard 9659), issued in August 1907. Their first Columbia cylinder was "You Can't Give Your Heart to Somebody Else and Still Hold Hands with Me" (33088) and their first Columbia disc was "I'd Like to See a Little More of You" (3612), although before this Jones and Murray had joined Frank C. Stanley for "Whistle It" (3589).

Their most successful cylinder recording for Edison was probably "Rainbow" (Standard 10049), issued in January 1909. This Percy Wenrich composition with lyrics by Jack Mahoney made "Indian" songs fashionable for a few years, and Ada Jones recorded similar songs with Murray, including "Blue Feather" (Standard 10162), "Silver Star" (Amberol 940), and the very popular "Silver Bell" (Standard 10492; Amberol 576).

Other notable Jones-Murray recordings issued by various companies include "Be My Little Baby Bumble Bee," "The Boy Who Stuttered and the Girl Who Lisped," "Smile Smile Smile," "When We Are M-A-R-R-I-E-D," "Wouldn't You Like to Have Me for a Sweetheart?," "I'm Looking for a Sweetheart, and I Think You'll Do," and "I've Taken Quite a Fancy to You."

Another female recording artist that Murray took credit for "discovering" is Elida Morris, who had her first session on January 21, 1910. It was a Victor session, and Murray assisted on one number, though nothing from this session was issued. Morris and Murray had a second Victor session on May 16, which resulted in the release of "You'll Come Back" (16653) and "Angel Eyes" (5782).

Meanwhile, Murray assimilated new trends and styles. He continued to enjoy success with Jones. Moreover, he added much to a group formed in 1909, the American Quartet, called the Premier Quartet on the Edison label.

In early 1909 he signed a joint contract that limited his recording activity to Victor for discs (this included Zon-o-phone discs) and Edison for cylinders. The contract ran for ten years (to 1919) and the companies must have paid handsomely for his services to compensate for the loss of money he would have earned by working for various companies in a freelance capacity. Over the next decade he often cut the same songs for the two companies, with interesting differences in interpretation. In fact, Murray made changes even when cutting for one company new takes of a song. At least three takes of "Casey Jones" (16483), credited to Murray and the American Quartet, were issued. On takes one and three, Murray opens with the line, "Come all you rounders if you want to hear . . ." (take one has an orchestra interlude before the second verse, whereas on the third take Murray goes from the chorus to the second verse with no break) while on take twelve he opens with "Come everybody . . ." The song suited Murray's voice perfectly and he performed it often before audiences. Walsh claimed that it was the singer's biggest seller but this is unlikely since copies are not as easy to find as many other Murray records.

Some of the most popular recordings made between 1910 and 1920 with Murray as a solo artist or Murray working with others include:

- "Alexander's Ragtime Band" (Edison 10522; Edison Amberol 692; 1911)
- "All Alone" (Victor 5846; Edison 10509; Zon-o-phone 5750; 1911)
- "Oh, You Beautiful Doll" (Victor 16979; Edison 10545; Edison 921; 1911)
- "Moonlight Bay" (Victor 17034; 1912)
- "The Gaby Glide" (Victor 17077; 1912)
- "Waiting for the Robert E. Lee" (Victor 17141; 1912)
- "Be My Little Baby Bumble Bee" (Victor 17152; 1912)
- "The Wedding Glide" (Victor 17170; 1912)
- "Snookey Ookums" (Victor 17313; 1913)
- "He'd Have to Get Under—Get Out and Get Under (To Fix Up His Automobile)" (Victor 17491; 1914)
- "Just for To-Night" (Victor 17622; 1914)
- "When You Wore a Tulip and I Wore a Big Red Rose" (Victor 17652; 1914/1915)
- "On the 5:15" (Victor 17705; 1915)
- "The Little Ford Rambled Right Along" (Victor 17755; 1915)
- "Are You from Dixie? ('Cause I'm from Dixie Too)" (Victor 17942; 1916)
- "Simple Melody" (Victor 18051; 1916)
- "Pretty Baby" (Victor 18102; 1916)

- "There's a Little Bit of Bad in Every Good Little Girl" (Victor 18143; 1916)
- "Over There" (Victor 18333; 1917)
- "Good-Bye Broadway, Hello France!" (Victor 18335; 1917)
- "K-K-K-Katy" (Victor 18455; 1918)
- "They Were All Out of Step But Jim" (Victor 18465; 1918)
- "The Alcoholic Blues" (Victor 18522; 1919)
- "Take Your Girlie to the Movies (If You Can't Make Love at Home)" (Victor 18592; 1919)

The June 1918 issue of *Along Broadway*, an Edison trade publication, states, "We have yet to find the popular song Billy Murray can't put across . . . We recently added a few figures together and found that 'There Must Be Little Cupids in the Briny' is Billy Murray's 'Best Seller.' If you have never heard it, you've missed five minutes of high entertainment." This refers to Edison Diamond Disc 50248. The Victor Talking Machine Company stated in its record catalogs year after year, "Billy Murray is one of the most successful of all American singers of humorous songs, and probably entertains, through his Victor records, a larger audience than any other singer who has ever lived."

Murray was among the first to sing on discs marketed as dance records and was arguably a pioneer among dance band singers. In 1919 he contributed vocal refrains to Joseph C. Smith and His Orchestra performances ("Chong" on Victor 35684, "The Vamp" on Victor 18594), and in the early 1920s he sang refrains for various dance bands. Labels occasionally identify Murray but more often state "with vocal refrain." On January 2, 1923, for "Mr. Gallagher and Mr. Shean" (Victor 19007), Murray was the first vocalist to record with Paul Whiteman and His Orchestra.

His exclusive Victor contract ended at the beginning of 1919, and he then worked for a year as a freelance artist, covering some songs for a few companies. These include:

- "Wait Till You Get Them Up in the Air, Boys" (Columbia A2794, Victor 18628, Pathé 22262, and Empire 21135)
- "That Wonderful Kid from Madrid" (Okeh 4050, Emerson 10138, Vocalion 14019, and Lyric 5214)
- "I'll See You in C-U-B-A" (Victor 18652, Okeh 4079, Gennett 9029, Vocalion 14035, Pathé 22322, and Empire 421)

Page 103 of the January 1919 issue of *Talking Machine World* states, "The Columbia Graphophone Co. announced this week that Billy Murray, one of the most popular recordings artists of the present day, had joined the

Columbia recording staff. . . . He specializes on [sic] the rendition of Irish songs and rapid-fire comic songs . . ."

Page 60 of the February 1919 issue of the trade journal states, "The New York Recording Laboratories of Port Washington, Wis., announce that Billy Murray is to sing for Paramount records. . . . He will make his debut with Paramount in a comedy song: 'Can You Tame Wild Wimmin?' which, according to Musical Director Walter Rogers, of the company's New York studios, is well adapted to Murray's talents." Murray and Rogers knew each other well since Rogers had been Victor's musical director until 1916 and had supervised many Murray sessions. Page 138 of the September 1919 issue of *Talking Machine World* features a full-page Emerson Phonograph Company advertisement announcing a new Murray release on Emerson 1042, and it states that Murray is "a frequent visitor to the Emerson Recording Studios."

Among the rarest Murray discs from this freelance period are those issued in a series of hill-and-dale (or vertical) cut "long-playing" records issued in the summer of 1920 by Grey Gull Records. The first with Murray was Grey Gull H-2007, which features on one side the tenor singing "Profiteering Blues" and "Tiddle-Dee-Winks" (the former song is also on lateral cut Grey Gull L-2012; the latter is on Grey Gull L-2015). The other side features two songs performed by one Mel Eastman, probably a pseudonym for a well-known singer of that time. Priced at a dollar, the disc was issued in July 1920 along with three other Grey Gull discs promoted as "Long-Playing Two-in-One Records" (the others feature Henry Burr, Stetson Humphrey, and the Grey Gull Military Band). In October the company issued Murray on two more long-playing discs. On one side of H-2010 he sings "Chili Bean" and "There's a Typical Tipperary Over Here." On one side of H-2011 he sings "Oh! By Jingo" and "The Simple Simon Party." Mel Eastman again sings on the reverse sides of the discs. All songs covered by Murray on these long-playing discs were also made available on lateral cut discs. The company's experiment with long-playing records was short-lived.

"Oh! By Jingo!" on Emerson 10177 sold briskly in June 1920. In the August 1984 issue of *Hobbies*, Walsh repeats Murray's recollections from the early 1950s that the tenor had cut it for Victor, but a version cut by new artist Margaret Young on March 26 was made available in American shops in June, even though this comic song suited Murray's talents perfectly (his version was issued on Canadian Victor 216141). Director Eddie King had persuaded other executives that Young's version should be issued, Murray's rejected. Since the new song "Oh! By Jingo!" was so popular that summer—every record company covered it—expectations for Victor 18666 were high, but though a Murray performance was on the "B" side ("Profiteering Blues"), sales were disappointing. Victor dealers complained to company executives that they were losing money because record buyers were going to other stores to buy Murray's version on Emerson, also issued in June. Murray told Walsh, "It took my Emerson record of 'Oh! By Jingo!' to get me a good exclusive Victor contract!"

The July 1920 issue of *Talking Machine World* announced that Murray again had signed to be an exclusive Victor artist, the new contract going into effect on July 1, 1920. Pinpointing the year in which Murray's career peaked is difficult since he remained very popular from 1905 until the end of the acoustic era two decades later, but the fact that Victor executives paid enough to induce Murray in 1920 to sign a contract making him exclusive to that company suggests that his career at the time was as strong as ever. For two years after World War I, with wartime shortages over, the record industry enjoyed unprecedented sales, and Murray records sold well in 1919 and 1920.

But good years were followed in 1921 and 1922 by a recession in the national economy, and the record industry suffered accordingly. Some Murray records sold very well in this period, including "(Down by the) O-H-I-O," sung with Victor Roberts on Victor 18723 (this was really Billy Jones, who became almost a rival in the early 1920s since this tenor recorded for various companies many songs that Murray cut for Victor) and "Ten Little Fingers and Ten Little Toes," sung with Ed Smalle on Victor 18830. But the decline in Murray's career arguably began in the early 1920s. Some of his records sold as well as they had in previous years, but the industry had grown, with many more artists making records than ever before. Company executives for years had viewed Murray as indispensable, but by the early 1920s that was no longer the case.

Popular music changed in the 1920s, and fewer discs featuring Murray as a solo artist were issued by Victor. The company shifted Murray's session work from solos to duets, and Murray was increasingly assigned to sessions during which he contributed brief vocal refrains to dance band performances. He was engaged as a studio vocalist during many Paul Whiteman and His Orchestra sessions, which is noteworthy since the rise of dance bands such as Whiteman's essentially doomed the old-school type of singers, including Murray.

The duets of Murray and Aileen Stanley, which sold well throughout the 1920s, were stylistically varied. They cut blues-derived numbers ("You've Got to See Mama Ev'ry Night"; Victor 19431; 1923), straight-forward ballads ("It Had to Be You"; Victor 19373; 1924), and comic sketches ("Any Ice Today, Lady?"; Victor 20065; 1926). Their final duet, "Katie, Keep Your Feet on the Ground" (Victor 22040; 1929), was cut in

1929, after Murray's second exclusive Victor contract had expired. At this point he worked occasionally for Victor as a freelance artist.

One of Victor's first experiments with electrical recording was issued on a twelve-inch disc. Titled "A Miniature Concert" (Victor 35753) and credited to "The Eight Popular Victor Artists," it was recorded on February 26, 1925, and issued on May 29. It was one of the first electrically recorded performances available in shops, though Victor did not actually announce to the American public a switch to electric recording until November (an advertisement in the July 8 issue of the *Toronto Daily Star* does mention a "new electrical recording process" and lists "A Miniature Concert"). Robert Baumbach notes in *Look for the Dog* (Stationary X-Press, 1981) that the performance was one of several test recordings made both acoustically and electrically for comparison. Executives judged the electrical version good enough for regular matrix numbers to be assigned (CVE-31874-3 and CVE-31875-4). The recording begins with a chorus of voices, including Murray's:

> How d'ya do?
> We beg of you
> To listen once again.
> We're here because
> We're here to entertain you.
> "His Master's Voice" was calling
> So here we are again
> To demonstrate
> What's on the Victor menu.
> You will find our bill of fare
> Is flavored with some jazz
> Our chef is just a syncopated music man
> From Alabam'

This is followed by a dozen individual performances clearly tailored for the recording session, each lasting less than a minute, resulting in a true "mini concert." Murray provides terse yet fun introductions for artists, as in this example: "Mrs. Banta's boy Frankie will play 'Strut Miss Lizzie' by Henry Ford." Frank Banta then plays for seventeen seconds. Murray himself sings a bit of "Casey Jones" in twenty-six seconds and then ends side A by announcing, "We'll see you on the other side." The others intone, "Turn over!" For nearly a minute saxophonist Rudy Wiedoeft displays his talents. Monroe Silver delivers jokes for a minute (a typical one-liner is what he says of his boy in college: "He must be studying languages 'cause last week I got a bill—$60 for Scotch!"). John H. Meyer does not take a solo turn but sings only in the Sterling Trio and Peerless Quartet.

The introduction in 1925 of electrical recording with the use of a condenser microphone posed a challenge to Murray. The new process affected singers in different ways. Some singers adjusted to the new technology easily, especially those who, because of relatively "small" voices, already sang close to a crooning style. Others had to make significant changes in singing technique when recording. Murray initially had some trouble since he was used to singing in full voice, which had been suitable for acoustic recording. Moreover, Victor's early system for electrical recording itself had problems, causing grief for singers.

Murray appears on some of the earliest electrically recorded Victor discs, which suggests that executives had expected his transition to the new process to be smooth. He sings vocal refrains on both sides of Victor 19630, featuring "Let It Rain, Let It Pour" and "All Aboard for Heaven" performed by Meyer Davis' Le Paradis Band. This was Victor's first dance band recorded with the new process and then widely distributed (it was released on May 1, 1925). He sang refrains during some of the first electric sessions for Paul Whiteman and His Orchestra.

But he was instructed to alter his vocal techniques to suit the new process, such as for a session on November 4, 1925. For the electrically recorded "Roll 'Em Girls" (Victor 19838), Murray sings in a subdued manner, holding back—and the performance lacks the dynamics of previous recordings (he also sings a vocal refrain on "Roll 'Em Girls" when Jack Shilkret and His Orchestra cut a dance band version on December 31). In the June 1942 issue of *Hobbies*, Walsh summarizes the effect of the new recording:

> Many tenor voices, such as Billy's, suffered severely from the pioneer electric recording. It gave them a husky, raspy edge of a spurious baritonal quality. . . . By 1928 the crooner vogue had so taken the field that Billy, after 25 years of singing for Victor, was washed up with that company, aside from singing an occasional refrain or taking part in a minstrel sketch.

Walsh refers to a twelve-inch Victor disc featuring the "Minstrel Show of 1929" (35961), credited to the Victor Minstrels ("Male voices with orchestra") and cut in January 1929.

Other performances recorded with the early electric process show Murray in better form, such as "Oh Say! Can I See You Tonight?" (Victor 19757), cut on August 7, 1925. In the end electrical recording was not a problem for him. But it did bring about new musical trends, and Murray's diminishing stature as a recording artist during this new era is notable.

Duets made with Aileen Stanley sold well, but after the January 1926 release of "Roll 'Em Girls," neither Victor nor Edison issued records with Murray as a featured artist—that is, with credit on labels given to Murray alone—with an exception from 1928: on one side of Edison Diamond Disc 52448 Murray is given full credit for "Ho-Ho-Ho-Hogan," a type of comic number Murray cut often a decade earlier. On the other side, credit is given to Billy Murray and the 7 Blue Babies for "Doin' the Raccoon." Four Diamond Discs of the late 1920s are credited to Murray and His Merry Melody Men, or Murray's Melody Men. With the introduction of the electric recording process, he generally recorded duets, participated in trios (such as Billy Murray's Trio on Victor 20517—others in the trio were Carl Mathieu and Monroe Silver), and sang vocal refrains for dance bands.

In the first two years of electric recording, he contributed vocal refrains during sessions for Paul Whiteman and His Orchestra, Jean Goldkette and His Orchestra, the International Novelty Orchestra, Phil Spitalny and His Orchestra, and others. Some of these dance band records sold well, such as "Barcelona," performed by the International Novelty Orchestra (Victor 20113), but their sales were not determined by Murray's small contribution. By early 1927 Murray was no longer used for Victor dance band records, a Jean Goldkette session of January 28, 1927, being his last. He sings a refrain for "I'm Looking Over a Four-Leaf Clover" (20466). He performed the same song as a featured solo artist in Victor's New York studio on January 15 but the take was rejected.

Into the late 1920s Murray continued to tour with the Eight Popular Victor Artists and he sang increasingly on radio. He even performed off-Broadway, playing a number of parts as one of the principal cast members in *Bad Habits of 1926*, a revue held at the Greenwich Village Theatre. Featuring the music of Manning Sherwin, the lyrics of Arthur Herzog, and production by Irving S. Strouse, the show premiered on April 30, 1926, and ran for nineteen performances.

By June 1927, Murray's contract as an exclusive Victor artist expired, and thereafter Burr disbanded the Eight Popular Victor Artists. Working as a freelance recording artist for the first time in years, Murray with Monroe Silver cut "Mike and Ike in Politics," issued in late 1928 on Romeo and other labels (they cut it on September 19, 1928, for Columbia but the take was unissued). He also began providing vocal refrains for dance bands on small labels. He worked with The Detroiters Orchestra, Tuxedo Dance Orchestra, Golden Gate Orchestra (a name used for the California Ramblers), Fred Rich's Orchestra, The Seven Blue Babies, Dick Cherwin and His Orchestra, Bernie Stevens and His Orchestra, Al Dollar & His Ten Cent Band, and others.

Murray, Walter Scanlan (this is the professional name that Walter Van Brunt used from 1917 onward), and Monroe Silver began working together as the Three Wise Fools, but Silver soon dropped out, leaving Murray and Scanlan as a team. Their first Edison Diamond Disc, "My Blackbirds Are Bluebirds Now" backed by "The Twelve O'Clock Waltz" (52422), was released in November 1928. (Walsh states in the October 1978 issue of *Hobbies* that Murray identified Johnny Loesch as the recording engineer for most of Murray's Edison disc engagements.) The duo also worked for Victor (a single title in May 1929), Brunswick, Pathé, Crown, and several other labels. Following a formula used by the popular Happiness Boys, the records included comic dialogue in addition to singing. None sold especially well.

The Edison company began marketing lateral cut discs in August 1929 (labels state "Needle Type"), and the duo is on several. One release, "Sergeant Flagg and Sergeant Quirt" (14066), so impressed Edison executives that they offered the team a retainer fee of $6,000 per annum apiece with the proviso that the company be given the opportunity to record all similar sketches before they were made available to any other label. On October 14, 1929, Murray and Scanlan performed the novelty number on the radio show *The Edison Hour*. The record itself was announced on one of the last lists issued to Edison needle-cut dealers. List N-11, dated October 25, urges dealers to get "your standing order in." List N-12, dated November 1, promotes the disc heavily, as does the last list, N-13 for November 8. The Edison company then shut down its commercial record operations, after a sudden decision to abandon the commercial recording market. All needle-cut Edison discs are rare today. Despite the heavy promotion, the Murray and Scanlan duet did not sell well.

They made four double-faced Brunswick releases: "That's My Idea of Heaven"/"Building a Nest for Mary" (4408), "Last Night, Honey"/"The Whoopee Hat Brigade" (4513), "My Wife Is on a Diet"/"Icky, the Lollipop Song" (4597) and "Shut the Door, They're Coming Through the Window"/"Sergeant Flagg and Sergeant Quirt" (4611). The team of "Saunders and White," featured on the Romeo label for S. H. Kress & Company dime stores, was actually Murray and Scanlan.

The team also provided voices for a couple of cartoons. *Finding His Voice* (1929) featured Murray as the character "Talkie" and Scanlan supplying the voice for "Mutie." These characters were drawn to look like the two singers. The two characters were reprised in *Just a Song at Twilight* with Murray doing Mutie and his partner becoming Talkie.

In the early 1930s, Murray and Scanlan turned increasingly to radio. The two singers became associated with a comedienne named Marcella

Shields, whose singing style resembled Aileen Stanley's and whose conversational mannerisms were like Gracie Allen's. Murray and Scanlan had continued making records until 1932 when—with the Depression at its worst—demand all but disappeared, record sales bottoming out.

On November 19, 1935, Murray returned to the recording studio to do spoken character roles on an Aesop's Fables cycle released in early December, in time for Christmas sales. These children's recordings were made for the American Record Corporation's Brunswick label and issued on three ten-inch discs. Participants were Murray, Bradley Barker, and Loraine Leopold. Labels identified the artists as "Billy Murray, Bradley Barker & Company." In 1937 Murray sang the lead on "Mickey Mouse's Birthday Party," issued as Melotone 70106 and credited to the American Novelty Orchestra. The song paid tribute to the Disney character on the eve of the tenth anniversary of *Steamboat Willie*'s release.

In the spring of 1940, Leonard Joy, head of RCA Victor's New York recording studios, invited Murray to be lead vocalist for "It's the Same Old Shillelagh," which would be issued on the company's budget label as Bluebird 10811, in 1940. The label gives credit to Harry's Tavern Band but states in small print at the bottom, "vocal refrain by Billy Murray." He sang lead throughout—it was more than a mere refrain.

Murray returned to the Victor studios in October 1940. Two close friends, Jimmy Martindale and Jim Walsh, went with him and even participated in the session for "When Paddy McGinty Plays the Harp" as part of the ensemble providing background vocals ("Too roo loo! Too roo li!"). Murray did three takes each of "The Irish Were Egyptians Long Ago" and "When Paddy McGinty Plays the Harp," and the selected takes were issued on Bluebird 10926. This time Murray was given top billing on the label, with Harry's Tavern Band relegated to a smaller typeface. In late 1940 the singer returned to Victor to record "The Guy at the End of the Bar" and "The Beard in the Gilded Frame," issued as Bluebird 10980. In early 1941 he cut "I'd Feel at Home If They'd Let Me Join the Army" (this Albert Gumble and Jack Mahoney song about domestic disputes had been popular when first published in 1917 and Murray had recorded it for Victor during the World War I era) and "'Twas Only an Irishman's Dream," issued as Bluebird 10995.

Murray had one more session date with Victor in 1941, cutting "When I See All the Lovin' They Waste on Babies (I Long for the Cradle Again)" and "He Took Her for a Sleigh Ride (In the Good Old Summertime)." They were issued as Bluebird 11134.

He performed on the *National Barn Dance* for a short time during the 1941-1942 period as a replacement for Henry Burr, who had been forced to leave radio due to illness.

He might have recorded a little more in the World War II era had not a recording ban ordered by the American Federation of Musicians union gone into effect from mid-1942 to late 1944. The ban prevented studio musicians from accompanying vocalists, so vocalists themselves were restricted. It is not surprising that during the one session Murray had in 1943, he delivered comic dialogue, singing briefly only at the open and close of the two sides of the issued disc, accompanied by mouth organ. He was teamed with Monroe Silver for "Casey and Cohen in the Army," with Murray playing the Irish Casey while Monroe was the Jewish Cohen. Despite dialogue about World War II military service (when Casey asks who started the war, Cohen replies, "I think it was some girl out west by the name of Pearl Harbor"), the performance is a throwback to the early days of the record industry, when "Casey" and "Cohen" skits sold well. Issued on Beacon 2001, it was also the last record made by Murray, who received $50 for this work. Due to wartime shortages, at this time old records were melted down for the shellac needed for new pressings of records, and it is conceivable that old Murray discs were among those melted for Beacon releases! The Beacon label, owned by Joe Davis, would typically feature jazz performances after the recording ban was lifted, and the release of this comedy record was an anomaly for the company.

According to Murray's obituary published in *The Freeport Leader* a decade later, he worked at the Grumman Aircraft Engineering Corporation in Bethpage, New York, during World War II. His main duties were announcing and singing over the firm's intercommunication system. Walsh writes in the February 1947 issue of *Hobbies*, "Billy suffered an attack of coronary thrombosis early in 1944 that had his friends badly worried." But Murray recovered and enjoyed good health for a few more years.

His death came suddenly. On Tuesday, August 17, 1954, friends took the Murrays for a drive to Jones Beach. Murray proposed that the group attend Guy Lombardo's production of *Arabian Nights*. At the box office Murray purchased tickets but soon had trouble breathing. Murray attempted to ease the others' concern by saying, "You take your tickets and go in. I'll join you in a minute. I think I will go to the lavatory." The others stayed where they were as Murray entered the bathroom. Within fifteen seconds they saw people pouring into the facility. Murray's wife and her male companion dashed in to find Murray on the floor surrounded by a crowd. The friend tried to administer first aid, but it was too late. Murray died almost immediately.

His only survivors were his wife Madeline and brother Barton, who resided in Denver. He had been married twice before. The identity of his first wife is unknown. The couple was divorced by 1908. He married Grace Kathrine Brinkerhoff in November 1915 but they divorced in 1923. He married Madeline Funk in 1925.

A short Murray obituary appeared in *Billboard*, the music trade weekly. Walsh wrote Murray tributes for not only *Hobbies* but *Variety*, the latter piece published under the title "Victor's Billy Murray Dies at 77; Had Peak Phono Audience in His Era."

Myers, J. W. (c. 1864-c. 1919)

John W. Myers, usually identified on records as J. W. Myers, was arguably the leading baritone balladeer in the first decade of commercial recordings, working regularly from the early 1890s to 1904 or so, after which the dropoff in his output is dramatic. He is not to be confused with singer John Meyer, who sang first as bass and then as baritone for the Peerless Quartet.

Born in Wales, he emigrated to America at age twelve and worked at various jobs, eventually becoming a theatrical manager in New York. He resigned his managerial position in 1895 to tour with an opera company. Myers possessed a rich baritone voice and as far back as his youth was frequently asked to sing in concerts and at private gatherings. He had already been making cylinders for a few years by this time (he is identified as "the popular baritone" in an 1892 New Jersey Phonograph Company catalog described by Jim Walsh in the October 1958 issue of *Hobbies*), and when the tour was finished, Myers returned to New York City to concentrate on concert work there and to attend recording sessions.

He founded the Globe Phonograph Record Company by November 1896. That month's issue of *The Phonoscope* reported that Globe cylinders were priced at a dollar each. Globe folded after a short period.

A catalog issued in 1898 by Columbia's New England headquarters— the Eastern Talking Machine Company at 17 Tremont Street, Boston— lists over fifty Myers titles and states, "J. W. Myers, the famous baritone, whose records have achieved a wonderful popularity, has recently made a contract to sing exclusively for the Columbia Phonograph Company." Although Columbia's 1898 catalog identifies Myers as exclusive to that company, Myers cut dozens of titles for Berliner, having sessions as late as November 1897, March 1898, and December 1898. Columbia at that time made only cylinders, and it is possible that his contract allowed him to make discs for Berliner. On December 14, 1898, Myers cut "I Dreamt I

Dwelt in Marble Halls" from Balfe's *The Bohemian Girl*, which he had already covered for Columbia. It was issued as Berliner 1941. For a baritone to sing this is unusual since the song tells of rejecting marriage proposals by "knights upon bended knee." At that same 1898 recording session, Myers sang Moore's "The Last Rose of Summer," making him perhaps the only male to record this song.

Titles in Columbia's 1898 catalog include "Bedouin Love Song" (5601), "Twickenham Ferry" (5625), and "I Dreamt I Dwelt in Marble Halls" (5631). He recorded often for Columbia at the turn of the century, and other titles from this period include "In the Shade of the Palm" (cylinder 31620), "On a Sunday Afternoon" (cylinder 31755; disc 106), and "In the Good Old Summer Time" (disc 940). Columbia's June 1904 list of new records includes Myers singing Stanley Crawford's "In the Village by the Sea" on cylinder 32446. An October 1904 catalog shows he also cut it on ten-inch disc 1743.

The May 10, 1901, catalog of Zon-o-phone discs issued by the National Gramophone Corporation lists seven titles sung by Myers, including "Ma Charcoal Charmer" (9880), a rare instance of him singing a "coon" song. Another is "My Princess Zulu," (from *The Sleeping Beauty and the Beast)*, issued in 1902 on Columbia disc 73.

He recorded over 100 titles in the early days of the Victor Talking Machine Company, beginning on February 20, 1901, with many performances issued on seven-inch discs. For a couple of years, from August 1902 until early 1905, he cut no new titles for Victor, though he returned to the studio in 1902 to cut new takes of old titles. New titles recorded on February 8, 1905, include "The Wearing of the Green" and "Marching Through Georgia." His final Victor recordings were made on December 4, 1906. The two titles issued from this session are "The Bowery Grenadiers" (4968) and "The Land League Band" (5018). He recorded the same numbers for other companies.

For Edison he cut a couple of dozen titles, most of them in 1901, beginning with "Light of the Sea" (7820). He was a versatile artist, covering sentimental standards ("We'll Be Sweethearts to the End," 9498), bass-baritone classics ("Rocked in the Cradle of the Deep," 7840), and comic numbers ("Mamie, Don't You Feel Ashamie," 7821). "Bridge" (8010) was released in 1902, and he stopped making Edison records for a few years, finally returning with "Night Time" (9470), issued in February 1907. Announcing its release, the December 1906 issue of *Edison Phonograph Monthly* states, "Mr. Myers was always a favorite among admirers of the Edison Phonograph and Edison Records, and his re-enlistment in the Edison corps of artists will be pleasing news to them."

By this time, Myers recorded mainly sentimental numbers and songs of a previous generation. The February 1907 issue of *Edison Phonograph Monthly*, announcing the April release of Standard 9524, states, " 'The Bowery Grenadiers,' by J. W. Myers, is a revival of an old song that will awaken more than ordinary interest. It will recall by-gone days, when the late John W. Kelly entertained thousands with it. Thirty or more years ago it was one of the most popular songs of the day." His final Edison recording was "Land League Band" (9576), issued in June 1907. The April 1907 issue of *Edison Phonograph Monthly* calls this "a lively old march song popular a generation ago." Myers was issued only on two-minute wax cylinders, his recording career with Edison being over by the time four-minute wax Amberols were introduced in 1908.

He was popular abroad. The February 15, 1906, issue of the *Talking Machine News*, published in London, noted:

> The newsboys of London and New York whistle the same tunes, whether they are "Navajo," "My Irish Molly O," "Bedelia," or "In the Shade of the Old Apple Tree," because the talker has made them known on both sides of the ocean. . . . If George Alexander or Henry Burr or J.W. Myers were to advertise a concert in the Albert Hall next month, nine-tenths of their audience would be talking machine users.

Edison and Victor issued Myers recordings until 1907. One of his last Columbia recordings was a new take, with orchestra accompaniment, of "Where the Silv'ry Colorado Wends Its Way," issued in January 1909 on A610. This title had earlier been issued on single-sided disc 1092 as well as cylinder 32032, both with Myers accompanied by piano. His singing style was losing its appeal. He stopped recording for a few years, though Major H. H. Annand reports in a catalog of U-S Everlasting cylinders that J. W. Myers was among those who in 1908 started the U-S Phonograph Company of Cleveland, Ohio. If he did help establish the company, it is curious that Myers did not make U-S Everlasting cylinders.

He resurfaced as a Columbia, Rex, and Emerson artist. One late Columbia title is "Along the Yukon Trail" (A1614), issued in 1914. On Rex 5111 he sings Irvin Berlin's 1914 song "Follow the Crowd." Titles he recorded for Emerson are "Wearin' of the Green" (7136), "My Dad's Dinner Pail" (7115), and "Paddy Duffy's Cart" (7115). An Emerson catalog of 1917 gives his name as John W. Myers. Nothing is known of his death but Walsh concluded that he died around 1919.

Original Dixieland Jazz Band

The Original Dixieland Jazz Band, commonly called the ODJB, was the first jazz group to be recorded. Its debut record helped create a jazz craze in 1917. At that time the group consisted of cornetist Dominic James ("Nick") LaRocca, clarinetist Larry Shields, trombonist Edwin Branford ("Eddie") Edwards, pianist Harry W. Ragas, and drummer Anthony ("Tony") Sbarbaro—all white musicians from New Orleans.

The band evolved from an earlier one that included LaRocca, Edwards, Ragas, and clarinetist Alcide "Yellow" Nunez. Arriving in Chicago in early March 1916, these four New Orleans musicians worked under the leadership of drummer Johnny Stein and under the management of entrepreneur Harry James (not the big band trumpeter), opening at Schiller's Cafe on the city's South Side. This was not the first New Orleans band to play in Chicago. A predecessor was Tom Brown's Band from Dixieland, which accompanied vaudeville comic Joe Frisco. One member of Tom Brown's Band, Gus Mueller, would a few years later play clarinet on Paul Whiteman's first records, and another Brown member was Larry Shields. This may have been the first band to be called a jass band. The words "jaz" and "jazz" had appeared in print as early as 1913—the words meant vigorous, energetic—but the term "jass band" would not be used until New Orleans bands in Chicago identified themselves as such.

Stein's band was called a "jass" band at least by May 1916. Soon afterward the term "jass band" caught on in Chicago. William Howland Kenney reports in *Chicago Jazz, A Cultural History 1904-1930* (Oxford University Press, 1993) that the first use of "Jass Band" in the Chicago black press was in the September 30, 1916, issue of the *Defender*. Kenney writes that the word is used "to describe music produced by black pianist-songwriter W. Benton Overstreet in support of vaudevillian Estella Harris at the Grand Theater. Harris . . . was now accompanied by a 'Jass Band.' " Kenney also states, "Very soon thereafter, a variant spelling of the term—'Jaz'—was used in the Indianapolis *Freeman* to describe an instrumental group, John W. Wickliffe's Ginger Orchestra."

Reportedly fed up because the Schiller's Cafe owners refused to increase pay, the four musicians—LaRocca, Edwards, Ragas, and Nunez—

soon deserted Johnny Stein to form a new band. Needing a drummer, they sent for Tony Sbarbaro. In early June the Original Dixie Land Jass Band opened at Del'Abe's Cafe in the Hotel Normandy at Clark and Randolph streets. From July onward the band worked steadily at the Casino Gardens at Kinzie and North Clark streets. For personal and musical reasons, clarinetist Alcide "Yellow" Nunez was fired and replaced by New Orleanian Larry Shields.

Harry O. Brunn's *The Story of the Original Dixieland Jazz Band* (Louisiana State University Press, 1960) reports that upon hearing the ODJB in Chicago, Al Jolson enthusiastically recommended the band to agent Max Hart, who signed the band for Reisenweber's. Brunn cites no source for Jolson's involvement, but Edwards late in life recalled in an unpublished manuscript that Hart visited the Casino Gardens with Jolson, T. Roy Barnes, W. C. Fields, Don Barclay, Fanny Brice, and Will Rogers. Hart had made inquiries about a "Jas Band" as early as the autumn of 1916 and by the end of the year had traveled to Chicago to hear the band. In the possession of Gary Edwards, grandson of Eddie Edwards, is a telegram dated October 25, 1916, from the "office of Max Hart, 902 Palace Theatre Building, 1564 Broadway" to Chicago publisher Will Rossiter. The cable reads, "Dear Sir: Will you kindly give me some information regarding a 'Jas Band' which you have. Yours very truly, Max Hart." (Danish-born Max Hart, whose real name was Max Meyer Hertz, was father of Lorenz Hart, of the songwriting team Rodgers and Hart.)

Their engagement beginning on January 27 in the 400 Club Room of the new Reisenweber's Building at Columbus Circle (8th Avenue and 58th Street) was a sensation. The main restaurant, which was huge (elaborate revues entertained diners), formally opened on January 17, but a smaller restaurant in the building, the 400 Club Room, was not ready until January 27, and while waiting for it to open, the band played briefly at the Coconut Grove. A major record company contacted the ODJB two days after the 400 Club Room debut. Brian Rust possesses a photocopy of a January 29, 1917, letter (sent to Rust by Gary Edwards, grandson of Eddie Edwards) from a Columbia Graphophone Company executive addressed to "Jass Band, c/o Reisenweber's Restaurant, 58th Street & Columbus Circle, New York City." It invites the band to call on him "to discuss a matter which may prove of mutual benefit and interest." It is signed by A. E. Donovan, who had been appointed manager of Columbia's professional and personal record departments in early October 1916, according to page 45 of that month's issue of *Talking Machine World*. Edwards had scribbled a note on the letter: "Forbush—Wednesday afternoon, 2:00 p.m." It is likely that the band met Donovan or Walter A. Forbush (Columbia's recording engineer) on January 31, played an original composition (probably without record-ing it), and failed to impress Columbia executives with "jass" during this test. The band naturally would have pushed one of its original composi-tions as suitable for recording. Brunn had stated that the session was "ca. January 30." Donovan's letter establishes January 31—a Wednesday—as the date.

ODJB trombonist Eddie Edwards recalled early studio days for the May, 1947 issue of *Jazz Record*, which is reprinted in *Selections from the Gutter* (University of California Press, 1977), edited by Art Hodes and Chadwick Hansen. From his account and Brunn's book, the myth arose that the ODJB's Columbia disc features the first jazz recordings. Although Rust's *Jazz Records: 1897-1942* cites a January date for Columbia A2297, Rust has since called this an error, identifying May 31 as the real date for the performances. In "The First Jazz Record of All?" in *Victrola and 78 Journal* (Issue 6, Summer 1995), he states, "Discographies should be amended to read the Victor date *first*, and *then* the Columbia date (which produced probably the worst of all mementoes of the band)." In recalling for Brunn that they had visited Columbia first, some band members evi-dently confused a January audition with a May session, their memories of visiting a Columbia studio in late January being stronger than memories of returning.

Edwards gives a problematic account of recording for Columbia and Victor. He recalls Columbia studio carpenters building shelves and "ham-mering away while we tried to play," which is inconceivable if the band had been recording, though it is plausible if the band was merely audition-ing for Columbia executives. Edwards' account says nothing about the third company to record the band in 1917, the Aeolian Company.

A month after auditioning for Columbia, the band recorded for Victor, and takes from this February 26 session were issued relatively quickly. The first jazz record was Victor 18255, which featured "Dixieland Jass Band One-Step" (on the "A" side—"Composed and played by Original Dixieland 'Jass' Band") backed by "Livery Stable Blues." It is worth noting that "one-step" is in one title, and the other is characterized on the label as a fox trot. The phrase "For Dancing" is added to the right of the spindle hole on both sides of the disc (Columbia adds the phrase "Dance music" to the right of its spindle hole). Victor supplements stressed that ODJB records provided dance music. For example, announcing the release of "Broadway Rose" and "Sweet Mamma" on 18722, Victor's March 1921 supplement states, "Here are two numbers, which, if danced proper-ly, are guaranteed to keep the participant at least two jumps ahead of gloom and disaster." Announcing the release of "Dangerous Blues" and

"Royal Garden Blues" on 18798, Victor's November 1921 supplement states, "For those who demand humor in their dance records, these are assuredly 'good tunes.'"

The May 1917 Victor supplement, printed in late April, describes the ODJB's debut record and includes a photograph of the band. The May 1917 issue of *Talking Machine World* announces that Victor was distributing to dealers "an attention compelling poster listing two special Jass band ... selections."

The two compositions on the first jazz disc have complex histories, and legal difficulties led to some changes on the disc's label. The inclusion on the disc's A side ("Dixieland Jass Band One-Step") of a strain from Joe Jordan's 1909 "That Teasin' Rag" led to claims of copyright infringement. The earliest copies of the first ODJB disc do not cite the title of Jordan's rag; later copies say "Introducing 'That Teasin' Rag'" (curiously, the title on side A of the disc was changed to "Dixie Jass Band One-Step," the suffix "-land" omitted).

Also, a mixup with sheet music and song titles—"Livery Stable Blues" was supposed to have been called "Barnyard Blues" on the label—led to litigation. New Orleans trombonist Tom Brown claimed to be the writer of "Livery Stable Blues," and Nunez claimed the same.

Brunn states in *The Story of the Original Dixieland Jazz Band* that Victor's success with its first ODJB record inspired Columbia executives to release test recordings made months earlier: "It was not until 'Livery Stable Blues' had become a smash hit that Columbia recovered the master from its dead files and made pressings of 'Darktown Strutters' Ball' and 'Indiana' on A2297." However, Rust reports that the original recording card in the CBS files for both titles bears the date May 31, 1917. It reveals that four takes of Shelton Brooks' "Darktown Strutters' Ball" and three of James Hanley's "Indiana" were completed, two takes of each song used for pressings of Columbia A2297. In the Spring 1991 issue of the *Association for Recorded Sound Collections Journal*, Tim Brooks points out that the Columbia sides have May 1917 matrix numbers and that "notations on the original cards strongly indicate that [the Columbia sides] were recorded then as well, not renumbered from some earlier trial."

The disc was announced in Columbia's September 1917 supplement, though the July 1917 issue of *Talking Machine World* featured an advertisement listing the record as ready for issue on August 10. Columbia was beginning the experiment of issuing some records near the middle of a month. The advertisement states, "Here is the solution of one of your big problems—how to get more business from the 10th to the 20th—the ten dullest record days of the month!" It identifies "Indiana" as a one-step and

"Darktown Strutters' Ball" as a fox-trot, as does the disc's label. Brunn reports that the band learned "Indiana" in the publisher's office immediately before the session, humming "the tune en route so that it would not be forgotten." He reports that "Darktown Strutters' Ball" was likewise re-corded in a haphazard manner: "They had rehearsed the piece in the key of 'C,' but LaRocca, at the mercy of his peculiar musical memory, started off in 'D.' His colleagues had no choice other than to follow suit. . . ." Though the two performances issued by Columbia are less interesting than the two already issued by Victor, they are too polished for Brunn's accounts to be credible.

Shelton Brooks was grateful that the ODJB cut his "Darktown Strutters' Ball." In 1918 he supplied for his new song "When You Hear That Dixie-land Jazz Band Play," published by Will Rossiter, lyrics that celebrate the jazz pioneers: "At Reisenwebers' [sic] place they started, and cleaned up the whole darn town . . . They sway and play the 'Liv'ry Stable Blues.'"

It may seem odd that the band cut two numbers composed by others when it returned to Columbia on May 31. Given the success by late May of Victor 18255, which featured original compositions, Columbia executives were arguably shortsighted if they believed that "Indiana" and "Darktown Strutters' Ball" would appeal to record buyers more than original ODJB material. On the other hand, Columbia executives probably knew about legal disputes that followed the release of Victor 18255, and they must have concluded that material composed by others was safer than original ODJB compositions.

Before Columbia issued what the ODJB had recorded for the company on May 31, the band had signed a contract with the Aeolian Company of New York and had two sessions for that company. LaRocca's scrapbook or diary, which the musician late in life allowed Brian Rust to study, suggests that the first session was on July 29, 1917. The jazz artists were among the first musicians to record for the company. The Aeolian contract was for six months and was not renewed. The ODJB Aeolian-Vocalion discs, which are vertical cut, are incredibly rare, and it is not clear when they were issued nor how they were distributed. The Aeolian Company waited until mid-1918 to announce to the trade that it was making records. The May 1918 issue of *Talking Machine World* states, "The Aeolian Co., New York, is now ready to announce to the talking machine trade the new Aeolian-Vocalion record. The first list of records is now ready for general distribu-tion. . . . The Vocalion record will be merchandised through Vocalion representatives exclusively." The recording studio was not at the famous Aeolian Hall at 33 West 42nd Street but in a building at 35 West 43rd Street.

The band formed a vaudeville act with dancers Frank Hale and Signe Patterson, opening at B. F. Keith's Colonial Theater in late November 1917. They played in New York City vaudeville house for over a year. One of many acts in the popular revue *The Passing Show of 1918* at the Winter Garden was "Hale & Patterson and the original [sic] Dixieland Jazz Band."

With legal problems evidently resolved, the band returned to Victor in the spring of 1918. The band members would have naturally been eager to record again for the nation's most prestigious record company, and Victor executives undoubtedly looked forward to issuing more hit records. The five ODJB records issued by Victor in 1918 and early 1919 sold well, including "Tiger Rag" (18472). Sales would probably have been even greater had not wartime shortages limited the production of records at this time. Significantly, all ten titles issued from the 1918 sessions were original compositions.

Edwards was drafted in late July 1918, and trombonist Emile Christian joined. After a hiatus from Reisenweber's, on September 7 the band was again featured for a couple of weeks at the 400 Club Room (9:00 p.m. nightly), this time with Bert Kelly's Jazz Band as a second band. The next change in personnel was due to the influenza of late 1918: pianist Harry Ragas was a flu victim, dying on February 18, 1919. Composer-pianist J. Russel Robinson soon joined. Raised in Indianapolis, Robinson was the first ODJB member not from New Orleans (Sidney Lancefield played piano for the group too briefly in 1919 to count as a member).

The band traveled to London in March 1919. Brian Rust writes in *My Kind of Jazz* (Elm Tree Books, 1990, p. 140), "Just as the Original Dixieland Jazz Band was the first band to introduce jazz, at least under that name, to the United States, so it was also the first to bring real jazz to Europe when it arrived in Liverpool on April 1, 1919, to appear in London as an added attraction to the revue *Joy Bells* at the Hippodrome." Quickly removed from *Joy Bells*, allegedly because star attraction George Robey was jealous of the applause given the ODJB during its London debut on April 7, the band opened at the Palladium on April 12, weeks later opened at the Martan Club, two months later opened at Rector's, and then opened at the Palais de Danse.

J. Russel Robinson reported in an interview for the August 1947 issue of *The Record Changer*, "[W]e played for contract at the Martan Club which was located at 6 and 8 Old Bond Street . . . but our contract wasn't renewed. The rest of the fellows decided to go and play at the Palais de Dance at Hammersmith, but I thought this was the wrong sort of move and left." For several months, beginning in October, English pianist Billy Jones was a band member. When he returned to the United States, Robinson became a Palace Trio member, working with Rudy Wiedoeft and Mario Perry. He rejoined the ODJB when the others returned from abroad. Robinson was finally replaced by Frank Signorelli in 1921.

England's Columbia company engaged the band in 1919 and 1920 for seventeen numbers issued on twelve-inch discs. The band recorded eight original compositions (all with Robinson on piano) as well as nine non-original works, mostly popular tunes of the day (all with Jones on piano). The most important performances recorded in London were "Satanic Blues" and "'Lasses Candy." They were original compositions but ODJB performances of them were unavailable in the United States during the band's heyday. The band had recorded the two numbers for Victor before leaving for England and would record them again also upon returning, but no takes were judged satisfactory by Victor executives. The band did record "Satanic Blues" in 1936 for RCA Victor.

The band visited Victor's New York City studio soon after returning from England, making test records on September 13, 1920, including a take of "Singin' the Blues," written by pianist Robinson. The band never again recorded the entire song but included a chorus when recording "Margie," called a medley fox trot. After making tests in September, they did not return to the studio until late November, by which time Robinson had composed "Margie." The band would make fine records in its remaining sixteen months with Victor, but these ODJB records are more commercial, less wild, than discs of 1917 and 1918. It is significant that all selections issued by Victor before the England trip were ODJB compositions—one member or another took composer credit, sometimes two members working together, sometimes the entire band—and these compositions have since become jazz standards. But no recordings issued by Victor after the England trip were composed by original ODJB members. About half of these selections were composed by African Americans, the others by white songwriters. Robinson was co-composer of "Margie" and "Palesteena" (sharing credit with Con Conrad), but though these two songs proved popular, the New Orleans roots of the ODJB are obscured in these numbers.

Beginning with the September session during which only test records were made, Victor executives evidently wanted the ODJB to conform more to their own ideas of how a popular dance ensemble should sound. Saxophonist Bennie Krueger was added, the first time a non-ODJB member performed on ODJB records. Few jazz bands making records in the earliest years used saxophones, and the instrument was virtually never used in early New Orleans jazz bands. Saxophone was added undoubtedly at the insistence of a Victor recording manager—either John S. Macdonald, Eddie King, or Clifford Cairns. In late November and early December, the ODJB with Krueger recorded various takes of titles issued on what became their best-selling disc: "Margie" coupled with "Palesteena" (18717). Various versions of the two songs were also issued in February 1921 when the ODJB disc was released—Eddie Cantor's version of "Margie" on Emerson 10301, Cantor's version of "Palesteena" on Emerson 10292, Billy Jones' version of "Palesteena" on Okeh 4222 and his versions of both songs on Aeolian-Vocalion 14132, the Vernon Trio's version of "Margie" on Gennett 4658, Fred Whitehouse's version of "Palesteena" on Cardinal 2001, the Frisco Syncopators' version of "Margie" on Paramount 20037, the Crescent Trio's version of "Margie" on Cardinal 2005, and the Rega Dance Orchestra's version of "Margie" on Okeh 4211.

Announcing the new ODJB release, Victor's February 1921 supplement indicated that the sound on the record was different, the adjective "beautiful" used for the first time to describe an ODJB selection:

> The Original Dixieland Jazz Band is back on the stage this month with two superb fox trots. They are widely different from anything this organization has ever done. "Margie" is melting, soft, tender, romantic in spirit, but for all that has the dash and go, perhaps, which supply the only real romance in jazz music.... "Palesteena" ... is in similar style, with some lovely effects produced by the use of sustained tones against highly rhythmic "figures" in other instruments. These are beautiful and original recordings.

On August 10, 1920, black singer Mamie Smith supported by her Jazz Hounds recorded Perry Bradford's "Crazy Blues" for Okeh 4169. Half a year later, on January 28, 1921, the ODJB cut "Crazy Blues" as an instrumental (18729)—its kazoo solo was novel for the time. The ODJB's version of Bradford's tune probably sold more copies than any other of "Crazy Blues" (Victor had a more sophisticated network for the distribution of a hit disc than the relatively new General Phonograph Corporation, maker of Okeh discs).

Also cut during the January 1921 session were "Home Again Blues," "Broadway Rose," and "Sweet Mamma (Papa's Getting Mad)." The first two were conventional popular songs. Victor had already made a vocal recording of "Broadway Rose"—Henry Burr enjoyed success with this song—and that Victor executives viewed such material as suitable for the ODJB indicates they wanted the band to deliver a more commercial sound, or what supplements called a "beautiful" sound. Victor's March 1920 supplement, announcing its release, admits the song "was a beautiful sentimental song, but that does not prevent its becoming an equally beautiful fox trot." The band performs it at a quick pace, and it is a fine performance. The last song of the three, "Sweet Mamma (Papa's Getting Mad)," is noteworthy for being the first ODJB record to feature voices. Band members, along with executives Eddie King and Clifford Cairns, sing out "Sweet mama, papa's getting mad!" The performance ends with Nick LaRocca announcing in New Orleans dialect, "Yes, sir! Sweet mama, papa's getting mad!"

A few months passed before the next session. On May 3 the band recorded takes of Tom Delaney's "Jazz Me Blues" and W. C. Handy's "St. Louis Blues." An instrumental version of "Jazz Me Blues" was issued on 18772; the takes of "St. Louis Blues" from this session were rejected, as were takes of "Jazz Me Blues" featuring Lavinia Turner as vocalist—the only time a female recorded with the ODJB in the Victor studio, and also the only time an African American recorded with the band. The Delaney song, destined to become a jazz standard, was published in 1921 and was recorded around this time by Lillyn Brown for Emerson 10384. It had been introduced on record by Lucille Hegamin, whose version on Arto 9045 was issued in March. It was Hegamin's record debut.

During sessions on May 25 and June 7, 1921, Al Bernard added vocal refrains for "St. Louis Blues" (18772), "Royal Garden Blues" (18798), and "Dangerous Blues" (18798). Though the decision to add vocal refrains came from Victor executives, Krueger may have been instrumental in the choice of Bernard for the sessions. Bernard had added vocal refrains to Bennie Krueger and His Orchestra sessions beginning in early 1921, including "Royal Garden Blues" (Brunswick 2077). Around the time of the ODJB session, Bernard added refrains during Krueger sessions for Gennett, including "St. Louis Blues" (Gennett 4751). Like the ODJB members, Bernard was from New Orleans, and perhaps he was considered suited for the band since in 1919 he had recorded for different companies "Bluin' the Blues," an ODJB number. Closely associated with "St. Louis Blues" and other W. C. Handy tunes, Bernard was as close to a jazz singer in mid-1921 as any white singer making records at the time. (He worked closely with J. Russel Robinson around this time—this is another possible connection with the ODJB, though Robinson had left the ODJB by this point, pianist Frank Signorelli taking his place.)

Bernard's vocal contributions to these three numbers are lackluster, but band members, including saxophonist Krueger, are in fine form, with Shields delivering a memorable twenty-four-bar solo on "St. Louis Blues," which is the first time on record that a band member delivers an improvised solo of significant length. It is the first solo of distinction to be issued on a jazz record, and since this version of "St. Louis Blues" sold well, it must have influenced in the early 1920s many aspiring jazz musicians. Over a year passed before clarinet soloing on records—namely, Leon Rappolo's work with the New Orleans Rhythm Kings—would match Shields' performance.

The final Victor session was on December 1, 1921, which produced only "Bow Wow Blues (My Mamma Treats Me Like a Dog)" (18850), composed by Cliff Friend and Nat Osborne. For the first time, an ODJB performance was issued with another artist on a disc's reverse side, in this case the Benson Orchestra of Chicago performing "Railroad Blues." The ODJB's final Victor performance shared something with one of its first, "Livery Stable Blues"—the comic imitation of animals. "Livery Stable Blues" is far more significant since nothing like it or its companion piece, "Dixie Jass Band One-Step," had ever been recorded before. "Bow Wow Blues," though a fine performance, is indicative of the ODJB's inability after only a few years—at least partly due to studio interference—to remain innovative jazz artists. The song itself was composed by Tin Pan Alley writers, and dog imitations on jazz records were already becoming passé. The Louisiana Five enjoyed success with "Yelping Hound Blues" in 1919, and others who had recorded songs with "dog" themes around this time include Gorman's Novelty Syncopators ("Barkin' Dog" was issued in late 1919 on Columbia A2844) and Saxi Holtsworth Harmony Hounds ("Bow-Wow" was issued on Gennett 9039 and Emerson 10247). The ODJB was following rather than setting a trend.

Ominously, Shields quit in December 1921 to settle in California. Original members LaRocca, Edwards, and Sbarbaro were joined by clarinetist Artie Seaberg, pianist Henry Vanicelli, and saxophonist Don Parker for three Okeh sessions beginning in late 1922. Two Okeh discs were issued, both rare today. Among the four titles, "Toddlin' Blues" was the most significant since it was an original ODJB composition not recorded for any other company by that time. "Some of These Days" was a Shelton Brooks standard, and the two remaining titles, "Tiger Rag" and "Barnyard Blues" (also known as "Livery Stable Blues"), had already been recorded for other companies. Since no versions by the band of the original compositions "'Lasses Candy" and "Satanic Blues" had been issued in America, it is surprising that the band did not record these during the Okeh sessions.

The band would not record again until the mid-1930s. In 1935 a group called the Original Dixieland Jazz Band made two records for Vocalion, but the only original band member was Sbarbaro. In 1936 "Nick LaRocca and the Original Dixieland Band"—the name given on record labels—cut titles for RCA Victor. Sbarbaro played drums and Shields played clarinet, but this was not a true reunion of original members. A dozen additional musicians were used, and new arrangements were supplied for the old numbers. The resulting performances share little with the band's trademark sound and sold poorly.

Finally, on September 25 and again on November 10, 1936, four original members (LaRocca, Shields, Edwards, and Sbarbaro) along with J. Russel Robinson rerecorded numbers that the ODJB had introduced nearly two decades earlier, using old arrangements for the most part. The band, identified as The Original Dixieland Five, does not repeat early sections on "Original Dixieland One Step," which creates time on the record for Shields to take a solo. His fine solo had been worked out in advance (he had delivered the *same* solo eight months earlier when the augmented band had recorded "Original Dixieland One Step"). Band members were considerably older and the music must have seemed dated to audiences at that time, but the two sessions produced remarkable records, the microphone capturing nuances that no acoustic-era recording horn could. Drums and piano were finally prominent on ODJB records.

The four surviving original members never worked together again, but the name Original Dixieland Jazz Band was used for records made later. In 1938, Shields, Edwards, and Sbarbaro made Bluebird records credited to the Original Dixieland Jazz Band. Edwards and Sbarbaro continued to work together from 1943 to 1946, making various records credited to the Original Dixieland Jazz Band, with other musicians including Max Kaminsky, Eddie Condon, and Wild Bill Davidson. Commodore records of 1946 gave credit to "Eddie Edwards and His Original Dixieland Jazz Band."

Ossman, Vess L. (August 21, 1868-December 7 or 8, 1923)

Known as "the Banjo King," Vess Ossman was for two decades beginning in the 1890s the most popular banjoist to make records. It was a propitious time for being a master banjoist since no instrument recorded better than banjo in the early decades of the industry. Another nickname was "Plunks." Sylvester ("Vess") Louis Ossman was born in Hudson, New York, son of Frederick and Anna Ossman. His father owned a bakery. According to an obituary cited by Jim Walsh in the February 1949 issue of *Hobbies*, the young Ossman took his first music lesson from Fidell Wise of Hudson.

Only a few banjoists had preceded him in making commercial records. Allen Koenigsberg's *Edison Cylinder Records, 1889-1912*, reprints "The First Book of Phonograph Records," compiled by Edison employee A. Theo E. Wangemann (1855-1906), and it shows Will Lyle making "50 Banjo Records . . . on invitation" on September 4, 1889. Lyle made additional recordings later that year. Banjo players who recorded as solo instrumentalists in the 1890s include the Bohee Brothers, William Stanley

Grinsted (he would later cultivate a singing career, using the nom de disque Frank C. Stanley), Clark H. Jones, Parke Hunter, Rudi Heller, Stephen B. Clements, Ruben ("Ruby") Brooks, the team of Diamond and Curry, the team of Joseph Cullen and William P. Collins, and, in 1898, a young Fred Van Eps, who at that time spelled his name "Van Epps."

Ossman's first known cylinder was of Sousa's "Washington Post March," listed in a North American Phonograph Company supplement of 1893. Around this time he also cut "Love's Sweet Honor." He recorded several additional titles for the company in 1894 and within a couple of years became an important Columbia artist, from 1896 to 1899 cutting dozens of titles, sometimes accompanying Len Spencer.

From about 1896 to 1910, his services as a recording artist were in great demand, and he continued to record into the World War I era. Regarding Ossman's records at the turn of the century, Jim Walsh noted in the October 1948 issue of *Hobbies:*

> In keeping with the prevailing taste of the period, he recorded mostly negro songs, lively ragtime ditties and marches, but what he played was performed with true artistry. Probably his banjo solos of the late '90's and early 1900's express the go-ahead optimism and accelerated tempo of the American life of those days as effectively as anything could.

He made nearly seventy discs for Berliner, beginning in mid-1897. On August 19, 1897, he recorded two numbers that are noteworthy: "Rag Time Medley" (467) is one of the first recordings to mention the new phrase "rag time" (it was generally given as two words in the late 1890s); "L.A.W. March" (468) was actually composed by Ossman. Another Ossman composition that he recorded is "Sunflower Dance."

He made cylinders for Bettini in June 1898 and again around 1900. He made a dozen seven-inch Zon-o-phone discs at the turn of the century. Around this time a New York City musical instruments dealer, John A. Haley, reprinted letters by Ossman because they endorsed Haley's products. A letter written by Ossman on September 12, 1899, gives his address as "Banjo Studios, 121 West 125th St." A letter dated June 27, 1900, states, "Undoubtedly, your strings are the best strings I ever put on my banjo . . . Vess L. Ossman, Banjoist, Banjo Studio Room 52, A.B.C. Building, 67-69 West 125th Street."

On July 19, 1900, he began his long association with the company that would soon be famous as the Victor Talking Machine Company. On that day he recorded several numbers for Eldridge R. Johnson's Consolidated Talking Machine Company. Only one performance from that first session was issued: "An Ethiopian Mardi Gras" (seven-inch A-150). An RCA Victor advertisement in *Life* for October 26, 1946, commemorates the pressing of the company's one billionth record and announces, "The oldest master record in RCA-Victor's huge library was made on January 21, 1901. It is a banjo solo, played by Vess Ossman, 'Tell Me, Pretty Maiden.'" The take that Ossman cut of this selection from the musical *Florodora* on January 21, 1901 was originally issued on ten-inch Monarch 3049, which was one of Victor's earliest ten-inch discs (Ossman made seven-inch discs before this but masters from earlier sessions were no longer stored by RCA Victor). Ossman cut "Tell Me, Pretty Maiden" again for Victor on October 7, 1902. Celebrating the pressing of a billion records, RCA Victor in 1946 reissued "Tell Me Pretty Maiden" on a gold label record with new matrix number D6-CC-6167, the label stating, "From FLORADORA [sic] . . . Oldest RCA Victor 'Master' Record recorded Jan. 21, 1901."

By the early 1900s Ossman's fame was international. He made two concert tours of England—in 1900 and 1903, making records in London during both visits—and diversified his recording activities beyond solo and accompaniment work to include duets, trios, and a banjo orchestra. He led the Ossman-Dudley Trio, which also consisted of Audley Dudley on mandolin and a harp-guitar player.

Ossman often recorded the same titles for various companies. These include "Dixie Medley" (called "Turkey in the Straw Medley" on Victor 4424), "Cocoanut Dance," "Darkies' Patrol," "Rag Time Medley," "A Coon Band Contest," "Ragtime Skedaddle," "Hands Across the Sea," "Rusty Rags," "The Colored Major," "Whistling Rufus," "Keep Off the Grass," and "A Gay Gossoon." Victor 16266, featuring "Keep Off the Grass" and "Silver Heels," remained popular for years, and when new takes were required in the spring of 1919, Fred Van Eps was chosen to rerecord them. The Van Eps performances were issued under the old catalog number of 16266.

After 1910 his name appeared less frequently in company supplements whereas his chief rival on the banjo, Fred Van Eps, became increasingly prominent. As leader of Ossman's Singing and Playing Orchestra, Ossman provided dance music at hotels, often in cities far from recording studios, including Indianapolis and Dayton. He made no records in 1913 and 1914. He began recording again in late 1915, first for Edison and then for Victor. He cut some numbers every few months in 1916 and 1917 for companies as varied as Edison, Victor, Columbia, Operaphone, and Gennett.

He also joined by April 1917 the touring act of recording artists sometimes called the Popular Talking Machine Artists (the group was known by various names until "Eight Famous Victor Artists" was used regularly in the early 1920s, by which time Ossman had left). In the February 1965 issue of

Hobbies, Walsh describes a photograph of the Record Maker Troupe in Troop's Music Store at Harrisburg, Pennsylvania, in April 1917. The artists included Ossman, Albert Campbell, Byron G. Harlan, Arthur Collins, and songwriter-pianist Theodore Morse. A program that survives of the Peerless Record Makers appearing at the Williamsport High School in Pennsylvania on April 17, 1917, lists Ossman as performing the Percy Wenrich rag "The Smiler." The May 1917 issue of *Talking Machine World* identifies members of what is called the Phonograph Singers—Campbell, Burr, Collins, Harlan, Morse, Billy Murray—and the fact that Ossman's name is missing suggests he stopped touring with recording artists by this time. Walsh reported that Ossman did not get along with manager Burr.

He recorded for Columbia as late as 1917, with "He's Just Like You" as cut by Vess Ossman's Banjo Orchestra on May 1, 1917, being among the last issued performances (A2321). His final recordings for a major record company were made on December 14, 1917, for Columbia, accompanying singer Carroll Clark for two numbers that went unissued.

He wed Eunice Smith, who was born in Hyde Park, New York, on August 21, 1868 (she died around 1930), and the marriage produced three children aside from a few that died in infancy: Vess L. Ossman Jr. (he also became a skilled banjoist); Raymond; and daughter Annadele, who was born around 1908 (she wrote to Walsh, ". . . I was his youngest daughter and he died when I was fifteen").

Toward the end of his life, he worked most often in Midwestern hotels as a leader of his own dance orchestra and lived with his family in the Riverside apartment complex in Dayton, Ohio. In 1923 he began a long tour of B. F. Keith's vaudeville houses, his banjo-playing son, Vess Ossman Jr., being part of the act. The famous musician suffered a heart attack while playing a theater show in Minneapolis, Minnesota. He recovered in a hospital from the first attack and returned to stage work. He suffered another attack hours after performing in a vaudeville house in Fairmount, Minnesota. He is buried in Valhalla Cemetery in St. Louis. Most sources state that he died on December 8, 1923, but Bob Ault reports in the May 1986 issue of *Hobbies* that Valhalla Cemetery records state that he died on December 7. He had been scheduled to play, with his son, in St. Louis during Christmas week. Vess Ossman Jr. later worked for a theater agency in St. Louis and died in the city on January 22, 1942.

An Ossman performance appeared on a record list as late as 1926 when Edison reissued "Banjo Medley," cut in 1909 and originally issued on wax Amberol 250, on celluloid Blue Amberol 5377.

Peerless Quartet

The Peerless Quartet—the most successful and long lived of all groups that recorded during the acoustic era—was organized in 1906 by Frank C. Stanley. Stanley also served as its manager until his death from pneumonia at age forty-one in December 1910.

The Peerless was basically an offshoot of the old Columbia Quartet, of which Stanley had been a member, though it also evolved from the Invincible Quartet, one of several vocal groups that Stanley organized and managed. The Columbia, which had its origins in the late 1890s, underwent many personnel changes though Albert Campbell remained as first tenor. By 1904 the Columbia Quartet consisted of Campbell, second tenor Henry Burr, baritone Steve Porter, and basso "Big Tom" Daniels. When Daniels was succeeded by Stanley, the four original Peerless members were together. It was still the Columbia Quartet, but in time the members adopted the name Peerless in order to work for other companies.

Stanley did much of the lead singing upon joining, though it was unusual for a bass-baritone to lead in quartet singing, which is normally led by the "second tenor" ("first" and "second" indicate the relative pitch of tenors, not their importance to a quartet—"first tenor" sings the highest). In male quartet singing, the bass usually sings the foundation or root of a chord, the second tenor sings the melody, the first tenor sings harmony above the melody, and the baritone completes the chord by filling in the missing link somewhere between the bass and the first tenor.

The Invincible made Edison cylinders by 1902, and the Edison lineup for this was first tenor Byron G. Harlan, second tenor George Seymour Lenox, baritone Arthur Collins, and Stanley. On Columbia, American, and other disc releases, Campbell or Burr sang the lead in place of Lenox, who seems to have been exclusive to Edison. Managing the Invincible evidently gave Stanley the experience needed to manage the successful Peerless.

An early appearance of the Peerless Quartet name is in a February 1907 Zon-o-phone supplement announcing "Where Is My Boy Tonight?" (673), company literature identifying members as Burr, Porter, Stanley, and "Frank Howard" (the name often used for Campbell on Zon-o-phone releases). Jim Walsh states in the December 1969 issue of *Hobbies*, ". . . I suspect that the Universal Male Quartet, which began making Zon-o-phone records in 1906, was really the Peerless, and that, since Zon-o-phone records were the product of the Universal Talking Machine Company, the Quartet was at first called the Universal Quartet, just as it was the Columbia Quartet on Columbia discs and cylinders."

The Peerless made its Victor debut with "Women!" from Lehár's light opera *The Merry Widow* (single-sided 5392; later double-sided 16424). It was issued in April 1908. During the 1907-1909 period, the Peerless also had debut releases on Edison, Indestructible (as just "Quartet" or "Male Quartet"), U-S Everlasting, American, Imperial, and other labels. The first Edison cylinder to feature the name Peerless Quartette is Standard 10106, issued in April 1909. On it, the quartet performs a comic sketch called "A Meeting of the Hen Roost Club," which was written by Cal Stewart, according to the February 1909 issue of *Edison Phonograph Monthly*. Announcing the July 1909 release of "Call to Arms" by the Peerless on Amberol 171, the May 1909 issue of the trade journal states, "The sketch portion was written by Albert Campbell."

In 1909 Arthur Collins replaced Porter, who left the Peerless to join the new American Quartet. Collins became an important addition to the Peerless, singing lead on some numbers. With a voice well-suited for ragtime and other upbeat numbers, he contributed to the quartet's versatility. He was especially prominent when the Peerless worked as a minstrel troupe on records, going by such names as the Virginia Minstrels on Victor 35095 and North Carolina Minstrels on Victor 35307. Stanley served as interlocutor and is addressed as "Mr. Stanley," but otherwise the men call each other by their first names—"Arthur," "Albert," and "Harry" (for Burr, who was a stuttering minstrel). John Meyer, addressed simply as "John," later served as interlocutor.

The quartet was called the Columbia Quartet on Columbia records for years after other companies adopted the name Peerless. The Peerless name did not appear in a Columbia list until the release of "That Raggedy Rag" (A1177) in August 1912 (the Peerless also recorded it for Victor 17341). From that point onward the quartet was usually called the Peerless on Columbia labels, though the foursome was occasionally called the Columbia Quartet into the World War I period.

Following Stanley's death in December 1910, Burr took over as manager and engaged John Meyer, with whom Burr had been associated in church work, to sing bass parts. This new combination was very popular. Campbell later recalled that there was so much studio work to be done, especially after Burr formed the Sterling Trio (which was the Peerless minus Collins), that the group had to go three shifts a day to meet all recording commitments. The Peerless made so many records for Pathé that the company, eager to give the appearance that they had a large roster of artists, sometimes issued the Peerless under its old name of the Invincible Four. Group members toured as part of the Record Maker Troupe.

Around 1919 Collins departed the Peerless though as late as 1921 Columbia catalogs listed Collins as the quartet's baritone, or "first bass." Page 125 of the May 1919 issue of *Talking Machine World* identifies Collins as part of the "record makers on tour" throughout Ohio and Pennsylvania in May, though it is possible Collins left months earlier and that the trade journal had not been informed of the change. Columbia records made in 1917 feature Frank Croxton in Collins' place, which suggests Collins did not work regularly with the Peerless member as late as 1919. Campbell told Walsh, "It was a personal matter. He just couldn't get along with Burr." Walsh also suggested that Collins was dropped—along with duet partner Harlan—either because Victor and Columbia executives resented their giving "Tone Tests" across the country for Edison, or because Edison company executives insisted that they not sing for two large competitors in the months they were giving recitals designed to convince audiences that Diamond Disc technology was best.

Collins' departure created an opening for Croxton, who took over the bass parts; Meyer, who had been singing bass, took baritone parts. This lineup remained until 1925. Burr negotiated an exclusive contract with Victor in late 1920. Page 62 of the November 1920 issue of *Talking Machine World* states, "Of great interest to all Victor dealers and Victor record enthusiasts is the announcement made by the Victor Talking Machine Co. that the popular record artists Albert Campbell, Henry Burr, John Meyer and Frank Croxton will, after November 1, be exclusive Victor artists." Victor discs featuring the Peerless sold well in the remaining years of the acoustic era.

On February 26, 1925, the group contributed to "A Miniature Concert," the earliest performance on a Victor record made with the electric recording process. It was not Victor's first electric disc available in shops since a dozen Victor discs featuring performances cut after the February 26 session had been released by the time twelve-inch Victor 35753 was issued on May 29 (Victor did not announce to the American public that it had converted to the new electric process until November). Billy Murray, acting as master of ceremonies on the record, alludes to Prohibition when he introduces the Peerless Quartet as "Beerless."

Page 159 of the March 1925 issue of *Talking Machine World* reports that on March 12 the Eight Popular Victor Artists were featured on the sixth radio program sponsored by the Victor Talking Machine Company

(Victor's first radio program had been broadcast on New Year's Day, 1925). This program of popular artists including the Peerless Quartet, Billy Murray, and Rudy Wiedoeft must have seemed refreshingly different to at least some listeners since all previous programs had featured Victor's Red Seal artists. Also on the air on March 12 was the International Novelty Orchestra led by Nat Shilkret.

During the early electric era the Peerless cut again some numbers that had been popular in the acoustic era, but by this time the quartet's style of singing was becoming dated. The Revelers and other singing groups with a more jazz-oriented sound were becoming increasingly popular. Perhaps because Burr wanted a new sound, or tension was building among members, or he could hire others for less money, Burr disbanded the old lineup of the Peerless Quartet in 1925 and hired new singers. This happened sometime between mid-1925, when the old Peerless cut new takes of titles originally issued in the acoustic era (the electric takes were on 19870, 19877, 19883, 19885, 19887, and 19888), and early September.

Whatever the reason, Walsh surmised in the December 1969 issue of *Hobbies* that this "must have been a fairly sudden decision involving a great deal of ill feeling." On the other hand, Quentin Riggs reports that when Walsh met Campbell in 1940, the tenor spoke warmly and positively about Burr.

An advertisement in the September 1925 issue of *Talking Machine World* indicates that Campbell, Meyer, and Croxton were joined by tenor Charles Harrison to form a rival Peerless Quartet, Croxton serving as manager (they used the name Peerless Entertainers for Gennett discs issued in April and May 1926). This new group was available for bookings by November 1925 as part of a larger ensemble of artists called the Peerless Entertainers. *Talking Machine World* advertisements indicate that Arthur Fields filled the comedy spot that Murray occupied in the other company. Moreover, Rudy Wiedoeft left the Eight Popular Artists and joined the Peerless Entertainers.

For Burr's Peerless Quartet, replacements included first tenor and comedian Carl Mathieu (born February 3, 1894; died August 1973), baritone James Stanley (born May 22, 1881; died August 12, 1963—at times in his career he also performed as a bass), and bass Stanley Baughman (born December 18, 1892; died May 1963).

James Stanley came with considerable experience, having led his own group, the Stanley Quartet, since at least 1916. An advertisement in the May 20, 1916, issue of *Musical America* indicates the quartet consisted of James Stanley, who sings bass; tenor Joseph Mathieu; soprano Louise MacMahan; and contralto Flora Hardie. The quartet recorded for Pathé.

Eleanor Stanley is cited as pianist for the quartet. This was the former Eleanor Stark, whose father, John Stark, was a famous music publisher of ragtime music, including Scott Joplin's "Maple Leaf Rag."

Pierre Key's *Music Yearbook of 1926-27* mentions a Mendelssohn Quartet consisting of first tenor Joseph Mathieu, second tenor Carl F. Mathieu, baritone Harold Wiley, and bass Stanley Baughman, which suggests Mathieu and Baughman were singing in two quartets at the same time. A concert program for the Eight Popular Victor Artists dated May 7, 1927, for a performance in Grand Rapids, Iowa, states that Baughman "sang with the Mendelssohn Quartet for several seasons, is a pianist of ability and is musical instructor during summer seasons at Columbia University."

It also states that Mathieu "is soloist at St. Marks in the Bouwerie" and that Stanley "is baritone soloist at the Church of the Incarnation, New York." Stanley made records as late as 1928 as a member of the Dixie Minstrels (he sang bass, not baritone), which recorded for Romeo and related labels. Walsh quotes in the October 1959 issue of *Hobbies* a letter from tenor Lambert Murphy that suggests James Stanley suffered throat problems, like Murphy himself, late in life. Murphy wrote to Walsh, "Richard Crooks dropped in on us recently and told us that Jim Stanley . . . had the same thing happen to him as I had, and that we both make the same sort of noises. The handicap of having a loud whisper instead of a voice is considerable. . . ."

Victor signaled the change in its January 1926 record supplement by announcing a double-faced disc by "the new Peerless Quartet." The first record was Victor 19827: "It Must Be Love" backed by "Let Me Linger in Your Arms," recorded on October 23, 1925.

On October 22, 1926, Murray collaborated with Mathieu, Baughman, and Stanley—three Peerless members—for the last American Quartet performance. The four recorded "Bring Back Those Minstrel Days" by the electric process, but it was never issued.

Despite a new lineup delivering a fresh sound, Burr's Peerless did not last much longer. With control of the company in new hands (on December 6, 1926, Eldridge R. Johnson sold his 245,000 shares of stock in the Victor Talking Machine Company to the Wall Street banking firms of Speyer & Co. and J. & W. Seligman), Victor executives decided not to renew the contracts of many established artists, including Burr. The last Peerless Quartet title issued by Victor was "Old Names of Old Flames" (21079), recorded on November 11, 1927. With no contract and diminished interest in stage appearances (talking pictures undercut the popularity of touring acts), Burr disbanded the Peerless in 1929.

Around 1934, Peerless recordings of 1925—with Burr, Campbell, Croxton, and Meyer—were issued on Montgomery Ward M-4808 (in 1933 RCA Victor began making records to be sold through Montgomery Ward stores, at first using a red-on-buff label). The titles were "I'll Take You Home Again, Kathleen" and "Beautiful Isle of Somewhere." Labels give credit to "Henry Burr and Peerless Quartet." Other titles remained available for a longer period, such as "Where Is My Boy Tonight?," available in the Montgomery Ward catalog from fall 1933 to fall 1939 on M-8160.

Porter, Steve (c. 1862-January 13, 1936)

Baritone Steve Porter was born in Buffalo, New York, as Steven Carl Porter. Jim Walsh writes in the May 1952 issue of *Hobbies*, "Death notices gave his age as 73, so he probably was born in 1862." He began his show business career as a vaudeville comedian in the 1890s and eventually became best known, at least as a solo recording artist, for Irish humor. Perhaps his most important contributions to records was as a member of popular quartets, especially the Peerless and American.

Victor catalogs state, "Mr. Porter is one of the pioneer makers of talking machine records, having been engaged in this work since 1897." Porter's first known Berliner session was on July 29, 1897. One disc featured "Sally Warner" (1757), the disc's surface noting the date. This was followed by a session one day later, and he was in the studio again on August 13, 1897, to cut "Sweet Rosie O'Grady" (537) and other numbers. He made other Berliners in 1897, some when Porter sang as a member of the Diamond Four, which also featured Albert Campbell. As a solo artist Porter made two dozen Berliners, mostly hymns and popular ballads. The November-December 1897 issue of *The Phonoscope* lists Porter among the personnel of the Greater New York Quartet, which also included Roger Harding, Len Spencer, and a singer named "Depew."

Porter is not included in Columbia's June 1897 list, but over sixty Porter titles are in the 1898 list, which states, "Mr. Steve Porter is a valuable acquisition to the staff of Columbia Entertainers. He is possessed of a rich baritone voice." As on Berliner discs, he sings mostly songs of a sentimental, patriotic, or sacred nature on early Columbia cylinders. His comedic talents must have become evident to industry executives only after he had established himself as a recording artist.

The July 1898 issue of *The Phonoscope* refers to Porter as a member of the Ocean Yacht Club of Staten Island. Porter's yacht, the *Chiquita*, was forty-two feet long and had a fourteen-foot beam. That such information was published in a trade journal suggests he was by this time well known to industry insiders. The February 1899 issue of the trade journal states,

"Fred Hylands, Roger Harding, and Steve Porter are the enterprising young men who have recently organized a song publishing company under the name of the Knickerbocker Music Publishing Co." The involvement of Harding and Porter was brief. The April issue of the trade journal announces that it had been renamed Hylands, Spencer and Yeager—Len Spencer had taken an interest in the firm.

Quentin Riggs writes in the December 1969 issue of *Talking Machine Review:*

> Around 1899 Porter took part, along with S.H. Dudley and William F. Hooley, in the organization of the American Phonograph Company, which was formed by recording artists with the idea of selling cylinder records direct to the consumer. They offered to have the Haydn Quartet make records of any songs that the customers wanted, regardless of whether or not they were listed in the catalog. It was a novel idea, but the competition was too great and the company soon went out of business.

Porter's versatility as an artist is indicated by the range of material he cut during his first Victor recording session on June 12, 1901. Numbers include the comic "Backyard Conversation Between Two Irish Washerwomen" as well as Charles K. Harris's sentimental "Hello, Central! Give Me Heaven" (he also recorded the Harris number on Lambert cylinder 518, opening with the announcement that he is joined by "Master Hogan in the gallery"—really tenor John Bieling). At the same Victor session he recorded Paul Dresser's sentimental "On the Banks of the Wabash, Far Away" as well as a parody of Dresser's "The Blue and the Gray." These performances and others were issued by Victor on seven-inch discs.

Walsh reports in the January 1975 issue of *Hobbies,* "For a time in the late 1890s [Porter] and Russell Hunting were engaged in turning out the crude type of moving pictures made in those days. Both soon afterward went to England, where Porter became recording manager of a small recording firm—probably Nicole Frères." Porter recorded for the Nicole Frères company over twenty titles—American comic and sentimental songs as well as English songs such as "Varmer Giles" (evidently sung in a West Country dialect). Other titles include "Mr. Dooley," "Stay in Your Own Back Yard," "As Your Hair Grows Whiter," "Way Down Yonder in the Cornfield." He returned to America for more recording activities, but he again left to work abroad, this time as recording director at the HMV plant at Calcutta, India.

He returned to the United States from India around 1906 and resumed recording activities. He soon reached the peak of his popularity as a solo performer, his comic monologues of various Irishmen, especially "Flanagan," selling well. Typical titles are "Flanagan on a Farm" (Columbia A356; Victor 16141) and "Flanagan on a Broadway Car" (Victor 16015). "Flanagan at the Barber's" was issued on Zon-o-phone 985 in March 1908 and literature promotes it as "a selection of rapid fire wit and humor describing the haps and mishaps, experienced by our Hibernian friend, 'Mike Flanagan,' while in the hands of a 'Tonsorial Artist.'" Victor 17658 has an interesting coupling: on one side Porter performs "Mr. Dooley's Address to the Suffragists," which the label characterizes as "Irish specialty with orchestra," and the other side features "Fall in Line (Suffrage March)," composed by Zena S. Hawn and performed by the Victor Military Band. Another comic character created by Porter was Alderman Doolin.

The first of many Edison cylinders featuring Porter as a solo artist was issued in March 1907: "Flanagan's Troubles in a Restaurant" (9495). Most of his solo work for Edison's National Phonograph Company was issued on two-minute wax cylinders between 1907 and 1909, though he continued making solo recordings for Edison into the 1920s. Edison issued in July 1910 on Amberol 465 a potpourri of songs from Gilbert and Sullivan's *The Mikado*, and Steve Porter sang the role of Ko-Ko. As a featured artist he cut five performances issued on Edison Diamond Discs, the last being released in 1923—"Flanagan's Troubles in a Restaurant" (51010), versions of which he had recorded much earlier in his career. The reverse side of Diamond Disc 51010 features Porter performing "Arkansaw Traveler" with Ernest Hare.

Though he was not an original member of the Spencer Trio, formed by Len Spencer in the late 1890s, Porter was a member along with Billy Golden when the trio made three recordings for Victor on February 6, 1903: "The Mocking Bird Medley," "Alpine Specialty," and "In Front of the Old Cabin Door." The trio's last recording was made on September 27, 1904: "Amateur Night on the Bowery" (Victor 4093).

Porter was a member of the Rambler Minstrel Company, which also included Billy Murray, Arthur Collins, and Byron G. Harlan. Porter often played the role of interlocutor and is addressed as "Mr. Porter" by the others. He wrote much of the material he recorded. Various records, such as the "descriptive specialty" titled "The Old Time Street Fakir" (Victor 16903), credit Porter for the writing. This kind of sketch was popular in the early days of recording, with George Graham recording the monologue "Street Fakir" for Berliner in 1896.

A comic sketch written by Porter in 1907 titled "An Evening at Mrs. Clancy's Boarding House" was recorded by him several times for Columbia and Victor.

He wrote many rube sketches, such as "Hi and Si of Jaytown," performed by Porter and Byron G. Harlan on Edison Blue Amberol 1523. On Victor 16849, he and Harlan perform "Two Rubes Swapping Horses" (a four-minute version was also recorded for Edison). Harlan plays Cyrus Skinner and Porter plays Hiram. Although the sketch has jokes, it is not entirely a comic sketch—one goal of the performance is to capture in a realistic manner two Americans from a rural area (Jaytown is said to be in Ohio) exchanging dialogue. Cy—or "Si," as Edison literature spells it—jokes and laughs, but the talk turns serious as a swap is made: one mare for the other's horse and $4.22. A brief tune based on "The Old Grey Mare" is then sung with melodeon accompaniment. The sketch ends with the two characters descending to a cellar for cider. The Victor label gives Porter credit as writer.

He was a founding member of the Peerless Quartet, led by Frank C. Stanley. When the American Quartet was formed in 1909 for Victor (on Edison records the quartet is called the Premier Quartet), Porter left the Peerless to join it, Arthur Collins soon replacing Porter in the Peerless. Other members of the new quartet were tenors Billy Murray and John Bieling and bass William F. Hooley. Charles Hart, who worked with Porter in Edison's revised lineup of the Premier Quartet in the early 1920s, wrote in the December 1958 issue of *Hobbies*, "Steve Porter was jokingly called the 'silent baritone.' He would cup his right ear in his right hand and almost rest his chin on the horn. . . . Porter's voice must have blended in, for the records had a good vocal balance. But I don't believe that anyone actually ever heard Porter's voice."

Around 1923 to 1925, Porter continued to record rube and Irish sketches for small companies. An example is his recording of "Flanagan on a Trolley Car" on Grey Gull 4003, probably issued in early 1924. In the early electric era Porter made new takes of "Clancey's Wooden Wedding" and "Christmas Morning at Clancey's," issued on Victor 20299. He remade some of his sketches electrically for Grey Gull as late as 1928, sometimes working with Byron G. Harlan and Harlan Knight. The three perform "Greetings in Bingville" on electrical Grey Gull 4255 (also Radiex 4255), and the three perform "The Trial of Josiah Brown" on Grey Gull 4256. Harlan and Porter cut "Uncle Si and Hiram Swapping Horses" and "Uncle Si at [the] Village Barber" (Grey Gull 4230).

In the January 1975 issue of *Hobbies*, Walsh quotes a 1928 clipping from the *New York Herald Tribune* indicating that Porter worked with singer Al Bernard and New Zealand-born baritone Percy Hemus in minstrel shows that were broadcast weekly on radio, probably for a short time only. The radio show was called the *Dutch Masters' Minstrels,* and Porter played his old role of interlocutor.

After Porter left the recording business, he invented a commercially successful hearing aid called the Port-o-phone, which he had designed to help his deaf mother-in-law. According to *The New York Times,* Porter died on January 13, 1936, "at his home in the Hotel Oxford, 205 West 88th Street." He was survived by his wife, Emma Forbes, with whom he had made some records, such as "Mrs. Hiram Offen Discharges Bridget O'Sullivan," a vaudeville sketch written by Porter and first issued in 1906 as single-faced Columbia 3469, later on doubled-sided A379.

Prince, Charles A. (1869-October 10, 1937)

Charles Adams Prince was born in San Francisco. His father was a New Englander who headed a successful fruit canning company on the West Coast, and his mother a New York native. It has been said that he was a descendant of President John Adams, but Hugh Brogan and Charles Mosley's *American Presidential Families* (Macmillan, 1993) does not include Charles Adams Prince among the hundreds of descendants. It is possible he was a distant relative.

Prince's interest in music began in his youth when his mother took him to local theatrical productions. As a young man he took to the road, traveling for several years with circuses, minstrel shows, and legitimate comedies. Tim Brooks reports that Prince recorded for the New York Phonograph Company as early as 1891. At first he worked mostly as a piano accompanist, and he continued to provide piano accompaniment for artists a decade later: he provided accompaniment for the historically significant Columbia Grand Opera series of ten-inch discs recorded in late 1902 and issued in 1903. These were the first recordings made in the United States with big-name opera stars, preceding Victor's Red Seal series by a few months.

Jim Walsh reports in the January 1953 issue of *Hobbies* that Prince succeeded Fred Hager as director of Columbia's band and orchestral recordings, which Hager himself reported to Walsh. Prince was responsible for providing orchestral accompaniment for vocalists when piano accompaniment ceased to be standard.

Records of Columbia's house ensemble, called the Columbia Orchestra and Columbia Band, were issued regularly from the mid-1890s onward (an 1897 catalog states, "Every musician in this great orchestra has been selected by Mr. [Victor] Emerson with special reference to the creation of an organization representing the highest achievement in our art"). But its conductors, which included cornetist Tom Clark (advertising in the July

1898 issue of *The Phonoscope* states that he was director of the Columbia Orchestra) and then Fred Hager, remained unidentified on records until 1905 or so, around the time that the Sousa march "The Diplomat" (3053) was credited to Prince's Military Band. Thereafter many discs of Prince's Orchestra were issued. They featured overtures, snippets from operas and symphonies, arrangements of well-known concert songs and popular tunes, descriptive specialties, "trombone smears," and ragtime.

In the recording studio Prince led superb musicians, including Vincent Buono on cornet; Leo Zimmerman on trombone; George Schweinfest and Marshall P. Lufsky on flute and piccolo, respectively; Arthur Bergh and George Stehl on violin (Bergh would later serve as recording director for other companies, including Emerson and Okeh, and on November 15, 1924, succeeded Prince himself as general manager of Columbia's recording laboratories); Thomas Mills on xylophone and bells; Howard Kopp on xylophone, bells, and drums; Thomas Hughes and William Tuson on clarinet; and Charles Schuetze on harp.

Prince's versatility within the phonograph industry for much of the acoustic era was arguably unsurpassed. He often played the piano in duets or trios with other Columbia artists, and at times he provided organ accompaniment ("Adeste Fideles" on Columbia A1978 features Prince on organ and Thomas Mills on chimes). He did not often make solo records, but exceptions include performances of "Chacone" and "Amaryllis" (A2102) on celesta, credited on the label to Charles A. Prince. He also made bell and celesta records using the name Charles Adam. On Columbia labels his name is given in different ways, such as "C. A. Prince" on single-sided 3624 and "Chas. A. Prince" on A1854.

He sometimes acted as a foil or straight man for popular comedians such as Frank Tinney, Len Spencer, and Steve Porter. For example, he plays the "professor" in some of Porter's Irish specialties, such as "Flanagan at the Vocal Teacher's." On "Frank Tinney's First Record," made in 1915, Prince speaks often (Tinney calls him "Charley" and the label cites his assistance). Because Prince's voice is clearly identified on the Tinney record, we know for certain that Prince had served as an announcer on many Columbia records made years earlier—it is the same voice!

In addition to performing, arranging, and conducting, Prince composed. His works include "Edna Mazurka," "The Barbary Rag," "Around the Christmas Tree," "Bell Buoy March," "Cuckoo and Canary," "Medley Two-Step," "Panama Exposition March" and "Suffragette Militante March." Leading Prince's Orchestra, he recorded some of his compositions, such as "Children's Toy March" (A2996). Leading Prince's Band, he recorded some others, such as "Boy Scout" (A1412). For a few years, beginning around 1904, he also collaborated with Len Spencer in writing topical specialties that were recorded by the Columbia Band. Notable examples included "Cumming's Indian Congress at Coney Island" (1550), "Departure of a Hamburg-American Liner" (1563) and "The Capture of the Forts at Port Arthur" (1865/XP cylinder 32579).

Although the names Prince's Military Band and Prince's Orchestra were used on records by 1905—Prince's Symphony Orchestra was on some recordings of classical works though Columbia Symphony Orchestra was more common—his productions were issued under other names in the United States and abroad. Many firms used Columbia masters in the early years of the century—Aretino, Busy Bee, Climax, Consolidated, Cort, D & R, Diamond, Harvard, Harmony, Kalamazoo, Lakeside, Manhattan, Oxford, Remick Perfection, Royal, Thomas, Sir Henri, Square Deal, Star, Standard, United—and on most of these labels the performing ensemble is listed merely as Band or Orchestra, but sometimes a company name is added, such as the Cort Band or Harmony Orchestra.

In February 1918, Columbia released a double-sided twelve-inch disc featuring Wagner's "Rienzi Overture" (A6006), performed by the Columbia Symphony Orchestra comprising ninety instruments and directed by Prince. He never again recorded with so large an ensemble.

Many labels for Prince's dance band records state, "Under the supervision of G. Hepburn Wilson." Wilson was a noted dance instructor, Columbia's counterpart to Victor's dance expert Vernon Castle. One popular dance record was Prince's "Dardanella" (A2851), though sales did not match those of Selvin's Novelty Orchestra on Victor 18633.

In the early 1920s he led the Columbia Dance Orchestra, and labels cite him as director. Some labels give the name Prince's Dance Orchestra. In this period Columbia identified on labels artists who were exclusive to the company, at least "at pressing," and Columbia A3681 featuring Prince's Dance Orchestra identified the orchestra as exclusive. Brian Rust's *American Dance Band Discography* identifies Prince as director of the Columbia Dance Orchestra from late 1922 until July 15, 1924. The records were not especially popular. Columbia in the early 1920s had more success with younger bandleaders, including Ted Lewis, Paul Specht, and Frank Westphal. "My Dream Girl" and "San' Man," issued on Columbia 181-D, were among Prince's final Columbia performances.

After going into receivership in February 1922, Columbia underwent dramatic reorganization, and Prince left the company by the summer of 1923 or at least was no longer musical director. Page 144 of the August 1923 issue of *Talking Machine World*, in announcing the newly formed and short-lived Vulcan Record Corporation (15 East Fortieth Street, New

York City), states, "The orchestra for this [Junior Operetta] series of records was under the direction of Charles A. Prince, formerly musical director of the Columbia Graphophone Co. and nationally famous as an orchestra director." He also appeared on Puritan records of this period.

Page 66 of the October 1924 issue of *Talking Machine World* repeats an announcement made weeks earlier by the Victor Talking Machine Company regarding "the appointment of Charles A. Prince, formerly of New York, as associate musical director." He was with Victor as early as June 5, 1924, when he directed an accompanying orchestra for Billy Murray and Ed Smalle when the tenors cut "Hinky Dinky Parlay Voo." Later that year he worked with Murray at the same Camden, New Jersey studio during other sessions (Rosario Bourdon normally was conductor for sessions in the Camden studio; Nat Shilkret was director during this period at Victor's New York studio). Logs also establish that he provided piano accompaniment in June 1925 for Billy Murray and Ed Smalle sessions. Prince probably did not remain with Victor for much more than a year.

He eventually returned to California where he taught music. After an illness of three months in 1937, he died near San Francisco in the home of his sister, Hazel Prince Tuggle.

Rogers, Walter B. (October 14, 1865-December 24, 1939)

Walter Bowman Rogers was a key figure of the phonograph industry for three decades, first as a featured cornetist on records and then as a music director for companies, the two most important being the Victor Talking Machine Company and Brunswick.

He was born in Delphi, Indiana, to William and Nancy (Bowman) Rogers, both of whom had emigrated from Bradford, Yorkshire, England, around 1860 (Nancy's mother followed and lived next door to the couple in Delphi). Walter was one of four children. Little is known of his early years other than that his family moved to New York when he was about sixteen.

Victor catalogs from around 1910 through 1916 gave this biographical sketch:

The career of this brilliant young conductor has been one of uninterrupted success. After some years of study in the Cincinnati College of Music, he joined Cappa's Seventh Regiment Band of New York as cornet soloist, and during the years that followed he was one of the great features of that famous band. On the death of Bandmaster Cappa, Mr. Rogers became the leader of the band and served four years in that capacity. In 1899 John Philip Sousa made him a flattering offer and he became the cornet soloist of Sousa's Band. After five successful years with Sousa, the Victor Company induced Mr. Rogers to leave the band and become its general Director of Music. His work with the Company speaks for itself in the Victor Orchestra records and the artistic accompaniments which are provided for Victor singers.

After examining catalogs and advertisements of the 1890s, Jim Walsh concluded in the February 1959 issue of *Hobbies* that Rogers had assumed direction of the Seventh Regiment Band prior to 1894.

His first records were made about the time he was hired by Sousa, who permitted band members to make records as "Sousa's Band" under the direction of Arthur Pryor (the full Sousa Band never assembled for sessions since recording technology could not do justice to such a large ensemble) and also permitted members to make records as soloists. Rogers recorded cornet solos for Berliner in 1900 as a member of a Sousa recording group and is featured on two Berliner discs as cornet soloist accompanied by Sousa's Band: "Souvenir of Naples" (01187) and "Ah! 'Twas a Dream" (01188). On yet another Berliner, "The Three Solitaires" (01189), Rogers is included in a trio, the other two being the famous cornet soloists Herbert L. Clarke and Henry Higgins. (A distinctive voice makes announcements at the beginning of many Berliner and Victor discs—it could be the voice of Rogers, who was often in the Berliner and Victor studios from 1900 onward.)

On October 1, 1900, Sousa's Band under the direction of Pryor began recording for Eldridge R. Johnson's new company, the Consolidated Talking Machine Company (soon renamed Victor). The Victor record catalog for February 1902 noted Rogers had signed an exclusive contract with the company. It also included the following list of cornet solos by Rogers with accompaniment by Sousa's Band: "A Southern Dance," "A Soldier's Dream," "Auld Lang Syne," "Minne-ha-ha Waltz," "Souvenir of Naples," and "When You Were Sweet Sixteen."

Recordings made with piano accompaniment include "Absence Makes the Heart Grow Fonder," "Bonnie Sweet Bessie," "Concert Polka," and "German Sounds." He recorded duets with trombonist Pryor, such as

"Nearer, My God, to Thee" (3415), and joined flautist Darius A. Lyons on Titl's "Serenade" (3424). The 1904 catalog showed a significant increase in cornet discs. Most of Rogers' 1902 titles had been remade, and those that had earlier featured piano accompaniments now had orchestral support. Rogers was also included in Victor's $1.50 Deluxe series, introduced in 1903. Deluxe discs were the first twelve-inch discs to be marketed.

The 1904 Victor catalog lists more titles featuring Rogers as a cornet player than catalogs before or after. Soon afterward his responsibilities as recording director took so much time that he stopped recording as a soloist, and with each passing year the Victor catalog carried fewer of his records made earlier as a soloist. The 1909 record list included only six of his solos, three duets, and one trio—none of them were new titles.

Walsh writes in the February 1959 issue of *Hobbies*, "Walter Rogers' engagement as Victor's musical director in 1904 was the result of the company's deciding to establish its own permanent orchestra instead of engaging musicians by the 'date.' It also tied in with a new policy, established in 1903, of using an orchestra, rather than the piano, to accompany most vocal records."

The transition was more gradual than Walsh suggested. Before 1904, piano accompaniment for vocal numbers was standard during Victor sessions, with orchestral accompaniment provided only occasionally. In 1904 orchestral accompaniment was increasingly provided during Victor sessions and by early 1905 had become standard for popular singers, with orchestral accompaniment becoming standard for operatic singers by the autumn of 1905. Enrico Caruso was accompanied by piano during his first two Victor sessions—one in February 1904, the next in February 1905 (his pianists are unknown). For his third session, in February 1906, orchestral accompaniment was provided, and the orchestra may have been led by Rogers. Surviving ledgers clearly identify Rogers as leader during most of Caruso's sessions from 1907 to 1916.

A versatile arranger, Rogers was responsible for many novelties in the Victor catalogs. He arranged and directed most of the company's early dance records. He also conceived the idea of organizing a staff ensemble to sing "gems" or medleys from musical comedies (the Victor Light Opera Company) as well as grand opera (the Victor Opera Company). Various Victor catalogs, including the one dated November 1916 (it was printed in October 1916), state, "Mr. Rogers' skill in combining the most attractive bits of these musical works is most remarkable." After he left Victor, the wording was changed for the May 1917 catalog to this: "[T]he skill used in combining the most attractive bits of these musical works is most remarkable."

He directed the Victor Concert Orchestra, Victor Orchestra, Victor Military Band, Victor Band, and, for a few sessions, Sousa's Band. He led musicians who provided accompaniment for singers, from opera stars Nellie Melba and Luisa Tetrazzini to popular singers Billy Murray and Ada Jones. As late as March 20, 1916, he was conductor for Caruso recordings. On May 25, he was conductor for Geraldine Farrar and Johanna Gadski recordings. On July 12, he led the orchestra that accompanied various Victor singers who performed in Atlantic City's Hotel Traymore during a National Association of Talking Machine Jobbers convention. The concert opened with Rogers conducting the overture from the opera *Mignon*.

Around August 1916 Rogers left Victor as its musical director, soon afterward becoming recording manager of Henry Burr and Fred Van Eps' new and short-lived Paroquette Record Manufacturing Company. Josef A. Pasternack became Victor's musical director, leading the Victor Concert Orchestra and other ensembles. Rogers' reason for leaving Victor is unknown, but to go from musical director of the industry's most prestigious company—where he worked closely with performers of international renown—to that of a very small company was clearly a step downward. Relations between Rogers and remaining Victor executives were evidently acrimonious. References to Rogers were purged from catalogs printed from 1917 onward (Victor catalogs printed in 1916 had praised him in the sections "Rogers" and "Victor Light Opera Company"). The one reference that remained in catalogs after 1916 was a listing of "Miserere from Trovatore," recorded on January 13, 1905, by Rogers on cornet and Arthur Pryor on trombone (Victor 16794).

The first Par-o-ket discs were issued in December 1916, and several of these were credited to Rogers' Military Band. Paroquette released little more than 100 titles. On May 22, 1918, the company's assets were publicly auctioned.

According to page 83 of the September 1918 issue of *Talking Machine World*, around September 7 Rogers was appointed musical director of the newly established New York Recording Laboratories, maker of Paramount discs. The company's general offices were in Port Washington, Wisconsin, but its recording studio was at 1140 Broadway, New York City, according to page 88 of the March 1918 issue of *Talking Machine World*. Recordings credited to Rogers' Band and Walter Rogers' Band were issued by Paramount beginning in August 1918. Later he seems to have worked for the Emerson Company. The December 1921 Emerson supplement listed a record, "Kiddies' Patrol (Christmas Eve)"/"Kiddies' Dance (Christmas Morning)" (10459), both composed by Rogers, and performed by the Emerson Concert Band. (The same two Rogers compositions are on Banner 2063, with the name Walter Rogers under the titles, nothing more. Presumably he led the studio orchestra.)

The January 1920 issue of *Talking Machine World* officially announced Brunswick records to the trade, and an article identifies Walter B. Rogers as "General Musical Director." The article states about Rogers, "He has been director of several famous bands, among them being the New York Seventh Regiment Band. He was for some time cornet soloist with the noted band under the baton of John Philip Sousa. He was with the Victor Talking Machine Company from 1904 to 1916 as musical director."

Page 34 of the August 1923 issue of *Talking Machine World* indicates how Rogers and musical director Walter G. Haenschen divided duties, calling Rogers "director of classical recording" and Haenschen "director of popular recording." One of the first records made with Brunswick's "Light-Ray" electrical recording system features "Forge in the Forest" and "Anvil Chorus" performed by Walter B. Rogers and His Band. These were cut in July 1925 and issued on Brunswick 2932 in October. Rogers may have had difficulty adapting to the new system since he received unfavorable reviews in early issues of *Phonograph Monthly Review*, which was first published in October 1926. The May 1928 issue, however, gave a positive review: "Brunswick 3515. Stars and Stripes Forever and National Emblem Marches. Given a band of larger size, Rogers might put Creatore and Sousa to shame, so effectively does he handle his present small organization. An excellent disc on all points."

Rogers left Brunswick when the Depression caused record sales to drop dramatically. He did some teaching in Brooklyn and played in New York theatres until around 1932. After several years of apparent retirement, Rogers died on Christmas Eve of 1939 in his home at 182 68th Street, Brooklyn. He had been ill for three years with chronic myocarditis. His death certificate gives his wife's name as Florence.

Selvin, Ben (c. 1898-July 15, 1980)

Originally a violinist, Ben Selvin probably made more records than any other bandleader of the 78 rpm era, his career in the record industry spanning decades. He may be best known among record collectors not for specific recordings but for quantity. Page 145 of the January 1924 issue of *Talking Machine World* celebrates Selvin's 1,000th record, and this was early in Selvin's career. The same article states that Selvin was "twenty-five years of age."

Page 34d of the September 1927 issue of *Talking Machine World* gives this background information:

> Ben Selvin, a native of New York, started fiddling at the age of seven. He made his first public appearance at the Star Casino at the age of nine. Acclaimed a prodigy, and presented with a gold medal in recognition of his genius, it was planned to send him to Paris for further study. Reverses prevented, but Ben was determined to succeed, so kept on working in and around New York. In 1913 Mr. Selvin made his first appearance on Broadway. From there he went to Rector's, then to Reisenweber's and Healy's. When nineteen years old, Ben Selvin organized his own orchestra and played at the Moulin Rouge for Broadway's record orchestral run—a run of seven years.

Victor's November 1919 supplement credits Benjamin B. Selvin for arranging the two numbers on Victor 18614 performed by Selvin's Novelty Orchestra, "Mandy" and "Novelty One-Step." Another early Selvin recording became his best-selling record: "Dardanella," with lyrics by Fred Fisher and music by Johnny Black and Felix Bernard, was cut by Selvin's Novelty Orchestra for Victor 18633 on November 20, 1919, and was issued in February 1920.

The June 1921 issue of *Talking Machine World* announced that Selvin's Novelty Orchestra, featured at the time at the Moulin Rouge in New York City, "signed up exclusively for the making of Vocalion records." He must not have been signed as an exclusive artist for a long period since Brunswick and other companies continued to issue discs of Selvin's Orchestra. The September 1922 issue of the trade journal announced that Selvin would continue to be exclusive to the Vocalion label, and page 143 of the September 1923 issue of *Talking Machine World* announces that Selvin again signed to be an exclusive Vocalion artist, adding:

> Although only twenty-eight years old he not only directs the Selvin Orchestra at the Moulin Rouge, New York, but he directs and manages the Bar Harbor Society Orchestra and the Broadway Syncopators, both exclusively Vocalion combinations. . . . It is said, besides furnishing six records or twelve selections a month for the Vocalion list, his orchestra also accompanies most of the Vocalion artists in

their recordings of popular songs. . . . [H]e keeps three arrangers busy preparing effective and novel orchestrations.

He worked often in radio. Page 54 of the November 1924 issue of *Talking Machine World* describes WJZ programs sponsored by the Aeolian Company in New York City, and Selvin's orchestra was featured on the air: "The program on Monday was opened by several irresistible dance numbers by Ben Selvin's Woodmansten Inn Orchestra, Vocalion record artists . . ."

His status as an exclusive Vocalion artist evidently ended around September 1924, when he began recording for Columbia, Paramount, and the Plaza Music Company, which issued records on Banner and related labels. In 1926 and 1927 he also made Brunswick records—he had last recorded for Brunswick in 1922 before signing as an exclusive Vocalion artist. He continued to record for Vocalion, which became a Brunswick subsidiary in January 1925.

By the end of 1927 he was closely associated with Columbia. Page 34d of the September 1927 issue of *Talking Machine World* states, "Ben Selvin, besides being known as one of the greatest of American orchestral leaders, has accepted the post of Program Director of the Columbia Phonograph Hour, sponsored by the Columbia Phonograph Co., to be presented every Wednesday evening over the entire chain of the Columbia Broadcasting System, starting September 28." The Columbia Broadcasting System, a broadcasting chain controlled by the Columbia Phonograph Company, had been formed only months earlier.

Page 128 of the November 1927 issue states:

> The Columbia Phonograph Co. announces that it has secured a three-year contract with Ben Selvin and His Orchestra, by which this celebrated dance orchestra and its leader will record exclusively for Columbia. The first release under the new contract is a coupling of "Playground in the Sky" and "Wherever You Are," both of which are from the new musical comedy success, "Sidewalks of New York." Ben Selvin has the distinction of recording the famous phonograph record of "Dardanella" back in 1919, the record which sold more copies than any other up to the recent phenomenal success of Columbia's "Two Black Crows" records. Another early great hit of Mr. Selvin's was "Three O'Clock in the Morning." Ben Selvin has recorded more than 3,000 selections for various phonograph companies in the past.

This article's claim that "Dardanella" was the industry's best-selling record prior to 1927 is probably not true, though the disc was genuinely popular.

A few recordings among his thousands are "I'm Forever Blowing Bubbles" (Victor 18603, 1919), "Yes! We Have No Bananas" (vocal by Irving Kaufman, Vocalion 14590, 1923), "Oh, How I Miss You Tonight" (Columbia 359-D, 1925), "Manhattan" (Columbia 422, 1925), "Blue Skies" (Columbia 860-D, 1927), "Happy Days Are Here Again" (Columbia 2116-D, 1930), and "When It's Springtime in the Rockies" (Columbia 2206-D, 1930).

In the early 1930s he led orchestras on various radio shows. For example, during the winter of 1933-1934 he directed The Taystee Breadwinners over New York City's WOR on Monday, Wednesday, and Friday at 8:15 p.m. on a show sponsored by the Taystee Bread Company and starring Jones and Hare, who were called "The Taystee Loafers."

Joseph Lanza reports in *Elevator Music* (St. Martin's Press, 1994, p. 46), "Selvin was Muzak's chief programmer in its early years; he supervised its first New York City transmission in 1936 and had helped the company devise its first standardized programming."

George T. Simon writes in *The Big Bands* (Schirmer Books, 1981, p. 53) about Selvin's connection with James Caesar Petrillo, president of the American Federation of Musicians, who was worried about musicians being put out of work due to radio broadcasts as well as jukeboxes reproducing music from records:

> . . . [P]erturbed by the possible adverse effects of recording on his membership, he hired Ben Selvin, a highly respected recording executive and orchestra leader, to conduct a thorough study of the entire recording field as it affected musicians. Selvin's report was exhaustive. Presented at the annual convention of the musicians' union, it received a standing ovation from the delegates . . .

Selvin argued against a ban on recording, pointing to other ways to address the problem of large numbers of musicians being unemployed, but Petrillo ordered that a ban go into effect on August 1, 1942. The ban was arguably a disaster for working musicians—for example, it contributed to the decline of big bands or the "swing" era—but in the end the major record companies did agree to pay the union a royalty for released records.

Around 1947 Selvin worked for Majestic Records as chief of artists and repertory. In the mid-1970s he was reunited with his one-time Brunswick recording director Walter Haenschen ("Carl Fenton") for a taped interview at Lincoln Center. The unpublished interview is part of the Haenschen collection at Ithaca College in upstate New York.

Shannon Four, Shannon Quartet, and Revelers

Bass singer Wilfred Glenn organized this quartet in early 1917. It relieved the work load of Victor's Orpheus Quartet, which recorded less regularly by 1917 for various reasons, including Harry Macdonough's heavy duties as a recording director (Macdonough was second tenor of the Orpheus) and the increasingly busy schedule of baritone Reinald Werrenrath as a concert performer. The Shannon and the Orpheus Quartets were related in that Glenn was a frequent substitute for Orpheus bass William F. Hooley and replaced him when Hooley died on October 12, 1918. Glenn did not record often as a solo artist but worked steadily as member of various ensembles, and by 1917 he had the experience, confidence, and industry contacts needed to form a new quartet.

The Shannon Four originally consisted of first tenor Charles Hart, second tenor Harvey Hindermyer, baritone Elliott Shaw, and Glenn. Tenors changed—for example, by the spring of 1918 Lewis James replaced Hindermyer, and various tenors substituted for James when he left the quartet for a couple of years in the early 1920s—but Glenn always remained as bass and Shaw remained as baritone aside from a short time when he was ill, at which point Phil Duey substituted.

The group's Victor debut was "I May Be Gone for a Long, Long Time" (18333), issued in September 1917. It was followed a month later by the release of "Wake Up, Virginia" (18355). For the next few years Victor issued a new Shannon Four title nearly each month, often with an American Quartet performance on a disc's reverse side. In December 1917 three titles were issued while nothing from the Orpheus Quartet was offered. The Orpheus would continue to record, but the Shannon was already recording material that ordinarily would have been judged suitable for the Orpheus.

The group was credited on some records for assisting featured soloists, such as Elizabeth Spencer on "Sweet Little Buttercup," issued in March 1918 as Victor 18427. Occasionally a quartet member is the featured soloist. For example, a performance of the patriotic song "Paul Revere" on Victor 18481, issued in August 1918, is credited to "Charles Hart and Shannon Four." "When the Autumn Leaves Begin to Fall," issued on Okeh 4410 in November 1921, is credited to Lewis James and the Shannon Four.

Victor 18488 is credited to "Harry Macdonough and Shannon Four," which is unusual since Macdonough at this time was generally assisted by his own Orpheus Quartet. More unusual is Victor 18428, "There's a Vacant Chair in Every Home Tonight," since it is credited only to the Shannon Four yet Macdonough is soloist and second tenor.

Glenn told researcher Quentin Riggs that he chose the name Shannon Four because in 1917 anything Irish seemed to be popular, especially Irish songs and singers (around this time Walter Van Brunt changed his performing name to the Irish-sounding Walter Scanlan). The quartet recorded some Irish songs, such as "Katy Mahone" (Diamond Disc 80436). Glenn also told Riggs that Hindermyer was dropped because his voice did not blend well with the others.

The January 1919 issue of *Talking Machine World* reports the success at a Victor dealership of a January 2 concert in Pottstown, Pennsylvania, featuring Ada Jones as well as the Shannon Four, which according to the trade journal consisted of the four original members—Hart, Hindermyer, Shaw, and Glenn. The inclusion of Hindermyer in the list is curious since a full-page Paramount Records advertisement in the May 1918 issue of *Talking Machine World* includes a photograph of the Shannon Four, and James—with his distinctive moustache—is one of the four, not Hindermyer. It is likely that James was unable to sing that evening and Hindermyer filled in.

In contrast to the Orpheus Quartet, which was exclusive to Victor, the Shannon Four recorded for most American companies, sometimes under the names Gounod Quartet, Aeolian Quartet, Vocalion Quartet, and Shannon Four Quartette, depending upon the company (the name Trinity Quartet was even used on a Canadian Victor disc). Emerson, Columbia, Vocalion, Emerson, Arto, and a few other companies for a long time used the original name, Shannon Four. Pathé at first used the name Shannon Four but then used the name the Acme Male Quartet.

Beginning in 1917 the group made Edison recordings and used the name the Shannon Quartet, never the Shannon Four. It made four Edison Diamond Discs as the Shannon Quartet and an additional Diamond Disc featuring Helen Clark and the Shannon Quartet (80386). Five Shannon Quartet titles were dubbed to Blue Amberols, with the first issued in November 1917: Von Tilzer's "I May Be Gone for a Long, Long Time" (3319). It was later called the Lyric Male Quartet when recording for Edison.

After working steadily for Victor from 1917 until 1921, the quartet made no Victor records. "College Days" (18792) had been issued in October 1921, and when the group returned with "Kentucky Babe" and "Little Cotton Dolly" on Victor 19013, issued in April 1923, a name change from Shannon Four to Shannon Quartet signaled a new phase with Victor. At least on one occasion thereafter Victor did use the name Shannon Four. On New Year's night, 1925, Victor sponsored the first of a planned biweekly radio concert series. It was broadcast from New York by station WEAF and performers included tenor John McCormack with the Shannon Four assisting on "Adeste Fideles." The Shannon Four, using various names, worked steadily in radio into the 1930s.

The group performed on radio for the first time in October 1921, broadcasting from a Westinghouse factory in Newark, New Jersey. Many radio engagements followed, the sponsors changing often. Page 182 of the December 1923 issue of *Talking Machine World* states, "As part of the policy of the Columbia Phonograph Co. to have semi-weekly radio broadcasts of its artists through Station WEAF, the owners of radio receiving sets were delighted to hear the Shannon Four through the air on Tuesday evening, December 11."

It recorded as the Shannon Four for "Wond'ring," issued in 1920 on Brunswick 2039, one of the earliest Brunswick discs issued in the United States. Later, Brunswick sometimes used the name White Way Quartet. Whereas the quartet made no Victor records in 1922, it recorded often for Brunswick from mid-1922 to early 1923, using different names, and Billy Jones replaced Lewis James on most of these recordings, including those of the White Way Quartet on Brunswick 2320, 2343, 2331, 2349, and 2373. Some labels emphasize Billy Jones's contribution, such as Brunswick 2127 ("Billy Jones and Strand Trio"), 2140 ("Billy Jones and Male Trio"), and 2321 ("Billy Jones and Male Quartet"). On Brunswick 2364, credit is given to "William Reese and White Way Quartet." Reese was a pseudonym for Jones—more precisely, it was the singer's first and middle names (he was born William Reese Jones). Jones even sang with Charles Hart and Elliott Shaw in the Crescent Male Trio on Brunswick 2098 and 2110. The Crescent Trio normally consisted of Lewis, Hart, and Shaw.

The absence of Lewis James on Shannon Four records from late 1921 to 1923 is puzzling. James recorded often in this period (sometimes as member of the Crescent Trio), as did the Shannon, but they did not work together though they worked for the same labels. Issued in 1922 were records credited to Sam Ash and the Crescent Trio (Okeh 4472, issued in February 1922, and Okeh 4526, issued in April), Byron G. Harlan and the Crescent Trio, and Theo Karle and the Crescent Trio, which are quartet records (two tenors, a baritone, and bass) made without James. It is possible that the tenor had a temporary falling-out with manager Glenn.

The quartet recorded often for Columbia. One popular number was "When You're Gone, I Won't Forget" (A3318). Issued in January 1921, it remained in the Columbia catalog throughout the 1920s.

Columbia continued to use the name Shannon Four until 1924. On Columbia A3606 and A3641, issued in 1922, Billy Jones is the tenor instead of Lewis James. Billy Jones was only a temporary replacement for

Lewis James, who soon returned to the quartet. Charles Hart left the group in 1923 so he could study operatic singing in Germany, and Franklyn Baur took his place. In mid-1925, around the time electrical recording was established, the quartet went in a new direction, singing in a more modern, upbeat, jazzy style. Glenn was encouraged by Clifford Cairns, one of Victor's recording managers, to rename the group the Revelers when it cut modern arrangements of new songs. A name change was needed if only because the old Shannon name identified the group as a quartet, and Revelers performances often included a fifth voice, Ed Smalle. Smalle also provided piano accompaniment and arrangements. Later, beginning around November 1926, pianist and composer Frank Black provided accompaniment and arrangements. In 1928 Black was appointed musical director of the National Broadcasting Company, but he continued to coach the vocal group and served as accompanist on some recordings as late as 1930. Most Revelers labels state "male voices," though many state "male quartet."

That the Shannon Quartet was not associated with the upbeat, jazzy sounds of that era is exemplified by such typical recordings as "America, the Beautiful" (19242), "The Sidewalks of New York" (20128), and "Rainbow" (20173). The group, whether named the Shannon Four or Shannon Quartet, more often recorded traditional fare than new songs of the 1920s, though exceptions include Isham Jones' "Swinging Down the Lane" backed by Wendell Hall's composition "Underneath the Mellow Moon," issued on Columbia A3938 in September 1923. This disc and a few others were harbingers of the Revelers' sound.

In the early 1920s the Shannon Quartet's vocal arrangements were not strikingly different from those used by the Peerless and other quartets. On the other hand, the Revelers used not only clever and sometimes elaborate arrangements that must have sounded fresh to audiences in the 1920s but almost always recorded new songs. Their composers include George Gershwin ("Strike Up the Band"), Dietz and Schwartz ("Dancing in the Dark"), Louis Alter ("Blue Shadows"), and Cole Porter ("I'm in Love Again").

In the mid-1920s Victor issued Shannon Quartet discs as well as Revelers discs, such as in July 1926. Victor 20082 credits the Revelers for singing the new Hart and Rodgers song "The Blue Room" while another disc, Victor 20072, features the Shannon Quartet singing Maude Nugent's "Sweet Rosie O'Grady," a hit of the 1890s. It seems likely that an older generation bought Shannon Quartet records while a younger one bought Revelers discs.

The first Revelers disc featured songs recorded on July 20, 1925: "Just a Bundle of Sunshine" backed by "Every Sunday Afternoon" (Victor

19731). It was issued in October 1925 and was followed in November by the release of "Collegiate"/"I'm Gonna Charleston Back to Charleston" (19775). Neither disc sold well. The next release, "Dinah"/"Oh, Miss Hannah" (19796), issued in January 1926, proved extremely popular. Issued at the same time was Victor 19791 with the Shannon Quartet singing far more traditional fare—"Jingle Bells" and "The Quilting Party (Seeing Nellie Home)."

The Revelers in the electric era rerecorded only two numbers issued years earlier on a Shannon Quartet disc. Released in April 1923, Victor 19013 features the Shannon Quartet singing, without accompaniment, "Kentucky Babe" and "Little Cotton Dolly." On Victor 22249, the Revelers—identified as "male quartet" instead of the more typical "male voices"—perform the two songs using the old arrangements, Frank Black accompanying on piano. The new takes were made electrically in late 1929, when James Melton was one of the quartet's two tenors, and the disc was issued in 1930.

On Victor 35772 the Revelers sing "Gems from Tip-Toes," a potpourri of tunes from George Gershwin's successful show. This is noteworthy since performances in Victor's "Gems From . . ." series are typically credited to the Victor Light Opera Company (or Victor Opera Company), as is the case on side B of Victor 35772. At this February 12, 1926 session soprano Gladys Rice was considered a member of the Revelers. Labels give credit only to "The Revelers" (Rice is not named) and state to the spindle hole's right, "Mixed Voices with pianos," not the customary "Male Voices." A year later Rice worked again with the group for "Vocal Gems from Oh, Kay!" (35811)—again, label credit is given only to "The Revelers," Rice being considered an actual member. On April 5, 1928, the Revelers contributed to another musical show potpourri, this time featuring Victor Arden-Phil Ohman and Their Orchestra. Labels for "Selections From 'Good News'" (35918) state "with male chorus."

For years the name Revelers was used only by Victor. The name Singing Sophomores was used on Columbia records, with the ensemble identified as a male quintet on some Columbia labels, such as 652-D and 1257-D (Ed Smalle, cited as arranger on 652-D, provides the fifth voice and piano accompaniment). However, the first Columbia disc of the Singing Sophomores (485-D) identifies the group as "male quartet." For hymns, traditional numbers, and even the occasional vocal refrain on a dance band record, the quartet recorded sometimes from the mid- to late-1920s for Columbia as the Shannon Quartet. As with Revelers records, Singing Sophomores performances have sparse accompaniment if any at all—only a piano on "Show Me the Way to Go Home" (485-D), only a guitar on "Chloe" (1257-D)—whereas most Shannon Quartet performances for Columbia have fuller, more traditional accompaniment.

By early 1926, Charles Harrison worked with Shannon members in mixed choruses, and this led to Harrison briefly joining the Revelers in 1927 when Baur left. When Brunswick's musical director Gus Haenschen ("Carl Fenton") organized sessions for a mixed chorus in late January and early February 1926, Harrison worked with Glenn, Baur, and Shaw, among others (James was absent). For Brunswick the Shannon members recorded as the Merrymakers. When the group recorded "The Merrymakers' Carnival" for Brunswick 20044 on March 6, 1926, the singers were Franklyn Baur, Ed Smalle, Elliott Shaw, and Wilfred Glenn. Months later, on July 21, 1926, "The Merrymakers in Spain" and "The Merrymakers in Hawaii" were recorded (Brunswick 20049), and for this session Charles Harrison replaced Smalle.

Page 119 of the August 1926 issue of *Talking Machine World* reports, "A group of American radio artists headed by Wilfred Glenn, basso of the Eveready Hour, which has been a popular broadcast feature in the United States for several years, will be featured in London at a fashionable night club at the opening of the season in September, according to an announcement by the National Carbon Co., Inc. manufacturer of the Eveready line of batteries." In London in October 1926 the Revelers recorded two titles for England's Columbia company.

Page 72 of the March 1927 issue of *Talking Machine World* lists artists who performed during a Brunswick Hour of Music program and identifies the Merrymakers on its March 4 broadcast as Lewis James, Franklyn Baur, Elliott Shaw, and Wilfred Glenn. In the summer of 1927 the group again visited England and recorded for England's Columbia, Frank Luther replacing Baur for the duration of the visit. During another trip abroad, James Melton was one of the tenors (Harrison replaced Baur by mid-1927, though Luther took his place for the trip; in late 1927 Melton replaced Harrison). The Revelers completed at least three European tours.

The four singers on Victor 22036—issued in September 1929 and featuring "Ploddin' Along" and "Wake Up! Chillun, Wake Up!"—were Shaw, Glenn, James, and Melton, with Frank Black at the piano. RCA Victor stopped issuing new Revelers discs after the group cut "When Yuba Plays the Rumba on the Tuba" and "Dancing in the Dark" for Victor 22772. This session was on July 24, 1931, and shortly afterward the Revelers sang a part of the "Yuba" song for a long-playing ten-inch disc (DL-5) that promoted Victor's newly launched long-playing "program transcription" discs. Melton dropped out around 1932 and was replaced by

Robert Simmons, who was married to Patti Pickens, a member of the Pickens Sisters recording trio.

For a few more years the Revelers drew large radio audiences, earning $1,000 a program, according to the December 1933 issue of *Radioland*. Later in the 1930s the Revelers recorded hymns for Decca, and catalogs identify the singers as first tenor Robert Simmons, second tenor Lewis James, baritone John Herrick, and bass Wilfred Glenn. The Revelers disbanded around 1939, but Glenn later organized another Revelers group, which did not make records. According to the February 1948 issue of *Musical America*, members were first tenor Glenn Burris, second tenor Nino Ventura, baritone Rand Smith, and Glenn (Paul Vellucci was pianist-arranger). Personnel frequently changed during the late 1940s and early 1950s.

Shilkret, Nathaniel (December 25, 1889-February 18, 1982)

Nathaniel Shilkret shaped the musical sound of the Victor Talking Machine Company in the 1920s perhaps more than any other musician, and he was important in the early years of RCA Victor, formed in 1929. This classically trained clarinetist served as bandleader, composer, piano accompanist, and musical director for countless popular Victor discs as well as many Red Seal, or classical, discs. From the mid-1920s onward his name was often on labels, but much of his work conducting Victor's "house" orchestras went uncredited. He was most influential in Victor's early electric era of recording but had recorded prolifically in the acoustic era. He was especially successful at giving popular tunes of the day a semiclassical treatment, tunes being sometimes arranged for a small ensemble of instruments, other times for a symphonic orchestra.

Several reference books erroneously cite 1895 as Nat's year of birth. He was born in Queens, New York as Naftule Schuldkraut on December 25, 1889, according to his birth certificate. Researcher Bob Arnold also located the birth certificate of Jack Shilkret, who was born on October 9, 1896, and the family name on Jack's birth certificate is given as Skilkrout, which means the name had already changed in the six years since Nat's birth. The family's address is given as 32 Columbia Street.

During an interview in Nat Shilkret's home in Massapequa, New York, on October 7, 1963, he told Brian Rust, "My folks came from Austria . . . I'm another famous Jew born on Christmas Day." They probably came from Galicia, at that time in Austria but in present-day Poland. Citing Arnold's findings, Peter Cliffe in the British journal *The Historic Record* (Issue 28, July 1993) gives the parents' names as Wulf and Krusel Shuldkraut and writes, "When Jack (shown as Jake) was born in New York on

October 9, 1896, the family's surname seems to have become Shilkraut, on its ways to Shilkret . . . The mother is recorded as Katie Geiger. It is almost certainly the same woman: of Austrian birth and having five other children." According to descendants of Jack Shilkret, "Geiger" here is a misprint for "Zeiger," and the mother would later be known as Rose, the father as William. Her other three children were Lou, who played piano; a girl named Ray; and Harry, who played cornet on many recordings directed by older brother Nat as well as on Jack Shilkret records (Harry later had a career as an allergist).

Beginning in 1926, Shilkret wrote a series of autobiographical pieces for *Phonograph Monthly Review*, and he states in the February 1927 issue that he began to study music with lessons by his father on the clarinet, adding, "After school—or I should say kindergarten, since I was a little over five years old at the time—my father and I would sit side by side and practice for hours . . . Piano, however, was the instrument I liked most and I started to play by watching my older brother at his lessons."

The young Shilkret was evidently skilled at the piano since he was accepted as a pupil by Charles Hambitzer (1881-1918), who also taught a young George Gershwin.

Shilkret states in the November 1929 issue of *Phonograph Monthly Review:*

> [A]t the age of seven I played in a boys' orchestra, where the blood of the seventy boys would curdle at the strains of "Raymond Overture" or "William Tell" . . . [A]fter six years of playing both as soloist and instrumentalist in the boys' orchestra, which meant, in an impressionistic age, about 100 or 300 programs per year, I was immediately accepted in major orchestras, at the age of thirteen. I joined the Russian Symphony [led by Modest Altschuler] and the Volpe orchestra at that time, and two years later, the Philharmonic, and then later, [Walter] Damrosch and the Metropolitan orchestra. . . . A few years later, at the age of 23, I joined the Victor Talking Machine Company as musical director, and it was there that I became acquainted with the music all over the world, not only the latest music, but traditional and folk music, which was the backbone of our foreign catalogue.

Page 38 of the March 1924 issue of *Talking Machine World* states that Shilkret was fifteen—not thirteen—when he joined the Russian Symphony Orchestra, which seems the more likely age since that ensemble was founded in 1904.

A summary in the *1937-38 International Motion Picture Almanac* of the early years of Shilkret, who has an entry because he was music director for many films in the mid-1930s, states that he studied music from the age of four and "joined [a] major symphony orchestra at 12," which undoubtedly refers to the Russian Symphony Orchestra, whose guest conductors and soloists included Jean Sibelius, Mischa Elman, Jascha Heifetz, and Josef Lhévinne. This almanac, which incorrectly cites 1895 as his year of birth, gives the parents' names as "William and Rose Shilkret." The Austrian-Jewish origins had been obscured.

He also played in concert bands led by John Philip Sousa, Arthur Pryor, and Edwin Franko Goldman. According to surviving August 15, 1903, concert programs, "Nathan Schildkraut"—identified as the "10-year old clarinet phenomenon" though he was actually thirteen at the time—played as a member of the Boys New York Symphony Orchestra, under the direction of A. F. Pinto, at a Willow Park Concert in Philadelphia.

About his education, he states on page 22 of the November 1926 issue of *Phonograph Monthly Review,* "I had taken my freshman exams at college and decided that I was to take my music seriously, in other words, make it my profession. Up to then my ambition was to be a civil engineer. I quit college, but retained one of the instructors to give me private tuition for two years." Music would always provide his livelihood. He states in the same November 1926 article, "At the age of seventeen, I began to play piano for vocal teachers. I coached singers, helped the teachers and here is a secret. I studied and practiced singing for two years. Conductors are notorious for their terrible vocal talents and I am no exception . . ." He received an honorary doctor's degree in music in 1935 from Bethany College in Kansas.

The 1929 and 1930 Victor catalogs state, "At twenty-four he entered the service of the Victor Company." Shilkret himself states on page 7 in the October 1926 issue of *Phonograph Monthly Review,* "At the age of twenty-four I was engaged by the Victor Talking Machine Company as Musical Director. And now, although only thirty-four years old, looking back over my phonograph experiences makes me feel like a veteran." Shilkret implies here that he was hired around 1916.

Page 72 of the September 1927 issue of *Talking Machine World* states:

At the age of twenty-four, because of his ability, amounting to genius, as an arranger and musician, he was made a conductor in the company. In addition to this, he is also manager and musical director of the foreign language department, where records in thirty-five different languages are made. Publications sent in for examination are left to the judgment of Mr. Shilkret and many of these selections are arranged by him. . . . Very often he is accompanist for many famous artists who made Red Seal records.

The October 1926 issue of *Phonograph Monthly Review* began running his autobiographical series "My Musical Life," and he is introduced to readers as Victor's manager and musical director of the U.S. Foreign Department. He wrote in his debut article:

> My first recordings were mostly foreign records. Always a lover of folk music, this gave me chance to study the music and the languages of thirty-five various nationalities. . . . Some of my happiest experiences have been spent in the many years of study and contact in the Foreign Department. . . . To merge myself into the spirit of a Russian Gypsy Orchestra, a German Concert Director, or an Argentine Typical Tango Orchestra and find that each nationality accepted me as its own was sufficient payment for the many hours spent in orchestral arrangements and conducting in the laboratory. . . . I became Manager of the Foreign Department, but my musical activities were not confined to that alone, having conducted the great artists and orchestras on the extensive Victor list.

Shilkret wrote in the November 1929 issue of *Phonograph Monthly Review:*

> It was my great pleasure to form orchestras of various nations and to feel that they accepted me as one of their own—to practically engage artists, make your own programs, and conduct, and finally list on the average of 70 selections per month, was a great experience. I did this for more than 5 years. Then came the experience in the operatic recordings and later on, the Spanish Department where my International Orchestra became the most popular of the Pan-American nations—then the Popular Department, which is the busiest part of our musical palates of America.

Shilkret probably did not recognize the session as significant at the time, but he provided piano accompaniment on July 1, 1922, for fiddler A. C. ("Eck") Robertson during recordings of "Done Gone" and "Sallie Johnson/ Billy in the Low Ground," issued on Victor 19372. During this Texas fiddler's two Victor sessions of mid-1922 (June 30 and July 1), "hillbilly" music was being recorded for the first time, though that adjective was not used at first. However, Robertson's first disc did not include Shilkret's accompaniment but instead featured two selections cut on June 30 (on

Victor 18956 he plays unaccompanied on "Sallie Gooden" and is joined by Texas fiddler Henry C. Gilliland on "Arkansaw [sic] Traveler").

Ensembles that Shilkret conducted in the 1920s, relying on a more or less stable pool of trained studio musicians who worked regularly for Victor, include the Victor Salon Orchestra, International Novelty Orchestra, International Concert Orchestra, Victor Concert Orchestra, Victor Symphony Orchestra, International Symphony Orchestra, Victor Schrammel (Viennese) Orchestra, Shilkret's Rhyth-Melodists, the Troubadours (this was also led at times by Hugo Frey), the All Star Orchestra, the Eveready Radio Group, and the Hilo Hawaiian Orchestra. He was often assisted by Leonard Joy. Many records in the late 1920s were issued under the name Nat Shilkret and the Victor Orchestra.

For a few 1927 sessions, he even used the name the Virginians, which might have confused the record-buying public since a Ross Gorman group with that name had made records in the early 1920s for Victor, and Ross Gorman and His Virginians recorded for Columbia's budget label Harmony in early 1927. Likewise, it is curious that a performance of "Dream House" from a Shilkret session in New York on April 19, 1928, was issued on Victor 21392 under the name Art Hickman's Orchestra. The final Hickman session had been a year earlier, on April 29, 1927, and all Hickman sessions in the mid-1920s had been recorded on the West Coast.

In 1924 he formed the Victor Salon Orchestra. Victor's August 1924 supplement, announcing the release of Victor 19364 ("Eleanor" and "Out of the Dusk to You"), calls the ensemble the Victor String Orchestra, but Victor's 1925 catalog lists this debut record under the name Victor Salon Orchestra. He writes in the October 1926 issue of *Phonograph Monthly Review*, "I thought of a concert orchestra that would play popular music in novel arrangements so that no person could help being touched by either the music or the method of performance. The result was the Victor Salon Orchestra. The success of this orchestra was truly great."

To promote "Just a Cottage Small" (Victor 19972), cut on February 15, 1926, Shilkret wrote about his orchestra for *Metronome*. His account was reprinted on pages 154-156 in the January 1927 issue of *Phonograph Monthly Review*. Referring to himself in the third person, he states:

> The Victor Salon Orchestra does represent a new idea in the orchestra . . . The story of the Victor Salon Orchestra is inextricably associated with the personality of Nathaniel Shilkret, who conceived the idea and made it what it is today. . . . It is Shilkret who welded the organization together, made the arrangements which embodied his idea, who rehearsed and conducted the orchestra into the commanding position it holds today. . . . What he wanted was a straightforward, honest ar-

rangement of a popular number in which he would take nothing away from the original composition and would add some elements of beauty which might not be inherently part of it. . . . It was Shilkret's intention to treat popular music in the classic manner and bring to its rendition all the resources of the classic styles.

According to Shilkret's article, Victor Salon Orchestra musicians included violinist Lou Raderman, violinist Pete Eisenberg, cellist Bernie Altschuler, pianists Jack Shilkret and Leroy Shield, flutist William Schade, cornetist Charles Del Staigers, and xylophonist Joe Green. Shilkret writes, "[I]t is only natural that there should have been a bid for the orchestra's services on the radio. Last summer [1925], they played a series of concerts for the celebrated Eveready Hour . . . This season they are known as Hire's Harvesters . . ."

His name was rarely given on acoustically recorded discs. Exceptions include an International Concert Orchestra disc issued in 1923 featuring items from Strauss's *Gypsy Baron* and Lehár's *Gypsy Love* (35725); a Victor Symphony Orchestra disc featuring a Rossini overture (19331); and a Victor Salon Orchestra disc (19505). Labels state, "Under the Direction of Nathaniel Shilkret" and "Nathaniel Shilkret, Director."

The first performance on disc credited to Shilkret's Orchestra is "Africa" (Victor 19394), recorded on June 4, 1924, but this was conducted by younger brother Jack Shilkret, a pianist, band conductor, and composer (most successful was "Make Believe," widely recorded in early 1921). Jack Shilkret's name was on labels even earlier, such as on Brooke Johns and His Orchestra discs from 1923 ("Under the direction of Jack Shilkret"). Members of Jack Shilkret's Orchestra included brother Harry Shilkret on trumpet, trombonist Harry Raderman, Harry's brother Louis Raderman on violin, Harry's brother Al Raderman on saxophone, Lee Conner on saxophone and banjo, and saxophonist Jack Wasserman, formerly with Joseph C. Smith's Orchestra. Page 162 of the September 1924 issue of *Talking Machine World* includes a photograph of eight band members. Jack Shilkret and His Orchestra played regularly at the Pelham Heath Inn, upper New York City. Jack provided piano accompaniment for some artists during Victor's early electric era, including saxophonist Rudy Wiedoeft on Victor 21152.

Jack and Nat Shilkret worked closely throughout the 1920s. In 1920, Leo. Feist, Inc. published "April Showers Bring May Flowers," with music by the two brothers (words are by Leo Wood). In the years when Nat was musical director for Victor's New York studio, Jack at the piano often assisted vocalists when piano instead of orchestral accompaniment was required. Whereas Nat worked only for Victor in the 1920s, Jack worked for some other companies, including Columbia ("Aileen" and "Jack and Jill" are instrumental performances on 1414-D featuring Jack at the piano and Andy Sannella on saxophone) and Grey Gull (he led the Jack Shilkret Trio). Jack Shilkret and His Orchestra recorded in the 1930s, and Jack worked with Frank Crumit and Julia Sanderson on the *Bond Bread Radio Show*. He was in a number of "soundies," or musical film shorts of the 1940s made for coin-operated machines, and wrote background music for some FitzPatrick Traveltalks, a series of one-reelers shown in movie houses. In the early 1920s Jack married Rose Isaacs (originally "Eisig"), whom he met in the Catskills while leading his band at a resort, and they had two children, Marilyn Millicent and Warner Neil (he changed his legal name to Neil Warner—his daughter, Julie Warner, is a successful TV and movie actress). Jack died on June 16, 1964, in New York after spending a day at the World's Fair.

In abbreviated form Nat Shilkret's name was on a Victor label in 1921 after the Shilking Orchestra recorded "Bring Back My Blushing Rose" (18797) and "When the Sun Goes Down" (18804). Shilking blends the names of Nat Shilkret (along with brother Jack) and Eddie King. Arthur Shilkret, son of the musician, wrote to Barry Cheslock in a letter dated July 6, 1982, "My father and Mr. King combined their names to set a new style of sound and arrangement. Of course, my father did the arranging and musical direction." Eddie King, who played percussion instruments and even recorded bell solos, was a veteran at making discs, making solo records for Zon-o-phone as early as 1905 (Jim Walsh states in the April 1966 issue of *Hobbies* that King became Zon-o-phone's artists and repertoire manager) and performing in Columbia ensembles before that. In the 1920s both musicians had important responsibilities at Victor, presiding over countless recording sessions of dance numbers and other forms of popular music in the company's New York studio. In November 1926 Eddie King left the company to work for Columbia.

In the Bix Beiderbecke biography *Bix: Man & Legend* (Quartet Books, 1974), by Richard M. Sudhalter and Philip R. Evans, Shilkret is contrasted with Victor executive Eddie King, who opposed "hot" music. It was King who insisted that Jean Goldkette's dynamic band of 1926 record such saccharine numbers as "Idolizing" and the waltz "Hush-a-bye." King gave instructions on how instruments should be played, even showing pianist Irving Ruskin what piano vamp introduction was appropriate for "Dinah," which was "ever so corny," Ruskin recalled in a 1962 letter quoted in Philip R. Evans and Larry F. Kiner's *Tram: The Frank Trumbauer Story* (Scarecrow, 1994). Shilkret, on the other hand, gave musicians more freedom. In a 1982 interview published in *The Mississippi Rag* (December

1988), arranger Bill Challis stressed that only some bandleaders were allowed to select for themselves material for a recording session, and Shilkret was among those few: "We had to take the tunes that were assigned to us [Goldkette's orchestra]. Roger [Kahn] was around New York, you know, and Whiteman got anything he asked for. Nat Shilkret . . . used to do whatever he wanted."

Shilkret writes in the November 1929 issue of *Phonograph Monthly Review* about his duties as head of Victor's "Popular Department":

> This meant hearing all the premieres of the new shows written by popular writers, listening to all the new "gags," as Tin Pan Alley called them, for the coming season. Competition is keen and one has to be on his toes to pick hits and be able to feel the pulse of the people. Sometimes it meant writing sketches on a new idea. All this was my experience before I began my concerts in radio.

From 1923 to 1925 Shilkret conducted Sousa's Band during Victor sessions (in 1926, Arthur Pryor led Sousa's Band for Victor sessions; in 1929 and 1930, Rosario Bourdon conducted Sousa's Band).

The December 1926 edition of the *Q.R.S. Monthly Catalog* lists Shilkret for the first (and possibly only) time as a player piano roll artist. He performs "Danube Waves" on QRS 3730.

Shilkret began working regularly on radio in 1925. On December 23, 1924, Victor president Eldridge R. Johnson, along with AT&T's vice president, issued a statement that Victor was turning to radio as a publicity medium. Page 18 of the January 1925 issue of *Talking Machine World* states that Victor was broadcasting "primarily for the purpose of popularizing the company's records." On New Year's night, 1925, Victor sponsored the first of a planned biweekly radio concert series. It was broadcast from New York by station WEAF and performers included tenor John McCormack (with the Shannon Four on "Adeste Fideles"), soprano Lucrezia Bori, and the Victor Salon Orchestra led by Nat Shilkret. Artists were introduced on the air by Calvin G. Child. Victor placed half-page advertisements in newspapers on the 31st announcing "The beginning of a new era in radio broadcasting." Shilkret led Victor musical groups on subsequent radio programs. Page 159 of the March 1925 issue of *Talking Machine World* reports that on March 12 the Eight Popular Victor Artists were featured on the sixth radio program sponsored by the Victor Talking Machine Company. Featuring on the program such artists as the Peerless Quartet, Billy Murray, and Rudy Wiedoeft was a change since previous programs had featured Red Seal artists. For this occasion Shilkret led what the trade journal identified as the International Novelty Orchestra.

The April 2, 1927, issue of *Roxy Theatre Weekly Review,* published for patrons of the Roxy Theatre in New York City, announces that artists for an April 6 radio broadcast would be Vernon Dalhart, Carson Robison and Rex Schepp, supported by the Maxwell Concert Orchestra, under the direction of Nathaniel Shilkret. It states, "The program will be made up of Hill Billy, Negro dialect spirituals, Indian and Southern tunes, all well worth hearing."

Page 19 of the November 1927 issue of *Talking Machine World* states:

> The Victor Talking Machine Co. announces that, after several months of negotiations, arrangements have been completed with the Mark Strand Theatre, New York City, whereby Nathaniel Shilkret and the world-famous Victor Salon Orchestra will make their first appearance as a permanent feature of the Mark Strand program on November 5. . . . For the Mark Strand he has augmented the Salon Orchestra, bringing together an organization composed of several of the most popular Victor orchestras now playing under his baton.

Shilkret's increasing importance to Victor may have contributed to Paul Whiteman's decision to leave Victor in 1928 for Columbia, though Whiteman's greatest incentive to switch companies was undoubtedly the astonishing sum of money Columbia offered. Sudhalter and Evans assert (*Bix: Man and Legend,* p. 233) that Whiteman seemed to leave Victor for Columbia because of "rivalry with Nat Shilkret over who recorded what material. Whiteman had for years assumed first crack at whatever songs he wanted, and the fact that Shilkret was more and more often recording many of the same selections, thus undermining what Whiteman saw as his personal market, angered the 'King of Jazz.'"

Thomas A. DeLong's biography of Paul Whiteman, *Pops* (New Century, 1983), gives more details about the conflicts between the two men. When Whiteman suffered setbacks during the April 21, 1927, session for the electrical remake of *Rhapsody in Blue* (Gershwin evidently disagreed about interpretation, feeling Whiteman was speeding passages too much in order to obtain a "jazzy" effect, and horn players failed to show up), Whiteman left the studio in a huff, later returning to find Shilkret on the podium—Whiteman left again. Nat Shilkret reported to Brian Rust during an unpublished 1963 interview, "It was poor old Nat who conducted!" The performance led that day by Shilkret was issued with Whiteman's name on the disc since it was, after all, Whiteman's orchestra.

On May 28, 1928, the Victor Talking Machine Company formally announced a contest for new symphonic and popular concert works, offering $25,000 for the best work of a symphonic type appropriate for a full symphony orchestra, $10,000 for the best new work in the jazz or symphonic jazz idiom, and $5,000 for the second-best work in the latter category. Shilkret conducted the winning symphonic jazz compositions on radio in December 1928 (winners in the symphonic jazz categories were picked by this time whereas the $25,000 winner would not be picked until mid-1929) and also led the Victor Concert Orchestra during recordings of the two works. Thomas Griselle's "Two American Sketches" (a nocturne and a march) won the $10,000 prize. Born in Upper Sandusky, Ohio, and trained at the Cincinnati College of Music, Griselle (1891-1955) had once toured as piano accompanist for Nora Bayes and then Alice Nielsen, provided accompaniment on Starr Piano Company records as early as January 1917, and beginning in August 1922 was musical director in Gennett's New York City recording laboratory. Rube Bloom's "Song of the Bayou" won the $5,000 prize. Playing time for each of the two winning compositions is less than five minutes, and the recordings were issued on twelve-inch Victor 36000.

In 1932, he conducted a Victor orchestra during sessions that rerecorded the voice of Enrico Caruso, who had died too soon to be recorded by the electrical process. Shilkret's sessions produced seven sides that combine Caruso's voice as recorded during the acoustic era with a modern orchestral sound.

As an arranger and composer, Shilkret was important to Victor. He was musical arranger for the wildly popular "The Prisoner's Song," cut by Vernon Dalhart on July 13, 1924 (Victor 19427). Believing he deserved composer credit for it, Shilkret late in life referred to Dalhart as a man who stole a song from him. He did receive composer credit for "The Lonesome Road," another folk song newly arranged for the popular record market. It was first recorded on September 16, 1927, by the song's lyricist, Gene Austin, whose real name was Eugene Lucas, along with a handful of studio musicians led by Shilkret (Lou Raderman plays viola—he had played the same on "The Prisoner's Song"). It was issued as Victor 21098 on January 20, 1928. Sam Coslow, of the publishing firm Spier and Coslow, may deserve some credit as co-author. In his book *Cocktails for Two* (Arlington House, 1977), he recalls performing "necessary surgery" on the song prior to publication. Coslow recalls that Shilkret and Austin "had . . . revised and dressed up an obscure old spiritual." Shilkret recorded it again on April 29, 1929, this time arranged for the Victor Symphony, with Willard Robinson contributing a vocal refrain. "The Lonesome Road" became a standard among jazz musicians.

Another popular Shilkret composition was "Jeannine, I Dream of Lilac Time." Lyrics were provided by L. Wolfe Gilbert. Written in 1928, it served as theme song for the motion picture *Lilac Time*, starring Colleen

Moore. Shilkret composed with Robert Lewis Shayon the song "If I Should Send a Rose," sung by Red Seal tenor Richard Crooks on RCA Victor 1760. More ambitious compositions include a symphonic poem titled *Skyward* (1928) and a trombone concerto (1942). In 1945 he commissioned Arnold Schoenberg, Igor Stravinsky, Darius Milhaud, and others to write a movement each for a biblical cantata titled *Genesis,* Shilkret himself contributing the opening movement ("The Creation"). *The Genesis Suite* was recorded for the Artist Records label (JS-10) by the Werner Janssen Symphony of Los Angeles, with Werner Janssen conducting and Edward Arnold narrating. A performance with the same conductor and narrator was given by the Utah Symphony on February 8, 1947.

Shilkret moved to Hollywood in 1935 to work as an arranger, conductor, and musical director (according to the *1937-38 International Motion Picture Almanac,* he was "general musical director" of RKO Radio Pictures) but continued to work for RCA Victor though he was evidently no longer exclusive to the company. While still in New York on April 4, 1935, he provided orchestral accompaniment for Irene Dunne when she recorded for Brunswick two numbers from the film *Roberta.* In the mid-1930s he conducted for Nelson Eddy records that sold well (a session on March 11, 1935, was held in New York City whereas sessions in 1936 and 1937 took place in Hollywood). The last record conducted by Shilkret to enjoy great success was "The Donkey Serenade," sung by tenor Allan Jones on RCA Victor 4380. Jones had sung it in the 1937 MGM film *The Firefly,* and under Shilkret's direction he recorded it for RCA Victor in Hollywood on January 13, 1938.

He arranged and conducted music for a couple dozen films from the mid-1930s onward, beginning with RKO Radio Pictures productions. Perhaps the most notable is the 1936 *Swing Time,* which features the dancing team of Fred Astaire and Ginger Rogers as well as the music of Jerome Kern. Shilkret composed the score for *Mary of Scotland,* directed in 1936 by John Ford and starring Katharine Hepburn and Fredric March. *Winterset,* released in late 1936, also brought Shilkret recognition due to its outstanding musical score. The Laurel and Hardy film *The Bohemian Girl* (1936) credits Shilkret with "musical direction." Another popular film with music conducted by Shilkret is *Shall We Dance* (1937), featuring Gershwin songs.

He worked steadily on radio shows, including *Camel Caravan* and *Relaxation Time.* As mentioned earlier, Shilkret in the 1930s began to lead orchestras on records issued by companies other than RCA Victor, and in the 1940s Capitol issued for the children's market a series titled *Bible Stories for Children,* each new release consisting of two records. The stories are narrated by actor Claude Rains, and jackets for the sets state, "with Nathaniel Shilkret's full concert orchestra providing a thrilling musical background." The jacket of a Columbia LP from the early 1950s titled *Paris 90 with Cornelia Otis Skinner* (ML 4619) names him musical director, and the label credits him for conducting.

In 1940 the Nathaniel Shilkret Music Company was established. One of his most ambitious compositions, "Ode to Victory," was the basis for a short film of that name made by MGM during World War II. This is mostly an orchestral work inspired by well-known patriotic tunes. It concludes with a chorus. He worked intensely on films in the years 1944-1946, earning credits for music on at least seven features, such as *The Hoodlum Saint*. He was still working with film as late as 1953 since he is credited for work on a short film about fishing called *Flying Tarpons*.

Shilkret died in Franklin Square, Long Island, New York. He was married to a woman named Anna, sometimes Ann. Their son, Arthur Shilkret, wrote a letter to Barry Cheslock on July 6, 1982, from his home at 632 Smith Street in Franklin Square listing manuscripts left by his father, including "a fully typed ms. for an autobiography of some 1000 pages" but that manuscript has never been published.

Smith, Joseph C.

Joseph C. Smith's Orchestra was successful from 1917 to 1921, reaching its peak popularity around 1919-1920, with Victor issuing new Smith recordings almost every month. The labels on many Smith records have the phrase "for dancing" or "dance music." It recorded fox-trots, one-steps, and waltzes, a few featuring a vocal refrain contributed by a Victor studio singer. Although musicians varied, generally eight instruments were used in the band, a combination of violin (Smith was a violinist), viola, piano, cello, trombone, cornet, and drums.

Smith's Orchestra began recording for the Victor Talking Machine Company on September 25, 1916. From this session came twelve-inch 35593 featuring Stewart James's "Songs of the Night" (the Victor Dance Orchestra is on the reverse side). It was issued in December 1916, and Victor's supplement for that month calls the orchestra "a new organization . . . popular with New York dancers." "Money Blues" was also recorded at this session but was held for a few months, and that session's take of a Cole Porter song went unissued.

The record number of Smith's first ten-inch Victor disc—18165—suggests it was intended for a December 1916 release, but Brian Rust's *American Dance Band Discography* shows that the orchestra returned to Victor on January 8, 1917, to rerecord Cole Porter's "I've a Shooting Box in

Scotland," a number introduced in 1914 in a Yale University Dramatic Association production and used again in the 1916 show *See America First*. It was the first Porter composition to be recorded (Prince's Band soon afterward recorded it for Columbia A5950, issued in June 1917). It is a curious choice for a dance record without vocals since the song's lyrics had charmed theater audiences, not the music. But the choice of a Porter song may be viewed as an appropriate beginning for Smith since he would go on to record many songs from popular Broadway shows, as well as medleys from shows. "I've a Shooting Box in Scotland" was backed by "Money Blues" on Victor 18165, which was issued in April 1917. Recording a song with "blues" in its title was an anomaly for Smith.

Two other performances recorded at this second session were issued on twelve-inch 35615: "Havanola" (also recorded by Prince's Band around this time for Columbia A5938 and by Jaudas' Band for Edison Blue Amberol 3298), and "Waltz from Drigo's Serenade." The disc was also issued in April, and Victor's supplement for that month gives "Havanola" the subtitle "Have Another," calling this "a very bright and cheerful number."

The next ten-inch Smith disc featured "Poor Butterfly" backed by "Allah's Holiday" (18246), both recorded on February 19, 1917. Raymond Hubbell's "Poor Butterfly" was recorded by a handful of Victor artists at this time—Frances Alda, Fritz Kreisler, and Elsie Baker (as "Edna Brown"). The Record Bulletin in the April 1917 issue of *Talking Machine World* notes that the disc was announced in March as a "dance special" along with the Original Dixieland Jazz Band's first disc (recorded on February 26).

In May 1917 "Evensong Waltz" and "Get Off My Foot" were issued on 18247. Victor's May supplement states, "The waltz is coming into its own again, and all dancers will welcome the dreamy 'Evensong' ([by] Easthope Martin), which is rich with color."

At this time the orchestra was featured at New York's Plaza Hotel. It is uncertain who the musicians were, but Hugo Frey was probably the pianist at the first session since Frey's composition "Money Blues" was recorded. Frey was a regular member of Smith's ensemble and its most important one aside from director Smith because Frey was a skilled composer as well as a talented pianist (on a few labels Frey is credited for his piano work— for example, the phrase "Piano passage by Hugo Frey and Frank Banta" is on Victor 18816). Other Frey compositions recorded around this time— not by Smith—were "Uncle Tom," played by Howard Kopp and Samuel Jospe on Columbia A2058 (issued in October 1916), and the sentimental Irish song "Molly Dhu" (written with Wilbur Weeks), recorded by Charles Harrison and issued in March 1917 on Victor 18154. The Van Eps Banta

Trio perform Frey's "You're the One That I Want" on Emerson 1023, issued in August 1919.

Along with the previously mentioned "Money Blues" and "Havanola," Frey compositions recorded by Smith's Orchestra include "Calicoco" (18478), "My Dough Boy" (18478), "Rockin' the Boat" (18521), "Happy" (18715), "Mary" (18500; cowritten with George L. Stoddard), and, on twelve-inch 35676, the waltz "Dódola" (Prince's Orchestra recorded this for Columbia A6010, issued in February 1918).

Jack Wasserman played saxophone during at least some sessions. When Wasserman in 1924 recorded with Jack Shilkret's Orchestra, advertisements placed in trade journals by the Buescher Band Instrument Company described Wasserman as "formerly with Joseph C. Smith's Orchestra. . . . He is rated one of the best players of the High Soprano Saxophone and rates with the very best players on three other sizes of Saxophone."

In previous years dance records had a different sound, and Smith's music must have struck many dancers as fresh, original, different. For dancing, Victor recordings made by the Victor Military Band, Conway's Band, and Pryor's Band, among others. Dance music evolved so that military bands gradually went out of fashion, and Smith's music—with violin and piano—became increasingly popular (predecessors on the Victor label include Europe's Society Orchestra and McKee's Orchestra). Victor's June 1917 supplement, announcing two new Smith discs (one ten inch, one twelve inch), states, "Smith's Orchestra has a quality of sound peculiar to itself, and one that is especially ingratiating with dancers." In July 1917 four dance records by the Victor Military Band were issued (none by Smith), but in August, two Smith dance records were issued, only one by the Victor Military Band. Gradually a new era in dance music was ushered in, the way paved for Paul Whiteman and His Ambassador Orchestra, the Isham Jones Orchestra, and others of the 1920s. After 1919 no new Victor Military Band titles were issued.

The December 1917 supplement, announcing the release of two Smith discs (one ten inch, another twelve inch), again stresses the novelty of the sound: "Both these medleys are full of striking instrumental effects which almost compel one to dance, even if one doesn't know how. Joseph C. Smith and His Orchestra manage to produce a tone quality peculiar to themselves. It haunts you like the tone of a saxophone."

The ensemble recorded a couple dozen titles for Victor within a year of its recording debut in September 1916. Nobody today would mistake it for a jazz band but the August 1917 Victor supplement states, in announcing a new Smith disc, "'Dance And Grow Thin' . . . has some sounds in it that would not disgrace a Jass Band—one observes particularly the sighing of the trombone and a mouse-like twitter in the treble that defies analysis." By September 1917, when Earl Fuller's first disc was issued, Victor used the spelling "jazz" instead of "jass."

On November 20, 1917, Smith's Orchestra recorded two titles for Columbia disc, both being Frey compositions: "Calicoco" and "When You Come Back" (A2460). Announcing the disc's release, Columbia's March 1918 supplement states, "For fifteen years, Mr. Smith has been an important factor in Metropolitan dancing circles."

Since Smith's first Victor session had been in September 1916 and his one Columbia session was fourteen months later, it is likely that Smith initially had a one-year contract with Victor. Evidently nothing issued up to the end of that first year had been successful enough for Victor to care much that Smith turned to a rival company soon after the end of that year—clearly Victor had not induced Smith to remain exclusive to Victor. Perhaps to the surprise of Smith and Victor executives, a song recorded at the end of Smith's first year, "Missouri Waltz" (35663), proved to be extremely popular when finally issued in February 1918. When Smith returned to Victor again for a May 8, 1918, session, he remained exclusive to Victor for four years.

Half a year passed between the recording of "Missouri Waltz" on October 29, 1917, and the session on May 9, 1918, that began Smith's second phase with Victor. Among other numbers, the orchestra recorded "Calicoco," which it had recorded for Columbia. On June 3, 1918, Smith's Orchestra recorded "Smiles," with vocal by tenor Harry Macdonough (Victor 18473), and this proved enormously popular. This may be the first dance record to feature a vocal refrain, and several Smith records that followed would feature vocal refrains, a novelty at the time. Vocals on "Mary" (18500) were provided on July 29, 1918, by Charles Harrison, Lewis James, and Harry Macdonough.

Harry Raderman's distinctive trombone playing is featured on Smith's popular "Yellow Dog Blues" (18618), recorded on October 1, 1919. The label of this disc even identifies Raderman as soloist—"Harry Rederman [sic] and his Laughing Trombone." It was the most popular recording of a W. C. Handy composition up to this time.

The orchestra recorded a few titles for Victor every month or two for the next few years. "Hindustan" (Victor 18507) was popular, as was the waltz "Alice Blue Gown" from *Irene*. "Peggy," recorded on September 25, 1919, and issued in February 1920 as Victor 18632, is notable for being a late recording with a contribution by tenor Harry Macdonough, who sings a refrain. Macdonough in this period supervised recording sessions held in Victor's New York City studio and would have determined what Smith numbers should include vocal refrains, always provided by studio singers—Henry Burr was used on some occasions, Billy Murray on others.

On October 1, 1919, Macdonough sang the refrain for a waltz number titled "Lovely Summertime," composed by Smith himself. The take featuring a vocal refrain was rejected. "Lovely Summertime" was instead issued as an instrumental on Victor 18681.

Though in 1920 Smith's Orchestra was Victor's most important dance band ensemble, by 1921 Victor depended as heavily on the Benson Orchestra as well as Paul Whiteman for dance music. By 1922, larger dance orchestras were in fashion along with smaller semi-jazz ensembles, such as the Virginians. New dance records often featured choruses dominated by banjoists and saxophonists. Moreover, numbers were more carefully arranged, allowing for greater variety in instrumentation during a performance. Smith's arrangements, by comparison, were monotonous, with long musical sections repeated without variation (a percussionist limited to woodblocks does add variety to the sound on occasion).

To keep up with musical trends, Smith experimented when cutting some of his later Victor records, relying less on strings, even adopting a reed section. "It's You" (18827), recorded on October 20, 1921, features a long cornet solo by Ernest Pechin—unusual for a Smith performance. Smith's music was going out of fashion. The February 1922 Victor supplement, in announcing the release of two fox trots conducted by Smith on Victor 18845, states, "'Joe' Smith's dancers swear by him—so do every other Victor conductor's." In other words, Smith had a following, but other Victor conductors had their own loyal fans—this is no great praise for Smith. His last Victor recording was made on March 16, 1922.

Though Smith's sound was becoming dated, one of his best-selling discs was made at the end of his Victor tenure: "Three O'Clock in the Morning" (18866), recorded on January 27, 1922. Around the time Smith left Victor, Paul Whiteman recorded the song (on August 22, 1922), and this became Whiteman's best-selling record. Victor did not ordinarily have two dance orchestras cover the same number—though there are differences, the Smith and Whiteman performances would have seemed very similar to most dancers—and it is likely that Whiteman was permitted to record the popular waltz only because Smith had left Victor by this time. It is not known why Smith left the company, though it would be understandable if he had envied the popularity of Paul Whiteman and His Orchestra, whose records outsold Smith's dance records.

In the late summer of 1922, Smith's Orchestra began making Brunswick records, none of which sold well. Smith is listed in the 1923 Brunswick catalog as an exclusive Brunswick recording artist. Smith's Orchestra continued making Brunswick recordings into 1923. Smith is included in a photograph of Brunswick orchestral leaders—others include Walter C. Haenschen (Carl Fenton), Isham Jones, Benny Krueger, Arnold Johnson—on page 35 of the February 1923 issue of *Talking Machine World*. "Un Tango Dans la Nuit (A Tango in the Night)" backed by the Argentine tango "De Cinq à Sept" was issued as Brunswick 2393 in April 1923. In May, Brunswick issued "Love and the Moon" and "Wonderful You" (2402). Four additional Smith sides were issued in August 1923.

Hugo Frey was no longer Smith's pianist. In the early 1920s he directed, or codirected with Nat Shilkret, such studio dance bands as The Great White Way Orchestra (some records feature piano duets by Banta and Frey, just as some Smith discs had), the Manhattan Merrymakers, and the Troubadours. Labels for some records credited to these orchestras cite Frey as director. He worked steadily in Victor's New York studio from 1922 through 1925 and even directed a Troubadours session as late as June 30, 1927 (Victor 20922 and 35831). As a music arranger for the publisher Robbins Music Corporation, he was responsible in 1926 for transcriptions and arrangements in the song books *Famous Negro Spirituals* and *Celebrated American Negro Spirituals*. He continued to work for Robbins into the 1940s.

By the fall of 1924 Smith led the Joseph C. Smith and His Mount Royal Hotel Orchestra for CKAC radio broadcasts in Montreal. Smith's final recordings were made in Montreal for HMV in early 1925. According to Brian Rust, Smith brought his band to London from Montreal in the autumn of 1925, and when he returned to the United States, he left behind his drummer and xylophonist Teddy Brown, who went on to become a popular solo entertainer in Great Britain. Smith's recording career was over by the time of electrical recording.

It is not known when or where Smith was born. Little is known of him after he made his final recordings in 1925, although Rust reports owning an Okeh disc issued in March 1925 (40251—it features Jimmy Joys' St. Anthony Hotel Orchestra) with a sticker suggesting that Smith owned a music store in La Porte at that time. Rust also reports that Smith lost his savings in the Wall Street crash of 1929 and spent his last years in Florida.

Frank Kelly wrote in his "Where Are They?" column for *Record Research* (January 1970, Issue 103), "Another big old-timer who was hit hard in his later years was JOSEPH C. SMITH whose orchestra recorded scores of tunes for Victor. . . . Smith ended up as a doorman in Florida in recent years." But Kelly provides no source for this. Subsequent *Record Research* issues featured letters by Smith fans, but few shed light on the man himself. One letter mentions that Smith's orchestra played the Mount

Royal Hotel in Montreal from June 1923 to October 1925 and made six records for Canadian Victor in March and June 1924. One writer reported that he had corresponded with Hugo Frey, who had commented that "Smith was very popular in his time but slipped . . . when Paul Whiteman came on the scene." Issue 105 (May 1970) reports, "Joseph C. Smith is listed in the 'In Memoriam' list for 1964-65 published by the Associated Musicians of Great New York, Local 802, A.F.M."

He is not to be confused with the Joseph Smith who appeared in motion pictures. One generation earlier, a Joseph C. Smith (1878-1932) was well-known as an exhibition dancer and choreographer, but it is unlikely that this is the bandleader. Victor promotional literature would have mentioned it if the bandleader had been famous in this way.

Sousa, John Philip/Sousa's Band

John Philip Sousa was born on November 6, 1854, in Washington, DC. Known as "The March King," he was the composer of many memorable marches, especially during the last quarter of the nineteenth century, along with songs and operettas, including *El Capitan* (1896). He was the author of a novel, *The Fifth String* (Bobbs-Merrill Company, 1902), and an autobiography, *Marching Along* (Hale, Cushman & Flint, 1928).

He played violin in a number of orchestras prior to assuming, at age twenty-six, the post of U.S. Marine Band director (1880-1892). The first recordings associated with Sousa were made by the U.S. Marine Band in 1890. It was not the full band since recording technology at the time could accommodate little more than a dozen players. It went on to record at least 229 titles for Columbia by the summer of 1892, when the conductor left to form Sousa's New Marine Band, soon renamed Sousa's Grand Concert Band. Records identify the ensemble simply as Sousa's Band.

James R. Smart's *The Sousa Band: A Discography* (Library of Congress, 1970) lists over a thousand recordings credited to Sousa's Band. It also lists records made in the early 1890s by the United States Marine Band—that is, it lists records made by the ensemble during the period when Sousa headed the band. Sousa himself was not present at these sessions. His famous name brought much-needed prestige to the fledgling recording industry, and he was presumably paid well for this (certainly band members must have welcomed the supplementary income), but Sousa must have concluded that records brought no prestige in return since he openly expressed disdain for the medium. "The Menace of Mechanical Music" is the title of an article he wrote for the September 1906 issue of *Appleton's Magazine*, and it contained this line: "Canned music is as incongruous by a campfire as canned salmon by a trout stream."

It is understandable if Sousa in the 1890s viewed records with such contempt that he declined to conduct during sessions since recording and playback technologies were decidedly crude throughout that decade. Brown wax cylinders and Berliner discs hardly did justice to Sousa's Band, whose concerts thrilled audiences. By 1906, technology had advanced significantly, but records still could not deliver the rich sounds of live performances (companies naturally stressed that record buyers could hear Sousa's Band in their homes at any time, which is not a point addressed by Sousa). Sousa mainly worried that mechanical music—records and player pianos—threatened the livelihood of musicians, which was a genuine problem, but that he openly criticized recorded music after taking so much money from various record companies is remarkable. No other famous artist had been so closely linked to the industry for so many years, and he continued his association with companies, the name Sousa's Band being put on many records even after he had coined the phrase "canned music"!

In any case, Sousa did not conduct during a recording session until December 21, 1917, and thereafter attended only three others—on September 6, 1918; March 29, 1923; and September 4, 1926 (during this one session of the electric era, he led the Philadelphia Rapid Transit Company Band).

Sousa's attack on mechanical music in *Appleton's Magazine* alarmed some in the record industry, but others took advantage of it in advertising. Page 17 of the January 1907 issue of *Edison Phonograph Monthly* features an advertisement (designed for Edison dealers to duplicate in local newspapers) stating:

> Even John Philip Sousa, who has no use for phonographs, has been forced to recognize the Edison Phonograph as a formidable competitor. The two-step king says that people will no longer go to concerts if they can have music in their own homes so easily and so cheaply as they can with the Edison Phonograph. This is an unwilling tribute, but it nevertheless is a tribute.

On page 76 of the April 1921 issue of Victor's trade journal *Voice of the Victor* is the article "Victrola and I," credited to the band leader. A headline above the article title states, "A Special Article Written For 'The Voice of the Victor' By John Philip Sousa." This publication of a Sousa article in this trade journal was obviously calculated to signal to Victor dealers that Sousa's views about talking machines had changed (the bandmaster actually says little about machines or records). That it was written by Sousa cannot be certain but it was clearly published with his cooperation and approval since details in the article about his recent experiences in South

Africa could only have come from him. It was reprinted in the September 1921 issue of the trade journal. Sousa was giving concerts at the time with an organization of eighty-five pieces, his touring season lasting from July 14, 1921, to March 10, 1922.

Trombonist Arthur Pryor led many sessions from the late 1890s until he left the band in 1903 (the first Victor recordings of Pryor's Band were made on November 24, 1903). Other band members or former band members who conducted at sessions were cornetists Henry Higgins, Herbert L. Clarke, and Walter B. Rogers. Some pre-1899 Berliner discs give credit on the label to Higgins for conducting (Pryor seems to have conducted regularly in 1899 and 1900). Clarke led the band for most records made from 1904 to 1906, after Pryor's departure, and probably conducted for Edison sessions in 1909 and 1910—he recorded "The Bride of the Waves" as a cornet solo for Edison around this time, and the October 1909 issue of *Edison Phonograph Monthly*, in announcing Amberol 310, identifies Clarke as "the assistant leader of Sousa's Band."

Walter B. Rogers left the band to become Victor's musical director and conducted most Sousa Band sessions for Victor from 1907 to 1916. Joseph Pasternack, who succeeded Rogers as Victor's musical director, had never been a member of Sousa's Band but conducted a handful of band sessions from 1919 to 1925. Rosario Bourdon conducted two Sousa's Band sessions in 1919 and another two sessions a decade later. Nat Shilkret as a young man had briefly been a member of Sousa's Band and later conducted the band during some Victor sessions, mostly in 1923 and 1924.

Records were made for most of the early companies, including small ones such as the Chicago Talking Machine Company and D. E. Boswell and Company, also of Chicago. Hundreds of takes were made for Victor, beginning on October 1, 1900, when the new company was known briefly as the Consolidated Talking Machine Company. Curiously, no Sousa's Band discs issued by Victor open with spoken announcements, though such announcements were standard for all other performers in the company's earliest years, including soloists from Sousa's Band who made discs. Famous soloists who made recordings as featured artists include Walter B. Rogers, Arthur Pryor, and Emil Keneke.

Edison's National Phonograph Company recorded Sousa's Band for about a year, beginning in the summer of 1909. The July 1909 issue of *Edison Phonograph Monthly* states:

> The actual work of making Records by Sousa's band will not begin until August and the Records themselves cannot be issued for two or three months later. The fact, however, that Mr. Sousa has entered into this arrangement is little less than noteworthy. . . . Mr. Sousa has

been more or less opposed to talking machines and this arrangement indicates a decided change in his attitude.

This is misleading since Sousa's "arrangement" with the Edison company was essentially the same as those made with other companies in earlier years (Sousa himself did not conduct during Edison sessions). Issued in November 1909 were "Stars and Stripes Forever March" (Amberol 285) and "Powhatan's Daughter March" (Standard 10237).

Dozens of Sousa compositions were recorded by the band, including "El Capitan March" (Columbia, 1895), "Washington Post March" (Columbia, 1895), "The Stars and Stripes Forever" (Columbia 532, 1897), and "The Invincible Eagle" (Victor 844, 1901). The band in concerts and on recordings helped popularize works by other composers, such as Neil Moret's "Hiawatha," introduced by the band in public performances in the summer of 1902 and recorded on August 14, 1903 (Victor 2443) as well as on later dates. Virtually every performance by Sousa's Band on recordings is an instrumental. The sole exception appears to be the popular "In the Good Old Summer Time," first recorded by the band on December 17, 1902, and again cut on October 27, 1905 (Victor 1833). A vocal refrain is sung by Harry Macdonough and S. H. Dudley (the label states only "Vocal Chorus"), a rare instance of a military band performance featuring a vocal refrain.

No new Sousa Band records were made from December 1912 to November 1915, and thereafter sessions were irregular, with only one or two during most years up to the final session on July 1, 1930, and usually with only two or three titles cut per session. Sousa did not lead his own band in late 1917 or 1918 but was instead a trainer of bands at the U.S. Naval Training Station at Great Lakes, near Chicago. Labels of some Victor discs of the World War I period identify the composer as "John Philip Sousa, U.S.N.R.F" to reflect his new status as a lieutenant in the United States Naval Reserve Force.

From the mid-1920s onward, with the advent of the microphone and the marketing of equipment that played electrically recorded performances, military bands on records sounded far better than in the old days of the acoustic process, but by this time military bands were passé. It appears that some records of the early electric era credited to Sousa's Band were in fact Arthur Pryor's Band.

The first Sousa Band records made with the electric process were conducted by others, but Sousa himself presided over a session on September 4, 1926. He led not his own band but the Philadelphia Rapid Transit Company Band, which existed from 1922 to 1947 and was otherwise led by Albert E. Eckenroth. The issued disc is rare. Sousa is given label credit on Victor 20192 only as composer. One side featured "The March of the Mitten Men," dedicated to Thomas E. Mitten, chief executive officer of the company that provided trolley transporation from Philadelphia to Willow Grove Park, where Sousa played many concerts (Mitten owned that company and had built Willow Grove Park, which is five miles outside the city). The reverse side featured "The Thunderer."

Sousa died on March 6, 1932, in Reading, Pennsylvania.

Spencer, Len (January 12, 1867-December 15, 1914)

Leonard Garfield Spencer was born in Washington, DC. The middle name was given in honor of Senator James A. Garfield, a friend of the Spencer family before he became a U.S. president. Len's mother, Sara, was a leader in the women's suffrage movement. His father Henry Caleb Spencer—son of Platt Rogers Spencer, co-inventor of the Spencerian style of penmanship—operated the Spencerian Business College located in the nation's capitol at Ninth and D Streets until he died in 1890.

Len's younger brother—Henry Caleb Spencer Jr., born on February 14, 1875—also became a recording artist. Harry Spencer worked mostly for Columbia but did record for other companies, even making Zon-o-phone discs in 1901. He mostly cut recitations, such as the popular "President McKinley's Address at the Pan-American Exposition." By the early 1900s Harry was Columbia's chief announcer and his voice can be heard at the beginning of many cylinders and early discs. Jim Walsh states in the October 1958 issue of *Hobbies* that Harry later was a train caller in Lancaster, Pennsylvania, as reported to Walsh by Joe Belmont. Harry suffered mental illness late in life and died on August 29, 1946, in St. Elizabeth's Hospital in Washington, DC.

Len Spencer himself did announcing for other Columbia artists of the 1890s. Listing titles of the Columbia Orchestra, Columbia's June 1897 catalog states, "The announcements are as loud and distinct as only Mr. Spencer can make them, and his quaint negro humorisms, laugh, shouts, etc., so familiar to talking machine patrons, add much to the popularity of these records." Only Len Spencer is identified elsewhere in the catalog, so the "Mr. Spencer" here undoubtedly refers to Len, not Harry. Columbia Orchestra numbers that include "shouts" and "laughs" include "Alabama Walk Around" (15086), "Old Nigger Wing" (15088), "Tapioca Polka" (15091), and "Frolic of the Coon" (15092).

Working as a junior instructor at the Spencerian Business College, the young Len Spencer frequently visited the sales office of the newly formed Columbia Phonograph Company, at that time with headquarters at 919 Pennsylvania Avenue in Washington, DC, to get information, have parts serviced, and purchase cylinders. The college used an office graphophone, or dictaphone. He expressed a desire to record his own voice, and company executives discovered he had a rich baritone and the ability to put his character into a song.

Frank Dorian, a Columbia official who began working for the company in 1889, recalled in later years for Walsh that Spencer's career as a recording artist began either in late 1889 or early 1890. Dorian wrote in the January 1930 issue of *Phonograph Monthly Review:*

> Spencer's earlier records were made by grouping four or five phonographs on top of an upright piano with their horns converging towards the key board, on which Spencer played his own accompaniment while he sang. He received the munificent sum of ten cents for each accepted record. If he was fortunate enough to get three out of every four records accepted, it was possible for him to make as much as $3.00 or $4.00 for each full hour of singing.

In this era of slot machines and ear tubes, no method of producing "master" cylinder records had been invented, so artists were required to perform the same numbers over and over by the wearisome "round." Spencer possessed the three qualities needed to excel at this line of work: endurance, patience, and versatility. In early days he sometimes used the nom de disque Garry Allen.

Although Spencer became known as a comedian—especially in speaking roles—in his early years he was comfortable singing numbers of all genres. In the 1890s he recorded many sentimental songs and hymns.

After making early Columbia recordings, he worked exclusively for Edison's United States Phonograph Company, located in Newark, New Jersey. During this period he continued to live in Washington, DC, and traveled to New Jersey to make records.

The March 1897 issue of *The Phonoscope* identifies Spencer as having been with the United States Phonograph Company for several years but announced that he had begun to make Columbia records (he was actually returning to the company). By February 1897 he was also making Berliner discs, such as "Nearer My God to Thee" (915). According to the trade journal, by late 1897 he was a member of the Greater New York Quartet, which also consisted of Roger Harding, Steve Porter, and a singer named "Depew" (the trade journal gives only last names for the quartet members).

By 1898, Spencer was most valued as an interpreter of what companies characterized as "Negro" material. A Columbia catalog issued in 1898 by its New England headquarters, the Eastern Talking Machine Company, gives these subheadings for Spencer cylinder titles: "Negro Songs," "Negro Love Songs and Lullabys," "Negro Songs and Dance—with Shouts, Asides, and Clogs," "Pickaninny Songs," "Old Man Negro Songs—Interspersed with Pathetic Sayings, Very Characteristic," "Comic and Topical Songs," and "Gospel Songs."

Spencer was the first singer to record on a regular basis songs with "rag" and "ragtime" in the title, evidently specializing in such material before Arthur Collins. In the Eastern Talking Machine Company catalog of 1898 the phrase "rag time" is used after two Spencer titles: one is "You'll Have to Choose Another Baby Now (rag time)," 7363; the other is "My Coal Black Lady (a new hit in rag time)," 7420. A third Spencer selection has "rag time" in its actual title: "The Wench with the Rag Time Walk," 7422.

A Kansas City Talking Machine Company catalog of this period adds the phrase "popular rag time" to the title "You've Been a Good Ole Wagon, but You're Done Broke Down" (7309), sung by Spencer. One other Spencer selection, "I Love My Little Honey" (7311), is characterized as a "rag time melody."

He often recorded the speeches of famous men, usually in abbreviated form. Edison Standard 8154, issued in 1902, features Spencer reciting "Lincoln's Speech at Gettysburg."

He was closely associated with the comic skit known as "The Arkansaw Traveler," which he recorded for various companies (Tim Brooks reports that Harry Spencer—not Len—was responsible for the frequently found Columbia versions). It is a character study of an Arkansas native who sits before his cabin playing his fiddle and giving witty answers to a stranger who passes by the cabin. Spencer recorded it several times for Victor, beginning on November 23, 1901 (seven-inch A-1101; ten-inch M-1101). He provided voices for both the stranger and Arkansas native, and Charles D'Almaine played violin. In 1902 Spencer recorded the first of a few versions for Edison (Standard 8202).

On May 1, 1898, he signed an exclusive contract with Columbia, but this arrangement lasted only about a year. He had made Berliners beginning in 1897 and when his status as exclusive Columbia artist ended, he returned to make Berliners in April 1899. Spencer was one of Victor's most frequently recorded artists in the company's earliest years, his first session for the company taking place on May 17, 1901. He also recorded for Zon-o-phone, Leeds & Catlin, and other early disc manufacturers as well as various cylinder companies.

Spencer collaborated with many other recording artists. He performed many duets with Vess L. Ossman, "The Banjo King." He organized the

Len Spencer Trio, which included Steve Porter and Billy Golden, led the Imperial Minstrels, and was a member of many minstrel ensembles. A typical performance is on Edison Standard 8672, titled "Georgia Minstrels," credited to the Edison Minstrels, and issued in April 1904. After the company exchanges jokes, Spencer sings (or "introduces") "Uncle Billy's Dream."

Spencer was a successful entrepreneur. He organized companies for recording purposes, especially minstrel companies; he managed and promoted artists, including George W. Johnson for a time; he ran a booking agency. An 1898 Columbia catalog shows that Spencer managed the Spencer Trio and Imperial Minstrels. The September 1898 issue of *The Phonoscope* states:

> Early in November Len Spencer's Greater New York Minstrels will open in Orange, NJ, under the management and proprietorship of the genial "Len." The roster of the company embraces many artists prominent in the talking machine business. Among others are the Diamond Comedy Four, Billy Golden, comedian; Vess L. Ossman, banjoist; Steve Porter, in illustrated songs; Roger Harding, tenor balladist; the Three Murray Brothers, musical experts . . . and in conclusion Golden, Spencer and Harding in their great plantation act entitled: "In Front of the Old Cabin Door."

The team of Ada Jones and Len Spencer, popular from 1905 to around 1910, recorded many skits written by Spencer, with Jones often concluding with the chorus of a popular song. The skits—companies used the terms "vaudeville specialty" and "descriptive specialty"—are not especially clever, the many jokes being mere variations of ones told in countless minstrel companies and vaudeville shows, but they sold well.

Billy Murray reported in the January 1917 issue of *Edison Phonograph Monthly*, and then later to Walsh, that he was responsible for Jones making her Columbia recording debut in 1904. The catalyst was a recording session involving Murray and Spencer. Victor Emerson, then supervisor of Columbia recording sessions, was appalled by Murray's imitation of a female and insisted upon a woman playing the female role. Murray states in the Edison trade journal, "I told the director about the girl I had heard in the Fourteenth street museum [Huber's] and suggested that she be given a try-out. He told me to bring her around. I did, and she made just as big a hit with everybody else as she did with me."

The first Jones and Spencer recording was titled "Heine," issued as Edison 8982 in May 1905. The April 1905 issue of *Edison Phonograph Monthly* characterizes it as a "Dutch vaudeville specialty" during which the Ted Snyder song "Heine" is introduced. Other successful Jones-Spencer duets include "Pals," "He's Me Pal," "Mr. and Mrs. Murphy," "Peaches and Cream," and "Coming Home From Coney Island." They did a series of "Jimmie and Maggie" recordings.

A new Jones and Spencer performance would be issued regularly by Edison—nearly every month—from the time she made her debut with the company through the next few years. By 1910 Spencer and Jones titles were issued less frequently, though for another decade the Edison company occasionally issued Spencer and Jones skits on Blue Amberol cylinders (a total of eight), usually performances that had earlier been available on wax Amberol cylinders. For example, in October 1919 Edison issued "A Race for a Wife, a Racetrack Sketch" on Blue Amberol 3857. It had earlier been on Amberol 335.

In April 1904 Edison issued Standard 8656, which featured Spencer performing "Uncle Tom's Cabin (Flogging Scene)." He plays both Uncle Tom and Simon Legree, and the melodramatic performance includes incidental music from an orchestra. The scene is taken from a popular play instead of directly from Harriet Beecher Stowe's novel *Uncle Tom's Cabin*. Spencer often recorded the same material for different companies, and Victor also issued a version of "Uncle Tom's Cabin (Flogging Scene)." Perhaps because it is based on a respected literary work, Victor labels give credit to "Leonard G. Spencer" instead of the less formal but more customary "Len Spencer" or "Mr. Spencer." He recorded takes on March 3, 1904, for a ten-inch disc (2674) and a twelve-inch disc (31196). He performs it also on ten-inch Zon-o-phone 464 as well as Columbia 1783. "Our National Airs" on Victor 4075 and "Lincoln's Speech at Gettysburg" on Victor 2113 are likewise credited to "Leonard G. Spencer."

On Edison Standard 8879, issued in January 1905, Spencer undergoes the transformation from Dr. Jekyll to Mr. Hyde, basing his performance on the transformation of actor Richard Mansfield in a popular play of the time. Spencer performs the same on Columbia 1908.

His home was in Washington, DC, for much of his career as a record artist, and since most studios were in New York City, he spent much time away from his family. Around 1904 he moved his family to Dyker Heights near Coney Island. In a series of articles about Spencer in 1958, Walsh reported in *Hobbies* that when Spencer was in his late thirties—perhaps around 1905-1906—he lost the sight of his right eye after an accident involving a recording studio's swinging door. Walsh learned this from Spencer's second daughter, Ethel, who also described her father as over six feet tall with "a powerful well-built physique."

By 1910 or so the popularity of descriptive sketches—a form at which Spencer excelled—declined significantly, and Ada Jones began devoting much of her time to recording duets with other artists, particularly Billy Murray. In contrast to many black wax Edison cylinders made in the Gold-Moulded era—not to mention the many made in the brown wax era—only four Blue Amberols feature performances credited only to Len Spencer, all of them issued posthumously. This includes a performance of "Arkansas Traveler" (3745—the spelling is no longer "Arkansaw"), issued in June 1919. Another, issued in August 1919, was a skit written by Elizabeth D. Boone titled "Hezekiah Hopkins Comes to Town" (3793).

Spencer continued to work as a booking agent as well as a sketch writer, though by 1910 such sketches were becoming dated. His last record was "Uncle Fritz and the Children's Orchestra," a sketch composed by F. X. Chwatal and released on Edison Diamond Disc 50196 in December 1914. It was his only Diamond Disc. Spencer plays the role of a German uncle who has brought toys to a group of children.

He suffered a cerebral hemorrhage on December 15, 1914, while talking with a performer who had come into Len Spencer's Lyceum, the name of his booking agency's office at 245 West 42nd Street (in 1912 it was at 46 East 14th Street and was previously at 46 East 14th Street, 16 West 27th Street, 44 West 28th Street, and other Manhattan locations). He died in the office in the arms of friend Arthur Dowling, according to a death notice in the December 16, 1914, edition of *The New York Times*, which also notes, "He was well known in Masonic circles, being a member of Dirigo Lodge, the Royal Arch Masons, and the Knights Templars." His daughter Ethel was also with him when he slumped over his desk on that day. He was forty-seven. He was cremated at North Bergen, New Jersey, and buried in a family burial plot in Glenwood Cemetery in Washington, DC. Brother Harry took over the Lyceum for several months until the business folded.

In 1885, he married Margaret Agnes Kaiser, who died in 1891. His second wife was Elizabeth Norris, whom he married in 1892 and then remarried in 1895 after a long separation. She died in 1941. His three surviving children from this marriage were Myrtle, who sang with her father on a few recordings; Ethel; and Clara (a daughter named Constance died in childhood). Ethel, later Mrs. James A. Yarbray of San Antonio, Texas, supplied Walsh with details about her father, which Walsh reported in the July and August 1958 issues of *Hobbies*.

Stanley, Aileen (March 21, 1893-March 24, 1982)

Her real name was Maude Elsie Aileen Muggeridge. She was born in Chicago, so it is fitting that she was among the first singers—in January

1923—to record Fred Fisher's newly published "Chicago" (dance bands recorded it months earlier but Stanley's Okeh 4792 was the first by a vocalist). Her father and mother had emigrated from England though her father died of typhoid several months before she was born, contracting it from another daughter, who also died of the disease. Her mother, Maria, encouraged young Aileen and her brother Stanley to develop their singing and dancing talents. Another brother was named Robert.

They formed a brother-and-sister team called Stanley and Aileen, also the Peerless English Juveniles, even the Premier Versatile Entertainers. They toured the Midwest and West Coast by 1904, playing Nickelodeons and burlesque houses, but after Stan ran off with a chorus girl and began a new act, Aileen chose to perform solo in vaudeville, forming a new stage name (Aileen Stanley) by reversing the name of the old act (Stanley and Aileen).

It is not known when she began working alone in vaudeville, but the February 22, 1915, issue of *Billboard* included this review of her debut at New York City's Palace Theatre: "Aileen Stanley was splendid to look at and sang four songs with excellent effect. She was making her first bow to Times Square and produced applause galore and laughs for her comedy incidents . . ." By 1919 she toured the Orpheum Circuit. In 1920 she was in a New York show called *Silks and Satins*. Written and produced by William Rock, this was basically a revue, and in it Stanley sang some numbers.

She made a test record for Columbia at 229 West 46th Street in New York City. A pressing now owned by Dick Carty is dated "Oct. 1919," gives the number 63236-1 (matrix and take), and indicates that piano accompaniment was provided by "Bob," undoubtedly Robert Buttenuth. The name "Donovan" on the white label indicates that the test was supervised by A. E. Donovan, manager of the company's professional and personal record departments. Stanley delivers a song (title unknown) about returning home to Dixie, the singing style close to Marion Harris's.

Advance Record Bulletins in the June 1920 issue of *Talking Machine World* announced the July release of a Stanley disc: "Ding Toes" backed by "I'm a Jazz Vampire" on Pathé 22389. Ross Laird states on page 513 in *Moanin' Low: A Discography of Female Popular Vocal Recordings, 1920-1933* that these "two titles were advertised as due to be issued on Pathé 22389, but this was never released. Instead the second title was remade and eventually issued." It appears that she made her recording debut on Pathé 22393 with "Alibi Blues," issued in August 1920 (the reverse side features Ernest Hare). It was followed by the release in September of "I'm a Jazz Vampire" and "Ding-a-Ring-a-Ring" on Pathé 22407.

She recorded other titles for Pathé in 1920, and in the early 1920s she performed for Pathé, Olympic, Vocalion, Brunswick, Gennett, Okeh, Edison, and Operaphone. But Stanley discs issued by these companies are rare. Her best-selling records of the 1920s were made for the Victor Talking Machine Company.

Her first Victor recordings were made on August 10, 1920, around the time "Alibi Blues" was issued by Pathé and following her success in *Silks and Satins.* "Broadway Blues" and "My Little Bimbo Down on the Bamboo Isle" were issued on Victor 18691 in November 1920 (the same month as Paul Whiteman's debut discs—Victor was introducing many new artists at this time), and the disc sold very well. The chorus of the Walter Donaldson-Grant Clarke song "My Little Bimbo" features the words of a bragging sailor, Bill McCoy, who was once shipwrecked on a Fiji, or "Fee-jee-ee-jee," Isle. Stanley sings words that are slightly changed from the song as copyrighted. In the first verse she identifies the sailor as "Dan McCoy," which is problematic since in the second verse she uses the name as given by the songwriters, "William" (and "Bill"). Sheet music gives these lines in the chorus:

I've seen wrecks,
Plenty of wrecks,
Out on the stormy sea
But by heck there never was a wreck
Like the wreck she made of me
For all she wore was a great big Zulu smile
My little bimbo down on the Bamboo Isle

Stanley sings these words:

You know, I've seen wrecks,
Plenty of wrecks,
Out on the deep blue sea
But by heck there never was a wreck
Like the wreck she made of me
And all she had was a great big Zulu smile . . .

The change of "stormy" to "deep blue" is inconsequential, but other changes—substituting "and" for the coordinator "for," and "had" for "wore"—weaken the song. Grant Clarke's original lyrics are not exactly risqué but do hint at nudity ("all she wore was a great big Zulu smile"), which was daring for 1920. Stanley's changes make the song less suggestive. On August 12 she recorded "My Little Bimbo" for Edison (Diamond

Disc 50707; Blue Amberol 4147), with the lyric changes she had used two days earlier for Victor. It was the song most identified with her in the early 1920s, and her photograph was on the cover of the sheet music.

In the early 1920s she was known in vaudeville as "The Personality Girl." Edison promotional literature announcing new Blue Amberols for April 1922 calls "Boo-Hoo-Hoo" (4487), "A serio-comic song, which suits the style of Aileen Stanley to perfection. In vaudeville, Miss Stanley is known as 'The Phonograph Girl,' because of her popularity on records." For any company to dub Stanley "The Phonograph Girl" as early as 1922 was bold given the relatively few Stanley records released at this time— more records were being sold of Marion Harris, Nora Bayes, and possibly Mamie Smith. Stanley's popularity did increase and by 1923 may have been the most popular female singer making records, but it is more likely that those of blues singer Bessie Smith, new to the industry in 1923, sold in larger quantities. By 1926 Stanley was dubbed "The Victrola Girl" (after cutting two final titles for Gennett in the fall of 1924, Stanley had sessions only for Victor and British affiliate HMV).

In the early 1920s she was identified on some labels as a contralto, on others as a soprano, but most labels identified her only as "comedienne," a term used on labels throughout the 1920s for a wide range of female artists who sang popular material, including blues singers Clara Smith and Bessie Smith.

On January 4, 1922, she married Robert Buttenuth in Minneapolis. Page 135 of the June 1922 issue of *Talking Machine World* identifies Buttenuth as her piano accompanist and manager. He was cocomposer of "I'm a Lonesome Cry Baby," recorded by Stanley for Victor 19144 on June 26, 1923.

In her early recording years, Stanley sang blues and a few songs also recorded by jazz ensembles. Her performance of "Singin' the Blues" (18703) was issued in January 1921, and the Victor supplement for that month states, "Through this Miss Stanley sings with an excellent negro accent." She recorded it on October 27, a few months before the Original Dixieland Jazz Band (ODJB) incorporated a verse of the song into their performance of "Margie," which would become the ODJB's best-selling disc. On August 26, 1920, Columbia artist Nora Bayes had been first to record Conrad and Robinson's "Singin' the Blues." The song was famously revived by Frank Trumbauer in a 1927 Okeh session that captured Bix Beiderbecke and Trumbauer himself at their best.

Other early Stanley discs on Victor that sold well include "Home Again Blues" (18760, 1921), which had been recorded a few months earlier as an instrumental by the ODJB, and "Sweet Indiana Home" (18922, 1922). In late 1921 she recorded for Okeh the song "Bow Wow Blues (My Mama Treats Me Like a Dog)," recorded a few months earlier for Victor as an instrumental by the ODJB.

In the early 1920s Edison Diamond Disc jackets promoted Stanley as a blues artist. The jacket for "Where-Is-My-Daddy-Now Blues" (50736) states, "Aileen Stanley is among the foremost 'Blues' singers of the day, and conveys their peculiar atmosphere." This was also issued as Blue Amberol 4204. Incredibly, in 1921 she was issued on Black Swan 14116 ("Honey Rose" and "Mandy 'n' Me") as Mamie Jones. At least some record buyers must have believed they were hearing a black artist when listening to this Black Swan disc. The same take of "Honey Rose" was issued on Olympic 14109, along with "Mimi," and the same take of "Mandy 'n' Me" was issued on Olympic 14113, along with "Ma!" Olympic labels give credit to Stanley, not Mamie Jones.

She recorded "Anna in Indiana" for Edison (50804; issued as Blue Amberol 4349 in October 1921) as well as for Pathé. Her last performance for Edison was "On the Isle of Wicki Wacki Woo," recorded on June 14, 1923, and issued on Diamond Disc 51207.

On January 30, 1925, she recorded with Gene Austin a song composed by Austin (with Jimmy McHugh and Irving Mills) titled "When My Sugar Walks Down the Street" (Victor 19585). This was Stanley's last recording made with Victor's acoustic process (she soon afterward performed in England and made recordings by the electric process for HMV). Nat Shilkret supervised the session and provided orchestral accompaniment— Shilkret and Austin would work together on many more recordings. It was Austin's first Victor recording (he had already made Vocalion and Edison records), one of several that Austin made with Victor's acoustic process. Austin's "crooning" style was extremely popular during Victor's Orthophonic period.

Stanley returned to the Victor studios in August and made her first Orthophonic recordings. She was immediately paired with Billy Murray, though early efforts at "If I Had a Girl Like You" were rejected, as were most takes from her first session using a microphone. Only "You're in Wrong With the Right Baby" was issued. It was not unusual to make several takes in the early days of electric recording. Stanley was more successful in making the transition from acoustic to electric recording than most other singers who had enjoyed success in the early 1920s. Her career arguably peaked in the late 1920s.

On September 22, 1925, Murray and Stanley recorded "If I Had a Girl Like You" with enough success for a take to be issued. On Victor 19795, it was backed by "Keep Your Skirt Down, Mary Ann," with Murray singing as an Irish mother.

In the Victor studio she worked regularly with Murray. Their first duets were "When the Leaves Come Tumbling Down" (19026) and "You've Got to See Mamma Ev'ry Night" (19027), cut on February 15, 1923. Murray's partnership with Stanley resulted in a wide stylistic range of recordings during the last years of Victor's acoustic era and then during the Orthophonic years. They include blues-derived numbers ("You've Got to See Mamma Ev'ry Night," (19027), comic sketches ("Nobody's Sweetheart," 19373), and ballads ("It Had to Be You," 19373). In 1926 they recorded "Bridget O'Flynn (Where've Ya Been?)" (20240), and on this Murray truly holds back in a way he never could in the acoustic era by literally whispering sweet nothings during an opening comic skit. Stanley also recorded with Johnny Marvin during Victor's Orthophonic period, their version of "Red Lips—Kiss My Blues Away" (20714) selling especially well.

In the Orthophonic era Victor executives used Murray most often as a partner for the younger Stanley. The two voices blended well in comic duets about sweethearts—at least on all issued takes. A surviving test pressing of "D'ye Love Me?," cut on November 6, 1925, shows that the musical key appropriate for Stanley was much too low for Murray, the tenor often straining, at times sounding like a baritone (weeks later Murray cut this song with Gladys Rice, who sang it in a higher key).

Murray and Stanley duets sold very well, but it was an odd pairing. Murray, born in 1877, was significantly older, and though in some duets he sings in an Irish accent as Stanley's mother, in other songs Murray plays a lovesick teen, most notably "Whaddya Say We Get Together?" (20065) and "Does She Love Me? (Positively-Absolutely)" (20643). Murray again plays a teen in "I'm Gonna Dance Wit de Guy Wot Brung Me," made on June 27, 1927 (20822).

On June 13, 1929, Stanley and Murray had their final session as a team. Victor issued "Katie, Keep Your Feet on the Ground" (22040) but rejected "Please Don't Cut Out My Sauerkraut."

Stanley performed as a torch singer for "Broken Hearted," made on August 5, 1927 (20825), and "I'll Get By, As Long As I Have You" (21839), made in 1929. Her last two Victor discs were issued in 1930, neither of which sold well. Her success as an American recording artist began in the early 1920s and ended with that decade. She made some records in England in the mid-1930s.

From 1937 to 1959 Stanley and ex-husband Bob Buttenuth ran a coaching studio for developing singers. One contralto adopted the name Aileen

Stanley Jr. and performed with her coach Aileen on a nostalgic radio show titled *Music Hall Varieties* (also featured were Beatrice Kay, Joe E. Howard, and Irving Kaufman). Five numbers sung by Aileen on July 25, 1946, were pressed on Record 1352 of the NBC-produced Thesaurus Orthacoustic, and these radio transcription discs were sold to stations. Identified as a contralto, she is accompanied by the Music Hall Varieties Orchestra. The songs are "Row Row Row," "I Was Born in Michigan," "My Home Town Is a One-Horse Town," "Let It Rain, Let It Pour," and "The Nights Are Six Months Long." Only two of these songs had been recorded by Stanley in earlier years: "I Was Born in Michigan" and "My Home Town Is a One-Horse Town."

Songs recorded by student Aileen Stanley Jr., also called a contralto, were made available on Record 1482, and they include "Down in Jungle Town" and "I Want to Go Back to Michigan." Promotional literature for the radio show states, "Like millions of others, Aileen Stanley lost her personal fortune in 1929, but her interest in the entertainment world was of far greater importance. Although she is no longer on the stage, Miss Stanley is in still another venture connected with show business—coaching young women who'll be the stars of tomorrow."

When Bob died, the studio was closed and Stanley moved to a house on Hammond Street in Hollywood.

Stanley, Frank C. (December 29, 1868-December 12, 1910)

This important bass-baritone was born William Stanley Grinsted in Orange, New Jersey. His father was Augustus T. Grinsted, an educator who was at one time the president of Orange's Board of Education. An obituary printed soon after the singer's death states that William had a bass voice that was fully trained during his boyhood, whereas another suggests he did not have vocal lessons until later. Victor generally identified Stanley as a bass, Columbia and Edison usually as a baritone.

In high school he entertained classmates during recess with his banjo playing. In the early 1890s he made North American Phonograph Company cylinders as a solo banjoist and used his real name. A booklet titled "The First Book of Phonograph Records," compiled by Edison employee A. Theo E. Wangemann and duplicated in Allen Koenigsberg's *Edison Cylinder Records, 1889-1912*, shows Grinsted recording twelve titles on October 22, 1891. Titles include "Lumber Yard Jig" and "The Long Island Jig." He had at least one session in 1892 and another in 1893, and that may have ended the first part of his recording career. Perhaps none of these early brown wax cylinders featuring the work of banjoist Grinsted have survived. Around 1900 the banjoist accompanied Arthur Collins on a few

Edison cylinders, and in this capacity he was given the name George S. Williams. Perhaps the last recording on which he provides banjo accompaniment for Collins is Edison Standard 7779, issued in 1901: "I've Got a White Man Workin' for Me." A molded black wax cylinder from around 1902 features Collins with George S. Williams, the latter accompanying Collins on banjo and also singing "Negro Recollections" (7665). This is either a case of Edison reissuing on black wax a performance that had originally appeared on brown wax or evidence that Grinsted was playing banjo as late as 1902 as "George S. Williams," cutting new takes of old selections.

Playing banjo for a handful of recording sessions brought him extra income. He worked full-time as a clerk in Orange's Second National Bank from around 1890, when it opened, to 1902, finally resigning to devote himself to a musical career.

He began singing on records by 1898 and for this phase of his recording career he adopted the name Frank C. Stanley. The August 1898 issue of *The Phonoscope* states that Stanley's "second effort" at recording for the Norcross Phonograph Company (this was run by Ike W. Norcross Jr.) resulted in forty-five good master records. The journal says that Stanley had "made a good start" in the record-making business and adds that his only vocal teacher was Frederick G. Handel.

Nearly all recording artists before this time used their real names since before 1898 or so artists who recorded regularly were not prominent as concert artists and had no reasons for disassociating themselves from recorded work. But by the end of the century some trained musicians new to the industry adopted pseudonyms—many wished to sing in prominent churches, for example, and records at this time did not enhance any singer's reputation. Others who used pseudonyms by the end of the century include baritone Alberto De Bassini (known as "Albert Del Campo"), tenor John S. Macdonald (known on records as "Harry Macdonough"), and baritone Emilio De Gogorza (known as "E. Francisco").

The name W. Stanley Grinsted was used by the singer for concerts, including one at the Waldorf-Astoria on December 6, 1910, a week before his death. As explained in the program for a concert called The Frank C. Stanley Testimonial Concert, given on March 8, 1911:

> When Mr. Grinsted began his career as a professional record maker, he was engaged in concert work and was active as a singer in church choirs. In those days it detracted from a singer's standing to be known as a singer for Phonograph records, and Mr. Grinsted was compelled to assume the nom de plume of Frank C. Stanley.

The singer's widow later informed Jim Walsh that the first name was adopted because Frank Banta, Edison's house pianist, urged the singer to combine the names of Frank Banta and W. Stanley Grinsted. The middle initial ("C.") must have been added simply because several prominent record artists of this period included middle initials in their professional names, including Dan W. Quinn, Will F. Denny, George J. Gaskin, Vess L. Ossman, and William F. Hooley.

In 1898 he sang as soloist on a dozen Edison cylinders, all patriotic numbers (5000 to 5011). Selections on later two-minute wax cylinders include musical comedy hits such as Victor Herbert's "I Want What I Want When I Want It" (9307), hymns such as "Abide with Me" (5019), and sentimental parlor tunes such as "She Was a Good Old Soul" (8821). Announcing the release of "The Stars, the Stripes, and You" (9363), the August 1906 issue of *Edison Phonograph Monthly* states, "Some of Mr. Stanley's most popular Records have been of patriotic songs, his fine baritone voice being peculiarly fitted to the music of these compositions."

Many who made Edison cylinders in the 1890s also made Berliner discs, but this was not true for Stanley, who recorded sporadically in the 1890s. Working for Edison was obviously convenient since the company had a recording studio in his hometown. His banking job must have limited his opportunities to record for other companies. After Stanley quit his bank job in 1902 he recorded steadily for nearly every company until his death.

The singer was on rare occasions issued under the pseudonym "George S. Williams," such as on cylinders issued in 1899 by the firm Harms, Kaiser, and Hagen. Several years later the name "Fred Lambert" was used on Zon-o-phone discs when selections were of a light-hearted or comic nature, with single-sided examples including "Since Father Went to Work" (420), "That's Gratitude" (921), and "She Couldn't Keep Away from the Ten Cent Store" (1027). As "Fred Lambert," he also recorded two Irving Berlin songs issued in September 1909 on double-sided Zon-o-phone 5526: "My Wife's Gone to the Country (Hurrah! Hurrah!)" and "No One Could Do It Like My Father." On at least one American Record disc ("Fear Not Ye, O Israel," 030822) he is identified as D. H. Poppin. American also used the name "Howard Blackburn" for the singer.

He went on to manage the Peerless Quartet. This succeeded two other groups that Stanley had organized in the early 1900s, the Invincible Quartet, which made Edison cylinders by 1904, and the Columbia Quartet.

The Peerless Quartet under Stanley's leadership consisted at first of bass Stanley, baritone Steve Porter, second tenor Henry Burr, and first tenor Albert Campbell. Stanley generally sang the lead. When Porter left for the American Quartet around 1909, Arthur Collins replaced Porter. Jim Walsh believes the quartet first recorded in 1906 under the name Universal Male Quartet, though it was also known as the Columbia Male Quartette around this time. As the Peerless, its first Victor record was "Women!" from *The Merry Widow* (5392), issued in April 1908. Its first Edison recording was a two-minute cylinder, the comic "A Meeting of the Hen Roost Club" (10106), issued in April 1909.

Stanley's speaking voice was resonant, and he recited for Edison two-minute Standard 7982 (available briefly around November 1901) excerpts of President William McKinley's speech at the Pan-American Exposition in Buffalo, New York. McKinley had delivered the speech on September 5, 1901, a day before his assassination. Other companies issued similar recitations—William F. Hooley, Len Spencer, and Harry Spencer made records of the speech—but companies did not always identify speakers, so some listeners in the early part of the century undoubtedly believed they were listening to the voice of the president himself.

In late 1910 the Columbia Phonograph Company issued a ten-inch "Special Demonstration Double-Disc" designed to promote Columbia double-sided discs as having superior tone quality. (The company began selling some doubled-sided "Climax" discs in 1904, stopped issuing these around 1907 because of a legal dispute, and then sold double-sided Columbia discs in the fall of 1908, beginning its "A" series.) One side of the 1910 promotional record featured the Columbia Male Quartette—what other companies called the Peerless Quartet—singing "Kentucky Babe," with Stanley taking the lead.

Stanley speaks at length on the other side, extolling the quality of Columbia discs:

> The purpose of this record is to demonstrate the Columbia double-disc record. It is not offered for sale. Columbia double-disc records! Music on both sides! A different selection on each side! Two records at a few cents above the price of one! They may be played on any disc machine—the Columbia Graphophone or the Victor talking machine.

Stanley then introduces instruments from the studio orchestra. Cut in late 1910, this advertising talk is among Stanley's last recordings. In late 1913 Columbia replaced the first demonstration record with another, this time with solo artist Henry Burr on one side singing "Good Night, Little Girl, Good Night," the other side featuring an unidentified man giving a brief version of Stanley's talk.

He enjoyed success working with other artists. Stanley met contralto Corinne Morgan while the two were engaged for church singing and he evidently suggested they make recordings together. Their first Edison recording appears to be the duet "O That We Two Were Maying," issued in November 1902 as Standard 8256. Along with other songs, they recorded the same for Victor on October 28, 1903. The last Morgan-Stanley recording session for Victor was on March 20, 1906. The Morgan-Stanley partnership from late 1902 to early 1906 was one of the most successful in these years.

Stanley began recording with contralto Grace Nelson, whose real name was Grace Hornby, because Morgan was abroad by mid-1904 (using the names "Ethel Clarke" and "Helen Haydn," she cut eight titles for England's Gramophone and Typewriter company on August 22, 1904). He had earlier worked with Nelson for the Edison version of the Florodora Sextet. The September 1904 issue of *Edison Phonograph Monthly* announced the October release of Stanley and Nelson singing "What Colored Eyes Do You Love?" (8814), and two other duets followed, including a "coon" duet written by Cole and Johnson: "Sambo and Dinah" (Edison 9043).

In January 1905, a new duet featuring Stanley and Morgan was issued: "By the Old Oak Tree" (8876). A solo number featuring Grace Nelson was also issued in January, after which the contralto made no other Edison records. Stanley and Nelson recorded four duets for the Victor Talking Machine Company on February 20, 1906, again performing the Cole and Johnson song "Sambo and Dinah" (4653). Stanley and Nelson also recorded for the American Record Company.

The Victor Talking Machine Company at first recorded Stanley in duets and finally used him as a solo artist on October 3, 1904, when he cut versions of "Birthday of a King" (ten-inch 4079; twelve-inch 31315). One week later, on October 10, he was paired with Byron G. Harlan for Civil War duets and rube sketches. "Marching Through Georgia" and "The Battle Cry of Freedom" proved so popular that Stanley and Harlan were called into the Victor studio again in 1907 and 1909 to cut new takes of these numbers. Harlan and Stanley—both residents of Orange, New Jersey—worked regularly together in the early years of the century, recording rube skits and Civil War standards for various companies. Presumably that partnership ended because Harlan was even more popular when paired with Arthur Collins. Stanley recorded duets with Harry Macdonough in several Victor sessions.

On November 17, 1905, Stanley as a solo artist recorded four numbers for Victor, perhaps the most popular being "Battle Hymn of the Republic" (4784). Nearly two weeks later, on November 29, he recorded "Down Deep Within the Cellar" (single-sided 4572; reissued on double-sided

16063), which was popular. Among his most popular Victor records was "Rocked in the Cradle of the Deep."

Meanwhile, Stanley worked regularly for Edison, though the March 1904 issue of *Edison Phonograph Monthly* explains why no Stanley titles had been issued during the previous month: "No. 8670, 'General Hardtack—On Guard,' is the first solo Record that Frank C. Stanley has made for us in two months, he having just recovered from a severe attack of pneumonia." Announcing the October release of Standard 8821, the September 1904 issue of the Edison trade journal states, "'She Was a Good Old Soul' . . . is made by Frank C. Stanley, and is the first one of this kind that we have listed. Mr. Stanley has not heretofore made sentimental Records, but after hearing this one all will admit that he can make them as well as anything else that he does." Part of this statement is inaccurate since Stanley had recorded sentimental numbers before this, at least for other companies. For example, Harlan and Stanley sang Paul Dresser's "On the Banks of the Wabash, Far Away" on Columbia brown wax cylinder 8410.

Beginning on June 12, 1906, Stanley and Elise Stevenson worked together during Victor sessions. Their first duet was "Cross Your Heart" (4776), from *The Umpire*. They recorded many duets for nearly all companies until his death. His main tenor partner after Harlan was Henry Burr. Victor issued its last record featuring Stanley in March 1911, a duet with Burr titled "Norine Maureen" (16712).

Songs recorded a few months before his death include "Hurrah for Our Baseball Team!" and "Mary, You're a Big Girl Now," issued on Zon-o-phone disc 5644 under the pseudonym Fred Lambert. Stanley's last Edison solo record was Ernest R. Ball's "Boy O'Mine" (521), issued in October 1910. The August 1910 issue of *Edison Phonograph Monthly* calls it "a sentimental song, leaning towards the pathetic." Stanley took part in a few ensemble pieces also issued around this time.

Stanley's life was cut tragically short by pleurisy and pneumonia. He died in his home at 199 High Street in Orange on December 12, 1910. His last professional engagement was on December 6 at the Waldorf-Astoria in New York City. Performing with Elizabeth Spencer, Harry McClaskey (this was Henry Burr using his real name), and others, he was the featured basso in a concert called "An Evening of Song with the Well-Known Composers Caro Roma and Ernest R. Ball." The January 1911 issue of *Edison Phonograph Monthly* states that Stanley caught a cold at the recital. His funeral was on December 15 at Orange's First Presbyterian Church. He was buried in Rosedale Cemetery.

In Orange on June 11, 1894, he had married a teacher named Elizabeth A. Griffing. Born in Wickford, Rhode Island, she had moved to Orange when a girl. They had two sons (William Stanley Jr. and Alan Douglas) and two daughters (Elizabeth and Elaine).

For the benefit of Stanley's family, a Frank C. Stanley Testimonial Concert was given in minstrel show form on March 8, 1911, at the New Amsterdam Opera House in New York City. It was organized by songwriter Ernest R. Ball and executives from various companies for which Stanley recorded. They were Walter H. Miller (Edison), Victor H. Emerson (Columbia), John S. Macdonald (this was the real name of singer Harry Macdonough—on this occasion he represented Victor's Calvin G. Child), and John Kaiser (U.S. Phonograph Company). Steve Porter served as interlocutor, and musical directors were Charles A. Prince, Ernest R. Ball, Walter B. Rogers, Albert Benzler, and Eugene Jaudas. Singers included Harvey Hindermyer, Edward Meeker, William H. Thompson, Elizabeth Spencer, Frank Coombs, William F. Hooley, Ada Jones, Henry Burr, Albert Campbell, Collins and Harlan, Walter Van Brunt, Will Oakland, Billy Murray, and others.

Stanley found time to serve in 1906 as a public school commissioner of West Orange and in 1910 served Orange as an elected alderman. An obituary in the Orange newspaper refers to him as "a loyal Democrat" and an obituary in the *Newark Evening News* identifies him as "an active Free Mason." An obituary in the *Newark Star* published on December 13, 1910, begins with this statement: "Orange was shocked today to learn of the death of Councilman W. Stanley Grinsted, member of the Orange Common Council from the Fifth ward, one of the best-known men in musical circles in the State and a popular resident of that city." It states that at the time of his death "he held the position of choirmaster of the Central Presbyterian Church, Fifty-seventh street, New York." An article from *The Music Trade Review* states, "In connection with Mr. Stanley's death, the Mayor of Orange ordered all public buildings of the city draped in mourning for thirty days."

He wrote some rube sketches and was also given credit for the music and lyrics of "In the Golden Afterwhile," recorded by friends for various companies. On Columbia A1111, it is sung by the Columbia Quartette, and the same group, using the Peerless Quartet name, cut it for Victor 16991, issued in December 1911. (John H. Meyer took Stanley's place in the ensemble—the Peerless also cut it for Edison, Blue Amberol 2021 being issued in October 1913.) Victor catalogs for a few years stated, "NOTE— The author's royalties on this ballad by the late Frank C. Stanley . . . are being paid to his widow and children." One of his four children was only five years of age when the singer died.

Announcing the release of "Somewhere" on Amberol 643, featuring Henry Burr (called Irving Gillette) with the assistance of the Peerless Quartet, the February 1911 issue of *Edison Phonograph Monthly* states, "A melancholy feature of the Record is the fact that in it the late Frank C. Stanley sang the bass part, this being the last work he did at our Recording Laboratory." It was later issued again as Blue Amberol 1772.

Stewart, Cal (1856-December 7, 1919)

Cal Stewart was famous for comic monologues in which he spoke as Uncle Josh Weathersby, resident of an imaginary New England village called Pumpkin Center, sometimes spelled Punkin Center (the letterhead on Stewart's personal correspondence read "Cal Stewart and his Punkin Center Folks"), others times Pun'kin. This was also home to the fictitious characters Jim Lawson (a ne'er-do-well with a peg leg and red whiskers), Ezra Hoskins (owner of the Pumpkin Center Grocery and General Store), Deacon Witherspoon, Lige Willet, Hiram Wood, Hank Weaver, Si Pettingill, and a "widderwoman" called Aunt Nancy Smith who married Josh in the popular "Wedding of Uncle Josh and Aunt Nancy Smith" (Victor 5071; Columbia A1717).

Uncle Josh's most distinctive mannerism is a laugh given after he speaks a few lines. Most monologues open with, "Well, sir . . ." and hereafter many sentences begin, "Well, . . ." or "Wall, . . ." In the late 1890s Stewart's recordings were characterized as "Yankee dialect stories" and "laughing stories." Later, some Victor labels used the terms "Yankee Talk" and "Rural Comedy."

Jim Walsh writes in a preface to Ronald Dethlefson's *Edison Blue Amberol Recordings 1915-1929* that Calvin Edward Stewart "was born in 1856 on a worn-out farm near Charlotte Court House, Virginia" and notes the irony of this Virginia native impersonating a New England character so successfully during a long career.

His death certificate reports that his parents were William and Helen (Douglas) Stewart, both from Scotland. According to Cal Stewart himself in a small book published in 1903 by the Charles C. Thompson Company of Chicago and titled *Punkin Centre Stories*, his early life was spent working on trains and in circuses, medicine shows, and vaudeville. Columbia's December 1919 supplement states that he had been "a stage-coach driver, a locomotive engineer and an actor."

In its April 5, 1904, edition, *The Portland Daily* published comments made by Stewart following a performance in Portland, Maine. He claimed that at age seven he performed in Baltimore as a black child in a play titled *The Hidden Hand.* He stated to his newspaper interviewer:

I left Virginia in 1872 and in 1875 began my . . . professional career with B.F. McCauley who was playing Uncle Daniel in The Messenger from Jarvis Section. I was the village boy but understudied Mr. McCauley for several years. I have since devoted my time to old age characters and liked them the best.

Later Stewart worked as an understudy for Denman Thompson (1833-1910), who played Uncle Josh Whitcomb in an extremely popular play titled *The Old Homestead,* which opened in Boston in 1886. The Boston Theatre program for April 5, 1886, announces that *The Old Homestead,* written by Thompson and George W. Ryer, was a sequel to the play *Joshua Whitcomb.* That play, which opened in 1876, was supposedly based on a real person, Joshua Holbrook, of Swansea, New Hampshire. Though he wrote other plays, Thompson never duplicated the success of this one, and he was in productions of *The Old Homestead* for decades. The play—with characters named Cy and Reuben, among others—inspired a vogue toward the end of the nineteenth century for plays that celebrated rural America, and Uncle Josh Whitcomb was clearly the model for Stewart's Uncle Josh Weathersby.

Stewart had reached forty by the time he began recording, probably in 1897. His earliest Berliner appears to be "A Talk by Happy Cal Stewart, the Yankee Comedian" (690), recorded in New York City on July 9, 1897. He made twenty Berliners in the next few years. He made brown wax Edison cylinders in 1897, with "Uncle Josh's Arrival in New York" (3875) having the lowest catalog number. He also made brown wax Columbia cylinders around this time, such as "Uncle Josh at Coney Island" (14003) and "Uncle Josh at a Baseball Game" (14005). They were recorded too late in the year to be included in Columbia's June 1897 catalog, but ten selections are included in the company's 1898 catalog, listed under a section titled "Uncle Josh Weathersby Series—Laughing Stories by Cal Stewart."

The January 1899 issue of *The Phonoscope* includes this paragraph about how Stewart promoted his Uncle Josh character:

"Uncle Josh Weathersby" (Cal Stewart) is certainly to be congratulated for the manner in which he is introducing himself to the public. He has spared no expense in getting up his printed matter. His latest venture is a card 11 × 14 inches upon which is an elegant half-tone of himself in Yankee costume, as he appears before an audience, together with a half-tone bust picture, which is a very true likeness. This work is from the press of Imandt Bros. Mr. Cal Stewart will be pleased to furnish these cards upon request. It may be said of his stories that they are strictly refined and full of the quaint humor peculiar to the New England character and are especially adapted to the family circle.

In early recordings the role of Uncle Josh's wife, Nancy, was played by Stewart's own wife. Labels give credit to "Mr. and Mrs. Cal Stewart." Later, Ada Jones performed as Aunt Nancy. Especially popular was "Uncle Josh and Aunt Nancy Putting Up the Kitchen Stove," recorded by Stewart and Ada Jones for several companies. When posthumously reissued on Radiex 4082 and Grey Gull 4082 it was oddly renamed "Uncle Josh and Aunt Mandy Put Up the Kitchen Stove." Since the original performance was taken from an earlier Emerson master, the actual performance on Radiex and Grey Gull speaks of Nancy, not Mandy. On Radiex and Grey Gull, Stewart is identified as "Duncan Jones," perhaps the only pseudonym used for Stewart aside from "Uncle Josh."

With Byron G. Harlan assuming the role of Jim Lawson, he recorded "The Village Gossips" (Victor 17854), identified on the label as a "rural specialty." It ends with Stewart singing about a trip to "New York Town" and then some laughter. Stewart recorded "Village Gossips" with Steve Porter for Edison Blue Amberol 1594 and Diamond Disc 50249.

Nearly all Stewart recordings feature the character Uncle Josh, but there are exceptions. In the late 1890s he recorded "Uncle Sam to George" for Edison brown wax cylinder 7252, which Allen Koenigsberg's *Edison Cylinder Records, 1889-1912* indicates was deleted from the Edison catalog on September 30, 1899. For Edison on a large size ("Concert") cylinder he recorded the comic song "Three Little Owls and the Naughty Little Mice" (481). He also sings it on seven-inch and ten-inch Victor discs.

The April 1909 issue of *Edison Phonograph Monthly* indicates that "A Possum Supper at the Darktown Church," issued on wax Amberol 142 in June, is not an Uncle Josh skit: "This descriptive coon sketch, written by Cal Stewart, demonstrates that his ability is not confined to writing Yankee drollery and reproducing it on Records . . . The story on this Record is very realistic of darkey life in the South." It is performed by the Cal Stewart Company.

He recorded songs that include hearty laughing, and some of these make no direct reference to the Uncle Josh character. On March 30, 1899, he cut "Laughing Song" for Berliner 046. The song "Ticklish Reuben," written by Stewart himself, was popular on Victor 1637. Other "laughing songs" recorded by Stewart include "And Then I Laughed" (Victor 5101) and "I Laughed at the Wrong Time" (Columbia A2923).

The popular "I'm Old But I'm Awfully Tough," issued by several companies, is both an Uncle Josh number and a laughing song:

"The belles they do say
Uncle Josh-u-waaay [Joshua]
You're old but you're awfully tough."

The character's age is given as "near 73."

Recordings made between 1897 and 1903 include "Uncle Josh on the Spanish Question" (Berliner 6005, 1898), "Uncle Josh's Arrival in New York" (Columbia 14000, 1898), "Uncle Josh at a Base Ball Game" (Columbia 14005, 1898), "Jim Lawson's Horse Trade with Deacon Witherspoon" (Edison 7847, 1901), "Uncle Josh's Huskin' Bee Dance" (Edison 7861, 1901), and "Uncle Josh on an Automobile" (Columbia 1518, 1903).

Stewart's "Fire Department," issued in February 1902 as Edison Standard 8003, was perhaps the first commercially available gold-molded black wax Edison cylinder (no new titles were issued on Edison brown wax cylinders after January 1902—the first black wax molded cylinders did not have the white titles on the rim, which were added in 1904). For a long time it was the only gold-molded cylinder by Stewart, who would not record again for Edison for a few years. In this monologue Uncle Josh recalls mistaking a fire-alarm box for a mailbox during a visit to New York City. He recorded it as "Uncle Josh and the Fire Department" for Victor 16931.

He made Victor recordings as late as October 20, 1903, and then became exclusive to Columbia for a few years. Companies were eager to have Stewart as an exclusive artist since this left rival companies with mere imitators. Len Spencer (helped by George F. Schweinfest on fiddle) recorded "Uncle Josh's Huskin' Bee" for Columbia disc 19, an early example of another artist cutting an Uncle Josh monologue, because Spencer was unavailable. His exclusive status with Columbia ended by December 13, 1906, since he was in a Victor studio on that day cutting several titles. He recorded often for Victor for the next few years.

In 1905 Edison executives were eager to have popular Uncle Josh material re-recorded, presumably because masters had worn out. Since Stewart was exclusive to Columbia, Andrew Keefe was hired to record Uncle Josh material, beginning with the song "I'm Old But I'm Awfully Tough" (9152), which Stewart had recorded for companies as early as 1898. Keefe's debut record was issued in December 1905, followed by Keefe's versions of "Uncle Josh in a Chinese Laundry" (9466) and "Uncle Josh in a Department Store" (9221).

Keefe's recording career was over before Stewart returned to Edison's National Phonograph Company in 1908. That return, announced in the September 1908 issue of *Edison Phonograph Monthly*, coincided with the introduction of a new Edison product, the four-minute wax Amberol cylinder. "Uncle Josh and the Sailor" (11) and "A Busy Week at Pumpkin Center" (43) were issued on October 1 in the first batch of Amberol releases. They were followed by the December release of "The Country Fair at Pumpkin Center" on Amberol 59, and the trade publication announces that this monologue consists of 650 words. In December, performances were also issued in the old two-minute format: "Uncle Josh's Arrival in New York City" (Standard 10016) and "Last Day of School at Pumpkin Center" (Standard 10021).

Within a few years Stewart was exclusive to the Edison company. Announcing the release of "I Laughed at the Wrong Time" on wax Amberol 830, the September 1911 issue of *Edison Phonograph Monthly* states, "From now on, Cal Stewart ('Uncle Josh Weathersby') will make Records for the Edison Company exclusively. His friends, who are legion, will be glad to learn that he is to be with us regularly." He was exclusive to Edison for five years.

A census in 1910 recorded that Stewart resided on West 95th Street in New York City. In 1916 Stewart and his young violin-playing wife, Rossini, made a home on Daniels Street in her hometown of Tipton, Indiana. Performing on vaudeville stages, the couple entertained audiences. Rossini Waugh Stewart died in New York City on November 25, 1943. The couple had no children.

Because Stewart cut some of the same monologues for various companies, studying different takes for variations in delivery is easy—however, the variations made by Stewart are rarely significant. One noteworthy exception was a change made to "Uncle Josh in Society." A take cut on November 9, 1908, was on double-sided Victor 16145. He cut a new take of the monologue for Victor on July 31, 1919, which was issued on discs bearing the old catalog number. In the 1919 version he states, "One lady asked me if I danced the jazz, and I told her, no, I danced with my feet." Some listeners have concluded that this use of "jazz" on Victor 16145—a record number first used in 1909—is the earliest known use of the word. They fail to take into account that Victor sometimes reused old record numbers when issuing new takes.

Stewart's last recording session may have been for Columbia on September 9, 1919, or for Emerson around that time. The October 1919 issue of *Talking Machine World* announced that Stewart had joined the Emerson

Phonograph Company, and he probably cut material for the company in September (no Emerson recording logs have survived).

At an earlier Victor session for "Train Time at Punkin Center," Stewart suffered what seemed to be a seizure, as Billy Murray later reported to Walsh. Prior to that attack he recorded "Uncle Josh Buys a Victrola," issued posthumously in February 1921. The monologue begins:

> Well, while I was down in New York I wanted to bring Nancy something for a wedding present. Every time I go anywhere I bring Nancy something for a peace offering—at least that's what the neighbors call it. So I got her all the good music there was in the world. Yes, I got her a Victor Victrolly. Well, sir, I wish you could have seen Nancy when I brought it home. We got it up in the living room. We would have got it up in the parlor only Nancy said all the neighbors would be coming in to hear it and she warn't goin' to have them trackin' mud all over her new ingrained carpet . . .

In early October 1919 Stewart fell ill while traveling to his home in Indiana after a tour. On October 14 he was taken to Chicago's American Hospital and on November 4 was transferred to Cook County Hospital, where he died on December 7. Walsh quotes in the April 1951 issue of *Hobbies* a letter from a records librarian at Chicago's American Hospital:

> He came to the hospital suffering from an incurable brain disease [a brain tumor], and was operated on by Dr. Max Thorek to alleviate his suffering, but this was only temporarily successful. . . . There is nothing to indicate whether or not he has any relatives or where he was born. This, I feel sure, was because he was very critically ill and for the most part delirious.

His cremated remains were buried in the Fairview Cemetery in Tipton, Indiana.

Noting his death, the January 1920 issue of *Talking Machine World* states, "As 'Uncle Josh,' Cal Stewart made records for all the leading companies, and although his death will be sorrowful news to dealers everywhere, it is a slight satisfaction to know that his rare art and kindly humor will live forever through the medium of his records." Uncle Josh material as recorded by Stewart continued to be issued into the 1920s, even on Columbia's budget Harmony, Diva, and Velvet Tone labels.

Probably the last Cal Stewart disc issued in the 78 rpm era was "Uncle Josh Buys an Automobile" on Montgomery Ward 4365, the label of which cites only the title, not the artist. Featuring a performance that had been issued two decades earlier on Victor 17854, it remained available until 1936.

One artist to make Uncle Josh recordings after Stewart's death was Billy Golden, whose "Uncle Josh's Birthday" was issued on Emerson 10291 in September 1922. During a period in which partner Arthur Collins was recovering from an injury, Byron G. Harlan was another to cut Josh monologues, including "Uncle Josh Buys an Automobile" and "Uncle Josh at the Circus," issued on Okeh 4517 in March 1922. He performed "Uncle Josh on the Radio" (writing credit is given to Cal Stewart and Fred Hager) and "Uncle Josh Patents a Rat Trap" (credit is given to Jack Baxley) on Okeh 4686, issued in December 1922. He also recorded Josh skits for the Brunswick label in the early 1920s. In July 1923, Brunswick issued Harlan performing "Uncle Josh at the Circus" and "Uncle Josh Buys an Automobile" (2431).

In 1903 Uncle Josh monologues were gathered in the book *Uncle Josh Weathersby's "Punkin Centre" Stories*, and a second collection, *Uncle Josh Stories*, was published posthumously in 1924.

Van and Schenck
(August Von Glahn: August 12, 1887-March 12, 1968; Joseph Thuma Schenck: 1891-June 28, 1930)

The duo Van and Schenck was popular in vaudeville beginning in the early 1910s, in Broadway shows, and on radio. The team made records from 1916 to 1929, enjoying their greatest success as recording artists from 1917 to 1924.

Van's real name was August Von Glahn. According to his obituary in the March 13, 1968, issue of *The New York Times*, he was born in Brooklyn's Ridgewood section. Another obituary in the *Star Journal* (March 14, 1968) states that he was raised on a farm near Hillside Avenue and 168th Street in Queens' Jamaica section, which is several miles from Ridgewood. Articles in *The Ridgewood Times* indicate both Van and Schenck had strong ties to Ridgewood. A fan club met regularly at a house at 70-12 Cypress Hills Street in Ridgewood, Gus Van often providing entertainment.

His parents were Charles and Lois (Lotz) Von Glahn, both of whom had been born in Germany. The Twelfth Census of the United States reports that August was born in 1886 but several later documents, including his marriage certificate and death certificate, state 1887. The Twelfth Census identifies him as a "printer's errand boy."

Joseph Thuma Schenck was born in the same neighborhood and the future partners attended the same school, though given the age difference it is unlikely they were close as schoolmates. His name was pronounced "Skenk" by his contemporaries. Billie Burke, wife of Flo Ziegfeld, pronounced it this way while paying tribute to the memory of the tenor on the April 3, 1932, broadcast of *Ziegfeld Follies of the Air*, a recording of which has survived. Mae West, also from Brooklyn's Ridgewood section, wrote in her autobiography *Goodness Had Nothing to Do with It* (Prentice-Hall, 1959) that Schenck was her first beau in long pants.

For years Van was a Brooklyn Rapid Transit Company employee, and his marriage certificate, dated August 12, 1909, gives "motorman" as Van's occupation. He married Margaret Baumgarten, also from Brooklyn, at St. Leonard's of Port Maurice Church. She died in 1949, and Van then married a woman known as Vi.

According to an obituary in the March 13, 1968, edition of *The New York Times*, Van "worked for the trolley company, but his singing ability led him into places where people paid to hear him . . . [H]e began singing in the back rooms of some saloons on the Brooklyn and New York waterfronts. Mr. Van related that he was having difficulty with his pianist, so he dismissed him . . ." Around 1905 Schenck was hired as Van's accompanist. The obituary states, "At first, Mr. Schenck functioned solely as a pianist because his voice was changing. But later, as it settled into a tenor, it blended well with Mr. Van's, and in 1910 they became a vocal team." Page 86 of the October 1927 issue of *Talking Machine World* reports that the two were presented with a silver loving cup by Brooklyn citizens on the "eighteenth anniversary of the first vaudeville engagement of the team," which suggests they performed in vaudeville for the first time in 1909.

In 1912 their composition "Teach Me That Beautiful Love" was published by Will Rossiter. The cover includes a photograph of the two with the caption, "Originally introduced by Van and Schenck in vaudeville." Song credit is given to "Joe Schenck and Gus Van"—that is, the names are reversed.

In 1916 they had a break when asked to substitute for a trained but temperamental chimpanzee scheduled to entertain at a dinner party hosted by Florenz Ziegfeld and Charles B. Dillingham. Van and Schenck evidently did well at the dinner party since they were soon featured in Ziegfeld shows, beginning with *The Century Girl.*

Invitations to make records evidently followed their successful appearance in *The Century Girl.* Their first recordings were made for Emerson in late 1916: "It's a Long, Long Time Since I've Been Home" (7107) and "Hawaiian Sunshine" (7198). Their first Victor recordings were made on December 29, 1916: "Yaddie Kaddie Kiddie Kaddie Koo" and "That's How You Can Tell They're Irish" (18220). Their next Victor disc was very popular: "For Me and My Gal" coupled with "Dance and Grow Thin" (18258).

The comic duo may be regarded as successors to Collins and Harlan, who were losing popularity around the time the younger and more jazz-oriented Van and Schenck began recording. Baritone Gus Van often sang the melody, and Schenck's high tenor voice harmonized—or he sang phrases that echoed Van's leading vocal (on a few records Schenck sings the melody). Their delivery on "For Me and My Gal" is similar to the style of Collins and Harlan. Another parallel is that Van and Schenck often performed songs in dialect—Italian, Yiddish, Southern, Chinese. The dialogue they exchange in "Ragtime Moses Oldtime Bomboshay" (Columbia A2630, 1918) would fit in a typical Collins and Harlan performance.

The duo left Victor for Columbia in early 1918, recorded exclusively for Columbia for over ten years, then returned to Victor in 1929. Popular Columbia recordings include "Ain't We Got Fun?" (A3412, 1921) and "Carolina in the Morning" (A3712, 1923).

Joe Schenck played accompanying piano when the team performed on stage for audiences but the duo is generally accompanied by orchestra on recordings. Van and Schenck wrote or co-wrote some numbers they recorded, including "Mulberry Rose" (Victor 18318), "I Miss the Old Folks Now" (Victor 18429), "Open Up the Golden Gates to Dixieland" (Columbia A2820), "All the Boys Love Mary" (Columbia A2942), "All She'd Say Was Umh Hum" (Columbia A3319), "That Red-Headed Gal" (Columbia A3905), "That Bran' New Gal O'Mine" (Columbia 6-D), and "Promise Me Everything, Never Get Anything Blues" (Columbia 78-D).

In 1920 they wrote the music of "Green River" to lyrics supplied by fellow Ziegfeld Follies performer Eddie Cantor, and sheet music identifies Van and Schenck (at 25 East Jackson Blvd, Chicago) as the song's publisher. In the 1920s various artists recorded Van and Schenck compositions (most were written with at least one other composer). "Who Did You Fool After All?" was recorded by the Virginians (Victor 19001) and Cal Smith's American Orchestra (Gennett 5011). "That Red Headed Gal," written in 1923 by the two with Henry Lodge, was recorded by Marion Harris on

Brunswick 2434 and Isham Jones Orchestra on Brunswick 2412. Two of their compositions were recorded in late 1923 by the team of Aileen Stanley and Billy Murray: "Big-Hearted Bennie" (Victor 19221) and "Promise Me Everything, Never Get Anything Blues" (Victor 19231).

Each singer made a handful of solo recordings. For Victor, Gus Van recorded "I Don't Think I Need a Job That Bad" and "If I Was As Strong As Samson" (Victor 18363), issued in November 1917. Joe Schenck recorded "Sally, Won't You Come Back?" (Columbia A3478), a song by Dave Stamper and Gene Buck that pays tribute to musical comedy star Marilyn Miller, who starred in *Sally*. Another "Sally" song they recorded was "I Wonder What's Become of Sally" (Columbia 148-D), issued in 1924.

They made their radio debut in 1923. In the late 1920s they made MGM Movietone shorts (opening credits bill the team as the "Pennant Winning Battery of Songland") and Vitaphone shorts, and in 1930 they starred in an MGM feature film, *They Learned About Women*, about major league baseball players who toured in vaudeville in the off-season. While in Hollywood they made their last Victor recordings to be issued: "Dougherty Is the Name" backed by "Does My Baby Love" (22352). Both songs were featured in the film.

Schenck was married twice. His first wife was named Amelia and around 1914 a daughter, Peggy, was born. The second wife was named Lillian (weeks after Schenck's death, Amelia filed a lawsuit alleging that the marriage to Lillian was not legal). He died of a heart attack in the Book Cadillac Hotel in Detroit, where Van and Schenck had an engagement at the Fischer Theatre.

The Ridgewood Times on August 15, 1930, includes an article about legal disputes that arose after Joe died, stating:

> Mrs. Amelia Schenck, first wife of the late Joe Schenck . . . is planning an action in the Surrogate's Court, Jamaica, to have Mrs. Lillian Broderick Schenck, the comedian's widow, dismissed as executrix of his estate, charging they were never married. Despite the one-time Lillian Broderick's contention that she married Schenck three times to make sure all was legal, the first Mrs. Schenck said Schenck never married Miss Broderick at all, and only a few weeks before he died sought a reconciliation with her.

Mrs. Lillian Broderick Schenck also filed a suit against Gus Van. The singer told the newspaper, "She declared I collected $25,000 insurance and owed Joe $27,000. She's right about the first part. We had a $50,000 joint policy to protect our contract and I collected my half when Joe died, naturally. I was entitled to it. As for the $27,000—I never heard about it before."

Gus Van then worked as a solo artist, appearing in vaudeville and performing on radio. In January 1931 he joined the cast of *Ballyhoo*, a musical comedy starring W. C. Fields. Also in 1931 he made a few recordings that were issued on Perfect and Banner. Four performances issued in 1933 on two Bluebird discs (5015 and 5046—related are Montgomery Ward discs 4257 and 4258) did not sell well. Starting in 1935 he made Universal motion picture shorts. He starred in "Gus Van's Garden Party," a ten-minute comic film released in September 1936 by Mentone Productions, Inc. In 1948 he was elected president of the American Guild of Variety Artists. According to his obituary in *The New York Times*, he moved to Miami Beach in 1949 and played in nightclubs and hotels there. He was struck by a car on March 5, 1968, and died in Mount Sinai Hospital in Miami Beach a week later.

Victor Light Opera Company

The group of singers who recorded for Victor, from 1909 into the 1930s, medleys from popular light operas, musical comedies, revues, and even early musical motion pictures was known collectively as the Victor Light Opera Company. Typically a chorus of voices opens a performance, a few soloists or duos are given less than a minute each to deliver the chorus of a hit song from the featured musical show, and the chorus returns to deliver the finale. Soloists are not identified on labels for Victor Light Opera Company productions, which is curious since the individual soloists were well known to record buyers. Had individuals been identified on labels, the company might have been more widely regarded as an all-star ensemble of record artists.

Singers changed almost from session to session, though in early years a handful of singers were featured regularly as soloists, especially Harry Macdonough, Reinald Werrenrath, Elizabeth Wheeler, and Lucy Isabelle Marsh. Uncredited soloists throughout the acoustic era were usually exclusive to Victor. Freelance artists such as Henry Burr and Arthur Collins were not included in light opera medleys. Some productions included singers who seem to have made no other records. For example, Victor logs show that the obscure Frances Hosea sang on some productions (she sang with several better known Victor artists on July 12, 1916, during a convention for talking machine industry executives in Atlantic City's Traymore Hotel, as reported in the July 29, 1916, issue of *Musical America*).

Titles from 1909 include "Gems from *Havana*" (31744), "Gems from *The Beauty Spot*" (31745), "Gems from *The Dollar Princess*" (31751),

"Gems from *A Broken Idol*" (31757), and "Gems from *The Golden Girl*" (31758). Other typical titles are "Gems from *The Country Girl*" (31838, 1911), "Gems from *Naughty Marietta*" (Victor 31852, 1912), and "Gems from *Leave It To Jane*" (Victor 35666, 1918).

Many discs in Victor's "Gems" series make available the only recordings of songs from shows that were once popular but are now mostly forgotten except by music historians. It is worth noting that the "Gems" series began at a time when American musical theater was becoming distinctly American, with fewer musical comedies being mere imitations of European models. Around 1910 Viennese operetta remained a powerful influence on American musical theater, and the Victor Light Opera Company did record medleys of shows by Franz Lehár, Emmerich Kálmán, Oscar Straus, and similar composers. However, composers offering musical scores with a distinctly American flavor were also emerging, Jerome Kern making his special contributions to American musical comedy within a few years. Medleys of several Kern shows are performed by the Victor Light Opera Company, beginning with *The Girl from Utah* in 1914.

Each show that was given a medley treatment by the Victor Light Opera Company was genuinely popular in its time, and not many hugely successful shows produced between 1910 and 1930 were spared the medley treatment. Notable exceptions include *Watch Your Step*, which was the first musical show with a score entirely by Irving Berlin, as well as *Robinson Crusoe, Jr.* and *Sinbad*, both of which had starred Al Jolson (Jolson himself recorded for Columbia the shows' best numbers). Many musical works featured in the "Gems" series had been first performed on stage decades earlier, with Wallace's *Maritana* being the oldest work to be given a medley treatment. It opened in 1848.

Nearly all Victor Light Opera Company performances were issued on twelve-inch discs. An exception is "Hello, People!" (ten-inch 16326), a single number from Leslie Stuart's *Havana* instead of a medley. The label calls this an "English operatic record" and gives no credit to Frank C. Stanley, who sings with a chorus of female voices (Stanley gives a stronger performance with female singers on Columbia A708, the label of which gives him credit). The B side, featuring "The Yama-Yama Man," called an "English specialty," gives credit to "Ada Jones and Victor Light Opera Company." That the label of one side gives no credit to a soloist and the other side does is curious. Issued in August 1909, Victor 16326 may be the first disc to refer to the new ensemble.

Another instance of the company assisting a featured solo artist is ten-inch purple label Victor 60031 featuring "Italian Street Song," which gives credit to "Lucy Isabelle Marsh with Victor Light Opera Company."

Ten-inch Victor 19897 from the electric era features "Song of the Vaga-bonds" (recorded on December 10, 1925) and gives credit to "Dennis King and Victor Light Opera Company."

For several years Walter B. Rogers supervised light opera recordings as well as those credited to the related Victor Opera Company, which per-formed medleys of grand opera. Many of the same singers were used for the two ensembles. Until November 1916, Victor catalogs stated, "Mr. Rogers' skill in combining the most attractive bits of these musical works is most remarkable." The wording was changed for the May 1917 catalog: "[T]he skill used in combining the most attractive bits of these musical works is most remarkable." This reflects Rogers' departure from the com-pany. From 1916 to the mid-1920s, Nat Shilkret conducted most recording sessions. Shilkret and Rosario Bourdon shared conducting duties in the Orthophonic era.

When the company was formed in 1909, its roster consisted of S. H. Dudley, Frederick Gunster, William F. Hooley, Harry Macdonough, Billy Murray, Frank C. Stanley, Elise Stevenson, and Elizabeth Wheeler. Princi-pal soloists from 1909 to 1924 include Harry Macdonough, Lucy Isabelle Marsh, Reinald Werrenrath, William F. Hooley, Elise Stevenson, Elizabeth Wheeler, William Wheeler, Billy Murray, Wilfred Glenn, Olive Kline, Marguerite Dunlap, Elsie Baker, Lambert Murphy, Charles Hart, Royal Dadmun, Charles Harrison, and Richard Crooks. From this pool of singers various ensembles were formed, such as the Lyric Quartet, Trinity Choir, Mixed Vocal Quartet, and Orpheus Quartet. As Jim Walsh writes in the February 1959 issue of *Hobbies*, "After 1912, the personnel [of the Victor Light Opera Company] was mostly a blending of the Orpheus and Lyric Quartets—Olive Kline, Elsie Baker, Lambert Murphy, Werrenrath, Mac-donough and Hooley."

When a performance called The Frank C. Stanley Testimonial Concert was given in minstrel show form on March 8, 1911, at the New Amster-dam Opera House in New York City, an ensemble billed as the Victor Light Opera Company performed the Sextette from Donizetti's *Lucia di Lammermoor*. It consisted of Lucy Isabelle Marsh, Marguerite Dunlap, Harry Macdonough, William Wheeler, Reinald Werrenrath, and William F. Hooley.

In the February 1961 issue of *Hobbies*, Walsh lists artists whose pho-tographs are in the Victor Light Opera Company section in Victor's 1913 catalog: Werrenrath, Marsh, Hooley, Dudley, Baker, Stevenson, Mac-donough, Dunlap, William and Elizabeth Wheeler, John Bieling, Steve Porter, John Barnes Wells, Harriette Keyes, Ada Jones, Murray, George M. Carré, Frederick Gunster, and Inez Barbour. (Victor's 1914 catalog does not include photographs of the light opera singers.) The inclusion of Ada Jones's photograph is misleading since she was not a regular participant. Her sole connection with the company appears to be "The Yama-Yama Man."

Singers who participated regularly were highly trained musicians. Tempos changed abruptly, and a single error by any one singer meant that an entire take was ruined. On nearly every production, singing dominates from beginning to end. A notable exception is "Gems from *Rainbow Girl*" (35677), which sold well when issued in September 1918. After a Harry Macdonough-Olive Kline duet of "I'll Think of You" and before the finale (a chorus sings the same) is a musical interlude titled "Mister Drummer Man." Characterized as a "Jazz orchestra," a handful of musicians play wildly and close to the recording horn, the volume of music noticeably louder than preceding numbers, the whistles and trombone slurs creating a sound found in no other Victor Light Opera Company production.

For short comic numbers Billy Murray was used in over a dozen productions. For example, Murray sings "Good-a-bye John" on "Gems from *The Red Mill*" (35329), and later in the electric era contributed the short "Monkey Doodle Doo" to "Gems from *Cocoanuts*" (35769). Though he possibly contributed to the opening chorus and finale on "Gems from *The Pink Lady*" (35423), Murray's most distinct contribution is stating, rather than singing, "No, I didn't!" three times during "Donny Did, Donny Didn't."

In Victor's "wing" label era, labels identify, on the spindle hole's right, most productions as "Operetta Medley with orchestra" even though the original American stage productions, such as Jerome Kern's early works, are better characterized as musical comedies. Victor supplements do use the term "musical comedy," as in this description of "Gems from *Oh Lady! Lady!*" from the June 1918 supplement: "Guy Bolton, P.G. Wodehouse and Jerome Kern can always be depended upon to produce musical comedy lyrics and melodies of fascinating daintiness. They have succeeded better even than usual in "Oh Lady! Lady!"[,] the musical comedy recently produced at the Princess Theatre, New York."

Several European operettas were the basis for Victor Light Opera Company productions, including Strauss' *Die Fledermaus* (called *The Merry Countess* when adapted for the American stage), Franz Lehár works, and Gilbert and Sullivan's most famous works.

Some productions are called "Vocal Medley with orchestra" (an example is "Gems from *Follies of 1914*") and others "Mixed Chorus with orchestra" (an example is "Gems from *Apple Blossoms*"). Victor Opera Company productions, which are medleys of grand opera instead of light opera or musical comedy, are usually identified as "Operatic Potpourri with orchestra" though "Gems from *In a Persian Garden*" is identified as a "Song Cycle with orchestra."

Victor Light Opera Company productions sold well when first introduced in 1909 and remained popular throughout World War I and into the 1920s. Victor's 1922 catalog, printed in late 1921, lists nearly sixty Victor Opera Company or Victor Light Opera Company productions available, some being several years old by this time. Victor's 1923 catalog shows only thirty-four titles, suggesting that demand for such medleys was declining. In 1920 six new productions were issued on three discs (35694, 35697, and 35697). From 1921 until the end of Victor's acoustic era in 1925, eight new productions were issued: "Gems from *Mary*" and "Gems from *Night Boat*" (35702); "Gems from *Honey Girl*" and "Gems from *Jimmie*" (35705); "Gems from *Blossom Time*" and "Gems from *Yankee Princess*" (35722); a new production of "Gems from *Sweethearts*" backed by a new production of "Gems from *Naughty Marietta*" (35736).

The advent of electric recording gave new life to the "Gems from . . ." series. Two of the best-selling Victor Light Opera Company discs were made at the beginning of the electric era: "Gems from *Rose-Marie*" backed by "Gems from *No, No Nanette*" (35756), and "Gems from *The Student Prince in Heidelberg*" backed by "Gems from *The Love Song*" (35757). Sessions were in April 1925.

Principal soloists from 1925 to 1930 include Lewis James, Franklyn Baur, Richard Crooks, Elliott Shaw, Wilfred Glenn, Lambert Murphy, Della Baker, Olive Kline, Gladys Rice, Elsie Baker, Royal Dadmun, and Billy Murray. The singers who made up the Revelers were invariably used, and in the electric era a couple of "Gems from . . ." productions are credited to the Revelers instead of to the Victor Light Opera Company.

An uncharacteristic moment in a Victor Light Opera Company production comes from Johnny Marvin in "Gems from *Honeymoon Lane*" (35811), first singing "Jersey Walk" and then performing a chorus in "scat" while playing a ukulele. Marvin was in the stage production of *Honeymoon Lane*, which opened on September 20, 1926, and the Victor recording was made a few months later, on December 16. Also unusual from the electric era is "Gems from *Rio Rita*" (35816), credited to "J. Harold Murray and Victor Light Opera Company." Murray starred as Captain Jim in Ziegfeld's successful stage production of *Rio Rita*, which opened on February 2, 1927. Not all record buyers would have known this since the label does not identify Murray as such, but it is noteworthy that one medley featured a guest artist who was a cast member of a show and who received credit on the label (the medley's other soloists are Virginia

Rea and Richard Crooks). In the early 1920s Murray, whose real name was Harry Roulon, made several recordings for Thomas A. Edison, Inc. and cut two titles for the Aeolian Company, maker of Vocalion discs. In 1930 he made a Brunswick record (4836).

Johnny Marvin (in 1926) and J. Harold Murray (in 1927) are the only original cast members from shows who participated in Victor Light Opera Company medley productions. Dennis King, a cast member of *The Vagabond King*, sings "Song of the Vagabonds" on Victor 19897 with the assistance of the Victor Light Opera Company, but this is not a medley arrangement.

When highlights from Jerome Kern's *Show Boat* were first recorded (on March 1, 1928), the production was credited to Paul Whiteman and His Concert Orchestra and issued as "Selections from *Show Boat*" (35912). Soloists included regular Victor Light Opera Company members Olive Kline and Lambert Murphy, and the choral group is the same as on Victor Light Opera Company productions, but in other ways this productions is distinctly Whiteman's, such as the solos taken first by Henry Busse and then Bix Beiderbecke after Kline sings "Why Do I Love You?" Years later Leonard Joy directed the Victor Light Opera Company in a *Show Boat* medley included in a set devoted to the music of Kern.

The elaborate productions of the Victor Light Opera Company are little appreciated today, perhaps partly because tempos are taken at a very quick pace and lyrics are nearly impossible to understand when sung by an ensemble singing into a recording horn (Victor helped matters, decades ago, by printing lyrics for productions in its monthly supplements). Nonetheless, they proved influential, inspiring other companies to organize similar groups. Columbia formed the Columbia Light Opera Company for this potpourri approach to musical works popular on the stage, usually using the phrase "Vocal Gems, from . . . ," in contrast to Victor using "Gems from . . ." On several twelve-inch Columbia discs, "vocal gems" are on one side and, on the other, Prince's Orchestra performs selections, in contrast to Victor's practice of putting different "Gems from . . ." productions on the two sides of a double-sided disc. A notable exception is Victor 35491, with "Gems from *The Lady in Red*" on one side and an Alice Green-Harry Macdonough duet on the other, "They Didn't Believe Me" from Jerome Kern's *The Girl from Utah*.

In July 1910 Edison's National Phonograph Company issued on wax Amberol 465 "Favorite Airs from *Mikado*" as performed by the Edison Comic Opera Company, consisting of Harry Anthony, Steve Porter, and three fairly obscure female singers (Edith Chapman, Edna Stearns, and Cornelia Marvin). The influence of the Victor Light Opera Company became clear a year later when *"Pinafore* Airs—No. 1" was issued on wax Amberol 795 as performed by the similarly-named Edison Light Opera Company (*"Pinafore* Airs—No. 2" was issued on Amberol 820 in November 1911, followed in successive months by "No. 3" and "No. 4"). Curiously, the Anvil Chorus from Verdi's *Il Trovatore* is performed by the Edison Light Opera Company on wax Amberol 834. Victor never used the name Victor Light Opera Company for numbers such as this from grand opera.

Medleys performed by the New York Light Opera Company were issued on Diamond Discs by the Edison company. Singers include Billy Jones, Gladys Rice, Joseph Phillips, John Young, Frank Mellor, Don Chalmers, and Helen Clark. The Edison company actually adopted the phrase "Gems From" for one of its last discs. On August 21, 1929, the Edison All-Star Ensemble recorded "Gems from *On with the Show*" for lateral cut Needle Type record 14060, issued on October 11, 1929. This was a medley of songs from not a stage production but a musical motion picture.

A similar ensemble was the Brunswick Light Opera Company. Pathé called its company The Imperial Light Opera Company. Even the small Empire Talking Machine Company, maker of Empire discs, had an Empire Light Opera Company.

The last Victor Light Opera Company disc issued in a black label series featured performances recorded on February 2, 1930: "Gems from *The Love Parade*" and "Gems from *Sunny Side Up*" (36008). Thereafter some productions led by Nathaniel Shilkret were issued on Red Seal, such as the five-disc set *Gems From Romberg Operettas*, with singers including soprano Helen Marshall, contraltos Helen Oelheim and Risé Stevens, tenor Morton Bowe, and baritone Tom Thomas. Leonard Joy led the company for *Gems from Jerome Kern's Musical Shows*. It appears that the last time the Victor Light Opera Company name was used was in 1942 on a set of ten-inch records featuring *H.M.S. Pinafore* selections.

Victor Military Band

From 1911 to 1919, Victor Military Band releases helped the Victor Talking Machine Company satisfy high demand for dance records. This Victor "house" band consisted of about a dozen musicians who also recorded as members of the Victor Band and Victor Concert Orchestra, and the band was especially popular during the years such dances as the turkey trot, the tango, and the fox trot were introduced to Americans. Many labels state "For dancing." Victor 17550, featuring "Thanks for the Lobster—Trot or One-Step," even adds, "60 bars per minute."

It also met a demand for patriotic music during World War I, recording such numbers as Sousa's 1918 march "The Volunteers" (dedicated to American shipbuilders) as well as the march "Liberty Forever!" composed by operatic tenor Enrico Caruso. These two titles were issued on Victor 18471. About "The Volunteers," the July 1918 supplement states, "Right at the start you hear the sirens blowing to call the men to work. Later comes the sound of the mallet pounding on blocks of wood, anvils, and lastly—just before the close—an extraordinary effect from the cymbals, suggesting an electric riveting machine." About "Liberty Forever!": "The instrumentation is a brilliant one, and clothes the melody in a colorful dress in which the xylophone, drums and trumpets play a conspicuous part."

The Victor Military Band recorded some ragtime and blues numbers of interest to music historians today. It appears to have been first to record W. C. Handy's classic "St. Louis Blues"—it included part of the song when it recorded, as a "medley fox trot," Handy's "Joe Turner Blues," issued in December 1916 as Victor 18174. Similar upbeat selections include Stewart's "Stomp Dance" (17508), Handy's "Memphis Blues" (17619), Chris Smith's "Ballin' the Jack" (35405), and Eubie Blake's "Bugle Call Rag" (35533).

The band recorded some selections for the educational market, with numbers such as "Old Zip Coon" (better known as "Turkey in the Straw") and "Arkansaw Traveler" marketed to elementary schools.

By 1919 Joseph C. Smith's and other society orchestras employing string instruments had become popular, and the music of so-called "military bands" (recording bands such as this one and Sousa's were in fact bands made up of professional musicians who were civilians) was no longer fashionable for dance purposes. A growing number of jazz ensembles also made military bands less fashionable. One of the band's last recordings, issued in the spring of 1919, was "Madelon" (Victor 18534), which features an uncredited vocal by French bass and operatic star Marcel Journet. The name Victor Military Band was revived in the 1940s for records conducted by Leonard Joy, including "Anchors Aweigh" and "Semper Paratus" (RCA Victor 27812).

The band was nominally under the direction of Victor's musical director Walter B. Rogers until he left the company in 1916 and was then under the nominal direction of the Polish-born Josef A. Pasternack, who replaced Rogers. But the work of recording popular tunes was usually delegated to others, and for some sessions Eddie King was director of the Victor Military Band. King, a fine drummer, had considerable experience as musical director for Zon-o-phone discs, and King began to work regularly in Victor's New York studio after Victor stopped the operation of its Zon-o-phone subsidiary in mid-1912.

Werrenrath, Reinald (August 7, 1883-September 12, 1953)

In the World War I years and into the 1920s, until the rise of Lawrence Tibbett as a concert and opera personality, Reinald Werrenrath was America's most prominent homegrown baritone. This was despite almost no operatic experience. His Victor records made his name well known to phonograph owners (he also contributed to hundreds of records that give no label credit to him), and for many years his concerts were well-attended. He enjoyed great success with parlor room ballads and songs with music set to Kipling verses—"Danny Deever," "Gunga Din," "Boots," "Fuzzy-Wuzzy," "The Gypsy Trail," "On the Road to Mandalay." Had this type of music remained popular, he might be better remembered today.

He was born in Brooklyn. His father was George Werrenrath, an operatic tenor based in Copenhagen who had traveled to Brooklyn to sing at Plymouth Church and subsequently married one of the choirmaster's daughters. Reinald attended public schools in Brooklyn, graduated from Boys High School in 1901, and graduated from New York University in 1905. (NYU granted him a Doctor of Music degree in 1932 as well as an alumni award for meritorious service in 1945.) He had begun singing in Brooklyn churches and male quartets in 1899.

He made his recording debut in 1904 with Edison's National Phonograph Company as the baritone of the Criterion Quartette, which recorded Macy's "Little Tommy Went a-Fishing" (8866), issued in January 1905. This Criterion group also made Zon-o-phone and Columbia records.

In August 1907, Edison released Werrenrath's first solo record, Ernest R. Ball's "My Dear" (9604), and for four months afterward a new Werrenrath record was issued, totaling five Standard cylinders. A duet made with new Edison artist Reed Miller (whose real name was James Reed), "Honey Boy" (9679), was issued in November along with the baritone, as a solo artist, performing Charles K. Harris's "Yesterday" on Standard 9694. The final two-minute cylinder, "Two Blue Eyes" (9716), which was issued in October 1907, was followed in February 1908 by a second (and final) duet recording with Reed Miller, "Don't Worry" (9751).

He sang at the Worcester, Massachusetts, Festival of September 1907, when he shared billing with Ernestine Schumann-Heink, George Hamlin, Emilio de Gogorza, and other opera and concert artists. The inclusion of de Gogorza on the bill was fortuitous for the younger singer since the older baritone was an artistic director for the Victor Talking Machine Company, and he arranged an audition.

Within a few years, Werrenrath became exclusive to Victor and was closely associated with the company for two decades, many of his records selling very well. His Victor debut as a solo artist was a twelve-inch, single-faced disc, "Danny Deever" (black label 31738), which would become one of his longtime concert staples. It was listed in Victor's July 1909 supplement. Early in his Victor career he also recorded Tin Pan Alley hits. On November 3, 1910, he recorded "Dreams, Just Dreams" (5809), by Irving Berlin and Ted Snyder.

Along with cultivating a recording career, he worked hard as a concert performer. By spring of 1909 he was a soloist on tour with the Chicago Symphony. In early March 1916 he was a featured soloist for the American premiere of Gustav Mahler's *Eighth Symphony,* performed by the Philadelphia Orchestra and 958 singers under Leopold Stokowski's leadership. Following the work's debut in Munich in 1910 and a 1912 production in Berlin, this was the third performance of the Mahler symphony. In 1917 he often worked at recitals in a quartet consisting of other Victor artists—Sophie Braslau, Mabel Garrison, and Lambert Murphy. He had joint recitals with Garrison as late as 1922.

For solo recitals, Werrenrath's accompanist was usually Harry Spier. They lived in the same New York City neighborhood. Page 33 of the October 1917 issue of *Talking Machine World* describes an incident that occurred when the singer was rehearsing in Spier's home on University Heights. A frustrated neighbor tried to drown out the rehearsal by playing a loud record. Werrenrath was startled because the record turned out to be his own "Flag of My Heart" on Victor 45124.

He continued to work for Edison into the wax Amberol period, with "Asthore" (Amberol 602) issued in February 1911. Two Blue Amberols feature Werrenrath, but they are reissues of wax Amberol records: "Asthore" (2055) and "Goodbye, My Love, Goodbye" (5415). Some of his Edison sessions included assuming baritone parts with the Knickerbocker Quartet, whose personnel varied according to whatever singers were scheduled for or available to the studio. Around 1910 he made U-S Everlasting cylinders, including "Invictus" (391).

He recorded with many singers, with some duets selling as well as his popular solo records. For a time he had a steady duet partner in tenor Reed Miller. For years he worked closely with tenor (and recording manager) Harry Macdonough—as a duo, they often cut hymns, but they also worked together in trios, quartets, or even larger vocal ensembles. Female partners include Elizabeth Wheeler, Lucy Isabelle Marsh, Elsie Baker, Olive Kline, Mabel Garrison, and Inez Barbour (Victor 17224, featuring the two singing "Every Little Movement" from the 1910 show *Madame Sherry*, sold well). He was paired with Christie MacDonald when this star of Victor Herbert stage productions had two recording sessions in 1911 and another two in 1913. His distinctive voice is heard on three of her five issued recordings—he shares label credit with the soprano on Victor 60060, 60102, and 70099—and he contributes to a fourth (60061) as a member of the Lyric Quartet.

He served as baritone of the Haydn Quartet (later spelled Hayden) for several years, beginning in 1909, replacing S. H. Dudley, who had been the Haydn's first manager. Werrenrath told Walsh:

> You may not know that in my earliest days with the Victor Company, Sam Rous, the baritone of the Hayden Quartet, was made editor of [the label's] catalog. [Because] his new job was a busy one, I was made the baritone, with Johnny [Bieling], Jack Macdonald [Harry Macdonough] and Bill Hooley, and sang with them for several years.

Victor never announced that the quartet personnel had been changed, and Victor catalogs into the 1920s continued to identify Dudley as the Hayden's baritone.

He was a founding member of the Victor Light Opera Company in 1909 and recorded often with that ensemble, finally dropping out around 1922, after which Royal Dadmun became the ensemble's leading baritone. Along with Lambert Murphy, Macdonough, and Hooley, he was a regular member of the Orpheus Quartet, formed in 1912, basically evolving from the Haydn. He also sang in the Trinity Choir and, taking the place of Frank C. Stanley, in the Lyric Quartet (quartet members changed but usually the others in the quartet were Macdonough, Olive Kline, and Elsie Baker).

He achieved a feat matched by no others in that he was first issued on Victor's black label records and worked his way up to the more prestigious purple label series (he was given credit on a handful of such records as a solo artist and in duets with Lambert Murphy—he was given no label credit when a member of the Victor Opera Trio, Victor Opera Quartet, and Victor Opera Sextette), moved to the blue label series that gradually replaced the purple label, then was elevated to Red Seal status. Soprano Lucy Isabelle Marsh and Scottish comic Harry Lauder also had performances issued at different times on Victor discs with black, purple, blue, and red labels, but they joined others in the catalog's Red Seal section only because the blue label series was discontinued in 1926. Werrenrath became a Red Seal artist long before this.

After he was first issued on blue label records, his real name was never again used on black label records with the exception of the 1940 reissue of "Rose in the Bud" on black label 26570. Instead, the pseudonym Edward Hamilton was used. The choice of this name may have amused some Victor employees since one Edward T. Hamilton was a company executive in charge of shipping.

In 1914 his name was on two Red Seal records, which in this period was unusual for a singer who had not made a name for himself on operatic stages. He participated in a recording of the famous Act III quartet from Verdi's *Rigoletto*, working with soprano Lucrezia Bori, mezzo-soprano Josephine Jacoby, and tenor John McCormack. It was cut on April 8, 1914, and issued on Victor 89080. A day later Werrenrath and McCormack cut "The Moon Hath Raised Her Lamp Above," issued on Victor 64440 (on this day the two male singers along with Marsh cut the trio from Verdi's *Attila* but it was unissued). In 1917 his name was again on a Red Seal disc—"Crucifix," sung with McCormack on Victor 64712, was popular. He is on some Red Seal records as a member of the Orpheus Quartet, which occasionally assisted Alma Gluck, among others (his name was not cited on such discs).

As a solo artist, he was first issued on Red Seal with the Victor Herbert song "Molly" (64830), and in Victor's 1920 catalog he was listed for the first time in a catalog's pink pages, among Red Seal artists. Announcing the disc, Victor's December 1919 supplement states, "With this number Reinald Werrenrath enters the Red Seal class and takes a well-earned seat beside the Immortals of modern music" (the records made a few years earlier with McCormack are overlooked). Werrenrath recalled being told by Victor staff that among higher-priced records his sales lagged behind only McCormack's, but this is an exaggeration since the discs of Enrico Caruso, Amelita Galli-Curci, and even Alma Gluck are more plentiful today than those of Werrenrath.

His elevation to Red Seal status did not lead to the recording of many operatic arias since this fare was generally reserved for such Red Seal baritones as Tita Ruffo and Giuseppe De Luca, with other prominent Red Seal baritones at this time including Emilio de Gogorza, Renato Zanelli, and Clarence Whitehill. As an artist on the cheaper blue label series, he was given more opportunities to sing opera. On Red Seal Victor 74610 he does sing in the original French "Vision Fugitive" from Massenet's *Hérodiade;* on Victor 87569 he sings "La Ci Darem La Mano" from Mozart's *Don Giovanni* with Mabel Garrison; on Victor 6563 from the electric era he sings in English "Evening Star" from Wagner's *Tannhäuser.*

His career arguably peaked around 1919-1920, when this new member of the Metropolitan Opera Company was elevated on Victor record labels to Red Seal status. On February 19, 1919, he made his Metropolitan Opera Company debut as Silvio in *Pagliacci* alongside Enrico Caruso and Florence Easton. On the afternoon of March 26 he appeared as Valentin in *Faust* (another baritone who made many records in this period, Thomas Chalmers, had made his Metropolitan debut as Valentin on November 17, 1917), and the April 5, 1919, edition of *Musical America* notes that the baritone earned "overwhelming applause," though this musical journal aggressively promoted American artists, and this account may be somewhat flattering to the baritone. He repeated the role of Valentin nearly a year later, on February 23, 1920, and again on March 15.

As a Met singer he had only the supporting roles of Silvio (Tonio is the major baritone role in *Pagliacci*) and Valentin (this character is important in *Faust* but appears in only two scenes). Moreover, he sang at the Met only on a few occasions. He did not cultivate an operatic career, perhaps because he lacked the temperament and dramatic flair to pursue operatic roles successfully or, more likely, he was unwilling to sacrifice work as a popular recitalist and festival soloist to pursue in earnest an operatic career. He already enjoyed prominence as a concert artist, as indicated by many notices in *Musical America* and *The Musical Leader*. No other American baritone's name was as well-known, in this country and abroad (he toured Europe several times as a concert artist).

Victor's trade journal, *The Voice of the Victor*, establishes that Werrenrath maintained a fuller schedule of concert engagements than most other Victor artists. In fact, the March 1919 issue indicates that he had one scheduled in Detroit on March 27, only a day after his March 26 performance at the Metropolitan.

Concerts and recording work earned Werrenrath far more than an operatic career would have done. According to an article by Allison Gray in the May 1922 issue of *The American Magazine*, Werrenrath earned in 1921 in royalties alone "about $40,000," which was independent of his Victor salary. Werrenrath himself was interviewed for the article, "A Ghostly Knock That Spoiled an Expensive Record," which is about the difficulties of making records. He told Gray:

> When I am making a record, I put up my left hand and curve it back of my ear, because I can hear myself better that way. And sometimes, as I put my hand down at the end of the song, feeling that at last it is perfect, the ring which I always wear on that hand strikes against the horn, making a sharp "ping"—and the record is spoiled. I've known everything to be going along beautifully, when all of a sudden some-

one would sneeze, or cough. That settles it! We simply stop, wait for a new disk, and start all over again.

In the early years of electric recording, many Victor artists again recorded songs that had been popular during the acoustic era, and Werrenrath cut electric takes of "Gypsy Love Song," "Duna," "Kashimiri Song," "Smilin' Through," and "Rose in the Bud," among others. His voice is on at least one noncommercial Columbia disc made with the early electric process. On Personal Record 146-D, processed by Columbia, he sings as a member of the Phi Upsilon Quartette.

He recorded less frequently by the mid-1920s and had relatively few sessions in the electric era. An unusual selection in the electric era was "The Prisoner's Song" (1159), which had been a surprise hit for Vernon Dalhart after being placed on the "B" side of Victor 19427. Werrenrath did not normally cover songs that pseudo-hillbilly artists and dance bands of the day also covered. Executives must have chosen it for Werrenrath in hopes that this new song delivered in a concert style would duplicate the success of the Dalhart disc (Dalhart's voice was also trained, but he delivered the song in a hillbilly manner). It did not sell well. With the exception of Victor 1280 featuring electrical remakes of "Gypsy Love Song" and "Duna," no Werrenrath discs with electrical remakes of songs popular in the acoustic era sold especially well, though several remained available until the 1940s.

In the acoustic era, few baritones who sang ballads and light music had voices that recorded so well as Werrenrath's, but in the electric era his voice had no such advantage. After two decades as a recording artist, his popularity was in decline. In 1926 Lawrence Tibbett became Victor's leading baritone, enjoying great success with recordings of arias but also nonoperatic material. Other American baritones who soon surpassed Werrenrath in popularity were John Charles Thomas and Richard Bonelli.

The Victor company had new owners in December 1926, and contracts for many longtime artists were not renewed in the following year. This must have included Werrenrath's since he had few sessions after 1926. A noteworthy disc from this period is Victor 1344 featuring "Rose in the Bud" and "The World Is Waiting for the Sunrise" (1344), issued on October 26, 1927. These two late performances were reissued around 1940 on black label 26570, one of a short-lived group of "classical" recordings offered at the price of black label records. His final disc for the company was Victor 1595 featuring "Homing" and "Last Night." Issued in 1932, it did not remain long in the catalog.

In October 1930 he took part in a private recording titled "Neysa McMein Memorial Record," made by Columbia on matrix No. W-170543-3. The three participants were Werrenrath, critic Alexander Woolcott, and Harpo Marx. The record was made as a Christmas greeting for McMein, an illustrator who was part of the Algonquin Hotel "Round Table." Werrenrath sings "Mighty Lak' a Rose" with Harpo Marx providing accompaniment on harp.

Werrenrath was among the first singers to make Vitaphone motion picture shorts, making two by October 1926. The first to be screened—during the second Vitaphone show at the Colony Theater in New York City (the feature film of that program was *The Better 'Ole*)—was Vitaphone Varieties 361: "Reinald Werrenrath, Famous Concert Baritone, Sings 'On the Road to Mandalay' [and] 'Duna.'" The second was Vitaphone Varieties 365: "Reinald Werrenrath, Concert Baritone, Sings 'The Long, Long Trail' [and] 'When You Look at [sic] the Heart of a Rose.'" No copies of the films are known to have survived.

"Werry," the nickname he used among friends, traveled widely throughout the 1920s to give concerts. As late as February 15, 1929, he gave a concert at San Francisco's Scottish Rite Auditorium, which followed a February 7 concert at the large Civic Auditorium. He sang occasionally on radio. He was in the long-running Broadway production of Jerome Kern and Oscar Hammerstein's *Music in the Air* (1932-1933, 342 performances) and served as a member of NBC's music staff during that period.

Around 1940 he became a charter member of the New York chapter of SPEBSQSA (Society for the Preservation and Encouragement of Barbershop Quartet Singing in America, formed in 1938). In the 1940s he maintained a studio at Carnegie Hall (advertisements in *Musical America* state, "Singer and Teacher of Singers"), taught at a musical institute in Washington, DC, and was director of the Albany Mendelssohn Club in Albany, New York. His last public appearance was in a joint recital with Tom Donahue at Carnegie Hall, October 1952. Toward the end of his life he suffered a stroke but recovered enough to record, in the spring of 1953, a ten-inch long-playing record titled *Reinald Werrenrath Favorites* (Gavotte LPG 104). Few other artists had a recording career extending from the two-minute cylinder era to the LP era. He died in Plattsburgh, New York, on September 12, 1953.

Whiteman, Paul (March 28, 1890-December 29, 1967)

In the last few years of the acoustic recording era, Paul Whiteman and His Orchestra was the most popular and influential dance music ensemble in the United States, and the orchestra remained incredibly popular throughout the 1920s, adapting well to the new electric recording process.

Whiteman continued leading dance orchestras for decades—in concerts, on radio, on records—but is most closely associated with the Jazz Age.

He was born in Denver, Colorado, into a musical family. His father, Wilberforce J. Whiteman, was superintendent of musical education for Denver schools. His mother sang in choirs. He had a sister, Ferne.

Paul became a violinist and violist, playing in the Denver Symphony Orchestra's string section and, by the time of San Francisco's Panama-Pacific Exposition of 1915, in various San Francisco ensembles, including the San Francisco Symphony Orchestra, the People's Philharmonic Symphony, and the Minetti String quartet. Programs for the June 27, 1915, Exposition concert under Camille Saint-Saëns' direction list "P. Whiteman" as one of eight viola players. He learned about jazz—or "jass," as it was often spelled in 1917—in San Francisco's cafes.

In 1918 he served in the U.S. Navy. Stationed twenty-five miles from San Francisco at Mare Island, he organized and trained musicians in the Naval Training Camp Symphony. Moving back to San Francisco, he organized a dance band, soon playing in the city's prestigious Fairmont Hotel. He formed another band when given the opportunity to play in Santa Barbara's Belvedere Hotel, which required moving to the southern part of the state. He soon opened in Los Angeles' Alexandria Hotel, the eight musicians under his direction being pianist Charles Caldwell, trombonist Buster Johnson, tuba player J. K. Wallace, trumpeter Henry Busse, drummer Harold McDonald, saxophonists Leslie Canfield and Charles Dornberger, and banjoist Mike Pingitore.

Only some of those men took part in Whiteman's first recording session, which was on August 9, 1920. By the time the orchestra reached the East Coast, Caldwell had left, pianist Ferde Grofé taking his place. Also gone were the two saxophonists. (Dornberger would form his own orchestra, his first record, Victor 19128, being issued on September 28, 1923—it was soon followed by Victor 19151, a Dornberger selection on one side, a Whiteman performance on the other.) Added by the time of the first session were Gus Mueller, Hale Byers, and Sammy Heiss. Soon after the August sessions, Ross Gorman, who could play all reed instruments, replaced Mueller. Whiteman mentions on page 241 in his book *Jazz* (J. H. Sears & Company, 1926—his co-author is Mary Margaret McBride) that Mueller, a New Orleans musician, was unable to read music and refused to learn, afraid that this would diminish his ability to "play jazz." Mueller had been frustrated because he was unable to play the "pretty music" that was characteristic of the orchestra and because, as he told the bandleader, "you fellers can't never play blues worth a damn!"

The first recording session of August 9, 1920, was arranged by Victor executives who had heard Paul Whiteman and His Ambassador Orchestra five weeks earlier at S. W. Straus's Ambassador Hotel in Atlantic City (the hotel had been open for only a year, since July 1, 1919). Whiteman's orchestra was "discovered" during that year's National Association of Talking Machine Jobbers' convention, which was held on June 28, 29, and 30. Whiteman writes in *Jazz*, "Even though we eventually did well at the Ambassador and began to pay Mr. Straus back, we might have gone home if the Victor Phonograph Company had not held a convention at Atlantic City. A representative of theirs, Calvin Childs, happened to lunch at the Ambassador and heard us play" (p. 65).

Sadly, the book *Jazz* is unreliable. Even in this passage Whiteman and co-author Mary Margaret McBride fail to give the correct name of the Victor Talking Machine Company and of recording director Calvin Child. Strictly speaking, the company did not hold the convention, but company representatives attended a convention held nearby at the Hotel Traymore for an association of talking machine dealers.

In three sessions in August, various takes of six titles were recorded, and these six titles would be on Whiteman's first three discs.

Victor's November 1920 supplement announced the release of a twelve-inch disc (35701) featuring, on one side, "Avalon—Just Like a Gypsy" (the label describes it as a "Fox Trot Medley" of songs) backed by "Best Ever Medley." The supplement states:

> These are the first records by Paul Whiteman and his orchestra from the Ambassador Hotel, at Atlantic City. They exhibit a new type of dance record—a new and singularly beautiful type, which must be heard to be taken at its true value. This orchestra has its own methods of scoring . . . "Best Ever" [Medley] is rather a startling record, even to anybody who knows music; for it introduces, first, a melody that seems strangely familiar and yet won't quite place itself. It is the "Dance of the Hours," from Ponchielli's opera, *La Gioconda*—and maybe it doesn't make some one-step!

The supplement's claim that the records "exhibit a new type of dance record" is not exaggerated. Whiteman's early records were different from most being issued by Victor, especially in instrumentation—a combination of saxophones, brass instruments, strings (banjo and violin), and percussion. Also, Whiteman's orchestra used nine musicians, making it larger than the typical dance orchestra of 1920. Joseph C. Smith's Orchestra at that time employed six musicians, sometimes seven. But it is worth noting that Selvin's Novelty Orchestra in late 1919 recorded the carefully arranged

"Dardanella" (Victor 18633), with nine musicians playing most of the same instruments that Whiteman used one year later for his first session. "Dardanella" was a huge hit in 1920 and arguably a harbinger of dance records to come, including Whiteman's. Though Selvin would make many more records, with performances issued on many labels, no other Selvin performance duplicated the success of "Dardanella." Whiteman, in contrast, enjoyed hit after hit as an exclusive Victor artist.

On "Avalon" a novel instrument is heard, described this way by the writer of Victor's November 1920 supplement: "One of [the orchestra's] weirdest effects is produced by an instrument that looks like a tire-pump, works like something between a slide trombone and a bosun's whistle, and sounds not unlike an ocarina magnified." Issued in November was another Whiteman performance featuring this instrument, "Whispering," on ten-inch Victor 18690. The song was composed by John Schonberger and Vincent Rose but only Schonberger's name is on the record—Richard Coburn wrote lyrics but Victor labels usually omit lyricist credit if selections are performed without vocals. The other side features "The Japanese Sandman," a Richard Whiting-Raymond Egan song (only composer Whiting is credited on the label).

The record was incredibly successful, and Whiteman was thereafter associated with the two songs. Working decades later as an artist for Decca's subsidiary label Coral, Whiteman again recorded "Whispering" (61228) and "Japanese Sandman" (61254), leading the "New" Ambassador Hotel Orchestra.

He did not introduce the songs on record. Versions of "Whispering" had been issued in October, a month before Whiteman's ten-inch Victor disc was released. Presumably others recorded it because Whiteman enjoyed great success with the new song in Atlantic City. Ensembles with versions issued in October were Harry A. Yerkes' Dance Orchestra (Aeolian 14100), the Van Eps Specialty Four (Emerson 10242), Nicholas Orlando's Orchestra (Pathé 22422), and the Vernon Trio (Brunswick 2049). A paragraph dated November 2 in the November 1920 issue of *Talking Machine World* stresses that the song was composed by a Los Angeles composer and adds:

> Phonograph companies were all urged some months ago to record this selection, but it takes some little time to persuade the East that good things sometimes originate in places removed from "Little Old New York." Thousands of "Whispering" record[s] have already been sold here. . . . The honor of "first out" goes to the Emerson Co., and its dealers are correspondingly elated.

"The Japanese Sandman" as sung by the Orpheus Trio on Pathé 22422 was issued in October, a month before Whiteman's dance band version appeared. When Whiteman's disc was issued in November, at least six other versions of "Whispering" and three of "Japanese Sandman" were also issued. The two songs were among the most popular of late 1920 and early 1921. Whiteman's were the most popular among recorded versions.

Victor's November 1920 supplement states about "Whispering," "Every instrument in the orchestra has its chance, even the whistle, which can speak as much romance as any of them." Victor promotional literature suggested that this instrument contributed greatly to Whiteman's early success. The novel instrument is heard again on twelve-inch Victor 35703 featuring "Grieving for You." Announcing that disc's release, Victor's January 1921 supplement states, "This record reintroduces the bosun's-pipe-slide-trombone-whistle instrument made famous in the first Whiteman records." Another selection to feature the instrument is "Oh Me! Oh My!" (18778). Victor's August 1921 supplement states, "The middle part introduces quaint rhythms, first in the saxes, then in the bosun's pipe whistle that first helped make the Whitemans famous." Another selection to feature the instrument is "Linger Awhile" (19211).

The two debut discs, available in November, were followed a month later with the release of Victor 18694 featuring "Anytime, Anyday, Anywhere," composed by Max Kortlander, backed by "Wang-Wang Blues," composed by Whiteman band members Mueller, Johnson, and Busse (other artists who recorded "Wang-Wang Blues," such as Van and Schenck, included lyrics provided by Leo Wood). Victor also issued in December vocal versions of the two songs Whiteman performed on his first ten-inch disc: John Steel sings "Whispering" on Victor 18695, and Olive Kline sings "The Japanese Sandman" on Victor 45201. Also noteworthy is that in December Victor issued the first records of the Benson Orchestra of Chicago. Like Whiteman's, this orchestra consisted of nine musicians (within a couple of years Whiteman's recording unit grew to twelve musicians, the Benson Orchestra to eleven). Victor would regularly issue dance records made by these two orchestras, and because instrumentation was similar, their sound was often similar. Competition by the Benson Orchestra and others pushed Whiteman toward increasingly innovative arrangements.

The first four Whiteman discs to be issued, from November 1920 through January 1921, are credited to Paul Whiteman and His Ambassador Orchestra. For the remaining years of the acoustic era discs would be credited simply to Paul Whiteman and His Orchestra. In Victor's electric era, some twelve-inch discs were credited to Paul Whiteman and his Concert Orchestra (early pressings of Victor 20514 give the name Whiteman's Orchestra but this was soon corrected, later pressings giving the name Paul Whiteman and His Orchestra). For four years the orchestra was featured almost nightly in Manhattan at 48th and Broadway at the Palais Royal, which Whiteman in his book *Jazz* calls the "largest café in New York City." It was owned by brothers named Thompson, who ran a number of similar establishments. The ensemble was called Paul Whiteman and His Palais Royal Orchestra even as late as 1924 when appearing at Aeolian Concert Hall, but the name Palais Royal was never used on discs.

In the autumn of 1921 the orchestra was featured for the first time in a vaudeville house, the prestigious Palace Theatre. To play to an audience that had no floor space for dancing was daring, but the engagement was very successful, proving that audiences were satisfied when simply listening to Whiteman's dance band. Victor discs left no doubt that Whiteman's records were for dancers. Virtually every ten-inch Whiteman record of the acoustic era has, after the song title, the simple phrase "Fox-Trot." The exceptions are "Medley Fox-Trot," "Oriental Fox-Trot," "Waltz," "Medley Waltz," "Medley One-Step," and "Blues Fox-Trot." Victor 18744, featuring "Down Around the 'Sip, 'Sip, 'Sippy Shore," is characterized as a "Medley One-Step" and may be the first Whiteman recording to feature a human voice: someone supplies square dancing calls. Whiteman records issued through most of 1921 have the redundant phrase "For dancing" at the right of the spindle hole.

Whiteman began recording at a time when the one-step was losing favor, dancers instead preferring to fox-trot. In an article titled "Why the Fox-Trot Flourishes," the October 1920 issue of *Talking Machine World* states:

> It was not so long ago that the fox-trot was an unknown quantity. Shortly after its initial appearance it divided honors about equally with the one-step, but today it seems to have monopolized the dance field, with the exception of an occasional waltz. . . . Those who attack this dance are prone to call it "jazz," thinking thereby to bring it into disrepute. There have been jazz fox-trots, but the best fox-trots can in no wise be termed "jazz."

An ambitious businessman, he formed in late 1921 the company Paul Whiteman, Inc. for the purpose of supplying dance bands throughout the New York City area. Whiteman served as president and opened an office at 158-160 West 45th Street. Page 147 of the December 1921 issue of *Talking Machine World* announced the appointment of Hugh C. Ernst as vice president and treasurer. Ernst was Whiteman's business manager.

Victor promotional literature often stressed that Whiteman's sound was new. Announcing Victor 35704, the February 1921 supplement states, "In both numbers there are many new and beautiful ideas—in rhythm, harmony and orchestral scoring." Important to the orchestra's success were imaginative arrangements. Whiteman's arranging staff during the acoustic era consisted of Ferde Grofé, Ross Gorman, and Albert Casseday. Grofé was especially important in shaping the Whiteman sound.

In the sense that his musicians followed carefully prepared arrangements, Whiteman took a symphonic approach to popular music. His men were proficient at reading music, with opportunities for improvisation given only to selected soloists (in the early 1920s solos were generally straightforward expositions of the melody). Program notes for the February 12, 1924, concert at Aeolian Hall state, "Paul Whiteman's orchestra was the first organization to especially score each selection and to play it according to the score. Since then practically every modern orchestra has its own arranger or staff of arrangers."

Walter Haenschen, a Brunswick director identified as "Carl Fenton" on discs, described in an unpublished 1973 interview with researcher Cecil Leeson how arrangements evolved in the Brunswick studio: "I spent practically every day with these boys and somebody would hit a good lick and he'd repeat it . . . many of these arrangements were never put on paper." He then identifies Whiteman as first "to really get legitimate arrangements."

The orchestra sometimes played, in dance time, melodies taken from what was regarded as "serious" music. Whiteman's first twelve-inch disc features music from Ponchielli's *La Gioconda* and, in "Avalon," a melody from Puccini's *Tosca* (in 1921 Puccini's publisher, Ricordi, actually sued Jerome H. Remick & Co., publisher of "Avalon," for copyright infringement). Two later examples are found on Victor 18777: the label for "Cho-Cho-San" states, "On melodies by G. Puccini arranged by Hugo Frey," and the label for the reverse side featuring "Song of India" states, "Adapted from Rimsky-Korsakov's Chanson Indoue [sic] by Paul Whiteman." "Oriental Fox-Trot" on Victor 18940 "introduces" a melody from Saint-Saëns' opera *Samson and Delilah*. The popular "So This Is Venice" (19252), performed by the orchestra in the *Ziegfeld Follies of 1923*, was adapted from Ambroise Thomas's "Carnival of Venice."

Whiteman was not the first popular music artist to borrow from established composers. Ragtime composer George L. Cobb had gained some notoriety after modifying Grieg's *Peer Gynt* Suite for his "Peter Gink." For his "Russian Rag," Cobb adapted a famous three-note phrase from a

Sergei Rachmaninov prelude. A decade earlier Irving Berlin borrowed from the classics for his popular "That Mesmerizing Mendelssohn Tune."

But few borrowed with as much commercial success as Whiteman. Some in the music industry expressed alarm. An editorial in the February 1923 issue of *The Musical Observer* deplored the trend of "jazzing the classics" and applauded a recent article by Richard Aldrich in *The New York Times* complaining that "jazz draws the line nowhere." Even worse, the editorial states, is "jazzing the 'spirituals' of the American negroes." It cites organizations, including the National Association of Negro Musicians, that protested in 1922-1923 the "jazzing" of "Deep River."

Though Whiteman is not cited in *The Musical Observer*'s editorial, he was the most prominent dance bandleader to conduct, for fox-trot dancing, melodies taken from the "classics" and "spirituals" (he never applied the same treatment to hymns). Readers at the time would have understood that Whiteman was chief target of the criticism, especially since "Deep River" was incorporated in the Creamer and Layton composition "Dear Old Southland," played by Whiteman on Victor 18856. Announcing its release, Victor's March 1922 supplement stated, " 'Southland' is based on American folk or negro tunes, the lamented Coleridge-Taylor's 'Deep River' prominent among them."

Whiteman was directly criticized by some, including *London Times* critic Ernest Newman. Whiteman responded to Newman's objections with counterarguments, undoubtedly aware that the exchange of opinions, covered in the October 2, 1926, issue of *The Literary Digest*, was excellent publicity.

On August 22, 1922, Whiteman recorded what would be his biggest hit of the acoustic era, "Three O'Clock in the Morning" (18940), a waltz composed a few years earlier by Julian Robledo and originally published as a piano piece. The song, with lyrics by Dorothy Terriss, who was really Theodora Morse (Terriss later shared composer credit with Whiteman and Grofé for the popular "Wonderful One"), was recorded by many others, including John McCormack on Red Seal 66109. For Victor to have a song recorded on one occasion by a dance band and during another session by a vocalist was not unusual.

Remarkably, Whiteman cut "Three O'Clock in the Morning" even though Joseph C. Smith's Orchestra had recorded it for the same company months earlier, on January 27, 1922. Issued as Victor 18866 in April 1922, Smith's version sold extremely well. That Victor issued competing dance band versions of the same song—an unusual practice—is testimony to the song's incredible popularity. Smith's Orchestra, which had been recording for Victor since 1916, had been the company's most popular dance band prior to the beginning of Whiteman's recording career, but with Whiteman's fox-trots being issued regularly in 1921, Smith's Orchestra began recording more waltzes than fox-trots, and Smith's popularity waned. Smith's Orchestra left Victor in 1922 to work for Brunswick, and this defection probably created the opportunity for Whiteman to record what was proving to be the most popular song of the year. Victor's November 1922 supplement, announcing the release of Whiteman's version of the waltz, states, "We have already made a record of it, but Whiteman's admirers have insisted that he record it too. So here it is. The various melodies are skilfully [sic] split up among new combinations of instruments." Smith's version as well as Whiteman's remained in the Victor catalog for the next few years. Using the electric recording process, Whiteman recorded it again in August 1926 (Victor 21599).

Also popular in 1922 was "Hot Lips" (18920), composed by two orchestra members, Henry Lange and Henry Busse, along with nonmember Lou Davis. Labels characterize it as a "Blues Fox-Trot."

Whiteman was among the earliest "name" bandleaders on radio, leading his orchestra as early as February 12, 1922, from the WJZ studio in a Westinghouse building in Newark, New Jersey (one year later the tower that transmitted WJZ's signals was moved to New York City—to Aeolian Hall's roof). Record executives did not yet view broadcasting as a threat, but by 1923 Victor's policy was that artists exclusive to the company could not perform for radio audiences, as Ward Seeley reported in "Will the Great Artists Continue?" in the June 1923 issue of *The Wireless Age* (Brunswick had a similar policy). Victor soon changed that policy, beginning on New Year's Day in 1925 a biweekly radio concert series featuring Victor artists. From 1925 through the 1940s, Whiteman worked regularly on radio.

On August 28, 1922, the orchestra was in New York's Globe Theatre pit for the introduction of George Gershwin's hastily written one-act opera *Blue Monday*, with singers on stage performing in blackface. It was a second-act opener for George White's *Scandals of 1922*. Though *Blue Monday* was withdrawn from White's revue after this single performance, it helped establish a working relationship between Gershwin and Whiteman, one that led to the creation and first performance of *Rhapsody in Blue*. In 1925 Whiteman revived a newly orchestrated *Blue Monday*, using the title *135th Street*, but it was not successful.

In the early 1920s the occasional dance band record issued by Victor and other companies included the brief contribution of a vocalist, and by the mid-1920s the practice of including a vocal refrain was common. At first Victor executives selected vocalists to be used for Whiteman sessions.

By using non-orchestra members for vocals, Whiteman followed the practice of the Original Dixieland Jazz Band and Joseph C. Smith. In the acoustic era Whiteman records featured Billy Murray more than any other vocalist. Other singers on Whiteman records made from 1923 to 1926 include the American Quartet, Ed Smalle, Lewis James, Gladys Rice, Franklyn Baur, Jack Fulton, Elliott Shaw, Wilfred Glenn, and the Southern Fall Colored Quartet. Whiteman had been using non-orchestra members on recordings as early as 1921, including whistler Margaret McKee as well as Hawaiian guitarist Frank Ferera. The use of whistling on early Whiteman records such as "Honolulu Eyes" and "Some Little Bird" probably owed something to the success of "Whispering," the whistling providing novelty to dance numbers.

The first vocal refrain to be included on a Whiteman recording was given by Murray on January 2, 1923, for "Mister Gallagher and Mister Shean" (Victor 19007), issued in March 1923. It is characterized as a "Fox-Trot," the label nowhere indicating that it features a vocal refrain. The orchestra's next recording to feature a vocal was "Last Night on the Back Porch" (19139), made nine months later on September 4. The American Quartet, which included Murray, was used on this occasion as well as on February 1, 1924, for "Why Did I Kiss That Girl?" (19267). Murray was again used for "Walla Walla" (19389), made on June 18, 1924, and "Doo Wacka Do" (19462), made on September 5, 1924. In 1925 Murray sang on a few more Whiteman records, including on some of Whiteman's early electric recordings.

Like Edgar Benson, Paul Sprecht, Jean Goldkette, and a few other astute businessmen in the 1920s, Whiteman controlled various dance bands. In his book *Vagabond Dreams Come True* (Grosset & Dunlap, 1930, p. 16), Rudy Vallée explains how prominent bandleaders came to control various dance bands:

> The big orchestra leaders, such as Whiteman, Lopez, Bernie, Olsen and the rest, find that their own individual bands are the means of bringing a great deal more work than can be performed under their personal leadership. It is quite obvious that, when people desire to give an affair at which they require a dance orchestra, one of the above names usually comes to their minds; and after phoning the office they find, of course, that the personal outfit of Paul Whiteman is either on tour or at some place where they play nightly. They are told, however, that the office supplies replicas of the original band called units and that these units may vary in size from three pieces to one hundred. . . . Thus springs up what is known as the Whiteman office . . .

Page 174 of the April 1923 issue of *Talking Machine World* announced, "Paul Whiteman, Inc., which controls the activities of a great many dance orchestras, has changed its name to United Orchestras, Inc. This change in no way affects the name of personnel of the famous Whiteman Orchestra, Victor artists, which will continue to be known as Paul Whiteman and His Orchestra."

For over two years, beginning in August 1920, the orchestra entered Victor studios on a monthly basis. Then, after it cut several titles in February 1923, there was a gap of seven months because the band toured England from March to August. During the summer months the orchestra recorded four titles in Hayes, Middlesex, at the HMV headquarters. The orchestra toured England again in 1926.

Paul Whiteman was first called "King of Jazz" in 1923, and the title is perhaps now infamous. Whiteman has long been used as a scapegoat by jazz historians who resent white musicians of the World War I era and 1920s for popularizing music that had originated with African-American musicians. Overlooked by critics is the strong evidence in newspapers and music trade journals that by 1923 the word "jazz" had become synonymous in music circles with "dance music." (As late as 1930, Rudy Vallée would write in his book *Vagabond Dreams Come True* [p. 163], ". . . Today 'jazz' is applied to almost any form of orchestra or band music which is not strictly classical . . .") Given the vague meaning of "jazz" throughout the 1920s, the epithet King of Jazz arguably fit this leader of the nation's most popular orchestra.

Whiteman exploited the title insofar as it helped him as a businessman and entertainer but made no extravagant claims about what he contributed to the art form. He wrote in his book *Jazz*, "It is a relief to be able to prove at last that I did not invent jazz. I took it where I found it. . . . All I did was to orchestrate jazz. If I had not done it, somebody else would have" (p. 20). In this statement Whiteman seems to acknowledge that "jazz" is not synonomous with dance music. The premise that Whiteman used jazz as a raw material is questionable. After all, in giving a song such as "Whispering" a full orchestral treatment, Whiteman only worked with a popular song of the day, not jazz. In arranging for modern dancers "Dance of the Hours" from Ponchielli's *La Gioconda*, he was not using jazz as a raw material. But some songs in the Whiteman repertoire, such as "Wang-Wang Blues" and "Hot Lips," did share qualities with the music popularized by the Original Dixieland Jazz Band and others.

The event during which Whiteman was first called "King of Jazz" is covered in the September 1923 issue of *Talking Machine World*. The "crowning" occurred on August 13, 1923, when Whiteman and his musicians returned from their first tour of England. The Buescher Band Instrument Company of Elkhart, Indiana, coordinated the event—Whiteman had just begun endorsing Buescher instruments in advertisements. The ship *S. S. Leviathan* was met, according to the trade journal, at the dock by "representatives of the music industries in New York." The article states:

> [A] reception was held on the "Leviathan" dock, in the course of which Paul Whiteman was crowned "King of Jazz." The crown for the coronation was made by the Buescher Band Instrument Co. . . . [T]he crown bore replicas of . . . various instruments, including, of course, the popular saxophone. The coronation address came over the long-distance telephone . . . sent by F. A. Buescher. The golden crown is inscribed "To Paul Whiteman in appreciation of his art and artistry and his aid to self-determination in the music of the nation."

Whiteman's homecoming was a media event, with a boatload of celebrities meeting Whiteman's ship "down at the Quarantine station about twenty miles below the city." Overhead, "a big army bombing plane" carried Charles Dornberger and His Orchestra, which provided music for the occasion. The band, led by a former Whiteman musician, had just begun to make Victor records and was enjoying success in George White's *Scandals*.

Another account of the event is on page 16 of the August 14 issue of *The New York Times*. Whiteman is called "Jazz King of America" in the opening paragraph and a later paragraph calls him "King of Syncopation" (the now-familiar phrase "King of Jazz" is not used). According to *The New York Times*, "six orchestras combined in a serenade from the deck of the steamship Tourist, which went down the bay filled with jazz fans." It reported that six musicians "in life-saving suits" performed in the water at the side of Whiteman's ship (a photograph in *Talking Machine World* shows more than six). *The New York Times* identifies two of the musicians: saxophonist Harvey Hauser and clarinetist Frank Winkler. According to *The New York Times*, "Whiteman and His Orchestra were the guests of honor at a banquet and reception given at the Waldorf-Astoria." Celebrities who welcomed Whiteman home included Victor Herbert, Irving Berlin, George M. Cohan, and John Philip Sousa.

Whiteman's book *Jazz* says nothing about when or where the bandleader was crowned King of Jazz but includes a photograph of an opera singer placing a crown on Whiteman's head, the caption stating, "Jeanne Gordon of the Metropolitan Opera, crowning the King of Jazz." Another photograph of Whiteman in cowboy attire features the caption, "The King of Jazz Dons His Chaps." The photographs and captions suggest that

Whiteman did not take seriously the title "King of Jazz." Nonetheless, the title had excellent publicity value. Announcing the release of Victor 19139, Victor's supplement of October 19, 1923, states that Whiteman "has been crowned 'King of the Jazz,'" and the October 26 supplement includes a photograph of Whiteman with a crown. Victor dealers exploited the title. The June 1924 issue of *Talking Machine World* reports that the Chubb-Steinberg Music Shop in Cincinnati created a special window display at the time Whiteman visited the city. The article states, "A regal-looking chair was placed in the center of the window and on the chair were placed a crown and a scepter to designate Whiteman as the 'king of jazz.'"

Upon its return from England, the orchestra played in *Ziegfeld Follies of 1923*, which ran at the New Amsterdam from October 20, 1923, until May 10, 1924.

On the afternoon of February 12, 1924, at Aeolian Concert Hall at 34 West 43rd Street, Paul Whiteman and his Palais Royal Orchestra ("assisted by Zez Confrey and George Gershwin") gave a concert billed as "An Experiment in Modern Music." The printed program listed two dozen selections under eleven section headings, including "True Form of Jazz," "Comedy Selections," "Contrast—Legitimate Scoring vs. Jazzing," "Recent Compositions with Modern Score," "Zez Confrey," and "Flavoring a Selection with Borrowed Themes."

The concert was recognized as an important musical event, notwithstanding mixed reviews, and is best remembered for introducing *Rhapsody in Blue* (program notes call it "A Rhapsody in Blue"), composer George Gershwin himself at the piano. That work, much appreciated at its debut, was recorded by Whiteman's orchestra and Gershwin a few months later on June 10, 1924, and issued on Victor 55225. Labels state "The Composer at the piano." The record, priced at $1.50, did not sell well, copies being rare today. The only other Whiteman disc in Victor's semiprestigious blue label series featured "Suite of Serenades" on 55226, also cut in June and also rare (this work by Victor Herbert—his last—was likewise introduced during the Aeolian Hall concert). In the electric era *Rhapsody in Blue* was cut again with Gershwin at the piano (Nat Shilkret directed Whiteman's orchestra) and issued on Victor 35822, in a popularly priced black label series. This sold well.

The February 15, 1924, issue of *Talking Machine World* cites these observations by one concert attendant:

> At Aeolian Hall on Tuesday, February 12, there was presented a program of American music that because of its uniqueness, marked a distinctly new development in the concert field. It was none other than the much-advertised concert offered by Paul Whiteman and his

Palais Royal Orchestra, which records exclusively for the Victor Talking Machine Co. It ably demonstrated the fact that it was quite competent to elevate popular songs above the ranks of so-called jazz and at the same time render capably compositions of a higher order. The demonstration, too, proved that a typical dance orchestra of the Whiteman caliber, with the addition of a string section, can give a thoroughly interesting interpretation of compositions ordinarily confined to the field of the full symphony orchestra.

(The phrase "a typical dance orchestra of the Whiteman caliber" implies other dance bands of 1924 matched Whiteman's in terms of musicianship, but it is unclear what those other bands were.)

The concert's program notes do not celebrate jazz, and it is unsurprising that this *Talking Machine World* writer stresses Whiteman's talent for elevating popular songs "above" jazz. The concert notes, after vaguely describing the evolution of jazz, state, "Attaching the name Jazz to all modern music is a gross injustice to composers of modern music and directors of modern orchestras." The song "Whispering" was played at the concert first in a straightforward manner, then "with Jazz treatment," serving as an example of a song "ruined" by the latter approach. Program notes state, "We hear a melodic, harmonious, modern theme jazzed into a hideous nightmare." Whether Gershwin himself believed he was contributing an original composition to a "jazz concert"—as opposed to a concert of modern music—is unknown. He did write over a year later in his article "Our New National Anthem" for the August 1925 issue of *Theatre Magazine*, "The blatant jazz of ten years ago, crude, vulgar and unadorned, is passing. In my *Rhapsody in Blue* I have tried to crystallize this fact by employing jazz almost incidentally, just as I employ syncopation."

Historians have called the Aeolian Concert Hall presentation a jazz concert, as did Whiteman years after the event—but it was not called that in 1924. It was promoted only as "An Experiment in Modern Music." Program notes take an ambiguous stand on jazz. A section of the program notes, written by Whiteman's business manager Hugh C. Ernest (later in the 1920s F. C. Coppicus managed the orchestra), questions whether Whiteman's music should be called jazz: "The experiment is to be purely educational. Mr. Whiteman intends to point out, with assistance of his orchestra and associates, the tremendous strides which have been made in popular music from the day of the discordant Jazz . . . to the really melodious music of today, which—for no good reason—is still called Jazz."

Evidently nobody knew ahead of time exactly what would take place on February 12. Page 6 of the January 15, 1924, issue of *Talking Machine*

World announced that a goal of the concert to be given within a month was to "increase the respect in which the so-called dance orchestra is held by music enthusiasts who are inclined to look down upon the work of this type of artists." It also stated that Whiteman would offer "a program of classical music," including Tchaikovsky's *Nutcracker Suite* (it was not performed). The word "jazz" is not used. The announcement that classical music would be played is significant, suggesting that Whiteman's intentions at one point were to establish mainly that his men had the skills of concert musicians.

Only later in the 1920s would the performance be characterized—perhaps incorrectly—as a jazz concert. For example, Alfred V. Frankenstein writes in his "Music and Radio" column in the September 1929 issue of *The Golden Book*, "Jazz was the music of places of popular entertainment until the afternoon of February 5 [sic], 1924. On that occasion Paul Whiteman gave his first concert, and jazz fell into the category of Art with a capital A. There had been jazz concerts before, but they had no tag of sophistication to them." Whiteman himself in his 1926 book *Jazz* made the concert seem more of a jazz event than it really was, undoubtedly because his book was ostensibly about jazz.

In reviewing the concert for *The New York Times* on February 13, music critic Olin Downes uses the word "jazz" only twice, once in summarizing the printed program's attitude toward "Livery Stable Blues" (Downes states that this opening number was "introduced apologetically as an example of the depraved past from which modern jazz has risen"), the other as an adjective for the hefty Whiteman ("a piece of jazz jelly").

One measure of the orchestra's popularity as a recording ensemble is the sheer numbers of releases by 1924. In March, six titles were issued on four discs; in April another six were issued on four discs (the reverse side of one disc features the Virginians—a group of Whiteman musicians); in May another four titles were issued on two discs. Around this time Victor issued twelve-inch Victor 35744, which was specially promoted as a "four-in-one" record. Paul Whiteman and His Orchestra performs "Where Is That Girl of Mine?" and "Driftwood" on one side, "Mandalay" and "Step! Henrietta" on the other. Page 29 of the June 1924 issue of *Talking Machine World* devotes an article to this "distinct innovation in dance records designed for those who protest against repetition," calling it a record with "two different dance numbers on each side." It was not a significant innovation since for years the company had been issuing twelve-inch dance records that featured medleys, the music arranged so dancers would not grow weary of a single melody. In any case, this Whiteman disc did not sell well.

By issuing sixteen Whiteman titles in the three months following the Aeolian Hall concert, the Victor Talking Machine Company took advantage of that concert's success. Meanwhile, Whiteman repeated the concert, with some modifications, in Aeolian Hall (March 7), Philadelphia's Academy of Music (April 13), Carnegie Hall (April 24), and concert halls of various cities in a whirlwind tour in the autumn. The tour led to a relatively long gap in Whiteman's recording activities, lasting from September 18 until November 17. According to the October 1924 issue of *Talking Machine World*, it was Whiteman's "first important concert tour."

Whiteman's musical training enabled him to adopt a symphonic approach for popular tunes, but his success sprang from a number of talents—a flair for publicity, an ability to get the most from his outstanding musicians, an ability to recognize talent in relatively unknown musicians (he hired some who would have remarkable careers), an instinct for hits, and a willingness to change his sound as times changed. The most impressive records were those of the late 1920s when the orchestra—far larger than that of the early 1920s—included such outstanding musicians as Bix Beiderbecke, Frank Trumbauer, Joe Venuti, Eddie Lang, and Bing Crosby. But Whiteman's influence was arguably greatest in the early 1920s when his group helped establish—more so than Victor predecessor Joseph C. Smith—an *orchestral* sound as standard for dancing, with elaborate and imaginative arrangements provided for popular tunes of the day.

Whiteman began recording only a year or two after most record companies ceased relying heavily on military bands for dance music. In time, Whiteman's innovations made the sounds of Joseph C. Smith's Orchestra and similar society dance ensembles seem quaint and simplistic. With his rising popularity in the 1920s, even the music of small groups that first recorded jazz, notably the Original Dixieland Jazz Band, was considered dated by the record buying public. Paul Whiteman and His Orchestra, during its first eight years with the nation's most prestigious record company, the Victor Talking Machine Company (Whiteman switched to Columbia in 1928, returning to RCA Victor in the early 1930s), was incredibly influential. His orchestra was unquestionably the most popular dance band of the decade.

Whiteman died in Doylestown, Pennsylvania, and his library of over 3,000 arrangements was bequeathed to Williams College in Williamstown, Massachusetts. Only one Whiteman biography has been published. Thomas A. DeLong's *Pops* (New Century, 1983) gives a satisfying account of some parts of the bandleader's career, though the book is without documentation and says little about the recordings.

Whitter, Henry (April 6, 1892-November 10, 1941)

William Henry Whitter was a pioneer in what would eventually be called "hillbilly" and much later "country" music (the June 1924 issue of *Talking Machine World* actually calls it "Hill Country Music," while Edison literature of early 1926 used the term "Mountaineer and Rural Ballads" for the genre). He sang songs that would become folk standards, and he was the first folk guitarist to make records. He was also on records a pioneering harmonica player, sometimes playing to his own guitar accompaniment, sometimes recording it as a solo instrument. Harmonicas were rarely heard on discs at this time—Columbia had issued in 1918 one record featuring the work of harmonica virtuoso Arthur Turelly, and in 1924 Ernest Thompson also played harmonica during Columbia sessions.

Whitter had sessions within a year of Arkansas-born fiddler A. C. ("Eck") Robertson, who had cut in mid-1922 for the Victor Talking Machine Company such instrumental numbers as "Arkansaw Traveler," "Sallie Gooden," and "Done Gone." (On two early selections Robertson is joined by fiddler Henry C. Gilliland.) Robertson's records sold well in Southern regions, probably better than industry executives had expected from old-time fiddling performances from a musician unknown in New York City, but Victor did not record more of this type of music until other companies enjoyed even greater success with similar material. Sales of Okeh records featuring Fiddlin' John Carson (the first singer in this genre), Whitter (the second singer), Ernest Thompson, and a few others made clear to the industry that a market existed for traditional music cut by rural musicians.

He was born in Virginia's Grayson County near the town of Fries (he worked in a cotton mill there) and lived in Cliffview during his years as a performer and later in Warrensville, North Carolina. According to Whitter himself, in March 1923 he traveled to New York to visit the recording headquarters of the General Phonograph Corporation, maker of Okeh records, but test pressings made of Whitter in that year were shelved.

Later in 1923 Fiddlin' John Carson enjoyed success with Okeh recordings (in *Talking Machine World*'s September 1923 Advance Record Bulletins, Carson's Okeh 4890 was listed under "Novelty" records, the two other categories being "Dance" and "Vocal"—the term "hillbilly" was not yet used), and Whitter was invited to return to the New York studio to record again. He made various vocal recordings for Okeh, made seven recordings of solo harmonica, and cut three titles as leader of Whitter's Virginia Breakdowners (others in this trio were fiddler James Sutphin and banjoist John Rector).

His first Okeh disc featured "The Wreck on the Southern Old 97," recorded on December 12, 1923, and issued in early 1924 on Okeh 40015, with "Lonesome Road Blues" on its reverse side. Lyrics are about a Southern Railroad mail express train that derailed on September 27, 1903, on the outskirts of Danville, Virginia, killing several people. The tune was based on Henry C. Work's "The Ship That Never Returned," published decades earlier and in the public domain by the time lyrics about the train accident were written.

Whitter took credit for the lyrics and may have been inspired by a poem written by a young Charles W. Noell, who lived in 1903 near the site where the train wrecked, or by a set of lyrics written by Fred J. Lewey. In 1930 one David Graves George argued in court, unsuccessfully, that he was responsible for the lyrics. Jim Walsh reported that Fred Hager shared royalties with Whitter. As Okeh's music director, Hager would have presided over Whitter's Okeh session of early 1923, from which nothing was issued, and possibly Hager and Whitter worked on the song during this session. Hager had left Okeh by the time Whitter returned in late 1923.

On April 26, blind musician Ernest Thompson of Winston-Salem, North Carolina, followed in Whitter's footsteps by cutting "The Wreck of the Southern Old '97" (the preposition "on" was changed to "of," and an apostrophe was added before "97"), and his version on Columbia 130-D was advertised on page 17 of the June 1924 issue of the trade journal *Talking Machine World*. Thompson's performance was issued again by Columbia in a budget series as Harmony 5120-H, the name Ernest Johnson given on the label. For Aeolian-Vocalion 14809, George Reneau also cut the song in April (the label gives this blind musician credit, but Gene Austin provides a vocal to Reneau's guitar accompaniment). Envying Whitter's success and believing he could sing it better, Vernon Dalhart recorded it for Edison in May 1924 and for Victor in July. Learning the words from the Whitter disc (the Thompson and Reneau versions were not yet out), Dalhart misunderstood some phrases, resulting in slightly different lyrics on his records. When the song was backed with "The Prisoner's Song," the combination proved irresistible: Victor 19427 was probably the best-selling disc issued up to that time.

Around August 1925, Virginia musician Kelly Harrell (1889-1942) cut the song during a session in Asheville, North Carolina, and this record—Okeh 7010, one of a dozen twelve-inch discs in Okeh's 7000 series of 1925—provided two opening stanzas missing on the Whitter disc. The label and Okeh's catalog state, "Guitar and Harmonica by Henry Whitter." Whitter himself had a record issued in this rare twelve-inch series: Okeh 7005 features Whitter's Virginia Breakdowners performing "Mississippi

Sawyer" and "Sourwood Mountain," both identified as "Square Dance" numbers.

Curiously, Whitter's "The Wreck on the Southern Old 97" on Okeh 40015 is not listed in Advance Record Bulletins published in *Talking Machine World*, though the release of Whitter's "The Old-Time Fox Chase" backed by "Lost Train Blues (Lost John)" on Okeh 40029 is in the February 1924 issue as being scheduled for March release, being listed with over two dozen other records in Okeh's new 40000 series also scheduled for March release. The 40000 series was not "hillbilly" related but was instead a general series that followed Okeh's 4000 series—early records of Whitter were issued in the same series as those of dance bands and popular singers such as Charles Harrison and Billy Jones. Whitter's Okeh 40029 was followed in May by the release of his third record, "Little Brown Jug" and "She's Coming Around the Mountain" on Okeh 40063.

Other Whitter discs were issued by Okeh in 1924. A full-page advertisement in the June 1924 issue of *Talking Machine World* includes a drawing of Fiddlin' John Carson and also one of Whitter holding a guitar, a harmonica near his mouth. It states:

> Another mountain star is Henry Whitter. Throughout his native hills he is acclaimed the most novel entertainer for he plays a harmonica and a guitar at the same time and never misses a note and in between accompanies himself when he sings those quaint, "Old Time Pieces." The craze for this "Hill Country Music" has spread to thousands of communities . . .

Whitter is called "the novelty entertainer from the sky country."

Page 35 of the May 1925 issue of *Talking Machine World* reports:

> Henry Whitter, exclusive Okeh artist, was a recent visitor to New York, where he was engaged in making several new records of "Hill" country music. Mr. Whitter is a real specimen of the Hill country, coming from Galax, Va., and on his first few trips to New York could not be induced to stay over night, coming in to the city in the morning, making what recordings were necessary and leaving before midnight arrived. Although he has overcome this shyness to some extent, he is still averse to what might be called "seeing the town." He insists that his trips from the railroad station to the hotel and thence to the recording laboratories are sights enough for him. . . . Mr. Whitter sings the old-time tunes of the Hill country, many of them of his own composition.

During a 1925 session in Atlanta he provided accompaniment for singer Roba Stanley (1910-1986), daughter of Georgia fiddler Rob Stanley. She was among the first female artists featured on country records (the first were banjoist Samantha Bumgarner and fiddler/singer/banjoist Eva Davis, a team that recorded for Columbia in April 1924) and was almost certainly the first teenager. Whitter played during Stanley's second and final Okeh session. Her fledgling career ended months later when she married at the age of fifteen.

When joined in mid-1927 by the nearly blind Appalachian fiddler Gilliam Banmon Grayson, Whitter generally served as a guitar accompanist. Gennett and Victor labels gave credit to Grayson and Whitter but G. B. Grayson was the dominant musician on the few dozen records they made from 1927 to 1929, being a better singer and more accomplished instrumentalist. In Memphis on September 30, 1929, this team was the first to record "Tom Dooley" (Victor V-40235), a song that became famous three decades later because of a best-selling record made by the Kingston Trio. Five titles were cut at this time, and it was Whitter's last session. Grayson's death within a year—on August 16, 1930, he was hurled from the running board of a car when it collided with a log truck—was a terrible blow for Whitter. Their few dozen recordings influenced subsequent generations of players, especially bluegrass musicians.

Jim Walsh wrote in the August 1929 issue of *Phonograph Monthly Review:*

> Though probably the world's worst singer, he is really good upon his chosen instruments. He is also, I hear, a peculiar combination of simplicity and shrewdness and has his own business ideas, one of which is to stand on a street corner, announcing his identity and distributing photographs of himself. I was informed by a local photographer that Whitter once introduced himself to him somewhat as follows: "Howdy do . . . I'm the celebrated Mr. Henry Whitter, of Okeh recording fame. I made 'The Wreck of the 97' what it is today. They's been millions of copies of it sold. Okeh give me a good contract and that record made me barrels o' money. I got money to burn, by G—!"

Whitter's recording career ended within weeks of Walsh writing those words, though Grayson and Whitter's record of "Going Down the Lee Highway" on Victor 23565 was issued as late as July 1931 and performances were reissued on Victor's Bluebird label. The musician died of diabetes in a mental institution in Morganton, North Carolina.

Wiedoeft, Rudy *(January 3, 1893-February 18, 1940)*

From the World War I years through much of the 1920s, Rudy Wiedoeft was very popular, his records and concerts inspiring others to learn the instrument. One Wiedoeft fan named Hubert Prior Vallée even adopted the name Rudy when devising a stage name—he would win fame as Rudy Vallée. In his book *Vagabond Dreams Come True* (Grosset & Dunlap, 1930), Vallée wrote, "I ate, drank and talked Rudy Wiedoeft so much that it earned for me the nickname of 'Rudy.' " Georgie Auld, a tenor saxophonist who became popular in the big band era, studied under Wiedoeft.

Saxophonists were recorded in the earliest days of the industry, with Bessie Meeklens making Edison cylinders in April 1892. In 1896 Eugene Coffin made Columbia cylinders. A saxophone quartet from Sousa's Band made a Berliner disc around 1897 and cut titles for the Victor Talking Machine Company on August 7, 1902 (nothing was issued), and on September 30, 1903 (again, nothing was issued). However, saxophone recordings did not enjoy great popularity until the World War I period, with the Six Brown Brothers enjoying success as Victor artists. In fact, after issuing the Bessie Meeklens cylinders, the Edison company did not make saxophone records again until 1910, when H. Benne Henton made a two-minute cylinder.

Wiedoeft was born in Detroit into a musical family. His father, Adolph, headed an orchestra, and brothers Adolph, Herbert, and Gerhardt also became proficient musicians. Rudy played clarinet in his father's orchestra before he was a teen, the Wiedoeft Family Orchestra playing mostly in cafes and hotels. He later took up saxophone. According to the 1923 Gennett catalog, he switched from clarinet to saxophone in 1914, but did not give up on clarinet altogether since he plays it on some early records. He generally performed on a C melody saxophone, which is now obsolete, though it was common at that time. At some point the Wiedoefts resettled in Los Angeles.

Wiedoeft headed eastward from Los Angeles in late 1916 in the pit orchestra of Oliver Morosco's production of *Canary Cottage*. That show opened in New York City at the new Morosco Theatre on February 5. Within a few weeks of his arrival he quit the show and was engaged at the Montmartre. For this midnight cafe on Broadway he pieced together a dance band, the Frisco "Jass" Band. In the band's name the word "jass"—new to the record buying public—was often placed in quotation marks, though by October 1917 Edison literature called it the Frisco Jazz Band. As the band's leader, Wiedoeft began his association with Thomas A. Edison, Inc. and was among the first to contribute to records marketed as jazz. Titles cut on May 10, 1917, were "Johnson 'Jass' Blues" (Wiedoeft plays clarinet) and "Canary Cottage," the latter issued in August on Blue Amberol 3241 (later on Diamond Disc 50440). The band toured the Orpheum Circuit in late 1917.

As a featured soloist accompanied by orchestra, Wiedoeft recorded for Edison his own waltz composition "Valse Erica," issued on Blue Amberol 3276 in October 1917. This was followed in February 1918 by another original waltz, "Valse Llewellyn" on Blue Amberol 3393. "Saxophone Sobs," composed by Erdmann, was issued on Blue Amberol 3421 in March.

Wiedoeft was carefully promoted by Edison's trade monthlies. The cover of the January 1918 *Edison Amberola Monthly* features a photograph of him holding his instrument, and the August 1918 issue of this trade journal includes a photograph of Wiedoeft in a U.S. Marine uniform, noting that he "voluntarily gave up a number of profitable theatrical engagements to join Uncle Sam's Sea Soldiers. He is now a sergeant stationed at Mare Island, California." Paul Whiteman, in the Navy, was also assigned to Mare Island in 1918.

From Mare Island the saxophonist was transferred to the prestigious Marine Corps Band in Washington, DC. Page 181 of the September 1919 issue of *Talking Machine World* lists Wiedoeft among new Emerson artists, and the trade journal discusses the months he was in uniform:

Rudy Wiedoeft is a native of Los Angeles and after appearing as a headline act on the Orpheum Circuit joined the Marine Corps Band. His saxophone playing with this band won for him an enviable reputation, and he then became a member of the famous Washington Band [at Mare Island], where he made such a record that he was transferred to the President's Marine Band at the Capital. During the early part of the war [that is, when America entered it] Mr. Wiedoeft organized a company of Marine Band musicians, and toured the West for the Red Cross, netting $50,000.

Upon his return to New York City after serving as a Marine, he recorded his composition "Saxophobia" for Columbia (on December 27, 1918), Edison (on February 4, 1919), and Pathé (for this company in early 1919 he led the Master Saxophone Sextet, with the spelling Saxaphone used on some labels). Pathé 22068 was issued in May 1919 but Columbia and Edison rejected takes of "Saxophobia." He dazzled audiences with "Saxophobia" at concerts and in time other companies issued versions of it. When issued on the rare Concert label in September 1920, "Saxophobia" was characterized as "A Saxophone Riot." It became, along with

"Valse Erica," his most influential composition. A version cut for Paramount 33071 was issued in December 1920.

Page 123 of the April 1920 issue of *Talking Machine World* reports that Wiedoeft was among the "famous talking machine stars" who performed on April 11 at New York City's 44th Street Theatre "under the auspices of the Emerson Phonograph Co."

Months later, he recorded "Saxophobia" for the Victor Talking Machine Company, and it was issued in April 1921 coupled with his composition "Valse Erica" on Victor 18728. The label identifies each number as "saxophone solo with orchestra." Two years later, this popular disc inspired an imitation from fellow saxophonist Clyde Doerr: Victor 19028 features Doerr performing his own compositions "Valse Hilda" and "Saxanola." Each is identified as "saxophone solo with orchestra."

Rudy Vallée states in his autobiography *My Time Is Your Time* (Obolsenky, 1962, p. 22), "There was a recording that was to change the whole course of my musical career as well as my name. It was a Victor record entitled 'Valse Erica' by a saxophonist named Rudy Wiedoeft. . . . The beauty of Wiedoeft's tone, the terrific speed of his tonguing, his clean-cut execution all hit me with a thunderclap." From his college in Maine, Vallée traveled in 1922 to New York City to meet Wiedoeft as well as to make a personal record at the Columbia recording studio. A friendship grew between the famous performer and his admirer. Vallée indicates that his idol as early as 1922 had a drinking problem, but alcoholism would not hurt Wiedoeft's career for a few more years.

Wiedoeft made his Victor debut in 1920. As member of the Wiedoeft-Wadsworth Quartet, he cut "The Crocodile" on March 1, 1920. It was issued on Victor 18663 in May. Fellow musicians were saxophonist F. Wheeler Wadsworth and pianists J. Russel Robinson and Harry Akst. Wiedoeft also played on a Joseph C. Smith's Orchestra record issued that month, "Karavan" (Victor 18662). Wiedoeft composed the song with Abe Olman, and it was recorded by several other dance bands. Around this time he also worked as a member of the Palace Trio, with Phil Baker on accordion (Mario Perry soon succeeded Baker) and J. Russel Robinson on piano.

Another Wiedoeft composition is "Llewellyn Waltz," performed by the saxophonist on Emerson 1050. He cowrote a song popular in 1921, "Na-Jo," sharing credit with one "Walter Holliday," who was really Walter Haenschen. The Benson Orchestra of Chicago cut it on April 15, 1921 (Victor 18779), and others recorded it.

In the early 1920s he made many Brunswick recordings. When Ernest Hare sang "Saxophone Blues" for Brunswick 2040, Wiedoeft provided accompaniment on his instrument. With orchestra accompaniment, he performs his own composition "Saxema" on Brunswick 2044. For the company he made many dance records, some issued under the name Rudy Wiedoeft's Californians, with orchestral arrangements credited to Walter Haenschen (Rudy Wiedoeft's Californians began making Edison records in late 1921). He also recorded as a member of the Wiedoeft-Wadsworth Quartet and the Palace Trio (with Mario Perry on accordion and J. Russel Robinson on piano).

On August 20, 1924, his composition "Sax-o-phun" was recorded by a new Victor dance band, George Olsen and His Music, and the label for Victor 19509 states, under the band's name, "Laughing Saxophone by the Composer." Here, Wiedoeft was following a trend set by other musicians. Nathan Glantz had already won fame for getting laughing effects while playing saxophone, and as early as 1919 Harry Raderman was known for his laughing trombone.

When banjoist Fred Van Eps left the touring group known as the Eight Famous Victor Artists, Wiedoeft joined as a featured instrumentalist. The change was announced on page 138 of the July 1922 issue of *Talking Machine World*. Five members of the touring group—Billy Murray, Henry Burr, Albert Campbell, John H. Meyer, and Frank Croxton—were exclusive to Victor, but Wiedoeft, pianist Frank Banta, and comic Monroe Silver were not. In fact, Wiedoeft and Banta worked closely together during sessions for various companies. Page 54 of the November 1924 issue of *Talking Machine World* lists Wiedoeft and Banta among Aeolian Company artists who performed together on radio broadcasts. With Banta accompanying, Wiedoeft recorded his own "Saxema" for Columbia 84-D in early 1924.

On February 26, 1925, the saxophonist contributed to the first electrically recorded performance to be eventually issued by Victor, "A Miniature Concert" (35753), featuring eight Victor artists who take turns performing. On this he plays at breakneck speed about a minute of "Saxophobia." Around late August 1925 the personnel of the touring group managed by Burr changed dramatically. Wiedoeft left Burr's touring group, and xylophonist Sam Herman became the group's featured instrumentalist.

Pages 184 and 196 of the October 1925 *Talking Machine World* announced that Wiedoeft had joined a new group of artists called the Peerless Entertainers, available for bookings in the New York City area. It consisted of the Peerless Male Quartet (Albert Campbell, John Meyer, Frank Croxton, Charles Harrison), pianist-composer Lieutenant Gitz Rice, baritone Arthur Fields, and Wiedoeft.

His final Victor records were made in New York on December 2, 1927. He was accompanied by pianist Jack Shilkret for four numbers, with Carson Robison and Arnold Brilhart joining on two numbers. As a solo artist he made Columbia records in the mid-1920s. "Valse Mazanetta," issued on 761-D in December 1926, includes Oscar Levant on piano (Levant had served as accompanist when Wiedoeft toured England in the spring of 1926). "Song of the Volga Boatmen" backed by "Melody" was issued in August 1927 (1053-D). Columbia's 1928 and 1929 catalog cite him as an exclusive Columbia artist, but the company did not record him often in these years.

He died in Flushing Hospital, Queens, New York, and was survived by his wife Mae.

His brother Herb Wiedoeft, a trumpet player, led the successful Cinderella Roof Orchestra, of the Cinderella Roof Dance Palace in Los Angeles. The dance band cut its first Brunswick records in August 1923 in Los Angeles. Members included brothers Ad (or Adolph) on percussion and xylophone, and Gay (or Gerhardt) on string bass. Herb Wiedoeft recorded exclusively for Brunswick until his death on May 12, 1928, caused by his car skidding off the Medford-Klamath Falls Highway near Medford, Oregon (earlier in 1928 Herb had married Esther Rineholdt, of Oregon). Band member Jesse Stafford assumed leadership of the band and it continued to record for Brunswick into the 1930s.

Williams, Bert (November 12, 1874-March 4, 1922)

Bert Williams, the first African American to become a Broadway headliner, was born Egbert Austin Williams to Frederick and Julia Monceur Williams in New Providence, Nassau, in the Bahama Islands. He and his partner George Walker made their stage debut as a duo in San Francisco in the mid-1890s and remained a popular comedy team until Walker became too ill to perform. Walker, who played the dandy to Williams' bumpkin, gave his last performance in Louisville, Kentucky, in February 1909 and died of syphilis on January 6, 1911, in Islip, New York. Williams continued to work in vaudeville, in the Ziegfeld Follies (1910-1919), and as a recording artist.

The January-February 1897 issue of *The Phonoscope* states that Williams as a solo artist had recorded "Mammy's Little Pickaninny Boy." The company is unnamed, and no copy of the brown wax cylinder is known to have survived. The duo began their recording career for the Victor Talking Machine Company on October 11, 1901. Williams, accompanied by piano, performed several numbers as a solo artist, and he was joined on other selections by Walker. Two titles from the popular show *Sons of Ham* were recorded during this first session, "The Phrenologist Coon" and "All Going Out and Nothing Coming In." "My Little Zulu Babe," also from the show, was recorded on November 8 by Williams alone (issued as ten-inch 1084) and again on November 10 by Williams with Walker (issued as seven-inch A-1086 and ten-inch Monarch 1086). Other songs recorded during the first session include "I Don't Like That Face You Wear," "Good Morning, Carrie," Cole and Johnson's "In My Castle on the River Nile," "The Ghost of a Coon," and "Where Was Moses When the Light Went Out?" All selections are announced in the discs' opening grooves.

Williams was a more subtle comic artist later in his recording career than at the beginning. "The Phrenologist Coon" is a crude "coon" song, with references to razors, chickens, and pickpocket artists ("By just feelin' in your pocket I can tell what's in your head"). Mabel Rowland's *Bert Williams: Son of Laughter*—published in 1923 in England, where Williams had a following—recounts how songwriter Ernest Hogan wrote the song after Williams had described to Hogan his dabbling in phrenology, astrology, and palmistry.

In "All Going Out and Nothing Coming In," Williams uses a surprisingly upbeat melody to rail against hard times:

Money is de root of evil,
Everywhere you go,
But nobody have any objection
To de root, now ain't dat so?
You know how it is wid money,
How it makes you feel at ease,
Things look bright all around,
And your friends am thick as bees.
But, oh! When yo' money is a-runnin' low,
An' you clinging to a solitary dime,
No one can see where you come in,
Dat am de awful time

George Walker sings "My Little Zulu Babe" with Williams making background noises and helping with the chorus. It parodies an African tribal chant.

Early Victor catalogs stated:

The most popular songs of the day are the "Rag Time" or "Coon Songs." The greatest recommendation a song of this kind can have is that it is sung by Williams & Walker, the "Two Real Coons." Their selections are always from the brightest and best songs with the most catchy and pleasing melodies. Although Williams & Walker have been engaged to make records exclusively for us at the highest price ever paid in the history of the Talking Machine business, and although their records are the finest thing ever produced, being absolutely the real thing, we add them to our regular record list with no advance in price.

In 1906 Williams made his debut with the Columbia Phonograph Company and for his remaining years made records only for that company. Of ten songs recorded in 1906, most were issued on cylinder as well as disc, and three had been featured in the Williams and Walker show *Abyssinia:* "Nobody," "Let It Alone," and "Here It Comes Again." Williams did not return to a Columbia studio until 1910, a year after Columbia stopped issuing titles on cylinder. In 1910 he cut four titles, and nearly three years passed before he again returned to a studio, but from 1913 onward he visited a studio at least once a year, sessions being much more frequent in his last three years.

Williams' signature song was his own composition, "Nobody." It was first recorded by Arthur Collins on Edison 9084, issued in September 1905. The August 1905 issue of *Edison Phonograph Monthly* states, "The song fits Mr. Collins like a glove. The story is of a coon for whom nobody does nothing, therefore he does nothing for nobody. . . . The music of this song is by Bert A. Williams and the words by Alexander Rogers."

For Columbia, Williams recorded "Nobody" in mid-1906 (single-sided disc 3423 and double-sided disc A302; cylinder 33011). Williams wrote in the January 1918 issue of *American Magazine:*

> Before I got through with "Nobody," I could have wished that both the author of the words and the assembler of the tune had been strangled or drowned or talked to death. For seven whole years I had to sing it. Month after month I tried to drop it and sing something new, but I could get nothing to replace it, and the audiences seemed to want nothing else. Every comedian at some time in his life learns to curse the particular stunt of his that was most popular.

He tried to repeat the success of "Nobody" with other songs that intoned one- or two-word catchphrases. These include "Unexpectedly," "Somebody," "Constantly," and "Not Lately," and each one avoids the snail pace of the signature tune. "Unexpectedly" tells in the second verse of a thief harshly punished not for stealing but for stealing too little. The judge objects that there isn't enough loot worthy of a bribe:

Got some work in a swell cafe
And I took me home a little fresh meat every day—
Just a small piece
And the boss got wise to me in some kinda way—unexpectedly
On next morn the judge says,
"What have you to say about that?
Your boss says he caught you
With two pork chops under your hat"
I said "not guilty, sir"
He says "Take 6 months for that"
And it came so unexpectedly, whee!
'Twas then I found out, yassir, whole lot of meaning
In that little word—unexpectedly
It seems like I never knew till then
Of things could happen so unexpectedly
He said, now, had I taken a steak and a ham or goose, then
"I mighta found some way that I could of let you loose
But for two measly pork chops—let you free?
Officer, take him and throw away the key"

In 1910 Williams for the first time was in a Ziegfeld Follies show. That show, which opened on June 20 at the Jardin de Paris, was simply titled *Follies of 1910* ("Ziegfeld" was added to the name of shows beginning in 1911). From that time through 1919 he was in each new Follies production with the exception of the *Ziegfeld Follies of 1913*. In 1916 Williams starred in the silent motion picture short *A Natural Born Gambler*, directed by G. W. Bitzer. During the last minutes of the film he performs the poker game routine that he made famous in the *Ziegfeld Follies of 1914* as a pantomime routine that followed his singing "Darktown Poker Club."

He recorded several numbers that he had introduced in the Follies. Typical is "No Place Like Home" from the 1917 Follies, with lyrics by Ring Lardner about a home suffering as much turmoil as European battlefields:

My wife is a pacific [pacifist]
She says, "Cut it out or somebody's bound to get hurt."
And I says, "Yes, madam, I'm with thee—
Cuz that somebody's first name is Bert."
Ah, home sweet home—I think that's where the real war is

It was recorded on September 14, 1917, and issued on Columbia A2438 in February 1918.

On December 1, 1919, he recorded what would become his best-selling record: "The Moon Shines on the Moonshine," issued on A2849 in March 1920. He introduced it in *Ziegfeld Follies of 1919*, which opened at the New Amsterdam Theatre on June 16, 1919.

Musical arrangements on Williams' discs are distinctive, with trombones and bassoons making comic noises, including "raspberries." Williams created a few distinct characters in his careful comic delivery. In "I Want to Know Where Tosti Went (When He Said Goodbye)" (A3305), the singer proudly rattles off what he knows, and the joke is that one who can say what he or she knows in a few lines of song cannot know much. The singer announces that one of the very few things he does not know is where F. Paolo Tosti was going when he wrote the popular song "Good-Bye" (Tosti was only the composer of the music; lyrics were by F. G. White-Melville). He brags about knowing all that "Mr. Wagner" wrote but fails to pronounce the composer's name in the familiar German manner. He is proud of his knowledge of the Bible and astronomy:

> I know about Peter and Paul
> 'Course, I don't know it all
> Know all about them planets, though,
> Up in the sky

Williams' delivery suggests that knowing that planets are "up in the sky" is the same as knowing "all about them planets."

Many songs recorded by Williams make use of racial stereotypes common at that time, with most characters coming off as naive, luckless, or shiftless. The character in "Samuel" (A1909) complains of his job at a hotel but insists he cannot leave because the hotel serves good fried chicken.

In contrast is "Save a Little Dram for Me" (A2979), which evokes a sharp parson who cajoles his congregation into sharing gin they sneak into a church service. The humor is gentle, as in these lines:

> He closed his Bible gently
> In the middle of the psalm
> And started thinking mentally
> Where that smell was coming from

This determined parson shares qualities with the indignant deacon who emerges in "It's Nobody's Business But My Own" (A2750). Williams makes a proud parson.

Although many Williams songs employ common racial stereotypes, direct references to Williams' race are rare after the "coon" songs recorded for Victor in the earliest years ("coon" is in two titles recorded during the early sessions). In the 1910 song "Play That Barber Shop Chord" (A929) Williams does speak of a "colored" family and "a kinky-headed lady they call Choc'late Sadie," but by 1910 the derogatory term "coon" is mostly abandoned ("How? Fried!" uses the term—the monologue was recorded in 1913 but was released posthumously in August 1922) and the crudest stereotypes are gone. A rare reference to skin color is in a later song, "I'm Neutral" (A1817), recorded in 1915, at a time when many Americans were worried about being drawn into the European conflict. Describing individuals in a mob, Williams comments, "A Russian saw my color and he hollered, 'Kill the Turk!'" In the context of the song, this reference to skin differences establishes that white Americans were antagonistic toward Turks (allied with the Germans), not toward blacks.

References to skin color are also made in the 1921 "Brother Low Down" (A3508) in which an itinerant preacher speaks of different shades of color:

All you satin blacks and chocolate browns
When I pass this hat around
If you want to keep from sin
Drop your little nickels in
And help poor Brother Low Down

The earlier "Borrow from Me" (A1354) describes ways to cast a stage production of *Uncle Tom's Cabin*: the Czar of Russia could "blacken up" to play Uncle Tom and another role could be played by "a brother who doesn't come too dark."

There are indirect references to racial tensions in some Bert Williams selections. In "I'm Gone Before I Go" (A2078), the singer speaks of a friend who volunteered to spy in Mexico rather than enlist with regular troops, but the pal's plan backfired: "Since then I have heared [sic] that they hung my friend from a sour apple tree. Oh-oh! I'm gone before I go." The title of "The Darktown Poker Club" (A1504) identifies for listeners the part of town in which Williams places the song's card game. The song does not directly refer to blacks, but "brothers" are depicted as too eager to gamble, cheat, and wield razors.

Williams tells of a blues singer in "You Can't Trust Nobody" (A3589):

That dark brown lady sang a wicked blues
I said a wicked blues
Full of moanful news
It ain't no use to arguefy

For the blues is blues
And you can't deny it
It's hard to listen to such sad tales
But to everyone that lady would wail

Although recorded on October 25, 1920, around the time Mamie Smith enjoyed success with "Crazy Blues" on Okeh 4169, it was not issued until June 1922. Williams himself recorded songs with "blues" in the title, such as "Unlucky Blues" and "Lonesome Alimony Blues," but worked strictly within a vaudeville and Tin Pan Alley tradition, giving no hint of what was to come in the records of blues artists such as Bessie Smith and Ma Rainey. A third Williams recording with "blues" in the title is a mouthful: "I'm Sorry I Ain't Got It You Could Have It If I Had It Blues" (A2877).

His final show, *Under the Bamboo Tree*, opened in Cincinnati on December 4, 1921. A week later the show played in Chicago for a long run at the Studebaker Theater. In that city in February 1922, Williams, whose health had been declining for some time, caught a cold that developed into pneumonia, which was complicated by heart troubles. He refused to take a rest from the new show in which he starred, unwilling to throw others out of work. He took the show to Detroit but was unable to complete a performance on February 27. The very sick entertainer traveled by train back to New York. He died in his home, leaving his estate to his wife Lottie.

Two biographies of the entertainer are Ann Charters' *Nobody: The Story of Bert Williams* (Macmillan Company, 1970) and Eric Ledell Smith's *Bert Williams: A Biography of the Pioneer Black Comedian* (McFarland & Company, 1992).

Wills, Nat (July 11, 1873-December 9, 1917)

Nat M. Wills, "The Happy Tramp," was probably born Edward McGregor in Fredericksburg, Virginia, although a *New York Times* obituary gives his real name as Louis Magrath Wills. As a child, he was on the stage with Neil Burgess in a play called *Vim*. He acquired theatrical training as a member of the stock company at San Francisco's Grand Opera House. During the 1890s Wills was end man of the Ideal Minstrels in Washington but by the turn of the century was well established as a vaudeville headliner. A partner in early years was Dave Halpin. Their act was billed "The Tramp and the Policeman."

He first assumed the role of a tramp in Washington, DC. During a dress rehearsal for the play *A Black Game,* scheduled for the old Globe Theatre, a drop fell from the fly gallery, seriously injuring an actor who had been playing a hobo role. The December 10, 1917, issue of *The New York Times* noted, "Wills stepped into the breach with such success that tramp parts became his dramatic allotment from that time on." He went on to star in the B. F. Keith and Orpheum Circuit of theaters for eight years. He also performed in the *Ziegfeld Follies of 1913*, and on September 22, 1913, cut for Victor songs he had introduced in the show, including "If a Table at Rector's Could Talk."

In the June 1951 issue of *Hobbies*, Jim Walsh notes this serious side to the comedian:

> When vaudeville performers, tired of being cheated and otherwise ill-treated by many theater managers and booking agents, organized a protective union, the White Rats of America, in 1900, the 27-year-old Wills was one of the leaders. He delivered a fiery address at an overflow meeting in a fraternal hall situated above Koster and Bail's [sic—Bial's] museum. After he spoke, the air was filled with the shout of "One for All and All for One!" . . .

Wills recorded material that had proved successful on stage. His first session was for Victor on October 14, 1908. His debut release, " 'No News' or 'What Killed the Dog' " (5612; reissued on 17222), tells of a conversation between a "colored servant" (Wills uses black dialect when speaking the part of Henry) and his employer, who begs for news from home upon being picked up at the train depot after having been away for weeks. The servant's initial observation that there was nothing to report except "yo' dawg died" leads to further questioning which reveals that the dog died from eating burnt horseflesh; the man's horses died in a fire that destroyed his barn; the barn caught fire from sparks of the fire that destroyed his home; the house fire was caused by candles around a coffin containing the body of his mother-in-law, who had died of shock because the man's wife had run away with a chauffeur.

It was Wills' most popular recording, remaining in the Victor catalog until 1927, when it was remade by Frank Crumit. Other monologues cut for Victor include "Hortense at the Skating Rink" (31734; 1909) and "Darky Stories" (17768; 1915). He was a skilled comic singer, and the baritone cut for Victor such songs as "Saving Up Coupons for Mother" (5700; 1909) and "Parody on Eight Familiar Songs" (17894; 1913), which is backed by the monologue "A Father of 36." Curiously, "A Father" was recorded in 1915 but is backed by a performance recorded in 1913, which is uncharacteristic of Victor's normal practice of coupling performances from the same year. Another oddity is Wills' 1915 recording of "A New Cure for Drinking" being backed on Victor 17915 (issued in February

1916) by Al Jolson's 1911 performance of "Parody on Asleep in the Deep." Evidently the disc was supposed to feature a second Wills performance, a talk on "Christian Science," but this was judged unsuitable at some point and the Jolson performance was issued as a substitute.

His contract with Victor for years precluded him from making discs with other companies, but Wills was free to make Edison cylinders, and he began with a parody on "Down in Jungle Town" (Standard 10178). Announcing its August release, the June 1909 issue of *Edison Phonograph Monthly* states:

> In making his initial appearance in the ranks of Edison Record makers, Mr. Wills has chosen for his first selection, a parody on the well-known monkey song, "Down in Jungle Town," and he sings it to the music of that selection. The words, however, treat of the Roosevelt hunting trip to Africa in a facetious way. . . . Mr. Wills is one of the best known artists on the vaudeville stage. His Tramp Act has made him famous from coast to coast.

Wax Amberol 176, featuring "The Flag He Loved So Well," was issued at the same time as the two-minute "Down in Jungle Town" parody, and the trade journal announced, "This is Mr. Wills' first Amberol Record. It is twice as funny as the one in the two-minute list, for it is twice as long." Edison promotional literature stressed that Wills wrote the material featured on his cylinders.

His first Columbia disc, "The Drink Cure" backed by "A Comic Medley Song" (A1352), was issued in September 1913. His other Columbia disc featured "No News" backed by "Two Negro Stories: (a) The Head Waiter; (b) The Colored Social Club," released on A1765 in July 1915. In 1916, for the newly formed Emerson Company, he recorded yet another version of "No News" backed by a condensed version of "Hortense at the Skating Rink," the latter a monologue that had been previously issued on a twelve-inch Victor disc. Wills' last Victor release, "Automobile Parody," was issued in February 1917. A few other Emerson discs were issued later in 1917, including "To Europe on a Cattle Boat" (7193, released July 1917) and "War Stories" (7253, released November 1917).

On December 9, 1917, he died at his home in Woodcliffe-on-Hudson, New Jersey, from what appeared to be accidental suffocation, though some have concluded it was suicide. The following day's issue of *The New York Times* noted:

> Wills, whose hobby was automobiles and gas engines, went to the garage back of his home in the afternoon to tinker with the engine of

his car. Two weeks ago thieves who broke into the garage smashed two top bolts which held the heavy doors shut when they were not held by the ordinary patent lock. Because of the cold, Wills locked himself in the garage so the doors would stay shut while he worked. He lifted the hood of the car, started the engine racing idly and crawled underneath to make adjustments. The tight little garage soon began to fill with the deadly fumes of partially consumed gasoline. Wills must have realized the danger, for he crawled from under the car and, not even stopping to halt the engine, struggled to the doors. If he cried out, no one heard him. . . .

Wills married four times. His widow, the former May Day (she was in the Ziegfeld Follies as May Harrison), who was twenty-three at the time of his death, squandered within five years her share of the large inheritance and died of a cerebral hemorrhage at age fifty in a shabby hotel room.

Selected Bibliography

General

Baumbach, Robert. *Look for the Dog: An Illustrated Guide to Victor Talking Machines*. Woodland Hills, CA: Stationery X-Press, 1981.
Brogan, Hugh and Charles Mosley. *American Presidential Families*. New York: Macmillan, 1993.
Charosh, Paul (comp.). *Berliner Gramophone Records: American Issues, 1892-1900*. Westport, CT: Greenwood Press, 1995.
Collier, James Lincoln. Jazz. In *The New Grove Dictionary of Jazz*. New York: St. Martin's Press, 1988.
Dethlefson, Ronald (comp.). *Edison Blue Amberol Recordings 1912-1914*. Woodland Hills, CA: Stationery X-Press, 1997.
Dethlefson, Ronald (comp.). *Edison Blue Amberol Recordings 1915-1929*. New York: APM Press, 1981.
Dethlefson, Ronald and Raymond R. Wile. *Edison Disc Artists and Records 1910-1929*. New York: APM Press, 1985.
Fagan, Ted and William R. Moran (comps.). *The Encyclopedic Discography of Victor Recordings: Matrix Series*. Westport, CT: Greenwood Press, 1986.
Fagan, Ted and William R. Moran (comps.). *The Encyclopedic Discography of Victor Recordings: Pre-Matrix Series*. Westport, CT: Greenwood Press, 1983.
Hardy, Phil and Dave Laing. *Faber Companion to 20th-Century Popular Music*. London: Faber and Faber, 1990.
Harvith, John, and Susan Edwards Harvith. *Edison, Musicians, and the Phonograph*. Westport, CT: Greenwood Press, 1987.
Hodes, Art and Chadwick Hansen (eds.). *Selections from the Gutter*. Berkeley, CA: University of California Press, 1977.
Jasen, David. *Tin Pan Alley*. New York: Donald I. Fine, 1988.
Koenigsberg, Allen (comp.). *Edison Cylinder Records, 1889-1912*. New York: APM Press, 1987.
Koenigsberg, Allen. *The Patent History of the Phonograph*. New York: APM Press, 1990.
Laird, Ross (comp.). *Moanin' Low: A Discography of Female Popular Vocal Recordings, 1920-1933*. Westport, CT: Greenwood Press, 1996.
Lanza, Joseph. *Elevator Music*. New York: St. Martin's Press, 1994.
Marco, Guy A. (ed.). *Encyclopedia of Recorded Sound in the United States*. New York: Garland Publishing, 1993.

Proceedings of the 1890 Convention of Local Phonograph Companies. Nashville: Country Music Foundation, 1974. Reprint.

Raymond, Jack. *Show Music on Record: The First 100 Years.* Washington, DC: Smithsonian, 1992.

Rust, Brian. *The American Dance Band Discography, 1917-1942.* New Rochelle, NY: Arlington House, 1975.

Rust, Brian. *The Complete Entertainment Discography, 1897-1942,* Second Edition. New York: Da Capo, 1989.

Rust, Brian. *Jazz Records, 1897-1942,* Fifth Edition. Chigwell, England: Storyville, 1982.

Rust, Brian. *The Victor Master Book, II (1925-1936).* Stanhope, NJ: Allen, 1970.

Settel, Irving. *A Pictorial History of Radio.* New York: Grosset & Dunlap, 1960.

Simon, George T. *The Big Bands.* New York: Schirmer Books, 1981.

Sutton, Allan (comp.). *A Guide to Pseudonyms on American Records, 1892-1942.* Westport, CT: Greenwood Press, 1993.

Whitburn, Joel. *Pop Memories: 1890-1954.* Menomonee Falls, WI: Record Research, 1996.

American Quartet

Walsh, Jim. "The (Premier) American Quartet," *Hobbies.* (February 1970) 38-40, 50, 130; (March 1970) 38-40, 44, 124.

Walsh, Ulysses ("Jim"). "The Coney Island Crowd: John Bieling," *Hobbies.* (July 1942) 12; (August 1942) 15.

Bernard, Al

Walsh, Jim. "Favorite Pioneer Recording Artists: Al Bernard," *Hobbies.* (March 1974) 37-38, 120-121; (April 1974); (May 1974) 35-38; (June 1974) 35-38, 119-121; (July 1974); (August 1974) 37-38, 120; (September 1974) 37-38, 117, 126; (October 1974) 37-38, 120; (November 1974) 37-38, 119-121; (December 1974) 37-38, 119-120; (January 1975) 37-38, 119; (February 1975) 37-38, 119-121.

Borbee's "Jass" Orchestra

Collier, James Lincoln. *Jazz: The American Theme Song.* New York: Oxford University Press, 1993.

Burr, Henry

"Henry Burr Music Co.," *New Amberola Graphic.* n49 (Summer 1984) 10.

"Henry Burr on the Radio," *New Amberola Graphic.* n75 (January 1991) 4-5.

Walsh, Ulysses ("Jim"). "Favorite Pioneer Recording Artists: Henry Burr," *Hobbies.* (April 1943) 12-13; (May 1943) 15, 21; (June 1943) 33, 129.

Collins, Arthur

"Arthur Collins, Baritone," *Talking Machine News.* 5:59 (June 1907) 169-171, bio, il.

Collins and Harlan

Gracyk, Tim, and Frank Hoffmann. "Collins and Harlan," *Victrola and 78 Journal.* n8 (Spring 1996) 28-34, bio, il.
Hamm, Charles. *Irving Berlin.* New York: Oxford University Press, 1997.
Kidd, Alec. "The Things I Say About the Records I Play No. 21: 'Bake Dat Chicken Pie'; Collins & Harlan," *Hillandale News.* n39 (October 1967) 156-158.
"Something 'Different': America's Favorite Duo of Entertainers: Arthur Collins, Baritone, and Byron G. Harlan, Tenor . . . ," *New Amberola Graphic.* n73 (July 1990) 8. Reproduction of the four-page Edison Tone Test program, dated March 22, 1921.

Dudley, S. H.

Riggs, Quentin. "S.H. Dudley," *Hillandale News.* n45 (October 1968) 64-65.
Walsh, Jim. "Reminiscences of S.H. Dudley," *Phonograph Monthly Review.* 6:4 (January 1932) 62-64.
Walsh, Jim. "S.H. Dudley," *Hobbies.* (January 1944); (February 1944); (May 1946).

Favor, Edward M.

Walsh, Ulysses ("Jim"). "The Coney Island Crowd: Edward M. Favor," *Hobbies.* (March 1942) 12.

Fenton, Carl (Walter Haenschen)

Ponselle, Rosa and James A. Drake. *Ponselle: A Singer's Life.* New York: Doubleday, 1982.

Fields, Arthur

Walsh, Jim. "Favorite Pioneer Recording Artists: Arthur Fields," *Hobbies.* (June 1953) 24, 37, 43, 45; (July 1953) 25-28, 38; (August 1953) 26-28, 33.

Earl Fuller's Famous Jazz Band/Rector Novelty Orchestra

Schuller, Gunther. *Early Jazz*. New York: Oxford University Press, 1968.

Gaskin, George J.

Walsh, Ulysses ("Jim"). "Favorite Pioneer Recording Artists: George J. Gaskin," *Hobbies*. (October 1944) 32-33.

Golden, Billy

Walsh, Ulysses ("Jim"). "Favorite Pioneer Recording Artists: Billy Golden," *Hobbies*. (June 1944) 25-27.

Harlan, Byron G.

"Byron G. Harlan, American Tenor," *Talking Machine News*. 5:63 (October 1, 1907) 369, bio, il.

Harris, Marion

Gracyk, Tim and George Wagner. "A Tribute to Marion Harris," *Victrola and 78 Journal*. n8 (Spring 1996) 2-9.

Hunting, Russell

"Back From 'South Ameriky': An Interview with Mr. W. Ditcham, of the Russell Hunting Co.," *Talking Machine News*. V:3 (October 1, 1907) 409.
"Round and About: Russell Hunting," *Talking Machine News*. 5:63 (October 1, 1907) 395-396.
"Russell Hunting Annual Dinner," *Talking Machine News*. 4:51 (January 1, 1907) 709.
Walsh, Ulysses ("Jim"). "Favorite Pioneer Recording Artists: Russell Hunting, Sr.," *Hobbies*. (November 1944) 27-28; (December 1944) 26-27, il.; (January 1945) 24-25; (February 1945) 26-27.

Jones, Ada

Jones, Ada. "Singing to the World," *Edison Phonograph Monthly*. 15:2 (February 1917) il.
Petty, John A. "Milford Fargo—A Tribute," *New Amberola Graphic*. n56 (Spring 1986) 15.

Riggs, Quentin. "Ada Jones," *Hillandale News*. n41 (February 1968) 201-203, il.
Walsh, Ulysses ("Jim"). "Favorite Pioneer Recording Artists: Ada Jones," *Hobbies*. (June 1946) 18-19, il.; (July 1946) 17-18; (August 1946) 18-19; (September 1946) 24; (October 1946) 26; (November 1946) 26-27; (December 1946) 25-26; (January 1947) 22.
Walsh, Jim. "Favorite Pioneer Recording Artists: Ada Jones and the Shannon Four Give a Concert in Roanoke, Va," *Hobbies*. (June 1954); (July 1954) 26-28, il.
"Whistle It," *The Talking Machine News*. 5:66 (November 15, 1907) 527.

Jose, Richard

Clark, Walter Van Tilburg (Ed.). *The Journals of Alfred Doten, 1849-1903*. Reno, Nevada: University of Nevada Press, 1973.
Gracyk, Tim. "Richard Jose: Countertenor and Recording Pioneer," *Antique Phonograph News*. (January-February 1994) 3-5+.

Kaufman, Irving

Riggs, Quentin. "Irving Kaufman: Passing of a Pioneer Artist," *New Amberola Graphic*. n16 (Winter 1976) 6.

Macdonough, Harry

Walsh, Ulysses ("Jim"). "Favorite Pioneer Recording Artists: Harry Macdonough," *Hobbies*. (November 1943) 34, 129; (December 1943) 26.

Murray, Billy

Carty, Dick. "Billy Murray—Jimmy Martindale; The Final Chapter," *New Amberola Graphic*. n85 (July 1993) 6-7.
Hoffmann, Frank. "Billy Murray: The Early Years," *Victrola and 78 Journal*. n8 (Spring 1996) 35-40, il.
Hoffmann, Frank. "In the Land of Harmony; A History of the American Quartet," *Victrola and 78 Journal*. n7 (Winter 1996) 22-27, bio, il.
Hoffmann, Frank, Dick Carty, and Quentin Riggs. *Billy Murray: The Phonograph Industry's First Great Recording Artist*. Lanham, MD: Scarecrow, 1997, il.
Hoffmann, Frank, and Peter Dilg. "The Sammy Herman Interview," *Victrola and 78 Journal*. n6 (Fall 1995) il.

Myers, J. W.

Walsh, Ulysses ("Jim"). "Favorite Pioneer Recording Artists: John W. Myers," *Hobbies*. (July 1944) 26-27.

Original Dixieland Jazz Band

Brunn, Harry O. *The Story of the Original Dixieland Jazz Band.* Baton Rouge, LA: Louisiana State University Press, 1960.
Kenney, William Howland. *Chicago Jazz: A Cultural History 1904-1930.* New York: Oxford University Press, 1993.
Rust, Brian. "The First Jazz Record of All?," *Victrola and 78 Journal.* n6, (Summer 1995) 9-10.
Rust, Brian. *My Kind of Jazz.* London: Elm Tree Books, 1990.

Ossman, Vess L.

"Sylvester Louis ("Vess L.") Ossman," In: *The Banjo on Record: A Bio-Discography,* edited by Uli Heier and Rainer E. Lotz (Discographies, Number 52). Westport, CT: Greenwood Press, 1993, pp. 305-331.

Peerless Quartet

Walsh, Jim. "Favorite Pioneer Recording Artists: History of the Peerless Quartet," *Hobbies.* (December 1969) 38-40, 130.

Porter, Steve

Riggs, Quentin. "Steve Porter," *Talking Machine Review.* n1 (December 1969) 3-5.
Walsh, Ulysses ("Jim"). "Favorite Pioneer Recording Artists: Steve Porter," *Hobbies.* (July 1943) 21-22; (October 1943) 15-16.

Prince, Charles A.

Walsh, Jim. "Favorite Pioneer Recording Artists: Charles Adams Prince," *Hobbies.* (December 1952) 29-30; (January 1953) 23-26, 31. il.

Rogers, Walter B.

Walsh, Jim. "Virtuosos of the Cornet: Walter B. Rogers and Jules Levy," *Hobbies.* (February 1959) 34-40.

Shannon Four, Shannon Quartet, and Revelers

Riggs, Quentin. "The Revelers," *Talking Machine Review.* n6 (October 1970) 158-163, 175-176, il.

Shilkret, Nathaniel

Coslow, Sam. *Cocktails for Two.* New Rochelle, NY: Arlington House, 1977.
DeLong, Thomas A. *Pops.* Piscataway, NJ: New Century, 1983.
Evans, Philip R. and Larry F. Kiner. *Tram: The Frank Trumbauer Story.* Metuchen, NJ: Scarecrow, 1994.
Sudhalter, Richard M. and Philip R. Evans. *Bix: Man & Legend.* New Rochelle, NY: Quartet Books, 1974.

Smith, Joseph C.

Jones, David L. "In Appreciation of Joseph C. Smith," *New Amberola Graphic.* 7:4/n28 (Spring 1979) 9-11.

Sousa, John Philip/Sousa's Band

"John Philip Sousa—A Tribute on Television; A Review by Peter Lawrence," *Hillandale News.* n54 (April 1970) 93-94.
"A Momentous Musical Meeting: Thomas A. Edison and Lt. Comm. John Philip Sousa Meet for the First Time and Talk Upon Music," *The Etude.* (October 1923) Reprinted in *New Amberola Graphic.* n30 (Fall 1979) 5-6.
Smart, James R. *The Sousa Band: A Discography.* Library of Congress, 1970. il.
"Sousa's Farewell Tour," *The Sound Wave and Talking Machine Record.* 5:3 (January 1911) 155.

Stanley, Aileen

Folkart, Burt A. "Vaudevillian Sold 25 Million Records; More Than Caruso," *Los Angeles Times.* (March 29, 1982) il. Reprinted in *New Amberola Graphic.* n40 (Spring 1982) 10.

Stanley, Frank C.

"Death of Three Prominent Talking Machine Artistes," *The Sound Wave and Talking Machine Record.* 5:4 (February 1911) 218, il.
"Frank C. Stanley, American Baritone," *Talking Machine News.* 5:58 (May 1907) 128-129, bio, il.
Hegarty, Michael. "Cylinder Stars on Disc," *Hillandale News.* n147 (December 1985) 291.

Stewart, Cal

"Cal Stewart's Last Letter to the Edison Co., September 22, 1919," *New Amberola Graphic.* n40 (Spring 1982) 10-11.

Dethlefson, Ronald, with David R. Crippen. "Visiting Edison's Recording Artists," *New Amberola Graphic*. n47 (Winter 1984) 5-9.

McNutt, Randy. *Cal Stewart: Your Uncle Josh*. Fairfield, OH: Weathermane, 1981, il.

Nace, N.E. "The Travels of Uncle John," *Hillandale News*. n35 (February 1967) 78.

Petty, John A. "Cal Stewart—The Acoustic King of Comedy," *New Amberola Graphic*. n11 (Fall 1974) 1-8.

Petty, John A. "The Cal Stewart File at the Edison National Historic Site, West Orange, New Jersey," *New Amberola Graphic*. n31 (Winter 1980) 6-8, 15, il.

Petty, John A. "A Look at a Phenomenal Recording Schedule: Cal Stewart's 1919 Columbia Matrices," *New Amberola Graphic*. n16 (Winter 1976) 3-5.

Petty, John A. "Uncle Josh Gets Personal!," *New Amberola Graphic*. n43 (Winter 1983) 10.

Petty, John A. "Uncle Josh on Zonophone," *New Amberola Graphic*. n42 (Autumn 1982) 16-17.

Riggs, Quentin. "Cal Stewart," *Hillandale News*. n31 (June 1966) 139-140.

Stewart, Cal. *Uncle Josh Weathersby's 'Punkin Centre' Stories*. Fairfield, OH: Hamilton Hobby Press, 1987. il. Reprint with foreword by Randy McNutt.

"Uncle Josh at the Statue of Liberty," *New Amberola Graphic*. n55 (Winter 1986) 3, 7.

Walsh, Jim. "Favorite Pioneer Recording Artists: Cal Stewart I," *Hobbies*. (January 1951) 20-22, 35.

Walsh, Jim. "Favorite Pioneer Recording Artists: Cal Stewart II," *Hobbies*. (February 1951) 20-25.

Walsh, Jim. "Favorite Pioneer Recording Artists: Cal Stewart III," *Hobbies*. (March 1951) 19-23.

Walsh, Jim. "Favorite Pioneer Recording Artists: Cal Stewart IV," *Hobbies*. (April 1951) 20-24.

Werrenrath, Reinald

Walsh, Jim. "Favorite Pioneer Recording Artists: Reinald Werrenrath," *Hobbies*. (August 1948) 32-33, 37.

Whiteman, Paul

DeLong, Thomas A. *Pops*. Piscataway, NJ: New Century, 1983.

Vallée, Rudy. *Vagabond Dreams Come True*. New York: Grosset & Dunlap, 1930.

Whiteman, Paul and Mary Margaret McBride. *Jazz*. New York: J.H. Sears & Company, 1926.

Wiedoeft, Rudy

Phoil, Tyn. "Thumb Nail Sketches No. 2; Rudy Wiedoeft Playing His Own Composition 'Saxema' on C-Melody Saxophone. Edison Blue Amberol 4005," *Hillandale News*. n40 (December 1967) 192.

Vallée, Rudy. *Vagabond Dreams Come True*. New York: Grosset & Dunlap, 1930.
Vallée, Rudy and Gil McKean. *My Time Is Your Time*. New York: Ivan Obolensky, Inc., 1962.
Walsh, Jim. "Favorite Pioneer Recording Artists: Rudy Wiedoeft and Other Saxophone Players," *Hobbies*. (November 1973) 37-38, 122-123, il.
Walsh, Jim. "Favorite Pioneer Recording Artists: Rudy Wiedoeft and Other Saxophone Players, Part II," *Hobbies*. (December 1973) 37-38, 119-123, il.

Williams, Bert

Charters, Ann. *Nobody: The Story of Bert Williams*. New York: Macmillan, 1970.
Debus, Allen. "Bert Williams on Record," *Hillandale News*. n154 (February 1987) 154-157.
Gracyk, Tim. "A Look at Bert Williams," *Antique Phonograph News*. (May-June 1994) 3-8.
Rowland, Mabel. *Bert Williams: Son of Laughter*. New York: English Crafters, 1923.
Smith, Eric Ledell. *Bert Williams: A Biography of the Pioneer Black Comedian*. McFarland, 1992.
Walsh, Jim. "Another Record by Bert Williams," *Hobbies*. (March 1951) 2.
"Williams, (Egbert Austin) Bert," In: *Encyclopedia of the Musical Theatre*, edited by Stanley Green. New York: Da Capo, 1976. p. 449.

Wills, Nat

Walsh, Jim. "Favorite Pioneer Recording Artists: Nat M. Wills, The Happy Tramp," *Hobbies*. (June 1951) 20-23, il.

Index

Berliner Gramophone Co.
 and George Broderick, 49
 and Arthur Collins, 67
 and Will Denny, 94
 and S. H. Dudley, 97
 and Edward Favor, 109
 female vocalists, 185
 and George Gaskin, 143
 and Billy Golden, 144, 145
 and Hayden Quartet, 27, 179
 and Harry Macdonough, 225
 and J. W. Myers, 250
 and orations, 18
 and Vess Ossman, 264
 and Steve Porter, 272
 and Walter B. Rogers, 280
Bernard, Al, **42-46**
 and Frank Ferera, 126
 and Walter Haenschen, 113
 and ODJB, 261
 and Steve Porter, 275
"Best Ever Medley," 358
Bethel, Tom, 107
Bible stories, 303-304
Bieling, John
 in American Quartet, 27-30, 180
 and S. H. Dudley, 98
 and George Gaskin, 143
 and Hayden Quartet, 178-180, 352
 and Harry Macdonough, 225
Biese, Paul, 173
"Big Chief Kill a Hun," 83
Big Four Quartet, 68, 164
Bill, Edward Lyman, 5
"Bill Simmons," 69
"Bird in a Gilded Cage," 200
"Bird Intermezzo," 153
"Birthday of a King," 329
Black, Frank, 290
Black dialect. *See also* Coon material
 and Al Bernard, 43
 and Arthur Collins, 66
  with Harlan, 73, 82
 and Billy Golden, 144, 145
 and Marion Harris, 173

Black dialect *(continued)*
 and Aileen Stanley, 322, 323
 and Nat Wills, 387
Blackburn, Howard. *See* Stanley, Frank C.
Blackface, 43
Blake, Eubie, 104-107, 209, 349
Bloom, Rube, 302
"Blue and the Gray," 67, 68, 163, 273
"Blue Bell," 152, 180, 225
"Blue Feather," 190, 239
"Blue Hawaii," 125
Blue Monday, 364
"Blue Shadows," 290
Blues
 and Al Bernard, 43
 and Marion Harris, 170, 171-172, 173
 and Ada Jones, 194
 and Billy Murray, 324
 and Aileen Stanley, 322, 324
 and Victor Military Band, 349
 and Bert Williams, 385-386
"Bluin' the Blues," 43, 44
"Bobby the Bomber," 165-166
Bonelli, Richard, 355
"Bonnie Sweet Bessie," 280
"Boo-Hoo-Hoo," 322
Booking offices, 101
"Boots," 350
Borbee's "Jass" Orchestra, **46-48**
Bori, Lucrezia, 353
"Borrow from Me," 385
Botsford, George L., 28
Bottleneck playing, 118
Bourden, Rosario, 312, 344
"Bow Wow Blues," 262, 323
Bowe, Morton, 348
Bowery accent, 188
"Bowery Grenadiers," 251, 252
"Boy and the Birds," 152
"Boy O'Mine," 330
"Boy Scout," 277
"Boy Who Stuttered. . . .", 190, 239

T - #0019 - 080222 - C0 - 212/152/24 - PB - 9780789012203 - Gloss Lamination